Ready-To-Wear Apparel Analysis

Second Edition

Patty Brown
Johnson County Community College

Janett Rice
Williams Sonoma, Inc.

Merrill,
an imprint of Prentice Hall

Upper Saddle River, New Jersey   *Columbus, Ohio*

Library of Congress Cataloging-in-Publication Data

Brown, Patty (Patricia Kay)
      Ready-to-wear apparel analysis / Patty Brown, Janett Rice. — 2nd
   ed.
            p.   cm.
         Includes bibliographical references and index.
         ISBN 0-13-606591-0
            1. Clothing trade. 2. Clothing factories—Quality control.
      3. Quality of products. I. Rice, Janett. II. Title.
      TT497.B74   1998
      687'.068'5—dc21   97–8726
                                                                      CIP

Cover Photo: Charles Feil/Uniphoto Picture Agency
Editor: Bradley J. Potthoff
Production Editor: Alexandrina Benedicto Wolf
Text Design and Production Coordination: Custom Editorial Productions, Inc.
Cover Designer: Russ Maselli
Cover Design Coordinator: Karrie M. Converse
Production Manager: Pamela D. Bennett
Director of Marketing: Kevin Flanagan
Marketing Manager: Suzanne Stanton
Advertising/Marketing Coordinator: Julie Shough

This book was set in Berkeley by Custom Editorial Productions, Inc., and was printed and bound by Courier/Kendallville, Inc. The cover was printed by Phoenix Color Corp.

 © 1998 by Prentice-Hall, Inc.
Simon & Schuster/A Viacom Company
Upper Saddle River, New Jersey 07458

Printed in the United States of America

10 9 8 7 6 5 4 3 2 1

ISBN 0-13-606591-0

Prentice-Hall International (UK) Limited, *London*
Prentice-Hall of Australia Pty. Limited, *Sydney*
Prentice-Hall of Canada, Inc., *Toronto*
Prentice-Hall Hispanoamericana, S. A., *Mexico*
Prentice-Hall of India Private Limited, *New Delhi*
Prentice-Hall of Japan, Inc., *Tokyo*
Simon & Schuster Asia Pte. Ltd., *Singapore*
Editora Prentice-Hall do Brasil, Ltda., *Rio de Janeiro*

Quality is never an accident. . . .
It is the will to produce a superior thing.
Attributed to John Ruskin,
nineteenth-century social critic

Preface

The purpose of this book is to provide a method for evaluating the quality of ready-to-wear apparel. The book takes an industry approach, integrating the study of traditional clothing construction with that of apparel mass production. The resulting body of knowledge and related vocabulary are important tools for anyone pursuing a career in the apparel industry. To make informed business decisions, one must understand how clothing is manufactured and appreciate the features that affect cost and quality.

A familiarity with apparel quality and how it is achieved enhances effectiveness on every level:

- Retailers and manufacturers establish standards that maximize quality while balancing cost limitations.
- Suppliers of equipment, materials, and services meet the manufacturers' requirements.
- Manufacturers communicate quality expectations to contractors.
- Wholesale representatives educate retail buyers about quality features.
- Retail buyers choose garments that perform as intended and deliver value to the consumer.
- Advertisers and marketers promote quality features to the target market.
- Retail salespeople communicate quality features to consumers.
- Consumers make informed purchase decisions.

In short, anyone can benefit from a knowledge of apparel quality.

WHAT'S NEW IN THE SECOND EDITION?

The biggest change in this edition is its organization. We have presented information about apparel analysis using an industry approach. The book is now organized in the same order in which apparel products and decisions about them are made. Thus, the study of apparel analysis reflects the apparel industry's approach to product development and product assembly. This edition incorporates commonly used industry terminology and the job titles associated with various functions. Readers learn to think, speak, and act like an industry professional and better understand the connections between different elements of the process. They are exposed to both merchandising and assembly decisions and the cost and quality results of those decisions. Thus readers receive an orientation to the complexity of the process of bringing apparel products to market.

The assembly portion of the mass production process is now organized according to the "4 Ps Formula: Parts, Panels, Pieces, and Products." This new feature helps readers focus on and remember the sequence of apparel construction while learning to recognize variations in the process.

An increased emphasis on standards and specifications and on how products are tested and inspected for compliance is another important change in this edition. Readers learn how to better communicate quality requirements and to fully understand how standards and specifications help create quality products. They also gain a sense of how testing and inspection enhance the quality of apparel products.

This edition contains a greater global focus, giving equal treatment to both imported and exported products. Readers gain experience in thinking more globally, an important skill in our increasingly global society. We have also covered more thoroughly the government regulations that affect apparel products and the apparel industry, allowing readers to understand how a company must function within its environment as required by law.

More photos and illustrations enhance the visual appeal of the text. A number of figures showing industry processes and equipment have been added, while the many figures showing close-ups of garment features that communicate much to readers about apparel cost and quality have been retained.

The first four chapters supply the background required for understanding the industry and the context within which decisions that affect product quality are made. Chapter 1 gives an overview of the apparel industry and explains its global nature and ever-increasing use of technology. Chapter 2 summarizes the regulatory climate within which the industry operates and explains both required and voluntary labeling. Chapter 3 defines apparel quality, establishes a framework for examining how consumers evaluate quality and value, and discusses costing and pricing. It also examines the quality methods employed by the apparel industry. Chapter 4 outlines the complete mass-production cycle.

The next six chapters explain the factors that must be considered when *planning* an apparel product. Chapter 5 explains how garments are shaped by darts and dart substitutes and supported by underlying fabrics and other devices. It also defines silhouette and style variations, with emphasis on garment lengths, waistlines, necklines, collars, sleeves, cuffs, pockets, and decorative details integral to the garment. Chapter 6 examines sizing and the evaluation of fit, crucial elements in formulating successful products. Chapter 7 reviews the influence of fibers, yarns, fabric structure, and finishes on the garment; its readers will benefit from a previous exposure to basic textiles. Chapter 8 covers the selection of the findings and trim items required to make garments. Chapter 9 introduces the stitch classes and types contained in U.S. Fed. Std. No. 751a: Stitches, Seams, and Stitchings. Chapter 10 discusses the seam classes and types contained in U.S. Fed. Std. No. 751a, seam defects and features that ensure seam integrity, stitchings, and other edge treatments.

The final two chapters explain the *execution* of the product plan through the assembly of the garments. Chapter 11 includes the steps performed during preliminary assembly; it covers the preparation of small parts, including the application of zippers, pockets, loops, and underlying fabrics, and the shaping, seaming, and hemming of garment panels. Chapter 12 follows the assembly process as garment pieces, including collars, sleeves, cuffs, waistbands, and linings, are constructed and become completed products.

Appendix A contains schematic diagrams of all the seam and stitching types in U.S. Fed. Std. No. 751a. Appendix B outlines the apparel production operations for which each seam and stitching type is used and lists the appropriate stitch types to use.

Throughout the book, the focus is on the functional and aesthetic performance of garments. Each chapter concentrates on identifying the physical features that produce desirable functional and aesthetic performance. At the end of each chapter, a quality checklist, a list of new terms, review questions, and related activities allow the reader to practice and apply the content of that chapter. The concepts come to life when applied to real garments. Related resources and a glossary are provided at the end of the text to aid in pursuing topics further. As readers explore the following pages, the authors hope they will develop a better understanding of apparel production and an increased appreciation of apparel quality.

— · — · — · —

ACKNOWLEDGMENTS

Thank you to Margaret McWhorter and Kitty Dickerson, who provided the original encouragement for the writing of this book. A special thanks to the many individuals who shared our enthusiasm for this project by offering their expertise. They include those who read the early drafts for the first edition: Lark Caldwell, Texas Christian University; Barbara Cunningham, University of Missouri Extension; Margaret McWhorter, Texas Christian University; Jerry Navlyt of Union Special Corporation Technical Training Center; and Jane Wilsdorf, Patty's mother. Reviewers of the second edition include Sue Barnhill, OshKosh B'Gosh; Ellen Goldsberry, Southwest Retail Center, University of Arizona; Mike Johnson, The Lee Company; Doug Kanies, Union Special Corporation Technical Training Center; Sandy Keiser, Mount Mary College; Jo Ann Pullen, ASTM D-13 Chairperson; Gail Raiman, American Textile Manufacturers Institute, Inc.; Lesley Rindosh, ACTS Testing Labs; Monica Schmid, Levi Strauss & Co.; Theresa Smith, Tultex; Mary Thompson, Brigham Young University; and Norma Willis, The Lee Company. Samples for photography were kindly lent by Texas Christian University, Johnson County Community College, The Fashion Group of Kansas City, and Jack Henry. Texas Christian University also deserves recognition for providing the grant that funded the research leading to this text.

Many individuals in the apparel and related industries have generously shared their expertise and resources: David Ayscue, Fieldcrest Cannon, Inc.; Sue Barnhill, OshKosh B'Gosh; Susan Black, *Bobbin Magazine;* Marilyn Borsari, U.S. Consumer Product Safety Commission; Gene Byrd, Angelica Image Apparel; Mary Jo Carroll, Carroll Associates; Susan Cowell, UNITE (Union of Needletrades, Industrial and Textile Employees); Darcy Crocker, The Wool Bureau; Gay Dawson, Aviano U.S.A.; Pauline Dellicarpini, Masters of Linen; Eric Essma, The Clorox Company; Ange Fatta, ACTS Testing Labs; Mary Fox,

Gerber Garment Technology, Inc.; Dorothy Fullam, Juki Union Special, Inc.; William Hamlett, Fieldcrest Cannon, Inc.; Jill Handman, International Fabricare Institute; Rod Helwig, Universal Fasteners; Kathy Hooper, American Society of Testing and Materials; Doug Kanies, Union Special Corporation Technical Training Center; Elizabeth Kellogg, Equest; Ira B. Livingston, Cotton Incorporated; Kyung Kim, Levi Strauss & Co.; Margaret MacBeth, Atlas Electric Devices Company; Tom Marxer, Angelica Image Apparel; Bill Mason, U.S. Customs Service; Robert Meltzer, American Society of Testing and Materials; Debbie Miller, Textile Industry Affairs; John Mueller, Juki Union Special, Inc.; Stephanie O'Neal, Kurt Salmon Associates; Ron Pacheco, Inchcape Testing Services; Pamela Patzke, Lands' End; Gary Peterson, Monsanto Chemical Company; Gail Raiman, American Textile Manufacturers Institute, Inc.; Jim Reid, Quik-Rotan; Del Rose, Gerber Garment Technology, Inc.; Linda Rosenberger, Coats American; Kathy Sargent, The Lee Company; Monica Schmid, Levi Strauss & Co.; Allen Short, Atlas Electric Devices Company; Beth Souther, Kurt Salmon Associates; LeeAnn Stevens, Winning Ways; Bob Swift, Crafted With Pride in U.S.A. Council; and Norma Willis, The Lee Company.

Thanks to Brad Potthoff, our editor at Merrill/ Prentice Hall, for his guidance and assistance in making this project possible. We also appreciate the fine work done by Laura Bofinger at Custom Editorial Productions, Inc. and by copyeditor Marianne Newman. Thanks to Patty's parents for all they have given through the years, and to the many colleagues, friends, and family who have lent support. And thank you especially to Patty's husband, Paul, who was patient and supportive through it all, and to her young children, Rachel and Adam, for sharing Mom with this book. Thanks to Janett's husband, Joe, who was encouraging and supportive during the preparation of this edition.

Patty Brown
Janett Rice

Contents

CHAPTER 1

Overview of the Apparel Industry: The Big Picture   **1**

HISTORY OF THE APPAREL INDUSTRY   1
TODAY'S APPAREL INDUSTRY   2
   Manufacturers   2
   Contractors   3
   Wholesale Representatives   4
   Retailers   4
   Branded versus Private Label   4
   Vertical Integration   5
GLOBAL TRADE IN
   THE APPAREL INDUSTRY   5
   Exports   6

   Imports   7
   Offshore Production   8
   Chapter 98 Production   8
   International Trade Policy   8
QUICK RESPONSE STRATEGY   10
   How Quick Response Works   11
   Benefits of Quick Response   11
COMPUTER USE   12
   How Bar Codes Work   12
   Benefits of Bar Codes   13

CHAPTER 2

Government Regulations and Labeling: Communicating to Consumers   **17**

REGULATIONS ON
   APPAREL LABELING   18
   Textile Fiber Products Identification Act   18
   Wool Products Labeling Act   20
   Fur Products Labeling Act   20
   Guides for Feather and Down Products   20
   Silk Labeling Regulation   21
   Care Labeling Rule   21
REGULATIONS ON APPAREL SAFETY   25
   Flammable Fabrics Act   25
   Regulations for Toys and Children's Articles   26
   Guidelines for Drawstrings on
      Children's Outerwear   26

REGULATIONS ON APPAREL
   INDUSTRY BUSINESS PRACTICES   26
   Occupational Safety and Health Act   27
   Fair Labor Standards Act   27
   Equal Employment Opportunity
      Commission Regulations   28
   Immigration Reform and Control Act   28
   Environmental Protection Agency
      Regulations   28
VOLUNTARY LABEL INFORMATION   29
   Trademarks and Brands   29
   Warranties and Certifications   30
   Union Made   32
   Size   32

CHAPTER 3

Apparel Quality: The Priority of Industry and Consumers   **37**

QUALITY FEATURES   38
   Physical Features   38
   Performance Features   38
   Selling Points and Buying Benefits   39

PRICE   39
   Price Lines   39
   Price as a Cue to Quality   41

HOW CONSUMERS
   PERCEIVE QUALITY   42
   Application of the Perceived
      Quality Model   42
   Determinant Attributes   43
VARIATIONS IN TARGET MARKETS   46
   End Use   46
   Demographics and Psychographics   46
VALUE: RELATING PRICE
   AND QUALITY   47
   Perceived Value Graph   48

Cost Per Wear   48
Apparel Life Expectancy   49
QUALITY PROCESSES USED
   IN THE APPAREL INDUSTRY   49
   Staffing the Quality Department   49
   Establishing Standards and Specifications   51
   Testing   56
   Inspection   58
   Analysis of Returns   61
   ISO 9000 Certification   62

CHAPTER 4

The Mass-Production Process: The Apparel Industry at Work   67

EVALUATION OF THE PREVIOUS
   LINE AND TREND ANALYSIS   71
DESIGN   72
   Line Development   72
   Preliminary Line Approval   73
   Fabric and Findings Research and
      Development   74
   Making of First Patterns   74
   Construction of Prototype Garments   74
SOURCING (CONTRACTING)   75
COSTING   75
   Precosting   77
   Production Costing   77
   Relationship of Cost to Price   80
   Balancing Cost and Quality   80
PREPRODUCTION   81
   Fabric Testing and Approval   82
   Writing of Garment Specifications   82
   Color and Shade Approval   82
   Findings Testing and Approval   82
   Care-Label and Other Label Approval   82

Making Preproduction Garments   83
Garment Classification with U.S. Customs
   (Imports Only)   83
Making Production Patterns   83
Grading   85
Marker Making   85
PRODUCTION   89
   Spreading   89
   Cutting   90
   Making Sample Garments   91
   Applying Decorative Details   91
   Assembly (Sewing) of Production
      Garments   91
   Wet Processing   92
   Pressing   95
   Finishing   96
   Final Audit   96
DISTRIBUTION   96
SALES TO CONSUMERS   97
THE ADVANCEMENT OF
   APPAREL PRODUCTION   97

CHAPTER 5

Shape, Silhouette, Style: Focus on Design Development   101

GARMENT SHAPE   101
   Role of Fabric Grain   102
   Shaping Methods   104
   Dart Equivalents   106
   Supporting the Shape   111
SILHOUETTE AND STYLE   115
   Garment Silhouettes   116
   Garment Lengths   116
   Edge Treatment Styles   116

Waistlines   116
Necklines   116
Collars   116
Sleeves   118
Cuffs   119
Pockets   120
Decorative Details Integral to
   the Garment   121
Design Considerations for Special Markets   124

CHAPTER 6

Sizing and Fit: The Keys to Competitive Advantage 131

SIZING 132
Numbered Sizing 132
Lettered Sizing 133
Childrenswear 134
Womenswear 136
Menswear 138

FIT 139
Controlling Fit 140
Five Elements of Fit 141
Evaluating Fit 145
Fitting Special Markets 151

CHAPTER 7

Fabric: The Essential Quality Indicator 157

FABRIC PERFORMANCE 158
Establishing Fabric Specifications 158
Aesthetic Performance of Fabric 162
Functional Performance of Fabric 164
Fabric Performance Testing 170

PHYSICAL FEATURES OF FABRIC 172
Fibers 173
Yarns 179
Fabric Structure 180
Dyes 184
Prints 186
Finishes 187
Leather and Fur 189

CHAPTER 8

Findings and Trim: More Quality Indicators 193

FINDINGS AND TRIM PERFORMANCE 193
Establishing Findings and
Trim Specifications 194
Aesthetic Performance of
Findings and Trim 194
Functional Performance of
Findings and Trim 195

PHYSICAL FEATURES OF
FINDINGS AND TRIM 196
Labels 197
Thread 197
Trim 199
Closures 202
Underlying Fabrics 210
Other Shaping and Supporting Devices 213

CHAPTER 9

Stitches: Holding the Garment Together 221

STITCH PERFORMANCE 221
PHYSICAL FEATURES OF STITCHES 222
Stitch Type 222
Stitch Length 236
Stitch Tension 239

Skipped Stitches 240
Stitch Width 240
Needles 240
Sewing Accuracy 241
Back Tacking and Latch Tacking 241
Long Threads 241

CHAPTER 10

Seams and Edge Treatments: Providing Structure 245

SEAM PERFORMANCE 245
Seam Pucker 246
Bulk 246
Seam Strength 247

PHYSICAL FEATURES OF SEAMS 248
Seam Type 248
Seam Allowance Width 257
Seam Stays 258
Sewing Accuracy 259

PERFORMANCE OF EDGE TREATMENTS 259
PHYSICAL FEATURES OF EDGE
    TREATMENTS   260

Edge Finish Stitchings 260
Other Edge Treatments 264

CHAPTER 11

Preliminary Garment Assembly: Parts and Panels   **275**

PARTS ASSEMBLY   277
    Serging Raw Edges 277
    Attaching Labels 277
    Adding Decorative Details 277
    Applying Zippers 283
    Constructing Pockets 286
    Adding Belt Loops and
        Miscellaneous Loops 288
    Applying Interfacing 289

Attaching Underlining 290
Applying Reinforcements 290
PANEL ASSEMBLY   291
    Shaping 291
    Seaming 292
    Attaching Elastic 294
    Hemming Garments and Applying
        Other Edge Treatments 296

CHAPTER 12

Garment Assembly and Finishing: Pieces into Products   **301**

PIECE ASSEMBLY   301
    Constructing Collars 302
    Setting Sleeves 306
    Adding Cuffs 308
    Constructing Waistbands 309
    Attaching Shoulder Pads 311
    Applying Linings 311

PRODUCT ASSEMBLY AND FINISHING 312
    Applying Buttons 312
    Applying Snap Fasteners 318
    Applying Hooks and Eyes 320
    Applying Miscellaneous Closures 320
    Finish Pressing 320

APPENDIX A

Seams and Stitchings   **331**

APPENDIX B

General Applications to Typical Operations   **337**

Related Resources   **325**
Glossary   **343**
Index   **359**

Overview of the Apparel Industry: The Big Picture

Chapter Objectives

1. Present the organization and structure of the apparel industry.
2. Explore the impact of global trading and international trade policy on the apparel industry.
3. Describe how the apparel industry uses Quick Response strategy and computer technology to maximize business efficiency.

Ready-to-wear apparel (RTW), * also called *ready-made* or *off-the-rack*, is clothing that is mass produced. To gain insight into the evaluation of ready-to-wear, an understanding of the past, present, and continuing evolution of the apparel industry is needed. The industry has grown during the past century into a complex manufacturing and distribution system to meet the demands of today's market.

Trends that impact today's industry and shape its future center around the expansion of global trading, resulting in increased competition, the reliance on Quick Response as a business strategy, and the advancement of computer applications and rapid communications networks.

HISTORY OF THE APPAREL INDUSTRY

The apparel industry is a relatively new one, with most of its growth in the nineteenth and twentieth

* In its broadest sense, the term *ready-to-wear* refers to any ready-made clothing. However, be aware that some people use the term specifically to refer only to women's clothing.

centuries. Clothing was hand produced before 1850. Virtually all of it was custom made for a specific individual. Sailors, soldiers, miners, and slaves wore low-quality ready-to-wear, but it was not considered proper attire for others. Ready-to-wear was known as *slops* and was worn only by the lower class.

Two main factors in the late 1800s contributed to the eventual acceptance of ready-made apparel by the general public (Kidwell, 1975). First, there was a demand for it. The middle class increased as a result of the same industrialization that made the sewing machine and mass production possible. These people wanted clothing to show their middle class status, but not at the cost of custom-made. Second, custom tailors responded to the demand by producing off-the-rack garments in their spare time. The Civil War created the need for military uniforms, which further spurred the development of ready-to-wear. Soldiers were measured and the results compiled to develop a sizing system so that uniforms could be mass-produced rather than custom made. Traditional tailoring methods were simplified to produce reasonably priced ready-to-wear uniforms. The establishment of size standards and relatively simple production methods paved the way for the mass-manufacturing of clothing for the general public.

The technology, labor supply, and distribution systems of the late nineteenth and early twentieth centuries were ripe for the growth of the mass-produced, ready-to-wear apparel industry in the United States. The Industrial Revolution was a major factor, with the advent of the sewing machine around 1850. Improved machines for cutting and pressing were developed at about the same time. Parallel advances in textile technology and the growth of a domestic textile industry made fabrics available in great variety and at reasonable prices. An influx of immigrants with sewing skills provided the labor force that made the mass production of apparel feasible. And as important as any other factor, the rapid expansion of department stores, specialty stores, and mail-order houses made possible the mass distribution of ready-to-wear apparel.

By 1860, the men's ready-to-wear industry produced everything from work clothes to formal wear. The women's ready-to-wear industry made slower inroads in the market, at first concentrating mainly on undergarments and cloaks. Women's dresses and other fashion garments of the era were complicated to construct and fit and underwent frequent style changes that made them unprofitable to mass-produce. However, when the simple skirt and shirtwaist became popular for women in the 1890s, ready-to-wear gained a firm foothold in the women's market. The trend toward simpler dressing continued into the twentieth century. By 1910 all items of women's clothing could be purchased ready-made.

TODAY'S APPAREL INDUSTRY

U.S. consumers alone purchase over $100 billion of apparel annually. The modern apparel industry is a global structure of firms, all intent on providing ready-to-wear to these and other consumers around the world. Textiles and apparel are often referred to as a single industry, but in fact they are two separate though closely related industries (Figure 1–1).

1. The **textile industry** is composed of
   a. fiber, yarn, fabric, and some findings producers
   b. converters that dye, print, and finish cloth
   c. wholesale representatives who may sell fabrics and findings to apparel producers
2. The **apparel industry** is made up of
   a. apparel manufacturers and contractors
   b. garment wet processors
   c. apparel wholesale representatives and direct importers who may sell garments to retailers
   d. apparel retailers, including department and specialty stores, chain stores, mass merchandisers, discount stores, mail-order and Internet retailers, TV retailers such as the Home Shopping Network (HSN) and QVC (Quality, Value, and Convenience), and direct sellers such as factory outlet stores.

Together, the textile and apparel manufacturing industries in the United States produce about $65 billion annually. The textile and apparel manufacturing complex includes about 5,000 textile mills and about 20,000 apparel plants. Along with related industries, it employs about 2 million people.

> **Note:** The concepts discussed throughout this textbook apply not only to the apparel industry but to many related textile products. Soft goods such as towels and sheets, footwear, handbags, belts, gloves, hats, hair accessories, furs, and luggage undergo similar processes in terms of production and are subject to the same planning and quality processes. Many of the concepts in this book also apply to the merchandising, manufacturing, and quality evaluation of non-textile fashion products such as cosmetics, fragrances, and jewelry.

Manufacturers

Apparel is produced by a manufacturer, a manufacturer using a contractor, or a manufacturing retailer using contractors. A traditional **manufacturer** has complete responsibility for the design, fabric and

Textile Industry

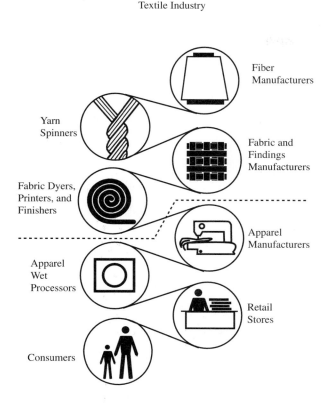

Apparel Industry

Figure 1–1 Progress of a garment through the textile and apparel industries.

Figure 1–2 Gerbermover® unit production system with overhead conveyor to transport garments from workstation to workstation. *(Courtesy of Gerber Garment Technology, Inc.)*

findings purchasing, production (Figure 1–2), and sale of finished garments to the retailer. The company profits from the difference between the cost of producing and distributing the garments and the price at which they are sold, usually to retailers. Retailers refer to manufacturers as **vendors** or **suppliers.** (Likewise, manufacturers refer to raw materials sources as their vendors or suppliers.) For more information on manufacturers, contact the **American Apparel Manufacturers Association (AAMA)** at 2500 Wilson Boulevard, Suite 301, Arlington, VA 22201.

When manufacturers operate their own factories, they are called **inside shops.** Manufacturers with in-house production have several advantages over those that depend on contractors, including

1. fewer communication problems
2. tighter control of quality
3. savings of time and transportation costs if garments are made exclusively at one location
4. more control over timing, making it easier to meet delivery dates.

Large companies with high volume dominate the jeans, basics (T-shirts, sweats, and underwear), and men's apparel industry. The basic nature of these products allows these manufacturers to steadily produce relatively unchanged products over extended fashion cycles. As a result, many of these companies have highly automated and specialized equipment. On the other hand, the women's and children's apparel industry, characterized by frequent style changes, consists of many small and often new companies that are constantly adjusting to the latest fashion trends.

Some of these apparel companies own no production facilities. They hire out part or all of the work to independent contractors. The flexibility contractors offer is critical to these manufacturers.

Contractors

Contractors primarily provide labor; they profit from their labor input. A contractor that performs all the production operations to produce a style is called a **cut, make, and trim (CMT) contractor.**

Companies that use independent contractors, or **outside shops,** have more flexibility because they have

1. no investment in plants and equipment, which enables them to present their products to the public with little initial investment

2. fewer employee training needs and fewer personnel problems and demands

3. no need to build factories as business grows, but merely to source additional contractors

4. no need to seek outside work and employ workers between seasons or if business slows, but simply to hire fewer contractors.

Subcontractors perform highly specialized functions for other contractors and manufacturers. They execute specialty work more quickly and economically than small firms or ones producing trendy fashions because they have purchased the specialized equipment and made a commitment to concentrate on jobs such as pleating, quilting, embroidery and screen printing. They spread the cost of the equipment over a number of different jobs, whereas many manufacturers cannot justify buying equipment that is only used for a single, occasionally needed operation, such as scallop edging or picot edging.

Wholesale Representatives

Wholesale representatives or **sales reps** are agents of the apparel manufacturing companies; they sell the finished garments to retailers. Apparel producers hire their own sales reps or contract independent sales agents. Wholesale representatives sell to retail buyers in showrooms at market centers and visit buyers to show them new lines. Wholesalers profit from the commission they earn on the goods they sell to retailers.

Some companies called **direct importers** sell and monitor production exclusively from other countries. These wholesalers often have a small staff located in the United States to monitor and track sales and production and another staff located in the country of origin responsible for sourcing and monitoring production.

Retailers

Retailers sell to the ultimate consumer. **Traditional retailers** buy finished garments from domestic manufacturers and/or direct importers and sell these goods to the consumer. They profit from the difference between the cost of buying garments from the manufacturer or importer and the price at which they sell them to the final consumer. For more information on retailers, contact the **National Retail Federation (NRF)**, Liberty Place, 325 7th Street N.W., Suite 1000, Washington, D.C. 20004. URL: http://www.nrf.com.

Many retailers today are **manufacturing retailers** for all or at least part of the goods they sell. A few examples are J.C. Penney, Sears, and The Gap.

A manufacturing retailer serves a dual role: that of the manufacturer responsible for producing private label brands and that of the traditional retailer selling the finished goods to the consumer.

> **Note:** From this point forward, whenever the term manufacturer is used it includes both regular manufacturers and manufacturing retailers responsible for private label products.

Branded versus Private Label

Private-label apparel is developed by or for a specific retailer, as opposed to **branded apparel**, which is developed by a manufacturer and sold to many retailers under the trademarked brand name. (For more information on trademarks and brands, see Chapter 2.) In the traditional **per sample buying** used to acquire branded merchandise, competing retail buyers often select merchandise from the same manufacturers' lines. In contrast, private-label merchandise gives retailers more control over the production of products they offer to consumers and allows for unique assortments.

The simplest form of private-label development occurs when a retailer hires a manufacturer to put a store label on merchandise the manufacturer already produces. Retailers employ **specification buying** whenever they request goods made to meet their requirements and standards rather than choosing from manufacturers' lines. At the other extreme, a retailer oversees the whole manufacturing process from design through production to create products unique to its store. In these cases, technically, retailers become manufacturing retailers that hire contractors to execute the design and production processes.

Private labels are nothing new. Large department stores and specialty store chains have carried them for years. The proliferation and popularity of national brands in the mid to late 1900s caused many retailers to move away from private-label merchandise, but now as stores struggle for unique images, improved profits, and expanding market shares, many of these stores are increasing their reliance on private labels again. Even small retailers may carry private labels; noncompeting retailers (for example, from different cities) band together to form buying groups large enough to share the costs of developing private labels. Some merchandise classifications lend themselves to the private-label strategy better than others. For example, the majority of men's and boys' underwear remains branded, while most sweaters in better department and specialty stores are sold under private labels. A few stores carry nothing but private labels.

Advantages of Private Labels. Retailers usually profit more from successful private labels than from national brands. National brands do little to build a unique reputation for a retail store, as many competing retailers sell the same merchandise. Customer loyalty belongs to the national brand and usually follows it to the store with the lowest price; offering a low price on national-brand merchandise builds store traffic, yet it hurts profits. Conversely, because private labels are exclusive, a popular one translates into loyalty to the retailer who sells it. Consumers cannot buy the same brand from a competing retailer, so they cannot directly compare it or its price at other stores. Without direct price competition, retailers carrying successful private brands sell them at attractive profits. The Limited is an example of a company that increased market share and profits by building brand recognition and customer loyalty to its products, first with their Forenza® brand and then with a number of other popular private labels. J.C. Penney's Worthington®, Hunt Club®, and Arizona® brands are other private-label success stories. Retailers that understand their target markets are well equipped to develop private labels.

Disadvantages of Private Labels. The downside of private labels for retailers is that initially the retailer must promote the private label to establish its popularity. Until demand grows, private labels are not very profitable. And private labels that never catch on with consumers pose great financial risks for retailers. On the other hand, highly advertised national brands with established reputations create in-store traffic immediately, as consumers seek out their favorite brands. And well-known national-brand merchandise commands higher prices than comparable merchandise with less well known private labels.

Another disadvantage is that building and running a successful private-label program requires a knowledge not only of customer wants and needs but of garment production and quality standards. Traditional buyers are not always equipped for the job. Some retailers hire independent product development consultants to formulate the right apparel products for their target customers. Others employ product development managers to assist buyers or substitute for buyers. Product developers establish quality specifications for design, materials, methods of construction, and sizing. They locate production sites and fabric sources that meet the demands of the product design. And they help make decisions about product features to upgrade or downgrade and how best to balance performance and cost limitations.

Vertical Integration

Vertical integration occurs when the same firm is responsible for multiple steps in the production or marketing of an apparel product. Examples of vertical integration include making the fiber and knitting or weaving the fabric, making the fabric and the garment, making the garment and selling it to the ultimate consumer, or any combination of these steps. Vertical integration can save a company time and money and allows it to profit from more than one step of the process. Increasingly, companies seek the benefits of the synergy resulting from vertically integrated organizations.

GLOBAL TRADE IN THE APPAREL INDUSTRY

Apparel manufacturers in the United States traditionally paid most of their attention to the domestic market. Today, however, the industry is a global one, and manufacturers are focusing on the world view. The world supply of apparel production capacity will continue to grow, exceeding world demand for the foreseeable future. Because manufacturers in approximately 200 countries worldwide compete for a piece of the global market, only the most competitive firms will survive.

In a global economy, more companies take advantage of opportunities to do business internationally, either to **import** (buy from other countries) or to **export** (sell to other countries). Recognizing, understanding, and respecting the national laws and customs and other cultural differences of trading partners fosters positive international business relationships. Most companies hire agents who speak the languages and understand the cultures of both parties to serve as intermediaries in international business negotiations.

Rather than exporting directly, many companies use export trading companies to simplify the export process. **Export trading companies (ETCs)** serve as intermediaries between the producers of the goods and the buyers of the goods in other countries. Export trading companies have experience in monitoring and coping with foreign markets, and they offer relatively low export costs due to the large volume of products they handle from many different producers. Doing business through a reputable export trading company is often as simple as a domestic transaction.

When importing, in addition to using a direct importer or other independent agent as an intermediary, many companies use a licensed **customs broker** to help them secure entry for the imported goods into the United States in the most time- and cost-efficient

Table 1–1 Internet Web Sites for Importers and Exporters

Sponsored by the U.S. Department of Commerce (DOC):

International Trade Administration (ITA) Dedicated to helping U.S. business compete in the global marketplace; offers extensive export assistance and lists trade information and services.
URL: http://www.ita.doc.gov

Office of Textiles and Apparel (OTEXA) Information on both imports and exports, including trade statistics and agreements such as GATT, WTO, and the HTSUS.
URL: http://www.ita.doc.gov/industry/textiles

The Trade Information Center (TIC) A comprehensive resource for information on all federal government export assistance programs.
URL: http://www.ita.doc.gov/how_to_export/itatic.html

Global Export Market Information System (GEMS) Information by country or region for American exporters.
URL: http://www.itaiep.doc.gov

Big Emerging Markets (BEMs) Information on markets with significant export potential.
URL: http://www.stat-usa.gov/itabems.html

Sponsored by the U.S. Customs Service (USCS):

U.S. Customs Service For general USCS information.
URL: http://www.ustreas.gov/treasury/bureaus/customs/customs.html

U.S. Customs Bulletin Board For trade information and customs news releases regarding global trade, currency conversion/exchange rates, quota thresholds, and federal register notices.
URL: http://www.ustreas.gov/treasury/services/cusbbs.html

---

manner. Table 1–1 contains a list of U.S. government web sites on the Internet offering both import and export information and assistance. For more information on importing and exporting, see Related Resources: Global Trade.

Exports

Exports help sustain and expand the U.S. economy. However, although there is high demand for U.S.-made goods in many foreign countries, the United States imports more textile and apparel products than it exports, leading to a **trade deficit.** The U.S. textile and apparel trade deficit, like other U.S. industry deficits, has been growing for many years (Figure 1–3). The relatively slow growth of exports compared to the rapid growth in imports is a major factor contributing to the trade deficit. An increase in exports would help reduce the trade deficit.

Some U.S. companies seek to meet the strong demand for U.S. products in many parts of the world by aggressively exporting products to other countries. These firms meet the challenge of competing in the global marketplace head-on. However, many U.S. firms, especially small- and medium-sized companies, having historically relied on the domestic market alone, fail to pursue opportunities in foreign markets, thus overlooking a major potential area for growth. Management in these firms might be uncertain about how to export

and may believe that exporting is too difficult, risky, and unproductive to attempt. In fact, fewer than 10% of all manufacturing businesses export regularly.

Advantages of Exporting. There are many benefits of exporting for the companies who pursue the challenge of selling their products in foreign markets.

1. Exporting expands the customer base and means greater sales, which translate to greater profit.
2. Demand in foreign markets is often countercyclical to American markets, offering market opportunities abroad when U.S. sales may have fallen off and extending the length of the demand for seasonal products. For example, Australia's seasons are the opposite of those in the United States.
3. Exporting often extends the life of a product that may be nearing the end of its popularity in the United States.
4. Exporting diversifies risk, creates new financing opportunities, and opens the way for further prospective business growth.

Disadvantages of Exporting. Exporting is not without its challenges, as with any business opportunity. Common problems include

1. difficulty in understanding foreign business practices
2. differences in product standards and consumer standards in foreign countries that make U.S.

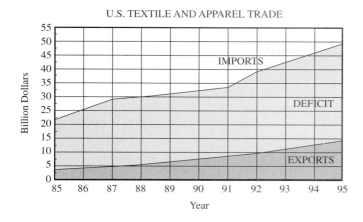

U.S. TEXTILE AND APPAREL TRADE

Figure 1–3 Growth in the U.S. textile and apparel trade deficit. *(Courtesy of American Textile Manufacturers Institute, Inc.)*

products unsuitable. For example, while black is considered a sophisticated color in the United States, in some other cultures it is the color of mourning or a color worn only by elderly women. Every aspect of the product—sizing and fit, color and styling, pricing—must be reconsidered for suitability to the export market.

3. problems in receiving payment for goods
4. difficulty in obtaining adequate representation in foreign markets
5. expensive foreign travel.

However, companies that tackle the inherent challenges of breaking into foreign markets often find the profitability of exporting outweighs the obstacles.

Imports

Throughout the early half of the twentieth century, U.S. companies produced the majority of the apparel sold in the United States. The trend toward obtaining apparel from countries with lower labor costs began in the latter part of the 1900s. Perhaps half of all apparel sold in the United States today is imported, accounting for about one in three dollars of U.S. apparel consumption. In the 1980s alone, textile and apparel imports nearly tripled. While the United States makes up only about 5% of the world's population, it is responsible for about 20% of the world's fiber consumption. Therefore, the lucrative U.S. market is a major target for apparel producers worldwide (Figure 1–4).

The chief reason for importing apparel is low cost, due primarily to the lower labor costs in many other countries. Although U.S. apparel workers (paid an average of about $8.00 per hour) are not highly paid by American standards, they earn more than apparel workers in most other parts of the world; in some poor, developing countries apparel workers earn as little as $.20 per hour. What seem like low wages to most Americans are very desirable to impoverished

people in these countries, who welcome any opportunity to raise their standard of living. A very labor-intensive industry, apparel manufacturing is an ideal industry for countries with little capital to invest but with plenty of unskilled workers willing to accept wages far below the U.S. minimum wage.

In the past, many importers placed orders with companies located in South Korea, Taiwan, Hong Kong, Singapore, and Malaysia. Orders for apparel made in some of these Asian countries are declining as manufacturing costs have risen and are becoming comparable with those in the United States. Instead, companies seeking low-priced apparel are placing orders in the Republic of China (mainland China), India, Pakistan, Bangladesh, Mauritius, and other African, Middle Eastern, and South American countries. Domestic manufacturers find it difficult to compete with foreign manufacturers that have the advantage of low labor costs. In addition, many foreign manufacturers have lower costs in other areas because they do not abide by the same safety and environmental

Figure 1–4 Crane unloading crates of cargo from ship in U.S. port. *(Courtesy of U.S. Customs Service. Photograph by Bill Mason.)*

standards of U.S. manufacturers. (For more information, see Chapter 2.)

Advantages of Importing. The competitive force of imports has kept apparel prices relatively low for U.S. consumers. Since the early 1970s, wholesale apparel prices have risen only about half as fast as the prices of other products. However, although imported apparel is purchased at a lower cost than domestic goods, it is not always sold at a lower price. Many manufacturers and retailers mark up low-cost imports more than domestic goods, selling them at the same or nearly the same price but making higher profits. The attractive initial cost of imports to the retailer continues to be the major reason for importing apparel. Apparel from foreign manufacturers also provides retailers expanded opportunities for putting together unique assortments compared to buying strictly from the same domestic suppliers as their competitors.

Disadvantages of Importing. Importing goods involves a number of challenges, including

1. expensive foreign travel
2. fluctuations in currency exchange rates, Third World instabilities, and filled quotas
3. higher shipping and insurance costs, agents' and/or brokers' fees, advance payment, and other "hidden" costs
4. longer lead times
5. inability to observe production without a long trip to the production site
6. less recourse on goods that do not meet quality standards
7. some consumers' negative reaction to imports.

All these problems with imports translate into lower sales and profits but may be offset by an attractive difference between the initial cost of imported and domestic goods. For information on U.S. government regulations on imported apparel, see chapter 2.

Offshore Production

Initially, U.S. apparel manufacturers complained about the dent imports make in the domestic apparel industry. They sought ways to limit imports, particularly through the enactment of protective legislation. However, as time went on, many U.S. apparel manufacturers began to take advantage of the benefits of importing themselves. They practice **offshore production,** either contracting with foreign producers to make goods or establishing their own sew-only plant in a foreign country. Because of lower labor costs, a number of well-known U.S. brands are mostly or entirely produced offshore according to their U.S. manufacturer's

specifications. About one third of all apparel imports results from this international **sourcing** (finding a contractor) by manufacturers. Another one third is accounted for by the international sourcing of retailers acquiring private label merchandise. (The majority of private label merchandise is made offshore.) Thus, only the remaining one third of apparel imports is marketed here directly by foreign companies (Glock and Kunz, 1995).

Chapter 98 Production

Some domestic apparel manufacturers cut fabrics in the United States and send the cuts to a low-wage country to be sewn, often in Central or South America because of their proximity. The assembled garments are then shipped back to the United States for finishing, pressing, and any needed wet processing. When the garments are shipped back, the manufacturer pays a tariff only on the value added—in other words, only on the labor costs of the production that took place outside the United States. This is allowed under **Chapter 98 (Provision 9802)** of the **Harmonized Tariff Schedule of the United States (HTSUS),** part of an international system of trade classification called the **Harmonized System (HS).** Chapter 98 takes the place of Item 807 under the former Tariff Schedule of the United States. Thus, you may still hear people say, "We 807ed those jackets," referring to sending the cut pieces offshore to be sewn. Products with high labor content and low weight (garments requiring little fabric or lightweight fabric) are ideal choices for Chapter 98 production. · Both Chapter 98/9802 and offshore production make it financially attractive for many U.S. manufacturers to utilize offshore labor.

International Trade Policy

Since 1947, an international agreement called the **General Agreement on Tariffs and Trade (GATT)** has promoted free world trade. Under GATT is the **Multi-Fiber Arrangement (MFA),** which seeks an orderly growth in the openness of world trade, allowing countries to encourage industrial growth in developing nations and at the same time minimize disruption of their domestic apparel industries. The MFA allows for treaties between two nations, called bilateral agreements, negotiated for the United States by the **Committee for Implementation of Textile Agreements (CITA)** of the U.S. Department of Commerce (DOC).

Tariffs. The GATT includes provisions for **tariffs,** otherwise known as **duties** or taxes, placed on imported apparel. The tariff or duty paid on garments entering the United States varies according to classification in the Harmonized Tariff Schedule of the United States (HTSUS). One of the three following rates of duty applies:

1. The *general* rate applies to countries with **most favored nation (MFN)** status, the designation for all U.S. trading partners who receive equal treatment (e.g., the United Kingdom).
2. Full or *statutory* tariffs, as much as 10 times the general rate, are charged to countries with which the United States does not favor trade (e.g., North Korea).
3. *Exemptions* from tariffs are granted to certain developing countries to encourage their economic growth under the **Generalized System of Preferences (GSP)** program and to countries with which the United States has specific trade agreements (e.g., Canada, Mexico, and Israel).

Tariffs are charged according to one of the following rates:

1. **ad valorem rate,** a percentage of the imported value of the merchandise
2. **specific rate,** a specified amount per unit of weight or other quantity (such as $.102 per dozen)
3. **compound rate,** a combination of ad valorem and specific (such as $.10 per kilo plus 5% ad valorem).

Quotas. The MFA allows **quotas,** which limit the quantity of items that may be imported. Quotas vary according to garment classification and country of origin. The United States applies strict quotas mainly to developed nations whose goods are considered a threat to the domestic apparel industry, such as Hong Kong, South Korea, Taiwan, and the Republic of China, who together account for over half of the apparel imported into the United States. More lenient standards are applied to poor, developing countries. Imported garments entering the United States must be accompanied by a **quota visa,** an endorsement by the U.S. Customs Service (USCS) granting entry and proving that they conform to quota limits for their classification and country of origin (Figure 1–5).

World Trade Organization. In 1995 the **World Trade Organization (WTO)** was established, and it gradually began phasing out and taking the place of the GATT (and thus the MFA) over a 15-year period. The Textiles Division of the WTO deals specifically with textile and apparel trade issues. The **Textiles Monitoring Body (TMB),** which replaces the Textiles Surveillance Body (TSB) of the MFA, oversees the administration of WTO policy concerning textiles and apparel. The end result of the phaseout of

Figure 1–5 Customs official examining garments destined for U.S. market. *(Courtesy of U.S. Customs Service. Photograph by Bill Mason.)*

the MFA will be freer world trade in textiles and apparel. One evidence of this new international economic order is the growth in multinational corporations such as Wal-Mart, J.C. Penney, and Benetton.

In the meantime, regions of the world are organizing their own free-trading blocs. For example, the **North American Free Trade Agreement (NAFTA)** created a single North American market for goods originating in the United States, Canada, and Mexico. Countries in the Caribbean Basin hope to achieve parity with NAFTA soon. This agreement may also expand to include Central and South American countries under the **Enterprise for the Americas Initiative (EAI).** Likewise, European countries, some of which are already united into a trading bloc known as the **European Union (EU),** are working on an agreement creating a free trade region to be known as "Greater Europe." And Asian countries have similar regional trading blocs at the same time as they work on additional trade agreements.

Circumvention. Tariffs and quotas enforced by the U.S. Customs Service are not entirely effective in controlling imports. Even after the tariff is paid, the cost of imported apparel is often still lower than that of goods produced domestically. Also, the regulations provide loopholes that allow imports to enter the United States at a higher rate than intended. For example, countries sometimes **transship** goods to a country with a more favorable tariff or quota position than their own; from there the goods are shipped to the United States. Illegal transshipment accounts for a substantial portion of the **circumvention** (avoiding) of trade regulations. As another example of trade rule circumvention, some foreign governments financially subsidize the production of apparel in order to establish an industrial economy in their countries. This allows manufacturers in those countries to dump goods; **dumping** occurs when manufacturers sell goods for a lower price than their cost of production in order to gain a foothold in a new market. This gives them an advantage over competing producers in other countries.

Free Trade and Fair Trade. There is one school of thought that importing apparel is hurting U.S. workers as their jobs in the apparel industry are being displaced and they are losing their source of income. These workers are a significant factor in the U.S. economy; along with workers in related industries, the U.S. textile and apparel industries account for almost 10% of the national industrial work force. The majority of workers in the apparel industry are women and minorities. They tend to have little education and few other employment options. Because the textile and apparel industries provide so many jobs, some believe the industry and its workers warrant protection.

On the other hand, while displacement is not easy, currently in our free-market economy there is a compensating high demand for workers in the food service, biotechnology, health services, and computer technology industries. Retraining is available to most displaced U.S. apparel workers, although service workers may earn less than manufacturing workers. On an international basis, U.S. apparel importers educate and train apparel workers in underdeveloped countries and therefore raise the standard of living in those countries. Thus, as members of the global community, U.S. companies help less fortunate people in other countries by providing them with skills and a source of income when apparel is imported from those countries. The debate is over whether or not this is at the long-term expense of U.S. workers.

There has been much political controversy over whether or not the United States should legislate greater control of textile and apparel imports. While the U.S. official position can vary from one government administration to another, the emerging era is one of *free* but *fair* trade. **Free trade** favors unrestricted imports in the interest of the free flow of goods between nations; if goods can be made better or at a lower cost in some other country, they should be. This view requires embracing the belief that the world is best served by a free-market, global economy. **Fair trade** focuses on the need for trade practices that provide a level playing field for all the global competitors, something that continues to be a challenge. Traditionally, retailers have favored free trade, while U.S. manufacturers and labor unions representing U.S. textile and apparel workers focused on the need for fair trade. The manufacturers and unions had some success in lobbying for legislation

to protect the industry against imports, but not enough to prevent the closing of factories and the displacement of many workers in recent decades. Gradually, as these same manufacturers have seen the opportunities open to them by participating in the global market, **protectionism** (using tariffs, quotas, and other means to restrict imports) has become less of an issue. Instead, they have begun working on gaining worldwide market access. Today a global market is replacing a world economy made up of relatively isolated national markets. Thus the merging of the free trade and fair trade views.

QUICK RESPONSE STRATEGY

The initial driving force behind the development of Quick Response was the U.S. textile and apparel industries looking for a way to gain a competitive advantage over foreign suppliers. Since then, however, the notion of Quick Response has become global. **Quick Response (QR)** is a comprehensive business strategy consisting of computer linkages and interindustry partnerships based on trust and cooperation that substantially speed up the production and delivery of goods while at the same time enhancing quality. Quick Response promotes responsiveness to consumer demand, encourages business partnerships, makes effective use of resources, and shortens the business cycle throughout the chain from raw material to consumer.

Originating with the idea that U.S. manufacturers could develop an advantage in this area over most foreign suppliers by capitalizing on their closer geographic proximity to suppliers and retailers and their greater ability to invest in new technology, Quick Response attempts to make domestically produced goods more profitable for U.S. retailers than imported goods, offsetting foreign manufacturers' advantage of low labor costs. The Quick Response movement has resulted in much more efficient U.S. textile and apparel industries. In addition, the Quick Response strategy and technology have established a global expectation about how industry partners (suppliers, manufacturers, and retailers) can cooperate. While the new open lines of communication between supplier, manufacturer, and retailer have had great impact on doing business more effectively, the need to be more responsive to the consumer is probably the most significant driving force behind Quick Response today. For more information, contact the **Quick Response Leadership Committee (QRLC)** of the American Apparel Manufacturers Association (AAMA), URL: http://www.tc2.com/qrlc or the American Textile Manufacturers Institute (ATMI), URL: http://www.atmi.org.

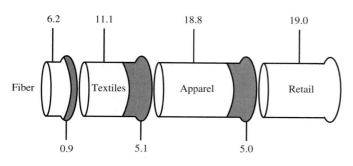

**THE APPAREL PIPELINE
66 WEEKS**

Inventory Time 55 Weeks (83%)

6.2   11.1   18.8   19.0

Fiber   Textiles   Apparel   Retail

0.9   5.1   5.0

Process Time 11 weeks (17%)

Figure 1–6 Traditional textile and apparel pipeline, showing inventory time (light sections) versus in-process time (dark sections). *(Courtesy of Kurt Salmon Associates.)*

How Quick Response Works

Quick Response concentrates on compressing the textile and apparel pipeline. The **textile and apparel pipeline** is the channel of distribution through which a garment passes, from the fiber producer all the way to the ultimate consumer. The pipeline consists of three main sections: (1) fiber/fabric producers, (2) apparel manufacturers and wet processors, and (3) retailers. Quick Response speeds the flow of goods through the pipeline by implementing advanced technology and efficient management practices. Figure 1–6 illustrates a typical textile and apparel pipeline of 66 weeks when traditional methods are used. Note that the garment is **in process**, or having work done on it, only 11 of those weeks. The remaining 55 weeks—or 83 percent of the time—the garment is in transit or **in inventory**, in the factory waiting to be processed or in a warehouse waiting to be sold. Quick Response commonly cuts the cycle from more than 60 weeks to fewer than 40 weeks. Incorporating Quick Response in all phases of the pipeline reduces the total length of a typical 66-week pipeline even more dramatically.

Quick Response management accomplishes these dramatic results by streamlining production and reducing both in-process time and inventory time. For example, without Quick Response, a T-shirt that requires under 3 minutes in-process time takes 2 to 8 days to flow through the production cycle; pants that involve 20 minutes in-process time often require 10 days in production; and a tailored coat requiring two hours in-process time takes up to 6 weeks to move through the factory.

Quick Response incorporates the use of improved computer and related technology to speed both planning and production and manage them more efficiently. It also incorporates the **just-in-time (JIT)** notion, signifying that there is no wasted time between the steps of production. Suppliers provide the right quantity and quality of materials "just in time" for the next process, reducing inventory and inspection costs. Figure 1–7 illustrates the shorter time frame for planning and manufacturing under the Quick Response system compared to traditional methods. Some apparel firms are achieving these feats today, but the concept of Quick Response is by no means an accomplished fact throughout the apparel industry. The pipeline contains numerous bottlenecks because some suppliers, manufacturers, and retailers have been reluctant to adopt the Quick Response philosophy and the technology required to execute it. However, many recognize the benefits of Quick Response and consider it a goal worth pursuing.

Benefits of Quick Response

Quick Response benefits retailers because buyers can purchase goods closer to the selling season, making it

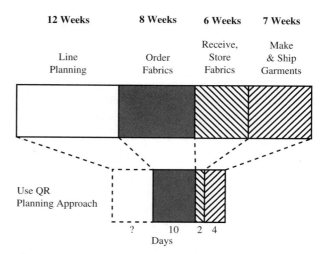

12 Weeks	8 Weeks	6 Weeks	7 Weeks
Line Planning	Order Fabrics	Receive, Store Fabrics	Make & Ship Garments

Use QR Planning Approach

?   10   2 4

Days

Figure 1–7 The shorter time frame required for planning and producing apparel using Quick Response. *(Courtesy of Kurt Salmon Associates.)*

easier to buy the "right" styles in the "right" numbers to meet customer demands. In fact, retail buying decisions may be made as late as two months prior to the selling season for domestic suppliers using Quick Response. In contrast, retailers must select apparel purchased abroad far in advance of the selling season to allow time for shipping and clearing U.S. customs. Five to six months or longer is normal for foreign suppliers. Shortening the **lead time,** the time from order placement to receipt of the goods, reduces the retailers' risks of making the wrong buying decision or missing out on a major trend. Prompt delivery of Quick Response merchandise translates into promptly filled reorders, reducing warehousing and inventory costs and retail **stockouts,** when a store runs out of an item. With a faster delivery time, retailers can increase their sales while simultaneously decreasing their inventories and markdowns. Thus, they are willing to pay a premium price for goods with fast delivery. This allows manufacturers to compete on time, not just cost.

COMPUTER USE

Computers and computer-linked technologies are revolutionizing the way the textile and apparel industries operate. The industries recognize the need for ever more sophisticated technology in order to remain internationally competitive. The ideal of many companies is **computer integrated manufacturing (CIM)**, in which all computerized facets of the business are electronically linked for efficient management. The computer improves the speed and accuracy of many production processes, such as design, patternmaking, grading, marker making, spreading, cutting, sewing, wet processing, and pressing (see Chapter 4). In addition, computers enhance management's ability to analyze situations, make cost-effective decisions, and communicate with others.

Computer communications are the leading trend of the day in the textile and apparel industries, impacting the way all companies do business. Companies are finding more and more new uses for electronic data interchange through computer modems. A **modem** converts information to audible tones that are fed through telephone lines and received by another modem at a remote location. **Electronic data interchange (EDI)** provides a vital link within companies and between companies by allowing the tracking of raw materials and finished garments at all phases of production, distribution, and sale. It creates greater coordination and cooperation between segments of the textile and apparel pipeline. The majority of major retailers and manufacturers currently use some form of electronic data interchange in their day-to-day operations; those

who do not will soon be left behind. Advances in computer communications and related technologies, such as the ability to send **faxes** (facsimiles of documents), have been a driving force behind the increased globalization of trade, enabling companies to conduct international business economically and quickly.

The use of the **Internet** (world-wide computer network) or direct company-to-company computer linkages provides inexpensive **e-mail** (electronic mail) communication, which has made communicating around the world as fast and simple as calling across town. The Internet's **World Wide Web (WWW),** also called simply "the Web," enables easy access and retrieval of documents containing text and graphics from web sites anywhere in the world. The growing potential of the Web for sourcing and marketing is a continuing revolution. Note throughout this book the **Uniform Resource Locators (URLs),** or web site addresses, for textile- and apparel-related organizations. (For a complete list, see Related Resources: URLs for World Wide Web Sites on the Internet.) Visiting these sites takes you on an exciting journey through the Web.

How Bar Codes Work

Bar codes are an essential element of the electronic data interchange enabling computer communications within the apparel industry. The price tags on most garments contain a **Universal Product Code (UPC),** a bar code like the ones used on groceries (Figure 1–8). A bar code is a "fingerprint" for a product. A laser beam reads the width of the black lines and the spaces between the lines of the bar code. It translates

① A number system character that identifies the product category. There are currently seven categories.

② A five-digit number that identifies the manufacturer...assigned by the Uniform Code Council, Inc.

③ A five-digit product code number that is assigned and controlled by the manufacturing company. This number is unique for each of the manufacturer's products, including each size, style, color, etc.

④ A check digit.

Figure 1–8   Universal Product Code (bar code).

that information into the 12-digit UPC number printed below the bar code. The first digit is a systems character; all apparel products start with a 0, 4, or 7. Digits 2 through 6 identify the vendor (manufacturer), and digits 7 through 11 identify a particular product of that vendor. The last number is a check digit. The *UPC Data Communications Guidelines for General Merchandise and Apparel* (1994) can be obtained for about $30 from the **Uniform Code Council (UCC)**, the not-for-profit membership corporation which administers the Universal Product Code, P.O. Box 1244, Dayton, OH 45401-1244, URL: http://www.uc_council.org.

Most major retailers, manufacturers, and trade groups have endorsed the Universal Product Code for use on apparel. Its use is also endorsed by the **Voluntary Interindustry Commerce Standards (VICS) Committee,** a group with representatives from all facets of the soft goods industry (including fabric and apparel, and bed and bath products) who determine the standards for electronic data interchange for the industry. However, a few retailers, during their transition to UPC, continue to use the older **Optical Character Recognition (OCR)** system, a series of computer-read numbers without a bar code. When both OCR and UPC are included on the same ticket, it is referred to as **Dual Technology Vendor Marking (DTVM).**

Benefits of Bar Codes

More and more retailers and manufacturers are equipped to take full advantage of all that bar codes offer. Even some small companies use hand-held computers equipped with scanners. The use of bar codes is expected to grow steadily because of their many possibilities for improving business efficiency. These include

1. substituting for each company's own numbering system of **stock-keeping units (SKUs),** creating uniformity throughout the industry
2. encoding of product features such as vendor, color, size, style, and price so that the information serves as a substitute for a verbal description of the item. This is extremely helpful to retailers; for example, a department store may have as many as two million different UPCs in stock, compared with only about twenty-five thousand for a large grocery store.
3. speeding up checkout time for retail customers. The retailer programs the computer so that the **point of sale (POS)** terminal (the computerized cash register) associates the garment's bar code with its current retail price, even if the garment is on sale or has been marked down.

4. providing all the necessary information for keeping track of inventory, subtracting sales and markdowns, adding new shipments and customer returns, and reordering items if and when necessary
5. making possible a fast and accurate **physical inventory,** or count of every piece of merchandise, by scanning each item's bar code
6. enabling manufacturers to mark goods at the factory, resulting in **floor-ready merchandise (FRM).** Manufacturers send floor-ready merchandise directly to the retail store with bar code tickets attached. The garments do not need to pass through a retail distribution center for marking; instead, the retailer puts them directly on the selling floor.
7. enabling manufacturers to gain speed and control accuracy in preparation of bar code tickets by creating them at the corporate site and electronically transmitting them to factory and contractor locations
8. improving communication between retailers and manufacturers regarding inventory levels (i.e., which items are selling well and which are not). For example, the retailer scans the bar code at the point of sale, and the electronic data from the bar code is transmitted via phone from the retailer's computer to the manufacturer's computer. This computer-to-computer communication provides immediate feedback to the manufacturer when a sale is made.
9. generation of automatic reorders for basic goods based on information about what sells. This reduces retail stockouts and replaces fast-selling items quickly.
10. tracking sales of basic goods and charting trends for the sale of fashion goods to forecast the ideal **model stock** for each store, adjusting the assortment automatically based on sales and anticipated demand in that particular store
11. enabling **shipping container marking (SCM),** marking the shipping boxes with bar codes for faster and more accurate handling of goods.

SUMMARY

The textile and apparel industries include both the textile industry (fiber, yarn, fabric, and other materials producers) and the ready-to-wear apparel industry (apparel manufacturers, contractors, subcontractors, wet processors, wholesalers, and retailers). Apparel manufacturers design, cut, assemble, and finish garments and sell them to retailers; retailers sell the finished garments to consumers. Contractors and subcontractors are hired to perform portions of the manufacturing process. Wholesalers sell the manufacturer's products to retailers for a commission. Traditional manufacturers produce branded apparel; manufacturing retailers produce their own private-label apparel.

The apparel industry is a global one. Some U.S. manufacturers exporting products to other countries meet the demand for American products abroad. Most U.S. retailers import at least some of their products from other countries, and many U.S. manufacturers take advantage of lower labor costs in foreign countries through offshore and Chapter 98 production. The World Trade Organization (WTO) is being phased in as the organization regulating global trade. World leaders are seeking free but fair trade in textiles and apparel. Currently, tariffs or duties are paid on garments entering the United States according to classification in the Harmonized Tariff Schedule of the United States (HTSUS); quotas limit the quantity that may be imported. Tariffs and quotas are enforced by the U.S. Customs Service.

The Quick Response strategy depends heavily on interindustry cooperation and new technology, specifically the use of the computer, to speed production and delivery and to enhance quality. Computer integrated manufacturing (CIM), computer communications such as e-mail and fax, and electronic data interchange between retailers and manufacturers through the use of the Universal Product Code (bar codes) are key components.

Checklist

The following questions are provided as a guide for evaluating the practices of an apparel producer. If you can answer yes to most of these questions on behalf of the producer you are evaluating, the producer is implementing good business management policies and procedures.

✓ Is the decision to use in-house production or contractors/subcontractors based on cost, quality, and lead-time considerations?

✓ Does branded apparel provide consistent quality and value?

✓ Does private label apparel build an image for consistent quality and value?

✓ Is the company vertically integrated when advantageous?

✓ Does the company take advantage of opportunities to import and export when advantageous?

✓ Is the most beneficial and profitable choice made regarding domestic, offshore, or Chapter 98 sourcing, or some mix of these?

✓ Are tariffs and other importing costs considered in cost estimates?

✓ Do imported garments conform to quota limits for their classification and country of origin?

✓ Does the company favor free but fair trade?

✓ Does the company refuse to transship, dump goods, or otherwise circumvent trade regulations?

✓ Does the producer build interindustry partnerships and invest in new technology to shorten lead times and improve quality?

✓ Are computers used to improve speed and accuracy in design, patternmaking, grading, marking, spreading, cutting, sewing, pressing, and wet processing? Ideally, is manufacturing computer integrated?

✓ Does the company link to suppliers and customers using electronic data interchange?

✓ Do employees have Internet access?

✓ Are individual products and shipping containers bar coded?

New Terms

If you can define each of these terms and differentiate between related terms, you have gained a good working vocabulary for discussing the topics in this chapter. The terms are listed in the order in which they appear in the chapter.

ready-to-wear apparel (RTW)
textile industry
apparel industry
manufacturer
vendor
supplier
American Apparel Manufacturers Association (AAMA)
inside shop
contractor
cut, make, and trim (CMT) contractor
outside shop
subcontractor
wholesale representative/sales rep
direct importer
retailer
traditional retailer
National Retail Federation (NRF)
manufacturing retailer
private label
branded apparel
per sample buying
specification buying
product developers
vertical integration
import

export
export trading company (ETC)
customs broker
trade deficit
offshore production
sourcing
Chapter 98 (Provision 9802)
Harmonized Tariff Schedule of the United States
 (HTSUS)
Harmonized System (HS)
General Agreement on Tariffs and Trade (GATT)
Multi-Fiber Arrangement (MFA)
Committee for Implementation of Textile
 Agreements (CITA)
tariff/duty
most favored nation (MFN)
Generalized System of Preferences (GSP)
ad valorem rate
specific rate
compound rate
quota
quota visa
World Trade Organization (WTO)
Textiles Monitoring Body (TMB)
North American Free Trade Agreement (NAFTA)
Enterprise for the Americas Initiative (EAI)
European Union (EU)
transship
circumvention
dumping
free trade
fair trade
protectionism
Quick Response (QR)
Quick Response Leadership Committee (QRLC)
textile and apparel pipeline
in process
in inventory
just-in-time (JIT)
lead time
stockout
computer integrated manufacturing (CIM)
modem
electronic data interchange (EDI)
fax
Internet
e-mail
World Wide Web (WWW)/Web
Uniform Resource Locator (URL)
bar code
Universal Product Code (UPC)
Uniform Code Council (UCC)
Voluntary Interindustry Commerce Standards
 (VICS) Committee
Optical Character Recognition (OCR)

Dual Technology Vendor Marking (DTVM)
Stock-keeping unit (SKU)
point of sale (POS)
physical inventory
floor-ready merchandise (FRM)
model stock
shipping container marking (SCM)

Review Questions

1. What factors were responsible for the growth and acceptance of the U.S. ready-to-wear industry in the 1800s?
2. Compare the advantages and disadvantages of inside and outside shops.
3. How does a manufacturer differ from a contractor?
4. Who is the vendor/supplier for a retailer? For a manufacturer?
5. Discuss the advantages and disadvantages of private label versus branded merchandise for retailers.
6. Why has the amount of apparel imported into the United States increased in recent decades?
7. Discuss the advantages and disadvantages of an unrestricted flow of imported apparel into the United States from the following points of view:

   a. U.S. manufacturer
   b. U.S. retailer
   c. U.S. consumer
   d. U.S. government
   e. foreign government of a developed country
   f. citizen of an undeveloped country

8. How is global apparel trade regulated? Specifically, how are imports into the United States controlled?
9. Explain the concept of Quick Response. How does it benefit U.S. manufacturers and retailers?
10. Discuss computer applications within the apparel industry. How does the use of UPCs/bar codes benefit apparel manufacturers and retailers?

Activities

1. Visit an historic costume collection to compare early ready-to-wear to modern ready-to-wear. Or, in a costume history book, compare fashions from the early and mid 1800s to fashions of the late 1800s and early 1900s. What are the most obvious differences? Which era's fashions lent themselves better to mass production?
2. Research a major apparel manufacturer. Write for an annual report, advertising brochures, and related information and read articles about the company. Conduct a phone or personal interview with

someone who works for the company, if possible. Answer the following questions:

   a. Who owns the company?
   b. Who is the target customer?
   c. What classifications of merchandise does the company produce?
   d. What price line or lines are produced?
   e. Is production done in-house or by contractors?
   f. Where, geographically, is the production done?
   g. What is the annual sales volume?
   h. In what countries are the company's products sold?

3. Visit a major market center. Investigate the relationship between the sales reps and the manufacturers they represent.

4. In a store where you work or shop, find out which items are private labels and which are branded. Approximately what percentage of each are present?

5. Where do you think the garment you are wearing right now was made? Check the label to see if you are correct. Compare results with other students.

6. Examine the labels of all the clothes in your closet. What percentage of your wardrobe is imported? Made in the U.S.A.?

7. If possible, ask a U.S. Customs Service agent to speak to your class. Find out how apparel products are processed for entry into the United States. Or ask the import coordinator for a manufacturer to visit and explain his or her job responsibilities.

8. Take a computer tour of the WWW via the Internet. Visit the sites suggested in this chapter. What useful information can you find?

9. Does a store where you work or shop record prices using bar codes? Ask how they use the information they gather. Are there other advantages?

Government Regulations and Labeling: Communicating to Consumers

Chapter Objectives

1. Discuss the requirements of federal laws for apparel labeling and safety.
2. Recognize standard care symbols.
3. Identify business practices required by federal laws that affect the apparel industry.
4. Understand the impact of voluntary label information on consumer perceptions of quality.

Government regulations on apparel products range from those requiring informative labeling on garments to those providing assurances to the consumer that products will not present hazardous risk.

In addition to regulations specific to apparel labeling, the U.S. government has laws governing safe and fair business practices that affect the apparel industry and its workers. Companies must stay abreast of federal regulations in order to comply with all requirements (see Related Resources: Regulations).*

Ready-to-wear garments contain a variety of labels that convey information to those evaluating apparel quality. Labels provide a means for the consumer to learn about the garment and assist the consumer in making informed decisions about selecting and caring for clothing. Beyond the voluntary information that may be included, clearly and accurately written labels reflect the requirements of a variety of government regulations written on behalf of the U.S. consumer. These regulations apply to all apparel products made in and imported into the United States. Apparel destined for other countries may need to meet the requirements of different labeling and other regulations. For example, some countries limit or prohibit the use of certain chemicals (for example, azo dyestuffs, formaldehyde, heavy metals, ozone depleting substances) in apparel products.

REGULATIONS ON APPAREL LABELING

U.S. law mandates that all apparel sold in the United States contain permanent labels that fulfill the requirements of the Textile Fiber Products Identification Act and the Care Labeling Rule. Garments made of wool or a wool blend must conform to the requirements of the Wool Products Labeling Act. Garments fully or partially made of fur must conform to the Fur Products Labeling Act. Garments containing feathers or down must meet the requirements of the Guides for Feather and Down Products Industry. Silk apparel must conform to the Silk Labeling Regulation. All these regulations are administered by the **Federal Trade Commission (FTC)**. To obtain copies of the regulations, contact the Federal Trade Commission (FTC), Washington, D.C. 20580. URL: http://www.ftc.gov.

Information may be woven in or printed on the label (see Chapter 8), and labels may be attached in a variety of ways (see Chapter 11). Care labels must be permanently affixed and must remain legible throughout the useful life of the garment. FTC regulations specify the location of fiber i.d. labels inside the center back neckline or, if the garment has no neck, in a conspicuous location elsewhere inside or

outside the garment; care labels usually share these locations. For packaged garments, both the garment and packaging must be labeled unless the garment's label is visible through the package. This primarily applies to packaged underwear and other accessories.

Textile Fiber Products Identification Act

The **Textile Fiber Products Identification Act** (16 CFR Part 303), or **TFPIA** became effective in 1960 (last amended in 1986). The TFPIA is commonly called "Fiber I.D. Regs" in the industry, but it involves more than just fiber identification. It requires labels to disclose three things to consumers: (1) fiber content, (2) manufacturer or importer, and (3) country of origin. TFPIA labeling must be permanently affixed to all garments sold in the United States.

Fiber Content Identification. A garment's **fiber content** affects its appearance, ease of care, comfort, durability, and cost (see Chapter 7). Labels meeting fiber i.d. requirements disclose the fiber content as a percentage of each fiber in the garment, in order of predominance by weight (Figure 2–1). The percentage must be accurate within 3% (with a zero tolerance for 100% contents). The label must list any fiber constituting less than 5% of the total weight as *other fiber* unless the fiber makes a significant contribution to the performance of the garment. For example, spandex, is identified because it affects elasticity even if present as only a small portion of the total fiber used. Garments of unknown fiber content must be so labeled; for example, *5% undetermined fibers*.

The fibers used in garment trim, such as lace or ribbon, need not be identified if they cover less than 15% of the garment's surface area, but the fiber content label must include the term *exclusive of decoration*. If fiber ornamentation, such as embroidery, constitutes less than 5% of the total weight, it need not be identified, but the label should read *exclusive of ornamentation*. The label should identify the fiber

---

* For more information, refer to the Code of Federal Regulations (CFR), the Federal Register, and other U.S. government publications. For a complete list of government publications, visit URL: http://www.access.gpo.gov/su_docs. For information on U.S. Customs Service regulations applicable to imported apparel, see Chapter 1.

Figure 2–1 Examples of apparel labels.

content of linings or interlinings separately from that of the garment.

The fiber i.d. regs require that labels refer to fibers by generic names, in English. A **generic name**, as established by the FTC, denotes a family of fibers with a similar chemical composition. Also allowed are non-English or non-U.S. names (for example *wolle* for wool, *coton* or *baumwolle* for cotton, *soie* for silk, and *polyamide* for nylon) as long as they appear in conjunction with the English generic name. Increased global trade makes this a common practice.

The law also permits a trademark to accompany the generic name. A **trademark** is the registered brand name for the generic fiber made by a particular producer. (Table 7-2 in Chapter 7 gives information on many generic fibers.) For example, *polyester* is a generic name; *Dacron* is a trademark for polyester fibers produced by DuPont. The trademark and generic name must appear in lettering of the same size and importance and on the same side of the label. In addition, labels may contain nondeceptive descriptions of fibers in conjunction with their generic names. For example, the words *combed* or *Pima* may be used to describe finer grades of cotton; the terms *worsted* or *Merino* to describe premium wools, and terms such as *HWM* or *viscose* to differentiate rayon fibers. The law forbids terms implying the presence of fibers which are not a part of the garment and terms which are promotional in nature. For example, the term *silky luster* may not be used to describe rayon fibers.

Most manufacturers accept the fiber content information provided by their domestic suppliers, and most consumers do not question the fiber content on the labels of the garments they buy. Imported fabrics, however, are generally tested to confirm fiber content due to U.S. Customs regulations. Occasionally, mislabeling occurs. For example, a garment labeled *cashmere* may contain sheep's wool instead of fibers from the Kashmir goat. Another form of mislabeling uses the correct fiber names but inflates the percentage of one of the fibers. An example is heather-toned fabric (such as the fleece used to make gray sweats), which gets its unique appearance from an intimate blend of different fibers. It is difficult to maintain control over the exact percentage of the different fibers from roll to roll. Some trade organizations, such as the Wool Bureau and Cotton, Inc., perform laboratory analyses of random garment samples to police the accuracy of fiber content labels. Likewise, stringent regulations are applied by U.S. Customs to the accuracy of labels on imported apparel products.

Country-of-Origin Identification. Labels on apparel sold in the United States must identify **country of origin**, or where the garment was produced.

Because of perceptions about the quality of imported apparel and the effect of apparel imports on the U.S. economy, country of origin is a noteworthy part of apparel labeling for customers who want to "buy American." On the other hand, many consumers, especially younger ones who identify closely with the concept of a global community, may not perceive country of origin as important in making a purchase decision.

Luxury imported apparel constitutes a limited portion of total imports. Unlike low-price imports, consumers perceive these goods to be of high quality because of the mystique of the label, for example, *Made in France* or *Made in Italy*. Many luxury imports indeed do possess high quality, especially those made of natural resources that are the specialties of certain nations. For instance, wools from Britain, silks from China, linens from Ireland, leathers from Italy, and cottons from Egypt are among the finest available. In other cases, luxury goods represent uncommon quality in labor, made possible by generations of experience in a particular craft and an emphasis on factors other than lowering costs and increasing production volume. For example, London is known for its exquisite menswear tailoring and Paris for its couture fashions.

Low-price imports constitute the majority of apparel imports into the United States (see Chapter 1). Consumers often associate these low-price imports with low quality and low fashion appeal. However, *country of origin is not a valid clue to quality*; no consistent evidence exists to show that one country of origin indicates higher or lower quality than another. The sophistication, fashion appeal, fit, and durability of low-price imported apparel have improved dramatically so that stereotypes about low-price imported apparel are no longer valid. By the same token, although many U.S. manufacturers have excellent quality records, others have low quality records. High quality and low quality result from conformity or nonconformity to quality standards, not from country of origin. By setting appropriate standards and maintaining them, manufacturers anywhere in the world can produce quality apparel.

Since 1984, garments made in the United States must bear a label reading *Made in U.S.A.* And garments made in the United States of non-U.S. materials are labeled *Made in U.S.A. of imported fabric*. To determine country of origin, the manufacturer is required to name the country where the garment (or fabric) was last substantially transformed. For example, if most of the garment is assembled predominantly in another country, the label must read *Made in (name of other country), finished in U.S.A.* Clothing made completely in other countries must be labeled *Made in (name of country)*. Chapter 98/Item 807 goods of U.S. fabric that are cut and sent offshore to be sewn are labeled *Made in (name of country where assembled) of U.S. materials*. Descriptions in mail-order catalogs also must disclose whether garments are made in the United States or imported and whether the fabric is domestic or imported. In today's global economy, the fiber, yarn, fabrication, and finishing of the cloth, and the cutting, sewing, and wet processing of the garment could take place in two or more different countries, muddying the country of origin issue.

Manufacturer Identification.   All garments must contain labels identifying their manufacturer. (For many imports, the name of the "Importer of Record" is substituted for the manufacturer.) The manufacturer's current identification number as registered with the FTC or brand if it is registered with the FTC must appear on the label; either can be used. The reputation of the manufacturer who produced the garment can influence the consumer's perception of the quality of the garment if the name is also listed, because consumers expect garments made by a specific manufacturer to be of consistent quality.

A manufacturer's, retailer's, or importer's registered identification number is the number you see following the letters **RN (registered number)** on garment labels. A manufacturer may have more than one RN for various divisions. Some older manufacturers have a WPL, or Wool Products Labeling, number instead of an RN number. The RN or WPL pinpoints the maker of the garment, although it can be confusing for a manufacturing retailer using a contractor. Does the contractor's number get used or the retailer's? Some manufacturers put their own RN on the label plus an additional number which denotes the contractor who sewed the garment.

RNs and WPLs enable consumers to determine the producer of a garment, should the need arise. Table 2–1 contains a list of a few prominent manufacturers and their RN/WPL numbers. The U.S. Department of Commerce plans to make the entire RN database available on the Internet soon. In the meantime, *The RN and WPL Encyclopedia* can be obtained for about $250 from Reed Reference Publishing, 121 Chanlon Road, New Providence, NJ 07974.

Wool Products Labeling Act

Since 1939 (last amended in 1986), the **Wool Products Labeling Act (WPLA)** has regulated the labeling of garments containing hair fibers. It is commonly called the "Wool Act" in the industry. The terms *wool* and *pure wool* refer to wool fibers that have not previously been made into a woven fabric.

Table 2–1   Examples of RN and WPL Numbers

Four-In-Hand Shop Ties Unl	RN39323
Four-O-Eight Fashion Inc	RN22921
Fourres Sport Walt Stielf Ltd	RN44959
Foursome Fashion Inc	RN49874
Fourteen Carrot Inc	RN 75117
Fourth Avenue Contemporary Sportswear	RN 70435
The Fourth Little Pig	RN 69904
Foushee Mfg Co	RN59188
Fowles & Company	WPL09511
Fownes Bros & Co Inc	WPL09522

New wool and *virgin wool* refer to fibers that have not previously been processed in any way. *Lamb's wool* comes from animals younger than seven months old; because it is the first shearing, it is finer and softer than other wool. *Recycled wool* refers to wool previously fabricated, possibly used, and then reclaimed into fiber form. Recycled wool, also called *shoddy*, represents lower aesthetic quality than new fibers; otherwise, it is as warm to wear as new wool. Recycled wool is confined to interlinings and, occasionally, outer fabrics for low-price coats.

Fur Products Labeling Act

The **Fur Products Labeling Act (FPLA)** regulates the labeling of garments made of fur still attached to the animal skin. It is commonly called the "Fur Act" in the industry. The act, in place since 1952 (last amended in 1980), requires fur products to carry a label bearing the English name of the animal and only that name. It also requires the label to indicate the country of origin of the fur. The label must disclose if the fur is waste fur or has been used, damaged, dyed, bleached, or otherwise treated to artificially change the color.

Guides for Feather and Down Products

The **Guides for the Feather and Down Products Industry** contains regulations for feather- and down-filled apparel. These guidelines, the latest set promulgated in 1971, establish definitions to be used in labeling feather and down products. For example, the terms *down* (the undercoating of waterfowl) and *feathers* (the outer covering of fowl) are clearly differentiated, as are related terms and tolerances. Products made of crushed, damaged, or used feathers or down must be so labeled. Labels also must not misrepresent the content of any filling by erroneously suggesting that it contains feathers or down, or that it contains feathers or down from a particular type of fowl, or that the product has been chemically treated to improve its performance, if such is not the fact.

Silk Labeling Regulation

In 1932, the **Silk Labeling Regulation** ruled that any product labeled *pure silk* or *pure dye silk* could contain no more than 15% weighting if black and no more than 10% weighting for other colors. Such weighting, once a common treatment done by soaking the silk in a solution of metallic salts, increases the weight and improves the hand and dyeability of silk. However, weighted silk is less durable and wrinkles more easily. Little silk on today's market is weighted.

Care Labeling Rule

The **Care Labeling Rule**, titled Care Labeling of Textile Wearing Apparel and Certain Piece Goods (16 CFR Part 423), has been in effect since 1972 (last amended in 1984). It requires that apparel carry a permanently affixed care label providing full instructions for the regular care of the garment. A care label is an implied warranty by the manufacturer that if the customer follows the care instructions, the garment will retain its appearance. The rule requires the manufacturer to recommend only one care method, although other methods may work as well. The care label must clearly and thoroughly tell the customer how to care for the garment. It must specify washing, bleaching, drying, ironing, and/or dry-cleaning procedures and warn against any part of the prescribed care procedure that would harm the garment or others being cleaned with it. The rule does not allow care labels that are promotional in nature; for example, *Never Needs Ironing* is unacceptable.

All ready-to-wear apparel sold to the public must be permanently care labeled, with the exception of garments that withstand any care method and items such as hosiery on which a label would detract from appearance or usefulness. However, such garments must provide care information to the customer on the product package or on a temporary care label. Garments consisting of more than one piece require only one care label, although a label in each piece is preferable. If the manufacturer locates care information on the back of a label, the front must state *Over For Care, Care Information on Reverse Side,* or a similar instruction.

Care or **refurbishing** plays an important role in maintaining the existing quality of a garment. Ideally, the care label recommends a care method that minimizes shrinkage, color loss, and deterioration of the garment. Manufacturers that impart an understanding of appropriate care procedures to consumers through appropriate care labeling avoid returns of garments that did not perform well because of improper care.

Some consumers use care labels in evaluating ready-to-wear for purchase. For example, one consumer avoids buying garments that require ironing or dry-cleaning, while another expects such care requirements. In either case, the care label affects the consumer's perception of the quality and/or performance of the garment. Care labels allow the consumer to estimate the maintenance costs for the garment, which influence the garment's ultimate cost and value.

Reasonable Basis for Care Labels. The Care Labeling Rule requires apparel manufacturers to have a reasonable basis for the care instructions they recommend. A **reasonable basis** includes evidence such as tests, current technical literature, past experience, or industry experience. For example, the manufacturer should have proof that washing will harm a garment that is labeled *Dry Clean Only*. However, if the label states *Dry Clean* without the *Only*, proof is not necessary.

Only the apparel manufacturer possesses complete information about the garment and all its components. Therefore, it makes sense that the apparel manufacturer is responsible for determining a safe care method for the garment. Testing the ability of the garment to withstand the recommended care procedure is important, even though testing increases costs. Accurate care labeling pays for itself in the form of fewer returns and more satisfied customers. Garments with inaccurate labels that suggest damaging care methods lead to dissatisfied customers.

Some manufacturers use care label instructions written for a particular fabric by its producer. This works if the only raw material required to make the garment is the fabric. When other fabrics or trim items are added to the mix, preparing care instructions becomes complicated. In these cases, the apparel manufacturer conducts research and makes a determination about the most appropriate care label instructions according to how the components interact with each other. For instance, do the interfacing and shoulder pads withstand the same care as the body fabric? Will the findings and trim accept the same care as the fabric? For example, the thread used to sew together the sweater shown in Figure 2–2 shrank when washed, distorting the armscye (armhole) seams. Although the care method suggested on the label did not harm the sweater fabric, it made the sweater

Figure 2–2 Sleeve and body of garment distorted by thread that shrank when garment was laundered according to the care method recommended on the label.

unwearable because the thread did not perform the same as the sweater.

Low labeling of care instructions is sometimes a problem, particularly for manufacturers and retailers importing apparel. **Low labeling** involves recommending a more conservative care method than the garment requires. Manufacturing personnel in other countries who do not have an extensive knowledge of U.S. care label regulations or U.S. consumer laundering practices do their best to write appropriate instructions, but this is difficult as they have little experience with U.S. laundering practices. For example, in some Middle Eastern countries fabric is often dyed using manual methods. Many of the dyestuffs will not retain color in warm- or hot-water laundering. For this reason all care labels for garments made of these fabrics are written with *Machine wash cold* instructions. This is low labeling as some of the fabric colors do not experience a color loss in warm- or hot-water laundering when tested.

Care Symbols. A voluntary standard that provides a set of **care symbols** and a system for their use has been carefully developed by ASTM Committee D-13.62 on Care Labeling to indicate to consumers the recommended care for apparel and other textile products (Figure 2–3). In 1996 the FTC approved the ASTM symbols as the official U.S. care symbols and allowed their use as of July 1, 1997 without any accompanying words on the label. During the first 18 months, while the use of symbols is phased in, detachable information that provides the corresponding written care instructions must be attached. Other countries are using similar care symbol systems, but a

single, consistent set of care symbols recognized internationally does not exist at the time of this writing, although that is the ultimate goal. Several countries participated in the development of the ASTM symbols, a step in the direction of true global interaction.

The ASTM voluntary system of care symbols consolidates the common elements from the systems of several different countries. The system uses five basic symbols—a washtub shape representing washing, a triangle representing bleaching, a square representing drying, an iron representing ironing, and a circle representing dry-cleaning. An *X* over the symbol means "do not use it" or "do not do it" *and may be used only when the procedure will damage the apparel item.* If dots are added to the symbols, the number of dots indicates the recommended temperature of the procedure, with more dots representing a higher temperature or heat setting. The machine cycles are represented by underlines, or "minus signs" below the symbol. "Minus signs" under the symbol reduce the action of the appliance from the normal cycle to the permanent press cycle (one underline or minus sign) and to the gentle/delicate cycle (two underlines or minus signs).

Care symbols overcome language barriers in providing care instructions for garments that are imported or exported, which is important as international trade in apparel continues to grow. These symbols are useful only to the extent that consumers understand them, which at the present time in the United States is not the case. The Federal Trade Commission is coordinating a multifaceted educational campaign to make consumers aware of care symbols and their meanings. This includes participation by educators at all levels, the extension service, ASTM, professional organizations, apparel and textile manufacturers and suppliers, retailers, the laundry products industry, and the home appliance industry.

Words Accompanying Care Symbols. ASTM Committee D-13 has developed a list of *Additional Words to Use With Care Symbols* (Table 2–2). This list provides supplemental information to be used with care symbols, when necessary. This allows all manufacturers to write consistent care labels and simplifies the production and use of care labels.

The Care Labeling Rule requires that all washing instructions suggest a particular method of washing— machine wash or hand wash. Drying instructions also must suggest a method—tumble dry, line dry, or dry flat.

The label must be specific about the variation of the method to use if other variations harm the garment or others being cleaned with it. For example, if a label says *Machine Wash,* the consumer can assume that any water temperature and cycle is safe. Otherwise, the label must state, for instance, *Machine*

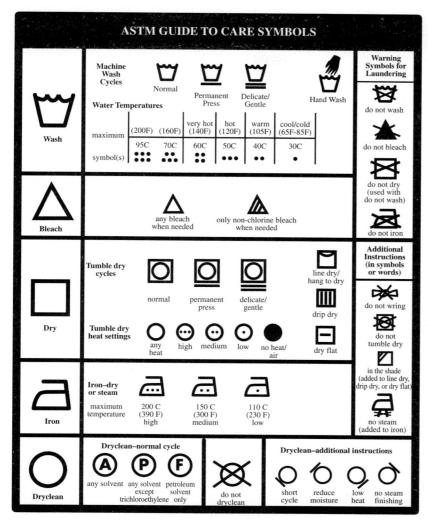

Figure 2–3   ASTM guide to care symbols. *(This chart has been reproduced by Prentice Hall under license from ASTM. The chart is reprinted from the ASTM Care Labeling System D 5489, Standard Guide for Permanent Care Labels on Consumer Textile Products, copyright 1996 American Society for Testing and Materials, 100 Barr Harbor Drive, West Conshohocken, PA 19428, USA (phone: 610-832–9585, fax 610-832–9555). Copies of the official standard should be obtained directly from ASTM.)*

Wash, Cold, Delicate Cycle. If the label does not prohibit bleach in conjunction with washing instructions, the consumer can assume that any form of bleach is safe. If the garment could harm other garments being washed with it, the label must so warn; for example, *Wash Separately* or *Wash with Like Colors.* The label qualifies the type of solvent or other aspect of the dry-cleaning process. If trim on the garment requires special care, the label must warn *Remove Trim.* Warnings about damaging the apparel need be given only for variations of the care procedure recommended on the label, not for all possible procedures. In other words, if the label states *Dry Flat,* it does not have to warn *Do Not Tumble Dry.*

Consumer Responsibilities.   Many consumers do not read care labels. Other consumers read care labels but do not trust them. They may have had an experience in which following the care label led to garment failure. Or they may have successfully used a care method other than the one suggested on the label. Although consumer "guessing" about the appropriate care for garments may meet with occasional success, it may also lead to ruining garments through inappropriate care. Consumers use information such as the fiber content of the garment to decide how to care for a garment. But variations in fibers, yarns, fabrications, and finishes that the consumer cannot see may cause the garment to require a different care method than the fiber content might suggest. For instance, although it is true that most cotton fabrics are washable, the dye in some cotton fabrics bleeds when washed at hot water temperatures and thus requires cool or warm water temperature. Or, a garment that might otherwise be washable may contain buttons, trim, or other components that are not washable. Consumers cannot tell these things from the fiber content label or by looking at or feeling a garment.

Based on the wording of the federal regulation and the small amount of space available on a care label,

Table 2–2 Additional Words to Use with Care Symbols

Federal Trade Commission Standard Terms	Terms in Common Usage
Preliminary and Laundering Instructions	
do not have commercially laundered	close zippers
Small load	do not pretreat
Separately	do not soak
With like colors	remove buttons
Wash inside out	remove lining
	remove shoulder pads
	remove trim
	wash dark colors separately
warm rinse	wash once before wearing
cold rinse	wash separately
rinse thoroughly	wash with like colors
no spin or do not spin	do not use fabric softener
no wring or do not wring*	remove promptly
no wring or twist*	rinse twice
damp wipe only	use oversize washing machine
Bleaching (all terms represented as symbols)	
Drying, All Methods	
no heat*	
remove promptly	tumble dry, air*
line dry in the shade*	do not tumble dry*
line dry away from heat	reshape and dry flat
block to dry	block flat to dry
smooth by hand	
Ironing and Pressing	
iron wrong side only	do not iron decal
no steam or do not steam*	iron reverse side only
steam only	iron right side only
iron damp	warm iron if needed
use press only	use press cloth
Wash or Dryclean (can be represented by symbols)	
Dry-cleaning, All Methods	
professionally dry-clean	use clear solvent
short cycle*	clear distilled solvent rinse
minimum extraction	
reduced or low moisture*	low heat*
tumble warm	
tumble cool	
cabinet dry warm	
cabinet dry cool	
steam only	
no steam or do not steam	no steam finishing*
steam only	
use fluorocarbon solvent	
Additional Instructions	
	Send to a professional leather cleaner. Do not wash or dry-clean by fabric methods.
	fur clean

Note. This guide uses symbols to represent many textile refurbishing procedures. Additional words may be needed to clarify specific care procedures. This table of additional words to use with care symbols includes the remaining terms listed in the Federal Trade Commission Care Labeling Glossary of Standard Terms and additional terms in common usage. These terms are illustrative only and are not meant to be an exhaustive list of all terms that might be appropriate or necessary. In general, whatever additional words are needed to state a care procedure that will result in the adequate refurbishment of the item should be used.

*=care instruction may be reported in words or a symbol.

apparel manufacturers list only one possible set of care instructions. Other safe care methods sometimes exist besides the one on the label. Consumers can use the one listed on the label or use an alternative method at their own risk. Rather than taking care decisions into their own hands, consumers should communicate with manufacturers and retailers regarding questions about or dissatisfaction with suggested care methods to encourage accurate and useful care labeling.

REGULATIONS ON APPAREL SAFETY

Unsafe clothing, especially clothing for infants and children, may cause serious injury and even death. The **Consumer Product Safety Commission (CPSC),** a division of the FTC, enforces the Flammable Fabrics Act, which regulates clothing flammability, and Regulations for Toys and Children's Articles, which govern sharpness and choking hazards. The CPSC's *Guidelines for Drawstrings on Children's Outerwear* suggests ways for manufacturers to reduce strangling and entanglement risks involving drawstrings. To obtain copies of the regulations, contact the **Consumer Product Safety Commission (CPSC),** East West Towers, 4330 East West Highway, Bethesda, MD 20814.

Flammable Fabrics Act

The **Flammable Fabrics Act,** established in 1953 (last amended in 1988), classifies fabrics according to how fast they burn under controlled testing conditions (ASTM D-1230). The regulations apply to clothing textiles, plastics, carpets and rugs, and mattresses and mattress pads. Title 16 CFR 1610 of the Flammable Fabrics Act sets forth standards for rating wearing apparel fabrics as follows:

- *Class 1*: normal flammability (suitable for clothing) Flame spread is 3.5 seconds or more for non-raised fiber fabrics and 7.0 seconds or more for raised fiber fabrics.
- *Class 2*: intermediate flammability. Flame spread is from 4 to 7 seconds and the base fabric ignites or fuses.
- *Class 3*: rapid and intense burning (unsuitable for clothing). Flame spread is 3.5 seconds or less for non-raised fiber fabrics and 4.0 seconds or less for raised fiber fabrics and the intensity of flame is such as to ignite or fuse the base fabric.

The purpose of these standards is to discourage the use of any dangerously flammable fabrics to make apparel.

The Flammable Fabrics Act, 16 CFR 1615 and 1616, establishes stringent requirements for infants' and children's sleepwear. Infants' and children's sleepwear includes clothing sizes 0–6X and 7–14 worn primarily for sleeping and related activities. Included are nightgowns, pajamas, robes, and other sleep-related accessories, excluding diapers and underwear.

The law requires that each garment be permanently labeled with a Garment Production Unit number (GPU) or style number and a Fabric Production Unit number (FPU) or style number to identify its producers in case of a fire-related incident. Manufacturers are required to retain records on each piece of children's sleepwear produced to verify compliance with the law. The law does not require labels on children's sleepwear to inform the consumer that the garment complies with federal regulations, but many manufacturers indicate compliance as a service to the consumer and to promote the garment.

Recent Amendment. In 1996, the CPSC voted to amend the children's sleepwear standard under the Flammable Fabrics Act. The amendments permit the sale of tight-fitting children's sleepwear and sleepwear for infants aged nine months or under, *even if the garments do not meet the minimum standards for flame resistance ordinarily applicable to such sleepwear.* The new amendments become effective in 1998.

For some time, many parents have been circumventing the intent of the children's sleepwear regulations by allowing their children to sleep in loose-fitting, 100% cotton T-shirts and other 100% cotton non-sleepwear garments such as underwear or daywear. The CPSC felt that parents should be given the option to buy tight-fitting, 100% untreated cotton sleepwear as opposed to the non-sleepwear garments, considering that the data show that no ignitions have resulted when children wear tight-fitting sleepwear. Most deaths and injuries are occurring when children sleep in loose-fitting, non-sleepwear garments, typically T-shirts. Tight fit appears to be a more important factor than the flame resistance of the fabric because (1) sleepwear that is tight fitting is less likely than loose-fitting sleepwear to come into contact with an ignition source; (2) even when ignited, tight-fitting sleepwear is not apt to burn readily because less air is available to feed the fire, and the proximity of the skin soaks up heat, retarding the spread of fire.

The new regulation exempts infant sleepwear garments from the sleepwear flammability requirements if they contain a label stating that they are sized for infants 9 months or under. The logic here is that such sleepwear is worn predominantly by infants 6 months old and younger, who are insufficiently mobile to expose themselves to sources of fire.

The changes will be accompanied by an information and education campaign to help consumers understand why the untreated cotton sleepwear garments being allowed on the market must fit children snugly; why certain types of sleepwear garments will remain flame retardant polyester or treated cotton; and why loose-fitting, untreated cotton garments should not be used as sleepwear. Proper labeling will remind consumers of the purpose of the regulations—to protect children. Retailers must understand why it is important to display complying sleepwear separately from noncomplying underwear and daywear that could be used for sleepwear, so that consumers will not inadvertently buy a product that is not deemed safe as sleepwear. The CPSC will continue to monitor fire injury data to insure that the relaxation of the standard does not reduce children's safety.

Regulations for Toys and Children's Articles

For the safety of infants and children, some manufacturers and retailers have adopted the CPSC **Regulations for Toys and Children's Articles** (in particular, Part 1501 Method for identifying toys and other articles intended for use by children under 3 years of age which present choking, aspiration, or ingestion hazards because of small parts; and Parts 1500.48/1500.49 Technical requirements for determining a sharp point/sharp edge in toys and other articles intended for use by children under 8 years of age). For consumer safety reasons, some apparel manufacturers and retailers have adopted these toy test methods and standards for nonfunctional or decorative trim items found on infants' and children's clothing due to the lack of similar regulations for apparel. Of particular importance are the size, pull strength, and sharpness of trim items. If the item is able to be pulled off a garment by a child it must be large enough to not be swallowed and choke the child and round enough to not scratch the child. For example, safety pins used to attach bows and flowers to infants' or children's garments (for easy removal when the garment is washed) could seriously injure a child. Ideally, items will be attached strongly enough to not be pulled off at all.

The CPSC regulations have been applied to decorative items only because buttons and snaps, while small and potentially dangerous, are considered necessary for ease of dressing. However, some manufacturers and retailers have adopted the regulations for functional small parts as well. In 1996, ASTM adopted a provisional standard for the determination of snap attachment strength, the first standardized test method to determine the number of pounds required to pull snaps from infants' garments. The new standard allows infants' garments to be tested consistently for this potentially serious choking hazard, using a special tool designed for this purpose.

Guidelines for Drawstrings on Children's Outerwear

In 1995, the CPSC issued **Guidelines for Drawstrings on Children's Outerwear** to help prevent children from strangling or getting entangled in drawstrings at the neck and waist or bottom of clothing such as jackets and sweatshirts. Drawstrings on children's clothing can possibly lead to injury or death when they catch on playground equipment, bus doors, fences, or cribs. *Note:* The drawstring guidelines are not mandatory as of this writing but many manufacturers voluntarily follow them. The guidelines suggest substitute closures such as snaps, buttons, Velcro®, and elastic as alternatives to hood and neck drawstrings. Hood and neck drawstrings in existing garments should be removed. The guidelines suggest waist/bottom drawstrings that extend no more than 3 inches out of the garment when it is fully expanded; shortening the length of drawstrings reduces the risk of entanglement. The drawstring should be sewn to the garment at its midpoint so the string cannot be pulled out longer on one side. The guidelines also recommend eliminating toggles and knots at the ends of drawstrings.

REGULATIONS ON APPAREL INDUSTRY BUSINESS PRACTICES

The U.S. government maintains jurisdiction over a number of regulations that affect business practices of American-based companies. These regulations affect not only individual workers but whole companies in the apparel industry as well as in other industries. The Occupational Safety and Health Act seeks to ensure a safe and healthy environment for U.S. workers. The Fair Labor Standards Act guarantees a minimum wage and prohibits unfair labor practices such as the use of child labor. The Equal Employment Opportunity Commission enforces the Civil Rights Act, the Age Discrimination in Employment Act, and the Equal Pay Act, which seek to eliminate discrimination in the workplace. The Immigration Reform and Control Act bars illegal immigrants from working in the United States. And the Environmental Protection Agency monitors and regulates the impact of companies' activities on the environment through the Pollution Prevention Act, the Clean Air Act, and the Clean Water Act.

Consumers may assume that products labeled *Made in the U.S.A.* were made in compliance with

U.S. laws. (The rare exceptions are federal violations.) However, many garments are produced in foreign countries, where expectations may be much lower and legislation governing manufacturing may be limited or nonexistent. Although not required, responsible and ethical U.S. manufacturers and retailers voluntarily comply with the spirit and intent of U.S. laws when conducting business abroad. Potential buyers must clearly communicate to contractors their "standards of vendor engagement" and monitor foreign contractors periodically to ensure compliance with human rights and environmental impact standards. More and more companies are recognizing their responsibility in screening contractors. Recent news attention to **sweatshops** (factories in which the owner reaps profits from the sweat of the workers, who are under compensated), both in the United States and abroad, has made this a hot topic.

Occupational Safety and Health Act

The **Occupational Safety and Health Act** of 1970 seeks to ensure safe and healthful working conditions for every working man and woman in the United States. The **Occupational Safety and Health Administration (OSHA)** enforces the act. Each state has the right to establish and manage its own occupational safety and health programs as long as its rules are "at least as effective" as those enacted by the federal program. About half the states have opted to institute their own programs; therefore, some requirements vary from state to state. For more information, contact the Occupational Safety and Health Administration (OSHA) of the U.S. Department of Labor, 200 Constitution Avenue, N.W., Washington, D.C. 20210. URL: http://www.osha.gov.

Some retailers and manufacturers conduct factory or site audits to ensure that U.S. contractors comply with OSHA regulations. A quality engineer or auditor makes an on-site visit to a contractor to survey the facilities and working conditions before reaching an agreement to do business. The auditor usually has an extensive checklist of health- and safety-related items such as uncluttered fire exits, appropriate number of fire exits per total number of employees, clean and uncluttered work and walk areas, adequate ventilation to ensure indoor air quality, and adequate lighting. If a contractor does not comply with OSHA regulations, the retailer or manufacturer might require the improvements be made before agreeing to a purchase contract, or in the case of excessive violations, not conduct any business with the contractor at all.

Ergonomics, the study of people in relationship to their working environment, has become one of the most prominent health and safety issues in the textiles and apparel industry. OSHA regulations require that manufacturers provide every possible way to reduce work-related injuries. In particular, OSHA has increased its emphasis on reducing cumulative trauma disorders (CTDs) in the work force. CTDs include a number of injuries, such as chronic back pain, tendonitis, carpal tunnel syndrome, bursitis, and tennis elbow, related to repetitive strains. Two particular job categories in the textile and apparel industry are prone to CTDs—certain sewing machine operator jobs and jobs requiring extended computer use. To protect the health and productivity of their workers, to reduce workers' compensation claims, and to avoid OSHA fines for willful violations, apparel manufacturers are paying attention to ergonomics. While a program of ergonomics may require an investment in new equipment and training, this pays off many times over by reducing the costs associated with employee injuries.

Ergonomics and safety engineers concentrate on the design of equipment and tools (computer information displays, sewing work aids, pressing aids, hand tools), organization of work (arrangement of tasks into jobs, work/rest cycles, and length of work shifts), work environment (noise, illumination, vibration, temperature), and other factors to reduce injuries. Ergonomic solutions include, for example, workstations, work-surface heights and angles, and chairs adjustable to fit individual workers (to avoid postures that cause excessive muscle fatigue and strain) and tool and handle designs requiring natural finger, hand, and arm positions. Tasks should be accomplished without excessive gripping, pinching, and pressing with the hands and fingers. Engineering solutions to ergonomic problems may be as simple as raising the foot pedal of a sewing machine so the operator can reach it better while maintaining a comfortable posture. Or they may be more complex, such as tilting a sewing machine toward the operator to allow the operator to sit up straight and still see the work in progress (Figure 2–4). In many cases, workers themselves are the best source of effective suggestions for ergonomic changes that are needed. For example, patternmakers observe work/rest cycles to avoid overuse of the wrists while creating patterns using the computer. They alternate patternmaking, which requires extensive computer mouse use, with specification writing, which requires planning, measuring, and measurement recording.

Fair Labor Standards Act

Since 1938, the **Fair Labor Standards Act (FLSA)** has required manufacturers to pay at least the minimum wage, to pay overtime for hours worked in excess of 40 hours per week, and to keep records on each employee regarding hours worked and pay. The

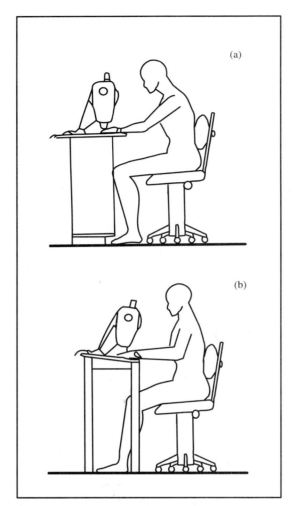

Figure 2–4 Operator in (a) adopts poor posture to see work, while ergonomic solution of tilting machine bed in (b) enables operator to sit up straight and still see work.

law prohibits oppressive child labor, minors under 16 from working in any manufacturing areas, and minors under age 18 from working in any hazardous occupation. The law also prohibits uncertified homework to make women's apparel. Selling or shipping **hot goods,** products made in violation of these regulations, is a federal offense. For more information, contact the Department of Labor (DOL), Wage and Hour Division, 200 Constitution Avenue N.W., Washington, D.C. 20210. URL: http://www.dol.gov.

Equal Employment Opportunity Commission Regulations

The **Equal Employment Opportunity Commission (EEOC)** oversees compliance with the **Civil Rights Act** of 1964, which prohibits employment discrimination based on race, color, religion, sex, or national origin. The EEOC also enforces the **Age Discrimination in Employment Act** of 1967, which protects employees 40 years of age or older, and the **Equal Pay Act** of 1963, which protects men and women who perform substantially equal work for the same company from sex-based wage discrimination. For more information, contact the Equal Employment Opportunity Commission (EEOC), 1801 L Street N.W., Washington, D.C. 20507.

Immigration Reform and Control Act

The **Immigration Reform and Control Act** of 1968 ensures that all employees of a company are either citizens of the United States or aliens authorized to work in the United States. Most textile and apparel companies use this act as the basis for their own internal policy requiring all potential employees to show proof of citizenship. In some widely publicized cases, certain apparel contractors have ignored this act and hired illegal aliens at low wages to work in unsafe and unhealthy conditions, in an attempt to produce apparel at low costs. The **Immigration and Naturalization Service (INS)** imposes substantial fines on both on the contractor and retailers who purchase apparel from such contractors, placing responsibility on both parties. For more information, contact the Immigration and Naturalization Service (INS) of the U.S. Department of Justice, 425 I Street N.W., Washington, D.C. 20536. URL: http://www.doj.gov.

Environmental Protection Agency Regulations

The **Environmental Protection Agency (EPA)** oversees compliance of the industry with laws including the **Pollution Prevention Act** of 1990, designed to reduce pollution at its source, the **Clean Air Act** of 1970, and the **Clean Water Act** of 1972. To conform to these requirements and to respond to consumer demand for environmentally friendly products, the apparel industry has implemented a number of so-called *green activities,* business practices that "help keep our planet green." Suppliers seek to reduce chemical emissions at every step of the textile and apparel pipeline—from the herbicides and pesticides used to grow natural fibers to the components used in dyeing, finishing, wet processing, laundry detergents, and dry-cleaning. Manufacturers continue to look for new ways to reduce the energy consumption required during the production process. And they seek to minimize the packaging of finished goods and to use packaging that can be recycled or that degrades rapidly. The development of new methods to recycle post-consumer-use clothing have recently made the news. Because most clothing eventually ends up in landfills, this area has much potential for reducing waste disposal. For more information, contact the Environmental Protection Agency (EPA), 401 M Street S.W., Washington, D.C. 20460. URL: http://www.epa.gov. Each state government also has its own environmental office.

- - - - - -

VOLUNTARY LABEL INFORMATION

Apparel labels contain a variety of information beyond that which is required by federal law, for example, brand, trademark, logo, warranty, certification, union label, and size. The following sections discuss voluntary label information and its impact on consumer perceptions.

Trademarks and Brands

A **trademark** is any brand name, word, or symbol such as a graphic logo used to identify and distinguish one manufacturer's products from another's. Trademarks registered with the **U.S. Patent and Trademark Office** include the ® symbol. The ™ symbol is sometimes used if the trademark is unregistered or state registered. For more information on trademarks, contact the U.S. Patent and Trademark Office of the U.S. Department of Commerce, Commissioner of Patents and Trademarks, Washington, D.C. 20231. URL: http://www.uspto.gov.

A registered trademark or identifying brand name on a garment often influences how the consumer perceives the quality of the garment. Manufacturers and retailers invest considerable effort in establishing stringent specifications and standards to produce high-quality branded products. If a producer builds a deserved reputation for quality apparel, a trademark or brand name serves as a cue to quality. Perhaps this explains in part the popularity of brand names, as they are one of the few point-of-sale cues customers have to predict functional performance at the point of sale (see Chapter 3). However, consumers may incorrectly associate a well-known brand name with a certain level of performance, just because the brand name is currently fashionable. A little-known brand name may provide equal or better quality than a well-known brand name, but some consumers hesitate to purchase the little-known brand name. Becoming familiar with brand names and the quality level with which they are generally associated is appropriate, but actual quality must be evaluated objectively.

Brands. Manufacturers develop **brands,** also called **name brands** and **national brands,** and make them available to any retailer who wants to buy them for resale to consumers. Brands became dominant in the ready-to-wear industry during the mid to late twentieth century. Examples of brand names include Lee, Levi's, Guess, Osh Kosh, and Liz Claiborne (Table 2–3).

Private Labels. Retailers develop and sell merchandise exclusive to their stores under **private labels,** also called **private brands** and **store brands** (see Chapter 1). A private label represents the retailer rather than a manufacturer. In many cases, customers are unaware that a particular private label belongs to the retailer because the names of most private labels sound just like national brands. Examples of private labels include J.C. Penney's Worthington® brand of womenswear, The Gap's Gapsport® brand of sportswear, and Hartmarx's Hickey-Freeman® brand of men's suits. Private labels featuring celebrity endorsements, such as Kathie Lee Gifford for Wal-Mart or Jaclyn Smith for KMart, are referred to as *signature labels* or *signature brands.*

Retailers have a great stake in ensuring the quality of private label merchandise, because consumers associate

Table 2–3 **Examples of Brand Names for Various Merchandise Classifications**

Levi's (jeans)
Lee (jeans)
Bali (bras)
Gunne Sax (dresses)
Chaus (women's sportswear)
Leslie Fay (dresses)
Jessica McClintock (bridal)
Campus Casuals (women's sportswear)
Izod (sportswear)
Ocean Pacific (sportswear)
Jockey (underwear)
Hanes (underwear)
Pendleton (wools)
Health-tex (children's)
London Fog (raincoats)
Esprit (junior's sportswear)
Vassarette (women's intimate apparel)
Guess (jeans)
Danskin (leotards)
Olga (women's intimate apparel)
Catalina (women's swimwear)
Van Heusen (men's shirts)
Carter's (children's)
Liz Claiborne (sportswear)

the quality level of the merchandise with the retailer, not the manufacturer. Retailers retain or lose customers depending on the strength or weakness of their private labels.

Licensing. Items that bear a famous name are not necessarily designed or manufactured by that individual. Designers and other individuals or companies may **license** their names, trademarks, or logos for use on merchandise produced by others. In a licensing agreement, the individual or company (*licensor*) is paid a fee by a manufacturer (*licensee*) for the privilege of affixing the licensor's name, trademark, or logo to the licensee's products. Licensors may or may not have input into the actual design of such products. However, they are usually concerned about the quality of the merchandise because it is a direct reflection on their names in the eyes of the public. Accessories, fragrances, and home furnishings are examples of products frequently bearing the licensed names of famous apparel designers. In fact, some high-fashion designers make more money from their licensing agreements than from the apparel segment of their business. The names of sports figures, movie and music stars, cartoon characters, and products such as the Coca-Cola soft drink and Crayola crayon brands are commonly licensed for use on apparel.

Counterfeit Goods. **Counterfeit goods** are fakes or copies of currently popular branded apparel, accompanied by the illegal use of the rightful producer's brand name or trademark. Counterfeit goods steal the profits of the legitimate manufacturer, diluting the reputation for quality and reducing the value of the brand name or trademark. If officials detect counterfeit goods, they confiscate the merchandise and prosecute those responsible.

Hang Ten's two feet, Izod's alligator, and Osh Kosh B'Gosh, Inc.'s triangle on the back of their overalls are all trademarks, registered with the U.S. Patent and Trademark Office; they cannot be copied legally. Some companies, such as Lee and Levi's (both known for the unique trademarked stitching on the back pockets of their jeans), Nike (known for the trademarked Swoosh design on the sides of their athletic shoes), and Ocean Pacific (with the registered OP trademark), have resorted to "fingerprinting" their labels. They print them with information that is invisible to the eye but readable by laser, enabling them to easily confirm suspected counterfeit goods bearing look-alike labels. If you walk the streets of New York City, you will see counterfeit Rolex brand watches, Gucci brand purses, and other counterfeit merchandise sold by street vendors. Many of these goods are produced overseas and sold through nontraditional outlets. However, occasionally a reputable retailer is

duped into buying counterfeit merchandise. This happened, for example, during the peak popularity of Calvin Klein brand jeans, when retailers were desperate for the product and some did not investigate their sources.

Knock-Offs. Knock-offs are entirely different from counterfeit goods. A **knock-off** is the copy or near-copy of a design under a different brand name. Firms that specialize in knock-offs often use less costly materials and streamline the design for fabric and labor efficiency, to produce designs resembling the original but at a much lower cost. For example, designer Victor Costa readily acknowledges knocking off the evening wear styles of couture designers. He produces his interpretations of the couture originals at a fraction of the cost, making dresses more affordable. No law prohibits knocking off the general idea of a design, a common practice in low- and moderate-price lines. In fact, to some extent, knock-offs enable consumers at all price levels to enjoy new fashion trends. Apparel designs are rarely patented or copyrighted; however, they are protected under fair trade rules. Thus, a knock-off that is an exact copy may not be legal, but a "near knock-off" that is substantially different than the original is permitted.

Warranties and Certifications

A warranty is a form of guarantee. All products come with an **implied warranty** that the product meets acceptable levels of performance. A garment must be suitable for the purpose for which it is marketed; for example, a competition swimsuit must not fall apart when it is worn in a swim meet. Beyond this, some products come with a **written warranty** on the label or hang tag stating that the product will perform at a certain level, for example, *Will not shrink more than 2%* or *Guaranteed not to fade*. Such written warranties are legally binding.

A **certification**, or **seal of approval**, indicates that the garment has met the certifying agency's standards for quality. Usually, no information about the standards is included on the label, only the fact that the certifying agency approved the garment. Therefore, a certification is only as good as the standards and the reputation of the agency issuing it. Some certifying agencies are independent; others exist to promote a specific fiber. Figure 2–5 contains examples of some well-known certification labels.

The *Woolmark* and the *Woolblend Mark* registered trademarks certify that the wool fibers contained in a garment meet the Wool Bureau's standards of quality for fiber content, colorfastness, abrasion resistance, tensile strength, dimensional stability, and other factors. The Wool Bureau also awards its *Superwash*

Figure 2–5 Certification labeling. *(Woolmark and Woolblend Mark courtesy of the Wool Bureau. Cotton Seal Symbol and NATURAL BLEND symbol courtesy of Cotton Incorporated. Masters of Linen symbol courtesy of Masters of Linen. Wear-Dated logo courtesy of Monsanto Chemical Company. Crafted With Pride registered certification mark courtesy of Crafted With Pride in U.S.A. Council. Approved Color Safe Identifier symbol courtesy of The Clorox Company (Textile Industry Affairs).)*

trademark label to washable wool apparel that meets quality standards.

The *Cotton Seal*, a registered trademark of Cotton Incorporated, identifies products made of 100% Upland cotton (a high-quality variety). The *NATURAL BLEND* trademark identifies products containing a minimum of 60% Upland cotton. The symbols certify a garment's naturalness and comfort. The

Cotton Seal is used only on products sold in the United States.

The *L* trademark symbol of the Masters of Linen certifies garments made from pure Western European linen and assures customers that the fabric has met rigid quality standards set for construction, colorfastness, dimensional stability, and strength.

Wear-Dated, a registered trademark of Monsanto, is a seal of approval that indicates the garment, which contains fibers made by Monsanto, has passed a series of laboratory tests. *Wear-Dated Apparel* meets standards for seam strength, colorfastness, shrinkage, and abrasion resistance. Monsanto fully guarantees the garment, not just the fabric, for one year.

The U.S. apparel industry promotes domestically made apparel by drawing attention to country of origin and relating it to quality. The impetus for promotional *Made in the U.S.A.* labeling resulted from surveys that suggested a majority of consumers perceive U.S.-made apparel to be of higher quality than foreign-made apparel. Several of these studies also suggested that many U.S. consumers did not notice country-of-origin labels when shopping. This prompted the implementation of advertising to focus consumer attention on country of origin in order to capitalize on some consumers' expressed preferences for domestically produced goods and to enhance the image of U.S.-made goods in the eyes of others. The *Crafted With Pride in the U.S.A.* registered certification mark campaign is the work of the **Crafted With Pride in U.S.A. Council.** It appeals to the patriotism of consumers as well as to their desire for value. The Crafted With Pride in U.S.A. Council also coordinates the advertisement of Miss America's and other celebrities' endorsements of U.S.-made apparel, featuring the theme *Made in the U.S.A.—It Matters to Me* and *What a Feeling—Made in the U.S.A.* Evidence suggests that since the Crafted With Pride campaign began, the amount of attention consumers pay to country of origin labeling has increased, and so have sales. For more information, contact the Crafted With Pride in U.S.A. Council, 1045 Avenue of the Americas, New York, NY 10018.

The Clorox Company recently introduced a new certification label called the "Color Safe Identifier." This label, designed primarily as a marketing tool for manufacturers and retailers, also functions as a consumer certification of bleaching safety. Manufacturers and retailers, whose garments comply with all FTC care labeling regulations, may enter into a licensing agreement with the Clorox Company for the use of the Color Safe Identifier symbols. These symbols, when used on a hang tag, call attention to the fact that any garment displaying the symbols may be washed in detergent and color-safe bleach. The program helps manufacturers and retailers to market the perception of quality, value, and durability while providing consumers with increased confidence in accurate, affirmative bleach instructions on care labels.

Union Made

Union labels are sewn into garments produced in union shops, or factories where the workers are union members. Union labels indicate that a garment was produced under fair labor practices as defined by the union. They offer assurance that the workers who made the garment were not mistreated or misused, as sometimes happens in apparel factories around the world where employees have few rights. And union labels represent the union members' pride in their work. According to consumers' attitudes toward labor unions, union labels affect their perceptions of a garment's quality.

Unions arose out of the factory system in the United States during the early part of the twentieth century. The factories that sprang up to meet the rising demand for ready-to-wear apparel in the late 1800s and early 1900s often operated as sweatshops. The factory owner reaped profits from the sweat of the workers, many of whom were newly arrived immigrants, both children and adults. Some owners took advantage of workers, who had few other employment options. People were overworked and underpaid in crowded, poorly lit, unsafe, and unsanitary conditions.

Labor unions were formed in the 1800s to organize apparel workers, but invariably they were small, isolated, and weak local entities that did not succeed in winning rights for workers. The first national union, the International Ladies Garment Workers Union, or ILGWU, was founded in 1900, uniting the many small unions into one. In 1914, a union formed to represent workers in the men's ready-to-wear industry. This union later joined with unions in the textile and shoe industries to become the Amalgamated Clothing and Textile Workers Union of America, or ACTWU. In 1995, the ILGWU and ACTWU merged to become the **Union of Needletrades, Industrial and Textile Employees**, or **UNITE**. UNITE is the fourth largest manufacturing union in the nation, powerful enough to fight for rights and job security for workers in the textile and apparel industries. Figure 2–6 shows the label of UNITE. For more information, contact the Union of Needletrades, Industrial and Textile Employees (UNITE), 1710 Broadway, New York, NY 10019.

Size

Manufacturers and retailers use sizes and size classifications as an assortment-planning device and as a

Figure 2–6 Union label. *(Courtesy of UNITE, the Union of Needletrades, Industrial and Textile Employees.)*

marketing tool; consumers use them in trying to locate a garment that fits. The industry offers a variety of sizes and size classifications to fit and appeal to the full range of consumers.

Size labeling suggests to consumers the suitability of a garment for their body dimensions. The labeled size of a garment is intended to help determine whether or not that particular garment will fit a particular individual. Sizes are grouped together into size classifications, according to the sex, age, and/or body type of consumers.

There are no officially recognized standards for apparel sizes in the United States. (For an in-depth discussion of sizing and fit, see Chapter 6.) Thus, sizes are unique to each company. Variations in size standards from company to company are partly the result of each firm's effort to develop a distinctive fit that differentiates their goods in the marketplace and fits their target consumers better than garments produced by the competition. Although the lack of size standardization often irritates consumers, it has advantages. The variety of cuts and fits produced by different manufacturers translates into such a variety of cuts and fits that consumers with any body type can find apparel that fits. If all clothing conformed to the same strict size standards, anyone with an other-than-average figure could not find clothing that fits.

SUMMARY

Federal laws require certain label information on all apparel products. Labels fulfilling the Textile Fiber Products Identification Act disclose the garment's fiber content, manufacturer, and country of origin. Labels list the fiber content by percentage in order of predominance by weight. The manufacturer's, retailer's, or importer's name, registered trademark, or RN (registered number)/WPL (Wool Products Labeling) number is shown. The country where the garment was last substantially transformed is listed as the country of origin, and the origin of the fabric, if different, also must be disclosed. The Care Labeling Rule requires the manufacturer to suggest a suitable care method for the garment. Only one method need be suggested, but the manufacturer should have a reasonable basis for it. Consumers should follow the care label, not make a judgment about how to care for the garment based on fiber content. Care symbols help overcome language barriers in communicating suggested care methods. The Wool Products Labeling Act, the Fur Products Labeling Act, the Guides for Feather and Down Products Industry, and the Silk Labeling Regulation provide for accurate labeling of those products.

Some label information on garments is voluntary. Voluntary labels include trademark and brand, warranty and certification, and union and size labels. These labels help consumers gain additional information about the garment and help retailers sell the garment. The information on apparel labels provides an important tool for evaluating apparel quality. Responsible manufacturers and retailers provide accurate and informative labels; alert consumers express their concern about labels that are inaccurate or inadequate.

Besides labeling, government regulations also pertain to apparel safety. The Flammable Fabrics Act establishes stringent flammability requirements for infants' and children's sleepwear. Regulations for Toys and Children's Articles help prevent the use of decorative trim that poses a choking or scratching hazard. Guidelines for Drawstrings on Children's Outerwear help prevent the use of potentially dangerous drawstrings on children's clothing. Sound business practices require compliance with all federal regulations pertaining not only to products but to the safe and fair treatment of workers and the impact of the company on the environment.

Government Regulations and Label Checklist

If you can answer yes to the following questions regarding garments you evaluate, they meet mandatory labeling and other requirements.

✔ Are fibers identified by their generic name, in order of predominance by weight?
✔ If the trademark name of the fiber is used, does it appear on the same side of the label and in the same size type as the generic name?
✔ Is the manufacturer, retailer, or importer of the garment identified by name, registered trademark, and/or registered number (RN or WPL)?
✔ Is the country of origin identified on the label?
✔ If the garment is made of wool, is the type of wool identified according to the Wool Products Labeling Act?
✔ If the garment is made of fur, is the type of fur identified according to the Fur Products Labeling Act?

✔ If the garment is made of feathers or down, is the type of plumage identified according to the Guides for Feather and Down Products?
✔ If the garment is made of silk, does any metallic weighting of the silk fall within the limits imposed by the Silk Labeling Regulation?
✔ Does the label clearly specify the washing, bleaching, drying, ironing, and/or dry-cleaning method that should be followed to care for the garment?
✔ Does the suggested care method have a reasonable basis?
✔ Is infants' and children's sleepwear, sizes 12 months–6X or 7–14, tight-fitting or does it meet the requirements of the Flammable Fabrics Act? Does the label contain a GPU and FPU number or style number? Does the label warn against care procedures that damage any flame resistant finish on the garment?
✔ Does any nonfunctional, decorative trim on children's garments meet the requirements of the Regulations for Toys and Children's Articles?
✔ Does children's clothing conform to the Guidelines for Drawstrings on Children's Outerwear?
✔ If made in the United States, does the production of the garment conform to the Occupational Safety and Health Act, Fair Labor Standards Act, Equal Employment Opportunity Commission Regulations, Immigration Reform and Control Act, and Environmental Protection Agency Regulations?

If you can answer yes to the following questions regarding the garment you are evaluating, the labels contain voluntary information.

✔ Does the garment label feature a trademark, branded, or private label?
✔ Does the garment have a warranty, certification, or seal of approval label?
✔ Does the garment have a union label?
✔ Does the garment have a size label?

New Terms

If you can define each of these terms and differentiate between related terms, you have gained a good working vocabulary for discussing the topics in this chapter. The terms are listed in the order in which they appear in the chapter.

Federal Trade Commission (FTC)
Textile Fiber Products Identification Act (TFPIA)
fiber content
generic name
trademark
country of origin
registered number (RN)
Wool Products Labeling Act (WPLA)

Fur Products Labeling Act (FPLA)
Guides for the Feather and Down Products Industry
Silk Labeling Regulation
Care Labeling Rule
refurbishing
reasonable basis
low labeling
care symbols
Additional Words to Use With Care Symbols
Consumer Product Safety Commission (CPSC)
Flammable Fabrics Act
Regulations for Toys and Children's Articles
Guidelines for Drawstrings on Children's Outerwear
sweatshops
Occupational Safety and Health Act
Occupational Safety and Health Administration
 (OSHA)
ergonomics
Fair Labor Standards Act (FLSA)
hot goods
Equal Employment Opportunity Commission
 (EEOC)
Civil Rights Act
Age Discrimination in Employment Act
Equal Pay Act
Immigration Reform and Control Act
Immigration and Naturalization Service (INS)
Environmental Protection Agency (EPA)
Pollution Prevention Act
Clean Air Act
Clean Water Act
trademark
U.S. Patent and Trademark Office
brand/name brand/national brand
private label/private brand/store brand
licensing
counterfeit goods
knock-off
implied warranty
written warranty
certification/seal of approval
Crafted With Pride in U.S.A. Council
union label
Union of Needletrades, Industrial and Textile
 Employees (UNITE)

Review Questions

1. What label information is required on all garments sold in the United States? What information is voluntary?
2. Explain the specifics of the Textile Fiber Products Identification Act for disclosing the fiber content of a garment.
3. Discuss the purpose and requirements of country of origin labeling.
4. How is the manufacturer of the garment identified on the label?
5. What are the specific requirements of the Care Labeling Rule?
6. Why should consumers follow care labels rather than choose a care method of their own?
7. Who enforces federally mandated apparel labeling?
8. Discuss federal regulations on apparel safety.
9. List the federal regulations on business practices that affect the apparel industry.
10. What is a trademark? What perceptions about a garment's quality do consumers form, based on trademark or brand?
11. What information does a certification label or seal of approval provide?
12. Name the union representing apparel factory workers.

Activities

1. Examine the labels of 10 different garments in your closet or in a retail store for conformance to the TFPIA and the Care Labeling Rule. Do all the garments comply with TFPIA requirements? If so, explain. Do you find any violations? If so, explain.
2. Survey five friends your age and five people your parents' age. Which do they think is of higher quality, apparel made in the United States or in other countries, or is there no difference? Have them name three countries that come to mind when you mention high-quality apparel and three countries that come to mind when you mention low-quality apparel. What are the perceptions of your friends versus people your parents' age regarding the relationship between quality and country of origin?
3. Survey five friends. Do they always, sometimes, or never read care labels before purchasing apparel? Does the care label influence their likelihood of purchasing the garment? Do they always read the care label before caring for a garment? Do they always follow the suggested care procedure on the label? In your opinion, how could they improve their use of care labels?
4. Explain the use of care symbols to a group of consumers.
5. Visit an apparel manufacturer. Ask:

   a. what testing is done to ensure accurate labeling
   b. what labeling concerns the manufacturer has

6. Write to the Federal Trade Commission and obtain copies of apparel labeling manuals for your professional or school library.

7. Talk to a group of parents about safety regulations on children's apparel and help them understand their role in choosing safe clothing.

8. Contact quality assurance personnel for a large apparel manufacturer or retailer. Ask how they ensure safe and fair business practices that conform to federal requirements on the part of their contractors.

9. Invite a union representative to your class to talk about the role of unions in apparel production.

Apparel Quality: The Priority of Industry and Consumers

Chapter Objectives

1. Define apparel quality.
2. Examine how consumers evaluate quality.
3. Explore the relationship between price and quality.
4. Understand the quality processes used in the apparel industry, and discuss the contribution to product quality made by each of these processes.

Quality is a key factor in the production, marketing, buying, and selling of ready-to-wear apparel. A career in the fashion industry requires a clear understanding of apparel quality. Success in this industry depends upon the ability both to recognize degrees of quality and to know how quality standards can be met. Everyone involved in the apparel industry is influenced by the need to achieve an appropriate balance between quality and price. The ultimate goal is to provide apparel products that best meet consumers' expectations.

Both buyers and sellers are conscious of **apparel quality,** its degree of excellence and conformance to requirements or the extent to which a garment meets expectations. ISO, the International Organization for Standardization, defines quality as "the totality of characteristics of an entity that bear on its ability to satisfy stated or implied needs."

A quality-conscious company produces products that meet the wants and needs of consumers, and its business grows as satisfied customers make repeat purchases. Therefore, everyone benefits from an emphasis on quality. Apparel companies include both manufacturers, who produce garments and sell them to retailers; and retailers, who buy apparel from manufacturers or contract out their own designs and sell directly to consumers. These firms must pay attention to quality to maintain and build their business. And the suppliers of raw materials to the industry must be able to meet the apparel producer's quality requirements. Regardless of the company's type, product quality knowledge equips management and employees to deliver products that meet the wants and needs of the company's targeted customers.

No one is *against* quality, though some place it on a priority level below other business concerns. Some of these people argue that paying attention to quality increases the costs of doing business. However, the combination of manufacturing **rework** (the repair of defective items), customer returns, complaints, ill will, and lost sales caused by lack of quality all add up to cost more in the long run.

Successful businesses consistently offer consumers at least one of three things: *something different, something better, or something cheaper.* Consumers become loyal to certain brands because they can depend on that brand to deliver the same features every time. To generate sales, many manufacturers and retailers provide ready-to-wear that reflects the latest fashion trends (something different) or the lowest price (something cheaper), with little concern for other aspects of apparel quality and value. Although color, style, price, and fit initially "sell" a garment by attracting attention, other features determine the consumer's ultimate satisfaction. This phenomenon calls for a focus on the overall quality and value of the product (something better).

QUALITY FEATURES

Apparel quality has two dimensions: (1) physical features, or what the garment *is*; and (2) performance features, or what the garment *does* (Solinger 1980). *The physical features of a garment determine its performance* (Figure 3–1). Therefore, consumers purchase garments with specific physical features that they believe will fulfill their performance expectations. For example, a consumer chooses a blouse made of silk (a physical feature) because silk typically produces desirable performance (e.g., lustrous beauty and comfort). For more information on quality, see Related Resources: Quality.

Physical Features

A garment's **physical features** provide its tangible form and composition. Physical features include the

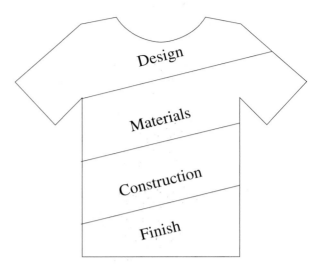

Figure 3–1 The physical features of a garment (design, materials, construction, and finish) determine its performance.

garment's design, materials, construction, and finish. **Design** provides the plan for the garment's style. For example, is the skirt slim or full? **Materials** include the fabrics and other components used to produce the garment. For instance, are the overalls made of denim or corduroy? **Construction** refers to the methods used to assemble the garment. For example, what types of stitches are used? **Finish** involves any garment wet processing. For instance, is the garment stone washed or durable press?

A garment's physical features are **intrinsic attributes;** they cannot be altered without changing the product itself. This text concentrates on intrinsic cues that can be used to evaluate the quality of textile and apparel products.

Performance Features

A garment's **performance features** determine the standards it meets and how it benefits the consumer. Performance features include the garment's aesthetic performance and functional performance.

Aesthetic performance refers to *attractiveness.* Do the design, materials, and construction of the garment fulfill appearance expectations? Do the design elements (color, line, shape, form, and texture) of the garment reflect good design principles (balance, proportion, emphasis, rhythm, and unity)? Does the garment possess classic or current fashion trends desired by consumers? And does its appearance fulfill the wearer's emotional needs, such as wanting to impress or be accepted by others? These questions are important to ask when evaluating ready-to-wear because design impacts the visual appeal of clothing and therefore consumer acceptance of it. However, a thorough discussion on evaluating design aesthetics is outside the focus of this text (see Related Resources: Design and Style).

Functional performance includes performance features other than appearance, namely the garment's utility and durability. *Utility* refers to usefulness. For example, does the garment fit? Is it comfortable? Is it easy to care for? Does it function appropriately for the intended use? *Durability* or *serviceability* refers to how well the garment retains its structure and appearance after wear and care. Does it resist shrinking? Do the seams remain intact? Does the zipper continue to zip?

Aesthetic and functional performance occasionally overlap. For example, fit may be an aesthetic feature (attractive fit versus unattractive fit) or a functional feature (comfortable fit versus uncomfortable fit).

Selling Points and Buying Benefits

Emphasizing a product's quality by enumerating its benefits to the consumer is a valuable sales and marketing technique. Today's increasingly well-educated shoppers appreciate information about the quality of the apparel products they buy.

Selling points are the physical features of a garment that make it desirable. However, effectively promoting a textile product involves more than merely citing a list of selling points. Ideally, selling points are interpreted to the consumer in terms of buying benefits. **Buying benefits** are the performance advantages that result from the garment's physical features. They explain how each feature fulfills the consumer's wants and needs. For example, the statement "This shirt is 100% cotton" is a selling point, but not nearly as meaningful to consumers as the statement of an associated buying benefit, for example, "Because this shirt is 100% cotton, it is cool and comfortable." The more technical the selling point, the more important to translate it into buying benefits that the consumer can readily understand and relate to their lives.

Knowing the selling points of the merchandise and understanding the buying benefits the consumer is seeking enhance business success on every level, from personal selling to marketing and manufacturing. Lands' End catalogs use this technique effectively. Note the use of selling points and the associated buying benefits to promote the quality of a man's tie in Figure 3–2. Be alert to selling points and buying benefits throughout this text but especially in the chapters dealing with product raw materials and garment assembly methods.

PRICE

In addition to intrinsic features, apparel products have **extrinsic attributes,** those that can be altered without changing the garment. Like intrinsic cues, extrinsic cues influence quality evaluations. Extrinsic cues include the price of the garment, image and reputation of the manufacturer, brand name, country of origin, image and reputation of retailer, and hanger, hang tags, and packaging. All these cues are visible at the point of sale. They carry connotations of quality and influence the consumer's perception of the garment's quality, either positively or negatively.

Of the extrinsic cues, consumers pay the most attention to *price*. Price is a major determinant of consumers' apparel purchase decisions for several reasons. First, consumers rely heavily on price as a quality cue. Second, they compare a garment's price and perceived quality to determine value. Third, whether or not a consumer can afford to purchase a particular garment depends upon price.

Price Lines

Ready-to-wear is categorized according to price lines (Figure 3–3). **Price lines** are clusters of merchandise at various price levels, from most expensive to least expensive. Price lines categorize retailers, departments within retail stores, and manufacturers as "high end," "low end," or somewhere in between. **Off-pricing** or **discounting** can occur within any price line; off-price retailers sell goods at lower prices than the manufacturer's suggested retail price. They profit by selling large quantities of merchandise at lower margins and/or by keeping operating costs low.

Mass Merchandise Price Lines.   Important ready-to-wear price lines are budget, moderate, and better, often equated with the retailer's lingo of "*good, better, and best.*" Such marketing tactics encourage consumers to associate quality and price by using references to quality and price synonymously in this manner. The majority of apparel falls into one of these price lines. Budget, moderate, and better constitute the *mass market,* where large volumes of goods are sold. These price lines are dominated by brand names as opposed to designer names. The French term for ready-to-wear, **prêt-à-porter** (pret´ ah por tay´) or **prêt** for short, refers to goods in the mass merchandise price lines. It means, literally, "ready to carry."

Better represents the highest of the mass merchandise price lines. Notice how "better" quality is suggested as associated with higher prices. Better

At Lands' End, the back of a tie is every bit as important as the front.

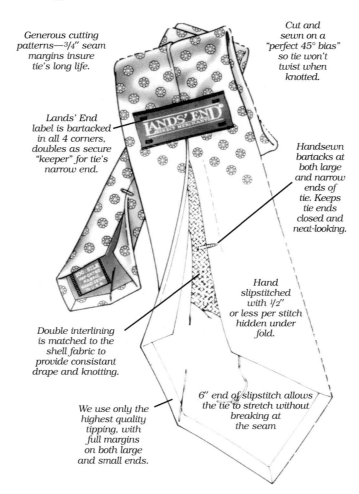

Generous cutting patterns—³/₄″ seam margins insure tie's long life.

Cut and sewn on a "perfect 45° bias" so tie won't twist when knotted.

Lands' End label is bartacked in all 4 corners, doubles as secure "keeper" for tie's narrow end.

Handsewn bartacks at both large and narrow ends of tie. Keeps tie ends closed and neat-looking.

Double interlining is matched to the shell fabric to provide consistant drape and knotting.

Hand slipstitched with ¹/₂″ or less per stitch hidden under fold.

We use only the highest quality tipping, with full margins on both large and small ends.

6″ end of slipstitch allows the tie to stretch without breaking at the seam

Figure 3–2 Use of selling points and buying benefits to promote the quality of a man's tie. *(Reprinted courtesy of Lands' End Catalog. © Lands' End, Inc.)*

lines frequently feature well-known brands and relatively low-price designer names. In some stores, a price line called **bridge** falls between better and designer merchandise, "bridging" the gap between the two; bridge may also refer to goods between better and moderate. **Moderate** price lines serve as a middle ground—moderate-price goods associated with moderate quality standards, for the average consumer. **Budget** is the lowest of the mass merchandise price lines. Consumers usually assume that budget goods meet lower quality standards than other price lines. Therefore, for marketing purposes, budget goods are often given a more appealing name such as *popularly priced, value priced, or bargain.*

Remember that price lines are relative. For example, "moderate sportswear" in an exclusive department store may be "better sportswear" to a mass merchandiser. Brands such as Liz Claiborne and Pendleton may be considered as moderate merchandise in one store, better merchandise in another, and bridge merchandise in a third. **Price points** are the specific prices to be charged within each price line. For example, a retailer might plan $19.99, $29.99, and $39.99 price points for its moderate-price-line shirts.

Exclusive Price Lines. Couture and haute couture are the highest price lines of ready-to-wear. In its purest sense, **couture** (koo tur´) refers to high-quality

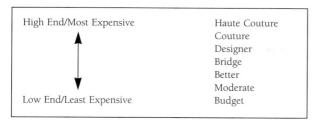

Figure 3–3   Ready-to-wear price lines.

clothing *custom made,* or made to measure, for a specific individual. It originated in Paris, where designers made couture clothing (literally "fine sewing" in French) for their private customers. **Haute couture** (öt koo tur´) is a term reserved for the most fashionable and exclusive couture apparel. True couture and haute couture are associated with exceptionally fine fabrics, careful and detailed construction, excellent fit, and very high prices, often $10,000 or more for a dress. **Bespoke** is a comparable term for high-quality, custom-made men's suits, usually from London.

Some designers, mainly in Europe, still have couture houses where they make true couture clothing for a few wealthy clients. But these same designers also produce ready-to-wear lines, from which they make far greater profits due to larger sales volumes and mass-manufacturing techniques. Thus, *couture* has become a diluted term, often used to describe high-price, designer-name ready-to-wear rather than custom-made clothing. For example, *American couture* usually refers to ready-to-wear. Although expensive, these garments cost much less than true couture.

In its highest sense, **designer clothing** is synonymous with couture or haute couture. As a price line, however, it includes work by popular designers who make only ready-to-wear; although they may make high-quality garments, they are not considered among the ranks of the couture designers. In fact, the term *designer* as a price line has been so overused that it sometimes refers to merchandise that bears the name of a designer, not necessarily a famous one. Designer names have experienced such popularity that some so-called designer apparel carries the name of a nonexistent person and is equivalent to an ordinary brand name. Because of these variations, designer merchandise differs widely.

Price as a Cue to Quality

Price influences the consumer's perception of apparel quality. Most consumers believe that there is a positive relationship between price and quality; they assume that a garment with a high price meets high quality standards. Sayings such as "You get what you pay for" perpetuate this idea. A high price often lends an aura of quality to a garment; if a price seems too low, the quality of the garment is suspect. However, a high-price garment may actually be less serviceable than a lower-price garment. Of course, remember that "quality" involves much more than just serviceability. A costly skirt made of fine silk might not be as serviceable as a less expensive one made of a sturdy cotton denim, but one cannot infer that the quality of the denim skirt is higher.

While not necessarily related to quality, extrinsic cues such as price, brand, and manufacturer's and/or retailer's reputation are nevertheless used by consumers in assessing quality. Consumers are especially likely to use price as a cue to quality because, unlike the performance of a garment, price is visible and known. And price is a number that can be easily compared to the prices of other garments, unlike the difficulty of comparing elusive characteristics such as durability.

This is not to say that price and other extrinsic cues are more important than the intrinsic aspects of the product. However, especially in the absence of other information, price is important to the consumer's quality evaluation. When the consumer cannot readily see other differences in two similar garments, price is the main piece of information available for use in evaluating quality. It appears that consumers rely on price as a quality indicator because they are trying to make an informed decision. However, the more additional quality cues are available, the less likely it is that price influences quality judgments.

One would think the higher the price of the garment, the better the quality of its design, materials, construction, and finish. However, cost of production does not by itself determine price (see Chapter 4), and price does not necessarily reflect quality. High-quality goods can be found at relatively low prices and low-quality goods can be found at high prices. Research studies show that reliance on price to evaluate apparel quality yields inaccurate results.

Consumers rely on price as a quality indicator because *sometimes* price aids them in making a successful quality evaluation. For some garments a high price reflects superior design, materials, construction, and/or finish. Sproles (1977) found support for this general idea when he investigated the relationship between the prices of various products and their inherent quality as determined through objective tests and established standards. Sproles' findings indicate a positive relationship between price and quality for about 50% of the products studied. For those products, when the price was higher, the quality was higher, and when the price was lower, the quality was lower. However, the other half of the products studied did not demonstrate such a relationship. In fact, over 10% actually appeared to display negative relationships between price and quality; when price went up, quality went down! For the products Sproles studied, if consumers based their quality evaluations entirely on price, they would make many poor decisions.

HOW CONSUMERS PERCEIVE QUALITY

Successful apparel manufacturers and retailers understand how consumers evaluate apparel quality both at the point of sale and in use. One of a consumer's main questions when making a purchase decision is, "How will the garment perform for me when I wear it?" Before shopping for apparel, consumers establish the aesthetic and functional performance standards they think the garment should meet. While shopping, they compare possible purchases to these standards. However, because these processes usually happen informally and subconsciously, many consumers are unaware of *how* they decide what to buy. For more information, see Related Resources: Consumer Behavior.

Figure 3–4 features the **perceived quality model**, which illustrates the process consumers use to evaluate the overall quality of a garment. The perceived quality model quantifies a consumer's evaluation of the *desirability*, or overall quality, of a garment. Although the actual process is not formal and conscious, the model shows how consumers form perceptions about apparel quality.

The model demonstrates that no two purchase decisions are made in exactly the same way. It contrasts how different consumers evaluate the same garment, and how the same consumer evaluates two different garments or types of garments. You may find the model useful in examining your own purchase motivations and those of others.

Application of the Perceived Quality Model

Table 3–1 illustrates how two hypothetical consumers, A and B, evaluate the same T-shirt using the perceived quality model. To evaluate a garment using the model, follow these steps:

1. *Select* the features that affect the quality of the garment you are evaluating. Consumers consider different characteristics to assess quality, so the features vary from person to person and depend on the type of garment being evaluated. Any number and combination of factors may be used. Note in Table 3–1 that Consumer A considers more features than does Consumer B when evaluating a T-shirt.*

2. *Weight* each performance feature to reflect its *importance* in determining quality. The weights represent the percentage of the feature's influence on your quality evaluation. Adding the weights should total 100%, illustrating that, together, the features account for the overall quality evaluation of the garment. Different consumers value some things more than others, so the weights vary from person to person and with the type of garment. Note the

---

* Because most consumers use price as a cue to quality, it may be included as a feature in the model. However, doing so technically changes the model from one that measures perceived quality to one that measures perceived value (see discussion concerning Figure 3–5).

$$Q = \sum_{f=1}^{n} w_f r_f$$

Overall quality score =
Sum of (weight of each feature × rating of each feature)

Q = overall quality score; a number ranging from 0 to 100 representing a consumer's evaluation of a garment's quality, with 100 as maximum quality and 0 as absence of quality

Σ = sum

n = number of features used in the evaluation; varies depending on consumer and garment

f = feature used in evaluating a garment's quality; the features used depend on the consumer and the garment

w = weight; a percentage ranging from 0 to 100 representing the contribution or importance of the feature to the overall quality evaluation, with the weights of all features totaling 100%

r = rating; a number ranging from 0 to 100 representing how well the garment performs on that feature, with 100 as maximum performance and 0 as absence of performance

Figure 3–4 Perceived quality model. *(Adapted from models in* Understanding Attitudes and Predicting Social Behavior *by I. Ajzen, and J. Fishbein, 1980, Upper Saddle River, NJ: Prentice Hall; and* Decision-Making for Consumers: An Introduction to Consumer Economics *by E.S. Maynes, (1976, New York: Macmillan.)*

Table 3–1 Comparison of Two Consumers' Evaluations of a T-Shirt Using the Perceived Quality Model

Consumer A's Perceived Quality Evaluation:

Feature	Weight (Importance)		Rating		Contribution to Quality
Brand name	10%	x	70	=	7
Color	10%	x	60	=	6
Comfort	5%	x	20	=	1
Country of origin	5%	x	70	=	3.5
Durability	2.5%	x	10	=	.25
Ease of care	2.5%	x	10	=	.25
Fabric	5%	x	40	=	2
Fit	10%	x	60	=	6
General appearance	20%	x	60	=	12
Shrinkage	5%	x	60	=	3
Style/fashion	15%	x	80	=	12
Price	10%	x	50	=	5
Total	100%				58
					Overall Quality Score

Consumer B's Perceived Quality Evaluation:

Feature	Weight (Importance)		Rating		Contribution to Quality
Color	30%	x	70	=	35
Fit	10%	x	90	=	9
General appearance	15%	x	60	=	9
Style/fashion	25%	x	80	=	20
Price	20%	x	80	=	16
Total	100%				75
					Overall Quality Score

different weights assigned to various performance features by Consumer A and Consumer B.

3. *Rate* how well the garment meets expectations for each performance feature on a scale of 0 to 100, with 100 as the highest rating. The ratings depend entirely on your attitudes about the garment's performance. Thus, ratings vary from person to person. Note the different ratings assigned to the T-shirt by Consumer A and Consumer B.

4. *Multiply* the weight, or importance, of each feature by its rating to determine the contribution of the feature to the quality evaluation.

5. *Add* the contribution of all the features to calculate the *overall quality score* for the garment. There is no "minimum" quality score, above which all consumers think a garment is high quality and below

which all consumers agree that a garment is low quality. The overall quality score that constitutes an acceptable level depends upon the individual consumer. However, if we establish an overall quality score of 70 as average, Consumer A finds the T-shirt unacceptable (overall quality score 58) and Consumer B finds it acceptable (overall quality score 75). A consumer who likes the T-shirt very much would have an even higher quality score for it.

Determinant Attributes

A consumer's overall satisfaction with the quality of a garment may be measured (1) at the point of sale, (2) later, when the garment is in use, or (3) when the garment is discarded. The features that have the greatest effect on the consumer's satisfaction at any of these times are called **determinant attributes**. At the point of sale, the aesthetic features of the garment are typically determinant. However, if functional features are unsatisfactory when the garment is worn, they eventually replace aesthetics as determinants of the consumer's satisfaction (or more accurately, at that point, dissatisfaction). The following sections illustrate the differences in quality perception at the point of sale and when the garment is in use. The examples of the perceived quality model, for the sake of brevity, include only the broad categories of "aesthetic performance" and "functional performance." These features represent the multiple aesthetic and functional features that a real consumer would evaluate separately.

Point-of-Sale Evaluation.   Consumers easily judge a garment's aesthetic performance at the point of sale just by looking at it. The attractiveness of a garment affects consumers emotionally and psychologically; a consumer is unlikely to purchase a garment that does not meet his or her aesthetic standards. Aesthetic features of a garment initially attract or repel consumers. *In fact, color, style, and fit, all aesthetic features, are three of the four most common determinants of consumers' clothing purchase decisions;* price is the other (Galbraith, 1981). Yet evaluation of these aesthetic dimensions is subjective; beauty cannot be quantified. Aesthetic judgments are largely influenced by personal tastes and current fashions. Also, the wearer's height, weight, figure type, and coloring interact with the appearance of the garment, making it more eye-pleasing or less so.

Consumers cannot accurately evaluate a garment's functional performance at the point of sale. They may estimate some features of functional performance, such as comfort or freedom of movement, by trying on the garment. Or they may try to predict functional performance based on the designs, materials, or construction of the garment, especially if they have had experiences with similar garments. Customers associate well-known brand, manufacturer, and retailer names with a certain level of functional performance. Choosing garments from these sources may help customers feel more confident about the functional performance they can expect from the purchase.

However, most aspects of functional performance are *latent,* or hidden until the consumer wears and cares for the garment. The first laundering or dry-cleaning often brings out the majority of latent defects. Galbraith (1981) determined that most consumer dissatisfaction with apparel results from problems involving size/fit, seams that pucker and burst, buttons that fall off, improper choice and application of interfacings, uncomfortable and inaccurate care labels, fabric shrinkage, color change, pilling, snagging, edge abrasion, holes in pockets, and stain/soil retention. Consumers can see and accurately predict few, if any, of these functional defects at the point of sale. They buy a garment *assuming* that it will function adequately in use, without really knowing whether it will or not. Therefore, because functional performance is largely unknown at the point of sale, it does not greatly influence most consumers' purchase decisions, unless they have had prior bad experiences.

In the example in Table 3–2, the hypothetical consumer bases most of a decision about suit quality on aesthetics, assigning it a weight of 70%. The remaining 30% of the quality judgment is based on functional performance. The consumer rates aesthetics low (10) for a hypothetical gray suit and high (90) for a hypothetical blue suit. Because aesthetics is visually determined at the point of sale, the suits are rated so differently because of differences in their appearances. However, the consumer cannot visually determine the functional performance of the two suits at the point of sale, so the expectation is that both will function adequately and each suit is given a rating of 70.

Table 3–2   Point-of-Sale Quality of Two Suits, as Evaluated by a Hypothetical Consumer

Feature	Weight	Gray Suit Point-of-Sale Rating	Blue Suit Point-of-Sale Rating
Aesthetics	70%	x 10 = 7	x 90 = 63
Function	30%	x 70 = 21	x 70 = 21
	100%	28	84
		Overall Point-of-Sale Quality Score	Overall Point-of-Sale Quality Score

When the ratings are totaled, the blue suit achieves a higher overall quality score at the point of sale than does the gray suit. If a score of 70 is established as average, or acceptable, it can be concluded that the consumer views the gray suit as being of "high quality." As in most cases, *aesthetic performance determines the apparel purchase decision.* In some cases, functional performance rather than aesthetics is determinant at the point of sale. For instance, a serious runner is more concerned about comfortable exercise clothes than attractive ones. However, in most cases, aesthetics is predominant.

In-Use Evaluation. Although not accurately predicted by customers at the point of sale, the functional performance of the garment becomes obvious in use. For example, customers can determine how warm a garment is, how much it fades, and how easily it tears, but only after they use the garment. At that time, the consumer reevaluates the garment, comparing actual performance to point-of-sale expectations about performance. Because aesthetic performance is accurately predicted by customers at the point of sale, its influence on the in-use quality evaluation remains constant. However, because customers cannot predict functional performance accurately at point of sale, they may rate in-use quality differently than they did at the point of sale when they evaluate the garment. Therefore, functional performance on the in-use quality evaluation becomes critical to keep consumer satisfaction.

Reconsider the consumer, who was discussed previously, evaluating the gray and blue suits. Table 3–3 shows how the quality judgment of the consumer may change after the suits are put into use. After wearing and caring for the suits, the consumer gathers "data" on their functional performance, which affects the customer's in-use quality evaluation of the suits.

In use, the consumer rates the function of the gray suit high (90) and the function of the blue suit low (10). Note the impact of these ratings on the overall quality scores of each suit. Poor function in the presence of excellent aesthetics creates dissatisfaction with the blue suit (in-use quality score = 66). However, excellent function in the absence of excellent aesthetics does not create satisfaction with the gray suit (in-use quality score = 34). This leads to the realization of an important fact: *Adequate aesthetic performance is required to create satisfaction, and adequate functional performance is required to prevent dissatisfaction* (Swan and Combs, 1976).

Another phenomenon causes the in-use quality score of a garment to differ dramatically from the point-of-sale quality score. The importance, or weight, assigned to each performance feature *may change* when the garment is worn. This occurs because some features, depending upon their in-use performance, increase or decrease in importance. For example, durability might be weighted low at the point of sale. If the garment quickly wears out, however, durability becomes a very important feature in evaluating the in-use quality of the garment, and the weight assigned to durability is raised accordingly, increasing its influence on the overall quality score.

Achieving in-use consumer satisfaction is as important to an apparel manufacturer and/or retailer as is delivering satisfaction at the point of sale. Granted, satisfaction at the point of sale determines whether or not the consumer buys the garment. But in-use satisfaction determines whether he or she keeps it or returns it. And in-use satisfaction affects the consumer's feelings of good will or ill will toward the manufacturer and/or retailer and determines whether or not the consumer makes repeat purchases. Therefore, companies that ignore functional performance and rely exclusively on the aesthetic appeal of their products ignore their own futures. In other words, to quote the Siemens Quality Motto, "Quality is when your customers come back and your products don't."

Consumers assess their ultimate satisfaction with a garment at the time they remove it from service.

Table 3–3 In-Use Quality of Two Suits, as Evaluated by a Hypothetical Consumer

Feature	Weight	Gray Suit In-Use Rating	Blue Suit In-Use Rating
Aesthetics	70%	x 10 = 7	x 90 = 63
Function	30%	x 90 = 27	x 10 = 3
	100%	34	66
		Overall In-Use Quality Score	Overall In-Use Quality Score

When consumers discard items they no longer wear, they objectively evaluate how well each garment performed compared to their original expectations for it. A garment that ultimately fulfills the consumer's expectations of quality leads to satisfaction that translates into an increased loyalty to the manufacturer and/or retailer. A garment that ultimately fails to meet the consumer's expectations leaves the consumer dissatisfied, eroding loyalty to the manufacturer and/or retailer. Therefore, providing garments that meet or exceed consumer's quality expectations contributes to long-term business success.

VARIATIONS IN TARGET MARKETS

Manufacturers use **market segmentation** to divide consumers into groups with common characteristics. Consumers in the same market segment tend to have the same wants and needs and exhibit similar buying behavior. A **target market** consists of the consumers in a particular market segment that a manufacturer aims to please with a particular product, for example, professional working women, aged 45–55, with income above $65,000, as the target for better career apparel. Through market research, discovering the motivations of consumers in the target market for a product helps the manufacturer or retailer determine consumer requirements and expectations for the garment—style, color, and fit preferences, price willing to pay, and value expected. Understanding the target market enables the manufacturer or retailer to satisfy customers by predicting the selling points and buying benefits that are important to them. (For more information on target markets, see Chapter 4.)

Many consumers lack the ability to objectively evaluate quality. Although everyone has experience in wearing clothing, the average consumer is not trained to evaluate it. However, consumers do not necessarily base their quality judgment on the *inherent* quality of a garment but instead upon their *perception* of its quality. Thus, *in the consumer's mind,* the perceived quality *is* the real quality of the garment. Successful manufacturers and retailers tune into the standards expected by their target market in order to satisfy the bulk of their customers.

End Use

The **end use**, or intended use, of a garment helps determine the target market for a product and affects how consumers evaluate quality. For example, the target market for bridalwear is brides-to-be. The typical target consumer is looking for a garment appropriate to wear at her wedding. The bridalwear manufacturer targets some styles to first-time brides and others to previously married brides. Some styles are targeted to brides having large, formal weddings and others to those having small, casual weddings. For any bride, a high-quality wedding gown possesses aesthetic characteristics—it is beautiful and flattering to the wearer. A functional characteristic, such as ease of care, has little or no importance to a bride who wears the dress only one time. On the other hand, ease of care is a major quality indicator for children's play clothing and is important to most parents.

In another example, young teenage consumers typically want the latest apparel fashions (an aesthetic characteristic). Durability (a functional characteristic) is relatively unimportant to them because fashion will probably make their wardrobe obsolete before it wears out. In contrast, adults tend to be interested in **investment dressing,** the purchase of classic apparel such as coats and suits that can be worn several seasons; thus, utility and durability are important to them. Manufacturers and retailers consider end use to determine appropriate performance standards. For example, wearers expect different performance characteristics from a man's flannel work shirt and a child's flannel nightgown, even though both are made in the same fabrication.

Demographics and Psychographics

The demographics and psychographics of the consumers in a target market help manufacturers and retailers determine the wants and needs of those consumers. **Demographics** are statistics that describe a population, including age, income, education, occupation, race, geographic location, and other factors that affect a consumer's product preferences. As the demographics of the population change, so does the behavior of consumers. Tracking demographics and psychographics helps apparel industry professionals plan appropriate business strategies. There is no "average" consumer in the United States, but companies can find commonalties in their target market. For example:

- Demographics indicating the aging of the U.S. population led Levi's to develop their popular Dockers brand pants for men. The loose fit of Dockers is more comfortable and more flattering to the expanding waistline of a person approaching middle age than are tight pants. By 2010, one in every three Americans will be over 50, a fact that is sure to strongly influence future apparel product development.
- Rising education levels in the United States mean more high-income, sophisticated customers

interested in better quality garments, who expect more information about selling points and associated buying benefits.

- The vast number of women in the workforce require clothing appropriate for the office.
- The trend toward casual-professional dress in the workplace has increased the demand for shirts, slacks, and unstructured jackets in casual, easy-care fabrics.
- The increase in families having few children but earning high incomes creates a demand for luxury children's clothing, such as leather jackets instead of cloth coats for toddlers.
- The population shift in the United States to the South and West increases the need for casual warm-weather clothing year round.
- The growth of racial minorities as a percentage of the population leads manufacturers to develop products that meet the particular needs of these market segments. One in three U.S. children is African American, Hispanic, or Asian, pointing to the future of minority marketing, most applicable when a minority group is geographically concentrated. One example is an emphasis on petite sizing for clothing destined for a predominantly Asian community. Also, design preferences may vary according to subcultural differences. Several ethnic groups in the United States traditionally buy young girls' dresses with puff sleeves, close-fitting bodices, and full ruffled skirts needing petticoats for holidays and special occasions. Other groups perceive this style of apparel to be out of date and therefore unacceptable. Manufacturers and retailers must be aware of the cultural and subcultural differences in the way their target market perceives quality.
- In international trade, cultural differences make it possible for a garment considered of high quality in one culture to be considered of low quality in another because of varying standards and expectations. An example is garments made of madras-plaid cotton fabric imported to the United States from India. At first, U.S. consumers perceived the garments to be low quality because the natural dyes faded and ran when the garments were laundered. A carefully conducted marketing campaign convinced U.S. consumers that the fading was normal for the type of dyestuff used and a desirable characteristic of genuine Indian madras cloth. This change in perception upgraded the perceived quality and value by U.S. consumers of products made in madras plaids, even though the majority of Indians still consider the cloth of low quality and therefore undesirable.

- The features used to define apparel quality change over time and according to fashion trends. Hand-stitched seams and boned bodices, important in a high-quality garment a hundred years ago, are not relevant to modern definitions of ready-to-wear quality. And the stone washed, abraded, and torn jeans popular in the early 1990s would have been abhorrent to quality-conscious consumers in the 1950s.

Demographics are most useful when considered along with psychographics. **Psychographics** characterize people according to their lifestyle values—interests, attitudes, and opinions. Understanding these things about consumers helps predict what they expect and desire of a garment because their values influence their clothing behavior. For example:

- Groups of consumers valuing beautiful clothing consider aesthetic features such as color and design most important in judging quality.
- Consumers with the attitude that clothing should be comfortable make quality judgments based on features such as the roominess or light weight of a garment.
- A refocus on the home and on family values in the 1990s after the 1980s emphasis on workplace success is reflected in fewer apparel purchases, more feminine womenswear styling, and a wider variety of casual styles for men.
- An interest in preserving the environment shared by many consumers today creates a demand for environmentally friendly products.

Although consumers tend to act like other consumers in the same target market, the individual standards of particular consumers may vary. Consumers with high standards are dissatisfied when a garment does not meet their expectations; others with lower expectations might be relatively pleased and satisfied with the performance of the same garment. For example, if one consumer expects to wear a pair of shorts four years, but they last three, the consumer is dissatisfied. But if another consumer expects to wear the shorts only two years, and they last three, the consumer is satisfied. In other words, the product meets or exceeds expectations.

VALUE: RELATING PRICE AND QUALITY

The relationship between quality and price is expressed in terms of **value.** An item of apparel is a *fair value* if it delivers quality comparable to the price

Figure 3–5 Perceived value graph illustrates the relationship of price and perceived quality.

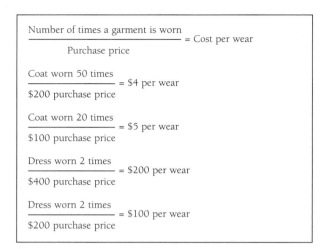

Figure 3–6 Formula for calculating cost per wear, and examples.

paid. An *overpriced* garment furnishes little quality for the price, and a *bargain* offers high quality compared to the price paid.

Perceived value is a determinant factor in a consumer's decision whether or not to purchase a garment. If the garment seems a fair value or a bargain, the consumer's perception of value motivates buying. Perceived value is also assessed when the garment is removed from use, as the wearer appraises his or her ultimate satisfaction with the garment compared to the price paid.

Perceived Value Graph

The perceived value graph in Figure 3–5 represents how consumers make decisions based on the *price* of a garment relative to *perceived quality*. Notice the position of the various points on the graph. The points representing garments with high perceived quality/low price fall into the bargain sector. The points representing garments with high price/low perceived quality fall into the overpriced sector. The points representing equal price and perceived quality are on the fair value line. Luxury goods are at the upper end, where both price and perceived quality are high. So-called "sleazy" or cheap merchandise is found at the lower end, where both price and perceived quality are low. The value graph illustrates that the consumer must perceive the quality of a garment as equal to or greater than the price before making a purchase.

Cost Per Wear

In purely economic terms, the value of a garment depends on how much it costs to wear it. The purchase price divided by the number of times the garment is

worn determines the **cost per wear.** An expensive garment is a better cost-per-wear value than an inexpensive one *if* the expensive item is worn more frequently or over a longer period of time. For example, if a $200 coat is worn 50 times before being discarded, it is a better value than a $100 coat worn only 20 times. The $200 coat costs $4 per wear; the $100 coat costs $5 per wear (Figure 3–6). However, an inexpensive garment is a better cost-per-wear value than an expensive garment if neither is worn much.

Consumers commonly apply the cost-per-wear formula when durability is important. However, it can also be used when other factors, such as comfort or styling, affect the relationship between the purchase price of a garment and the number of times a garment is worn. For example, evening dresses are usually worn only a limited number of times because the wearer is unwilling to be seen in the same evening dress more than a few times, or because the dress goes out of fashion before it physically wears out. A $400 evening dress worn two times costs $200 per wear, whereas a $200 evening dress worn the same number of times costs only $100 per wear. If a garment requires dry-cleaning, the cost of care influences the cost per wear; for example, a washable sweater has a lower cost per wear than a *Dry Clean Only* sweater of the same price.

Paying a high price to obtain a high-quality product is a poor use of economic resources if it does not lower the cost per wear. However, a high price that translates into a low cost per wear is a good economic choice. Of course, the decision to purchase a garment is often based on factors other than the best use of economic resources. For instance, if a child looks charming in a fancy party dress, the emotional appeal of the dress to a grandparent may make the cost per wear irrelevant, even if the child wears the dress to only one event before outgrowing it. A wedding dress is another example of a garment not usually subject to cost-per-wear analysis.

Apparel Life Expectancy

The **International Fabricare Institute (IFI)**, an association of professional cleaners and launderers, promotes the *Fair Claims Guide for Consumer Textile Products*. It defines the value of clothing of various ages. The *Fair Claims Guide* suggests that certain apparel categories imply certain life expectancy rates if the garment is cared for as recommended (Table 3–4). It estimates how long a garment reasonably may be expected to last, considering normal wear, care, and fashion change. The *Fair Claims Guide* is widely used in the arbitration of apparel serviceability disputes; for example, replacement value is calculated based on the degree to which the garment's life expectancy has been used up and the condition of the garment. In addition, the *Fair Claims Guide* is useful as a yardstick to which all garments may be compared. Individuals responsible for manufacturing and selling ready-to-wear apparel should be aware of these guidelines and be sure that products meet or exceed them. For more information, contact the International Fabricare Institute (IFI), 12251 Tech Road, Silver Spring, MD 20904. URL: http://www.ifi.org.

QUALITY PROCESSES USED IN THE APPAREL INDUSTRY

The apparel industry constantly pursues quality in the production of garments that meet consumer expectations. Determining the wants and needs of consumers helps manufacturers and retailers establish appropriate quality standards for the merchandise they produce and sell. Companies that offer products most closely meeting the expectations of their target market have the greatest chance for success in selling to and satisfying consumers.

Consumers' aesthetic expectations are easier to discern than their functional expectations. Shoppers cast their votes in the form of dollars at the cash register for the colors and styles they prefer; sales figures send a clear message to the industry regarding which aesthetic characteristics they like and dislike.

However, the apparel industry does *not* get a clear message regarding functional performance preferences. Consumers are neither satisfied nor dissatisfied with the utility or durability of a garment at the point of sale; they cannot identify garments that meet or fail to meet functional performance standards until

after wear and care. Companies that pursue and acquire an understanding of functional performance expectations have a clear advantage in ensuring that they provide the level of in-use performance that consumers want. Some quality-conscious companies do this by not approving a product until it has successfully passed normal home laundering processes. Another way for a company to acquire and utilize functional product knowledge is for employees to wear and use the product. In fact, everyone at The Lee Company has the opportunity to wear jeans to work every day so they get to know their product better. This company policy enables the employees to clearly see the consumer's perspective on their product and to pinpoint and correct in-use performance problems rather than concentrate only on point-of-sale aesthetics.

Staffing the Quality Department

Many large manufacturers and some retailers establish **quality departments** that monitor and maintain quality standards. These departments, called **quality assurance (QA)** or **quality control (QC)**, constantly refine methods and procedures to consistently achieve the company's desired level of quality. The company determines the quality level that will reflect the expectations of the target consumer. The quality organization, no matter what the title or structure, is staffed by individuals with varying responsibilities that contribute to maintaining this product-quality level.

Quality personnel in apparel manufacturing organizations promote the principle that quality is *built into* the manufacturing process; it is *not* a separate function. Quality cannot be "inspected into" the product; all inspection can do is detect products that do not meet standards and prevent them from reaching consumers. Therefore, it is the responsibility of all employees to "do it right the first time." Quality-conscious companies support the philosophy that employees at all levels of planning and production are expected to participate in identifying the causes of defects and proposing solutions to problems. Planning for quality and building it into the product at every step are the only ways to ensure a consistent quality level.

Instilling a commitment to quality in employees throughout the company, from corporate management to factory workers, is essential. If workers get the idea that management talks about quality but rewards volume production, they concentrate on production. But if workers believe that management genuinely cares about quality and recognizes efforts to maintain and improve quality, they will care about quality too.

Table 3–4 Average Life Expectancy of Textile Items in Years
(Reprinted with permission of International Fabricare Institute, the association of professional cleaners and launderers; Fair Claims Guide for Consumer Textile Products; Copyright 1988. All rights reserved.)

Apparel		Household Furnishings
Bathing suits. 2	Fabric, lined & unlined. 3	Bedspreads. 6
Bathrobes	Rubber and plastic 3	Blankets
Lightweight 2	Shirts	Heavy wool and
Heavy or quilted 3	Dress 3	synthetic fibers 10
Wool 3	Sports 2	Lightweight. 5
Blazers	Wool or silk. 2	Electric 5
Cotton and blends 3	Ski jackets	Comforters. 5
Imitation suede* 3	(including down) 2	Down 5
Wool 4	Skirts 2	Curtains
Coats and jackets (outerwear)	Slacks	Sheer 3
Children's 2	Lounging and active sport. 2	Glass fiber 3
Cotton and blends 3	Dress 3	Draperies
Down 3	Socks 1	Lined 5
Fur. 10	Sport coats	Unlined 4
Imitation fur or suede* 3	Cotton and synthetic	Sheer 3
Leather and suede 5	blends. 3	Glass fiber 4
Plastic 2	Imitation suede* 3	Sheets & pillow cases 2
Wool 4	Wool and wool blends. 4	Slipcovers. 3
Blouses 3	Suits	Table linen
Choir robes. 6	Cotton and synthetic 2	Fancy 5
Dresses	Summer-weight wool. 3	Other 2
Casual 2	Imitation suede* 3	Towels 3
Office 3	Silk. 3	Upholstery fabrics 5
Silk 2	Washable 2	
Evening	Winter-weight wool. 4	
High fashion 3	Sweaters 3	
Basic. 5	Ties 1	
Formal wear 5	Underwear	
Gloves	Foundation garments 1	
Fabric 1	Panties. 1	
Leather 2	Slips. 2	
Rainwear & windbreakers	Uniforms 1	
Film & plastic coated 2	Vests 2	

Note. *Nonwoven only. Life expectancy for coated or flocked articles is two years.
Author's note: The life expectancies in this table reflect those of garments cleaned by commercial launderers and professional dry cleaners. Also, the figures provided may be conservative if factors such as infrequent use, classic styling, and durable fabrication and construction are taken into account.

Large manufacturers establish performance standards and perform extensive quality tests to ensure conformance to standards as part of routine procedure. They evaluate raw materials as well as assembled apparel products for adherence to standards. Smaller manufacturers often do not have the staff or equipment to perform quality analysis at this level. They send the raw materials and assembled apparel products to independent testing labs that provide these services. No matter what the size of the company and what limits are placed on resources, it is possible to monitor and maintain quality.

There are some firms that do not care about consistent quality and try to get by with the lowest possible investment in their products. Not creating repeat, brand-loyal consumers eventually takes its toll on these manufacturers. These companies represent a minority of manufacturers. However, they indirectly tarnish the reputation of legitimate, honest, quality-conscious companies.

Retailers with quality departments recognize the importance of maintaining a consistently positive image by selling quality apparel to their customers. Rather than relying solely on manufacturers to deliver high-quality apparel to them, they monitor the quality of the products they buy and sell to ensure that all goods meet the standards of their organization. At the very least, most retail quality departments measure products to check conformance to fit specifications and they launder the products to confirm appropriate end use performance. Some retailers have quality requirements as comprehensive as those of the most sophisticated manufacturer. For example, they might require boys' denim jeans to achieve specified levels of shrinkage, tensile strength, tear strength, crocking, weight, colorfastness to light, laundering, and bleaching. A specified number of samples from all incoming shipments is tested to ensure conformance to these standards.

Establishing Standards and Specifications

Standards and specifications, although related, serve different purposes (Table 3–5). **Standards** are general guidelines established by companies to reflect the overall quality level of their products. Standards answer the question, "At what level must these products perform?" For example, a company might set a standard for seam strength; all seams must be at least as strong as the standard. Standards are often written as *minimum standards* to establish a "base line." Standards guide the decision-making process, because all decisions must result in products that meet company standards. Standards must be communicated throughout the company, to all suppliers, and to the appropriate independent contractors and testing laboratories. Standards are not proprietary or secret; they must be open and available to anyone who needs them if a company is going to achieve its quality goals.

Specifications or **specs** define specifically *how*, for a particular style of garment, to meet the company's standards. Specifications serve to inform suppliers and staff about how a particular product is to be made. For example, to meet the seam strength standard mentioned in the previous paragraph, stitch and seam type, number of stitches per inch, and thread size are specified, or "spec'ed". Unlike standards, which are general to all products, specifications are specific to one product and are written *exactly* as needed to ensure conformance.

Both standards and specifications must balance required levels of aesthetic and functional performance with the cost limitations of the price line on the design, materials, construction, and finish (Figure 3–7). This is vital for the final product to be not only of the desired quality but also a good value. An integral part of establishing product performance standards is determining the target market and target price point of

Table 3–5 Distinguishing among Fabric Standards, Garment Standards, Fabric Specifications, and Garment Specifications

Document	Purpose	Used By	Example of Content
Fabric standards	To maintain product quality level desired by selected target market	Testing Technicians, Quality Engineers, Buyers, Merchandisers	% shrinkage (-4 × -4) lbs. tensile (200 × 140) lbs. tear (10 × 6)
Garment standards	To maintain consistent sewing practices on all products	Quality Auditors, Sewing Operators, Sewing Engineers, Costing and Quality Engineers	No broken stitches No holes No raw edges Oversew length = 1 inch
Fabric specifications	To specify desired raw materials to supplier during purchasing process	Buyers, Merchandisers, Purchasing Agents, Costing and Quality Engineers	8 oz. per sq. yd. denim plain weave indigo dyestuff
Garment Specifications	To specify how product is to be made	Designers/Merchandisers, Patternmakers, Sewing Engineers, Costing and Quality Engineers	8 spi 301 inseam 401 bandset

Note. For fabric term definitions, see Chapter 7. For stitch, seam, and edge treatment definitions, see Chapters 9 and 10.

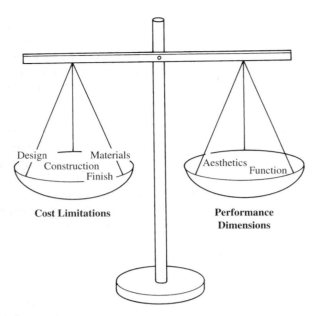

Figure 3–7 Manufacturers must balance aesthetic and functional performance with cost limitations.

a product. A picture must be painted of the "typical" customer for this product. (See discussion of Variations in Target Markets.) Average life expectancy of the product needs to be determined. Once all these characteristics are defined, steps can be taken to establish standards.

The first step in developing standards is to conduct research on the same or a similar product on the market. Manufacturers establish a database by surveying the market to obtain data on like products from price points both above and below the target price point. They consult industry standards such as those established and published annually by the American Society for Testing and Materials (ASTM). Most companies also find a way to obtain their direct competitors' standards for comparison purposes. They analyze this information with input from the company's designers, merchandisers, buyers, quality engineers, production engineers, technicians, and operators. Careful consideration of all the information gathered enables a company to set standards that are realistic and appropriate for the target market.

Some companies use oral agreements on standards and specifications. A manufacturer may call a contractor and request that a certain seam type be used on the garments the contractor is making. As long as both parties remember the agreement accurately, no problems will arise. However, for greater documentation and clarity and to reduce errors, the current trend is to use formal, written standards and specs. The written standards and specifications leave no

room for error, and they can be electronically transmitted in less time than it takes to make a phone call.

The more detailed the standards and specifications, the less room for misunderstanding. Of course, a balance should be struck between documents that are complete enough to cover all the pertinent points and documents that are unnecessarily tedious. Both standards and spec sheets need to be comprehensive, clear, and concise. Fabric standards and specifications are usually short and used by a relatively small number of people. Garment (product) standards and specifications are more lengthy and are used by a larger group of people. They also are more likely to be sent outside the company to contractors. In-house documents may take on an abbreviated format that is clearly understood by employees of a company, but documents sent to contractors should not be abbreviated to avoid misunderstandings.

Standards should be updated on a regular basis. Specifications are written for a particular product and are therefore always current, but standards tend to be generic and apply to many products. It is easy to take standards for granted and forget to update them. New technology or new fashion trends can cause a standard to become permanently or temporarily obsolete. An example is found in the "grunge look" popular in the mid 1990s. Clothing intentionally was designed to be baggy and worn-looking. Normal colorfastness and fit standards were ignored.

The U.S. government recognizes the importance of standards and specifications in communicating quality requirements. In the past, the government established extensive standards and specifications for the production of apparel for the armed services. The Federal Acquisitions Streamlining Act of 1995 caused the federal government to adopt industry standards and specifications instead of developing their own. This change allows the government to more efficiently maintain current and consistent quality standards, with the entire industry benefiting from the government's participation in the process. Even with the change in procedures, government standards and specifications still ensure that all manufacturers bidding on a contract submit a bid based on the production of exactly the same design, using the same quality and quantity of materials and comparable construction methods. The quality monitoring process and the clarity with which government standards and specifications are written make possible clear-cut rejections of any products deviating from standards. Consequently, military garments are of consistent quality, regardless of the manufacturer, which highlights the benefits of detailed, written specifications.

When designing products, instead of thinking about standards and specifications for each particular component of a uniform, the U.S. government recently began working from an integrated **systems approach**. For example, consider a firefighter's uniform. The uniform consists of a helmet, mask, jacket, pants, and boots. These items of apparel must all work together to perform the needed function. The government considers all these items as an integrated system, and all parts of the system must function well with the other parts. Standards are being written for the complete system instead of each separate part. This is a unique approach and one that undoubtedly will trigger related approaches in industry.

Standards. Companies write standards for two separate aspects of apparel production: (1) fabric and findings, or raw material, standards and (2) garment or product standards. Both fabric and findings and garment standards must be strictly enforced to protect the image of a quality-oriented business. Manufacturers and retailers who grow "too fast" or become complacent can become plagued by quality problems. Successful companies meet the challenge of maintaining the quality standards that originally made them popular, but for a vastly increased volume of goods. Firms that do not establish and enforce strict and realistic methods to assure quality tarnish their reputations by offering low-quality apparel to the public, eventually damaging their business.

Fabric and Findings Standards. *Fabric and findings standards* communicate with suppliers about the performance of the raw materials to be purchased. Raw materials include not only fabric but also findings such as zippers, thread, and buttons. During the planning phase of apparel development, when a company is investigating many possible fabrications, standards are discussed at great length with suppliers. Products are tested to determine if the sample performs as the supplier indicates. If any test result falls below the specified level, negotiations take place between the two companies. Usually the supplier is asked to improve the product but there can be situations when it is acceptable for a product to deviate from standards. One such example was the fashion trend of blue jeans with holes that was popular in the early 1990s. Several fabric mills approached this fashion trend by shooting the denim with buckshot. When the fabric has small holes throughout, the tensile strength of the product is significantly reduced. Because of consumer demand for a hot fashion trend, most companies allowed temporary deviations from their normal tensile strength standards on that single product. It was done on the basis that a trendy, short-lived-fashion jean would not require the strength or serviceability needed of a classic jean expected to last for many years.

Garment (Product) Standards. *Garment* or *product standards* communicate the correct diagnostic tool for measuring the quality of assembled apparel products. Garment standards, frequently called **defect guides,** aid in the monitoring and maintenance of quality levels during production and inspection. Most defect guides are generic and pertain to any style of garment produced by a particular company. They usually are written in terms of majors and minors. A **major defect** is not acceptable in any situation (for example, a raw edge, a place in a seam where one ply of fabric has not been caught in the stitching). A **minor defect** will not affect the use of the product but needs to be corrected on future production (for example, a stitch length that is too long). Table 3–6 contains a list of major and minor garment defects. Any producer, inspector, or tester of garments must have a copy of and understand the company's product defect guide.

Specifications. Specifications, as used by apparel producers and retailers, take two forms: (1) fabric and findings specifications and (2) garment or product specifications. If accurately written, both fabric and garment specifications allow products to be conceptualized on one side of the globe and produced on the other side exactly as designed. As more companies do business on an international level, language and cultural differences increase the chance for misunderstanding. Written specifications contribute to clear communications and prevent production failures which create a "lose-lose" situation—the manufacturer receiving unfit products and the contractor not getting future orders. Time restraints, great distances, and high shipping costs make it difficult or impractical to return goods that do not meet quality standards, so specifications are vital in getting products right the first time (Figure 3–8).

Fabric and Findings Specifications. The *fabric and findings specification* is primarily used when making a "buy". The buy can be the purchase of any component of the apparel product, such as zipper, thread, or buttons. Fabric weight and type of fabric construction (weave or knit type) are essential to a fabric spec. Other features often specified include color, width of cloth, yarn size, yarn construction, and type of dyestuff. Any buy made without a clear understanding of these features may cause problems at later stages of production. Carefully spelling out all the desired characteristics in a fabric specification ensures consistency, especially when more than one mill supplies the fabric for the same production run of garments. As garments are produced, manufacturers continue to use fabric specifications as a reference in routinely monitoring the consistency of the fabric throughout all production lots of a large-volume style.

Table 3–6 General Guidelines for Grading of Visual Defects
(Courtesy of ACTS Testing Labs.)

Defects	Major	Minor
1. Materials		
Hole, tear cut, fabric run, dropped stitch	X	
Permanent crease	X	
Permanent stains	X	
Washable stains		X
Loose threads	Per Severity	
Frayed edges	Per Severity	
2. Seam and stitching		
Open seams (More than 2 sewing stitches)	X	
Understitching (no. of stitches/ under the specified requirement)		X
Overlap stitching	Per Severity	
Double stitching	Per Severity	
3. Shade and color		
Off shade	Per Severity	
Color mismatch	Per Severity	
4. Sewing label		
Missing	X	
Misplaced		X
Incomplete label	X	
Wrong label	X	
Insecurely attached		X
5. Pocket		
Not in specified location, more than 1/4"	X	
Not in specified location, less than 1/4"		X
Sewn in crooked way	Per Severity	
Size and shape not to specified requirement	X	
6. Pressing		
Overpressed	Per Severity	
Distorted	Per Severity	
Wrinkled	Per Severity	
7. Buttons		
Missing functional buttons	X	
Missing decorative buttons		X
Misaligned, lead to bulge when buttoned	X	
Functional buttons insecurely sewn	X	
Decorative buttons insecurely sewn		X
Size type not to specified requirement	X	
Damaged buttons	X	
8. Buttonholes		
Missing function buttonholes	X	
Missing decorative buttonholes		X
Added functional or decorative buttonholes	X	
Misaligned, lead to bulge when buttoned	X	
Broken or skipped stitches in buttonholes	X	
9. Embroidery		
Missing embroidery	X	
Misplaced embroidery	X	
Size shape or color not to specified requirement	X	

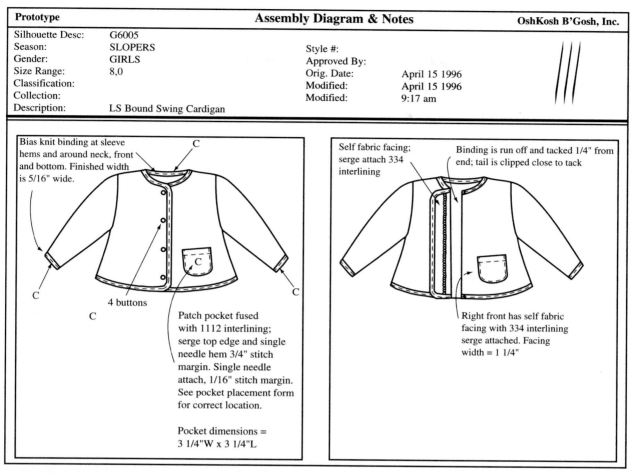

Prototype	**Assembly Diagram & Notes**		OshKosh B'Gosh, Inc.

Silhouette Desc:	G6005		Style #:	
Season:	SLOPERS		Approved By:	
Gender:	GIRLS		Orig. Date:	April 15 1996
Size Range:	8,0		Modified:	April 15 1996
Classification:			Modified:	9:17 am
Collection:				
Description:	LS Bound Swing Cardigan			

Bias knit binding at sleeve hems and around neck, front and bottom. Finished width is 5/16" wide.

C

4 buttons

C

Patch pocket fused with 1112 interlining; serge top edge and single needle hem 3/4" stitch margin. Single needle attach, 1/16" stitch margin. See pocket placement form for correct location.

Pocket dimensions = 3 1/4"W x 3 1/4"L

Self fabric facing; serge attach 334 interlining

Binding is run off and tacked 1/4" from end; tail is clipped close to tack

Right front has self fabric facing with 334 interlining serge attached. Facing width = 1 1/4"

Figure 3–8 Garment specifications regarding assembly details. *(Courtesy of OshKosh B'Gosh.)*

Garment (Product) Specifications. Garment or *product specifications* note every operation used in making a garment in sequential order. They can be lengthy documents, depending upon the complexity of the product. A simple T-shirt might have only 6 operations while a pair of jeans might have 20 or more operations. (Specifications for a variety of garments are shown in Chapters 9, 11, and 12 in Figures 9–1, 11–1, 11–2, 11–16, and 12–1.) The specs note the size and color of thread and the stitch type for each operation. Many stitch types and sizes of thread can be used in a single garment, each carefully chosen for a specific purpose. If a manufacturer is making the same style garment at several locations or is sending it out to different contractors, they all can produce exactly the same garments by carefully following the construction specifications.

Tolerances. Some construction standards and specifications include plus-or-minus tolerances. A **tolerance** is the difference between the allowable minimum and maximum of a specification or standard.

Allowable tolerances establish the limits within which the product can vary yet still be of acceptable quality. For example, specifying that seams be stitched using *exactly* 12 stitches per inch (12 spi) is a realistic *goal* but an unrealistic specification, considering the nature of soft goods and the equipment and procedures used to handle them. A realistic specification is 12 stitches per inch, plus or minus 2 stitches per inch (12 ± 2 spi). This provides the more reasonable range of 10 to 14 stitches per inch, achievable in the varying conditions of a soft goods production line yet still reflecting acceptable quality standards.

Unreasonable standards have little chance of being met, making them unenforceable and useless. For instance, a too-rigid standard is that the side seam and sleeve seam must meet exactly where they intersect under the arm. This standard sets an impractical goal that is frustrating to the production staff and hurts the credibility of the individual who wrote the standard. However, if a tolerance of plus-or-minus 1/4 inch is established, so that the seams meet within 1/4 inch of one another, the goal is achievable. Making the tolerance stricter, plus-or-minus 1/8 inch, tightens quality standards. Or making it more lenient, plus-or-minus 1/2 inch, loosens quality standards.

Tolerances provide a realistic way to control quality when mass-producing products. However, tolerances apply only to operations where some variance is acceptable (this includes most operations). An example of a specification not needing a tolerance is the number of buttons on a shirt. If seven buttons are specified, seven buttons must be on the shirt. What does need a tolerance, however, is the placement of those same buttons. They need to be placed as specified plus-or-minus 1/8 inch (written "as specified ± 1/8 inch").

Testing

The primary purpose of **testing** fabric, findings and trim, and apparel is to determine or confirm that the appropriate product quality level is maintained. Testing functions vary depending upon whether they are being conducted by a manufacturer or a retailer. The retailer is primarily concerned about how the product will perform in the store and when used by the consumer. Examples of store performance are mainly in the area of colorfastness to light and colorfastness to gases in the air. Poor performance in these areas causes uneven fading of the garment while still in the store. Once the consumer buys the apparel product, characteristics such as shrinkage and *crocking* (the rubbing off of dyestuffs) become very important. Standardized tests can measure these characteristics, but many retailers conduct only a simple wash test based on the assumption that the manufacturer conducted all the necessary standardized tests before the products were assembled.

Manufacturers test to verify the quality performance of incoming raw materials, both to meet retailers' and consumers' needs and to determine impact on manufacturing processes. Fabric characteristics such as excessive weight, stiffness, and elongation affect how the cloth handles in a production line. A fabric that crocks excessively can shut a plant down if the dyestuff redeposits itself on the operators, the machines, other products in process, and in the air. Comparing products from different suppliers verifies similarities and differences in raw materials from various sources. For more information on raw materials, see Chapters 7 and 8.

Manufacturers continue to monitor the quality of raw materials during apparel production, by cutting fabric swatches from the spreading table at random and sending them for testing. Test results are compiled into monthly or quarterly reports that rate the overall performance of each supplier.

Testing departments often participate in new product development. They conduct **product comparison research**, sometimes called **comparison shopping**, in which they evaluate competitors' products by measuring the dimensions, conducting physical tests, comparing prices, and analyzing the results to determine value. Testing departments also conduct **wear tests**, in which individuals wear apparel products to determine in-use performance. Short production lead times often prohibit in-depth wear tests, which require several months of repeatedly washing and wearing the same garment. Also, finding subjects willing to wear the same garment several times a week for several months is difficult. Consequently, manufacturers often conduct informal or abbreviated wear tests that last for a week or two and then project the results over a longer period of time. Thus, testing brings vital input to the merchandising/product development process.

Testing Process. In the normal testing process for apparel raw materials, a one- or two-yard piece of fabric or several samples of a finding item are sent to the testing laboratory, where lab personnel test the item using standardized test methods (Figures 3–9, 3–10, 3–11). (Additional examples appear in Chapter 7, Figures 7–6, 7–8, 7–9, 7–10.) Many of the

Figure 3–9 Technician using stitch counter to determine weave density of fabric. *(Courtesy of Levi Strauss & Company.)*

Figure 3–10 (a) Atlas Fade-ometer® and (b) specimens loaded inside Fade-ometer® to test colorfastness of the fabric to light exposure. *(Courtesy of Levi Strauss & Company.)*

tests require a temperature- and humidity-controlled environment to ensure results comparable to those of other labs (such as a supplier lab) performing the same tests. The testing department sends the lab report to the merchandiser, buyer, or quality staff member, who discusses the results with the supplier. If the product meets standards or they agree on needed corrections or allowable deviations, the fabric or finding is ordered and production can begin.

After the apparel production process begins, the testing lab repeats some of the same tests on fabric selected at random from production lots in addition to performing some new tests on production garments. If all processes have been carried out correctly, these tests will confirm the acceptability of the product. If testing uncovers problems at this stage, production is stopped and corrections made as soon as possible. Existing production is either reworked or marked as second quality and sold at a discount or destroyed.

The current trend in the industry is to move at an ever faster pace yet still deliver appropriate quality. One way to achieve shorter lead times is through the **certification** of supplier (mill) laboratories. This certification means the apparel manufacturers or retailers accept performance test data from the supplier in lieu of performing the tests themselves. Not only does this eliminate the transportation and testing time on the part of the manufacturer but it increases the reliability and cost effectiveness of the test data. Instead of basing purchasing decisions on a one- or two-yard sample, the decision is based on mill data encompassing a much larger sample size. Using a supplier certification system frees in-house testing personnel for other responsibilities. Many companies require that their suppliers send fabric and garments to independent laboratories for

verification of performance characteristics. In the past, these lab reports were delivered to the vendor of the product and then mailed or faxed to the buyer of the product, who originally requested the tests. Now computer technology makes it possible to transmit the reports directly from the independent lab simultaneously to the vendor and the buyer. This not only speeds up the process but increases the confidence in the accuracy of the test data as unacceptable test results cannot be falsified.

More and more manufacturers and retailers are establishing testing programs as part of the company quality program. Mills and large manufacturers and retailers have found in-house labs indispensable for a

Figure 3–11 Crockmeter for determining the colorfastness of materials to crocking (rubbing abrasion). *(Courtesy of Atlas Electric Devices Company.)*

long time. Small manufacturers and contractors now also participate through the use of independent laboratories. Thus, they do not have to incur the expense of setting up a lab but can still enjoy the benefits that a lab brings to maintaining a consistent quality level.

Test Methods. Testing labs use standardized test methods whenever possible. Standardized textile and apparel test methods are written by industry volunteers through two professional organizations—the American Society for Testing and Materials (ASTM) and the American Association of Textile Chemists and Colorists (AATCC). For the application of these test methods to fabrics and findings, see Chapters 7 and 8.

The **American Society for Testing and Materials (ASTM)** involves producers, users, consumers, and those having a general interest (representatives of government and academia) in writing standards for materials, products, systems, and services for a number of different industries. ASTM Committee D-13 meets twice a year to write and revise standards and specifications for textiles and apparel. A careful balance is maintained on the voting membership of each D-13 subcommittee so that one type of member does not control any particular area of interest. ASTM has no technical research or testing facilities; such work is done voluntarily by its technically qualified members. In the *Annual Book of ASTM Standards*, ASTM publishes the resulting standard test methods, specifications, practices, guides, classifications, and terminology. For example, ASTM provides 14 different standards relating to zippers alone (Table 3–7), just a small sample of the many standards provided by ASTM. ASTM also publishes a monthly periodical, *Standardization News*, providing technical information to the industry. For more information, contact the American Society for Testing and Materials (ASTM), 100 Barr Harbor Drive, West Conshohocken PA 19428. URL: http://www.astm.org.

The **American Association of Textile Chemists and Colorists (AATCC)** is commonly referred to in the industry as *A-Squared*. AATCC technical committee members, professional volunteers from a variety of organizations, meet three times a year. They write test methods relating to chemical processes and materials used in the textile industry, and AATCC publishes the test methods annually in the *AATCC Technical Manual*. For example, AATCC provides over 35 test methods and procedures for colorfastness alone (Table 3–8), just a small sample of the many test methods and procedures provided by AATCC. AATCC also conducts industry seminars and workshops designed to disseminate information quickly about industry concerns and common problems. AATCC also publishes a monthly periodical, *Textile Chemist and Colorist*, providing technical information. For more information, contact the American Association of Textile Chemists and Colorists (AATCC), One Davis Drive, P.O. Box 12215, Research Triangle Park, NC 27709.

Inspection

To monitor and regulate quality, most quality programs include **inspections**, the careful examination of fabric, garment parts, and completed garments at varying stages in the production cycle.

Table 3–7 ASTM Standards Relating to Textiles—Zippers

D2050-87 Terminology Relating to Zippers

D2051-86 Test Method for Durability of Finish of Zippers to Laundering

D2052-85 Test Method for Colorfastness of Zippers to Dry Cleaning

D2053-86 Test Method for Colorfastness of Zippers to Light

D2054-86 Test Method for Colorfastness of Zipper Tapes to Crocking

D2057-85 Test Method for Colorfastness of Zippers to Laundering

D2058-87 Test Method for Durability of Finish of Zippers to Dry Cleaning

D2059-87 Test Method for Resistance of Zippers to Salt Spray (Fog)

D2060-85 Methods for Measuring Zipper Dimensions

D2061-87 Test Methods for Strength Tests for Zippers

D2062-87 Test Methods for Operability of Zippers

D3657-88 Specification for Zipper Dimensions

D3692-89 Practice for Selection of Zippers for Care-Labeled Apparel and Household Furnishings

D4465-85 Performance Specification for Zippers for Denim Dungarees

Table 3–8 AATCC Test Methods and Procedures for Colorfastness

Method	Test Method
2-1988	Colorfastness to Fulling
3-1985	Colorfastness to Bleaching with Chlorine
6-1986	Colorfastness to Acids and Alkalis
7-1988	Colorfastness to Degumming
8-1988	Colorfastness to Crocking: AATCC Crockmeter Method
9-1988	Colorfastness to Stoving
11-1988	Colorfastness to Carbonizing
15-1985	Colorfastness to Perspiration
16-1987	Colorfastness to Light: General Method
16A-1988	Colorfastness to Light: Carbon-Arc Lamp, Continuous Light
16C-1988	Colorfastness to Light through Glass: Daylight
16D-1988	Colorfastness to Light: Carbon-Arc Lamp, Alternate Light and Darkness
16E-1987	Colorfastness to Light: Water-Cooled Xenon-Arc Lamp, Continuous Light
16F-1988	Colorfastness to Light: Water-Cooled Xenon-Arc Lamp, Alternate Light and Darkness
16G-1985	Colorfastness to Light: Determination of Fastness Above L-7
23-1988	Colorfastness to Burnt Gas Fumes
61-1989	Colorfastness to Laundering, Home and Commercial: Accelerated
101-1989	Colorfastness to Bleaching with Peroxide
104-1988	Colorfastness to Water Spotting
106-1986	Colorfastness to Water: Sea
107-1986	Colorfastness to Water
109-1987	Colorfastness to Ozone in the Atmosphere Under Low Humidities
116-1988	Colorfastness to Crocking: Rotary Vertical Crockmeter Method
117-1989	Colorfastness to Heat; Dry (Excluding Pressing)
125-1986	Colorfastness to Water and Light: Alternate Exposure
126-1986	Colorfastness to Water (High Humidity) and Light: Alternate Exposure
129-1985	Colorfastness to Ozone in the Atmosphere Under High Humidities
131-1985	Colorfastness to Pleating: Steam Pleating
132-1985	Colorfastness to Dry Cleaning
133-1989	Colorfastness to Heat: Hot Pressing
139-1985	Colorfastness to Light: Detection of Photochromism
157-1985	Colorfastness to Solvent Spotting: Perchloroethylene
162-1986	Colorfastness to Water: Chlorinated Pool
163-1987	Colorfastness: Dye Transfer in Storage; Fabric-to-Fabric
164-1987	Colorfastness to Oxides of Nitrogen in the Atmosphere Under High Humidities
172-1989	Colorfastness to Non-Chlorine Bleach in Home Laundering

Fabric Inspection. Fabric inspections occur at the mill and again immediately after the fabric has arrived at the apparel manufacturing facility. Inspections are performed on a percentage of all yardage. Inspectors note defects in terms of majors and minors. Usually a specified number of major defects are allowed but if the yardage contains more than the specified number of majors, it is rejected.

When time permits, the unacceptable yardage is returned to the vendor; however, in many cases time does not permit the return of the cloth. In this case, the manufacturer negotiates a discount, to be subtracted from the next fabric order.

Garment Inspection. Inspections of garment parts and completed garments are performed during and/or after the assembly process. Traditionally, sewing machine operators are paid according to the number of pieces they complete rather than by the hour. Varying rates are set according to the complexity of the operation; however, under this pay plan operators usually have more incentive to work rapidly than to work accurately. When using this system, management builds the desired quality standards, including tolerances, into the piece rate. The operator is then held responsible for both the quality and quantity of work performed as verified by inspectors. More progressive manufacturers are now incorporating the quality inspection area into piece rates and/or paying operators on a scale that is graduated according to quality levels produced.

The aim of any manufacturer's quality inspection system is more than to detect defective garments and prevent their shipment. It also is to detect the source of assembly problems, thus enabling the correction of the problem. When defective garments are found, inspectors send the garments back for rework and identify the source of the defectives on a log sheet. The log sheets are used to provide management with data on recurring problems. These are addressed in a variety of ways, including retraining and job repositioning. Inspection thus helps improve the quality of future production as it monitors the current production run. The manufacturer wants to catch any problems before reworks, shipping costs, and time delays occur.

Retailers that inspect incoming merchandise are better able to maintain a consistent image for quality than those who don't by preventing defective merchandise from reaching the sales floor. They also ensure that private label garments are consistently sized to meet fit specifications. Retailers that monitor the quality of the goods they sell are able to identify vendors that produce low-quality merchandise and to eliminate sources that are unable to meet quality standards.

Inspection Systems. Three types of quality inspection systems are commonly used in the apparel industry to verify garment quality: (1) in-line inspection, (2) trim and inspect at the end of the line, and (3) final audit. Quality is built into the product by using in-line inspections to catch defect causing problems early and preventing their recurrence. End-of-the-line inspections catch most defective garments missed in line or created in wet processing. And the final audit confirms the quality level and provides an acceptable quality level used for incentive and assessment.

In-Line Inspection. **In-line inspection** takes place *during* the production process as the garment is being assembled. *Quality* or *in-line inspectors* are responsible to the quality department and work among the sewing lines inspecting sections of garments as a bundle is completed. For example, one in-line inspector might be responsible for inspecting only the setting of pockets and zippers on a pair of pants. Another in-line inspector, at a later stage of production, inspects the sewing of the side and inseams. Instead of inspecting all pieces in a bundle, a **random sampling** or **statistical sampling** plan is used. With a statistical plan, a representative sample of the pieces is inspected rather than the entire bundle. For example, in a bundle of 36 pieces an inspector will look at 12 pieces and send the bundle back to the operator for repair if more than one defect is found. In-line inspectors are stationed at several places in the line depending upon the complexity of the garment construction. A simple garment style might have only one inspection station while a complicated garment style might have three inspection stations.

Trim and Inspect. The second type of quality inspection, found at the end of the production line, is often called **trim and inspect**. It is based on a **100% inspection** system, which means that each and every garment is inspected (Figure 3–12). The inspectors examine each garment for defects and trim any excessively long, dangling threads missed by the sewing operators. Any defective garments found are sent back for rework or repair. Statistics about defective garments are gathered to furnish trainers and supervisors information about problem machines, rates, or methods. If garments are wet-processed, trim and inspect occurs *after* wet processing. Although labor intensive and costly, 100% inspection is considered essential for wet-processed products due to the harsh agitation of wet processing. Some companies that make garments that are not wet-processed may use a statistical quality sampling plan in the final inspection, which is cost effective and can be appropriate for such products.

Final Audit. The last type of quality inspection, commonly called a **final audit** or **final inspection**, is either the last stage in manufacturing quality processes or the first stage in retailing quality processes. This function, like in-line inspection, is based on a statistical sampling plan. An *auditor* or *inspector* will examine a representative sample of the entire number of garments in a production lot. A certain number of defectives is allowed.

Figure 3–12 Inspection at end of production line. *(Courtesy of Winning Ways.)*

If a manufacturer is checking its own production and finds the lot contains more than the allowed number of defectives, the entire lot is sent back for 100% inspection and repair. If a retailer is performing the audit and finds more than the allowed number of defectives, the entire lot is sent back to the manufacturer. In either case, an **acceptable quality level (AQL)** is calculated to provide a numerical quality indicator. Sewing lines or companies with consistent AQLs of over 95% would be considered high performers. An important note is that a comprehensive final audit checks not only the quality of the garment but also accuracy of fold and pack, carton marking, case count, hang tags, and main labels.

Producers of high-quality garments tend to perform all three types of inspections. It requires a considerable investment in time and money but is considered worth it to achieve a quality level appropriate for their particular target market.

Some small manufacturers cannot afford the investment of all three types of inspection systems. They often use a combination of the three types. For example, one inspector will be used to conduct both random in-line inspections and final audits. This can be just as effective as the separate systems.

Analysis of Returns

It is a consumer's right and responsibility to communicate with the industry by returning unsatisfactory merchandise. However, consumers return only about 10% of defective garments to the retailer (Latture, 1981), even though they report dissatisfaction with over 20% of their clothing purchases (Best and Andreasen, 1976). The number of defective garments returned to manufacturers is even smaller. Because most people do not return garments with which they are dissatisfied, a return by a single customer may represent the dissatisfaction of many others. Some manufacturers consider each return representative of eight nonreturned defective garments. For this reason, each return is taken seriously. Defective garment returns benefit both consumers and the apparel industry. Consumers gain the benefit of having a defective garment replaced or their money refunded. Retailers and manufacturers benefit from the opportunity to win back the consumer's good will, and they can gain a better understanding of their products and consumer expectations. However, consumers fail to return defective garments for a number of reasons.

1. If the price of a garment is low, consumers may have low expectations for the garment and thus do not return it when it fails. If consumers pay a lot for a garment, they expect more from it and are more apt to return it when it fails.
2. If the price of a garment is low, the consumer may not consider it worth the time and trouble to make the return. Consumers are more apt to return high-price than low-price garments because their time and trouble are better rewarded.
3. Because most people own many garments, when one garment fails, a consumer is not forced to return the failed garment for lack of anything else to wear.
4. Consumers often accept the blame for choosing a defective garment even though the defect may have been latent at the time of purchase. They feel that somehow they "should have known better." As a result, consumers fail to return garments with performance problems that are the manufacturer's responsibility.
5. Some retailers' return policies (and sometimes retail employees' reception of returns) discourage returns. For example, if the consumer loses the receipt for a garment that turns out to be defective, he or she is not permitted or does not feel entitled to return it.

Retailers, however, are not as reluctant to **return to vendor (RTV)** defective garments to manufacturers. In most cases retailers pass on the individual garments returned by consumers, but in some cases retailers return bulk quantities of merchandise that did not sell well. A typical return by a retailer to a manufacturer could range from single garments in various styles to hundreds of garments in one style. Retailers should have a valid reason for the return of large quantities of merchandise and not try to pass the consequences of a bad buy on to the manufacturer.

Most retailers, manufacturers, and suppliers handle the financial aspect of defective merchandise returns as a chargeback system to simplify the paperwork. In a **chargeback** system, a running total of all defective merchandise is kept by the buyer, authorization for return is granted from the seller, and the appropriate amounts are subtracted from payments on future merchandise.

Conscientious manufacturers thoroughly analyze customer returns. Defective garments are sent to a central receiving location where trained associates study the actual garments and read the accompanying documentation. Records are kept according to garment style, location of production, and reason for return. Many of these quality-conscious companies continually review the returns report to identify manufacturing problems that can be corrected in future production. For example, a jeans manufacturer was experiencing large numbers of soiled jeans returned from retailers and consumers. The quality staff determined that the soil was coming from a variety of places within the plant where garments were coming in contact with oily and dirty equipment. A directive was issued for the plant to begin a major housekeeping program that involved regular cleaning of all equipment. In addition, spot cleaning stations were created and located near the inspection stations. Inspectors were trained to find spots and soils during the inspection process. Operators were trained to professionally spot clean any spots and soil found. These actions saved the manufacturing company thousands of dollars annually in customer returns and created an unmeasurable amount of good will with satisfied retailers and consumers. An analysis of returned goods is also an excellent way for retailers to find out about garment failures that occurred after the sale, in use by the consumer, and thus improve future products.

If the volume level of the retailer is too great to permit the actual return of the garments, reports are often substituted. In fact, in this age of high technology, some manufacturers prefer a report in lieu of garments. As long as the report contains the needed basic information, the manufacturer still benefits without the need to see the garments. On the other hand, if the garments are discarded without the creation of a report, the manufacturer is denied the feedback from consumers about the in-use performance of the products.

Retailers also benefit from analyzing customer returns. An analysis of merchandise returned by consumers helps retailers trace which vendors' goods are most frequently returned. They can reward vendors with good quality records by buying from them again and can eliminate sources of consumer dissatisfaction.

ISO 9000 Certification

There has been a push in recent years to establish international standards for quality practices and systems within a company, particularly through **ISO 9000 certification.** The ISO 9000 standards are a series of voluntary, private-sector standards against which individual companies may become certified. **ISO** is not, as many think, an acronym for International Standards Organization. Instead, it is short for the **International Organization for Standardization.** The word "ISO" comes from the Greek word "isos," meaning equal. U.S.-member organizations include the American Society for Quality Control (ASQC) and the American National Standards Institute (ANSI). **The American Society for Quality Control (ASQC)** is a professional organization for people interested in quality control. ASQC publishes annually the *ASQC Textiles and Needle Trades Division Transactions*, a series of papers relating to textile and apparel quality. For more information, contact the American Society for Quality Control (ASQC), Textile and Needle Trades Division, 611 East Wisconsin Avenue, P.O. Box 3005, Milwaukee, WI 53201. URL: http://www.asqc.org. The **American National Standards Institute (ANSI)** is a privately funded federation of leaders from both the public and private sectors that coordinates the U.S. voluntary consensus standards system. For more information, contact the American National Standards Institute (ANSI), 11 West 42nd Street, New York, NY 10036. URL: http://www.ansi.org.

The ISO 9000 series of standards is applicable to any kind of organization in any industry. It provides specific guidelines for establishing and maintaining a quality system within a company. The intent is to provide an international benchmark for in-house quality practices which allows the comparison of the procedures a company uses for meeting quality standards to those used by other companies, on a global basis. The ISO 9000 series of standards includes:

ISO 9000: Quality Management and Quality Assurance Standards: Guidelines for Selection and Use

ISO 9001: Quality Systems: Model for Quality Assurance in Design/Development, Production, Installation and Servicing

ISO 9002: Quality Systems: Model for Quality Assurance in Production and Installation

ISO 9003: Quality Systems: Model for Quality Assurance in Final Inspection and Test

ISO 9004: Quality Management and Quality System Elements: Guidelines

While the ISO 9000 series of standards contains many details, in essence the standards require a company to "document what you do" and then "do what you say you do." The company's trading partners, either suppliers or customers, can trust it to produce the same level of quality it says it does, each and every time. ISO certification serves as a reflection of a well-organized operation. Note that it does *not* provide a guarantee of product or service quality; it provides assurance that a company adheres to its own standards and thus produces a *consistent* level of quality. It is left entirely up to the individual companies as to what level of quality they choose to produce. Companies that achieve ISO certification provide this as evidence to both their suppliers and their customers that they have implemented a plan for achieving consistent quality (Lund, 1994).

There are many reasons for American companies to become ISO certified. They include

1. maintaining or gaining access to a market where ISO or equivalent compliance is required (particularly Europe)
2. meeting the requirements of a single customer (such as some government agencies that require ISO or equivalent compliance for large contracts)
3. matching the challenge of a competitor who has become certified
4. seeking the greater focus on and awareness of quality that comes about through the ISO certification process.

Independent test laboratories, due to the role of quality assurance in global trade, are the main examples of companies related to the textile and apparel industries that are in the process of becoming ISO certified. However, we should expect more and more companies (both manufacturers and retailers) to join this quality initiative in the future.

SUMMARY

Quality is important to building a successful apparel business. Quality is defined as the degree to which a garment meets expectations. Consumers perceive quality differently, depending on the target market, end use of the garment, and on demographics and psychographics. Quality apparel results when the intrinsic physical features of a garment—its design, materials, construction, and finish—produce the aesthetic (attractiveness) and functional (utility and durability) performance desired by the consumer. Enumerating the buying benefits related to each of the garment's selling points helps consumers understand how the garment fulfills their wants and needs.

Quality evaluation is quantified by the perceived quality model, in which the consumer weights the importance of and rates each of the features of the garment being judged to find out the contribution of each characteristic to the overall quality evaluation. The sum of the contributions of all the features yields an overall quality score for a garment that is useful in comparing two different garments or types of garments evaluated by the same consumer, or in examining how different consumers evaluate the same garment.

Aesthetic features generally determine the consumer's evaluation of the garment's quality, or desirability, at the point of sale. But functional features become more important when the garment is put into use. The apparel industry maximizes consumer satisfaction by providing garments with quality aesthetic performance and minimizes consumer dissatisfaction by providing garments with quality functional performance. Ultimate consumer satisfaction, rather than merely satisfying consumers at the point of sale, is the goal of forward-looking companies.

Extrinsic aspects, such as price, brand, and retail store reputation also influence the consumer's perception of quality. Price lines often cause consumers to associate price and quality. However, price is an inadequate predictor of apparel quality. The perceived value of a garment expresses the relationship between its price and its perceived quality.

A comprehensive industry approach builds quality into apparel products by establishing standards and specifications for both raw materials and garments, with reasonable tolerances, according to customers' expectations; laboratory testing ensures conformance. Manufacturers inspect 100% of production or a random sample, using in-process inspections, end-of-line inspections, and final audits. An analysis of returns provides feedback about customer dissatisfaction with the garment. Through such efforts, the apparel industry strives to provide apparel that not only attracts consumers but satisfies them.

Quality Checklist

If you can answer yes to each of these questions regarding the garment you are evaluating and the company that produced it, it has been produced using accepted quality processes.

✔ Does the company have a quality department dedicated to consistently achieving the desired level of quality? Does the company have a written quality philosophy statement?

✔ Does the company have raw materials and garment performance standards? Are these standards up to date, realistic, and appropriate for the target market?

✔ Did the company establish raw materials and product specifications which reflect the company's overall quality standards?

✔ Are standards and specifications written in detail? Are they communicated to and understood by suppliers, contractors, and throughout the company?

✔ Are realistic tolerances provided when variance is acceptable?

✔ Are standards monitored and enforced using measurement, testing, and inspection procedures? Are test methods standardized?

✔ Is the product compared to the competition? Is the product wear tested? Does it successfully pass home laundering processes?

✔ Does the inspection process include in-line inspection, end-of-line inspection, and/or a final audit?

✔ Does the company analyze returns of merchandise to pinpoint problems that can be corrected in future production?

✔ Does the company "document what it does" and then "do what it says it does" in terms of its quality processes?

New Terms

If you can define each of these terms and differentiate between related terms, you have gained a good working vocabulary for discussing the topics in this chapter. The terms are listed in the order in which they appear in the chapter.

apparel quality
rework
physical feature
design
materials
construction
intrinsic attribute
performance feature
aesthetic performance
functional performance
selling point
buying benefit
extrinsic attribute
price line
off-pricing/discounting
prêt-à-porter/prêt
better
bridge
moderate
budget
price point
couture
haute couture

bespoke
designer clothing
perceived quality model
determinant attribute
market segmentation
target market
end use
investment dressing
demographics
psychographics
value
cost per wear
International Fabricare Institute (IFI)
quality department
quality assurance (QA)
quality control (QC)
standard
specification/spec
systems approach
defect guide
major defect
minor defect
tolerance
testing
product comparison research/comparison shopping
wear test
certification
American Society for Testing and Materials (ASTM)
American Association of Textile Chemists and Colorists (AATCC)
inspection
in-line inspection
random sampling/statistical sampling
trim and inspect
100% inspection
final audit/final inspection
acceptable quality level (AQL)
return to vendor (RTV)
chargeback
ISO 9000 certification
International Organization for Standardization (ISO)
American Society for Quality Control (ASQC)
American National Standards Institute (ANSI)

Review Questions

1. Define apparel quality.
2. How do the physical features of a garment and the performance of a garment differ?
3. List the four main physical dimensions and the two main performance dimensions of apparel. Give examples of each.
4. Why are buying benefits more important to the customer than selling points?

5. Which performance dimension is more important at the point of sale? Which performance dimension becomes more important when the garment is in use?
6. How do consumers differ in their individual perceptions of quality?
7. What is the difference between the intrinsic and extrinsic features of a garment?
8. List, in order from most expensive to least expensive, the various price lines defined in this chapter. Discuss the meaning of each.
9. How is a price line different from a price point?
10. Discuss the relationship of quality, price, and value.
11. Explain the concept of cost per wear.
12. What is the role of a modern quality department?
13. Differentiate between standards and specifications. How are standards and specifications useful in the pursuit of quality?
14. Compare and contrast 100% inspection and random statistical sample inspection. What are the advantages and disadvantages of each method?
15. How are customer returns helpful to retailers and manufacturers?

Activities

1. Study the perceived quality model presented in this chapter. Do you think the model explains the way consumers actually make apparel purchase decisions? Why or why not?
2. Buy two similar garments for comparison (e.g., two T-shirts or two pairs of jeans).
   a. Evaluate the garments at the point of sale, using the perceived quality model.
   b. Wear and care for the garments over the course of a few months.
   c. Evaluate the garment in use, using the perceived quality model.
   d. What differences did you find in your point-of-sale and in-use evaluations? Explain.
3. Establish performance criteria for different types of garments. For example, what are the typical attractiveness, utility, and durability expectations for the following classifications of merchandise?
   a. wedding gowns
   b. baseball uniforms
   c. tailored suits
   d. infant sleepers
   e. swimsuits
4. Establish performance criteria for different target markets for the same type of garment. For example, what are the typical attractiveness, utility, and durability expectations of customers who buy the following classifications of merchandise?
   a. jogging shorts
   b. men's casual shorts
   c. women's casual shorts
   d. toddlers' shorts
   e. biking shorts
5. Using a catalog, list the selling points and buying benefits the retailer uses to promote three different products. Could the use of selling points and buying benefits be more effective? If so, how?
6. Visit a major department store. Identify the locations of their budget, moderate, and better goods. What terms does the store use to differentiate between these departments?
7. Survey five friends. Which do they use more in evaluating apparel quality, price or their own knowledge about quality? How much does the price of a garment tell them about the quality of the apparel they buy? Based on your findings, to what extent does price influence consumers' perception of apparel quality?
8. For two similar garments in your wardrobe, estimate the cost per wear of each. Determine which is the better value from a cost-per-wear standpoint. Compare your results with those of your classmates.
9. Visit the quality department of a manufacturer or major retailer.
   a. What are their product standards?
   b. What details do their specifications cover?
   c. How do they establish standards and specifications?
   d. How do they communicate standards and specifications?
   e. Do their specifications include tolerances?
   f. What inspection methods do they use?
   g. What testing methods do they employ?
   h. How do they analyze returned merchandise?
10. Visit the Internet WWW sites for ASTM, AATCC, ASQC, and ANSI. What useful information can you find?

The Mass-Production Process: The Apparel Industry at Work

Chapter Objectives

1. Describe in order the steps in the mass production of apparel.
2. Discuss the costing process and the relationship of cost to price.
3. Consider the impact of computers and related technologies on the apparel production process.

The mass production of apparel is accomplished through an amazing combination of human ingenuity and sophisticated technology and equipment. Most apparel is mass-manufactured in a series of steps which vary slightly from firm to firm. Each part of the process impacts the quality of the finished garment. The usual production sequence is as follows: (1) evaluation of the previous line and trend analysis; (2) design; (3) sourcing, including costing; (4) preproduction; (5) production; (6) distribution; and (7) sales. For details, see the **apparel production cycle** in Figure 4–1. Within each category many processes are happening simultaneously for different products and different selling seasons.

Line development or **lead time calendars** (Table 4–1) help in the scheduling of key activities during all stages of the production cycle. Separate calendars containing the deadlines for each selling season are developed for each product line and are distributed throughout the company.

The basic concepts in Figure 4–1 and Table 4–1 apply to most firms; however, the exact production cycle and line development calendar vary from company to company, based on the type of products

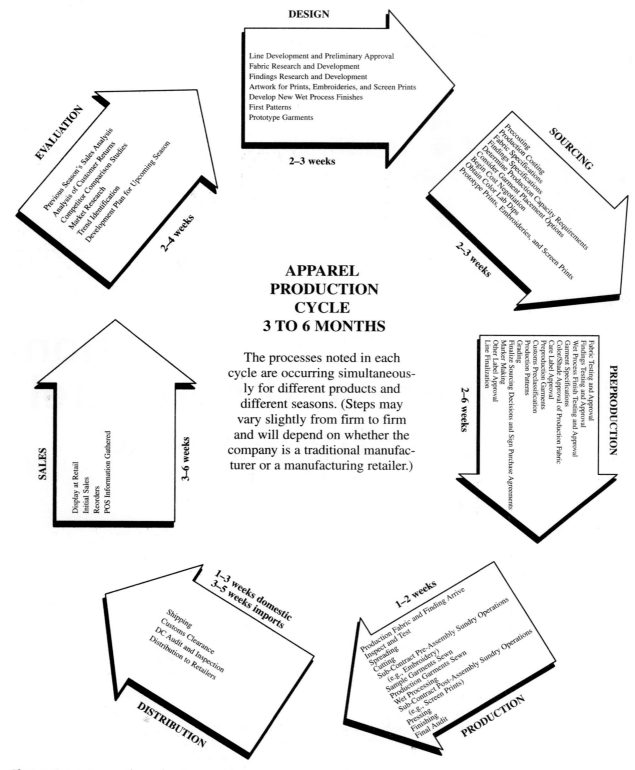

DESIGN

Line Development and Preliminary Approval
Fabric Research and Development
Findings Research and Development
Artwork for Prints, Embroideries, and Screen Prints
Develop New Wet Process Finishes
First Patterns
Prototype Garments

2–3 weeks

EVALUATION

Previous Season's Sales Analysis
Analysis of Customer Returns
Competitor Comparison Studies
Market Research
Trend Identification
Development Plan for Upcoming Season

2–4 weeks

SOURCING

Precosting
Production Costing
Fabric Specifications
Findings Specifications
Determine Production Capacity Requirements
Consider Garment Placement Options
Begin Cost Negotiation
Obtain Color Lab Dips
Prototype Prints, Embroideries, and Screen Prints

2–3 weeks

**APPAREL
PRODUCTION
CYCLE
3 TO 6 MONTHS**

The processes noted in each cycle are occurring simultaneously for different products and different seasons. (Steps may vary slightly from firm to firm and will depend on whether the company is a traditional manufacturer or a manufacturing retailer.)

PREPRODUCTION

Fabric Testing and Approval
Findings Testing and Approval
Wet Process Finish Testing and Approval
Garment Specifications
Color/Shade Approval of Production Fabric
Care Label Approval
Preproduction Garments
Customs Preclassification
Production Patterns
Grading
Finalize Sourcing Decisions and Sign Purchase Agreements
Marker Making
Other Label Approval
Line Finalization

2–6 weeks

SALES

Display at Retail
Initial Sales
Reorders
POS Information Gathered

3–6 weeks

DISTRIBUTION

1–3 weeks domestic
3–5 weeks imports

Shipping
Customs Clearance
DC Audit and Inspection
Distribution to Retailers

PRODUCTION

1–2 weeks

Production Fabric and Finding Arrive
Inspect and Test
Spreading
Cutting
Sub-Contract Pre-Assembly Sundry Operations
(e.g., Embroidery)
Sample Garments Sewn
Production Garments Sewn
Wet Processing
Sub-Contract Post-Assembly Sundry Operations
(e.g., Screen Prints)
Pressing
Finishing
Final Audit

Figure 4–1 Apparel production cycle.

being manufactured. It also will vary depending on whether the company is a traditional manufacturer with its own production facilities or a manufacturing retailer relying completely on contractors.

Table 4–1 Line Development/Lead Time Calendar
(Courtesy of OshKosh B'Gosh.)

Who is Responsible	Item to Complete	Trans	Fall	Holiday 1	Holiday 2	Spring 1	Spring 2
	Ready to ship to retailers	5/1, 6/1	7/1, 8/1	9/1, 10/1	11/1, 12/1	1/1, 2/1	3/1, 4/1
	Chinese New Year	*2/14–28*	*2/14–28*	*2/14–28*	*2/14–28*		
Merchandiser	Fabric direction, predip colors	7/11	9/19	11/19	1/25	4/4	5/21
Merch/Sourcing	Send costing packages: pre: artwork/specs/ sketch/overview	7/25	10/3	12/3	2/8	4/18	6/4
Merch/Sourcing	Finalize quotes/ placement	8/15	10/24	12/24	3/1	5/9	6/25
Pttn Engineers	Send final pattern packages/artwork/ construction	8/18	10/27	12/27	3/1	5/12	6/28
Manufacturer	Receive initial strikeoff's of artwork, lab dips	9/1	10/31	1/10	3/15	5/26	7/12
Manufacturer	Approval of scmprt/ emb/lab dips/ handlooms/proto's	9/15	11/14	1/24	3/29	6/9	7/26
Manufacturer	Start production of sample line	9/18	11/17	1/27	4/1	6/12	7/29
Merch/Sourcing	Samples/boards ready for sales mtg	10/13	12/12	3/3	4/26	7/7	8/23
	Sales meeting	11/1, 2	1/2, 3	3/13,14	5/16,17	7/24/25	
Sales Force	Present line to retailers	11/6	1/9	3/18	5/20	7/29	9/16
Sales Force	First tier quantities input by customer service	11/27	1/30	4/8	6/10	8/19	10/6
Merchandiser	Quantities to buy from knit timeline	11/27	2/5	4/8	6/10	8/19	10/6
Sourcing	Program placement from knit timeline	10/28	12/28	3/14	5/15	7/15	9/14
Manufacturer	Woven & Y/D fabric production (60 days)	10/16	12/16	3/2	5/3	7/3	9/2
Manufacturer	Printed knit fabric production (45 days)	10/31	12/31	3/17	5/18	7/18	9/17
Manufacturer	Fabric transit	12/15	3/1	5/1	7/2	9/1	11/1
Manufacturer	Cut	1/5	3/22	5/22	7/23	9/22	11/22
Manufacturer	Sew (30–45 days)	1/12	3/29	5/29	7/30	9/29	11/29
Manufacturer	Pack	3/13	5/13	7/13	9/13	11/13	1/13
Manufacturer	Xfactory	3/20	5/20	7/20	9/20	11/20	1/20
	In DC date	4/15	6/15	8/15	10/15	12/15	2/15

Note. Dates in italics are changed due to timing of Chinese New Year.

A number of different people pool their talents and coordinate their efforts to manufacture apparel.

Table 4–2 provides examples of job titles in a typical apparel manufacturing corporation. Exact job titles

Table 4–2 Apparel Manufacturing Job Titles

In-Plant Job Titles	Corporate Job Titles
Management Positions	*Management Positions*
Plant Manager	President (CEO)
Plant Supervisor	Various Vice-presidents
Line Supervisor	Various Directors
Apparel Engineer (Industrial or Sewing)	Various Managers and Supervisors
In-Plant Staff Positions	*Corporate Staff Positions*
	Merchandising Department
	Merchandise Manager
	Assistant Merchandise Manager
	Tracking Assistant
	Planning Assistant
	Trend Assistant
	Design Department
	Designer
	Assistant Designer
	Patternmaker
	Assistant Patternmaker
	Marking Technician-Prototypes
	Cutting Technician-Prototypes
	Sewing Operator-Prototypes
	Finishing Operator-Prototypes
	Material Control Department
	Grader
	Marker Technician
	Specifications Department
	Specifications Engineer
	Specifications Technician
	Product Engineer
	Product Analyst
	Apparel Engineering Department
Junior Engineer	Cutting Engineer
Engineer Analyst	Finishing Engineer
	Sewing (Industrial) Engineer
	Special Projects Engineer
	Safety Engineer
	Equipment Engineer
	Wet Process Engineering Department
Wet Process Engineer	Wet Process Engineer
Wet Process Preparer	Wet Process Technician-Prototypes
	Quality Assurance Department
In-line Inspector	Quality Engineer
Final Inspector	Quality Analyst
In-plant Auditor	Field Inspector
	Testing Technician
	Testing Engineer
	Claims Specialist

Table 4–2 Continued

In-Plant Staff Positions	Corporate Staff Positions
	Purchasing Department
	Purchasing Agent-Fabric
	Purchasing Agent-Sundries
Sourcing (Contracting) Department	
	Contract Coordinator
	Assistant Coordinator
Apparel Production (In-Plant)	
Marker Technician	
Fabric Inspector	
Spreader	
Cutter	
Shademaker	
Bundler	
Line Supervisor	
Sewing Operator	
In-line Inspector	
Repair Operator	
Thread Clipper	
Finishing Foreman	
Trim & Inspect Inspector	
Final Inspector	
Presser	
Fold & Pack Operator	
Quality Auditor	

and associated responsibilities differ slightly from company to company. Small manufacturers understandably collapse more job responsibilities under fewer job titles.

---·---·---

EVALUATION OF THE PREVIOUS LINE AND TREND ANALYSIS

Many people think the apparel production process begins with the design inspiration; however, that concept is more applicable to the haute couture design process. In mass production, the design process is guided by a **development plan** that is formulated before any actual "designing" begins. This development plan is based on an evaluation of last season's sales figures, on market research and trend identification (both U.S. and foreign), on analysis of customer returns, and on comparison of competitors' products. The development plan provides the general direction for the upcoming season in terms of color and style.

Formulation of the development plan begins with an analysis of the sales figures and customer return data from the previous line. This data indicates the styles that sold best—those most well received by the consumer. These styles serve as a good base for the next line. Many companies also conduct market research. They survey customers or include them in **focus groups** to discover their wants and needs. Classic-styled or basic garments such as turtlenecks or T-shirts undergo product **comparison studies**, in which designers or merchandisers shop the market and purchase examples of competitors' products, which are carefully scrutinized for fit, fabrication, physical performance, appearance, and price.

Fashion trends must be identified and included in the formulation of the development plan so that the new line reflects the trends popular with consumers in terms of silhouette, style, color, and detail. Companies research trend information in a variety of ways:

- Designers or merchandisers travel to places like Europe or New York City to view designer collections, survey the market, and collect trend information by observation.
- Some companies have in-house trend merchandisers responsible for continuously being on top of current trends. Other companies consult **fashion forecasters** and **color services**, who analyze fashion influences and predict fashion and color direction.

- Industry professionals read trade publications such as *Women's Wear Daily (WWD)* and *Daily New Record (DNR)* (for menswear), as well as consumer fashion magazines, to help them keep abreast of trends.

DESIGN

The design process includes (1) line development, (2) preliminary line approval, (3) fabric and findings research and development, (4) first patterns, and (5) prototype garments. In mass production, most large firms *combine the responsibilities of **designers** with those of* **merchandisers,** who formulate and build the line to satisfy the company's target market. (Similarly, large retailers developing lines of private-label apparel may call their product development people *buyers* or *merchandisers*.) Thus, the distinction between designers and merchandisers in many firms has become one of semantics, with the title *designer* perhaps bringing to mind creativity and the title *merchandiser* bringing to mind a business orientation and focus on the target market. In truth, regardless of the title, both designers and merchandisers must creatively focus on business goals *and* the wants and needs of the target market.

Line Development

During the design process, designers or merchandisers come up with a cohesive **color story** and design concepts that reflect the general ideas suggested by the development plan for the season. They take their inspiration from fabric, from the arts, from history, from current events, from people-watching, from suppliers and vendors, or from anywhere they can get a creative, marketable idea. A series of related designs produced by a particular manufacturer makes up a comprehensive package called a **line**, or a **collection**. Sometimes the line is divided into small **groups** of garments, coordinated together based on color, theme, fabric, or silhouette.

- Fashion-forward lines, such as junior sportswear lines, consist of the newest design concepts.
- Classic lines, such as men's suits, merely update standard designs.
- Firms producing staple or basic lines, such as underwear, may show little or no change from one season to the next.

Designers or merchandisers originate ideas for the creation of new styles by sketching (using computer aided design) or by suggesting changes in existing styles. Occasionally, in trendy or high fashion designs,

a designer will **drape** a design on a mannequin using fabric. Some companies' philosophy is to knock off or copy, with or without modification, the general idea of successful designs shown by other firms; apparel designs are rarely protected by copyrights (although fabric designs may be, and in some cases, manufacturers will buy exclusive rights to a fabric for a period of time). Small firms or those producing classic or basic garments may not have a designer or merchandiser; minor changes in design and fabrication are made in proven **bodies** or styles from season to season and are decided by the production manager, who oversees production.

Computer-aided design (CAD) systems aid the design and manufacturing processes. CAD maximizes designer creativity and speeds design and marketing in numerous ways. The majority of large manufacturing companies use CAD systems. Even for smaller firms, CAD is becoming commonplace, with systems available at a wide range of price points. For more information on CAD, contact the **Computer Integrated Textile Design Association (CITDA)**, P.O. Box 849, Burlington, NC 27216. URL: http://www.citda.org.

CAD systems offer tremendous possibilities, although few companies that own CAD systems take advantage of all their technological potential. For example, CAD can

1. eliminate time-consuming sketching by allowing the designer to draw an original design on-screen and make changes in it without redrawing it each time. Either a computer mouse or a digitizing pen and tablet are used for input.
2. allow the designer to use, recombine, or change elements of garments in memory to create new designs. These garments may be internally generated from past seasons or come from a purchased library of styles.
3. scan actual garments or pictures of garments into memory, where the designer modifies them as desired (Figure 4–2). Companies use this feature to adapt to their own use historical garments, competitors' styles, or samples bought in another country.
4. scan existing fabric swatches into memory, enabling the designer to duplicate print motifs that formerly took hours to draw by hand.
5. apply colors and prints to garment designs on-screen. The computer mixes literally millions of colors as directed by the designer and instantly applies them to the design. Colors can be lightened, darkened, or changed in hue at the touch of a button, eliminating time-consuming hand coloring of sketches. Special printers can print these designs directly onto sample fabric yardage.

Figure 4–2 Artworks™ computer-aided design system applies scanned fabric print to sketch on screen. (*Courtesy of Gerber Garment Technology, Inc.*)

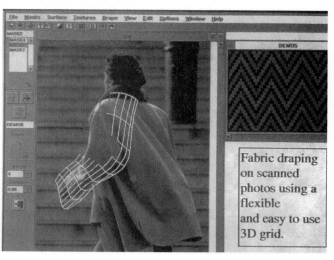

Fabric draping on scanned photos using a flexible and easy to use 3D grid.

Figure 4–3 Artworks™ computer-aided design system simulates 3-D draping of fabric on sketches and photos. (*Courtesy of Gerber Garment Technology, Inc.*)

6. allow the designer to experiment endlessly with the size, shape, orientation, and color of designs at a touch, and to store favorites for later access.

7. communicate designs to other locations via fax or on-line computer systems. The graphic output arrives, along with the written specifications, at the contractor's production facilities across town or around the world in a matter of seconds.

8. preview lines on-screen. Designers and merchandisers can edit and approve potential designs, refining and tailoring them to meet requirements. Buyers can see manufacturers' lines from around the world without leaving their offices. The main disadvantage of viewing a sketched line on the computer is that the garment may look different when made up in fabric. For example, the drape and hang of the cloth may vary from sketch to actual sample. This problem is addressed with the new digital imaging systems which can transmit images of actual garments being modeled live (Figure 4–3).

9. provide digital images for desktop publishing or advertisements and catalogs before the actual garments are produced. These features are helpful to mail-order retailers, who must plan their catalogs many months in advance.

10. require **prototype** (trial) garments to be produced only of the designs chosen for production. Traditionally, manufacturers make prototypes of many garments each season, some of which are not chosen for the line and others of which are not chosen for production. Prototypes ordinarily cost between $10 and $300 each to make, depending on the garment, due to fabric and labor

costs, and many prototypes are made several times before the design is approved. Because buyers can approve designs and see lines on-screen, sometimes prototypes are not needed until the design is tested in fabric for production. The need for fewer prototypes reduces costs. Also, eliminating early prototype making allows the line to be designed closer to the selling season—eight to ten weeks closer—so the designer or merchandiser can make more accurate decisions about what will sell well.

Preliminary Line Approval

Because of the demand for increasingly shorter lead times and the desire to be as close to the market as possible, many lines are almost finalized before any sewing is done. The lines are prepared as sketches (often CAD system output) on **line presentation boards** (groups of sketches on poster boards) and presented to a group of decision makers. Each design is discussed in detail. These meetings usually include designers, merchandisers, patternmakers, production engineers, production managers, and quality managers. Because each person represents a different aspect of the production process, their input can prevent problems from occurring during production. For example, if a new design detail needs a special attachment for a sewing machine, the production engineer informs the group about the needed device, gets it ordered, and schedules trial runs with it before production begins. The group decides on the most suitable production methods for each design presented. A true cost is then prepared and presented to the designers or merchandisers who make the final decision on whether to keep the style or drop it. They base their decision on lead times, product cost, production capabilities, expected sales, and markup of the style.

Fabric and Findings Research and Development

Manufacturers must seek out the right fabric and findings for the styles they plan to produce. (For more information, see Chapters 7 and 8.) Most fabric and findings suppliers send their sales reps to large manufacturers and retailers to privately show their product lines. "Mill week" is a common occurrence at some large companies where representatives from many major mills present their latest fabric lines to the buyers and merchandisers of a company. Companies also conduct fabric and findings research at trade shows such as the Bobbin Show™. Designers or merchandisers may use existing raw materials or ask suppliers to develop new, customized fabrics and findings to create unique looks for their products.

When designers or merchandisers like a particular fabric (or finding item), they have several yards (or samples) sent in for experimentation and testing. If the materials pass testing, they are used in a prototype garment to see how they look when "made up." If chosen, the fabric (or finding) is reordered in a larger quantity to make other prototypes.

At this point in the process, artwork must be developed and approved for any fabric prints, embroideries, or screen prints that will be used on the fabric or garment. Any new wet process finishes must also be developed and tested.

Making of First Patterns

Once the design ideas are finalized, some styles are selected to be made into garments (usually new styles or styles having significant change from the previous line). First, patternmakers convert these designs into **first patterns** that, when the fabric pieces are sewn together, create prototype garments. The patternmaker develops a pattern piece for each part of a garment, making the necessary changes in the company's basic pattern, the **sloper** or **basic block.** (An example of a basic block appears in Chapter 5, Figure 5-5.) A company derives its basic block through a process called **drafting,** in which a pattern is drawn using the body measurements of the typical target customer. A CAD **pattern design system (PDS)** speeds patternmaking and can improve its accuracy. An experienced production patternmaker efficient in the use of the PDS system drafts the block on the computer. Other patternmakers draft on hard paper

Figure 4–4 Computerized pattern design system with automated pattern grading. *(Courtesy of Gerber Garment Technology, Inc.)*

and later enter the block using a **digitizer** that converts the hard pattern into a computerized format. The patternmaker then directs the computer to make the changes in the pattern on-screen using standard *flat patternmaking* techniques (Figure 4–4).

Construction of Prototype Garments

Prototype garments are the experimental garments made from the first patterns. They seldom are constructed using mass production techniques or finished with finalized wet process formulas, but they nevertheless allow merchandisers and designers the opportunity to see the garment made in a comparable fabric and with a finish as close as possible to the actual production finish. This is necessary to perfect fit and silhouette concepts. Often multiple versions of the same style are made repeatedly depending upon the accuracy of the first pattern until the desired effect is achieved.

Highly skilled operators construct each prototype garment in a **sample room** or **prototype lab.** Instead of using a production assembly process, a single operator makes an entire garment. Sometimes sample yardage is available in the actual fabric; however, if the prototype development happens before the fabric is available, fabric representative of the desired final fabrication is used. If the merchandisers or designers are not satisfied with the prototype garment, it is reworked or remade; for example, a different sleeve style might improve the styling of the garment or changing the angle of the darts might improve the fit of the garment.

Prototype garments serve three additional purposes. The first is to help costing engineers accurately determine if the garment can be profitably produced at its target price point. The second is to help manufacturing develop production cost estimates. The third use is to provide a three-dimensional, on-site reference example to accompany written specifications sent to production locations, either in-house or outsourced.

SOURCING (CONTRACTING)

Manufacturers must reserve the necessary quantities of raw materials and decide who will cut and sew the garments at this stage in the production cycle. Cutting and/or sewing may be done in the manufacturer's own plants. If a manufacturer is going to **source out** or contract production to another company, the **outsourcing** process begins now (Figure 4–5). Contractors and fabric suppliers specialize in certain products or processes. When sourcing fabrics or garments, these specialties need to be targeted. Determining the lead time, production capacity availability, and negotiated cost are key ingredients in the garment placement decision. Once these factors are determined, then sourcing (often global and done on-line) can be enacted to find the optimum mill or contractor. Table 4–3 contains a list of Internet sourcing resources.

If production is not to be done in-house, there are a number of sourcing options to consider. (For more information, see Chapter 1).

- Contracted domestic production. No duties apply to domestic production, but wages in the United States are higher than in many foreign countries.
- 9802/807 production done in a foreign country (primarily the Caribbean Basin). No duty is paid on the cut fabric that is sent outside the U.S., but duty is paid on the assembled garment that is sent back. The advantage of 9802/807 production is cost savings due to the lower wages paid to factory workers in these countries.
- Global outsourcing, the sourcing of products from outside the United States. This includes buying from a domestic importer, a foreign producer, using a foreign contractor (the most common), or domestic ownership of a foreign factory (the most rare). Duty is paid on the entire garment when it is brought into the United States, but if the services of a domestic importer are used, the importer handles all the transactions.
- A mix of low-cost foreign sourcing and fast and flexible nearby manufacturing, or any other combination. In any of these cases, the fabric may be sourced domestically or abroad, independent of the garment sourcing. Duty is paid on fabric brought in for domestic apparel production.

Costs and lead times must be considered when making a production sourcing decision. Lead time consists of the length of time from design concept to transit of finished product to the retailer. The longer the lead time, the earlier fabric and findings buys must be made. Too long a lead time can be detrimental to sales as the consumer buying climate may change. In one example, a garment with extensive needle construction is needed in 9 months. In this case, because the lead time is generous, Far East or Middle East production would be the logical choice. Labor costs will be low on the extensive needle construction, and transport time will be moderate. In another example, a garment with moderate needle construction is needed in 3 months. 9802/807 or domestic production would be desirable; labor costs are higher but will not affect the price extensively as only moderate needle construction is required. Transport time will be low. In the case of sourced or contracted garments, lead times must be carefully planned and monitored. Any sourcing choice can be advantageous, if based on the company's objectives.

When the majority of textile and apparel companies are linked via computer, sourcing of products will become relatively quick and easy. Picture this scenario: A manufacturer interested in sourcing out a product prepares a costing package specifying all the characteristics needed in the garment. The manufacturer enters the fabric and garment specification data onto a preformatted screen on the computer and notes the desired price range. Then either the package is electronically transmitted to a preselected group of candidate suppliers or mass communicated to all suppliers in the system. Within a specified time period, interested suppliers send back any questions and their confidential quotes or bids on the product. The manufacturer selects a contractor or contractors from the group of respondents and transmits a purchase agreement and the finalized costing package to the chosen contractor/s.

COSTING

Costing is the process of estimating and then determining the total cost of producing a garment, including the cost of materials, labor, and transportation as well as the general expenses of operating the business. Two types of costing are done—precosting and production costing.

PRODUCT COSTING INFORMATION

Reference #	G 6006
Season:	spr1 (spr2) spr3 spr4 trans fall hol1 hol2
Description:	Solid Waffle Cardigan w/printed trim

Cost Due:	4/30	From:	OSHKOSH B'GOSH
Quota:	USA EEC		Far East Sourcing Manager
Proto Sample Due:	with quotation	Fax #:	(414) 231-0714

Base Fabric:

Type	jersey interlock fr.trry denim other_____
Content:	(100% Cotton) 80%C/20%P other_____
Finish:	stone enzyme bleach sanded brushed other____

Weight:	215-225 grm m²
Yarn Type:	20/1, cmbd 62/64" w
Shrinkage:	10x8

Print Detail: c=binding &pkt=print jersey (no puff)   gingham

# of Colors:	2	blotch:	yes (no)
% Coverage:	50%	dyestuff:	reactive pigment
Artwork Attached:	(yes) no	Ground Color:	(white) or _____

Trim/Other Information:

	Type	Color	Size	Amt
(Buttons)	(Sew Through) or E.L.	Pink Daisy	19L.	4
~~Snaps~~	Logo etched or _____			
~~Grippers~~	Ring or _____			
~~Piping~~				
~~Picot~~				
~~Collar~~				
~~Placket~~				
~~Welt~~				

	Type	Color	Size	Amt
Screenprint:				
Embroidery:				
(Applique:)	left frt	5 color	med	2
~~Patch:~~				
(Thread:)		white		
~~Elastic:~~				
~~Rib:~~	cttn/lycra or _____			
~~Other~~				

Quantity:

Sizes:(circle) layette(0-9M) (newborn)(infant) toddler 4-6X/7

Proto Size: 3/6   (12M)   3T   5

Packing Information:

Hangtag:	(yes) no
Hanger:	(w/sticker/sizer) w/o sticker none pant (shirt) piggyback
Carton:	packed by lot # in baler bag liner w/garments on hangers

SKETCH

Appliqué
Appliqué

In DC Date:	2/1/97	Total Proj. Pcs.:	3500
X Fac Date:	12/20/97	Target Cost:	
		Wholesale:	

Label (loop)	(baby b'gosh(0-24M)) b'gosh(2T & 4-6X/7) care (integrated)
Decorative Label	jean shirt rectangle vestback vertical (none) other
Misc:	

Pieced Dyed Color Detail:

1)	White	
2)		
3)		
4)		
5)		

Figure 4–5 Sourcing form used to solicit cost estimates from potential contractors. (*Courtesy of OshKosh B'Gosh.*)

Table 4–3   Internet Resources for Textile and Apparel Sourcing

---

Apparel Manufacturer's Sourcing Web   Publishes *The Agent,* since 1940, "the most trusted sourcebook for the Apparel and Sewn Products Industries."
URL: http://www.halper.com/sourcingweb.html

ApparelNet   "The OnLine Guide for the Apparel Industry: a comprehensive resource for apparel-related products, services, information and companies."
URL: http://www.apparel.net

Apparel Exchange   "Automatically matching buyers and sellers by e-mail and fax broadcast to over 26,000 companies in the textile and apparel industry."
URL: http://www.apparelex.com

Textile Information Management System (TIMS)   "A tool for searching and trading with the vast number of companies in the textile, apparel and fashion industry worldwide."
URL: http://www.unicate.com

Embroidery and Garment Screen Printing (ESPonline)   "A centralized on-line network for those in the embroidery and screen-printing industries."
URL: http://www.spyder.net/esp

Davison's Textile Blue Book   Publishes Davison's Textile Blue Book, "the most comprehensive listing of U.S., Canadian, and Mexican textile companies available anywhere," with more than 7100 textile companies listed.
URL: http://dama.tc2.com/sourcing/davisntb/davisntb.htm

America's Textiles International (ATI)   Publishes *The Textile Red Book International Buyers Guide* mill directory and database, including textiles, weaving, manufactured fibers, nonwovens, yarn preparation, spinning, fabric finishing, package dyeing, knitting, hosiery, and apparel manufacturing.
URL: http://www.billian.com/textile.htm

FabricLink   "The web resource for Fabrics and Textiles," providing trend and technology information; fiber, fabric, and clothing care education (including dictionary of fiber and textile industry terms), and mill and manufacturer directories.
URL: http://www.fabriclink.com

The Apparel Industry Sourcing Site   "A complete and up-to-date listing of domestic and import fabric and trim sources."
URL: http://fashiondex.com

Precosting

The first step in the costing process is precosting. A precosting package is developed and distributed to prospective contractors, often accompanied by a prototype garment and/or garment specifications. **Precosting** is a preliminary estimate, or "best guess" of what it will cost to produce the garment, based on judgment and past experience. This **quick cost** is usually accurate within 10 to 15% of the actual cost and gives the manufacturer some idea of whether the style can be produced and sold at a profit. The quick cost helps the manufacturer decide whether to reject the style, accept it as part of the line, or send it back to the designer or merchandiser for changes to reduce its cost.

Production Costing

After it is accepted as part of a line, a garment must be accurately costed. This detailed cost is known as **production costing**. Production costing is based on a sample or detailed sketch of the garment, accompanied by written specifications.

Production costing used to be a simple, straightforward process. Manufacturers calculated costs with great accuracy because they produced similar styles from year to year. Fashion, competition, and production methods changed relatively slowly. Today, frequent style changes, stiff international competition, and rapidly advancing technology make costing much more complex and accuracy more crucial than ever. Some large companies calculate each element of cost to the nearest $.0001 per garment to ensure accurate prediction of total costs. Other manufacturers merely calculate their costs to the nearest $.01 per dozen.

Most manufacturers cost garments manually; some use computers to assist them. To perform computerized costing, first the manufacturer stores the time and costs required to execute various sewing operations into the computer's memory. When a garment is costed, the

SEQ. NO.	ITEM CODE		ESTIMATE SHEET										
		60" Body		22.50 Yd. @	2.38	63.68	DATE			STYLE			
				Yd. @			8 / 17 / 90			Dress			
		60" Trim		2.25 Yd. @	2.90	6.53	INQ. NO.			PROD. NO. GG SUB INV			
				Yd. @			12560						
		60" Lining		1.25 Yd. @	1.615	2.02	FOR					SAMPLE	
						72.23						1501	
	B1000	BIAS	MAT. REQ. 7/8" UE (TRIM)	21 Yd. @	48.12	1.01	QTY.			SIZES			
		BIAS	MAT. REQ.	Yd. @	MY			150	DOZ. 0	EA	4-22		
		BIAS	MAT. REQ.	Yd. @			SIZE DEPENDENT			DESCRIPTION			
		DECT		Yd. @									
		ELAS		Yd. @						Make like sample			
	BN7	BTN	24/1/4 BALL NAVY	24 Ea. @	1.16	.19				made for the			
		BTN		Ea. @	gr.					customer.			
		FSTN		Ea. @									
		FSTN		Ea. @						To be assembled			
		CUFF		Ea. @						using type 512			
		TAPE		Yd. @						serge stitch			
		TAPE		Yd. @						seam.			
		VEL		Yd. @									
		VEL		Yd. @						To have 2			
	TH6XX	THD	70/3 Spun Poly	2000 Yd. @		.86				blindstitch			
	TROXX	THD	40/3	80 Yd. @		.05				bottom hem.			
		THD		Yd. @									
	ZP999	ZIP	24" CB Coil	12 Ea. @	24 ea.	2.88				To have front and			
	L5599	LABEL	Size Label #55	12 Ea. @		.15				back princess line			
		LABEL		Ea. @						gore seams.			
		EMB		Ea. @									
		MISC.								To have L/R inserted			
		MISC.								pocket bags cut			
	PF016	PKG	Poly bag	12 Ea. @		.18				from body			
	CN004	CTN	#4	33 QTY		.16				material.			
		OC											
			SUB. TOTAL			5.48							
	TOTAL MATERIAL COST					77.71							
	FACTORY												

SEW LABOR		20.55
CUTTING LABOR		2.25
TOTAL LABOR		22.80
VARIABLE OVERHEAD%		31.92
TOTAL MFG. COST		132.43
OVERHEAD		20.00
TOTAL COST PER DOZ.		152.43

Figure 4–6   Costing sheet. *(Courtesy of Angelica Image Apparel.)*

required operations are entered, and the computer then calculates the estimated labor costs of producing the garment. Overhead and materials are then added to reach the final cost.

A costing sheet is used for production costing (Figure 4–6), which is more detailed than precosting. Many companies use costing sheets containing a sketch of the garment, a style name, and a style number for identification purposes. The costing sheet may also record the size range, colors, selling season, and other pertinent information. The costing sheet includes the five main elements included in costing a garment: (1) fabric, (2) findings, (3) labor, (4) overhead, and (5) other.

Fabric Costs.   Fabric is generally the most significant factor in costing a garment. Fabric accounts for 60 to 70% of the total cost of basic-styled garments. In many cases, evaluating the quality and the amount of fabric used in a garment indicates better than any other factor the overall cost of producing it. The generous use of fabric; heavy or dense fabric (such as wool coatings); fabric with rare fibers, complex fabrication, or expensive finishes; fabric with patterns that require matching; amount of shrinkage anticipated; and fabric currently in high demand and low supply can all add significantly to the cost of a garment. Fabric specifications must be established by this point in the process in order to accurately estimate costs.

To determine fabric costs, the costing engineer estimates the consumption of fabric required to produce a style, including a waste factor, or **fallout**. Many companies use computer-generated material utilization calculations to determine yards needed and anticipated fallout. The total cost of the fabric equals the number of yards needed multiplied by the price per square yard since width is a variable from loom to loom, plus delivery charges, duty applicable to imported fabrics, and testing and inspection costs.

Findings Costs. **Findings**, **notions**, or **sundries** include all materials other than fabric required to produce a garment. For example, most cost sheets incorporate as findings such items as thread, trims, (ribbon and lace), closures (buttons and zippers), labels (care, brand, and size), and miscellaneous materials (elastic and shoulder pads).

The cost of findings significantly affects the cost of a garment and requires accurate estimation. For example, the yards of thread used for sewing may cost only a few cents per garment. However, a manufacturer that produces thousands of garments annually must account for thread costs to accurately predict total costs. Findings specifications must be established by this point in the process in order to accurately estimate costs.

Labor Costs. Labor costs include the spreading, cutting, sewing, pressing, finishing, and any wet-processing operations required to produce a garment. They may also cover the cost of designing, sample making, patternmaking, grading, and marker making. Retailers want floor-ready products, so manufacturers perform many of the operations formerly conducted in the retailer' distribution centers, for example, applying price tickets, hang tags, and hangers and preparing **prepacks,** predetermined groupings of different sizes as specified by the retailer. Labor accounts for a large portion, sometimes as much as half, of the total cost of garments produced in developed countries such as the United States. In low-wage countries, labor requirements have less impact on the total cost of the garment.

Each individual operation in the production of a garment contributes to its labor costs. To aid in costing, industrial engineers measure motions used by each operator and record the time required to perform each operation. These time and motion studies are compared to existing standards to determine cost-effective methods of apparel production. Automation reduces labor costs compared to manual production (although increased equipment costs may offset the reduction). Large production runs justify automation more than do small quantities; thus, basic goods can be produced with lower costs than can fashion goods. Even without automation, operators repeatedly working on the same styles (usually basic) work faster—translating into lower labor costs—than those learning to sew a new style every few weeks. To reinforce these ideas, examine a $30 men's basic dress shirt and a $30 women's fashion blouse. The dress shirt usually contains considerably more labor-intensive detail for the same price.

Overhead Costs. **Overhead costs** are the expenses of operating the business beyond the direct costs of producing garments. They include the factory, new equipment and technology; the cost of capital tied up in products, taxes, insurance, utilities; the salaries of supervisors, managers, and their staffs; employee benefits such as insurance and pensions; and community and charitable donations. In addition, overhead includes selling costs, such as advertising, marketing, discount terms (usually 8% of the wholesale price) offered to retailers who pay their bills on time, and the sales commissions (typically 7 to 10% of wholesale price) paid to the sales reps who sell the line to retail buyers. Distribution costs, covering items such as shipping and warehousing, are also considered a part of overhead.

Other Costs. Other associated garment costs include wet-processing chemicals, packaging materials, advertising labels, and contracted operations. Wet-processing chemicals can include bleaches, detergents, softeners, neutralizers, wetting agents, and resins. Complicated wet process finishes contribute a significant amount to the price of the product. Packaging materials include hangers, plastic bags, and packaging cartons. Though packaging is not a significant portion of garment cost, efforts are made to keep this expense minimal. Advertising label expenses include stickers, hang tags (dangling paper labels), *billboards* (paper labels, sometimes stapled to the garment and sometimes attached with swift tacks), *belly bands* (paper strips wrapped around shirts and other folded apparel), and the *swift tacks* (plastic devices used to hold advertising labels to apparel) or tape used in their application. Contracted operations are integral parts of the garment such as embroidery, screen print application, and pleating. These operations are often contracted to specialists.

Relationship of Cost to Price

It is important to remember that the terms cost and price mean different things, depending on the perspective. In general, cost refers to the dollar amounts paid to others. Price refers to the dollar amounts others pay.

Accurate costing helps manufacturers establish the **wholesale price** of garments, the price they charge retailers. Although the estimated cost of a garment does not automatically determine its wholesale price, manufacturers use cost figures as a guideline and rely on accurate costing to help them set profitable wholesale prices. For the company to make a profit, the wholesale price must be higher than the actual cost of producing the garment. But a too-high wholesale price discourages buyers. So how is the wholesale price decided?

When pricing apparel, producers are apt to price the garment according to "how much it looks like it's worth" more than any other factor. Thus, a familiarity with supply and demand in the marketplace is more important than cost in determining the correct price of a garment. A wise manufacturer determines the **market potential price** of a garment, the highest price that can be charged without dampening sales too much. For example, a company that produces a "hot" style that is in demand can sell the style for a high price, especially if the product has little competition. On the other hand, if a company offers a style that is plentiful, with many other manufacturers offering similar goods, the price of the item must be low enough to compete.

Generally, companies aim for an average profit margin, but the profit margin on particular garments may vary widely. For example, a manufacturer's target profit may be 6% of the wholesale price, but the company makes more profit on some garments, and less on others, and hopes to average out to 6% overall. In fact, sometimes firms sell a few garments at a loss to attract buyers to the line; such items are referred to as **loss leaders.**

When pricing garments, manufacturers also consider their companies' price line reputation. Most companies position their products in the same general price range from season to season so buyers know what to expect from them; consistency is important. Companies that produce one price line this season and another price line the next lose business because buyers want to count on the same resources for specific price lines from season to season. The wholesale price must allow an adequate retail markup and still result in a suitable retail price.

Like manufacturers, retailers also consider market forces when they establish the **retail price,** the price they charge the consumer. However, as a general rule, to cover operating expenses and still make a profit, retailers approximately double the wholesale cost to obtain the retail price of a garment, a practice called the **keystone markup.** Discounters take a lower markup and hope to profit by selling large quantities.

Balancing Cost and Quality

The many design, material, construction, and finish choices available are exciting, and knowledge of them is important, but in the real world these choices are not unlimited. A manufacturer has cost constraints to deal with on a daily basis. Shareholders want profits. Customers want quality clothing at low prices. The two concepts are in opposition. Many discussions about these issues take place in manufacturing companies on a daily basis. "How can we offer the features our customers want at the price our customers are willing to pay, and still turn a profit?" It presents great challenges.

Many manufacturers have internal programs called **profit improvement programs** to help meet these cost and quality challenges. Individual projects can be proposed by anyone within the company, but usually it is a direct job function of the industrial engineers. Each engineer tackles one or more profit improvement projects annually. These projects include improved work aids, development of new equipment, redesigning existing equipment, and eliminating unnecessary operations. This results in considerable cost savings to the company, enabling the company to offer its products at the best possible price while still pleasing the owners/shareholders.

Good management practices reduce overhead costs, but other cost reductions occur by making changes in the garment, thus reducing the cost of producing the garment. Producing a garment at or below a certain cost enables it to fit into a designated price line. Trade-offs or compromises in design, materials, construction, and/or finish are sometimes necessary to produce a garment at the desired cost. Discerning manufacturers compromise features that impact the overall performance of the garment least, or those which customers do not care about. Less quality-oriented manufacturers forfeit features that are not noticeable to customers at point of sale, but which contribute to quality. For example, low-quality shoulder pads look as good as high-quality shoulder pads at the point of sale but can shrink, curl, and twist after wear and care. A lower cost tempts some decision makers to sacrifice quality for profits. Other manufacturers lower the quality of their products without being aware of doing so. For example, shoulder pads might be offered from a new source at a lower cost. If the purchasing agent accepts the salesperson's word regarding the quality of the shoulder pads and does not have them tested, the quality staff may not find out about poor quality until their customers tell them. At this point it is too late; customer satisfaction has already been compromised.

In an ideal situation, desired performance balances with cost limitations, enabling the manufacturer to sell the garment at a reasonable price, make a profit, and satisfy customers. (Recall the performance-cost balance in Figure 3-7.) A garment that fulfills the consumer's expectations at a price he or she is willing to pay, without unnecessary features that inflate cost, represents this balance. But a perfect balance is difficult to achieve.

Reducing Materials Costs. Companies scrutinize fabric and other raw materials costs because of their significant contribution to total costs. For example, if a large company spends $50 million per year for fabric, a mere 1% savings translates into a half million dollars! Tactics for reducing fabric costs range from using a less expensive fabric or utilizing production methods that reduce waste to modifying the style, fit, or construction of the garment to require less fabric. Spec technicians may attempt to reduce costs by spec'ing seams that use less thread. Marker makers might try adding a slight tilt to fit more pattern pieces on the marker. Designers and patternmakers might employ techniques such as narrow seams and hems, shallow pleats, sparse gathers (a lower shirring ratio), and less-than-generous sizing to achieve lower fabric costs. These fabric-saving changes in a garment's style, fit, and construction, if taken too far, may affect quality adversely. For example, *skimpy* (less than generously cut) swimsuits for women hike up in back, unlike those cut long enough and full enough to provide better coverage. And wrap-around robes, skirts, and dresses that barely overlap expose the body more than those cut generously enough to fully overlap and wrap farther around the body. In another case, knit sport shirts often have too-short tails that come untucked easily. But shirts with *tennis tails* (cut longer in back than in front) stay tucked in when the wearer moves and reaches.

When attempting to reduce costs, manufacturers challenge all employees to devise new cost-cutting methods. Skilled employees reduce costs without sacrificing quality. They conduct research and study the proposed new methods carefully before submitting the ideas to management.

The cost of findings dramatically influences the cost of a garment. Designers and merchandisers use fewer and less costly findings to reduce costs. For example, a slightly less expensive button or a six- rather than seven-button shirt front reduces the manufacturer's

cost significantly when producing thousands of garments. Consumers may or may not notice such changes. Be sure to consider findings when comparing the quality of one garment to another seemingly identical garment, to detect differences that affect cost.

Reducing Labor Costs. Labor costs, especially in complex garments, significantly impact total costs. Naturally, garments requiring many construction steps have high labor costs. And operations requiring skilled operators have higher rates than those performed by less-skilled operators. Eliminating some steps and simplifying complicated, labor-intensive construction details, such as unusually shaped seams, pockets, and linings, reduce labor costs. For example, a row of stitches simulating a seam costs less to produce than an actual seam. Changing the type of stitches or seams affects production costs, because some stitch and seam types cost less to make than others. (For more information, see Chapters 9 and 10.) Sewing the garment faster also lowers labor costs. Some techniques for reducing labor costs affect the performance of the garment very little. In other cases, efforts to save on labor cause manufacturers to "cut corners," reducing the aesthetic or functional performance of the garment. Industrial engineers might change the methods or equipment used by the operators. Automation of procedures lowers labor costs (but raises equipment costs). Equipment purchases are studied carefully in terms of how many years it takes to achieve *payback* (when new equipment costs are balanced by savings in labor costs). Generally, major equipment is purchased if the payback period is less than 5 or 6 years. Lead times also affect costs. Reducing the number of in-process days it takes to make a garment helps reduce labor, overhead, and other costs.

–·–·–·–

PREPRODUCTION

During the preproduction phase of apparel manufacturing, many activities are being conducted simultaneously. It is an exciting time but also a confusing time as juggling many styles, each in varying stages of the production cycle, becomes challenging. Some companies have analysts who do nothing but track the styles to make sure no steps are left out. Other companies use technology for this function and develop computer systems to monitor and track production. If one step has been left out, the computer will send out a signal to alert personnel to not allow the style to proceed to the next step. Steps in preproduction include (1) fabric testing and approval, (2) garment specifications, (3) color (shade) and/or print approval, (4) findings testing and approval, (5) care label and other label approval, (6) making preproduction garments, (7) customs preclassification (imports only; can be done during production if manufacturer ensures that it already owns or can buy quota), (8) making production patterns, (9) grading, and (10) marker making.

Fabric Testing and Approval

Fabric approval is desired well in advance of garment production because fabric has to be made or finished and then shipped from the supplier, sometimes in another country, to the factory where it is to be cut. Fabric approval is finalized based on lab tests confirming compliance of prospective fabrics with company fabric performance standards. Written specifications for the approved fabric are sent to sew plants and contractors to enable monitoring for consistent quality. (For more information, see Chapters 3 and 7.)

Writing of Garment Specifications

Garment specifications include diagrams and instructions regarding stitch types, seam types, placement of buttons and pockets, and every other important detail to assure proper construction of the garment. (For more information, see Chapters 3, 11, and 12.) Garment specifications also include size and fit specifications. Spec technicians determine key points of measure and methods of measure and calculate the exact dimensions for the complete size range. Each company develops methods of measure for their own products and supplies them to contractors. (For more information, see Chapter 6.)

Color and Shade Approval

Color approval and **shade approval** are necessary for each fabric used in a garment, because different fabrics require different dye formulas to achieve the same desired color. Colors initially approved on a computer screen must be carefully converted to a like hue on an actual fabric, sometimes a real challenge. (Be aware that computer printers are not apt to print out the exact hue shown on the screen.) **Lab dips** (dyed color samples), **strikeoffs** (print samples), or hand-loomed samples (sample fabric, usually woven, made in the lab) are used to approve the final colors. **Shade bands**, long, narrow swatches of a fabric cut from different dye lots, all with acceptable variations of shade, are used to maintain consistency of coloration on incoming fabric. The bands are distributed to mills, sew plants, and contractors so all production personnel are aware of the desired fabric coloration.

Garments made in one fabric construction usually achieve color approval relatively quickly. However, shade approval can be time consuming if more than one fabric construction is involved. For example, a rugby shirt may have an interlock knit collar, a woven twill collar placket, and a jersey knit body, and all the components must be carefully matched. Or if the garment is part of a collection and there are a variety of fabric mills producing same color fabric for the collection, all colors need to match.

Color and shade approval is also important for findings and trim components of garments. Color samples are sent to the supplier and matched or, in the case of global production, the supplier sends color samples to the buyer and the buyer selects the desired colors. For example, a supplier sends embroidery thread samples to an apparel manufacturer where merchandisers choose the colors they want.

Garments that are wet processed after assembly also need shade or color approval. Wet processing is the technique of creating a unique fashion look by either dyeing or stripping color from a product when it is in garment form instead of fabric form. It is expensive to develop exact shades and colors when using assembled garments, so often final shade approval for wet processing takes place during preproduction or production using **fallout**, second or irregular quality garments, from the first lot of garments produced. Designers and merchandisers approve an acceptable light, medium, and dark shade and distribute samples of each to the appropriate wet-processing and quality personnel. These samples become the shade standard for that product. Whether the color is put in or taken out, shades must be within the acceptable standard range.

Findings Testing and Approval

Findings, the various sundries and trim items used on apparel, must also be approved before production can begin. Snaps, buttons, zippers, embroideries, screen prints, shoulder pads, and appliqués are among some of the trim items that must be tested and approved for color and overall appearance as well as performance. (For more information, see Chapter 8.)

Care Label and Other Label Approval

Garments usually have a variety of attached labels. Some of the labels are mandated by the federal government, some are for manufacturing and marketing purposes, and some are informational for consumer convenience. (For more information, see Chapter 2.) All of them must be written and produced early in the production cycle. Care labels cannot be written until the fabric and findings are tested and the refurbishing instructions have been determined. For this reason, testing of the actual fabric and other raw materials must be done as soon as they are available. The labels must be printed or woven (woven labels take longer to produce) before garment production begins because care-label insertion is one of the first assembly operations. *Joker labels*, the size labels ripped off by the consumer after purchase, cannot be printed until the size range to be produced is determined. Paper hang tags must be designed and printed in time to be attached before the garments leave the sew plant. Because application of these labels and tags occurs at the end of the assembly process, there is not the same sense of urgency as with the labels that must be sewn in.

Making Preproduction Garments

Trial units from every new style are made using actual production techniques in the manufacturing plant. These **preproduction garments** enable patternmakers, spec technicians, and quality engineers to verify size and fit dimensions after the garments have been assembled using production techniques. Two to five units are made in each size of the range. These garments normally are made in the correct fabric, but if correct fabric is not yet available, fabric as close as possible to the specified fabric is used. Often this step takes place before the correct labels and trim items are available; therefore, these details must be carefully checked later on the first production garments.

Garment Classification With U.S. Customs (Imports Only)

At this point in the production cycle, every detail about the line is finalized, sourcing choices are finalized, materials are ordered, and production is booked. If garments are to be imported, they may undergo preclassification at this time.

Classification of garments by the U.S. Customs Service (USCS) determines the tariff rate or duty of goods imported into the United States. (For more information, see Chapter 1.) Garments are classified according to the following criteria:

1. percent weight of each fiber in the finished garment
2. fabric construction (woven or knit)
3. gender of the intended wearer
4. item description.

Most apparel products clearly fit into only one classification. Some other unique products technically fit into more than one classification. For these unique products (men's boxer shorts designed to be worn as outerwear for juniors, or skorts, a combined skirt and shorts garment), importers try to slot the product into the available classification with the lowest duty rate. Incorrect classification can result not only in higher tariff costs but in an **embargo**, in which the goods are denied entry into the United States if the quota for that classification is filled for the country of origin. Due to its importance, many companies enlist the help of a licensed customs broker in filing for garment classification.

Preclassification with U.S. Customs involves classifying imported garments ahead of their arrival. Preclassification helps importers avoid costly delays and expensive misunderstandings about higher-than-anticipated tariff rates and filled quotas at the point of entry of the imported goods into the United States. The ideal time to determine apparel product classification is at the concept and design stage. Along with all pertinent information about the planned import transaction, the preclassification process requires the importer to furnish to U.S. Customs all necessary information for classification, plus a sketch of the item with **breakouts** (written explanations of details in sketches) where applicable and an accurate sample of the item; neither fabrication nor construction of the sample can vary from the goods when they arrive later (Figure 4–7). Using these factors, U.S. Customs classifies the garment and issues a **binding tariff classification ruling**, in effect for the garment for the life of its production as long as fabrication, construction, or style number does not change.

Computers streamline the preclassification process and make record keeping an ease. With computer spreadsheet programs, the importer records the style or part number and corresponding Harmonized System (HS) preclassification number, apparel quota category if applicable, and the U.S. Customs preclassification process number. This builds a "parts list" to be shared with U.S. Customs for accelerated entry processing. It is possible to electronically transmit a sketch of the garment, a photo of the fabric, and fabric and garment details for review by a U.S. Customs commodity specialist. The preclassification imagery and the commodity specialist's remarks are then electronically sent to U.S. Customs offices in New York City for a final review and binding approval. This process saves time and money for the importer because it eliminates the preparation of paper documents and the need for garment samples.

Making Production Patterns

When all the garments in the line are finalized and chosen for production, they are given to the production patternmaker or pattern engineer, who prepares

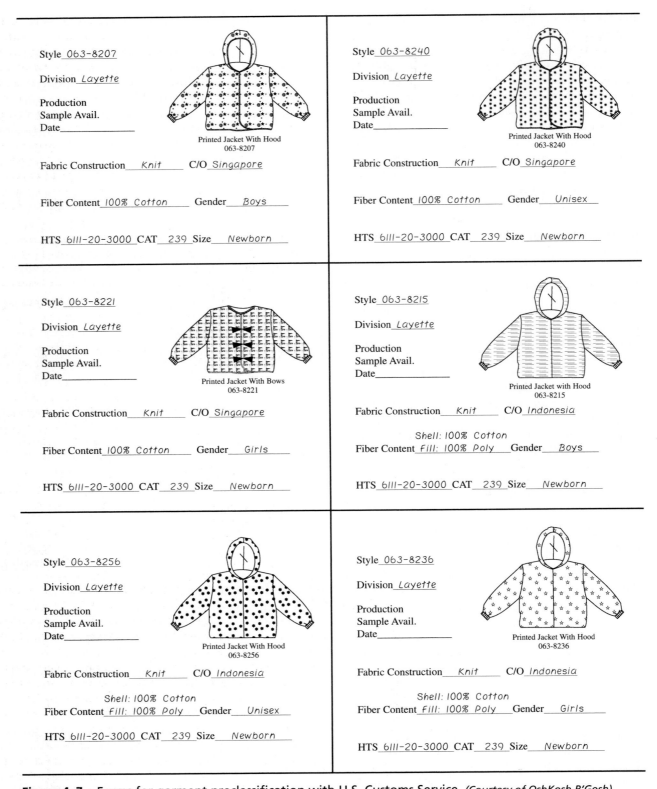

Style _063-8207_

Division _Layette_

Production
Sample Avail.
Date_____

Printed Jacket With Hood
063-8207

Fabric Construction___Knit___ C/O _Singapore_

Fiber Content _100% Cotton_ Gender___Boys___

HTS _6111-20-3000_ CAT __239_ Size ___Newborn___

Style _063-8240_

Division _Layette_

Production
Sample Avail.
Date_____

Printed Jacket With Hood
063-8240

Fabric Construction___Knit___ C/O _Singapore_

Fiber Content _100% Cotton_ Gender___Unisex___

HTS _6111-20-3000_ CAT __239_ Size ___Newborn___

Style _063-8221_

Division _Layette_

Production
Sample Avail.
Date_____

Printed Jacket With Bows
063-8221

Fabric Construction___Knit___ C/O _Singapore_

Fiber Content _100% Cotton_ Gender___Girls___

HTS _6111-20-3000_ CAT __239_ Size ___Newborn___

Style _063-8215_

Division _Layette_

Production
Sample Avail.
Date_____

Printed Jacket with Hood
063-8215

Fabric Construction___Knit___ C/O _Indonesia_

Shell: 100% Cotton
Fiber Content _Fill: 100% Poly_ Gender___Boys___

HTS _6111-20-3000_ CAT __239_ Size ___Newborn___

Style _063-8256_

Division _Layette_

Production
Sample Avail.
Date_____

Printed Jacket With Hood
063-8256

Fabric Construction___Knit___ C/O _Indonesia_

Shell: 100% Cotton
Fiber Content _Fill: 100% Poly_ Gender___Unisex___

HTS _6111-20-3000_ CAT __239_ Size ___Newborn___

Style _063-8236_

Division _Layette_

Production
Sample Avail.
Date_____

Printed Jacket With Hood
063-8236

Fabric Construction___Knit___ C/O _Indonesia_

Shell: 100% Cotton
Fiber Content _Fill: 100% Poly_ Gender___Girls___

HTS _6111-20-3000_ CAT __239_ Size ___Newborn___

Figure 4–7 Forms for garment preclassification with U.S. Customs Service. *(Courtesy of OshKosh B'Gosh).*

the final pattern for mass production. The pattern-maker converts first patterns into **production patterns,** or hard patterns, for optimum fabric utilization and ease of assembly and determines how each garment can be most economically mass produced using production techniques. Any unnecessary curves, fullness, seams, or details are eliminated from the first pattern to produce an efficient production pattern. A knowledgeable and skillful production patternmaker often consults production engineers about plant sewing techniques as they together reduce raw material waste and streamline designs without destroying their essence. As when making the first pattern, a PDS/CAD system speeds the process of making a production pattern and can improve accuracy.

Grading

Grading the production pattern involves increasing and decreasing its dimensions to reflect the various sizes to be produced. **Grade rules** may reflect even amounts of change between sizes, or different amounts. For example, a standard grade for misses sizes is a 1" circumference difference (at bust, waist, and hips) between sizes 6, 8, and 10; a 1 1/2" circumference difference between sizes 10, 12, 14 and 16; and a 2" circumference difference between sizes 16, 18, 20 and 22; and a 1/4" length difference between each two sizes. The **graded nest** consists of all the sizes of graded patterns, superimposed on one another. The nest allows a quick check of grading accuracy, to be confirmed by careful measurement. Graded patterns are evaluated to ensure that the garment's style has not been adversely affected by the grading process. For example, collar and cuff width, sleeve length, or skirt flare may be held constant across several or all sizes rather than being graded up or down, to preserve the design's intended appearance.

Another use for pattern nests that occurs later in the production cycle is in the researching of fit problems in finished garments. Quality engineers, when presented with a garment out of dimensional tolerance, might request a pattern nest to begin tracking down the sizing problem. The finished garment is carefully ripped apart, without stretching the cloth, and compared to the appropriate-sized pattern pieces on the nest. This allows the engineer to determine if the cloth was originally cut incorrectly or possibly trimmed excessively during certain operations.

Computer grading using a **computer-aided manufacturing (CAM)** system quickly and accurately grades the pattern to all the desired sizes automatically, eliminating the painstaking task of manual grading. For example, Figure 4–8 illustrates the computer-graded pattern pieces for a jacket front. This points out convincingly how valuable an integrated CAD/CAM system is. Manually distributing the grade throughout all these pieces would be extremely time-consuming. CAD/CAM does it automatically with the touch of a button. The computer changes the original pattern according to grade rules entered by the pattern grader for how much and where each incremental increase and decrease in size and shape is to be

made. Thus, the accuracy of the original or base pattern (usually made in a size from the middle of the size range) affects the accuracy of all the other sizes. Many companies have CAD/CAM systems for computerized pattern grading or contract out their pattern grading to firms that do. However, some firms still manually grade their patterns, often using a hand grading machine, essentially a very accurate set of rulers with knob controls, to increase speed and accuracy. Manual grading requires a skilled pattern grader for good results.

Marker Making

The **marker** indicates how all the pattern pieces of the garment are arranged on the fabric to achieve the most efficient layout. Sometimes even in ideal circumstances, 10 to 15% of the fabric is fallout, or wasted areas between the pattern pieces. Saving an inch of fabric here or an inch there over thousands of yards ultimately has a pronounced effect on company profits, so marker planning receives close attention. The goal is a tight marker, which uses the fabric efficiently with minimal waste. Large pieces are generally placed first, and small pieces are fitted in where possible. The marker maker moves the pieces around until a tight marker is achieved. To achieve better **material utilization (MU)**, the marker maker may allow some pattern pieces' edges to touch or slightly overlap. If the overlapping is slight (1/8" or less), it does not affect the dimensions of the finished garment. Another tactic for increasing material utilization involves tilting pattern pieces slightly rather than placing them perfectly straight on the fabric. Manufacturers of better garments avoid this practice because it causes the finished garment to be off grain and possibly hang crooked. (For more information, see Chapters 5 and 6.)

Making a marker manually involves the unwieldy task of shifting the pattern pieces around until they are squeezed together as closely as possible. The marker maker traces the pattern pieces onto the paper marker, which is the same width as the fabric, to provide guidelines for the cutter.

Many marker makers use CAM systems, which allow them to move small-scale pattern pieces around on the computer screen until the most efficient layout is achieved (Figure 4–9). Some of the features of computerized marker making are that it

1. allows marker makers to see the entire marker at the same time, allowing them to visualize a greater variety of possible arrangements of the pattern pieces
2. keeps track of the percent of material utilization at all times so the marker maker can readily assess various arrangements of the pieces

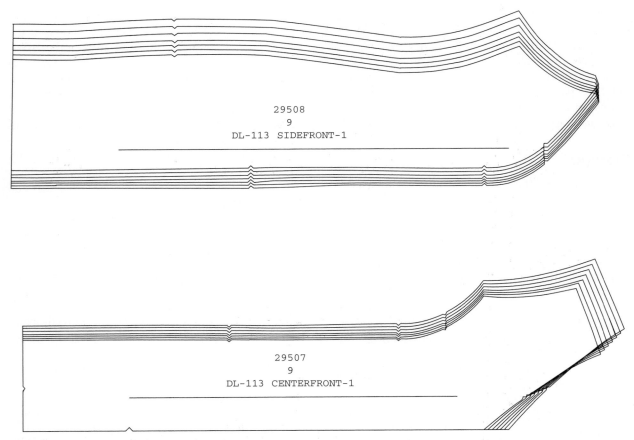

29508
9
DL-113 SIDEFRONT-1

29507
9
DL-113 CENTERFRONT-1

Figure 4–8 Computerized pattern graded nest for jacket front. *(Courtesy of The Lee Company.)*

3. positions pieces as closely together as possible where the marker maker indicates placement

4. automatically overlaps pieces a programmable amount if overlapping improves material utilization

5. automatically tilts pieces a programmable amount if tilting improves material utilization

6. arranges pieces so that patterns such as stripes and plaids match in the finished garment (for more information, see Chapter 11). This is important, because if matching is neglected at this stage, the patterns cannot be matched later in the assembly process.

7. color-codes pattern pieces on the screen according to size so the marker maker readily identifies smaller and larger pieces that otherwise appear identical

8. automatically superimposes the straight edges of side-by-side pieces; the shared cutting line saves fabric and speeds cutting

9. enlarges hard-to-see areas of the marker

10. plans ideal points for splicing the ends of fabric pieces

11. identifies locations where fabric defects can be placed without affecting the garment

12. stores markers for later use in nonbulky form compared to traditional paper markers. Marker recall system allows fabric-efficient markers to be used over and over again to make the same style of basic garment.

13. makes duplicate markers quickly and at low cost. This is important for producers of basic garments, who use the same marker over and over.

14. transmits markers electronically to remote factory locations.

The computer generally helps the marker maker achieve 1 to 4% higher fabric efficiency in companies producing fashion goods, where under ordinary circumstances 80% material utilization is not uncommon. Most companies producing basic goods have developed efficient markers over the years (often over 95% material utilization), so they realize a lower percentage of improvement when they change to computerized marker making. However, even small improvements in material utilization add up fast!

For companies cutting directly from a marker, the computer plotter generates a full-scale paper marker at the touch of a button. Other companies store the

Figure 4–9 Computerized marker making system. (*Courtesy of Gerber Garment Technology, Inc.*).

marker on tape and use the tapes to guide automatic computerized cutting, thus eliminating the need for manual cutting. Still other companies store the marker on a disk and send the disk to cutting locations.

The use of CAM systems for marker making is growing rapidly because of their accuracy, speed, and ultimate cost savings for apparel producers; computerized marker making systems provide quick pay backs in improved material utilization alone. Many companies that do not have computerized marker making contract out their markers to companies that do; others continue to rely on manual methods.

Matching Patterned Fabrics. Some fabrics have linear patterns, such as plaids, checks, and stripes, that require **pattern matching** or lining up at seams. (See Chapter 11, Tables 11–2 and 11–3.) Matching these fabrics is necessary to achieve an attractive finished garment. Computers are used to simplify the matching process during marker making and spreading (Figure 4–10). Because garment pieces must be placed on the fabric where patterns will match, and not where the panels fit closest together, material utilization is decreased when matching patterned fabrics. Because of increased fabric and labor costs, garments with matched patterns cost more than garments with unmatched patterns.

The larger the pattern, the more fabric required to match it. Typically, one extra repeat of the pattern is required for each major garment piece. Depending on the size of the pattern, matching can add significantly to raw material costs. And planning the use of patterned fabrics increases labor costs.

Even and Uneven Plaids. Matching plaids requires additional yardage. If the pattern is uneven, yet more fabric is needed. **Even plaids** contain a balanced arrangement of stripes on each side of the dominant horizontal and vertical bars. These types of patterns are easy to match. **Uneven plaids** vary in the arrangement of stripes on each side of the dominant horizontal and/or vertical bar. Uneven plaids require additional fabric for matching and sometimes limit the extent to which matching is possible. For example, uneven plaids printed on a fabric with a right and wrong side cannot radiate from center front but must move continuously around the body. This causes the two vertical halves of a garment to appear dissimilar; they are not mirror images. Stripes and other patterns may also occur as even or uneven.

Criteria for Matching. One important criterion for matching patterned fabric is that the dominant bars of the pattern be placed attractively on the garment. When a person squints his or her eyes, the dominant bars appear to stand out. Designers of high-quality

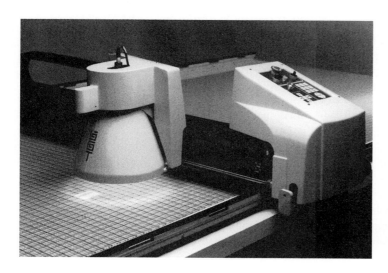

Figure 4–10 Automated plaid and stripe matching system. *(Courtesy of Gerber Garment Technology, Inc.)*

Figure 4–11 Plaids: (a) matched to form a chevron, and (b) unmatched.

apparel usually place the dominant vertical bar down the center front and center back of the garment and down the center of the sleeve. The dominant horizontal bar should be placed in a flattering position, at the hem line if it is straight or only slightly curved, perhaps avoiding the hipline, the fullest part of the abdomen, and the bustline. Different designers, given the same patterned fabric, may use it in different ways to create equally interesting and beautiful but unique garments.

The "V" formed when diagonal stripes are matched at seams, especially in skirts, is called a *chevron* [Figure 4–11(a)]. Chevrons can be created on bias-cut skirts or straight-of-grain skirts if they are flared. Even patterns are easier to chevron than uneven patterns.

Some fabrics do not lend themselves to matching. For instance, prominently woven twills angled at other than 45 degrees cannot be symmetrically matched.

Cost-Effective Ways to Minimize Matching. Simple garments with few pattern pieces, seams, and details require little additional fabric to match and are relatively easy to match compared to more complex garments. In many cases, simple garment designs made of patterned fabrics are more attractive than complex garment designs made from the same fabric. A simple garment design lets the pattern do the talking without fighting with it for attention. The larger or more uneven the fabric pattern, the more this general rule holds true.

Manufacturers producing low- and moderate-price lines sometimes make garments with unmatched patterns [Figure 4–11(b)]. A compromise is matching patterns in only the most noticeable places, for example, at the center front of a button-front shirt.

Figure 4–12 Pockets, pocket flaps, and yokes cut on the bias to minimize plaid-matching costs.

Other manufacturers take advantage of techniques to reduce the amount of labor and fabric required for matching patterns but still treat patterned-fabric garments attractively. They cut the garment or parts of the garment on the bias or from a coordinating solid-color fabric. Pockets, pocket flaps, collars, cuffs, yokes, button bands, and other small pieces are frequently handled this way. Bias-cut or solid-color details provide a suitably attractive alternative to matching patterns and reduce fabric and labor costs (Figure 4–12). They are superior to unmatched seams but do not reflect the same level of cost and quality as when the workers at every stage of the production process painstakingly match each piece of the garment.

Working with Fabrics with Large Motifs. Garments cut from fabrics with large motifs, such as prominent florals or paisleys, require thoughtful planning. Simple garments with limited numbers of seams tend to complement such fabrics. If highly visible seams are involved, matching of the motifs may be advisable to prevent a broken-up appearance. For example, lace fabrics with large motifs look better if matched at seams, important in bridal and formal gowns. Squinting at the fabric may help in checking the balance of the motifs on the overall garment. Prominent motifs should not be placed over the bust or buttocks without recognizing the unflattering effect. Motifs may be centered on the chest, sleeves, or other garment parts. Of course, positioning the motifs in this way lowers material utilization, increasing costs.

PRODUCTION

The actual production process begins when the fabric and findings arrive, after weeks or months of planning. The production process includes (1) spreading, (2) cutting the fabric, (3) making sample garments, (4) subcontracting decorative details if applicable, (5) sewing production garments, (6) wet processing if applicable, (7) pressing, and (8) finishing and inspecting.

Spreading

Spreading is the action of laying multiple plies of cloth on a table before the cloth is cut. Like marker making, spreading is a key factor in controlling product costs through efficient fabric utilization.

The *spreader,* either human or machine, layers the cloth back and forth on a long table. When spreading is conducted by human spreaders, they use a spreading device on wheels (also called a *spreader* or *spreading machine*) to smoothly carry the heavy rolls of cloth back and forth on the table. The human spreader moves the mechanical spreader and smoothes the cloth as it reaches the table. When a roll of cloth has been spread, the human spreader must carefully *splice* in the new roll of cloth to ensure no partial panels are cut. The human spreader must also watch for fabric flaw flags attached by the fabric mill and remove full widths of any fabric containing large flaws.

Mechanical spreaders are advancing with technology. Today's mechanical spreaders are electric and move themselves along a track on the spreading table. They have electronic sensors to determine the presence of mill flaw flags and automatically stop so the human spreader can remove the flaws.

Most companies cut many **plies,** or layers, of fabric at one time to save time and reduce costs. Most **lays,** or **lay-ups,** are stacked only a few inches high, with 24 to 32 plies. However, some are as high as 14 inches and contain nearly 500 plies. Such lays are possible because of the development of vacuum cutting tables.

Some fabrics are *directional;* they have a definite variance in appearance depending upon whether they are viewed from one direction or the other. Knowing that difference is important in spreading. Directional fabrics include napped fabrics such as velvet, velveteen, and corduroy, and pile fabrics such as fake fur.

Figure 4–13 These two children's corduroy overalls, made in the same fabric, were cut with the nap running in opposite directions, making them appear different in color.

All the nap or pile must lie in the same direction in the finished garment, usually the downward direction. This causes the least disturbance of the nap or pile during normal wear but may result in a less rich color. Directional fabrics also include *one-way* designs such as floral prints with all the flower stems pointing down, teddy bear prints with all the heads pointing up, and vertically uneven stripes, checks, and plaids. A patterned fabric should be carefully examined to determine if it has a one-way design versus an *all-over* design, which is nondirectional.

A directional fabric usually is spread with each ply of the fabric face up, a layout called **nap-one-way (NOW)** or **directional.** The manufacturer orients the tops of all the garment pieces in the same direction on the fabric. This does not allow as fabric-efficient a layout as **nap-either-way (NEW)** or **nondirectional,** the face to face layout for ordinary, nondirectional fabrics.

When the fabric has a direction that must be observed within the same garment but which can vary from garment to garment, the fabric may be spread **nap-up-and-down (NUD),** or **face-to-face.** Pieces from alternating layers are sewn together so that the direction of the fabric is consistent within each garment. For example, in Figure 4–13 the two children's corduroy overalls of the same style appear to vary in color—one appears light and the other dark; they were cut from alternating layers of a face-to-face layout. This causes them to reflect light differently, and the finished garments appear to have been cut from two different colors of fabric.

Cutting

Cutting affects the quality of the finished garment before assembly ever begins. Manual *cutters* are relatively well paid among apparel factory workers because of the skill and accuracy their job demands. If a manual cutter cuts a garment inaccurately, it cannot be sewn accurately; any poor cutting plagues the entire assembly process. Cutting is one of two production processes that is performed on many garments simultaneously. (Wet processing is the other process.) Thus cutting affects not just one but many garments.

Once the fabric has been spread, it is either moved to the cutting table or cut directly on the spreading table. Manual cutting is usually performed on the spreading table while automatic, computer-guided cutting is performed on a special vacuum cutting table. **Vacuum tables** use suction to compress and stabilize multiple plies of fabric and hold them in place (Figure 4–14). Vacuum tables allow the economical and accurate cutting of tall lay-ups, even on difficult-to-handle, slippery, and bulky fabrics.

Cutters in most factories use a *straight knife* with a straight, vertically vibrating blade. *Round knives* have a rotating, circular blade instead. These electric knives automatically stop to sharpen themselves during cutting to remain razor-sharp. A human or a computer guides the cutting knife around the outline of each pattern piece on the marker. Alternatively, a *band knife* is mounted in the cutting table and the cutter moves the fabric past it.

A human cutter follows the lines of the marker, but a computerized cutter guides the cutting according to a marker stored on tape. Faster than humans, computers accurately cut at speeds up to 800 inches per minute, and the computer plans the route the knife is to take for maximum efficiency. Safety issues and increasing fabric widths are forcing more and more companies to replace manual cutting with automated cutting.

A few factories have the capability to cut with computer-guided laser beams or high-pressure water jets. However, lasers can cut only one ply or a few plies at a time, and water jets can cut lay-ups no higher than about an inch. Companies specializing in small production runs find them useful, but these technologies are not practical for large runs.

Small, complex pattern pieces are sometimes cut out using a **die**, similar to a cookie cutter. For example, a cutter for a glove factory would have difficulty using a knife to cut accurately around the finger shapes of a glove piece. Instead, a heavy weight presses the sharp edges of the die, in the shape of the glove pattern piece, into the layers of fabric, cutting consistently every time. Dies cut out collars, cuffs, belt loops, and other small pieces for basic garments, such as men's shirts and slacks. Cutting for knit products is sometimes done with dies because the downward pressure causes less distortion to the knit cloth than knife cutting. Die cutting is used extensively for large-volume, classic products such as turtleneck tops. For fashion-oriented companies with new styles each season, however, the cost and lead time involved in casting new dies for each new style make die cutting impractical.

After cutting, the fabric is ply numbered and marked, if necessary. Ply numbering aids in maintaining shade consistency. All panels in a bundle are numbered. Operators sew only like-numbered panels together. Marks on the fabric enable **sewing operators** (workers who sew the garment together) to align seams of parts and panels properly and construct the garment accurately. For example, marks indicate pocket placement and dart tip locations. Notches at edges, hot or cold drill holes, needles carrying marking fluid or wax, or occasionally, thread marks (tailor's tacks) are used for marking. Marks need to be accurate, visible until the operation requiring them is complete, and not visible in the finished garment.

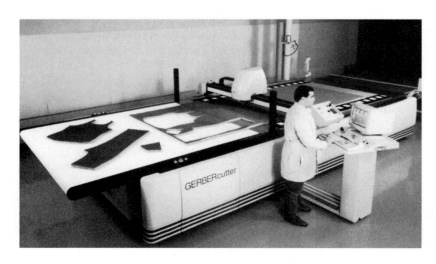

Figure 4–14 GERBERcutter® automated high-production cutting system. *(Courtesy of Gerber Garment Technology, Inc.)*

Making Sample Garments

Retail buyers view the line and place orders for the styles or numbers that they think will sell best in their stores. This is done by viewing sample garments. **Sample garments,** sometimes called salesmen's samples or duplicates, are the first garments made in the production process. Numbers can vary according to the size of the sales staff but usually a hundred or more units are made. Sample garments are made in the company's sample size and are made only in one color. Manufacturers plan for one or two samples for all the sales representatives plus a certain percentage for fallout. These garments are the first garments of a style to be produced, so there often is more fallout than in regular production as the engineers and operators "work out the bugs" in making a new style. Fabric is bought in *minimums* (the smallest amount of yardage a mill will sell) for sample garments. Any leftover yardage is used for bulk production.

Applying Decorative Details

Some decorative details such as embroidery are applied to garment panels before the garment is assembled. Advance scheduling of these processes (which are often contracted out) avoids holding up production. Other decorative details, such as screen printing on T-shirts, may be applied on completed garments. The garment construction and the decorative detail determine the best time for application. Some garments have multiple applications, both on panels and on the completed garment. There may not be enough time for sample garments to be embroidered or screen printed if those steps are being contracted out, so they may be produced without art. However, in the case of children's apparel, the artwork is what "sells" the garment, so time is allotted for its completion on the sample garments.

Assembly (Sewing) of Production Garments

Garments made domestically are generally assembled in an order referred to as **"parts, panels, pieces, products."** (For more information, see Chapters 11 and 12.) After cutting and marking, all **parts** (minor garment parts, such as portions of collars, cuffs, or pockets) and **panels** (major garment sections, such as fronts and backs) are tied together into **bundles** (stacks of like components). Panels not needed until later are sent to a holding area. Parts are sent to the parts line, sometimes called **preliminary,** where as many small parts as possible are prepared for assembly. For example, preliminary operations include hemming tops of patch pockets, adding decorative embroidery to front panels, partially assembling zippers, applying interfacing, and attaching labels. Once the parts line has completed a cut, the work is sent to the holding area and bundled in with the panels. The bundles are then sent to the appropriate lines for assembly of the major panels and **pieces** (semicomplete sections of the garment, such as sleeves, collars, and cuffs). Once the body of the garment is put together, final touches such as buttons and trim are added This completes the assembly of the **product,** the finished garment. The major production methods used to make apparel products include (1) the progressive bundle system, (2) the unit production system, and (3) modular manufacturing.

Many Asian factories in low-labor-cost areas specialize in sewing high-labor parts; then they send the parts to a high-labor-cost area for the low-labor operations. For example, parts may be assembled in China, and the major seams that transform the panels and pieces into garments may be sewn in Hong Kong, allowing for a *Made in Hong Kong* label.

Progressive Bundle System. Most factories produce garments on an **assembly line** in what is sometimes called the **progressive bundle system.** Identification tickets attached to the bundles contain information such as lot or cut number to help keep shade lots together, style number, operation to be performed on the bundle, and **piecework** rate for performing it. Piecework rates are expressed in **standard allowed minutes (SAMs),** which reflect the time required for a "100% operator" to perform the specified operation. Each operator completes the same task on each garment in the bundle before passing it on to the next operator. As operators complete a bundle, they save a portion of the bundle ticket, which is used to calculate the pay of each worker, based on the number of completed bundles. Garments are inspected during and after this process for quality. (For more information, see Chapter 3.)

Each garment passes through many different hands as it is assembled one step at a time. For example, a man's tailored jacket, generally considered the most complex garment to construct, requires at least 115 separate operations. On the other hand, a simple T-shirt requires as few as 8 operations (*Garment Construction Guide,* 1983).

Unit Production System. Some progressive manufacturers use modular manufacturing or unit production systems which replace the traditional assembly line and its bundles. **Unit production systems (UPS)** send garments to each operator's station via computer-controlled overhead transporters (An example is the Gerbermover® system depicted in

Figure 1-2.) Computers help track the progress of individual garments through the factory and direct them to operators who need work. Unit production systems improve the flow of garments through the factory and eliminate the time spent in handling bundles. Operators **cross-train** for several jobs so they can work where they are needed most. The unit production system optimizes operator productivity and reduces the time a garment spends in the sewing room from several weeks to less than a day! For example, in the traditional bundle system, if the collar setters finish more garments than the sleeve setters, bundles of collared garments wait for sleeves or more sleeve setters are added to the line. If the sleeve setters finish garments faster than the collar setters, the sleeve setters sit idle at their machines waiting for work or are sent home for the day. The unit production system sends each garment directly from a collar setter to a sleeve setter who needs work; if the sleeve setters get behind, a worker who was setting collars starts setting sleeves.

Modular Manufacturing. Modular manufacturing groups operators into teams, or modules. The team works on one garment at a time instead of a bundle of garments. The operators stand at their work stations and rotate to different machines as they work, becoming familiar with multiple steps in producing the garment. They also inspect their team's own work, catching and correcting mistakes as soon as they happen. Early experiments with modular manufacturing show that, besides inspiring teamwork and improving morale, it also enhances quality and reduces worker turnover. To make a garment using modular manufacturing or the unit production system takes as little time (sewing time only) as shown in these examples:

T-shirt 3 minutes

Pull-on pant 6 minutes

Zip-front pant 17 minutes

Unconstructed jacket 25 minutes

Lined blazer 40 minutes

Tailored coat 120 minutes

(Glock and Kunz, 1995; King, 1988).

Flexible Manufacturing. Flexible manufacturing refers to the combination of various manufacturing techniques based on the product being produced. For example, one product might lend itself to being made entirely by one operator, while the next might require the teamwork of modular manufacturing. Looking for ways to optimize the sewing process and reduce labor costs helps manufacturers remain competitive.

Automation. A wide variety of technologically advanced sewing machines, some computerized, help operators speedily and accurately execute the various steps in assembling a garment. Some sewing machines automatically or semiautomatically complete complex construction processes such as shirt collars and tailored jacket pockets. Sewing machine technology continues to de-skill many apparel manufacturing processes. But even automated sewing machines still require human operators, causing the apparel industry to remain very labor intensive. And although some operators use automated and semiautomated equipment, many use manual sewing machines that require considerable skill to operate.

To reduce the apparel industry's heavy reliance on human labor, **robotics**—the use of robots—is growing in importance. More than other industries, apparel production has defied full automation because of the soft, flexible nature of fabric, which prevents the production of uniform-quality goods by robots. But researchers are seeking and finding ways to overcome the problems inherent in handling cloth. Already, robots move rolls of fabric in mills and handle small parts and perform complex and repetitive sewing operations in some apparel factories. Vision systems and tactile sensing systems help robots locate fabric pieces and detect their orientation, enabling the robot to align and sew the pieces together within tolerances. For example, a robotics system sews a sleeve seam and vent over seven times faster than a manual sewing system. Although perfecting robotics for the apparel industry will require a huge investment in technology, an increase in the use of robots for garment production is expected.

Wet Processing

Garment **wet processing** is the most rapidly advancing phase of the apparel production process. Wet processing adds a finish to the assembled garments. It began in earnest in the 1970s with a few apparel manufacturers using small commercial washing machines to rinse sizing out of denim jeans to make the jeans more comfortable to wear. Consumers embraced the comfort and broken-in appearance of wet-processed garments. An added consumer benefit of wet processing is that because the garments are prewashed, they are essentially preshrunk already when they reach point of sale. When consumers try on wet-processed garments, they get a more accurate idea of in-use fit than with a garment that is not wet processed.

Wet processing has evolved into its own industry, with state-of-the-art wet-processing equipment handling up to 500 pounds of jeans at one

Figure 4–15   Industrial washer used in garment wet processing. *(Courtesy of The Lee Company.)*

time (Figure 4–15), new tunnel washers continuously rinsing garments without stopping, and computers controlling much of the work. Some jeans can be wet processed in basic formulas without ever being touched by human hands.

Wet processing softens, preshrinks, and creates a unique appearance before the garment goes to the consumer. Most jeans and many other styles of casual garments are wet processed *after* the garments have been assembled. While wet-processed apparel has wide consumer appeal, it requires extra skill and care on the part of the wet processor to achieve even coloring, without streaks or blotches. Wet processing can abrade the fabric and findings, eroding and causing holes. Any wet-processing errors are costly because not only are both the fabric and the garment ruined, but due to the large size of the wet process machines, dozens or hundreds of garments are ruined at one time. A number of other problems are inherent in wet processing. A few of them are unique to the wet process but most are common to a normal cut and sew process. The difference is that they become accentuated when wet processing is performed. Any metal fasteners applied before wet processing may rust or stain the garments if wet garments are allowed to sit for a considerable length of time before being dried. Bundle identity must be maintained to keep like shades together. Shading of parts becomes more pronounced if parts have been mismatched on the sewing floor. Holes develop in seams if the seam was not stitched properly. Threads break if the correct thread type and size was not used. If not chosen correctly, thread and other findings may not end up the same color as the body of the garment, and labels may become unreadable.

In general, wet processing magnifies any errors made in developing and sewing the garment, so manufacturers must make sure no mistakes are made. A company that produces garments that are unharmed by the wet process is producing excellent-quality apparel. The wet-processing system has forced manufacturers to produce a better constructed product. Previous to the demand for wet processing, construction defects manifested themselves after point of sale when the consumer laundered the products. These defects are now caught before point of sale by the manufacturer. Likewise, the mills have been forced to reduce defects, such as dye streaks and *set marks* (slight change in weave pattern due to stopping and restarting the loom), that do not show until the garment is laundered.

Wet processing takes place for one or more of four basic purposes—garment softening, color removal, color addition, and wrinkle prevention (Table 4–4).

Garment Softening.   **Garment rinsing** or **garment washing** is the most basic of all wet-process finishes. Finished garments are laundered using large washers and dryers to soften garments and give them that "broken in" look and feel that consumers desire. Garment rinsing primarily softens the fabric by removing the starches, sizing, and excess dyestuff used by the mill in the manufacturing process. It preshrinks the garment, giving purchasers an idea of the garment's true size and fit at the point of purchase, without significantly affecting the color. It is used most often on jeans used as work wear, washable silk shirts and blouses, and pigment-dyed garments.

Color Removal.   *Color removal* wet-process treatments are most commonly used in jeans. A basic indigo jean product is subjected to one of hundreds of color-alteration formulas. Most of the color removal formulas fall into one of three categories: (1) bleaching, (2) stonewashing and sandwashing, and (3) frosting. Of all the wet-process finishes, rinsing is the only process that does not damage the cloth. Each of the other processes reduces the tensile and tear strength of the cloth according to how strong the formula is and how long the garment is agitated in the machines. This is not a major concern for fashion garments as they have a relatively short life cycle. It is a concern, however, when a consumer is planning to make extended use of the product; it is not always possible to provide a unique fashion look via a garment finish and extended wear life at the same time. Again, it is a matter of achieving the correct balance for the end use.

Table 4–4 Basic Garment Wet-Process Finishes

Finish	Purpose	Description
Rinsing	Soften fabric without affecting color	Washing garments with water and detergent to remove starches and sizing
Rinsing on pigment-dyed fabric	Create aged look via color change	Rinsing pigment-dyed garments with detergent to remove excess pigment dyestuff
Bleaching	Remove color	Subjecting garment to chlorine bleach, potassium permanganate or other color-removing agent
Stonewashing/ Sandwashing	Soften fabric and create aged appearance via abrasion	Washing garments with stones, sand, enzymes or other products to remove starches and sizing and slightly abrade cloth
Acid washing or frosting	Remove color and add white highlights	Subjecting garment to potassium permanganate or other heavy salt (color-removing agent)
Dyeing	Add color	Dyeing of a white or natural garment
Overdyeing	Add color	Dyeing of a colored garment
Wrinkle-free	Reduce wrinkling of 100% cotton products	Treating garments or fabric with chemical resin formula.

Bleaching uses one or more types of color-removing agents to remove subtle or significant amounts of color. Bleaching is performed mainly on jeans and casual shirts. Softening and preshrinking effects are the same as in the rinsing process.

Stonewashing greatly softens the cloth, preshrinks it, and makes the garments look and feel used and comfortably broken in. It abrades the seams and edges. Originally, stonewashing involved the addition of actual stones to the wash cycle of a wet-process formula. More stones were added or the cycle was lengthened according to the desired degree of abrasion. Improved technology now allows this same look to be achieved with the use of artificial stones, chemicals, or enzymes at a lower cost and with fewer harmful effects to the environment. Closely related to stonewashing, **sandwashing** uses particles of sand to gently soften the fabric. It is a popular finish in casual men's wear.

Frosting or **acidwashing** is the most complicated of the basic wet-process finishes. Frosting uses a bleaching agent to remove color through a highlighting effect. It softens, preshrinks, and completely changes the character of the fabric through the loss of color in highlighted areas; dramatic light-dark effects result. Some garments totally change color depending upon the dyestuffs in the cloth and chemicals used in the wet-process formula.

Often wet-process formulas are developed that combine one or more processes. For example, it is possible to achieve a totally unique look with a stone-bleach formula or an acid-stone formula.

Color Addition. *Color addition* falls into two categories—dyeing and overdyeing. **Garment dyeing** involves the application of various colors, according to sales demand, to assembled garments made of a special white cloth called **PFD (prepared for dye)**. This garment dyeing process serves as a form of inventory control and is used most often on basic apparel such as casual shirts, T-shirts, and turtlenecks. **Overdyeing** involves dyeing one color over another to produce unique color and shading effects. If a blended fabric is used, one fiber, say cotton, accepts the color one way and the other fiber, say polyester, accepts the color differently.

Garment dyeing works best on knit fabrics made of cotton or other absorbent fibers, but it is used on a variety of fabrics. It is mainly limited to solid-color fabrics, although, occasionally, patterns are chemically imprinted on the greige goods. The patterns "pop," or appear, due to a reaction between the chemical imprinting and the dye formulation, when the garment is dyed. Garment dyeing shifts the responsibility for "color bugs" in the case of brand name products. The manufacturer dyes to order instead of trying to anticipate successful season colors.

Wrinkle Prevention. Another type of wet processing is the treatment of garments with **wrinkle-resistant** formulas that help garments maintain a pressed appearance after many washings and wearings. Such finishes are also called *durable press, permanent press,* and *wrinkle free,* although the finish is not permanent or totally wrinkle free. A variety of resin formulas are used, including a number of newly developed treatments for 100% cotton garments. This process is extremely complicated to execute correctly and results in **tender goods** (weak cloth) if not done carefully. The controls needed to monitor this process contribute to the high cost of garments treated with this formula.

The wrinkle-resistant finish is achieved in two ways; both involve applying chemicals to the cloth and baking the cloth in a curing oven. In one method the chemicals are applied directly to the cloth at the mill. In the other method the chemicals are applied to finished garments by the apparel manufacturer. Each method produces slightly different results. The *mill-cured* fabric is more wrinkle resistant than garment-cured but will not hold a crease. The *garment-cured* method allows a sharp, stable crease to be formed but is slightly less wrinkle resistant than the other.

Durable-press garments require little or no ironing; wrinkles fall out if removed promptly from the dryer. However, wearers of garments with a durable-press finish may notice some problems, depending upon the particular type of finish used. Some durable-press finishes attract oily stains while others repel them. Some have an odor before they have been laundered. The finishes sometimes cause the seams of the garment to pucker if the correct thread, seam, and stitch type have not been used. Strength generally is reduced, thus shortening the life of the garment. Consumers must make a decision as to whether they want ease of care or a long-lasting garment. Many consumers are willing to accept the limitations of the durable-press finish in exchange for time- and labor-saving convenience.

Pressing

After assembly, some garments (underwear and swimwear) require no pressing, but most require minimal pressing (T-shirts, slips, and nightgowns), or extensive pressing (tailored pants and jackets). Well-pressed garments make a good impression on consumers and command a higher price than unpressed or poorly pressed garments. (For more information, see Chapter 12.)

Pressing, often called **finish pressing** or **off pressing**, is conducted either with industrial steam irons or heavy pressing machines like the ones seen at dry-cleaning establishments. Heat and moisture, in the form of steam, combined with pressure work together to create a good press job. *Pressers* or *pressing operators* in companies that produce low-volume, high-fashion or highly structured clothing perform the pressing operation with small flat irons similar to those used by consumers at home. **Industrial flat irons,** however, are much heavier than consumer flat irons and are usually suspended from above for operator convenience and safety.

Pressing performed on high-volume ready-to-wear is conducted in an entirely different manner. These machines, no longer called irons, but *presses* or *pressing machines,* perform the pressing operation more efficiently than hand pressing. Generally, apparel is slipped over the machine; steam and pressure are applied automatically and then a vacuum extracts any excess moisture. These machines come in many shapes and sizes. **Flat-bed** or **buck presses** are large, flat, table-type presses where the presser positions and repositions sections of garments until the entire garment has been pressed. The garment might be repositioned as many as four times depending upon the type of garment being pressed.

Special **form presses** (sometimes called **Paris® presses**) are shaped like the garment. The garment is positioned once on the form, steam is blown into the garment, and slight pressure is applied through the force of blowing steam. Paris presses are useful on fabrics such as corduroy and velveteen that have a nap that would be crushed by pressure from a buck or flat-bed press. Because the only pressure applied is from the blowing steam, the nap of the fabric is not crushed or damaged. Paris presses are also used on tailored garments, such as wool jackets.

The last type of pressing machines are **upright presses** (sometimes called **Colmac® presses**). Upright presses are specially designed for specific types of apparel, such as jeans and jean jackets. Because of the high volume of these products, it is cost efficient to have special presses designed for each garment type. Upright presses use clamps, hangers, or both to hold the garment in position. The garment is positioned once, steam is blown into the garment, and then pressure is applied from the outside of the garment. As with form presses, excess moisture is extracted by suction.

Garments that have been treated with a resin finish to prevent wrinkling are subjected to heat during the finishing process in a **curing oven** or **heat tunnel**. The resin finish must cure in a controlled environment in order to be effective. Curing takes place after finish pressing.

Finishing

The **finishing** process refers to the final steps in the production of the garment. It includes adding finishing details, trimming and inspecting, repairing or reworking any defects, pressing, and folding and packing.

Adding *finishing details* after washing is a unique requirement of companies that wet process their products. After wet processing, buttons, labels, snaps, and other items that cannot withstand wet processing must be added. As a part of finishing, most manufacturers conduct 100% *trim and inspect*, in which every garment is inspected and long threads are trimmed. (For more information, see Chapter 3.) Any garments found to have spots or soil are sent to *spot cleaning operators* who clean the soiled areas. Any garments found with sewing defects are sent to *repair operators* who make the needed repairs.

After the garments are thoroughly inspected and any defects repaired, they are sent to the *fold and pack operation*. At this stage any accessory items such as belts, ties, or flowers are added; paper hang tags and size stickers are attached, and the garments are folded or hung on hangers. While packaging in plastic bags, commonly called **poly bags**, keeps garments clean and aids in reducing shipping damage, many manufacturers are responding to environmental concerns and are eliminating unnecessary packaging materials. If necessary to protect garments from soil, they use large *baler bags* that group several garments together in one bag; individual poly bags are used mainly for whites or when the retailer specifies them. Floor-ready merchandise, preticketed and on hangers but without individual bags, eliminates extra handling on the part of the retailers, saving them time and money. The garments are then placed either in cartons or on hanging racks and sent to the shipping area.

Final Audit

With the garments totally prepared for shipping, in-plant auditors perform a *final audit,* checking product quality and fold and pack-quantity accuracy. Using statistical sampling, they determine whether or not the *AQL (acceptable quality level)* has been met. If the product is found to be unacceptable, 100% inspection is performed and repairs are made; the product is not shipped until all rework is complete.

▬ ▪ ▬ ▪ ▬ ▪ ▬

DISTRIBUTION

Producers ship products in a variety of ways. *Air freight* is the most expensive and, therefore, least desirable method. *Vessel* (boat) is the most common method used for global shipments. Carriers offer two different routes—slow vessel or fast vessel. Fast vessel costs more but takes a more direct route to the United States. Train is used frequently in the United States and other countries, but truck is the most common land shipping method used for domestic shipments. A *shipping consolidator* makes the arrangements for global shipments. *Brokers* clear paperwork and imported products through customs and follow up on the results of shipments after inspection. The broker also ensures that quotas are not violated and duties are paid. Domestically, most manufacturers make their own shipping arrangements.

Distribution varies according to the size of the manufacturer and the buyer. Many domestic shipments leave the manufacturer and go directly to the retail store Most, however, make either one or two additional stops between the manufacturer and the retail store. Many large manufacturers have more than one location making the same product. This product must be consolidated at the manufacturer's **distribution center** (**DC**). When shipments arrive at the DC, the product is sorted and stored. Two stocks are maintained: forward and reserve. *Forward stock* is located convenient to the packing area and contains open cases that are pulled from to complete an order. *Reserve stock* is the excess product that is not being shipped immediately. Most companies operate on a *first in-first out (FIFO)* system so the reserve stock is always rotating into forward stock. The goal, of course, is to have low but adequate inventory as profits should not be tied up in excess inventory.

Most large retailers with multiple locations also have their own distribution centers. At these locations products are again consolidated if the product has been purchased from more than one source, but a retail distribution center's primarily purpose is to separate and ship stock in a mix appropriate to its stores. Large orders must be broken down and shipped to individual stores in the amounts appropriate for that store's volume.

Cycle time can be adversely lengthened if a product has to stop at two distribution centers. Pressure is continually being placed on employees of both manufacturers and retailers to reduce cycle time, and the elimination of unnecessary shipping time is one way to respond. A method used to reduce time and expense is **drop shipping**, the direct shipment to a store address. In the fashion business, as in other businesses, time is money.

Manufacturers that consolidate their products at their own distribution centers often conduct distribution center audits to monitor performance of individual manufacturing locations and objectively confirm product quality one last time. While quality cannot be inspected into the product, one final check can provide an increased confidence level and serve as a check on the system. In the case of extremely poor quality, finding the bad product at the distribution center allows the company to return the merchandise and prevent it from reaching the retailer or the consumer. Distribution center audits are frequently conducted to check packing methods and pack quantity, carton marking, and labeling accuracy. Retailers may also conduct inspections at their own DCs to provide an internal check on the **incoming acceptable quality level (IAQL),** or they conduct the same inspection at the manufacturer's factories or distribution centers, avoiding time delays and the cost of shipping unacceptable goods.

SALES TO CONSUMERS

At this point, the products which have been months in the planning and production stages finally hit the stores and are available for display and sale to the consumer. Some of these garments have literally been around the world in their journey from original inception to finished product. Most consumers viewing the racks of clothing in a retail store or the pages in a catalog probably would find it difficult to imagine the incredible coordination of effort that made it all possible.

Sales data captured by POS terminals and relayed back to manufacturers will be used in the formulation of the next line, and the cycle continues. At this point, high initial sales to consumers may trigger reorders of popular merchandise. Basic items generally are reorderable, but for most seasonal fashion merchandise it is too late.

Because the focus of this text is on understanding the production and quality evaluation of ready-to-wear, further information on retail sales, presentation, marketing, and advertising of mass-produced products should be acquired from other sources. Refer to Related Resources: Sales and Marketing.

THE ADVANCEMENT OF APPAREL PRODUCTION

A number of trade associations, related industry organizations, and publications contribute to the advancement and dissemination of mass-production research, technology, and philosophy. (See Related Resources: URLs for World Wide Web Sites on the Internet). For example, every fall in Atlanta, Georgia, apparel manufacturers gather for the **Bobbin Show™** (cosponsored by Bobbin Magazine and the American Apparel Manufacturers Association). The Bobbin Show showcases new apparel production equipment and technology and facilitates the exchange of ideas. For more information, contact **Bobbin Magazine,** P.O. Box 1986, Columbia, SC 29202. URL: http://www.bobbin.com.

The **Textile/Clothing Technology Corporation,** better known as **(TC)²** (tee see squared), is a coalition of industry, education, government, and labor concentrating on leading-edge manufacturing techniques and training to advance manufacturing technology and enhance competitiveness of the U.S. industry. $(TC)^2$ researches the practicality, productivity, and profitability of equipment and manufacturing systems. For more information, contact $(TC)^2$, 211 Gregson Drive, Cary, NC 27511. URL: http://dama.tc2.com/homepage.htm.

SUMMARY

Apparel is mass produced in a continuing cycle. The mass-production process begins with an evaluation of the previous line, analysis of customer returns, comparison studies of competitors' products, market research, and trend identification, all resulting in a development plan for the upcoming season. The design stage includes line development; preliminary line approval; fabric and findings research and development; developing artwork for prints; embroideries, and screen prints, developing new wet-process finishes, making the first patterns; and sewing prototype garments.

Sourcing involves precosting and production costing. The main factor affecting the cost of a garment is the quality and quantity of the fabric. Also considered when costing a garment are the quality and quantity of the findings, labor, and other costs, plus the overhead costs associated with conducting business. The price of the garment must be set higher than its cost to allow for a profit. Manufacturers often try to reduce the costs of producing a garment, trying to achieve a careful balance between cost and the desired quality. Sourcing also includes writing fabric and findings specifications; determining production capacity requirements; considering garment placement options; beginning cost negotiations with contractors; obtaining color lab dips; and making prototype prints, embroideries, and screen prints.

The preproduction stage includes fabric, findings, and wet process testing and approval; writing garment specifications; color/shade approval; care-label approval; sewing preproduction garments; making production patterns; grading the pattern; finalizing sourcing decisions; marker making; other label approval; garment classification with U.S. Customs

Service (imports only); and line finalization. Production includes arrival of the production fabric and findings, spreading, cutting, subcontracting of pre-assembly sundry operations, sewing sample garments, assembly of production garments, wet processing, subcontracting of postassembly sundry operations, pressing, finishing, and final audit. The computer is increasingly used in mass production, but the apparel industry remains very labor intensive. However, technological advancements bring continual improvements in efficiency.

Distribution includes shipping, customs clearance (imports only), DC audit and inspection, and distribution to retailers. Sales to consumers includes display at the retail store, initial sales, reorders when possible, and gathering of POS information.

Mass Production Checklist

If you can answer yes to each of these questions regarding the garment you are evaluating, it was produced using high-quality mass-production methods.

✔ Does the design reflect a carefully formulated development plan?
✔ Are prototype garments used to enable fine-tuning of the design?
✔ Does sourcing take into consideration costs and lead times?
✔ Does costing includes all fabric, findings, labor, overhead, and other costs?
✔ Is cost thoughtfully balanced with quality requirements?
✔ Are fabric and findings tested before approval?
✔ Are approved color and shade bands distributed to everyone who needs them?
✔ Do garment specifications include pertinent diagrams and instructions? Are they distributed to everyone who needs them?
✔ Are methods of measure distributed to all contractors?
✔ Are imported garments preclassified with U.S. Customs?
✔ Do production patterns reduce raw material waste and streamline designs without destroying their essence?
✔ Does grading preserve the design's intended appearance in all sizes?
✔ Does marker making maximize material utilization?
✔ Are patterned fabrics matched where possible? Are the dominant bars of fabrics with stripes and plaids and the dominant motif of fabrics with large motifs placed attractively on the finished garment?
✔ Is the finished garment free of noticeable fabric flaws?

✔ Are directional fabrics cut accordingly?
✔ Is cutting and marking accurate to enable accurate garment assembly?
✔ Does the mass-production method used maximize quality and minimize costs?
✔ Does wet processing enhance the aesthetic or functional performance of the garment without harming the garment?
✔ Is the garment protected by its packaging, without using unnecessary packaging materials?
✔ Do garments undergo additional inspections at the manufacturer's and/or retailer's distribution center?

New Terms

If you can define each of these terms and differentiate between related terms, you have gained a good working vocabulary for discussing the topics in this chapter. The terms are listed in the order in which they appear in this chapter

apparel production cycle
line development/lead time calendar
development plan
focus group
comparison study
fashion forecaster
color service
designer
merchandiser
color story
line/collection
group
drape
body
computer-aided design (CAD)
Computer Integrated Textile Design Association (CITDA)
prototype
line presentation board
first pattern
sloper/basic block
drafting
pattern design system (PDS)
digitizer
prototype garment
sample room/prototype lab
outsourcing
costing
precosting/quick cost
production costing
fallout (fabric)
finding/notion/sundry
prepack

overhead costs
wholesale price
market potential price
loss leader
retail price
keystone markup
profit improvement program
color approval
shade approval
lab dip
strikeoff
shade band
fallout (garment)
preproduction garment
embargo
preclassification
breakout
binding tariff classification ruling
production pattern
grading
grade rule
graded nest
computer-aided manufacturing (CAM)
marker
material utilization (MU)
pattern matching
even plaid
uneven plaid
spreading
ply
lay/lay-up
nap-one-way (NOW)/directional
nap-either-way (NEW)/nondirectional
nap-up-and-down (NUD)/face-to-face
cutting
vacuum table
die
sewing operator
sample garment
part
panel
bundle
preliminary
piece
product
assembly line
progressive bundle system
piecework
standard allowed minutes (SAM)
unit production system (UPS)
cross-train
modular manufacturing
flexible manufacturing
robotics

wet processing
garment rinsing/garment washing
bleaching
stonewashing
sandwashing
frosting/acidwashing
garment dyeing
prepared for dye/PFD cloth
overdyeing
wrinkle resistant
tender goods
pressing/finish pressing/off pressing
industrial flat iron
flat-bed/buck press
form/Paris® press
upright/Colmac® press
curing oven/heat tunnel
finishing
poly bags
distribution center (DC)
drop shipping
incoming acceptable quality level (IAQL)
Bobbin Show™
Bobbin Magazine
Textile/Clothing Technology Corporation/(TC)²

Review Questions

1. List the steps of the mass-production process, beginning with the evaluation of the previous line and ending with sales to the consumer.
2. Explain the factors that go into the formulation of a line development plan.
3. How are computers used to assist in the production of ready-to-wear?
4. What is the difference between a first pattern and a production pattern?
5. List the main options for sourcing garment production.
6. List the five main elements that must be considered when costing a garment. Which is generally the most significant?
7. List 10 examples of how a manufacturer might cut costs.
8. What part does the cost of producing a garment play in establishing its wholesale price?
9. Why is shade approval important?
10. Explain how a garment is classified with the U.S. Customs Service. What are the benefits of preclassification?
11. Compare and contrast the major production methods used to make apparel products.
12. Outline the main types of wet processing finishes.

Activities

1. Visit apparel manufacturers in your area. Compare and contrast their production processes from design through shipping the product. Or view videotapes on apparel manufacturing.
2. Compare blank copies of costing sheets from area apparel manufacturers. What elements do the cost sheets have in common? How are they different? Using the cost sheets, cost a garment. How could the cost sheets be improved?
3. Examine a garment and choose three features that you, as a manufacturer or retailer, would be willing to sacrifice to reduce costs. Choose three features that you, as a consumer, would be willing to sacrifice to reduce price. Are the features you chose as a manufacturer or retailer the same as those you chose as a consumer? Why or why not?
4. Examine two similar garments sold for different prices. What influenced the difference in the prices—fabric costs, findings costs, labor costs, or some other factors?
5. Take turns laying out a miniature marker, using half-scale pattern pieces, on a roll of paper. Who can achieve the best material utilization?
6. Study garments made of striped or plaid fabrics. What decisions did the manufacturer make about matching the patterns? Evaluate the results.
7. Obtain standards and specifications sheets from area manufacturers. Compare these and suggest how they might be improved.
8. Take a computer tour of the WWW via the Internet. Visit the sites listed in this chapter in Table 4–3. Explain how a manufacturer might use the information found at these sites.
9. As a group project, mass produce a small item using different mass-production methods (i.e., progressive bundle system, unit production system, modular manufacturing, and flexible manufacturing). Evaluate the impact of each method on costs and quality. (TC)[2] provides the "Pennville Plant" exercise for this purpose for about $400.
10. Examine various wet-processed garments and determine the type of wet processing performed on each.
11. Participate in a computer simulation using one of the models available from (TC)[2], such as The Textile/Apparel Process Simulator (T.A.P.S.), Line Balancing Decision Training, or Automatic Line Balancing Calculations.

Shape, Silhouette, Style: Focus on Design Development

Chapter Objectives

1. Examine the impact of design features on the performance and cost of the garment.
2. Understand the various ways of shaping garments to the human body, including the impact of fabric grain and the role of underlying fabrics and supporting devices in garments.
3. Present a vocabulary of style names, including garment silhouettes and variations in design features such as lengths, waistlines, necklines, collars, sleeves, cuffs, pockets, and decorative details.

Shape, silhouette, and style—these words capture the essence of apparel design. Decisions about shape, silhouette, and style guide the design development process. Designers and merchandisers give careful consideration to these fundamentals for even the most basic garments.

This chapter explains how flat, two-dimensional (2-D) fabrics are shaped and transformed into garments that fit three-dimensional (3-D) human bodies. This chapter also presents a menu of silhouettes and style options important for developing a professional vocabulary.

GARMENT SHAPE

Shaping a garment enables it to fit the wearer and achieve a desired silhouette and style or look. The skillful use of fabric grain, thoughtfully chosen shaping methods, and underlying fabrics and supporting devices that help a garment retain its shape often distinguish a high-quality garment from one of lesser quality. Attention to shape and support is important in all garments but especially in tailored clothing.

Tailored garments are carefully structured and detailed, for example, the classic business suit; they are often closely fitted and made of woven fabrics. Shaping methods, underlying fabrics, and supporting devices are critical to the aesthetic appearance of the garment; they affect the garment's functional performance as well, including fit, comfort, appearance retention, and durability.

Role of Fabric Grain

A major consideration in garment quality is the orientation of the fabric's grain. Just as furniture makers observe and use the grain of wood to create a desired effect, garment manufacturers use the grain in fabric to its best advantage. **Grain** is the orientation of the yarns that make up the fabric. Two sets of yarns interlaced at right angles to one another make up a quality woven fabric. Knit fabric has one continuous yarn instead of two sets of yarns. For this reason, knit fabrics do not technically have a grain, but most of the directional rules still apply in their use.

The appropriate handling of fabric grain affects the aesthetic and functional quality of the finished garment. Attention to grain is important throughout construction but is most critical during cutting. If cut incorrectly, trueness of grain cannot be restored to the garment.

Lengthwise Grain. The **lengthwise grain** or **warp** runs parallel to the **selvages,** the woven edges of the fabric (Figure 5–1). It consists of yarns that are held taut by the loom during weaving. Therefore, the lengthwise yarns are the strongest to withstand the tension of the weaving process. Lengthwise yarns tend to be stable, less apt to stretch or shrink, and more apt to hang straight than crosswise yarns. Designers plan most major pattern pieces to be cut with the length of the pattern piece parallel to the lengthwise grain. The lengthwise grain is then perpendicular to the floor when the garment is being worn.

In a few cases it is preferable to cut pieces on the lengthwise grain (with the warp), to intentionally have this grain run around the body instead of up and down. For example, waistbands require stability around the waist and should be cut so the lengthwise grain goes around the body. Collars, cuffs, and other minor pattern pieces may be cut this way for the same reason.

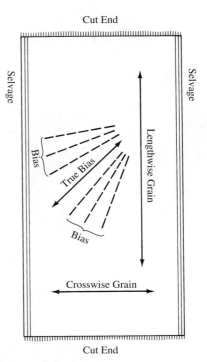

Figure 5–1 Lengthwise and crosswise grains, bias, and true bias.

Crosswise Grain. The **crosswise grain, fill, filling,** or **weft** of the fabric consists of the yarns woven over and under the lengthwise yarns. The crosswise grain runs at a 90-degree angle to the lengthwise grain and the selvages (Figure 5–1). The crosswise grain is less strong and has a slight stretch. Because designers place most major pattern pieces with their length running perpendicular to the crosswise grain of the fabric, this creates a softer look and provides comfort to the wearer.

If the producer cuts major pattern pieces on the crosswise grain, with the length of the pattern piece running in the same direction as the crosswise grain, the effect on the hang of the finished garment might be imperceptible depending on the fabric. But crosswise layouts are generally less desirable than lengthwise layouts because of the more stable and stronger lengthwise yarns.

Sometimes major pattern pieces are cut on the crosswise grain (with the fill) to maximize fabric usage or to create special effects. For example, on border print fabrics (with the design along one selvage edge), if a dress design calls for the border print to run around the hem, the skirt is cut on the crosswise grain. Generally these styles are not close fitting; adding fullness compensates for the otherwise stiff look of the garment when cut in the crosswise direction.

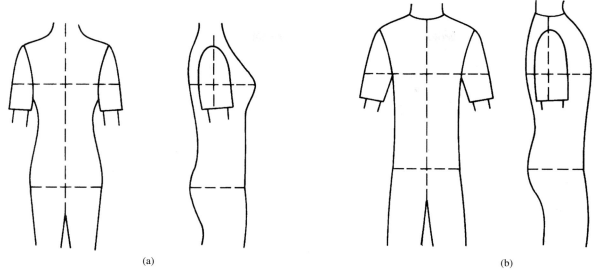

Figure 5–2 Correct positions of fabric grain on (a) female and (b) male bodies.

Straight-of-Grain. **Straight-of-grain** includes both the lengthwise and crosswise grains because they follow the straight yarns of the fabric. Unless there are design reasons for doing otherwise, marker makers place pattern pieces in the lengthwise direction, or straight-of-grain, of the fabric. Figure 5–2 shows the commonly accepted placement of grainlines on the human body for a basic garment. The lengthwise grain runs straight down the body at the center front and center back. The crosswise grain is perpendicular to the lengthwise grain at bust/chest and hip levels. For sleeves, the lengthwise grain runs straight down the center of the arm from shoulder to elbow. The crosswise grain is perpendicular to the lengthwise grain at bust/chest level. Straight-of-grain edges create seams with minimal stretch; for example, angled pants pockets gape less if the facing edge is cut on the straight of grain, to stabilize the bias-grain pocket edge.

To create various effects, a designer alters the position of the pattern in relation to the grainline to intentionally change the way the garment hangs. Pattern pieces cut on the lengthwise grain, crosswise, bias, or true bias create various results. Figure 5–3 illustrates how a skirt appears with the lengthwise grain placed at center front, side front, and side seam of the skirt.

In cut panels or finished garments, it may be difficult to distinguish between the lengthwise and crosswise grains unless you are familiar with the fabric. However, a close examination of the fabric usually reveals more warp yarns per square inch than fill yarns. (This does not hold true for all types of fabric, but is generally true.) Also, remember that if a woven fabric is stretched, the length generally stretches less than the width.

Bias and True Bias. The bias and true bias of a fabric are considered directions of the fabric rather than grain. Technically, any direction of the fabric that is not the lengthwise grain or crosswise grain may be referred to as **bias.** The **true bias** direction is at a 45–degree angle to the lengthwise and crosswise grains of woven fabrics. Usually when a garment is "cut on the bias," it refers to the true bias (Figure 5–1). The true bias of a woven fabric has several interesting features. (The bias direction on knit fabrics does not share these characteristics.) True bias is the most stretchy part of a woven fabric because its stretch is impeded by few yarn interlacings. Garments or pieces of garments cut on the true bias drape and roll beautifully and hang close to the body, emphasizing contours.

For these reasons, many high-fashion designers include bias cuts in their creations, especially for evening wear. Full skirts cut on the true bias can be flattering to the wearer and elegant. Bows, neckties, cowl necklines, and jacket and coat under-collars utilize the graceful drape and roll of the true bias. The stretch and roll of true bias makes it ideal as binding for curved as well as straight edges. Bias cuts are not frequently used in low-price apparel lines. A bias layout wastes considerably more fabric than a straight-of-grain layout for the same garment (Figure 5–4), sometimes as much as about 50 percent more. Also, bias-cut garments are difficult to sew because they tend to stretch out of shape during construction.

A garment cut on the bias is easily identified upon close examination. The fabric's straight-of-grain lies

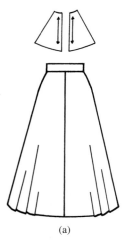
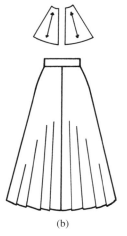
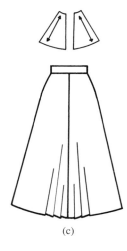

Figure 5–3 Different drape of skirts cut on various grains: (a) lenthwise grain at center front, (b) lengthwise grain in center of each gore, and (c) lengthwise grain at side seam.

on the diagonal, oriented at a 45-degree angle to the center front of the garment. *Do not* confuse the bias with the appearance of a twill weave fabric like denim. Examine a pair of denim twill jeans which are cut on the straight-of-grain, and notice that the diagonal ridges of the denim fabric result from its twill weave, not from being cut on the bias.

Garments Cut Off-Grain. Garments with proper grain alignment hang straight and maintain their shape in use. A close examination of the position of the warp and fill yarns of the fabric reveals the accuracy with which the garment was cut. Garments cut moderately off-grain do not hang straight and often affect comfort as they tend to pull toward the direction of lengthwise grain position. Garments cut extremely off-grain have a noticeably crooked hang. Evidence of the misuse of fabric grain includes twisted pant legs, twisted torsos, twisted sleeves, uneven hems, undesirable sagging and wrinkling in fitted garments, and pleats that fall open.

When making the marker, some manufacturers allow slight tilting of the pattern pieces (usually not more than 3%) to increase material utilization. How far off-grain the pieces may be cut depends on the type of fabric and the tolerances established for it. For low-price garments, several inches off-grain may be allowed. Off-grain fabrics also cause finished garments to have off-grain panels (see Chapter 7). Grain distortions and their effect on garment appearance are relative. Thus, garments cut slightly off-grain or from slightly off-grain fabrics may be acceptable if the problem is imperceptible in the final garment. However, manufacturers of quality clothing strive to produce "grain perfect" garments.

Shaping Methods

All garments contain **shaping methods** (darts or dart equivalents) that control the way the garment fits the contours of the body. The methods used to shape the garment and the location and amount of added shaping affect the garment's fit and style. Tailored garments and other apparel which fit closely to body contours are noted for the shape created by these methods, but even "shapeless" garments have their shape because of a choice of shaping methods. In low-cost garments, pattern engineers may have to change or eliminate shaping methods to meet pricing requirements. Pattern pieces might have to be designed slightly smaller or with straighter edges than pattern pieces in more expensive apparel. These changes often result in better material utilization and slightly lower sewing costs. However, the omission of shaping methods detracts from the design and ultimate fit of the garment. Again, balance comes into play. What price are the shaping features worth to the consumer?

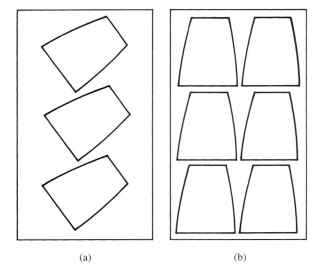

Figure 5–4 (a) Bias layout is less fabric-efficient than (b) straight-of-grain layout.

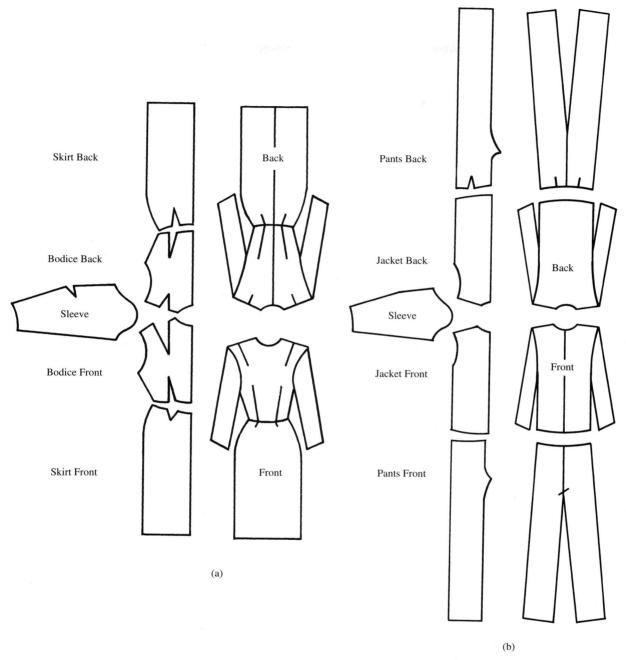

Figure 5–5 Basic blocks for (a) woman's dress and (b) man's suit.

A basic fitted garment is derived from a **basic block** or **sloper** pattern. Manufacturers have a basic block for each classification of apparel that they produce, for example, pants or jackets. Figure 5–5 shows the basic blocks for a woman's dress and a man's suit. The designer uses shaping methods to make changes in the basic block to produce style variations. Figures 5–19, 5–20, 5–21, 5–22, 5–23, and 5–25 later in this chapter illustrate a number of

styles, all originating from a basic block, with varying amounts of fullness added and controlled in different locations through various shaping methods. For more information about how shaping methods are used to create different clothing styles, see this chapter's section on styles.

Darts. A **dart** is a triangular fold stitched to shape the flat fabric to specific curves of the body. Notice

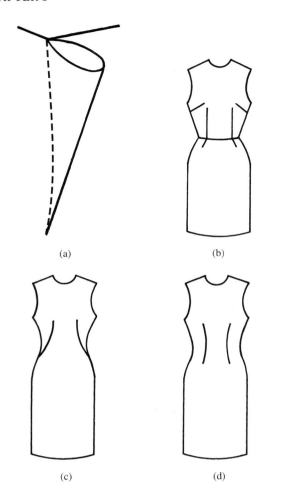

(a)

(b)

(c)

(d)

Figure 5–6   Darts: (a) stitched, tapering at the point, inside the garment, (b) single-pointed, (c) French, and (d) double-pointed.

the triangular *darts* in the basic blocks in Figure 5–5. Darts introduce shape into the garment, enabling a two-dimensional fabric to become a three-dimensional garment that fits a three-dimensional body.

Darts serve as a basic shaping method for apparel. They enable the garment to fit the body smoothly. However, a garment with darts does not usually fit as wide a range of sizes as do garments containing other shaping methods. Darts have relatively high labor costs but low fabric costs compared to other shaping methods.

Darts are almost always stitched inside the garment so that the triangular fold of the dart appears inside the garment. Occasionally, for style reasons, *decorative darts* are stitched so that the folded triangle appears on the outside of the garment.

Single-Pointed Darts.   Most darts are *single pointed* (Figures 5–6a and b). Designers use single-pointed darts vertically at the back neck or back shoulders of jackets; at the waistline of bodices, skirts, pants, and

dresses; and horizontally at elbows and at the bust-line of women's clothing. However, a dart can originate from any seam and occur at any angle so long as it points toward the fullest part of its assigned body curve. For example, *French darts* are diagonal bust darts that originate low in the side seams directed toward the bust curve (Figure 5–6c).

Double-Pointed Darts.   *Double-pointed darts* or *contour darts* look like two single-pointed darts joined at the wide ends to form one continuous dart (Figure 5–6d). Designers use double-pointed darts vertically at the waistline of jackets and dresses. Double-pointed darts nip the garment in at the waist while releasing fullness above and below it to fit the bust/chest and hip areas.

Size of Darts.   Narrow darts fit small body curves and wide darts fit large body curves. Each dart adds to labor costs, so in low-price garments one dart is often used per body curve where two or more narrow darts might yield smoother-fitting results. However, a single dart has the offsetting advantage of being less visually distracting than multiple darts. The wider the dart angle, the more angular the shape produced at the point. The more tapered the stitching near the pointed end, the more rounded the curve produced in the garment.

Dart Equivalents

Shaping can be accomplished by darts or by **dart equivalents** or **dart substitutes**. Dart equivalents substitute for darts by incorporating shape into the garment in a variety of ways. Dart substitutes include the following: shaped seams (including gores and yokes), style fullness (including released darts, added fullness, ease, gathers, shirring, smocking, elastic, and drawstrings) and other dart substitutes (including stretch fabrics, bias-cut pieces, pleats, tucks, godets, gussets, full-fashioned knits, and lacing).

All ready-to-wear garments contain shaping methods— either darts or dart equivalents. Darts or dart equivalents are required wherever the fabric of the garment fits a body curve. The bust, abdomen, buttocks, shoulder blades, and elbows are curves requiring shaping methods. For example, for a good fit in tailored jackets, a shoulder dart or dart equivalent is needed in the back shoulder seam of the garment to smoothly fit the shoulder blade area to the body. The absence of a shoulder dart or dart equivalent causes wrinkles to emanate from the neckline or armhole because fabric is pulled from these areas to accommodate the curve of the shoulder blades. In better jackets, ease may be substituted in the shoulder seam for the shoulder dart, yielding a smooth fit in the shoulder area. (See section on Ease later in this chapter.) In better shirts, a shaped seam joining the yoke to the body of the shirt serves as a shoulder dart substitute. When the shoulder darts or their substitutes are omitted, the area does not fit smoothly. For some garments, darts are completely released to fit body curves, although the fit is not smooth. (See section on Released Darts later in this chapter.)

The design of the garment helps determine which shaping methods are used. For example, loose styles are suited to the use of gathers or added fullness; close-fitting styles often feature darts or stretch fabrics. The fabric and price line of the garment also influence the choice of shaping methods. Because the female figure is naturally more curvy than the male figure, women's clothing features more shaping methods than men's clothing. In some cases, designers include shaping methods not for fit, but for comfort or aesthetic reasons.

Shaped Seams.   Not all seams are dart substitutes; many join flat fabric panels without imparting any shape. But *shaped seams* are a common dart equivalent, especially in close-fitting garments. Dart-substitute seams perform the same function as darts by shaping fabric panels where they are joined together. Figure 5–7 illustrates dart shapes incorporated in some shaped seams; fitted side seams, shoulder seams, fitted waistline seams, and set-in-sleeve armhole seams are examples of dart-substitute seams. **Princess seams,** which incorporate the bust and waist darts in fitted womenswear, are also dart-substitute seams. They add shape to the garment and enhance fit but cost more to cut and sew than other types of seams. Another example is better women's panties, which sometimes feature a center back seam to fit the buttocks better than ordinary panties. Yoke seams and gore seams often serve as dart substitutes.

Yokes.   **Yokes** are horizontal divisions within a garment; they are usually small, flat panels of fabric at the shoulder, waist, or midriff. When seamed to the garment, some yokes help the garment fit the body curve in the area near the seam (Figure 5–8). The yoke seam serves as a dart equivalent by incorporating the dart shape into the seam. Yokes called *risers* often substitute for darts at pants and skirt waistlines. *Midriff yokes* fit the garment close to the body below the bust. Yokes are frequently used in the backs of shirts and blouses to fit the garment through the shoulder blade area. They are also used in the fronts of shirts, as in Western-style yokes. In menswear these yokes are merely decorative features that provide no shaping, but in womenswear they often incorporate pleats or shirring to allow for a better fit through the bust area.

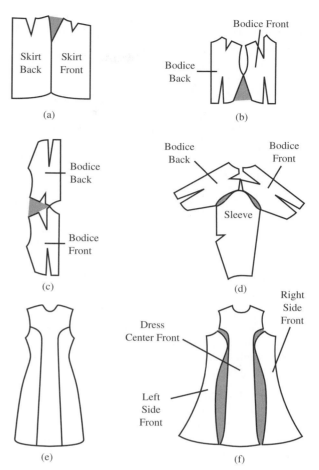

Figure 5–7   Shaded areas show dart-substitute effect of seams: (a) skirt side seam, (b) bodice side seam, (c) shoulder seam, (d) armscye (armhole) seam, (e) princess line dress, and (f) princess seams.

Split yokes feature a seam at the center back of the yoke. Split yokes (risers) in the backs of women's jeans can improve fit considerably. In custom-made shirts, a split yoke represents better fit because the center back seam is shaped to fit the individual. In ready-to-wear shirts, a split yoke serves no practical purpose, but manufacturers sometimes use them as a tool to create an impression of custom-made quality or to achieve better fabric utilization when planning the marker.

Gores.   **Gores** are vertical divisions within a garment, usually tapered panels seamed together to add shape to a garment. They serve as dart equivalents by incorporating the dart shape in the seams. Skirts are frequently gored (Figure 5–9). Two-gore skirts contain two panels, four-gore skirts contain four panels, and so on. The more gores, the higher the labor costs; however, the use of several small gores often achieves higher material utilization than a few large gores.

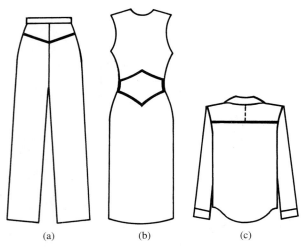

Figure 5–8 (a) Split yoke/riser in pants, (b) midriff yoke, and (c) back shoulder yoke in shirt (dotted line indicates seam placement for split yoke).

Gores are not always dart substitutes. Sometimes manufacturers add gores to narrow fabrics in order to widen them for cutting out garments with large pieces, for example, circular skirts.

Fullness. Garments may fit the body simply by allowing enough fullness in the fabric. Fullness may be the result of releasing darts or of adding extra fullness. This added style fullness may be controlled by ease, gathers, shirring, smocking, elastic, or drawstrings.

Released Darts. Sometimes fullness is achieved by releasing (not stitching) darts; **released darts** result in a straight silhouette rather than a fitted garment. A released dart allows the fabric to cover the intended body curve without fitting the fabric closely to the curve.

It is a common practice to release darts in today's ready-to-wear because of the popularity of loose-fitting clothing; darts are usually released in combination with the addition of extra style fullness to the area. Releasing darts reduces cost. However, it lowers quality to release the darts in close-fitting, tailored clothing unless the dart is substituted for by another shaping method

Style Fullness. Extra fullness, or *style fullness,* can be added to a garment, so that the additional fabric covers the body curves (Figure 5–10). When loose clothing styles are popular, extra style fullness is the most common dart substitute. Extra style fullness allows the garment to fit a wider range of sizes than many other shaping methods. Fabric panels are cut larger to introduce additional style fullness to the garment, adding significantly to the fabric costs of the

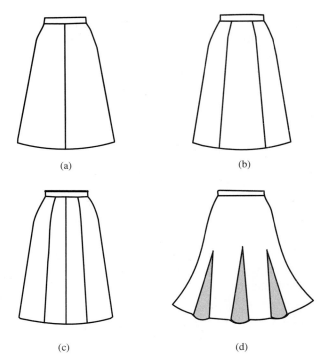

Figure 5–9 (a) Four-gore skirt, (b) six-gore skirt, (c) eight-gore skirt, and (d) skirt with godets.

garment. The extra fabric is eased, gathered, elasticized, pulled up with a drawstring, pleated, tucked, shirred, smocked, or left uncontrolled. Although it affects fit, extra style fullness usually is added for style reasons. (See section on Silhouette and Style later in this chapter.)

Ease. **Ease** is imperceptible fullness that is incorporated on one side of a seam and stitched in place (Figure 5–11). Designers use easing to join two fabric edges of slightly different lengths, easing the longer edge to fit the shorter edge. Easing aids the setting of fitted sleeves, sewing garments to waistbands, and sewing seams such as princess seams together, where the edges to be joined are not identical in length. Easing releases about the same amount of fullness as a dart for an area where the body curve is slight. For example, easing is used as a dart substitute at the elbow of fitted sleeves. Ease often substitutes for the back shoulder dart in tailored jackets. In low-quality garments, neither a dart nor ease is used at the shoulder, causing poor fit in the shoulder blade area. Easing requires the same amount of fabric and less labor than sewing a dart but is seldom used in mass-produced garments.

Gathers. Gathering is the drawing together of a series of small folds of fabric called **gathers**. The gathers are controlled and stitched in place. Gathers

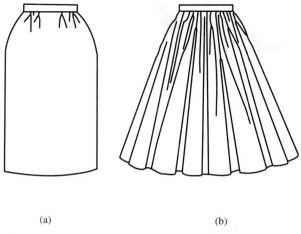

(a)   (b)

Figure 5–10 Gathers: (a) as dart equivalent, and (b) with extra style fullness.

Figure 5–11 Set-in sleeves: (a) eased into armscye, (b) slightly gathered, and (c) fully gathered.

provide visible fullness. Operators join two fabric edges of different lengths by gathering the longer edge to fit the shorter edge. Gathers serve as a dart substitute or to control added style fullness. The more style fullness added, the fuller the gathers (Figure 5–11). If very little style fullness is added, the gathers may look skimpy. Full gathers require two-and-one-half to three times as much fabric as a flat, ungathered panel. Full gathers are usually confined to high-price lines because of the added fabric costs. Less full gathers require only one-and-one-half to two times as much fabric as a flat panel. They may result in strained-looking gathers where the fabric releases minimal fullness over a large body curve. Lightweight fabrics must be much more fully gathered than heavier fabrics for a generous appearance, requiring more fabric. Gathers in bloused areas, such as puffed sleeves, require additional fabric length as well as width to avoid a pulled and taut lengthwise appearance.

Gathers can take the place of darts in fitting the garment to the body. For example, gathers at the front neckline of women's dresses provide fullness over the bust. Gathers in women's swimsuits at the side seams near the hips and/or along the leg openings provide fit and coverage for the buttocks.

Gathers provide a soft, feminine look. They are more attractive in lightweight fabrics than in heavy fabrics. Gathers do not distort geometrically patterned fabrics, such as plaids, the way darts do.

Shirring. **Shirring** incorporates parallel rows of gathers made in the body of the garment. Some people in the industry use the term shirring as a synonym for gathering. Shirring made with elastic thread stretches and helps shape the garment to the body (Figure 5–12b). Shirring may be done throughout the

garment, as in a woman's tube top, or in a limited area, as at the bustline of a woman's swimsuit. Some shirring is strictly decorative and provides no shaping.

Smocking. **Smocking** uses decorative stitches to hold the fabric in even, accordion-like pleats (Figure 5–12a). While mainly decorative, smocking may serve as a dart substitute. Smocking is popular in the chest area of infants' and girls' clothing; it gives slightly and enables the garment to "grow" with the child. Smocking is used occasionally in womenswear. Most smocking is done by machine. Smocking done by hand, found in high-price imported infantwear and childrenswear, is time consuming and costly.

Elastic. *Elastic* serves as a dart substitute by drawing up the longer fabric of the garment to the shorter length of the elastic. Thus, elastic applications often resemble gathering. The biggest advantage of elastic in ready-to-wear is its stretch. However, even though elastic stretches to fit a wider range of sizes than other shaping methods, that range has a limit; too-loose elastic does not hold the garment in place properly and too-tight elastic is uncomfortable for the wearer. Elastic serves as a closure because it allows the garment to stretch for dressing and undressing but draws up to fit closely when the garment is worn. A

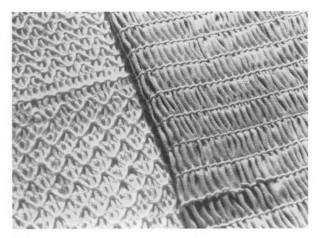

Figure 5–12 (a) Smocking and (b) shirring.

disadvantage of elastic is that it may lose its ability to recover from stretch over time and need replacing for the garment to remain wearable.

Applied elastic is stitched directly onto the garment to add shape where desired. (Examples are shown in Chapter 11, Figures 11–18 and 11–19.) Elastic is often used at the waistline of garments, at necklines, at the lower edges of sleeves and pant legs, and anywhere a gathered look and close fit are desired. It is especially suited for casual garments and childrenswear, and less suited to tailored garments. Applied elastic is usually found inside the garment. However, elastic is sometimes applied on the outside of the garment, mainly in sportswear or underwear. When elastic is applied on the outside of the garment, it is usually colorful or otherwise decorative, such as stretch lace in lingerie.

Casings are tunnels of fabric through which elastic or a drawstring is threaded to provide shape to the garment. (Examples appear in Chapter 11, Figures 11–19 and 11–20.) Although bulkier, casings are generally more comfortable to wear than applied elastic because fabric rather than elastic contacts the skin. Care must be taken to prevent the elastic from twisting inside the casing. Casings generally add more cost to the garment than applied elastic because of the additional fabric and construction steps required.

When elastic is attached at a specific distance from a garment edge, the fabric that extends beyond the elastic forms a ruffle when the elastic relaxes. This ruffle is called a *header*. (See Chapter 11, Figure 11–20.)

Drawstrings. **Drawstrings** are narrow tubes, cords, or strips of fabric inserted into casings in place of or in addition to elastic. (See Chapter 11, Figure 11–20.) They are pulled up and tied to shape the garment to the body. The drawstring controls garment fullness, pulling it up to fit or letting it out for dressing and undressing. Drawstrings are commonly used at the waist of sweatpants, windbreaker jackets, and men's swim trunks; they are also used to fit hood openings around the face. Remember that drawstrings are not appropriate for use on the hoods of infants' and children's garments, where they pose a potential strangling and choking hazard.

Miscellaneous Dart Substitutes. Besides darts, seams, and fullness, garments may get their shape from stretch fabrics, bias-cut pieces, pleats, tucks, gussets, godets, full-fashioned knits, or lacing.

Stretch Fabrics. *Stretch* fabrics stretch over body curves to help the garment fit. Fabrics that stretch only slightly may require the use of additional shaping methods; high-stretch fabrics need no additional shaping methods beyond the ability to stretch to the shape of the body. Therefore, no extra fabric or labor costs are required. Stretch fabrics allow the garment to fit a wider range of people than most other shaping methods. For example, most swimwear and dancewear fits closely through its ability to stretch to the size and shape of the wearer and to accommodate movement by stretching. *Bias-cut pieces* function like stretch fabrics by providing close fit but stretching over body curves and "giving" when the wearer moves.

Pleats and Tucks. *Pleats* are decorative, unstitched folds of fabric that often serve as dart substitutes, creating shape and releasing fullness. Trouser pleats are a good example of pleats that are dart substitutes. Not all pleats incorporate shape into a garment; many are merely decorative. *Tucks* are stitched folds of fabric that are usually ornamental. They occasionally serve as dart substitutes, as when used to shape the garment at the waist. For more information about tucks and pleats, see sections on Tucks and Pleats later in this chapter.

Gussets. **Gussets** are pieces of fabric set into a seam or seam intersection to provide body-conforming shape and fullness in a garment (Figure 5–13). Most gussets are triangular or diamond-shaped, although some dancers' costumes feature circular gussets to provide mobility. Gussets are used in the underarm seams of garments with kimono sleeves and in the crotch seams of sweatpants and in infants' and toddlers' clothes to make room for diapers. Karate pants and shirts feature huge gussets that provide freedom of movement for kicking and punching. High-quality gloves have gussets between the fingers for improved finger mobility. Gussets reduce strain and wrinkling, making the garment comfortable to wear and prolonging its life.

A good-quality gusset has sharp, even points; a poorly set gusset puckers or develops holes at the points. Gussets add to cost because of the extra fabric and skilled labor required.

Godets. **Godets** are triangular fabric pieces set into a seam or slash, usually at the hem of the garment

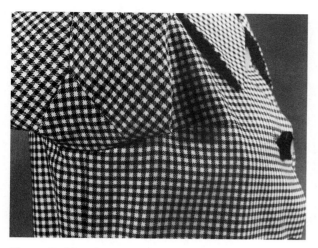

Figure 5–13 Gusset in underarm area.

(Figure 5–9d). Godets produce decorative fullness; they are mainly used in skirts but sometimes are used to cause pant or jacket hems to flare. A well-made godet has a sharp point and does not develop holes at the point.

Full-Fashioned Knits. Full-fashioned knits are a sign of quality shaping. **Full-fashioned marks** represent increases or decreases in the number of stitches in a knitted garment section, a result of shaping the piece. Each part of a full-fashioned knit garment is knitted to the desired size and shape, not cut from a large piece of fabric. The shaped pieces are sewn together for an accurately sized and shaped garment that maintains its shape and does not twist. But full-fashioned knitwear is slower and more costly to produce than are garments cut from knit fabrics. And it requires a longer lead time because the style of the garment must be determined before the knitting process begins. Sometimes manufacturers of garments cut from knit fabrics use stitches or fusing to create mock full-fashioned marks, which look similar but contain none of the real advantages of genuine full-fashioned marks. To identify full-fashioned garments, notice the increase or decrease in the number of stitches in genuine full-fashioned marks at shaped seams, for example, at the armscye seam of sweaters (Figure 5–14).

Lacing. **Lacing** operates on a principle similar to drawstrings. Cords or ties are threaded through eyelets, grommets, or buttonholes in the garment as in the lacing of a shoe. The lacing is pulled to shape and fit the garment and tied to fasten the opening.

Supporting the Shape

The shape of a garment is enhanced and preserved by underlying fabrics including interfacing, lining, underlining, and interlining. Other supporting methods may also be used to achieve or maintain the desired shape.

Underlying Fabrics. Most garments made from woven fabrics contain one or more underlying fabrics. (For more information on underlying fabrics, see Chapter 8.) Although not visible from the outside of the garment, these materials help maintain the garment's shape and/or lend it other qualities such as durability and warmth. Eliminating underlying fabrics to reduce costs results in limp garments that do not maintain their original shape; the garments tend to wrinkle and stretch out of shape.

The main, outer fabric from which a garment is made is called the **body, fashion,** or **shell fabric.** Underlying fabrics or supporting fabrics are inside the garment; they lend support to the garment and help maintain its shape. The four types of underlying fabrics include (1) interfacing, (2) lining, (3) interlining, and (4) underlining. These terms are used consistently throughout this text and are defined in this chapter. However, they are used loosely, sometimes interchangeably, in the apparel industry. For example, the terms interlining and lining are commonly used to refer to what is (technically) interfacing. And underlining (technically) is commonly called lining.

The presence of supporting fabrics in a garment is usually a sign of quality. Few consumers make a purchase decision based on the underlying fabrics of a garment, but ultimate satisfaction with the aesthetic and functional performance of any garment is affected by its supporting fabrics. The choice of underlying fabrics depends on the design, fabric, and end use of the garment. Waistbands that roll, collars and lapels that bubble, and knees, elbows, seats, and pockets that bag can be avoided if the manufacturer carefully selects and correctly applies supporting fabrics.

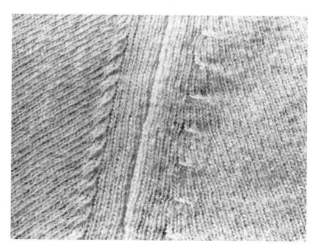

Figure 5–14 Full-fashioned marks at sweater armscye.

(a)

(b)

Figure 5–15 Shaded areas should be interfaced in (a) shirt and (b) jacket.

However, the addition of underlying fabrics to a garment increases production costs in terms of both materials and labor.

Interfacing. **Interfacing** is a supporting fabric used in almost all garments. Interfacing lends body, shape, and reinforcement to limited areas. Collars, collar bands, cuffs, buttons and buttonholes, pockets, waistbands, and other small design details are usually interfaced. In tailored coats and jackets, the shoulders and lapels are interfaced; in better coats and jackets, the designer or patternmaker also interfaces the armholes, patch pockets, sleeve hems, garment hem, and sometimes the entire garment front (Figure 5–15).

Interfacing is usually hidden between the garment and its facing, which explains the name "interfacing" (Figure 5–16). Rub the garment between thumb and fingers or separate the fabric plies to determine if there is interfacing enclosed between two plies; if

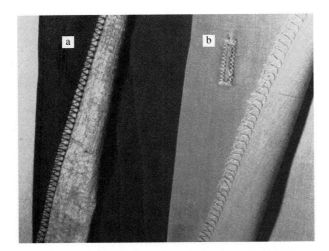

Figure 5–16 Blouses (a) with and (b) without interfacing at center front to support buttons and buttonholes.

fusible interfacing is used, one fabric ply will feel significantly stiffer than the other.

Lining. **Lining** is nearly a replica of the garment, constructed of lightweight fabric and sewn inside the garment with seam allowances reversed to provide a finished inside appearance. A lining

1. covers the garment's seam allowances, making the inside attractive when the garment is taken off
2. makes seam finishes minimal or unnecessary, because seam allowances are not exposed
3. makes the garment more comfortable to wear. The lining fabric acts as a buffer between the wearer's skin and the garment body fabric, seam allowances, and other inner construction details of the garment, especially important when the garment is made of a rough or scratchy fabric.
4. aids the wearer in slipping the garment on and off
5. extends the life of the garment by absorbing some of the stress, strain, and abrasion of wear
6. provides extra body, shape, and support, making the garment look smoother and less apt to wrinkle. The lining helps to prevent the garment from stretching out of shape, especially in stress areas such as elbows or knees.
7. provides opacity, an advantage for garments with sheer body fabrics
8. can provide extra warmth, which may or may not be an advantage, depending on the weather.

In general, garments with full linings are considered higher quality than those without. A fully lined garment requires nearly twice as much fabric and labor as an unlined garment, which increases manufacturing costs significantly. Manufacturers use partial linings in some garments; a partial lining extends only through the areas that require shaping and reinforcement rather than throughout the entire garment. Partial linings are common from the shoulder to the chest (called a ³/8

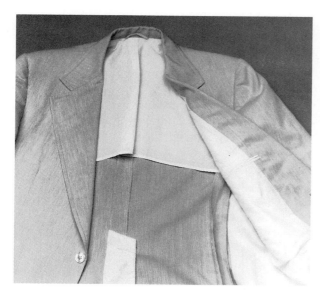

Figure 5–17 Partial lining in summer-weight jacket. Note ease pleat at center back of lining and booked seams.

Figure 5–18 Inside of an underlined dress.

lining) in the back of tailored jackets and from the waist to below the knees in slacks (Figure 5–17). Although partial linings cost less than full linings, they do not lower quality if they extend through the necessary areas. In fact, a partial lining may be more desirable than a full lining in clothing such as summer suits and sports jackets, because partial linings are cooler to wear and lighter in weight than full ones. High-quality men's jackets with a 3/8 lining usually have booked seams (see Chapter 10) and otherwise impeccable inner construction. Occasionally, partially lined garments are of higher quality than similar, fully lined garments, if the patternmaker used the lining in the fully lined garment to compensate for a low-quality fashion fabric and poor inner construction.

Detachable linings are installed so they can be zipped or buttoned in and out of garments, for example, all-weather coats and jackets. They make garments versatile for wearing in different kinds of weather but add significantly to cost because the main garment inner construction must be finished to withstand being worn without the lining and a method for attachment must be included.

Single garment pieces such as pockets, yokes, or bibs may be lined for added strength or support. Or a small piece of lining may be used in areas subject to abrasion, such as the inner thigh area of pants. This not only protects the fashion fabric from abrasion but improves the wearer's comfort, especially if the garment is made of a scratchy fabric.

Underlining. **Underlining** involves lining each major piece of the garment individually. Underlining a garment is less costly than lining it because underlining requires extra fabric but little additional labor (except in cutting). Underlining performs many, but not all, of the functions of lining. Like lining, an underlining provides body, strength, and support to the garment, making it look smooth and preventing it from sagging or stretching. In fact, underlining provides even greater support and body than lining since each piece of the garment is individually supported. Underlining provides opacity, preventing sheer or translucent fabrics from being seen through. Limp, unstable fabrics often require underlining, especially in stress areas or for construction details that demand extra body.

In some instances, underlining is preferable to lining. Underlining, unlike lining, prevents the seam allowances and other construction details from showing through to the outside of garments made of sheer or translucent fabrics such as lace. Therefore, underlinings, rather than linings, are often used in wedding and other formal gowns made of these fabrics. Underlinings are also used in areas prone to stretching, such as seats, knees, and elbows, where they are superior to linings in preventing stretch. Remember, an underlined garment has all seam allowances and other construction details exposed on the inside, whereas in a lined garment, inside details are covered by the lining (Figure 5–18).

Compared to lining, some disadvantages of underlining are that it

1. does not protect the skin from irritation by seam allowances of the garment body fabric

2. does not make the garment more attractive on the inside
3. does not make the garment easy to slip on and off
4. does not prevent seam allowances from raveling.

Interlining. An insulative **interlining** is applied strictly for additional warmth; these interlinings may incidentally add support and shape by their presence. Designers include interlinings in cold-weather clothing such as coats and jackets. Any material inserted for warmth between the garment body fabric and the lining constitutes an interlining. Interlining materials trap air, providing insulation from the cold. A garment's interlining cannot be seen unless the lining is lifted. Interlinings increase both material and labor costs.

Supporting Devices. Supporting devices are incorporated into garments to achieve or maintain the desired shape. Examples of devices that may support the shape of the garment and provide the fashion-correct silhouette include belts (although these may be strictly decorative), shoulder pads, chest pieces, sleeve heads, bridles and other seam stays, collar stays, bra cups, boning, hoops, bustles, horsehair

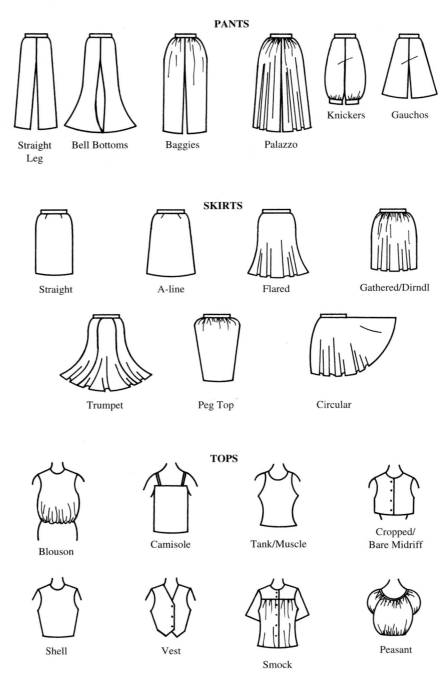

Figure 5–19 Examples of garment styles: pants, skirts, tops, jackets, and dresses.

braid, and weights. All add to material and labor costs. See Chapter 8 for definitions and more information about choosing these supporting devices.

SILHOUETTE AND STYLE

The silhouette and style of a garment are important aspects of quality because of their strong relationship to aesthetic performance. Whether or not a style exhibits the design principles of balance, proportion, rhythm, emphasis, and unity affects its acceptance. Current fashion trends, personal preferences, and end use also affect the evaluation of aesthetics. Though the aesthetic evaluation of garment style is beyond the scope of this text (see Related Resources: Design and Style), an introduction to the design features that are used to create styles is presented. A good vocabulary of style terms is necessary in all phases of apparel analysis because it enables accurate communication. The ability to use correct terminology is also important in designing, writing specifications and promotions, and selling apparel products.

The **silhouette** of a garment is its outline or shape. The **style** of a garment or garment part results from its silhouette and other identifying characteristics. "A particular style of garment usually refers to the cut of its structural lines in a manner that has become recognized, accepted and named" (Davis, 1996). Details added to the garment also help differentiate styles. In general, however, the color, fabric, and other details may change, but the style remains the same as long as its identifying style elements do not change. The key to identifying a style is knowing what characteristics make it unique.

Along with changes in fashions, style names tend to evolve over time; as a style loses favor, its name is dropped from common usage. When the style returns to popularity, whether it happens years, decades, or even centuries later, it often receives a new name. The popularity of various names for the same style changes as fashions change, with newer terms taking preference over more standard terms. Therefore, *always be alert to multiple names for the same style and to changes in and additions to your style vocabulary*. A few styles are illustrated in this chapter to provide an introduction to

JACKETS

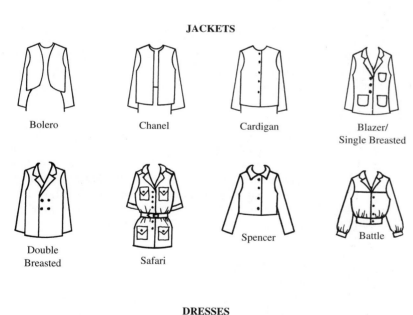

Bolero

Chanel

Cardigan

Blazer/
Single Breasted

Double
Breasted

Safari

Spencer

Battle

DRESSES

Shift/
Chemise/
Sack

Sheath

Trent/
Trapeze

Shirtwaist

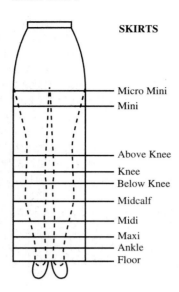

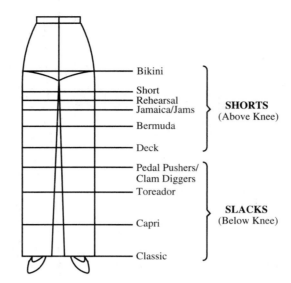

Figure 5–20 Skirt and pant lengths.

style names. However, to develop a comprehensive style vocabulary, refer to Related Resources: Design and Style at the end of the text.

Garment Silhouettes

Basic, fitted garments are illustrated in Figure 5–5. Varying the silhouette of a garment yields different styles. Silhouette is determined by the amount and location of fullness in the garment and the methods for controlling the fullness. (See sections on Shaping Methods earlier in this chapter.) The silhouette of a garment can take many forms. Figure 5–19 (pp. 114–115) illustrates a few silhouettes for pants, skirts, tops, jackets, and dresses, and the associated style names.

Garment Lengths

Historically, garment lengths have been a vital indicator of the current fashion and the popular silhouette. The terms for garments of various lengths are illustrated in Figure 5–20. Beyond the longest length, skirts extend into trains that drag on the floor when the wearer walks. Wedding dresses may feature chapel length or the longer cathedral length trains.

Edge Treatment Styles

For information on hem styles as well as other garment edge treatments such as facings, bindings, and bands, see Chapter 10. Plackets to finish openings on waistlines, sleeves, necklines, and pant legs are also discussed in Chapter 10.

Waistlines

Where the waistline of a garment is located in relation to the wearer's waist has a significant effect on the silhouette and style of the garment. Most waistlines fall at or near the wearer's natural waistline (Figure 5–21). Menswear waistlines typically fall at or near the natural waistline. Womenswear waistlines are much more variable and tend to rise and fall with fashion changes. Dropped waistlines fall between the waist and hips. In hip huggers, the waistline falls at hip level. (The term *hip huggers* applies to bottoms only.) High-rise waistlines occur slightly above the natural waistline. Empire waistlines occur under the bustline. (The term *empire* applies to female clothing only.) Current fashions help determine the level of the waistline.

Figure 5–21 illustrates a few common waistline styles. Waistlines within the body of the garment, as in a dress, can be fitted to the body by darts or dart substitutes such as pleats, seams, or elastic. Waistlines at garment edges may also be banded, faced, or finished by other edge treatment methods. (For more information, see Chapters 11 and 12.)

Necklines

Ready-to-wear apparel features a variety of neckline shapes and finishes. The neckline edge is cut into the desired shape, and the raw edge of the neckline is finished by any edge treatment such as facing, binding, or banding. Figure 5–22 illustrates a few common neckline styles.

Collars

A **collar,** or any band applied to the garment neckline, is mainly decorative, although it is sometimes functional in keeping the neck warm or dry or protecting it from the sun. A collar increases the cost of a garment because it requires additional fabric and labor. (For more information, see Chapter 12.)

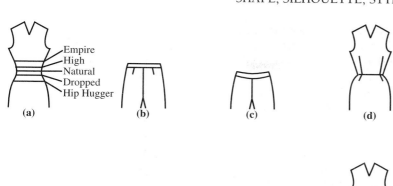

Figure 5–21 a) Waistline levels, (b) straight waistband, (c) contour waistband, (d) waistline seam, (e) faced waistline (dotted line represents facing inside the garment), (f) and (g) elasticized casings at garment edges, and (h) elasticized casing within body of garment.

There are three basic collar types: (1) flat, (2) standing, and (3) rolled (either full-roll or partial-roll). The shape of the collar's inner edge or neckline edge determines the collar type. The shape of a collar's outer edge determines its style. Figure 5–23 illustrates a few common collar styles.

A **flat collar** lies flat or nearly flat against the garment all around the wearer's neck. If the inner edge of the collar is shaped in a concave curve, matching the neckline edge, the result is a flat collar, for example, a sailor collar. Flat collars are used mainly on womenswear and childrenswear, rarely on menswear.

A **standing collar** is a band extending straight up from the neckline edge and standing up around the neck. If the inner edge of the collar is fairly straight, the result is a standing collar, for instance, a mandarin collar. A cowl is actually a standing collar cut high above the neckline so that it falls into folds.

A **rolled collar** is a band of fabric that rolls fully or partially around the neck. A full-roll collar rolls all the way around the neck; a partial-roll collar rolls at the back of the neck and lies flat or nearly flat at the front of the neck. Full-roll collars, such as turtlenecks, have a fairly straight inner edge. They are like a standing

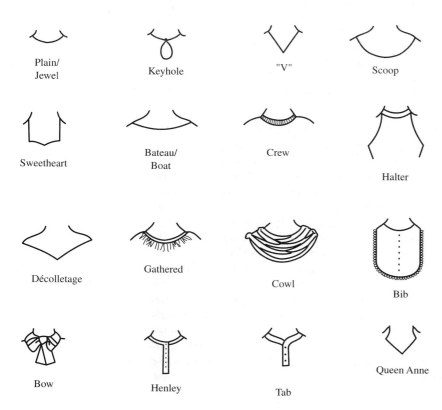

Figure 5–22 Examples of neckline styles.

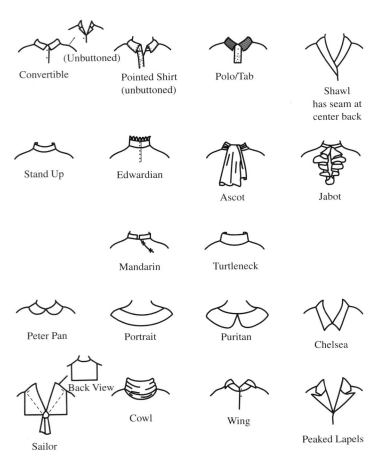

Convertible
(Unbuttoned)

Pointed Shirt
(unbuttoned)

Polo/Tab

Shawl
has seam at
center back

Stand Up

Edwardian

Ascot

Jabot

Mandarin

Turtleneck

Peter Pan

Portrait

Puritan

Chelsea

Sailor
Back View

Cowl

Wing

Peaked Lapels

Figure 5–23 Examples of collar styles.

collar, except that a full-roll collar is cut wider and folded down. The part of the collar that stands up next to the neck forms the collar stand, and the portion that is folded over forms the collar fall (Figure 5–24). If the inner edge of the collar is a concave curve somewhere between a straight line and the shape of the neckline, the result is a partial-roll collar, for instance, a convertible collar. The more concave the inner curve, the less the collar rolls. In a partial-roll collar, the fold at the back of the collar gradually tapers toward center front, where the collar lies flat or nearly flat.

The standard collar on a man's dress shirt is a mixture of two types; it consists of a standing collar with a full-roll collar inserted and sewn into the upper edge of the neckband to create the collar fall. Shirt collars are costly because of the extra labor and materials required; they are essentially the construction of two collars in one. However, the production of shirt collars is completely or partially automated so they can be accurately produced at a moderate cost.

Sleeves

A **sleeve** is a covering for the arm that is attached at or near the armhole, or **armscye**, area of the garment.

Sleeves are functional in providing modesty, warmth, or protection but are equally important for their contribution to the style of the garment; they are an important feature of the garment silhouette. They should be designed and constructed to flatter the garment and the wearer. (For more information, see Chapter 12.)

A sleeveless garment has no sleeves to finish its armhole edges. Consequently, the armholes of a sleeveless garment must be treated to finish the raw edges, usually by facing or binding.

All sleeve styles fall into one of three main types: (1) set-in sleeves, (2) raglan sleeves and (3) kimono sleeves. Figure 5–25 illustrates some sleeve styles; variations in sleeve length are also illustrated. **Set-in sleeves** are the most common type. A set-in sleeve resembles a tube hanging from the armhole. **Kimono sleeves** are cut as one with the body of the garment. A **raglan sleeve** is recognizable by its characteristic diagonal seam, which runs from the underarm to the neckline of the garment. The diagonal seam attaches the tapered sleeve panel to the body of the garment. (See Figure 7–2 in Chapter 7.) Raglan sleeves provide greater comfort and more reaching room than other sleeve types. They are a good choice for active sportswear and in clothing for people in wheelchairs or on

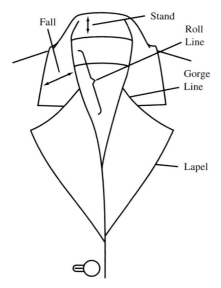

Figure 5–24 Parts of a classic, notched collar and lapels.

crutches, who require great range and freedom of arm movement. Because they do not restrain movement, raglan sleeves are also suitable in clothing for elderly people or others with limited mobility. Gussets in the underarm area of kimono sleeves can also add freedom of arm movement.

Cuffs

Cuffs are the banded or turned-back finishes at the lower edges of sleeve and pant legs. Crisp, well-made cuffs contribute to the overall appearance of a garment's quality.

Most cuffs are a band of fabric applied to the lower edge of a sleeve that extends or lengthens the sleeve as it finishes the lower edge. They control the fullness of the sleeve to fit the wrist, or the arm in the case of short sleeves. Cuffs may be decorative and of various widths and shapes. Wide cuffs and complex cuff shapes add to costs. On basic garments, the repetitive cuffing operation may be automated. This enables the manufacturer to achieve uniform results at a moderate cost. (For more information, see Chapter 12.)

Open-band cuffs have an opening so the wearer can fit the cuff band over the hand and then fasten it to fit snugly. Open-band cuffs include the following types:

1. *Barrel cuff* or *shirt cuff,* the most common type; it is a straight, open-band cuff style. Long-sleeved shirts and blouses usually feature barrel cuffs. The barrel cuff laps and buttons at the wrist. (Examples are shown in Chapter 10, Figures 10–34, 10–35, 10–36, and 10–37).

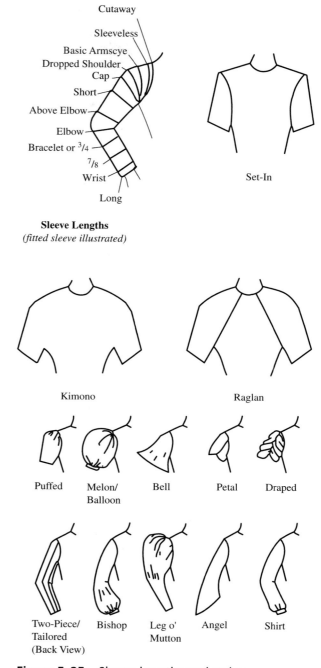

Figure 5–25 Sleeve lengths and styles.

2. *Convertible cuff,* an open band that fastens with layers superimposed to resemble a French cuff.
3. *French cuff* or *double-cuff,* the most formal style of open-band cuff (Figure 5–26). The French cuff is constructed like the barrel cuff but twice as wide. Then the cuff is folded back on itself so the cuff is doubled. The opening edges are superimposed rather than lapped and fastened with cuff links or studs through the buttonhole in each layer. French cuffs require considerably more fabric and

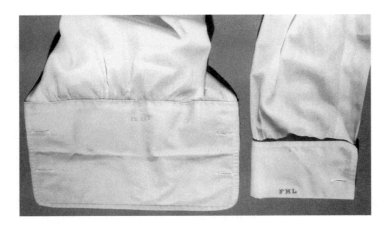

Figure 5–26 Monogrammed French cuff.

more labor than barrel cuffs. Because of their high production costs, French cuffs are mainly found in high-priced apparel and are most suitable to somewhat formal styles. For example, they are not used on button-down, oxford cloth shirts but on dressier shirts of fine broadcloth and on women's dresses.

A **closed-band cuff** is an unbroken ring of fabric large enough to fit over the arm. Closed-band cuffs are inexpensive. **Turned-back cuffs** on sleeves and cuffed pants are formed by turning back or rolling up the lower portion of the sleeve or pant leg.

Pockets

A **pocket** is a small pouch or bag sewn onto or into a garment and used to carry small items. Concealed pockets are strictly functional. Nonfunctional, "fake" pockets used to complement a garment's design are strictly decorative. However, most pockets are both functional and decorative. Functional pockets include special-purpose pockets, such as watch pockets in jeans, ruler pockets in carpenter's pants, game pockets in hunting clothes, ticket pockets in men's suit jackets, key pockets in jogging shorts, and hidden money pockets in travel clothing. These pockets are shaped, sized, and reinforced according to their special purposes.

For a pocket to be functional, it must be positioned at a convenient level and angle (for example, pockets in work uniforms). Pockets should be wide and deep enough to accommodate hands and/or items they are intended to hold. Pockets designed and placed to complement the garment design and to flatter the wearer contribute to aesthetics. If a garment features pockets on each side, pockets should be identical and level with one another. If the garment is made of a fabric with a pattern (e.g., plaid or stripe), a matched pocket reflects attention to quality but adds cost (see Chapter 4).

Pockets usually contribute to consumer satisfaction. Pockets are very important in work clothing and active sportswear, and children are especially fond of pockets in their clothing. Pockets may not seem vital at the time of purchase, but later the wearer may wish for a pocket when he or she needs a place to put hands, glasses, wallet, or keys. Pockets are sometimes left out of garments if they show through the garment or cause a ridge on the outside of it. However, the main reason for leaving pockets out of a garment is to reduce its price.

The cost of a pocket depends on its complexity, size, and the fabric used. Pockets often feature decorative trims, stitchings, or other details. These decorative touches add to the cost of the pocket. The addition of pockets must be balanced with cost. Because they require additional materials and labor, pockets add to the overall cost of a garment. Manufacturers can justify the cost of pockets if they are important to consumer satisfaction. There are three main types of pockets: (1) patch, (2) in-seam, and (3) slashed. (For more information, see Chapter 11.)

Patch pockets or **applied pockets** are pieces of fabric attached, like a patch, to the outside of the garment. (An example is shown in Chapter 9, Figure 9–16). Patch pockets tend to look more casual than other pocket types. Manufacturers routinely use them on the backs of jeans and the fronts of shirts and jackets, but patch pockets can be placed on sleeves, pant legs, or anywhere else. Patch pockets come in many shapes and sizes. Choosing and positioning them is very important because they have a great effect on the visual impression of the garment on the wearer. For example, large patch pockets at hip level draw attention to the wearer's hip size.

In-seam pockets are set into a seam of the garment, usually the side seams of skirts, pants, coats, and dresses. The pocket may be concealed or exposed. *Concealed* in-seam pockets are hidden in the seam of the garment. *Exposed* in-seam pockets are usually set into the side seam and waistline seam of the garment; they have a diagonal or curved opening edge offset from the side seam. Manufacturers use

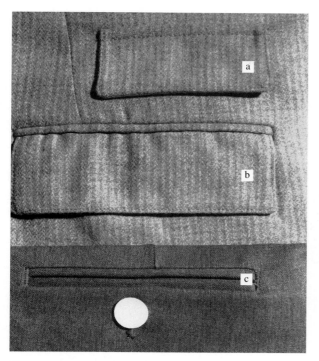

Figure 5–27 Pockets: (a) flap with no pocket, (b) flap on single welt, and (c) double welt.

Figure 5–28 Pockets: (a) upturned flap with piping, (b) upturned flap, and (c) single welt.

exposed in-seam pockets on the front hip of jeans (see Figure 5–31 later in this chapter) and men's pants (see Chapter 12, Figure 12–8), where they are often referred to as *quarter pockets*. Some women's skirts and pants also feature exposed front-hip pockets. Some jeans contain a *watch pocket*, a little patch pocket on the facing of an exposed in-seam pocket.

Slashed pockets are finished slits within the body of the garment, for example, on tailored jackets and on the back of men's dress pants. Slashed pockets are the most difficult pockets to construct. If made manually, precision is often low. In most cases today, slashed pockets are produced entirely by automation. Since automation became widespread, the overall consistency and quality of slashed pockets has vastly improved and the cost has become lower. But because of the complexity, slashed pockets remain more costly than other pocket types. The more pieces used to construct the pocket, the higher the fabric and labor costs. Nonfunctional, fake slashed pockets, with no opening, are found in low-price garments. Most slashed pockets are welt pockets (Figures 5–27 and 5–28). *Single-welt pockets* have a single lip usually no more than about 1/2 inch wide. A *double-welt* or *double-besom pocket* has two lips usually no more than about 1/4 inch wide each.

Flap pockets have a flap of fabric above the pocket. The flap extends down over the pocket opening. For patch pockets, the flap is sewn on above

the pocket. (Examples are shown in Chapter 4, Figure 4–12 and Chapter 10, Figure 10–28.) For in-seam pockets, the flap is sewn at the opening edge. For welt pockets, the pocket flap is placed above the single lips or between the double lips of the pocket. The breast pocket of many tailored jackets provide an example of an **upturned-flap pocket,** a flap that extends up (not down like a regular flap).

Decorative Details Integral to the Garment

Some decorative details are constructed as part of the garment. For example, fabric may be raveled out at the edge to form a fringe called *self-fringe*. In high-quality garments, a row of stitches just above the fringe prevents further raveling. Leather or vinyl may be slashed at frequent intervals to form self-fringe. Decorative details that are integral to the garment include tucks, pleats, creases, ruffles, bows and tabs. Many details constructed as part of the garment are functional as well as decorative. For example, tucks, pleats, gathers, style fullness, shirring, smocking,

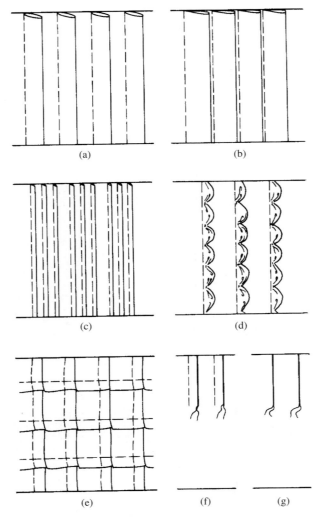

Figure 5–29 Tucks: (a) spaced, (b) blind, (c) pin, (d) shell, (e) crossed, (f) released, and (g) inverted.

seams such as gores and yokes, and darts decorate the garment as they help shape it.

Most decorative details integral to the garment are made with specialized sewing machine attachments. Thus, many operations that once required extensive skilled labor are now automated. (For more information, see Chapters 11 and 12.)

Tucks. A **tuck** is a stitched fold of fabric (Figure 5–29). The fold lies flat against the garment, but it can be lifted. Tucks can be made vertically, horizontally, and diagonally on a garment. Most tucks are stitched on the outside of the garment so the folds of fabric show on the outside.

Tucks require extra fabric and labor. If a designer uses numerous tucks in a garment, considerable fabric and labor are required. For example, a garment with tucks all the way across the front may require three times as much fabric as a garment with a plain front. Tucks also require skilled labor to carefully

space and stitch unless tucking folders or pretucked fabrics are used.

Besides the plain tuck, there are a number of variations, including these:

1. *inverted tucks*, stitched on the inside of the garment so the folds of fabric are not visible on the outside of the garment
2. *released tucks*, which are partially stitched, releasing fullness and introducing ease into the garment (see Chapter 6)
3. *dart-tucks* or *open-ended darts*, similar to released tucks. They are tapered like darts and the tips are left unstitched. Dart-tucks shape the garment, serving as a dart substitute.
4. *pin tucks*, narrow and closely spaced tucks, such as those in tuxedo shirts
5. *spaced tucks*, a series of tucks that occur at regular intervals
6. *blind tucks*, a series of tucks that meet, each one covering the stitches of the one preceding it
7. *scalloped tucks* or *shell tucks*, which feature decorative stitching at the edges that draw the tuck into a shell shape (similar to the shell hem in Chapter 10, Figure 10–26)
8. *crossed tucks*, two sets of tucks made perpendicular to one another
9. *corded tucks*, which have a cord inserted in the fold of the tuck to give a three-dimensional effect.

Pleats. A **pleat** is a fold of fabric folded back upon itself so the pleat is comprised of three layers (Figure 5–30). The top fold of the pleat hides the back fold; the pleat can be spread open to see the back fold. Pleats are not stitched to the garment throughout their length as are tucks, although occasionally pleats are partially stitched down at the upper edge to flatten them and hold them in place. Pleats can be pressed or unpressed throughout their length for different effects. Soft, rolled pleats are appropriate in soft fabrics. Sharp, pressed pleats must be made in a crisp fabric for the proper effect. Fabrics that can be heat set have the ability to maintain the creases of pleats. Pleats in other fabrics may be edgestitched along the folds for a crisp, well-defined look. Pleats hang vertically on the garment, secured at an upper edge; they cannot be made horizontally or diagonally. Pleat types include these:

1. *knife pleat*, the basic folded pleat; all pleats are variations of this pleat. (See Figure 5–31 later in this chapter.)
2. *box pleats*, two knife pleats folded away from one another. (See Chapter 12, Figure 12–2.)
3. *inverted pleats*, two knife pleats folded toward one another. Note the relationship between box and inverted pleats; when either occurs in a series, between every two box pleats an inverted pleat is created and vice versa.

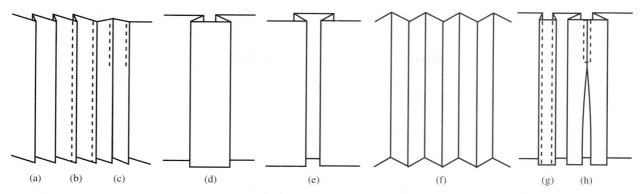

Figure 5–30   Pleats: (a) knife, (b) edgestitched knife, (c) partially stitched knife, (d) box, (e) inverted, (f) accordion, (g) edgestitched box, and (h) partially stitched box.

Knife pleats, box pleats, and inverted pleats may be used singly, in small groups (cluster pleats), or all the way around a garment. They are also used as a basis for the following:

1. *kick pleat*, a pleat at the hem of a skirt to give room to walk and sit; it may be a decorative feature as well
2. *vent*, an opening at the back hem of jackets, which allows the garment to expand for walking and sitting comfort
3. *gibson pleat* or *flange*, a pleat at the intersection of the shoulder and the armhole that releases fullness in the front and/or back of the garment
4. *accordion pleats*, repeated, evenly spaced, open knife pleats
5. *sunburst pleats*, smaller at the waist and larger as they near the hem. Accordion and sunburst pleats are used in skirts.
6. *crystal pleats*, extremely narrow accordion pleats used in formal gowns and some ruffle trims
7. *cartridge pleats,* also called *gauging*, accordion pleats drawn closed with rows of running stitches so that they resemble bold, even gathers. They are used in choir, academic, and clerical robes and in high-price garments.

Considerable labor is required to accurately space and press some pleat styles. Others, when made using specially designed work aids, require very little labor. When an entire fabric or garment requires pleating, the job is usually sent to a contractor that specializes in pleating. The cost difference between pleated styles depends upon the depth of the pleats. Shallow pleats require little fabric and are used in low-cost garments (Figure 5–31). Deep pleats require as much as three times the fabric needed for an unpleated garment. Full-depth pleats, with the back fold as wide as the front fold, look the same as shallow pleats when the wearer stands still but provide more attractive fullness when the wearer moves. They also provide plenty of sitting and moving ease. However, deep pleats are confined to high-price garments because of the cost.

Creases.   **Creases** pressed in pant legs are a decorative feature that adds a crisp look to the garment and slims the appearance of the wearer. Front creases start at the hem and end somewhere between the crotch level and the waist. Back creases extend from the hem to the crotch level. Fabrics that can be heat set maintain a sharp crease. In fabrics that cannot be heat set, stitching along the crease helps maintain a sharp crease line; this is done mainly in children's garments.

Figure 5–31   Pleats: (a) deep, and (b) shallow.

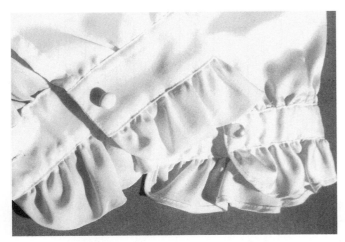

Figure 5–32 (a) Double-layer ruffle, and (b) single-layer, hemmed ruffle.

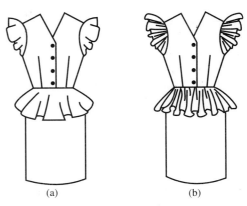

Figure 5–33 (a) Shaped shoulder ruffles and shaped ruffle peplum at waist, and (b) gathered shoulder ruffles and gathered ruffle peplum at waist.

Ruffles. **Ruffles** or **flounces** are decorative gathered, or pleated strips of fabric. Full ruffles are usually 2 1/2 times or more the length of the area to which they are gathered. They require more fabric than skimpy ruffles, which may be as little as 1 1/2 times the length of the area to which they are gathered. Full ruffles are found in high-quality garments. Soft, sheer, and lightweight fabrics need to be fuller than other fabrics to avoid a skimpy appearance. Ruffles should be even in width.

Bias-cut ruffles drape more gracefully than ruffles cut on the straight-of-grain. However, bias-cut ruffles are costly because of the amount of fabric required and because seaming the bias pieces together is time-consuming.

Ruffles are made by hemming the long edge of a single ply of fabric to make a single-layer ruffle, or by folding a piece of fabric in half lengthwise to make a double-layer ruffle (Figure 5–32). Double-layer ruffles require twice as much fabric as single-layer ruffles; however, double-layer ruffles require less labor because they do not require hemming. Most ruffles in low- and moderate-price lines are single-layer ruffles. Single-layer ruffles have less body than double-layer ruffles and are less attractive if the fabric has a right and wrong side and if the hem shows. However, although double layers are considered a mark of quality in many cases, they cause more bulk than single-layer ruffles and are not suitable for all applications.

Shaped ruffles are cut in a circle and straightened for sewing to the garment. This causes an attractive ripple at the outer, unsewn edge but they remain smooth where they are seamed to the garment (Figure 5–33). A shaped or gathered ruffle at the waistline is a *peplum*; peplums are a decorative style feature used in womenswear. Wide, successive rows of ruffles are called *tiers*.

Bows. A **bow** is a ribbon or fabric strip tied into a decorative knot with loops and streamers. Long, full bows require extra material, making them costly. Fabric bows cut on the bias tie and drape gracefully, but bias-cut bows are costly because they require extra material. Bows are either (1) an extension of the garment structure or (2) constructed separately and then tacked, glued, or pinned in place. Ribbon bows tend to ravel and become bedraggled when laundered; in such cases, the bows should be removable for laundering.

Tabs. A **tab** is a fabric strip that, when combined with a button, buckle, or d-rings serves as a functional closure as well as a decorative detail. (For examples, see Chapter 8, Figure 8–7.) Tabs are frequently seen at the wrist of the sleeves of all-weather coats. They are also used on pockets, necklines, back vents, and elsewhere as the design demands. *Epaulets* are tabs at the shoulders, often used on military uniforms, safari outfits, and trench coats. Although epaulets usually serve no function in normal consumer use, they may serve to keep shoulder bag or camera straps from slipping off the shoulder (e.g., safari shirts). Some tabs help shape the garment to the wearer, for example, buckled tabs on the back of vests.

Design Considerations for Special Markets

Some groups of consumers require special details in the clothing they wear. Special markets include childrenswear, maternity wear, clothing for mature figures, clothing for the physically challenged (for more information, see Chapter 6), and occupational clothing. Certain types of clothing, such as lingerie and active sportswear, also lend themselves to special details that make the garment more functional and well-suited to its purpose.

Childrenswear. Infants' clothing must help babies maintain constant body temperature because their natural body "thermostat" is not yet fully developed. Functional details in infants' and toddlers' clothing are the *snap crotches* and *inseams;* the snaps make diapering more convenient. The safety of details on clothing for these age groups is another major consideration. Buttons and snaps on infant and toddler clothing should be securely attached; if closures come off, the baby may swallow them. On infantswear, do not use drawstrings and avoid elastic around the neck or anywhere that a danger of strangulation exists. Also, materials used to make clothing for children size 2 and under must be nontoxic. Sleepwear should be tight-fitting to avoid catching fire; loose-fitting sleepwear in sizes larger than 9 months must meet federal flammability standards. For comfort, fabric for young children's clothing should be soft, lightweight, absorbent, flexible, extensible, and easy to launder.

Design features that accommodate a child's growth are appreciated by parents. Examples include deep hems, raglan or kimono sleeves, generous armholes for set-in sleeves, dresses with undefined waistlines, separates rather than one-piece outfits, long tails on shirts and blouses, stretch fabrics, sleeve cuffs that roll down (pant leg cuffs that roll down can trip the child), elasticized waistlines or waistlines with adjustable closures, and adjustable shoulder straps/suspenders. Horizontal **growth tucks** at the hem or waist of children's garments can be let out when the child grows. The main cost of growth tucks is the extra fabric required. Growth tucks are used to a limited extent in high-price line childrenswear. Because the garment has often faded more than the tucked area by the time the growth tucks are released, their value is questionable.

Self-help features that assist the child in dressing independently include conveniently placed, easy-to-manipulate closures and large, stretch, "pull-on" openings for neck, arms, and legs. The front of the garment should be easy to distinguish from the back; for example, marked with an appliqué. Extras such as belts, sashes, and bows should be pre-tied and attached to the garment. Buttons should be flat, smooth, and not excessively large or small but about one-half inch in diameter. Buttonholes should be large enough to accommodate the buttons easily. Large zipper pulls make it easy for a child to operate zippers. Openings should be down the front of the garment. Hook-and-loop tape rather than traditional fasteners should be considered.

Children's coats and snowsuits sometimes feature *mitten ties* that attach the mittens to the garment with a cord; they prevent the loss of the mittens. Knee and elbow patches add durability to play clothing that receives hard wear. Straps should be secured with loops at the shoulders so they do not fall off the shoulders.

Children like pockets. Pockets, cuffs, trims, and other details should be sewn on flat, not left dangling to catch on things or trip the child. Colors that stand out make children easier to see when they are playing, increasing safety. Nonslip (but breathable for comfort) soles on footed pajamas are another safety feature.

Maternity Wear. Maternity clothing features details that make garments expandable for the expectant mother. Excess fabric is the most common approach. Adjustable openings at the waistline accommodate the enlarging abdomen. *Stretch panels* may be inserted in the abdominal area of maternity-wear bottoms; stretch panels expand as the abdomen enlarges. They should be long enough and wide enough to avoid uncomfortable binding. They are usually concealed by long maternity tops.

Nursing garments have openings over the breasts for convenient breast-feeding. The openings are concealed by fabric overlays when not in use.

Clothing for Older Adults. Clothing for older adults, male and female, needs to be designed primarily for comfort. While people over 50 are still fashion conscious, they put increasing value on being comfortable in their clothing. Dissatisfaction with fit is more common among mature women than any other group. Safety features are very important for mature individuals who are not 100% mobile, as are features contributing to freedom of movement and ease and independence of dressing. Features meeting these needs include:

1. fabrics that stretch and give
2. roomy armholes
3. kimono and raglan sleeves
4. short or elbow-length sleeves
5. back fullness
6. unfitted or elasticized waistlines
7. large neck openings
8. V-necklines
9. long, front openings
10. closures that are easy to grasp, or elasticized openings that eliminate the need for hard-to-manipulate closures, especially for those with limited mobility brought on by strokes or arthritis.

Avoid long, loose sleeves that can catch fire on burners or heaters, short openings, back openings, small armholes, and very close-fitting garments.

Clothing for People with Physical Disabilities. For the most part, individuals with physical disabilities are just as fashion conscious as individuals without special needs. Their physical disability usually is not as significant or noticeable to them as it is to others. They have either been born with their special needs or have adapted to them. Therefore, people with disabilities do not choose clothing any differently than other people. We all want fashion, fit, and comfort.

Unfortunately, due to the uniqueness of each special need situation, it is not possible to mass produce appropriate apparel cost-effectively. Therefore, the selection of ready-to-wear special clothing is limited. For this reason, individuals with special needs who can afford to do so may have clothing custom made. Others may customize ready-to-wear on their own, learning techniques to adapt mass-produced apparel to their needs.

Clothing for people with special needs, whether mass produced or custom adapted, is characterized by functional details that vary according to the individual and the circumstances. Most details are kept as inconspicuous as possible, while some become a focal point of the item of apparel. (Clothing adapted for wheelchair users is illustrated in Chapter 6, Figure 6–13). The following are just a few examples of functional details for consideration in special need apparel.

1. *Mastectomy bras* contain special pockets to hold the prostheses or breast replacements in position for women who have had breast-removal surgery.
2. *Action-back pleats* are pleats in the back shoulder area of garments, for example, shirts, blouses, or jackets. They provide reaching room in otherwise fitted garments. Most action-back pleats are fairly inconspicuous. They are comfortable for crutch users and people in wheelchairs and for anyone involved in active sports, because they increase freedom of movement and reaching in the shoulder area.
3. *Underarm padding and reinforcement* in clothing for crutch users provide comfort for the wearer and extend the life of the garment.
4. For wheelchair users, *low pockets* (on lower pant legs, for instance) provide better access than traditional pocket locations.
5. For those with limited finger mobility, *hook-and-loop tape* sewn on behind buttons makes closures easier to manipulate.
6. *Loops* inside garments help with pulling them on.
7. *Openings that stretch* (for example, cuff buttons sewn on with elastic) simplify dressing and undressing.
8. *Zippered pant inseams and/or outseams* allow easy access to catheters.
9. For people with severe handicaps who cannot dress without assistance, clothing should be designed for *easy removal and replacement*.

Occupational Clothing. *Occupational clothing* for workers doing a particular job contains many practical features that protect the wearer, provide convenience and comfort, or improve the serviceability of the garment. For example, *hammer loops*

on carpenter's pants provide a place for hanging tools. Employees in a fabric store may wear aprons with *reinforced pockets* for scissors. Industrial workers require protective clothing. Police require *bulletproof* vests. Many companies embroider *workers' names* on their uniforms to help customers identify them. Other functional details of occupational clothing relate to fabric characteristics. For example, soldiers require *camouflage* prints; firefighters need *fireproof* clothing; surgeons wear gowns that have *antibacterial, static-free*, and *low-linting* characteristics. An in-depth coverage of occupational clothing is outside the realm of our discussion of ready-to-wear; to learn more, refer to Watkins (1984).

Lingerie. High-quality slips are sometimes constructed with shadow panels. A **shadow panel** is an extra layer of fabric at the center of the slip for modesty; it prevents the silhouette of the legs from showing through translucent fabrics. Shadow panels increase production costs.

Panties made of synthetic fibers usually feature a **cotton crotch.** This is a quality feature because of the absorbency of cotton, making the garment comfortable to wear.

Some bra and slip straps are made from elastomeric materials, which stretch with the wearer's movements for comfort. However, *stretch straps* may lose their elasticity over time, making the garment unwearable. A stretch strap that is also adjustable may be tightened if it loses its elasticity. *Adjustable straps* contain a mechanism for loosening and tightening, enabling them to fit a variety of figures.

Active Sportswear. Active sportswear often features functional details. The following are just a few of the many functional details that increase the usefulness of active sportswear.

1. *Reflective tape or designs* on jogging or biking clothing worn at night make the wearer visible to vehicles.
2. *Slits or laps* at the side seams of jogging shorts allow freedom of movement for running.
3. *Mesh-fabric vents* in the underarm area of football jerseys allow perspiration to evaporate.
4. *Grommets* (reinforced holes) in the pockets of swim trunks help water drain away and prevent pockets from ballooning out.
5. *Rubber buttons* on rugby shirts prevent contact bruises that result from hard plastic buttons.
6. *Pads* in biking shorts cushion the buttocks from the bicycle seat.
7. *Zippers* at the hems of ski pants and warm-up suits help the wearer put them on and take them off over ski boots and bulky athletic shoes.
8. *Trigger fingers* on mittens provide greater grasping dexterity.

SUMMARY

Garments are made from flat fabrics shaped to fit the human body. To hang straight, garments should be cut on the straight of the fabric's grain. They may be cut on the bias for special effects. All garments contain darts or dart equivalents that introduce shape into the garment. Darts are triangular folds stitched into the fabric that shape it to fit the body. The size, length, and angle of the dart should accommodate the body curve it is intended to fit. Shaped seams such as princess seams, gore seams in skirts, and yoke seams may incorporate dart shapes to help the garment fit the figure. Released darts and extra fabric add style fullness. Style fullness may be fitted to the body with ease, gathers, shirring, smocking, elastic, or drawstrings. Other dart substitutes include stretch fabrics, bias-cut pieces, pleats and tucks, godets, gussets, full-fashioned knits, and lacing.

Underlying fabrics provide additional shape, support, and smoothness to garments. Interfacing is used in detail areas. Lining covers the inner construction of the garment. Fully lined garments are generally more costly but are more durable, more comfortable, and more attractive than unlined garments. Underlining is constructed as one with the garment and has many of the same advantages as lining, except it does not cover inner construction details. (However, underlining does make inner construction details invisible from the outside of the garment.) Interlinings are applied strictly for warmth. Supporting devices are used to maintain shape as the design demands.

The identifying characteristics of a garment determine its style. Variations in silhouette, length, waistline, and edge treatments and in neckline, collar, sleeves, cuffs, pockets, and decorative details result in different styles. Style is evaluated based on fashion trends, personal preferences, appropriateness, function, and principles of aesthetic design.

Collars are either flat, standing, or rolled. Sleeves are one of three types: kimono, which is cut in one with the garment; raglan, which is attached to the garment with a diagonal seam; and set-in, which is attached to the armhole of the garment. Cuffs include open-band, closed-band, and turned-back. Pockets usually contribute to consumer satisfaction. The main pocket types are patch, in-seam, and slashed. Decorative details integral to the garment include tucks, pleats, creases, ruffles, bows, and tabs. Garments for special markets—childrenswear, maternity wear, clothing for mature figures, clothing for people with physical disabilities, and occupational clothing—may require special design features.

New Terms

If you can define each of these terms and differentiate between related terms, you have gained a good working vocabulary for discussing the topics in this chapter. The terms are listed in the order in which they appear in this chapter

tailored
grain
lengthwise grain/warp
selvages
crosswise grain/filling/fill/weft
straight-of-grain
bias
true bias
shaping method
basic block/sloper
dart
dart equivalent/dart substitute
princess seam
yoke
gore
released dart
ease
gathers
shirring
smocking
applied elastic
casing
drawstring
gusset
godet
full-fashioned marks
lacing
body/fashion/shell fabric
interfacing
lining
underlining
interlining
silhouette
style
collar
flat collar
standing collar
rolled collar
sleeve
armscye
set-in sleeve
kimono sleeve
raglan sleeve
cuff
open-band cuff
closed-band cuff
turned-back cuff

pocket
patch pocket/applied pocket
in-seam pocket
slashed pocket
flap pocket
upturned-flap pocket
tuck
pleat
crease
ruffle/flounce
bow
tab
growth tuck
shadow panel
cotton crotch

Shape, Silhouette, and Style Checklist

If you can answer yes to the following questions regarding the garment you are evaluating, it contains high-quality shape, silhouette, and style variations.

✔ Is the garment cut on the straight-of-grain (or on the bias for special effects)?
✔ Is an appropriate dart or dart equivalent used wherever there is a body curve?
✔ Are pleats full-depth?
✔ Are bows full and preferably cut on the bias?
✔ Do gussets have sharp, even, secure points?
✔ Does interfacing provide support where needed?
✔ Is the garment fully lined?
✔ Does the style meet fashion, personal, aesthetic, and end-use functional and appropriateness expectations?
✔ Are practical details included whenever they would enhance the function of the garment, particularly for special markets?

Review Questions

1. Why are most garments cut on straight-of-grain? Which grain is typically placed parallel to the length of the body and why? Describe the characteristics of garments cut on the bias.
2. Why are shaping methods like darts and dart equivalents needed in all garments? List the dart equivalents.
3. Compare and contrast
   a. gussets and gores
   b. gathers and ease
   c. yokes and split yokes
   d. smocking and shirring

4. What are the advantages and disadvantages of
   a. lining a garment?
   b. underlining a garment?
   c. interfacing a garment?
   d. interlining a garment?
5. List the various garment lengths.
6. What are the three main collar types? What determines a type of collar? Its style?
7. What are the three main sleeve types? How are they differentiated? List the various sleeve lengths.
8. Are pockets functional or decorative features of a garment? Support your answer.

Activities

1. Examine a low-price and a high-price example of the following garments for use of grain and grain trueness. Do you find any differences based on price? On classification?
   a. men's necktie
   b. jeans
   c. men's shirt
   d. skirt
   e. T-shirt
   f. jacket

2. Fold a dart in a piece of paper. How does this affect the shape of the paper? Try to closely conform a piece of fabric to a dress form or human body. What is required?
3. Examine a garment with darts. What body curve is each dart intended to fit?
4. Choose 10 different garments at random from a store, from a catalog or magazine, from a historic costume collection, and from your wardrobe. What shaping methods are used in each? Does the classification of the garment influence the type of shaping method used? Does fashion influence the popularity of certain shaping methods? Do you have a personal preference for some shaping methods over others? Explain your answers.
5. Visit an apparel manufacturer. Ask
   a. to see their basic blocks
   b. how they build shape into their garments
   c. what cost-cutting measure they take to eliminate costly shaping methods but ensure that garments still fit the customer.
   d. what types of supporting fabrics they use and why
   e. what other supporting devices they use.

6. Visit a high-price and a low-price source of athletic apparel. Examine the sweatpants for quality and quantity of shaping and supporting features.

For example, look for elastic, gussets, and drawstrings. Why are supporting fabrics and other supporting devices *not* used?

7. Find examples of the following neckline styles:
   a. plain/jewel
   b. keyhole
   c. V
   d. scoop
   e. sweetheart
   f. bateau/boat
   g. crew
   h. halter
   i. décolletage
   j. gathered
   k. cowl
   l. bib
   m. bow
   n. Henley
   o. tab
   p. Queen Anne

8. Find examples of the following collar styles:
   a. convertible
   b. pointed shirt
   c. polo/tab
   d. shawl
   e. stand-up
   f. Edwardian
   g. ascot
   h. jabot
   i. mandarin
   j. turtleneck
   k. peter pan
   l. portrait
   m. puritan
   n. Chelsea
   o. sailor
   p. cowl
   q. wing
   r. peaked lapels

9. Find examples of the following cuff styles:
   a. barrel
   b. convertible
   c. French
   d. closed-band
   e. turned-back

10. Find examples of the following sleeve styles:
   a. set-in
   b. kimono
   c. raglan
   d. puffed
   e. melon/balloon
   f. bell
   g. petal
   h. draped
   i. two-piece tailored
   j. bishop
   k. leg o'mutton
   l. angel
   m. shirt

11. Cut collars from paper with the following neckline shapes:
   a. straight
   b. slightly curved
   c. round

Try on the collars. What collar type does each produce?

Sizing and Fit: The Keys to Competitive Advantage

Chapter Objectives

1. Define the generally accepted size classifications and sizes used for childrenswear, womenswear, and menswear.
2. Consider the elements of good fit.
3. Understand the evaluation of fit.

Successful manufacturers and retailers spend a great deal of time and effort perfecting the sizing and desired fit for their target market customers. They conduct marketing studies to learn not only the buying habits of the target customers but their approximate sizes, shapes, and fit preferences. They use this data to design garments that suit the **sizing** (classification of the dimensions of garments) and fit needs of the target customer. For example, the target customer might be a woman between the ages of 25 and 35 with young children and a full-time job. The marketing data indicates she prefers loose, comfortable clothing that is easy to care for, she is less than 5'4", and weighs between 120 and 150 pounds. With this particular customer in mind, the designers plan basic blocks that are short in length but large in girth dimensions. The silhouettes will be loose on the body and made in cotton blend or synthetic easy-care fabrics.

A real-life example of unique fit success is The Lee Company's women's jeans line. Historically women wore men's jeans and struggled with the slim hips and large waists. When women began to wear pants on a frequent basis, design personnel at The Lee Company recognized that women's body shapes were different from men's and women should have a jean that comfortably fit their body shape. So instead of using a male basic block and converting it to a women's size, research was conducted on the differences between a man's and a woman's body shapes. Original basic blocks for jeans were then developed specially for the women's body shape. This resulted in a well-fitting women's jean that continues to impact the way women's jeans fit today.

SIZING

Size labeling suggests to consumers the suitability of a garment for their body dimensions. The actual dimensions of different brands and styles of garments of the same labeled size may vary considerably. In general, high-price lines tend to run large—larger than most other garments of the same labeled size; they are cut to fit generously because the high price allows for liberal use of fabric. Expensive lines that *run large* are sometimes referred to as being **vanity sized,** because they appeal to the vanity of customers who want to think of themselves as wearing a small labeled size. Generally, low-price garments tend to *run small*—smaller than most other garments of the same labeled size in an effort to conserve fabric. Conversely, some high-price lines run small because they aim at a target market that is small framed. When someone suggests that a garment runs *true to size*, it fits about the same as most other garments of the same labeled size.

Sizes are grouped together into **size classifications** according to the sex, age, and/or body type of consumers. (For more information, see Related Resources: Design and Style.) The old voluntary standard on apparel sizing encompasses the majority of variation of figure types within the population. However, many manufacturers do not make and most retailers do not carry all the sizes in a classification because few consumers require the extremely small and the extremely large sizes; the low volume does not justify the floor space. Retailers are also interested in limiting the number of special apparel departments, each requiring styles in a wide range of sizes. Catalog retailers and some specialty stores are more apt to carry the full range of sizes. Yet some individuals require sizes even smaller or larger than those included in the voluntary size standards. Manufacturers producing apparel for these people develop sizes using the extreme ends of the standards as a starting point, but due to the expense involved they do not make these sizes in the same number of color or silhouette choices as the more popular sizes.

Numbered Sizing

Numbered sizing is the most common method of sizing for the majority of mass-produced clothing, especially tailored and traditional clothing. Moderate and expensive clothing tends to be sized using numbers. Men's and women's sizing, while both numbered, are based on differing systems. Men's clothing sizes are stated in terms of body measurements while women's clothing sizes and most children's clothing sizes are stated in numbers that correlate to a set of body measurements The associated body measurements for womenswear and childrenswear are usually not published, the exceptions being measurement tables in some catalogs, height/weight charts on pantyhose packages, and some childrenswear labels.

Often consumers complain that not only do different brands and styles fit differently, but so do garments of the same numbered size and of the same brand and style. For example, it is possible to try on two pairs of the same brand and style size 12 slacks and find that they do not fit exactly the same; the two garments are not identical in actual dimensions. This may happen due to the unique characteristics of soft goods; fabric gives and stretches and changes characteristics according to changes in temperature and humidity. Also, most apparel is made by human beings who tend to fluctuate in skill level, mood, and temperament. Quality-conscious manufacturers set tolerances on all key garment dimensions. If an operator uses the plus tolerance in the morning when fresh and the minus tolerance in the afternoon when tired, it is possible that the same-sized garments hanging next to each other on the rack will have slight differences in measured size. While sometimes seen as a problem, this can also be an advantage. If a consumer likes a particular garment style but finds the waist somewhat snug, he or she can try on another garment and perhaps find a slightly more comfortable waist size.

Voluntary Standards. Sets of body measurements related to figure types serve as the basis for the numbered sizing of apparel. The American Society for Testing and Materials (ASTM) is currently working to update the standard tables of body measurements on which apparel sizes are based. Recently, the first database of body measurements ever collected for women aged 55 and older was completed and published. Body measurement standards for infants 0–18 months have been updated, and tables for the "average female" misses figure now depict only the measurements and proportions currently used by the U.S. apparel industry. ASTM is currently soliciting funds for a body measurement study to update all body measurements of women 18–55 years of age. While work is in progress, it will take considerable funding and several years to update all body measurement tables.

However, although outdated standards exist for body measurements, no current standards exist for the actual numbered label sizes themselves. The first voluntary standards for U.S. apparel sizing for men, women, and children were published in 1942 by the National Bureau of Standards (NBS), now the National Institute of Standards and Technology (NIST). The standards were slightly revised in 1970 to reflect some height and weight changes in Americans' bodies and were then withdrawn in 1983. At that time, the NBS turned over apparel sizing issues to ASTM for review and updating. The old sizing standard is still available from the **National Institute of Standards and Technology (NIST)** of the U.S. Department of Commerce, The National Center for Standards and Certification Information, Building 820, Room 164, Washington, D.C. 20899. URL: http://www.nist.gov. For the most current, updated information on apparel sizing, contact ASTM (see Chapter 3).

Although the measurements and proportions used by U.S. manufacturers today are still based on the withdrawn voluntary standards, each manufacturer has developed its own interpretation of apparel sizes for its specific market and target customer. Portions of the old voluntary standards are presented in this chapter because they are the only apparel sizing standards available. Review them to get a general idea about sizing and size classifications, but do not be surprised to see other marketed classifications in stores and catalogs, such as small, medium, large. Although most manufacturers use the old voluntary standards as a guideline for establishing sizes and size classifications, each interprets the numbers and categories differently. For the time being, "anything goes" in sizing, as manufacturers and retailers (especially mail-order firms) search for the best way to size garments and classify sizes.

Complicating the size issue further, with an increase in the international trade of apparel comes the difficulty of communicating the size dimensions of garments being imported and exported. Not only do language and the method of sizing vary in different countries, but the U.S. consumer measures the human body in inches and pounds rather than centimeters and kilograms. The three major sizing systems in the world are *U.S. sizes, British sizes,* and *European* or *Continental sizes* (Table 6–1). Most countries size using some variation of these three systems.

Sizing Expressed as Body Measurements. One of the problems with apparel sizing is not the lack of standardization, but that numerical size labeling has no real meaning for many female consumers. Sizing

Table 6–1 Comparison of Different Sizing Systems

Misses Sizes U.S. size	G.B. size	Continental size
6		34
8		36
10	32	38
12	33	40
16	35	42
18	38	44
20	39	48

frustrates many consumers, primarily women, instead of providing them with guidance in locating garments that fit. Women are more frustrated than men because the majority of women's clothing is not sized according to body measurements as men's is. Women have adapted by making it a standard practice to try on an assortment of styles and sizes before buying. Men do not experience the same need to try on apparel before purchasing. A possible solution to the sizing dilemma lies in labeling clothing with the body measurements the garment is designed to fit. Size labeling *expressed in terms of body measurements* gives useful information to consumers. It is used by mail-order retailers and some other retailers and manufacturers concerned with maintaining a quality reputation for providing good fit. Informative size labeling that relates directly to body measurements helps companies satisfy the fit needs of consumers.

Some countries convey size information without words, through **pictograms** (Figure 6–1). The body measurements critical to the fit of the particular garment are indicated on a sketch of the human body. Pictograms overcome language barriers and are easy for consumers to understand. At a glance, they give the shopper an idea of whether or not a garment will fit, if the shopper knows his or her measurements. Expect an increase in the use of pictograms for international trade; they are a practical solution to the size labeling of garments for import and export. They provide meaningful information about size because they are based on body measurements. Some mail-order retailers use pictograms to communicate size or measuring information to consumers in catalogs.

Lettered Sizing

Lettered sizing has grown increasingly popular in recent years. The stretch provided by knit fabrics and

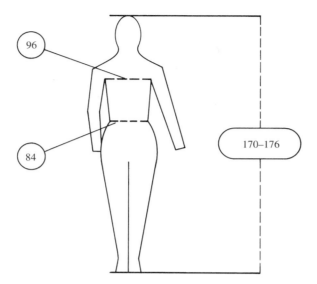

Figure 6–1 Pictogram size labeling for men's suit. Metric measurements convert to chest girth = 38″, waist girth = 33″, and height = 5′ 7″ to 5′ 9″.

the popularity of loose fits have encouraged this trend. **Lettered sizing** uses the size designations of *S* = small, *M* = medium, and *L* = large. It usually includes the extension *XL* = extra large, and sometimes *XXL* and *XXXL* for yet larger sizes and *XS* = extra small. Collapsing size categories into lettered sizes reduces the number of size divisions from seven or eight to just three or four, a move retailers like because it reduces inventory and simplifies display of merchandise on the sales floor. However, consumers cannot find an accurate fit within S, M, L, and XL as easily as they can within numbered sizes, which provide finer differences between sizes.

Lettered sizing is prevalent in low-price lines because it eliminates the need for precise sizing and because it is more economical to produce fewer sizes. Foreign manufacturers who have difficulty in achieving accurate sizing for the U.S. market turn to lettered sizing because of its simplicity. Many retailers like lettered sizing because, by eliminating the need to carry so many sizes, it allows them to carry a greater number of styles and colors. Consumers easily identify with lettered sizing, although it often gives them little real assistance in finding a garment that fits; S, M, L, and XL have little standardization from brand to brand and no consistent correlation to body measurements. In fact, S, M, L, and XL are used without any differentiation for unisex garments, menswear, womenswear, and childrenswear.

Sometimes garment length is also designated with lettered sizing. When they do not provide length in inches, manufacturers commonly use *P* = Petite or *S*

= Short, *A* = Average or *R* = Regular, and *L* = Long or *T* = Tall.

When lettered sizing is used internationally, it provides little information to consumers in another country unless it is designed with the foreign market in mind. For example, the average "small" person in the United States or Europe is significantly larger than the average "small" person in Asia.

One-size-fits-all sizing is an attempt by manufacturers and retailers to further collapse sizing by providing garments that have the ability to stretch to fit many figure types and sizes. But one-size-fits-all apparel cannot be expected to accurately fit figure types at either size extreme. Perhaps the more accurate label for these garments is "one size fits most."

Childrenswear

Although the voluntary apparel sizing standard for **childrenswear** bases sizes on age, consumers should *never base size selection on the age of the child*. For example, not all children are born the same size, so "newborn size" is a misnomer because some children are born too large to ever wear a "newborn size" garment. Children also grow at widely varying rates, requiring the use of *height and weight* rather than age to achieve proper fit. Most manufacturers of childrenswear now provide helpful charts on the label or on the package indicating the height and weight ranges that the garment fits. Always purchase clothing for children according to these guidelines rather than the garment's numerical or lettered size.

Childrenswear size classifications overlap somewhat. For example, a 24-month infants' size and a toddlers' size 2 fit approximately the same body dimensions, as do a toddlers' size 4 and a children's size 4. However, the garments differ in the amount of ease and length allowed for the differences in the locomotion of an infant, a toddler, and a child; also, infants' and toddlers' clothing bottoms are cut larger than children's to accommodate the thickness of diapers.

Like adult apparel, childrenswear is increasingly letter sized S, M, L, XL. This is common for garments such as sweaters, knit shirts, sleepwear, and underwear, and for all types of garments in low-price lines.

Infants' Sizes. Childrenswear begins with **infants'** or **babies' sizes**, for infants from birth to approximately 18 months or when the child is old enough to walk. The ASTM standard size designations range from 0–3 months to 12–18 months and correlate with *height and weight*. Many retailers carry infants' sizes up to 24 months (Table 6–2). But remember that age is not a good indicator of size; purchase garments according to the infant's height and weight. Lettered sizing for

Table 6–2 Infants', Toddlers', Children's, Girls', Boys', Womenswear, and Menswear Sizes

---

Infants' sizes *(correlate with height and weight):*
3 mo., 6 mo., 12 mo., 18 mo., 24 mo.

Toddlers' sizes (correlate with height and weight):
2T, 3T, 4T

Children's sizes (correlate with height and weight):
Girls: 4, 5, 6, 6X
Boys: 4, 5, 6, 7

Girls' sizes (correlate with height, weight, waist, and hip measurements):
7, 8, 10, 12, 14

Boys' sizes (correlate with height, weight, chest, and waist measurements):
8, 10, 12, 14, 16, 18, 20

Womenswear sizes (correlate with bust, waist, and hip measurements):
Misses figure type: 6, 8, 10, 12, 14, 16, 18, 20, 22
Women's figure type: 14, 16, 18, 20, 22, 24
Junior figure type: 3, 5, 7, 9, 11, 13, 15, 17

Menswear sizes:
Jackets (correlate with chest measurement and height):
32, 34, 36, 38, 40, 42, 44, 46, 48, 50 (Short, Regular, or Long)
Pants (correlate with waist and inseam measurements)
32, 33, 34, 36, 38, 40 waist/29, 30, 31, 32, 33, 34 inseam
Shirts (correlate with neck and sleeve length measurements)
$14\frac{1}{2}$, 15, $15\frac{1}{2}$, 16, $16\frac{1}{2}$, 17 neck/30, 31, 32, 33, 34 sleeve length

---

Note. The sizes listed do not reflect all the sizes in each of the ranges, but the most common sizes in each range.

infantswear usually consists of XS, S, M, L, and XL; sometimes NB (for newborn) substitutes for XS.

Toddlers' and Children's Sizes. Toddlers' sizes are for the child from 18 months to approximately 3 years of age, the early walking stage. Toddlers are characterized by short, round figures with undefined waistlines. The voluntary apparel sizing standard provides a range from 1T to 4T, although many retailers carry only sizes 2T to 4T (see Table 6–2). The sizes correlate with *height and weight*. S, M, L, XL may be used instead of numbered size designations.

Children's sizes, also known as *preschool, juvenile,* or *little boys'/little girls'* sizes, typically fit children approximately 3 to 6 years old. Children are taller and slimmer than toddlers but still have an undefined waistline. The voluntary apparel sizing standard provides a range from 2 to 6, plus 6X. Many childrenswear retailers carry only sizes 4 to 6 plus 6X for girls and 4 to 7 for boys (borrowing size 7 from boys' sizes). Children's sizes, like infants' and toddlers', correlate with *height and weight* (Table 6–2). S, M, L, XL also may be used.

Girls' Sizes. Girls' sizes fit girls approximately 7 to 11 years old. The bustline is undefined and the waistline slightly delineated. The voluntary apparel sizing standard provides a range from 7 to 18, although many retailers carry only 7 to 14 (Table 6–2). Girls' sizes correlate with *height, chest, waist, and hip* measurements in the voluntary standard. The standard also suggests the body-build categories of *slim, regular,* and *chubby.* Manufacturers and retailers usually choose more appealing terms than chubby; for example, *pretty plus* and *size up.*

Some retailers carry an additional size classification, not included in the voluntary standard. They call this classification *preteen, teen, junior high,* or *young juniors.* It is designed for girls with a more defined waistline who are not yet ready for junior sizes. These sizes typically run from 6 to 14.

Boys' Sizes. Boys' sizes fit boys approximately 7 to 17 years old. The boys' figure is characterized by developing shoulders and a delineated waistline. Voluntary apparel sizing standard provides a range from 2 to 24, although many retailers carry only the even-numbered sizes 8 to 20 (Table 6–2). The voluntary standard correlates boys' sizes to *height, weight, chest, and waist* measurements. It also suggests the body build categories, *slim, regular,* and *husky.*

Some retailers offer boys' sizes 8 to 14 and an additional size classification for sizes 16 to 20. Not included in the voluntary apparel sizing standard, they call this size classification *prep, student, teen,* or *cadet* to appeal to bigger boys not yet ready for young men's sizes.

Womenswear

Womenswear is clothing for adult females. Womenswear uses a complex sizing system. In theory, womenswear sizes are labeled with numbers that correlate with height, bust, waist, hip, and other measurements. In practice, womenswear sizes and grade rules vary widely among manufacturers and often bear little correlation to any standard. Perhaps rapid style changes in womenswear from season to season have made attention to sizing a low priority for manufacturers. However, women's former willingness to try on multiple garments to find one that fits may be ending as women have greater demands on their time; with less time available for shopping, they are forcing the apparel industry to improve the apparel sizing system.

Outerwear. **Outerwear** refers to clothing seen by others when it is worn; for example, dresses, blouses, pants, skirts, jackets, coats, sweaters, and sportswear (casual separates). Womenswear generally falls into four basic *merchandising* classifications: (1) junior, (2) misses, (3) petites, and (4) large sizes or plus sizes (and occasionally a fifth classification, talls).

These four classifications reflect three basic *body types/sizing classifications:* (1) junior, (2) misses, and (3) women's. These size classifications refer to general figure types (Figure 6–2). Ironically, the average "woman" does not wear "women's sizes" but "misses sizes." However, a few manufacturers refer to clothes sized for the average misses figure as "women's sizes" to differentiate them from "men's sizes."

Within the three womenswear body types/size classifications, the sizes used for outerwear are often referred to as **dress sizes.** When someone asks a woman, "What size do you wear?", usually the reference is to her dress size. Most dresses and other outerwear are labeled with these sizes (Table 6–2).

Outerwear is occasionally sized according to body measurements. *Bottoms* (e.g., pants and skirts) are sometimes labeled with waist or inseam measurements. In addition, other factors such as hip shape (slim, average, full) and leg length (short, regular, tall) may be used. *Tops* (e.g., blouses and sweaters) are sometimes labeled with bust measurement. Some producers use lettered sizing to label outerwear.

Misses Sizes. **Misses sizes** fit the adult woman of average proportions and average height; they are also commonly referred to as **missy sizes.** The ASTM

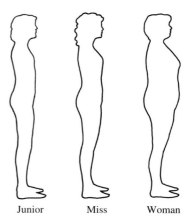

Figure 6–2 Womenswear body types and size classifications. (Petites and talls are available within each type.)

standard suggests misses sizes as even numbers from 2 to 20, although many retailers carry only sizes 6 to 14. Retailers often merchandise the larger misses size designations (for example, sizes 16 and over) as *plus sizes, large sizes,* or *women's sizes* (see next section). It is possible to find size 0; this may be an example of vanity sizing or an effort to fit women smaller than those included in the standard.

Petites are designed for the shorter woman (under 5'4") of otherwise average proportions. Petites are designated with a *P* after the misses size and typically run from size 2 to 12. Petites have been one of the fastest growing apparel categories in recent years, as manufacturers responded to the strong demand created by the significant number of shorter-than-average women looking for clothing that fits them appropriately. In many stores, petite departments are comparable in size to the regular misses clothing department. Thus, petites have become a major merchandising classification, although technically they are a subdivision of misses as far as sizing is concerned. Petite sizes generally reflect shorter proportions throughout the garment, and some designers also recognize the smaller frame typical of many petite women and adjust their basic blocks accordingly. **Talls,** for the taller woman (over 5'7") of average proportions, are designated with a *T* after the misses size.

Not all missy designs are produced in petites and talls. In part, this is due to the lower market potential of these figure types (especially true for talls). Also, some designs do not flatter a wearer of other-than-average proportions. For example, short jackets and small-scale details flatter the petite figure, whereas long jackets and bold details generally look better on the tall figure. Therefore, astute designers and merchandisers develop styles particularly suited to the petite and tall markets and do not treat them merely as subdivisions of misses.

Women's Sizes. **Women's sizes** fit the adult woman of average height who has a full, mature figure. Women's sizes feature less waist definition and longer sleeves than misses sizes. The voluntary standard lists women's sizes as even numbers 34 to 52, although these designations are now almost extinct. *Plus sizes, large size,* or *women's* departments and specialty stores are increasingly likely to designate women's sizes with what were formerly misses size designations, for example, even-numbered sizes 16 to 20 or 14 to 24. Thus, it is often unclear whether a garment was designed for a large misses figure type or a true women's figure type—the two do differ. Some manufacturers produce **tall women's** sizes, and *super women's* sizes (larger than size 52), more evidence of how size is a marketing tool as well as a fitting tool. At any rate, large sizes need to be designed in a greater variety which will flatter the full figure without sacrificing fashion.

Women's petites accommodate the shorter-than-average adult woman who has a full, mature figure. The old voluntary apparel sizing standard used the term *half sizes* and designations such as size 16½ to refer to women's petites, but that has gone by the wayside due to its negative connotations for consumers. Women's petites generally are merchandised in *plus size, large size,* or *women's* areas. This use of the word *petite* draws attention to the fact that petite means "short," not "small." Women's petites generally feature a lower, fuller bustline, shorter sleeves, and a higher, larger waistline than misses sizes. They should be designed to flatter the full, short figure.

The styling of women's petite apparel usually reflects the tastes and lifestyles of mature adults, suitable to the majority of wearers. (A young woman has difficulty finding clothing to reflect her age in a women's petite size.) Women's petites is an area ripe for growth with the aging of the U.S. population. In the past, manufacturers found it difficult to develop styles that both fit and flatter the short, stocky figure. Many designs had poor hanger appeal, which did not exactly make them "fly out the door." Successfully meeting the challenges of designing apparel for this market will be important as we enter the next century.

Junior Sizes. **Junior sizes** fit a short, slender, growing, youthful figure. They feature a higher bustline and a higher waistline than misses sizes. The voluntary standard lists junior sizes as odd numbers from 3 to 17, although many retailers carry only sizes 5 to 13. **Junior petite** sizes, designated by a *P* after the junior size, are for a woman shorter than the average junior; they are rather rare. A very few manufacturers produce **tall junior** sizes, designated by a *T* after the junior size. A tall junior size is not a division of the voluntary apparel sizing standard and, in fact, is a contradiction in terms.

Although it is true that, for example, "Junior is a size, not an age," there is some justifiable stereotyping of size classifications and ages. The majority of junior-size customers are young, so the styling of junior apparel is typically oriented to youthful fashion trends. However, there are exceptions to these generalizations, making it difficult for older junior-size women to find clothing styled appropriately for their age and lifestyle, in their size.

Double ticketing involves labeling clothing with both a junior size and missy size, for example, 3/4, indicating that it fits either a junior size 3 or a misses size 4. Because there are significant differences in the body types of juniors and misses sizes, it seems unlikely that double-ticketed garments fit both body types equally well unless the garment is one without exacting fit requirements.

Underwear. **Underwear** is clothing worn beneath outerwear. **Lingerie** or **intimate apparel** refers to underwear as well as loungewear and sleepwear. Because it is subject to repeat purchases, and because a smooth, comfortable fit is important, consumers expect consistent fit each time they purchase underwear. And because underwear is a fairly basic item, most manufacturers size it similarly. Low-price line underwear is often labeled with lettered sizing. However, numerical sizing allows an exact fit and is usually used in high-price lines.

Bras are sized by a two-part system. The first part, **bra size,** is a number. It equals the under-bust measurement (the rib cage just below the bust) plus 5 or 6 inches, whichever results in an even number. (Above a 38-inch under-bust measurement, add only 3 or 4 inches.) The second part, **cup size,** is a letter ranging from *AAA* to *F.* Measure the bust at its fullest point and determine cup size by finding the difference between this measurement and bra size, as shown in Table 6–3. For example, if the bust measurement is 1 inch different from the bra size, the

Table 6–3 Bra Cup Sizes

If bust measurement is	Cup size is
Same as or less than bra size	AAA
Up to ½ inch larger than bra size	AA
Up to 1 inch larger than bra size	A
Up to 2 inches larger than bra size	B
Up to 3 inches larger than bra size	C
Up to 4 inches larger than bra size	D
Up to 5 inches larger than bra size	DD/E
Up to 5½ inches larger than bra size	F

Table 6–4 Womenswear Panty Sizes

Hip measurement (in inches)	Panty size
33–34	4
35–36	5
37–38	6
39–40	7
41–42	8
43-45	9
46-48	10

customer requires an A cup; 2 inches, a B cup; 3 inches, a C cup; and so on.

Numbered sizes on panties correlate with hip measurements (Table 6–4). Half slips are sized by waist measurement and length from the waist in inches, full slips by dress size or bra size and length from the waist in inches, and camisoles and sleepwear by dress size or bra size. Girdles are sized by waist measurement and hip development (the difference between waist and hip measurement). The customer has straight hips if they are up to 8 inches larger than her waist, average hips if 8 to 10 inches larger, and full hips if 10 inches or more larger

Menswear

Menswear encompasses clothing for adult males. Men's figures have fully developed shoulders, a tapered waist, and slim hips. Menswear includes **men's clothing** (men's suits, jackets, pants, and coats), **sportswear** (casual separates), and **furnishings** (other items, such as shirts, ties, underwear, sleepwear, and accessories). Most menswear sizing is expressed in terms of body measurements, an example worthy of imitation by womenswear producers. The **men's sizes** classification includes clothing that fits the average adult man. Men's numerical sizes are expressed as body measurements; voluntary apparel sizing standards for menswear are listed by general figure types. Examples include *short* for the shorter man; *tall* or *long* for the taller man; *slim* for the slender build; *regular* for the average height and average build; and *big, portly,* or *stout* for the full build. Garments in all these categories are sized using the same numbering system as regular men's sizes. Lettered sizing is widely used within some men's merchandise classifications, especially sportswear, sweaters, sleepwear, and underwear.

Menswear sizing is considerably more consistent from manufacturer to manufacturer than is womenswear sizing. Granted, men's figures are somewhat more standard than women's, which have more curves. And perhaps the more basic, fitted nature of menswear has allowed its manufacturers greater opportunity to perfect sizing. Whatever the reason, menswear is more likely than womenswear to fit as indicated by its labeled size.

Young men's sizes are designed for young men with developing builds. A division of the voluntary apparel sizing standards, they are sized with body measurements just as men's sizes are. Young men's sizes contain the smaller men's sizes and reflect the youthful styling generally preferred by young men; they parallel the junior category for young women. They are cut proportionately smaller than men's sizes. Adult men with small statures sometimes experience difficulty in finding clothes appropriate for their age and lifestyle in young men's departments, or clothes their size in men's departments.

Jackets. Men's jacket and coat sizes are based on the wearer's *chest* circumference and overall *height*. A number denotes the chest measurement, typically an even number ranging from 32 to 50. Most men wear sizes 38 to 44; smaller sizes may be found in young men's and larger sizes in big and tall men's. Most retailers carry jackets with increments of 1 inch between sizes in the chest measurement up to size 44, with 2-inch increments thereafter; some carry only even sizes.

A letter accompanying chest measurement denotes height, with *S* for short, *R* for regular, and *L* for long. Thus, a 42R jacket, the most common size, represents a 42-inch chest and average height. Most retailers carry few shorts because it is easier to shorten garments than to lengthen them.

Pants. Men's pants sizes are based on two numbers. The first number correlates with the wearer's *waist* circumference, typically ranging from 32 to 40 inches. Waist sizes smaller than 32 inches are found in young men's and waist sizes larger than 40 inches in big and tall men's. Many retailers stock pants in 1-inch increments between sizes in waist measurement up to size 32, with 2-inch increments thereafter; some stock only even waist sizes. Few are willing to carry the large inventories required to stock every waist size.

The second number in a pants size represents the inseam measurement, typically ranging from 29 to 34 inches. The *inseam* is the length of the seam on the inside of the leg, from the crotch to the hem of the slacks. For example, a size 30/32 denotes a 30-inch waist and a 32-inch inseam. Some pants leave the factory unhemmed to fit a wider range of inseams.

Body build categories may be used to indicate the amount of fullness in the hips and thighs. Pants sizes

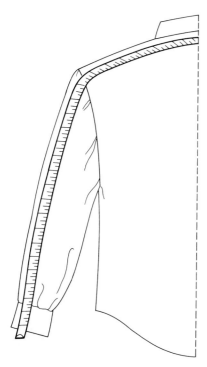

Figure 6–3 Measuring men's shirt sleeve length.

may also include *rise,* which is the measurement from crotch level to waist level (short, regular, or long).

Furnishings. Men's furnishings include shirts, ties, underwear, sleepwear, and accessories. Men's sport shirts are usually sized S, M, L, XL. Short-sleeved dress shirt sizes are based on neck circumference. Long-sleeved dress shirt sizes are based on two numbers, one denoting the wearer's *neck circumference* and the other denoting *sleeve length*. For example, a 15/34 shirt size indicates a 15-inch neck circumference and a 34-inch sleeve length. Neck sizes typically range from 14¹⁄₂ to 17 inches, with ¹⁄₂-inch increments between sizes. Smaller neck sizes are found in young men's and larger neck sizes in big and tall men's. Sleeve length is measured from the center back of the neck, across the shoulder, along the arm behind the elbow, and to the wrist bone (Figure 6–3). High-quality shirts meet exact standards of sleeve length with 1-inch increments between sleeve lengths, which typically range from 30 to 34 inches (with shorter lengths found in young men's and longer lengths in big and tall men's). So many different neck size/sleeve length combinations require the manufacturer to produce and the retailer to stock many different stockkeeping units (SKUs). In low-price lines, shirtmakers often lump sleeve lengths together. For example, a sleeve length of 32/33 denotes that the shirt sleeve fits a man with a sleeve length of either 32 or 33 inches. Two buttons are placed on the cuff; buttoning the cuff

tighter "fits" the shorter sleeve length; buttoning the cuff looser "fits" the longer length. (For an example, see Chapter 10, Figure 10–37.) This reduces the number of sizes and SKUs but provides less exact fit.

Manufacturers size undershirts, sweaters, and pajamas by chest measurement or S, M, L, XL. Undershorts (boxers and briefs) are sized by waist measurement or S, M, L, XL.

FIT

An awareness of fit is useful to anyone in the apparel industry. With fit in mind, designers and pattern-makers plan garments that fit the target customer as nearly as possible. However, much of the information on fit is equally pertinent to retailers who provide customer assistance with fit. Fitting a customer properly is becoming a lost art. Fewer retailers are offering this service any more. Offering a fitting and alterations program complements a retailer's merchandise assortment by delivering the service that many customers desire, building goodwill, and increasing customer loyalty to the store. Today some customers are willing to pay extra for these services, either directly for the service or indirectly in higher merchandise prices.

Fit refers to how well the garment conforms to the three-dimensional human body. Good fit is crucial to consumer satisfaction. However, it is often easier for consumers to find colors, prices, and styles they like than to achieve a good fit. The effects of a stunning design, gorgeous fabric, and exquisite workmanship are destroyed if the finished garment does not fit the intended wearer. Garments that fit well are not only more attractive than ill-fitting garments; they are also more comfortable. Garments that do not fit well are left hanging in the consumer's closet, seldom worn, or on the retailer's markdown rack. An estimated 70% of garments on markdown racks are there due to problems with workmanship and/or fit (McVey, 1984).

Fit problems may be caused by careless design or construction. However, many fit problems are the result of individual characteristics of the wearer. No two bodies are alike, and even the right and left halves of the same body are not mirror images of each other. New technology promises to overcome these problems. Computer systems can optically measure an individual's body in three dimensions. This data is then converted to a computerized, individualized pattern. A suit designed by this method can be cut out and ready to sew within 7 minutes of receipt of the measurement data (Friese, 1985). The resulting garments fit accurately because the computerized scanner detects subtle nuances in the shape of the body that normal measurement systems cannot detect. Garments manufactured in this way cost much less than traditional custom apparel. However, such systems are largely experimental, costly, and not yet in widespread use.

There are varying opinions on what constitutes good fit. For example, some people like the way tight pants look and feel, whereas others prefer looser pants. A long skirt may seem more attractive or more practical to one person, and another may prefer a shorter skirt. Personal preferences regarding fit are shaped by current fashion trends, cultural influences, age, sex, figure type, and lifestyle. The intended end use of a garment also affects the desired fit. For example, consumers expect active sportswear to fit more loosely than spectator sportswear to allow greater freedom of movement.

Closely related to fit is the concept of the appropriateness of a garment for a particular person's figure. In other words, does the garment not only fit but flatter the wearer? Retailers do customers a valuable service by steering them toward garments that are most suitable for their figures. Garment design can camouflage figure flaws or use optical illusion to make figure irregularities unnoticeable. For example, although both may fit equally well, a gently flared skirt probably will be more flattering to a person with large hips than will a straight skirt. For more information, see Related Resources: Design and Style at the end of the text.

Recently, manufacturers and retailers have become aware of the need for increased customer service. Consumers are demanding more product knowledge as they make purchase decisions. **Kiosks,** self-contained video units, have been placed in retail stores to provide consumers with more information about products and their attributes. For example, one major retailer operating a self-serve shoe department has placed kiosks containing videotaped programs explaining the different features of athletic shoes. This is one way retailers can meet the need for more product information and service while still meeting budget restrictions.

Controlling Fit

Manufacturers aim to produce apparel that consistently fits their target market because apparel that fits increases sales and customer satisfaction. Retailers try to offer garments that consistently fit their target market for the same reasons. Another challenge for manufacturers is to provide garments that continue to fit after wear and care. Consistent fit within a brand builds customer loyalty because the customer can rely on finding a good fit where he or she has

found it before. If fit is inconsistent within a brand, searching for a garment that fits becomes a frustrating and dissatisfying experience for the consumer. For these reasons it is important to understand the elements of fit. Sometimes consumers expect garments in the same brand but of varying silhouettes all to fit in the same manner. This is not possible due to the styling features. Thus, it is common for the same consumer to wear several different sizes in the same brand of clothing depending upon the silhouette variations. Retailers must deal with the inconsistency of fit of the same labeled size in not only the same but also in different brands.

Consistent fit is pursued at every step of the apparel production process. To achieve it, all production personnel involved must understand the implications their decisions have on the final product. Patternmakers who do not understand production sewing equipment and its limitations are unable to produce patterns that provide both smooth fit and operator efficiency. For example, eased and curved seams at the elbow of a two-piece sleeve fit the arm better than do straight seams. Contoured edges on collars and yokes fit better than those with perfectly straight edges.

The fit of a particular style is checked during development by testing the prototype garment on a live model. Prototypes are checked on models with measurements conforming to the desired body dimensions. Some companies go to the extreme of checking fit on several different live models who conform to the sample size body dimensions but vary in fullness. For example, many companies check fit on a size 12 model. They call in models that conform to the body measurements and proportions of their size 12, a small size 12, and a large size 12. A well-designed garment will fit all versions of the desired size. Testing a garment on a three-dimensional form (**form fitting**) is a more precise check of the fit of a garment than measuring but is less accurate than checking fit on a live model. The three-dimensional form cannot move or answer questions. Also, the cloth covering on the form is rough and garments do not easily slide over the surface. This can cause stretching of the garment and thus an inaccurate assessment of fit. The majority of mass-produced apparel is extensively fit on live models, commonly called **fit models,** during the design and development stage of the production cycle (Figure 6–4). During preproduction and production, fit is continually monitored using key measurements. If the measuring system detects a potential fit problem, garments are sent to the designers who evaluate the suspect garments on a live fit model. Live models may gain or lose weight, change

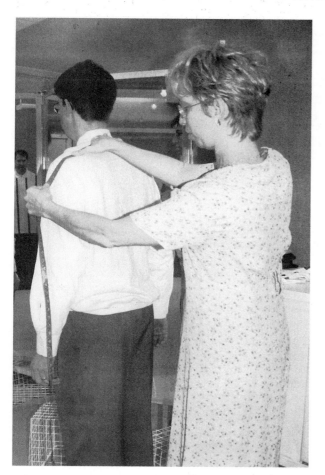

Figure 6–4 Fit modeling session. (Courtesy of Winning Ways.)

proportions, or become unavailable, making it difficult for a company to maintain consistent fit even when the company proactively maintains a current group of fit models.

Most manufacturers and retailers develop extensive and detailed fit specifications that finished garments must meet. Conformance to these specifications is checked in-line by quality inspectors who take length and width measurements of the garments at predetermined key points. Figure 6–5 shows an example of fit specifications for a sweatshirt. During inspection, the measurements of the garment must fall within the tolerance limits of the specifications for that particular size. Using measurements alone does not give the full picture of how well the garment will fit the body; therefore, they are used along with other measures. Taking measurements at inspection stations primarily helps eliminate garments with gross departures from specifications and detects garments that have been accidentally mislabeled for size. Mail-order retailers, such as L.L. Bean, Lands' End, and J.C. Penney, are noted for

their use of measurements to check fit. Consistent fit is especially important to mail-order retailers to avoid excessive returns of garments because of poor fit.

A simple linear sketch of the garment, known as a technical drawing or *flat* communicates the silhouette of the garment and may include "zoom" insets to focus on details. Sketches are kept as clear and simple as possible for ease in understanding the concepts. Tolerances are included where necessary. The methods of measure consist of precise definitions of various length and width measurements (for example, body length is measured from high point of shoulder, where neckline and shoulder meet, to lower edge; body width is measured from side seam to side seam 1" below armhole) (see Figure 6–5). A company's methods of measure must be understood not only within the company but by suppliers and customers in order for everyone to consistently agree upon measurement results. To establish or confirm dimensions, the garment is placed on a table for measuring as specified, the tape measure is placed on the garment as specified, and measurements of each area are performed as specified, with results carefully recorded.

Five Elements Of Fit

An evaluation of fit is based on five classic elements: (1) grain, (2) set, (3) line, (4) balance, and (5) ease (as originally identified by Erwin, Kinchen, and Peters [1979]). The five elements of fit are highly interrelated; they serve to describe different but related aspects of fit. For example, a garment with inadequate ease will, when worn, have poor set and distorted grain. If a garment is off-grain, it is also out of line and out of balance (Figure 6–6).

Grain. For good fit, the garment must be cut on **grain.** The lengthwise grain or yarns of the fabric need to run parallel to the length of the body at center front and center back, down the center of the arm from shoulder to elbow, and down the center front of each pants leg. The crosswise grain or yarns of the fabric should run perpendicular to the length of the body at bust/chest, hip, and upper arm at bust/chest level. The exception to these grain rules is a garment cut on the bias, with the bias of the fabric placed parallel to the length of the body to create special effects.

An on-grain garment hangs evenly and appears symmetrical. If the garment is off-grain, it will not hang straight. The garment and seamlines may twist or hang crooked because the fabric on each half of the garment behaves differently.

Deviations in grainline result when garments are not cut or sewn on grain or when the wearer's poor posture

Style #S111

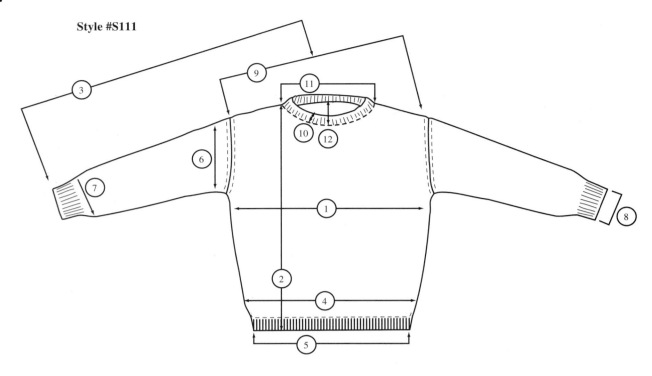

HOW TO MEASURE	SM	ME	LG	XL	TOL +/–
1. Chest (1" below armhole)	24	26	28	30	1 (total circ.)
2. Body Length	26	26³/4	27¹/2	28	³/4
3. Sleeve Length	32	33	34	35	³/4
4. Sweep (12" above waist)	22	23	24	25	1
5. Waist Relaxed	19	21	23	25	1
6. Armhole	12¹/4	13	13³/4	14¹/2	¹/2
7. Arm Width 2" above cuff	6¹/2	6¹/2	6³/4	7	¹/2
8. Cuff Opening	3³/4	3³/4	4	4¹/4	¹/4
9. Shoulder to Shoulder	22¹/2	23¹/2	24¹/2	25¹/2	³/4
10. Rib	⁷/8	⁷/8	⁷/8	⁷/8	¹/8
11. Neck Width (seam to seam)	9¹/2	10	10¹/2	11	¹/2
12. Neck Depth (seam to seam)	2¹/2	2¹/2	2¹/2	2¹/2	¹/4

Figure 6–5   Fit specifications and methods of measure. (Courtesy of Winning Ways.)

or figure irregularities interfere with the grain trueness of the garment as it hangs on the body. For further information on the role of fabric grain, see Chapter 5.

Set.   **Set** refers to a smooth fit without undesirable wrinkles. Wrinkles caused by poor set are not the type of wrinkles that can be eliminated by ironing the garment, but result from the way the garment fits the wearer. Set wrinkles usually occur because the garment is too large or too small, and the fabric pulls or sags where the garment does not fit. Occasionally, poor set is the result of the wearer's poor posture. Ideally, this could be corrected with improved posture, which eliminates the body curves and hollows that interfere with good set.

If a garment has poor set, the type of wrinkles and their location pinpoint the cause of the fit problem (Figure 6–7).

1. *Horizontal wrinkles under tension* indicate that the garment is narrower than the body just above or below the wrinkles. For example, skirts with horizontal wrinkles at hip level are probably too tight in that area.
2. *Loose, vertical wrinkles* indicate that the garment is too wide in that area. For example, vertical folds in the back of a jacket indicate that the garment is too wide across the back.
3. *Vertical wrinkles under tension* form when the garment is too short in an area. For example, tense,

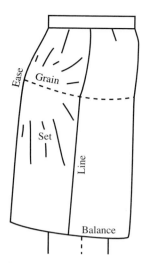

Figure 6–6 Fit problems.

vertical wrinkles in the bodice of a dress are a sign that the bodice area is too short for the wearer.

4. *Loose, horizontal folds* indicate that the garment is longer than the body. For example, a pair of pants on a swaybacked person will often exhibit loose, horizontal folds in the center back below the waistband because the pants are longer than the body in that area.

5. *Diagonal wrinkles* point to a particular body curve indicating that the garment is too small or lacks sufficient shaping to adequately fit that body curve. For example, large bust/chest or buttocks, abdominal curves, prominent shoulder blades, or a high shoulder all create diagonal wrinkles that point to the offending curve. Designing a garment with adequate darts or dart equivalents to fit the body curves solves the problem.

Line. **Line** refers to the alignment of the structural lines of the garment with the natural lines of the body. Some lines of the garment silhouette or outline the body. For example, side seams should hang straight like a plumb line down the center of the side of the body, perpendicular to the floor. Center front and center back lines should likewise fall straight down the center front and center back of the body. Darts and seams, such as shoulder seams, should

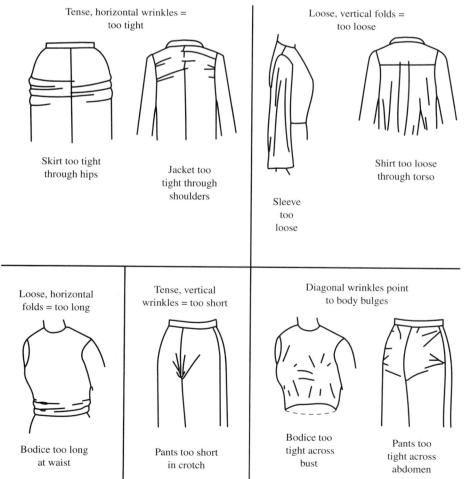

Figure 6–7 Wrinkles and folds indicate fit problems.

appear as straight lines that follow the body parts they are intended to fit. Other lines encompass the circumference of the body. For example, necklines, armholes, waistlines, and hemlines should be gradually curved lines that follow the circular lines of the body part they are intended to fit. Poor design or construction can result in an out-of-line garment, or figure irregularities can distort the lines of the garment.

Balance. **Balance** occurs when the garment is in equilibrium. The right and left halves of the garment appear evenly balanced, or symmetrical, when viewed from the front, back, or sides. For example, a skirt is balanced if the legs are in the middle of the skirt and not touching the front or back of the skirt. Balance relates to the elements of grain and line. Garments get out of balance if they are cut off grain, causing them to hang unevenly. Or, if the lines of a garment do not follow the lines of the body, the garment will hang out of balance. Poor posture or a lack of symmetry in the wearer's figure are likely causes of balance problems. Haphazard or uneven construction techniques may also result in an unbalanced garment.

Ease. **Ease** refers to the amount of roominess in a garment. (For a discussion of the term *ease* used as a shaping method, see Chapter 5.) Ease is the difference between the measurements of the garment and the measurements of the body of the intended wearer. There are two types of ease: fitting ease and design ease. The measurement of a garment should equal the measurement of the wearer's body plus fitting ease, plus design ease or style fullness (see Chapter 5), if any.

Fitting Ease. Even a garment that appears to fit the figure closely does not have the same dimensions as the body it fits. For example, a skirt measuring 36 inches at the hip line does not fit a person with 36-inch hips. A garment must contain adequate ease beyond the actual measurements of the wearer to allow room for ordinary movements like walking, sitting, reaching, and breathing. Ease in this context refers to *basic ease* or **fitting ease,** also called *movement ease, comfort ease,* or *garment ease,* the ease required for a comfortable, livable fit. Minimal fitting ease is required in *all* garments, no matter what the style. Without fitting ease, a garment is uncomfortable, appears tight and wrinkled, and wears out more quickly from the strain on seams and fabric. Table 6–5 lists the approximate minimum amounts of fitting ease required in the bust/chest, waist, and hips of garments to allow for simple movement. Fitting ease is also required vertically (shoulder to waist, waist to crotch, etc.) and elsewhere in the garment (around the neck, around the arm, etc.). Some garments require additional amounts of fitting ease beyond the minimum suggested, depending on the style and intended use.

Table 6–5 Fitting Ease (in Inches)

	Women	Men	Children
Bust/Chest	2½	2	1
Waist	1	½	1–1½
Hip	1½–2	½	1½–1¾

Gioello and Berke (1979)

For example, a baseball uniform requires more fitting ease for throwing and swinging than a business suit that is worn for sedentary activities. Clothing for toddlers generally contains fitting ease to accommodate diapers. Jackets and coats require more fitting ease than other garments because they are worn over several other layers of clothing.

Stretch fabrics substitute for fitting ease in a garment because the stretch makes up for the lack of ease. Very stretchy garments, such as rib knit shrink tops, may have negative fitting ease; for instance, a top may be cut 30 inches in circumference to stretch and fit closely to a 36-inch bust.

Design Ease. **Design ease** is extra style fullness added to fitting ease. All garments have fitting ease, but design ease is optional because it is added purely for the sake of appearance, giving a garment its "style." Basic-fitting garments have only fitting ease, but other garments have design ease in addition to fitting ease. For example, style fullness creates a full, pleated skirt rather than a straight one. It makes possible a gathered, puffed sleeve rather than a slim one. The amount of design ease in a garment depends on current fashion trends and the desired mood or style of the garment. (For examples, refer to Chapter 5, Figures 5–19 and 5–25.) Designers and pattern-makers create **oversized** garments by adding design or styling ease.

When loose-fitting styles with large amounts of design ease are popular, fit tolerances are often less strict. Leftover fitting ease goes unnoticed as extra design ease, or some of the design ease may be used as fitting ease. Although style fullness makes a garment roomier, it is not provided to enable a larger person to wear the garment. If the extra roominess created by the style fullness is used to accommodate a larger figure, the garment does not have the look the designer intended. For example, a fully gathered skirt with a lot of design ease might be able to go around very large hips, but it no longer appears gathered. Therefore, design ease should be excess ease that is not used to fit the body or allow for its movement. Likewise, the excess fitting ease in a too-large garment should not add to the style fullness, or again, the garment does not appear as the designer intended.

Evaluating Fit

Fit may be evaluated at many different points in the production cycle. However, the most important point for establishing good fit is in the development stage. By carefully evaluating the fit of prototype garments and making needed corrections, designers and merchandisers make it possible to produce garments with the desired fit. The following sections discuss the criteria for fitting garments at the prototype stage and for checking the fit of finished garments. These same concepts apply when fit research is being conducted on competitors' garments. The same criteria may also be applied by individual consumers as they try on garments, although that is not the focus of these sections on evaluating fit.

In evaluating the fit of a garment, all areas of the garment must be examined. The following sections trace the evaluation of fit from the upper body to the lower body, including the fit of the shoulders, bust/chest, neckline, collar, lapels, armholes, sleeves, waistline, hips, crotch, and length of the garment (Figure 6–8). Sections are included on fitting suits and foundation garments, which require special attention. Fitting people with special needs is also discussed.

During fit sessions, fit models wear undergarments and accessory items just as the consumer will do when wearing the garment. They also carry items appropriate for pockets (wallets, keys, and change) and stand and sit and make any other motions normally associated with a particular product. These actions simulate real-life wearing situations and help the designers and patternmakers achieve the desired fit. If changes are necessary, the patternmaker or designer ideally starts from the top and works down, taking care of the most obvious problems first. Making these adjustments first will often remedy other, more minor problems. The centers of the garment and the body are aligned throughout the process.

Shoulders. The shoulder area is the most critical when fitting upper-body garments like shirts and jackets. If the shoulders can be made to fit with a minimum of alteration at the initial fitting session, the rest of the garment can usually be altered without jeopardizing the style and drape of the garment.

In evaluating the fit of the shoulders, the shoulders should look smooth and feel comfortable. In classic garments, the armscye seam falls at the edge of the wearer's shoulder, where the bone of the arm hinges in its socket. The shoulders of the garment should be wide enough so that the sleeves hang smoothly. If the shoulders are too narrow, the sleeves will pull across the upper arm and cause wrinkles. If fashion requires shoulders that are narrower or wider, the pattern should allow sufficient ease for movement.

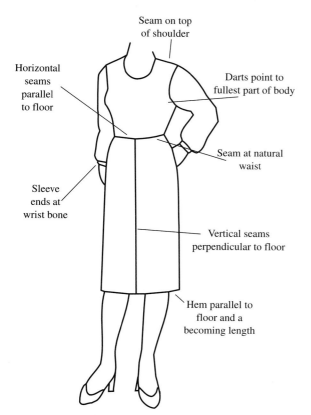
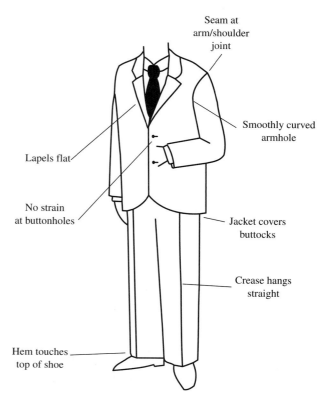

Figure 6–8 Characteristics of well-fitted garments.

The shoulder slope of the garment should match the shoulder slope of the wearer. The **shoulder slope** is the angle the shoulder seam makes as it slopes away from the neck. Individual shoulder slopes vary greatly. For example, standard shirt yokes accommodate two inches of slope from the base of the neck to the shoulder, but some manufacturers cut their shirts for squarer or more sloping shoulders. Shoulder pads in jackets make accurate fit in this area less critical because the pads fill in discrepancies in the two angles.

The shoulder seam should lie on top of the shoulder so that it is not visible from the front or back of the wearer when viewed at eye level. An exception to this is the *dropped shoulder* style, in which the shoulder seams are purposely brought forward to create a different look.

For good fit, a shoulder dart or dart equivalent is needed in the back of the garment to smoothly fit the shoulder blade area to the body. The absence of a shoulder dart causes wrinkles emanating from the neckline or armhole because fabric is pulled from these areas to accommodate the curve of the shoulder blades. In better jackets, ease may be substituted in the shoulder seam for the shoulder dart, yielding a smooth fit in the shoulder area. In better shirts, a shaped seam joining the yoke to the body of the shirt serves as a shoulder dart substitute. When the shoulder darts or their substitutes are omitted to speed manufacturing, the area does not fit smoothly.

Bust/Chest. The bust/chest of a garment is another area that is difficult to adjust; therefore, it is important to design a garment that fits smoothly through the bust/chest at the initial fitting. If the garment is too small, the seams or closures at center front and center back are likely to pull and gape open. For example, a large bust or highly developed chest often causes the button closure to gape at center front. Also, the garment may ride up because the larger bust curve takes up more length.

A well-fitted dart points toward the fullest part, or *crown,* of the body curve it is intended to fit; for example, bust darts should point to the tip of the bust. The tip of the dart should end about an inch before the fullest part of the body curve, or crown. Darts that are too short or darts that extend beyond the fullest part of the body curve result in a bubble at the dart tip. If two (or more) darts are used to fit the same body curve, they may be placed with their points equidistant from the crown or with one pointed directly at the crown and the other, usually the shorter and smaller one, placed near the edge of the curve. Darts occurring anywhere in the garment, as at the waist, shoulder, or elbow, should follow these same general rules. The current practice of eliminating darts to speed construction creates diagonal wrinkles on bodice fronts.

Neckline. Another critical area in fitting upper-body garments is the neckline. The circumference of the neckline of a garment should be large enough to fit without pulling or chafing but not so large that it does not lie flat against the body in front or back. Pullover necklines must be large enough to fit over the wearer's head. Even if banded with a stretchy rib knit, the neckline may not be large enough unless properly designed.

A basic neckline should cross the wearer's prominent vertebra at center back and the base of the throat depression at center front. The front of a basic neckline should be lower than the back to accommodate the natural forward tilt of the head. (For an example, see Chapter 9, Figure 9–8.) Patternmakers that do not distinguish garment fronts and garment backs in this way greatly compromise quality, fit, and comfort.

Collar. As for the neckline, the collar should be fitted carefully because it frames the wearer's face. The most important factor in the fit of the collar is neck circumference. The circumference of the collar should be about 1/4 inch larger than the neck measurement, or just large enough so that you can insert two fingers between the neck and the collar. A properly fitted collar is smooth and stays in place when the wearer moves. It should not be so tight that it pulls; a tight collar is uncomfortable and makes the neck look fat. But neither should the collar be so loose that it gapes (Figure 6–9).

The **collar slope** or vertical height also should be considered. The most flattering slope—low, medium, or high—depends on the wearer's neck length. Different designers and patternmakers plan garments with slightly different collar slopes, based on their target customer. When a shirt and jacket are worn together, the back of the shirt collar should extend about 1/2 inch above the jacket collar.

Popular collar styles generally depend on fashion. The length of the collar points also depends somewhat on fashion. However, narrow collar points are scaled to small people and wide collar points to large people. The **spread** of the collar, the distance from collar point to collar point, is a personal preference based on facial shape and the type of knot tied in the necktie, if one is worn.

Sometimes fabric wrinkles or bulges directly below the collar. A small ripple or bubble below the collar may be corrected in jackets by removing some of the shoulder padding. If the ripple or bulge is large, it may require resetting the collar deeper in the back neckline.

Lapels. Lapels should lie flat and smooth against the chest, without gaping or sagging. They should taper gradually from the neckline to the level of the top button.

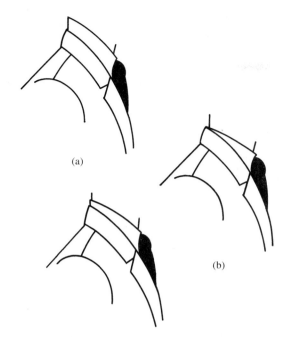

(a)

(b)

Figure 6–9 (a) Collars too loose and shirt collar slope too high for jacket, (b) collars too tight and shirt collar slope too low for jacket, and (c) collars fit correctly and shirt collar slope correct for jacket (about ½ inch shows).

Classic jacket lapels are 3 to 3½ inches wide. However, as fashions change, lapels become wider or narrower. The width of a man's necktie should be proportional to the width of the jacket lapels and shirt collar; wide ties are appropriate for wide collars and lapels, and narrow ties for narrow collars and lapels.

Armscyes. Armscyes (armholes) must fit well for the garment to be comfortable and attractive. The circumference of the armscyes should be large enough so they do not pull at the front and back of the garment, but not so large that they gape. In well-fit armscyes, the base of the armscye is cut close to the armpit, but not so close that it is actually felt—about an inch below the armpit. This provides adequate comfort, that is, room for movement without shifting the garment, and close fit without wrinkles in the armscye area. If armscyes are too snug, they bind and are uncomfortable. If sleeveless armholes are too loose, they may be comfortable but also gape, exposing a view of undergarments. When armscyes with sleeves are too large or low, they are actually less roomy and comfortable because movement is restricted in much the same way that a low crotch in a pair of pants impedes walking. Blouse or shirt armscyes generally are cut higher than jacket or coat armscyes.

Armscyes should be shaped so that the front of the armscye is less deeply curved than the back. This provides freedom of movement (because arm motions are usually in a forward direction) and smooth fit. Armscyes are enlarged by the patternmaker cutting the underarm curve lower. If the curve is cut around the entire circumference of the armscye, the garment will be too small in the front and back at chest level and across the shoulders.

Sleeves. Sleeves that fit well are attractive and comfortable. The circumference of a basic sleeve should be loose enough so that it does not bind or wrinkle horizontally around the arm. Tight sleeves are a problem for people like athletes with highly developed biceps and back muscles. Sleeves can be as loose as desired; the only limit occurs if a jacket is to be worn over the sleeves, in which case full sleeves will bulge under the jacket sleeve and look lumpy. The sleeve style affects the desired amount of design ease in a sleeve.

For set-in sleeves, the position of the sleeve in the armscye, often referred to as the set of the sleeve, is an important indicator of good fit. A well-set sleeve hangs at a slight angle toward the front of the body, much as the relaxed arm hangs at the side. The lengthwise grain of the sleeve is parallel to the length of the upper arm. The crosswise grain should be parallel to the floor and perpendicular to the lengthwise grain at bust/chest level. The underarm seam of a long sleeve should fall at the center of the underneath part of the wrist.

Waistline. Waistline fit is important for comfort. The circumference of the waistline is determined partly by the style of the garment, but it should not be so tight that it binds or rolls. It should return to its natural position after the arms are raised and lowered and should allow plenty of room for breathing and eating. It should not be so loose that it stands away from the body, droops, or adds excess bulk when a top is tucked in or worn under another garment. For example, men's tapered shirt styles are more fitted at the waist than traditional dress or formal shirts; thus, they fit closer to the waist and are less bulky when tucked into pants and worn under jackets than most sport shirts.

The narrowest part of the garment should fall at the wearer's waist. If there are buttons at the waist, the garment should not strain at the closures. (However, a slight indentation at the waist is permissible in men's jackets.) A jacket should be full enough so that the wearer can sit down with it buttoned. When fitting men's suits, the bottom buttons of single-breasted jackets and vests are left unbuttoned; the bottom or middle button of double-breasted jackets may be left open.

Pants and skirts should be supported at the waist, not the hips. If a garment rests on the hips, the waistline of the garment is too large or the hips of the garment are too small for the body. Hip-hugger styles are an exception.

Waistbands of men's pants are often constructed to allow for ease of alteration, with the final seam sewn through the seat and the waistband at center back. However, menswear waistbands usually can be taken in or let out at the center back seam no more than 1½ to 2 inches. Taking in the waist more than that brings the rear pockets too close together and can cause the legs to change position. Only a few women's garments are constructed to allow for easy alterations of the waistband. For this reason, most low- and moderate-price women's apparel, some men's apparel, and childrenswear at all price lines feature full or partial elastic at the waist to fit a wider variety of figures without alterations.

Hips. The fit of the hip area is critical when fitting lower-body garments like pants and skirts. If there is adequate room in the hip area (including widest hip and abdomen/upper hip curves), other parts of the garment usually can be altered to fit.

Garments with adequate room in the hip, thigh, and abdomen area fit smoothly without pulling, wrinkling (grinning), or riding up. Pockets, pleats, or vents that gape often indicate the garment is too tight in the hip or abdomen areas. If the garment has excess ease in the hip or thigh area, loose, vertical folds form. This is desirable in garments such as full, gathered skirts to which design ease was added for style purposes, but undesirable in a garment intended to fit closely.

Crotch. Pants and other **bifurcated** (having two parts) garments require a well-fitted crotch for comfort and durability. A properly designed crotch is one that does not cut or bind the wearer between the legs and conforms to the shape of the buttocks. It fits a majority of customers with the hip and waist size of the garment. There should be slight but not excessive ease in the crotch area.

Crotch Length. **Crotch length** refers to the measurement of the crotch from the center front waistline to the center back waistline as measured between the legs (Figure 6–10). Patternmakers allow approximately one inch for fitting ease. Crotch length includes both body length and body thickness; thicker bodies require longer crotch length and more deeply rounded crotch curves. The back of the crotch seam should be longer and more deeply curved than the front because the back and buttocks are generally more curved than the front of the body; the necessary shape and depth of the curve depend on the individual wearer. When garment fronts and backs are designed identically, quality fit is compromised.

Diagonal wrinkles radiating from the crotch area often result where the crotch curve is not long enough in the back to accommodate the size of the

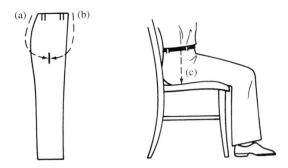

Figure 6–10 (a) Back crotch length and (b) front crotch length (a and b added together equal total crotch length), and (c) crotch depth, or rise.

buttocks. Or, if the wearer has a large abdomen, diagonal wrinkles may indicate the need for greater front crotch length. Patternmakers can adjust crotch length no more than about 1½ inches total in the inseam area; more can cause repositioning of the pant legs. Additional adjustment may be made at the waistline by raising or lowering the waistband. An alteration in crotch length is also referred to as changing the *thigh* or *stride*.

Rise. Crotch length is closely related to **rise** or **crotch depth** (Figure 6–10). However, rise constitutes only part of crotch length—the measurement from crotch level to the top of the waistband. (Rise can be measured on a seated figure by measuring from the chair seat to the wearer's waist level plus an inch or so for fitting ease.) Some better lines of pants offer a choice of rise: short, regular, or long. The desired rise depends on the length of the wearer's torso below the waist, and the waistline level and ease of fit desired. (The more fleshy the figure, the more the body spreads when seated, making additional ease desirable.) Men's suit pants generally feature a higher rise than men's sport pants and are usually worn just about even with the navel, so the waistline seam lies just above the hip bone. Men's sports pants usually have a shorter rise than suit pants and may be worn slightly lower on the hip. Unless fashion dictates otherwise, women's pants usually fit at the natural waist—the narrowest part of the female body.

Wrinkles emanating upward from the crotch area indicate a too-high, tight crotch, resulting in chafing and discomfort. Wrinkles emanating downward from the crotch indicate a low, loose crotch; it bags and sags, restricts walking, and has an increased probability of ripping from the strain of movement. If the rise must be lengthened or shortened, the waistband can be raised or lowered. Rise is also lengthened or shortened by changing the crotch length, but this sometimes causes a problem where none existed.

Garment Length. Garment length is an important fit factor in consumer satisfaction with a garment. Therefore, special attention should be paid to sleeve length, skirt length, jacket length, and pant length. The desirable length depends on current fashion trends, the end use of the garment, the body type and size, lifestyle, and opinion of the wearer. For example, childrenswear should be hemmed short enough so it does not pose a stumbling hazard or get underfoot when the child stoops. Skirt and jacket length varies widely with fashion, but basic sleeve length and pant length generally fall at customary locations on the body.

Length of Jackets. The appropriate length of a basic jacket is determined by the wearer standing with arms down and relaxed. If the fingers are curled up, the hem of the jacket should fall into that curl. The front of the jacket is usually about half an inch longer than the back. Men's jackets should cover the wearer's buttocks, and the hem should be parallel to the floor. If a vest is worn, it should cover the waistband of the pants or skirt.

Women's basic jackets follow the same rules, but the length of fashion jackets varies depending upon trends. Often, shorter jackets provide a pleasing proportion on shorter women and longer jackets on taller women. The length of the skirt also affects the desirable length of the jacket. Slightly shorter jackets may be in better proportion with skirts than with slacks. However, proportion rules are sometimes overruled by fashion trends. When selecting from various lengths of jackets and skirts and lengths of dresses, the proportions of the target customer should dictate which fashion trends will flatter.

Length of Other Upper-Body Garments. For upper-body garments such as shirts and blouses that have shirttails, the length of a shirttail should be at least 6 inches below the waist so that it will stay tucked when the wearer moves. If it is too much longer, it will add unwanted bulk and distort the pants or skirt into which it is tucked. The back tail may be cut longer than the front so it does not easily become untucked when the wearer bends or reaches. Shirts and blouses without tails may be any length prescribed by fashion.

The fronts of women's upper-body garments worn untucked should be cut longer than the backs to accommodate the bust curve and prevent the garment from riding up in front. Upper-body garments with waistline seams must have adequate length in the upper torso to prevent tense vertical wrinkles from forming at the waist. However, too much length will result in soft horizontal folds at the waist. Sometimes, this blousing is a desirable fashion effect, and extra length is added for style purposes. If the garment is

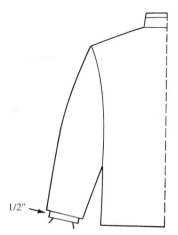

Figure 6–11 Sleeve length covers wrist bone when arm is bent slightly at the elbow, and shirt sleeve extends about 1/2 inch below jacket sleeve.

intended to blouse, the blousing should not be used up in fitting the length of the body.

Men's neckties should be tied with the *dimple* (indentation) centered under the knot. Methods of knotting a tie include the *four-in-hand, Windsor,* and *half-Windsor knots.* The knot chosen should complement the shirt collar spread; a smaller knot is generally dressier than a large knot. The end of the tie should reach the top of the belt buckle when tied. For tall men, this may necessitate a longer-than-average tie. Short men should tie a knot that takes up more of the length of the tie to achieve the proper fit. Standard ties range from 52 to 58 inches long. If a coordinating pocket square is worn, it should extend about half an inch above the breast pocket.

Sleeve Length. Sleeves can be any length but should flatter the wearer by not adding unwanted visual weight to the figure, especially at the bustline or hipline (for example, short, puffed sleeves on a large-busted woman). Long sleeves should cover the wrist bone when the arm is bent slightly at the elbow. When a shirt or blouse and a jacket are worn together, the shirt or blouse sleeves should extend 1/4 to 1/2 inch beyond the jacket sleeves (Figure 6–11). If the shirt or blouse has French cuffs, its sleeves may extend as much as an inch beyond the jacket sleeve to display the cuff links. Cuff width should be proportional to collar width.

Skirt Length. Skirt lengths generally are dependent on fashion trends. Skirt length is referred to in inches "below the band," from the lower edge of the waistband to the lower edge of the hem. The **sweep** of a skirt hem refers not to its length, but to its circumference at the hem. A skirt length should be chosen to flatter the wearer. In general, shorter-than-average skirts provide more pleasing proportions when worn by short women, and longer-than-average skirts are better for tall women. A flattering length for most people is with the hem of the skirt covering the fullest part of the leg and exposing the most slender lower leg and ankle. Basic skirts are often hemmed at or just below the knee. Floor length skirts generally are hemmed half an inch to an inch above the floor. All hems should be parallel to the floor unless they are unusually styled, for example, handkerchief hems. Large body curves, for example a protruding abdomen or buttocks, require additional overall length to go over the curve and maintain a level hem.

Pant Length. The proper length of pants depends greatly on fashion trends. However, for basic pants, there are two choices (Figure 6–12 a and b). The pants should either just skim the top of the shoe, or they should be slightly longer so they break. A **break** refers to the slight indentation that occurs between the knee and ankle when the pants hit the top of the shoe and are slightly longer. High-quality men's suit and sport slacks and some women's pants are sold unhemmed; the consumer is expected to have them altered to a precise fit.

Many men's dress pants and some women's pants are **canted** (Figure 6–12c). The backs of the slacks legs are cut from 1/2 inch to 1 inch longer than the fronts, causing the hem to fall at an angle from the front to the back of the pant leg. The lower back edge should fall where the heel and sole of the shoe meet. This ensures that the back of the shoe is covered better than if the pants were hemmed parallel to the floor.

Cuffed pants are hemmed straight rather than canted so that they are parallel to the floor. If cuffs are used on the bottom of pants, they should be similar in width to the waistband. Generally, wider pant leg cuffs and waistbands are used with wider jacket lapels, shirt collars, shirt cuffs, and neckties. Narrower-than-average cuffs or no cuffs flatter short people and wider-than-average cuffs are suitable for tall people.

Suits. A suit is usually a big investment and is worn daily in the business world and for important occasions. Therefore, most customers expect excellent fit as one of the most important criteria in purchasing a suit. Alterations at the point of sale are often done to perfect the fit of a suit by a customer who might tolerate the same imperfections of fit in more casual or sporty garments. The pants of a suit are usually fitted first, followed by the vest if any, and then the jacket.

The fit of women's jackets is largely determined by fashion trends. Fit, ranging from closely fitted to

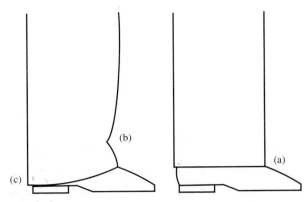

Figure 6–12 Pant leg: (a) skims top of shoe, (b) breaks slightly above the shoe, and (c) canted, about an inch longer in back than in front.

unconstructed styles, depends on current popular styling.

The fit of men's suits depends partly on the style. There are three basic styles: (1) American cut, (2) European cut, and (3) British cut. The differences between these styles are not clear. For example, some American-made suits may be more of a British cut than some British-made suits. However, there are some generalizations about the typical fit features of each cut.

American-cut jackets, called **standard cut** in the United States, are usually the most conservative in styling. They may also be the most comfortable. American-cut jackets are usually single breasted. The shoulders are padded only slightly; this jacket also is referred to as a *natural-shoulder style*. The jacket hangs from the shoulders and drapes loosely rather than fitting the body. The jacket tapers only slightly at the waist. The armscyes are cut slightly low for comfort. The lapels are notched, medium in width, and the jacket often features a single, center back vent. A type of American cut jacket is the *Ivy league* or *sack jacket*. It has a full body and unpadded shoulders. Pants worn with American-cut jackets may be cuffed or uncuffed. Less formal suits may feature jackets of a loosely fitted style referred to as *unconstructed*.

European-cut jackets are sleeker, more angular, and more highly shaped and closely fitted than American-cut jackets. They tend to flatter a slimmer man more than a heavier one. The shoulders are built up and padded heavily and squarely, and the jacket is fitted at the waist. The armscyes are cut high and tight, and the lapels often are peaked and either narrow or wide, depending on fashion. European-cut jackets are often double breasted and, if so, have two back vents or none at all. Pants worn with European-cut jackets seldom are cuffed. Vests usually are not worn with European-cut suits.

British-cut jackets fall somewhere in between American-cut and European-cut jackets. They have slightly padded shoulders like American-cut jackets and a somewhat fitted waist like European-cut jackets. British-cut jackets usually have two deep vents in the back of the jacket. They tend to fit the body more than merely hanging from the shoulders as an American-cut suit does. Pants worn with British-cut jackets often are cuffed and tend to have a shorter rise.

The fit of a man's suit is also determined by its drop. The **drop** of a suit is the difference between the measurement of the chest of the jacket and the waist of the pants. A 6-inch drop is fairly standard in men's suits in the United States. A greater-than-average drop of 7 to 9 inches provides a good fit for a man with a highly developed chest and trim waist (sometimes called an *athletic cut*). A smaller-than-average drop is recommended for men with larger waists than chests. Another designation is *gentlemen's cut,* with ample room to accommodate a figure with a spreading waistline.

Bras.   Well-fitted bras are essential for comfort and to provide a smooth foundation for outer clothing. Bras require special attention during fitting.

A well-fitted bra provides proper support for all the wearer's activities. Because bodies and busts come in many shapes and sizes, various styles and brands should be tried until good fit is achieved. Seamed bras provide more support than seamless stretch bras; generally, the more seams and stitchings, the firmer the support. A large bust often requires the support of an *underwire,* a plastic or wire support under the cup. *Minimizer* bras press the breasts to the sides rather than lifting them outward, making the bustline appear smaller. A small bust may be enhanced by *maximizer* bras with an underwire, light fiberfill lining, and/or foam padding. When fitting a bra, look for the following:

1. The support of a bra should come from under the cups, not from the straps. Bra straps should rest comfortably on the shoulders without digging into the flesh. The bra should stay in position when the wearer lifts her arms.
2. The lower edge, or *band,* of the bra should be straight around the body and parallel to the floor. If it rides up, it does not provide proper support.
3. The band should be snug but not so tight that it is uncomfortable. There should not be a bulge above or below the band.
4. The wearer should lean forward so the bust lies naturally in the cups of the bra. If the cups are not fully filled, a smaller cup size is indicated. If there is a bulge of flesh above the cup, a larger cup size

is needed. The center of the bra between the cups should lie flat against the sternum.
5. If the bra contains an underwire, it should rest against the rib cage, *not* the bust. Underwire bras should be carefully fitted, because a poorly fitted underwire is not only extremely uncomfortable but can damage delicate tissue.

Fitting Special Markets

From infancy to old age, the human body changes, often requiring special fitting. Various life circumstances also require special fitting for some people. Attention to the fit of one's clothing can increase self-confidence by flattering the wearer and provides greater comfort and convenience for people at all stages of life and in all circumstances. (For aesthetic and functional design details appropriate for these groups of individuals, see Chapter 5.)

Children.   Infants are born with heads two thirds their adult size. Rapid growth enables the infant to double its height and triple its weight in the first year of life, but the growth of its head continues to outpace the growth of its body. Because infants' and children's heads are disproportionately large in comparison to their bodies, their pullover (crew) necklines can frequently be too small. More than 5 pounds of pressure may occur when sliding a neckline over the head, and this causes discomfort (McVey, 1984). To avoid this problem but maintain a close fit at the neckline, lapped, snapped, or buttoned neckline openings may be added to facilitate comfortable dressing and undressing. Clothing must provide adequate ease to accommodate a diaper and ease for activities like learning to sit, crawl, and walk.

Toddlers also grow rapidly, but more slowly than infants. They grow faster in height than in circumference, causing them to lose their "baby fat" and become more muscular. They have short necks, round chests, and prominent abdomens. Clothing must provide enough ease in the seat, armscyes, pant legs, and crotch for the extremely active toddler without being so loose or long that it gets in the way.

Preschoolers continue to grow more in height than in circumference. Their abdomens decrease in size and their shoulders get broader. They require clothing that allows ease of movement for their constant activity.

Infants and preschoolers have short arms and legs in proportion to their bodies. Obviously, young children's bodies are not proportioned like those of adults. Patternmakers must recognize the differences in order to produce childrenswear that fits properly. Childrenswear is frequently cut in incorrect proportions for the child it is intended to fit; the arms and legs are cut in proportions that look right to adults when compared to the size of the garment, rather than in proportion to the body of the child. Such garments are purchased by consumers because they have proportions that look like clothing for miniature adults. These *grandmother clothes*, so-called because grandmothers are often the ones who cannot resist buying them, are often purchased as gifts without the child trying them on first. Such garments are rarely returned; therefore, the manufacturer does not receive many complaints and continues to produce the same ill fit in the next season's line (McVey, 1984).

Elementary school children are proportioned similarly to adults. Growth slows somewhat, with the child continuing to grow faster in height than in circumference.

Growth speeds up as children approach puberty. Their legs, arms, and feet grow most rapidly. As girls mature, their hips and shoulders broaden, their waistlines become smaller, and eventually their busts develop. Boys grow taller and broader in the shoulders and chest. Girls mature earlier than boys, but their growth slows or stops after sexual maturity. Boys mature later, but continue to grow in height and weight through their early twenties. The rapid growth of adolescents causes them to outgrow their clothing quickly.

Pregnant Women. Pregnant women have special fitting problems. During the first trimester, few changes are evident except for slightly larger breasts. During the second trimester, the waistline begins to rise and expand. As the waistline expands, the curvature of the lower spine increases to help balance the body. The waistline continues to rise until a few weeks before the baby is born, when it becomes lower. Hips and thighs increase in size. The hands, legs, and feet may swell. Garments for pregnant women must be larger in circumference through the bust, waist, hips, and thighs, and longer in front to accommodate the protruding abdomen and increased curvature of the spine.

Older Adults. The bodies of adults may continue to change as they age, although these changes depend somewhat on heredity and can be somewhat postponed by proper diet and exercise. Weight gain is typical of many middle-aged adults. The aging of women often is accompanied by an increase in bust, waist, hip, and thigh measurements, as the rib cage expands and the abdomen rounds out; this often occurs more dramatically due to hormonal changes following menopause. Also, due to changes in muscle tone, the bustline is often lower, but this can be controlled somewhat by a well-fitted support bra. The shoulders may round slightly or greatly. These changes require more length and width in the back bodice and less in the front to fit the figure smoothly. Men's aging often is accompanied by an increase in waist and hip measurements and a larger abdomen. As muscle tone decreases, men's and women's buttocks tend to flatten, requiring less length and width in the back of pants and skirts, with more in the front abdomen area. In fact, some elderly women have reported wearing elastic-waist pull-on pants *backwards* to achieve somewhat better fit.

Older adults may lose the weight they gained in middle age. Legs and arms may lose their shape as muscle tone decreases. Longer skirts, pants, and sleeves usually are preferred to short ones. Elderly people can become several inches shorter than their earlier adult height because of reduced cartilage in their spinal columns due to general aging and osteoporosis. Osteoporosis may lead to a dowager's hump, with the head forward, hollow chest, and increased neck circumference. *V* necklines, but not low ones, tend to be most comfortable and attractive. Women require lower bustline shaping in garments. Garments with soft fullness over the bust that do not accentuate the bustline are most flattering. Raglan or kimono sleeves provide maximum freedom of movement. Older adults find separates more comfortable than garments with waistline seams. Garments that pull on over the head or close in front are preferable to those that close in back. A garment should not fit so loosely that it catches on things or becomes a fire hazard near burners or heaters.

Heavy People. Heavier-than-average people, like anyone else, require clothing that looks good and fits well. Too-loose or too-tight clothing draws attention to a person's size. There is not a single solution for fitting heavy people because they may be large all over or they may be top heavy or bottom heavy. However, heavy men tend to be largest through the abdomen. Heavy women tend to have a lower bustline. They may find raglan and kimono sleeves without distinct armscye seams more flattering and more comfortable than set-in sleeves. Dresses without waistline seams eliminate the need to locate the less distinct waist and draw attention away from its circumference and the protruding abdomen. Garments that pull on over the head or close in front are preferable to those that close in back. Men and women may find slightly loose *V* necklines and open, flat collars more comfortable and more flattering than very high, closely fitted ones. Shoulder pads may help to visually balance people who are heavy.

People with Physical Disabilities. Other individuals who may have special fitting needs are those who have physical disabilities. They are not easily put into one category because their needs vary greatly; depending on their particular needs, they require clothing that adapts to their patterns of movement. For example, people using crutches or walkers require extra ease across the back shoulder area of the garment and through the upper part of the sleeves to allow them to move the crutches. Their shirts and blouses need to be cut longer to stay tucked; overblouses are perhaps a better choice. Skirts may need to be hemmed to correct the tilt caused by the changed posture. The garments of crutch users need to be cut high under the arm to prevent abrasion.

People who use wheelchairs also require extra ease across the back shoulder area of the garment and through the upper part of the sleeves. This gives them a longer reach and allows them to operate the wheelchair manually. Short jackets are more comfortable for the seated figure. Lower-body garments should be cut shorter in front and longer in back to accommodate the seated figure comfortably without bunching up in front in the lap area (Figure 6–13). If a person must use a wheelchair for years, the waist and hips enlarge, the front torso shortens, the back torso lengthens, and the shoulders may become broader from operating the wheelchair. The fit of their clothing needs to accommodate these physical changes. If necessary, clothing can be fit to smoothly cover leg or foot deformities or braces. However, clothing must not be so long or loose that it gets in the way of the operation of the wheelchair.

Nursing care patients require roomy clothing because they sit or lie down most of the time. Tight clothes may bind, cut off circulation, and restrict movement. However, clothing that fits too loosely can bunch up uncomfortably, catch on things, and not be pleasing to the wearer.

Thousands of people have a problem with incontinence, a partial or total loss of bowel and/or bladder control. Full garments are desirable because they conceal absorbent pads, waterproof pants, or other collection devices. If the wearer needs assistance in changing pads, clothing should be easy to remove and replace. Zippered pant legs or otherwise easy access to catheters is important.

Women who have had a mastectomy, or surgical removal of the breast(s), require garments with necklines and sleeves that fit to conceal the affected areas. Garments may require padding in addition to the prosthesis, or replacement body part, to fill in any hollow areas. Garments should be designed and constructed to allow moving and reaching without binding and chafing the sensitive surgical area.

1 Seated shape, with higher back, curved lap

2 Elasticized waistband for secure comfort

3 Inside wrist loops for easy pull-on

4 Deep fly zipper

5 Longer pant length

6 Low pocket

Figure 6–13 Clothing for wheelchair users. (Courtesy of Aviano U.S.A., 1199 Acaso, Suite K, Camarillo, CA 93012. 805-484-8138.)

SUMMARY

Manufacturers who develop consistent and meaningful sizing systems satisfy consumer expectations in the search for garments that fit. Most manufacturers loosely base their current size labeling on ASTM's standard tables of body measurements or the U.S. voluntary size standards that were established in the 1940s. Efforts are underway to update the tables of body measurements for both men and women aged 18–55. Childrenswear sizes are divided into infants', toddlers', children's, girls', and boys' categories. Use height and weight charts and body measurements when sizing childrenswear. Womenswear sizes are divided into four basic merchandising classifications:

juniors, misses, petites, and large sizes or plus sizes (talls is sometimes a fifth category). The three basic womenswear body types/size classifications include junior, misses, and, women's (with petites and talls available within each type). The numerical sizes within these categories correlate to a set of body measurements which often differ from one manufacturer to another. Men's sizes are usually expressed as body measurements, making them more meaningful to consumers than are women's sizes. For example, jacket sizes are based on chest measurements and height, shirt sizes on neck circumference and sleeve length, and pants sizes on waist and inseam measurements.

Lettered sizing (S, M, L, XL) is used in many apparel categories. It is more suitable to knit garments and those not requiring an exact fit than for woven and tailored garments. Lettered sizing eliminates fine differences in sizing and is more economical for the manufacturer and retailer because it requires the production and merchandising of fewer sizes.

Fit is influenced by fashion trends, personal preferences, and the intended end use of the garment. Fit is evaluated based on five elements: grain, set, line, balance, and ease. The lengthwise grain generally should run parallel to the center front and center back of the garment and the center of the sleeve. The crosswise grain should run perpendicular to center front and center back at the bust/chest and hip levels. Good set and balance refer to a smooth fit with no undesirable wrinkles. The lines of the garment should follow the silhouette and circumference lines of the body. Garments that are balanced appear symmetrical from side to side and front to back. Garments require adequate fitting ease to provide comfort and allow room for movement. Additional ease for style reasons is design ease.

Good fit is the result of the manufacturer's knowledge of target market characteristics and needs, careful engineering, design and production of garments, and quality assurance. The shoulder and chest are the most critical areas to fit in upper-body garments. The neckline, collar, and lapels should fit smoothly. Armscyes should be comfortable. The hipline and abdomen area are the most critical area to fit in lower-body garments. The waistline should be comfortable. Crotch length and crotch depth are important in bifurcated garments. The length of the garment, especially pant leg and sleeve lengths, is important to consumer satisfaction.

Fit must be adapted to the changes people experience as they age. Children are proportioned differently from adults, and their clothing should fit accordingly. Necklines should be large enough to fit over infants' heads without causing discomfort. Sleeves and pant legs should be relatively short in comparison to the body of the garment. Young children grow faster in height than in circumference. Adolescents grow rapidly throughout the teenage years, with girls gaining height faster than boys.

Special markets, including maternity, older adults, heavy people, and people with physical disabilities, also require fit adaptation. It is important that clothing for people with special needs appear similar to what the rest of the population wears.

Sizing and Fit Checklist

If you can answer yes to each of these questions regarding the garment you are evaluating, it fits well.

✓ Does the labeled size relate to the body measurements the garment fits?

✓ Does the garment set on the figure smoothly without wrinkling?

✓ Do the lines of the garment follow the lines of the body?

✓ Is the garment evenly balanced?

✓ Does the garment have adequate ease without having too much?

✓ Was the fit model dressed during the fitting as the customer will be when the garment is worn later (undergarments, shoes, etc.)?

✓ Does the shoulder slope of the garment match that of the wearer's shoulders?

✓ Does the armscye seam fall at the end of the wearer's shoulder?

✓ Does the shoulder seam lie on top of the wearer's shoulder?

✓ Does the garment contain darts or ease in the back of the shoulders?

✓ Do darts point toward, and end about one inch from, the crown of the body curve?

✓ Do the shoulders and chest of jackets and other upper-body garments fit smoothly and comfortably?

✓ Do the hips of skirts, pants, and lower-body garments fit smoothly and comfortably without pulling or riding up?

✓ Is the neckline/collar comfortably sized without gaping?

✓ Are pullover necklines large enough to fit over the head?

✓ Does the shirt collar extend 1/2 inch above the jacket collar?

✓ Are the armscyes fitted without chafing?

✓ Does the sleeve hang naturally from the armhole?

✓ Does the waist fall at the natural waist or desired waist level?

✓ Is the crotch high enough for the wearer to walk easily and low enough to avoid discomfort when sitting?

✓ Is the crotch curved the same shape as the wearer's body?

✓ Does the garment length flatter the wearer and reflect current fashion?

✓ Does the tip of the necktie reach the belt buckle?

✓ Do long sleeves hit at the wrist bone when the arm is bent slightly?

✓ Do the shirt sleeves extend about 1/2 inch beyond the jacket sleeves?

✓ Do the pant legs skim the tops of the shoes or break slightly?

New Terms

If you can define each of these terms and differentiate between related terms, you have gained a good working vocabulary for discussing the topics in this chapter. The terms are listed in the order in which they appear in this chapter.

sizing
vanity sized
size classification
numbered sizing
National Institute of Standards and Technology (NIST)
pictogram
lettered sizing
one-size-fits-all sizing
childrenswear
infants'/babies' sizes
toddlers' sizes
children's sizes
girls' sizes
boys' sizes
womenswear
outerwear
dress size
misses/missy sizes
petite
tall
women's sizes
tall women's
women's petite
junior sizes
junior petite
tall junior
double ticketing
underwear
lingerie/intimate apparel
bra size
cup size
menswear
men's clothing
sportswear
furnishings
men's sizes
young men's sizes
fit

kiosk
form fitting
fit model
grain
set
line
balance
ease
fitting ease
design ease
oversized
shoulder slope
collar slope
spread
bifurcated
crotch length
rise/crotch depth
sweep
break
canted
American/standard cut
European cut
British cut
drop

Review Questions

1. What are some of the problems consumers have with apparel sizing? What are some possible solutions?

2. Discuss the advantages and disadvantages of lettered sizing (S, M, L, XL) versus numerical sizing.

3. List and describe the four size classifications of women's outerwear.

4. List the body part/parts that are measured to size the following women's garments: dresses, coats, blouses, skirts, pants, bras, panties, full slips, half slips, and sleepwear.

5. List the body part/parts that are measured to size the following men's garments: jackets, slacks, shirts, sweaters, undershirts, and undershorts.

6. What are the major size classifications of childrenswear?

7. How is fit evaluated using the five elements of fit?

8. How are wrinkles used to diagnose fit problems?

9. Explain the difference between fitting ease and design ease.

10. What is the most critical area to fit when fitting upper-body garments? lower-body garments?

11. List the criteria for fitting:
   a. shoulders
   b. bust/chest
   c. neckline
   d. collar

e. lapels
f. armholes
g. sleeves
h. waist
i. hips
j. crotch
k. garment length of
  jackets
  other upper-body garments
  sleeves
  skirts
  pants

12. Compare and contrast the three basic suit cuts for men.
13. Trace the physical development of a person from infancy through old age and explain the impact of physical changes on fit.
14. What are the special challenges in fitting pregnant women? older adults? heavy people? people with physical challenges?

Activities

1. Measure three garments of the same numbered or lettered size and the same general style, but different brands. Take measurements in each area of the garment that is important for good fit. Compare the measurements of the three garments and explain any differences you find.
2. Survey five male and five female friends about their satisfaction/dissatisfaction with apparel sizing. Do you detect different levels of satisfaction between males and females?
3. Study size specifications and methods of measure from different manufacturers. Do the measured dimensions of the same labeled size differ? If so, by how much? How do methods of measure differ?
4. Visit a department store or look at a mass merchandiser's catalog. How are size classifications used as a marketing tool? How did they influence store or catalog layout?
5. Using a child you know, compare the size indicated by his or her age to the size indicated by his or her height and weight. Why should height and weight be used rather than age to decide a child's size?
6. Evaluate the fit of a classmate's clothing based on grain, set, line, balance, and ease.
7. Visit a nursing home or a center for people with physical disabilities. Select one or two individuals. Observe how the clients' clothing fits and ask them what their main problems are in trying to find clothing that fits.
8. Compare maternity clothes to regular clothes for women. What differences in fit, if any, are incorporated into the maternity clothes?
9. Compare the proportions of clothing for toddlers to those of clothing for adults. What, if any, are the differences and why?
10. Study a costume history book. How has fashion influenced the perception of good fit during the past 200 years? In what periods was a loose fit desirable? Tight fit? What variations have occurred in the length considered appropriate for various garments and garment parts?
11. Visit a store or a custom tailor shop where fine suits are sold. Find a suit in each of these cuts:
   a. American/standard
   b. European
   c. British
   d. unconstructed

   How are the suits the same? Different?
12. From a magazine or catalog, identify five examples of garments containing only fitting ease and five examples of garments containing both design and fitting ease.
13. Have five people who claim to wear the same labeled size try on the same garment. What variations in fit are found between these individuals? What challenges does this pose for the apparel industry?

Fabric: The Essential Quality Indicator

Chapter Objectives

1. Define the fabric performance features that affect garment performance, and understand the test methods used to evaluate these features.
2. Review the physical features of fabrics: fibers, yarns, fabrication, dyes, prints, and finishes.
3. Discuss the impact of a fabric's physical features on fabric performance.

Of all the components used to produce ready-to-wear, fabric makes the greatest single contribution to the cost and quality of a garment. There is a direct correlation between fabric quality and apparel quality (Mehta, 1984). Although high-quality fabric does not guarantee a high-quality garment, fabric provides a foundation for quality. The fabric interacts with other garment components and with the design and construction of the garment to affect overall quality. Therefore, the evaluation of fabric is integral to assessing apparel quality.

As discussed in previous chapters, fabric quality is assessed at all stages of apparel production. Testing is conducted before making a purchase to determine if the fabric meets appropriate specifications. A percentage of all incoming fabric is inspected as a routine quality inspection procedure. Informal inspection is conducted on the spreading table and as the garments are being assembled. Fabric is continually being assessed in one way or another during the entire apparel production process. This constant assessment is a key indicator to the important role fabric plays in maintaining quality.

Underlying fabrics found inside garments (interfacings, linings, underlinings, and interlinings) are discussed in Chapter 8. However, the aesthetic and functional performance considerations of the main body fabric discussed in this chapter apply to underlying fabrics as well as to other findings and trim items.

Although this chapter is no substitute for a basic textiles course, it serves as a review of the physical features and associated performance features of fabric and findings. It also relates fabric to garment performance. For detailed information on textiles, refer to a basic textiles book (see Related Resources: Fabric). For definitions of common textiles terms, refer to *ASTM Standard Terminology Relating to Textiles D-123* and *ASTM Standard Terminology Related to Fabric D-4850.*

FABRIC PERFORMANCE

Fabric is the textile material from which apparel manufacturers produce ready-to-wear garments. The performance of the fabric does not necessarily predict the performance of the finished garment, but the two are strongly related. The right fabric is required for the garment to meet aesthetic and functional performance expectations. Manufacturers establish the required aesthetic and functional performance standards for a fabric based on many factors (see Chapter 3). These factors include the design of the garment, the intended end use of the garment, fashion trends, consumer preferences, cost limitations, and the target market profile chosen by the company. For example, a loose, flowing design calls for a soft, fluid fabric. A work uniform requires a strong, durable fabric. Consumers may favor knits or wovens, depending on current trends.

Establishing Fabric Specifications

The apparel manufacturer purchases fabric from the supplier according to predetermined specifications. Establishing specifications for the fabric communicates expectations to the textile mill. In the absence of clearly defined specifications, the apparel manufacturer might receive raw materials that do not meet the desired end use performance standards of the garment. Most manufacturers establish their own performance standards for raw materials based upon their knowledge of and experience with the type of product they are producing.

ASTM Specifications. Other companies depend upon the fabric performance standards established by ASTM, commonly referred to as "industry standards." ASTM, through the efforts of Committee D-13, publishes performance specifications for selected textile fabrics; for example, men's and boys' woven dress shirt fabrics and women's and girl's blouse and dress fabrics (see Table 7–1). Some manufacturers and mills use these specifications as a starting point

for establishing their own specifications. Others use them exactly as written.

ASTM textile fabric specifications are updated on a regular basis and therefore can be considered relatively current. The term relatively is used due to the fast-paced nature of the fashion industry. Some fabrics, primarily those used in fashion fads, will not exist long enough for ASTM to develop specifications.

Worth Street Rules. Some apparel manufacturers depend upon the *Worth Street Textile Market Rules* for setting fabric specifications. The Worth Street Rules establish the procedures for buying and selling textiles by defining specifications and tolerances for standard types of fabric. Unfortunately the Worth Street Rules have not been updated in recent years and use of them for setting specifications is declining. *Worth Street Textile Market Rules* is available for about $6 from the **American Textile Manufacturers Institute (ATMI)**, 1801 K Street N.W., Suite 900, Washington, D.C. 20006. URL: http://www.atmi.org.

Ease of Production. In the labor-intensive apparel industry, raw materials must be as easy and convenient to work with as possible. Apparel manufacturers avoid many construction difficulties by establishing certain fabric specifications for the handling ease of the fabric. One example is fabrics cut with an automated cutter. The vacuum table used in this cutting process produces a considerable suction that stabilizes the cloth during the actual cutting process. Fabric cut in this manner needs to have enough sizing in it to prevent the cloth from being sucked into the suction table bristles and therefore stretched during cutting. An appropriate specification for hand or stiffness will prevent this stretching but will ensure the fabric is not too stiff for the operators to handle. Setting appropriate specifications requires careful study of all aspects of apparel production and consumer usage.

The ease or difficulty with which the manufacturer cuts, sews, and finishes a garment influences both quality and costs. For example, it is difficult to produce a garment from a fabric with a slick surface. Such a fabric causes production difficulties and requires extra time, skilled operators, and/or special equipment to achieve quality results. Weak fabrics, fabrics that ravel, and fabrics that build up static electricity pose additional production problems. Because of the effect on manufacturing costs and quality, a fabric's ease of production ultimately affects the consumer in the form of the retail price paid and value received.

The Kawabata System. In an effort to quantify the statement of difficult-to-measure fabric performance specifications, Sueo Kawabata of Japan developed the **Kawabata Evaluation System for Fabrics (KES)**

Table 7–1 Fabric performance specifications available from American Society for Testing and Materials (ASTM)

Standard	End Use
D 3135-87	Bonded, Fused, and Laminated Apparel Fabrics
D 3477-84	Men's and Boys' Woven Dress Shirt Fabrics
D 3562-83	Men's and Boy's Woven Dress Topcoat and Dress Overcoat Fabrics
D 3597-81	Woven Upholstery Fabrics—Plain, Tufted or Flocked
D 3600-81	Men's and Boys' Woven Rainwear and All-Purpose, Water-Repellent Coat Fabrics
D 3655-81	Men's and Women's Sliver Knitted Overcoat and Jacket Fabrics
D 3778-81	Women's and Girls' Drycleanable Woven Dress Coat Fabrics
D 3779-81	Women's and Girls' Woven Rainwear and All-Purpose, Water-Repellant Coat Fabrics
D 3780-79	Men's and Boys' Woven Dress Suit Fabrics and Woven Sportswear Jacket, Slack, and Trouser Fabrics
D 3781-79	Men's and Boys' Knitted Rainwear and All-Purpose, Water-Repellent Coat Fabrics
D 3782-79	Men's and Boys' Knitted Dress Suit Fabrics and Knitted Sportswear Jacket, Slack, and Trouser Fabrics
D 3783-79	Woven Flat Lining Fabrics for Men's and Boys' Apparel
D 3784-81	Men's and Boys' Woven Bathrobe and Dressing Gown Fabrics
D 3785-81	Woven Necktie and Scarf Fabrics
D 3819-81	Men's and Boys' Woven Pajama Fabrics
D 3820-81	Men's and Boys' Woven Underwear Fabrics
D 3821-81	Woven Terry Household Kitchen and Bath Towel Fabrics
D 3887-80	Knitted Fabrics
D 3994-81	Men's, Women's and Children's Woven Swimwear Fabrics
D 3995-81	Men's and Women's Knitted Career Apparel Fabrics: Dress and Vocational
D 3996-81	Men's, Women's, and Children's Knit Swimwear Fabrics
D 4035-81	Knitted Necktie and Scarf Fabrics
D 4038-81	Women's and Girls' Woven Dress and Blouse Fabrics
D 4109-82	Men's and Boys' Woven Coverall, Dungaree, Overall, and Shop-Coat Fabrics
D 4110-82	Men's and Boys' Knitted Bathrobe, Dressing Gown, and Pajama Fabrics
D 4114-82	Woven Flat Lining Fabrics for Women's and Girls' Apparel
D 4115-82	Women's and Girls' Knitted and Woven Dress Glove Fabrics
D 4116-82	Women's and Girls' Knitted and Woven Corset-Girdle-Combination Fabrics
D 4117-82	Women's and Girls' Woven Robe, Negligee, Nightgown, Pajama, Slip, and Lingerie Fabrics
D 4118-82	Women's Woven Coverall, Dungaree, Overall, and Shop Coat Fabric
D 4119-82	Men's and Boys' Knitted Dress Shirt Fabrics
D 4154-83	Men's and Boys' Knitted and Woven Beachwear and Sports Shirt Fabrics
D 4155-83	Women's and Girls' Woven Sportswear, Shorts, Slacks, and Suiting Fabrics
D 4156-83	Women's and Girls' Knitted Sportswear Fabrics
D 4232-83	Men's and Women's Dress and Vocational Career Apparel Fabrics
D 4233-83	Women's and Girls' Knitted and Woven Brassiere Fabrics
D 4234-83	Women's and Girls' Knitted Robe, Negligee, Nightgown, Pajama, Slip, and Lingerie Fabrics
D 4235-83	Women's and Girls' Knitted Blouse and Dress Fabrics

(Fortess, 1985). The Kawabata System can be used to objectively rate fabric properties, both aesthetic and functional. These ratings describe aesthetic dimensions that were formerly described only subjectively. Kawabata developed the system by correlating the physical measurements of various fabric attributes to the subjective perceptions of human judges. The Kawabata System ratings predict the suitability of a fabric for mass production, including its ease of construction and the finished appearance of garments made from it. However, the Kawabata System is a complex system of tests requiring considerable time, equipment, and training and therefore has not been generally accepted by the industry.

FAST. An Australian system called **Fabric Assessment by Simple Testing (FAST)** has been drawing attention as a less costly alternative to the Kawabata System. FAST measures only four main fabric characteristics critical to garment appearance and performance. The fabric is tested for these four factors: compression, bending, extension, and dimensional stability (these terms are defined later in the chapter). The tests require a minimum of time, equipment, and training. FAST can be used to estimate a fabric's hand and tailorability based on a computer's interpretation of the test results; thus, it is an economical approach. FAST helps manufacturers identify potential problems with fabrics and avoid costly fabric pitfalls such as stretching during cutting by testing a sample of the fabric before purchasing it. Preliminary data show FAST to be a satisfactory method, although not as sophisticated and detailed as the Kawabata System (Rees, 1990).

Defects. Most apparel manufacturers inspect incoming fabric for defects. Defects detract from the aesthetic appearance of a garment and sometimes from its functional performance. Common defects called **mill flaws** include broken, knotted, or thick *ends and picks;* barré (streaks); foreign material; spots; soil; and holes. Other defects include bowing and incorrect skewing; shading; and printing that is smudged, off-grain, or out of registration (these terms are defined later in the chapter). Also, part of the fabric inspection process is the verification of **put-up,** the amount of yardage on the roll.

In recent years, the implementation of the *just-in-time* process has made it more difficult to inspect raw materials at the apparel production location. Inventories are not being maintained on the premises; therefore the cloth is needed as soon as it arrives. This process has necessitated the development of new methods to maintain control over flaws and defects. Some manufacturers are negotiating with suppliers for increased sophistication in their suppliers' inspection systems. Some are eliminating inspection and depending totally on the supplier's existing inspection system. Others are monitoring the quantity of defects and flaws themselves and then charging excess amounts back to the supplier.

Flagging Defects. The majority of apparel manufacturers depend upon the fabric mills to identify and mark major defects in fabric. A **major defect** is defined as one that is longer than 9 inches and is located more than 2 inches away from the selvage edge of the cloth. The mills inspect all rolls of fabric before shipping them to the apparel manufacturers. It is not cost effective for the mills to locate and cut out all major defects. Therefore a **flagging system** is used to alert the apparel manufacturer so the spreaders can remove the flagged flaws as they spread the cloth. This system involves placing a flag along the selvage edge of the fabric wherever a major defect is located. The flags can vary from simple plastic tacks to sophisticated metallic markers that can be read electronically by a scanner.

The demands of spreading fabric correctly combined with the monotony of manual fabric inspection often allow flags to go by unnoticed. For this reason, sophisticated electronically scanned flagging systems were developed. As the fabric is being spread on the cutting table, an electronic eye on the spreader will emit a signal whenever a defect flag is found. The person operating the spreader can then stop spreading and remove the yardage containing the flaw.

Depending upon the type and quality level of cloth used, some manufacturers make no attempt to cut out flaws. Instead, they have found it more cost effective to inspect all the finished garments and reject those with major mill flaws. Small defects are not flagged for the same reason. It is more cost effective to either repair the flaw in garment form or classify the garment as a second than it is to stop a spreading machine and remove full width yardage from the lay.

Manufacturers of high-price apparel may consider any mill flaw unacceptable in the finished garment. Manufacturers of low- and moderate-price garments may accept minor flaws and flaws located in low-visibility areas. For example, a flaw in a shirttail is less objectionable than one on the collar or chest. Low-visibility areas can include seam and hem allowances and facings and interlinings. See Figure 7–1 for an example of acceptable mill flaw locations.

Some manufacturers have developed extensive Mill Flaw Repair programs. Mill flaw repair is commonly carried out in textile mills, hosiery plants, and jeans plants. In the apparel industry, it is the process of upgrading a second quality garment to a first quality garment. Highly skilled, specially trained operators repair selected, small mill flaws in finished garments. These repairs are permanent and cannot be detected when correctly performed.

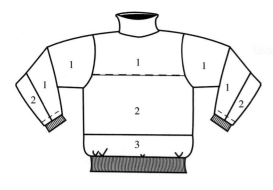

1) High-Visibility Area
2) Moderate Visibility Area
3) Low-Visibility Area

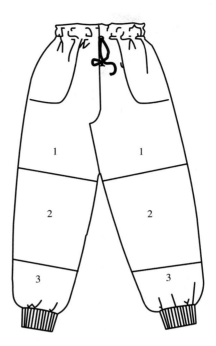

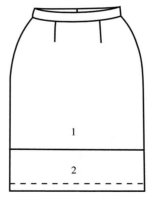

Figure 7–1 Fabric defect guide: level of visibility determines acceptability of fabric flaws; high-visibility areas should contain no visible flaws.

Four Point System. A number of fabric grading systems are used in the industry, including the *Four Point System, Ten Point System,* and the *Graniteville System.* All of these systems serve as methods to quantify the number and severity of fabric defects found during an inspection. The **Four Point System** is the most popular fabric grading system used in the apparel industry; it is endorsed by the American Society for Quality Control (ASQC) and the U.S. government. The system is used to assign penalty points to a fabric based on the number and size of defects. A fabric that receives four or fewer points per linear yard (or 40 points per 100 yards) is typically considered first quality. A fabric receives more points if it has more and/or more serious defects compared with a fabric that receives fewer points. Manufacturers producing high-price apparel usually specify fabrics with fewer points per 100 yards than do manufacturers of low-price apparel. If fabric inspectors detect more points per 100 yards than were specified, they may return the substandard fabric to the textile mill and acquire replacement goods. More commonly, because of short lead times, the apparel manufacturer will use the fabric and issue a chargeback to the mill for the excessive number of second quality garments created by the excessive number of mill flaws.

Apparel manufacturers communicate their standards to fabric mills. Mills *grade* or classify the quality level of their fabric and match the standards of the apparel manufacturer with the grade of fabric that meets those standards. This enables the mill to send piece goods of a known quality level to the appropriate customers.

Aesthetic Performance of Fabric

The aesthetic performance or attractiveness of fabric refers to the appearance of the fabric as it complements the appearance of the garment. Fabric plays an important part in the aesthetic performance of the garment. However, fabric must be considered in concert with the design and construction of the garment because design, materials, and construction interact to produce the total aesthetic effect of the garment.

Fabric aesthetics include color, pattern, color consistency, luster, opacity, and hand. All these elements of the aesthetic performance of a raw material are difficult to describe because of their subjective nature; they do not lend themselves to objective measurement. For example, it is more difficult to accurately specify the luster of a fabric than the strength of a fabric.

Color and Pattern. Color is perhaps the single most important feature in initially attracting consumers to garments. Merchandisers, buyers, and sourcers request fabric lab dips and samples from suppliers when considering various colored and patterned fabrics. However, the "beauty" or "goodness" of a color or pattern is subjective; there are no laboratory tests for evaluating the "quality" of colors or choosing the "best" design for a patterned fabric. The aesthetic evaluation of color and pattern depends on fashion trends, personal preferences, and an awareness of design elements and principles.

Color Consistency. Achieving *color consistency* within the same garment or ensemble is important. However, it is understandably difficult to buy or dye fabrics, trims, buttons, zippers, belts, and other components—all of different raw materials—to match. For example, dyeing an acrylic knit dress and a leather belt to match requires different formulas to produce the same color in each item.

Color consistency of fabric within the same garment or outfit is also important. Fabric producers can dye only a limited number of yards of fabric in each batch, or **dye lot.** Although they make every effort to exactly duplicate the dye "recipe" each time, there are slight shade variances from dye lot to dye lot. Each dye lot is numbered to differentiate it from other dye lots. After dyeing, swatches of the fabric are inspected under specific lighting conditions, and lots of the same shade are grouped together into matching **shade lots.** This is done either manually by human experts or partially manually and partially using computerized optical scanners called *colorimeters.* Low-volume apparel manufacturers can cut all the parts of a garment or coordinated outfit from a single dye lot, while high-volume manufacturers cut from a single shade lot.

Garment pieces from the same dye lot or shade lot must be shade marked (stamped, stickered, or otherwise identified) either during spreading or after cutting so the correct pieces can be bundled and sewn together. Stickers for this purpose are occasionally seen inside garments at the point of sale as it is not cost efficient for the manufacturer to remove them. Some makers of better goods attach hang tags with dye lot numbers to finished garments so consumers can select coordinated separates of the same shade.

Shading. **Shading** refers to the absence of color consistency, when sections of fabric rolls or parts of garments or outfits differ slightly in color from one another. Shading results when various parts of the same garment or outfit are made from rolls of fabric with color variation or from fabric dyed in different dye lots. Lines built on the modular dressing concept present special challenges to maintaining color consistency. Coordinating garments purchased months apart or in different stores are expected to match, even though they come from different dye lots. Manufacturers of these lines must pay special attention to shading from batch to batch. However, even within the same dye lot or same piece of fabric there may be differences in shade caused by uneven dyeing.

Dichroism occurs when light strikes the fabric differently from one end to the other, causing a difference in shade. Corduroy, velvet, and other napped fabrics display end-to-end shading of this type. (An example was shown in Chapter 4, Figure 4–13.) End-to-end shading occurs any time the color of the fabric appears different from one end of the fabric roll or one end of the lay to the other. Side-to-side shading, shading from one selvage to the other, may occur in some fabrics. Both types of shading are most prevalent in piece-dyed fabrics and must be monitored to achieve color consistency in the finished product.

Shading can be subtle or noticeable, depending upon its severity. If the sleeve of a garment is from a different dye lot than the body of the garment, or if the pants of a suit are cut from a different dye lot than the jacket, even a slight difference in fabric shade is

Figure 7–2 Shading evident in body and sleeves of sweatshirt.

noticeable in the finished garment or outfit. Shading detracts from the appearance of a garment, especially if it appears at a focal point like a front band, yoke, collar, or sleeve (Figure 7–2).

Although both sides of a fabric may look the same, most fabrics have a technical *face* (front or *right side*) and *back* (*wrong side*) that should be observed in the spreading and cutting of a garment. Most fabrics have a definite face and back; however, some fabrics must be examined closely to differentiate the two. If this difference is not observed when the fabric is spread, cut, and sewn, some or all of the garment pieces may be sewn together with the wrong side of the fabric on the outside of the garment. This can cause shading in the finished garment and is the reason a shade marking system is frequently used.

Metamerism. **Metamerism** refers to the apparent change in a color due to a change in lighting. For example, colors appear different in daylight than they do under incandescent or fluorescent light; components that appear to match under one light may clash under different lighting. This makes it difficult to control color consistency because consumers wear their clothing in many different types of lights. Mills can minimize the effects of metamerism through careful dye selection. To be on the safe side, however, it is recommended that consumers match colors under the type of light in which the clothes will be worn.

Luster. **Luster** is the amount of light the fabric reflects. Terms such as *dull, matte,* and *diffused* refer to fabrics with little or no luster; *shiny* and *lustrous* refer to those with high luster. Fabrics with smooth, flat surfaces tend to have great luster because a flat surface reflects more light than a surface with contours. Fiber shape, yarn construction, and finishes also impact luster.

Opacity. The **opacity** of a fabric refers to the amount of light that passes through it; opacity affects the appearance of the finished garment. Fabrics that have high light permeability and can be seen through are *sheer.* Fabrics that have low light permeability and cannot be seen through are *opaque.* Fabrics that have medium light permeability but cannot be clearly seen through are *translucent.* Fabrics with inadequate opacity for the end use of the garment require a lining or should not be used.

Hand. **Hand** is a broad term for the *kinesthetic* or movement aspects of a fabric. Hand refers not to the comfort but to the emotional sensations resulting from touching, moving, or squeezing the fabric with the human hand. Because of the difficulty in quantifying emotions, Kawabata concentrated on quantifying hand when he developed his evaluation system. The KES makes an invaluable contribution in this area because the hand of a fabric is critical to ease of garment production and to the aesthetic and functional performance of the finished garment. Apparel producers require the ability to equate various fabric hands with ease of production and to objectively specify fabric hand. Hand encompasses the following aspects of the fabric:

1. *drapability/flexibility,* or ease of bending, from *pliable/limp/fluid* (high) to *firm/stiff/crisp* (low). Drapability is the aspect perhaps most nearly synonymous with the concept of hand. It refers to how easily the fabric bends and consequently how it hangs, falls, clings, flows, sags, pleats, or gathers. Drapability is one of the most important characteristics of a fabric in achieving the desired design effect in the finished garment. The amount of drapability desirable in a fabric depends upon the garment design. For instance, tailored suits demand firm, crisp fabrics. Other designs, such as cowl necklines or harem pants, depend upon soft, drapable fabrics for the desired effect.
2. *compressibility,* or ease of squeezing, from *soft* (high) to *hard* (low).
3. *extensibility,* or ease of stretching, from *stretchy* (high) to *nonstretchy* (low)
4. *resilience,* or ability to recover from deformation, from *springy/alive* (high) to *limp* (low)
5. *density,* or weight per volume, from *compact* (high) to *loose/open* (low)
6. *surface contour/texture,* or variation in the surface, from *rough/coarse* (high) to *smooth* (low)
7. *surface friction/texture,* or surface resistance to slipping, from *harsh* (high) to *slippery* (low)
8. *thermal character,* or apparent temperature, from *cool* (high) to *warm* (low) (Annual Book of ASTM Standards).

Functional Performance of Fabric

The functional performance of a fabric refers to its utility and durability as a component of the garment. Utility includes the influence of the fabric on these garment characteristics: (1) shape retention, (2) appearance retention, (3) comfort, (4) ease of care, and (5) safety. Durability refers to the serviceability of the fabric regarding these characteristics of the garment: (1) strength, (2) abrasion resistance, and (3) resistance to degradation by chemicals and other elements of the environment.

As for aesthetic performance, the functional performance of a garment is not determined fully by the fabric. The design, materials, construction, and finish of a garment interact to determine utility and durability. For example, although fabric provides warmth, so can the design (a high collar to keep wind off the neck). And although fabric influences serviceability, so can construction (strong stitches and seams).

Dimensional Stability. One of the most important performance characteristics of a garment is **dimensional stability,** the ability of fabric and garments to maintain their original shape and size. Dimensional stability affects the function of the garment in terms of appearance retention and fit; for close-fitting garments it also affects comfort. Producing dimensionally stable garments, especially knitwear, is one of the big challenges in the textile and apparel industries.

Elongation and Elasticity. If a fabric is extensible, it **elongates** or stretches in use. (Use can be defined as during sewing or during wearing.) Permanent stretch occurs if the fabric does not return to its original dimension after refurbishing. **Elasticity** or **memory**, the fabric's ability to return to its original size after being stretched, helps maintain the garment's appearance. Elasticity is associated with quality, especially in knit fabrics. Without elasticity, garments stretch out of shape during wear and do not recover; for example, jackets with sagging elbows and pants with sagging knees exhibit a lack of elasticity. Other garments stretch when laundered; to avoid stretching they may require dry cleaning, or hand washing and *blocking* (arranging the garment in the original shape and size and allowing it to dry flat).

In general, extensibility or stretch is desirable in knit fabric and undesirable in woven fabrics. Woven fabrics remain stable in the warp direction and "give" (stretch) slightly in the fill direction. This type of stretch is appropriate and expected in woven fabrics. Garments made in woven fabrics are designed with these characteristics in mind. For example, most woven slacks are made with the leg panels and waistbands cut with the warp. This allows the cloth to elongate slightly in the fill direction, which circles the body.

Figure 7–3 T-shirts before and after multiple launderings. Laundered T-shirt exhibits shrinkage and loss of color.

The waistband, however, is placed on the body of the slacks with the warp yarns circling the body. This provides stability at the waist for a snug fit and smooth look.

Knit fabrics not only "give" in both lengthwise and crosswise directions, but they stretch considerably more than woven fabrics. Due to the structure of the knit cloth, the resulting stretch provides for a comfortable fabric that moves with the body. For this reason, knit fabrics are extremely popular today as consumers shift their emphasis from a fashionable appearance to fashionable *and* comfortable wearing apparel.

The amount of stretch or elongation in knit or woven fabrics can create problems in cutting apparel to the correct size. Excessive stretch or elongation will allow the cloth to stretch on the spreading and cutting tables or while the operator is sewing. For this reason, specifications for elongation need to be carefully planned, especially for woven garments. Knit garments, in basic styles, can be die cut instead of cut with a knife. The die cutting eliminates the horizontal force applied to the cloth as the cutting knife pushes its way through the cloth and thus prevents unnecessary stretching of the cloth.

Shrinkage. **Shrinkage** occurs when a garment or garment part becomes smaller, usually when it is laundered. Shrinkage is a major cause of consumer dissatisfaction because it not only affects the appearance of the garment but makes it uncomfortable and sometimes unwearable. Consumers have come to expect certain garments, for example, sweatshirts and T-shirts, to shrink when laundered (Figure 7-3). Many consumers attempt to compensate for shrinkage by purchasing an overly large garment so it will fit after laundering. But how much will the garment shrink? It is a guessing game.

The apparel industry recognizes that a 2 to 3% change in a garment of woven fabric, or a 3 to 5% change in a garment of knit fabric, represents a change of approximately one full size in a basic silhouette. Loose-fitting and oversized garment silhouettes are less affected. Garments that have been wet processed will shrink less after purchase than nonwashed garments.

Shrinkage results from either relaxation shrinkage or felting shrinkage. The majority of shrinkage in apparel is **relaxation shrinkage.** Fabrics can be stretched during finishing or as they are placed on rolls at the mill, as they are spread for cutting, or as the garment is sewn. Cotton fiber is easily elongated during processing but it relaxes back to its original length during laundering. Some manufactured fibers are also subject to relaxation shrinkage. As the fabric gradually relaxes to its original dimensions when the garment is washed and dried, relaxation shrinkage occurs. Relaxation shrinkage is the main reason why cotton fabrics tend to shrink as the T-shirts in Figure 7–3 did. Because they are more easily stretched in production, knit fabrics are subject to two to three times more relaxation shrinkage when laundered than are wovens (Hudson, 1988).

Another example of relaxation shrinkage occurs when the lengthwise direction of cotton garments becomes stretched during the garment finishing process. Most cotton garments are subjected to ironing or pressing after sewing. Unless the automatic presses are carefully adjusted or the manual pressing operators are careful as they smooth the cloth on the pressing machine, a considerable amount of lengthwise stretching can take place. The heat from the presses will temporarily set this stretch. This type of stretching, resulting in relaxation shrinkage, will be released once the garment is laundered. For this reason, consumers are advised not to make any alterations to garments that are too long until the items have been laundered. Quality and sewing engineers constantly battle this lengthwise stretching problem, due to variances in fabrication, pressing equipment, and human error. It is a difficult situation to control.

Felting shrinkage occurs when fibers mat together because of moisture, heat, and/or agitation. This form of progressive shrinkage is common in wool fabrics. Felting may cause a garment to shrink to half its original size, and the process is largely irreversible. Felting can be prevented by certain finishing processes.

The majority of laundering shrinkage, both relaxation and felting, occurs in the first laundering. Small amounts of additional shrinkage (called **residual shrinkage**) continue to occur in subsequent launderings, occasionally for as many as 20 or 25 cycles, but most end after 8 to 10 cycles. However, the majority of shrinkage overall takes place during the drying process, not the washing process.

It is difficult for the mill to control progressive shrinkage due to constraints in the manufacturing process. As fabric is woven, it is held securely along the selvage edges, but the beginning and end of the cloth are not secured in any way. This allows shrinkage preventative measures to be taken that control fill shrinkage more than warp shrinkage.

Torque and Skewness. **Torque** (in knits) and **skew** (in wovens) refer to fabric distortion that results when the crosswise yarns of a fabric slant from one selvage to the other rather than lying at right angles to the selvages (Figure 7–4b). Both conditions cause a rotation of the finished garment parts during laundering when the yarns relax and right themselves, returning to their original positions. Excessive torque in knits and skewness in wovens distorts garments so that they do not hang straight, sometimes to the point of causing the garments to be unwearable. Examples include twisted T-shirts and knit sweatpants with seams spiraling around the leg after laundering. Excessive torque and skew are most noticeable on pant legs due to the length of the seams involved.

Most fabric grain distortion happens when, during processing of a fabric, one selvage edge feeds faster than the other selvage edge; a *torqued* or *skewed* fabric results. Sometimes, the selvage edges feed faster than the center of the fabric. The result is a **bowed** fabric, in which the crosswise yarns arc across the fabric (Figure 7–4a).

A natural skewness occurs in 3 x 1 twill weave denim fabric—the fabric used for most blue jeans—created by the structure of the 3 x 1 twill weave. An artificial skewness is added during finishing to counteract the natural skewness. If the correct amount of skew is not added, "twisted legs" can result. Similarly, mills must compensate for the natural torque of some knits resulting from the circular knitting process to avoid twist in the finished garment (see Figure 7-5).

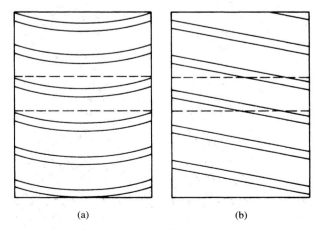

(a)   (b)

Figure 7–4 Grain defects: (a) bow and (b) torque or skew.

Figure 7–5 Torque in a knit shirt.

As with shrinkage, both torque and skewness problems do not become apparent until the garment is laundered. For this reason, it is especially important that apparel manufacturers routinely monitor the physical properties of cloth before cutting.

Appearance Retention. Fabric must maintain its original appearance for the garment to remain useful. The ability of a fabric to stay the same color; retain creases; resist wrinkling, snagging, and pilling; and withstand the heat of care processes determines whether the garment maintains its original appearance.

Colorfastness. **Colorfastness** is the ability of the fabric to retain its color (Figure 7–3). Colorfastness refers to color retention in reaction to laundering (bleach, water, detergent, heat), light, dry-cleaning solvents, sea and pool water, perspiration, and other chemicals. Colorfastness is a relative term; no garment is completely colorfast. Expect some loss of color because of the limitations of technology. However, some fabrics are much more colorfast than others. This is of particular concern when contrast colors are used on the same garment. Red fabric trim on a white windbreaker can bleed during washing if the correct red dyestuff is not used.

A loss or change in the garment's original color is a major source of consumer dissatisfaction. Consumers accept faded jeans, but most other items with colors that streak or fade are discarded as unwearable, even if structurally sound. More often color loss or change is so slight that the consumer does not notice unless it is compared back to the original color. For example, sometimes one part of a coordinated outfit is worn and laundered more than the other, causing it to fade. When the consumer wants to wear the pieces together again, they no longer match in color. Wise consumers wash both pieces together every time laundering is needed.

Lack of colorfastness may be expressed in a variety of ways

1. *Fading* refers to the lightening of a color because of the loss or breakdown of the dye. Clothes sometimes fade in the retail store under the bright lights on the selling floor or in display windows exposed to the sun. Most fading at the consumer level is due to repeated laundering, to sunlight exposure for garments worn outdoors, or to long-term storage in closets with windows.
2. *Frosting* occurs when color leaves the surface of the fabric due to abrasion. Notice it on the hems and pocket edges of denim jeans, especially those that have been stone washed. In this particular example, the frosting is a desirable characteristic. At other times, it is not desirable.
3. *Crocking* is the transfer of a fabric's color to another surface through rubbing; it occurs under dry or wet (moist) conditions. For example, the dye from a pair of unwashed blue jeans might crock onto a person's undergarments or skin.
4. *Bleeding* or *staining* is the migration of color from a wet fabric into water and sometimes from there on to another fabric. This can happen on the same garment or from one garment to another. It usually happens when the garments are left sitting in the wet condition for longer than an hour, such as when a load of clothes is left sitting in the washer for several hours before being dried.
5. *Yellowing* is the change of a base color to a very yellowed version of a color. It can occur in two ways. One is the incomplete rinsing of a garment after wet processing or home laundering. In this case, chemical or detergent residue accidentally left in the cloth causes the change in color as it reacts to heat and time. The other situation also involves chemicals left in the cloth, in this case, those introduced in the form of fabric softeners. When exposed to heat and time, some softener chemicals turn yellow. In both cases, thorough laundering of the garments removes most of the yellowed appearance.

As in dimensional stability, there are no regulations requiring the labeling of colorfastness of garments. Some garment labels include the word *colorfast,* but this has no objective definition and is a marketing tool used to appeal to consumers' desire for colorfast garments.

Wrinkle Resistance. Creases appear in most fabrics when pressure, heat, and/or moisture are applied to the folded or compressed fabric. *Wrinkle resistance,*

Figure 7–6 Random tumbling pill tester. Propeller-like blades tumble specimen to accelerate pilling. (Courtesy of Levi Strauss & Company.)

the ability of a fabric to avoid undesirable creases, is generally a desirable feature (except when a wrinkled look is fashionable). The fabric's resilience determines whether or not a garment that becomes wrinkled will remain wrinkled, affecting both appearance and ease of care. In other cases, *crease retention,* the ability of a fabric to retain creases, is desirable. Crease retention keeps the style crease on pant legs and the creases of pressed pleats sharp.

Synthetic fibers have a natural tendency for wrinkle resistance that natural fibers do not have. Often chemical treatments are applied to 100% cotton fabrics to make them more wrinkle resistant. This is effective if the process is carried out correctly. However, the chemicals used may cause the cotton fibers to become brittle. This brittleness decreases the strength of the cloth and shortens the life cycle of the garment.

Snag and Pill Resistance. Snagging and pilling detract from a garment's appearance and its usefulness. **Snags** are pulls in the fabric made when the yarns catch on a sharp object. **Pills** are fuzz balls, or balls of tangled fibers that form on the surface and are held there by one or more fibers (Figures 7–6 and 7–7). Pills may form all over a garment, but are likely to be the most noticeable where the garment receives abrasion for example, in the underarm area, inside collars, in the inner thigh area, and on sleeves and cuffs, (The collar in Chapter 12, Figure 12–11 shows pilling.) Some fabrics have a greater resistance than others to snagging and pilling.

Consumer focus groups have indicated that small pills over the entire surface of knit garments, while

not desirable, are acceptable and are worn on a daily basis. Pills on abraded areas of woven apparel are not as well accepted.

Heat Resistance. **Heat resistance** is the ability to withstand the high heat of washing, drying, and ironing temperatures without deforming the fabric. For example, some fabrics cannot withstand hot ironing temperatures, leading to *scorching,* the charring of the fabric evidenced by brown or black stains. **Thermoplastic,** or heat sensitive, fibers melt when exposed to high temperatures—a critical problem when the garment is tossed about in a hot washing machine or dryer or when it is pressed with a hot iron. However, fabrics made from thermoplastic fibers can be **heat set** to retain desirable creases such as pleats and the creases in pant legs. Heat setting also keeps garments made of thermoplastic fibers permanently wrinkle free. And melting can be desirable; for example, when fusible fabrics (made from thermoplastic fibers) are joined using heat instead of stitches.

Comfort. Many factors help determine comfort, for example, weight, hand, extensibility, insulation, and absorbency/wicking ability. The fabric's *weight* and *hand* are important influences. A stiff or heavy fabric or one with a rough, raspy texture, for example, makes the garment uncomfortable to wear. The extensibility of the fabric affects comfort and the ability of the garment to fit a variety of people. *Comfort stretch* is minimal stretch, which provides ease of motion. *Power stretch* or *action stretch* is a high degree of elongation, required in activewear, for example, dance leotards.

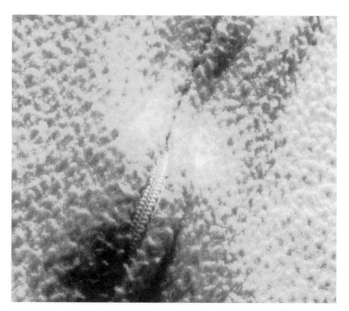

Figure 7–7 Overall pilling in children's sleepwear. Also note that zipper exhibits zipper hump (discussed in Chapter 8).

Insulation. The ability of the fabric to transmit air and heat also helps determine comfort. *Air permeability,* the rate at which air passes through a fabric, refers to the fabric's ability to "breathe." Air permeability and *thermal conductivity,* the rate at which heat passes through a fabric, both affect comfort. Fabrics with high air permeability and thermal conductivity are good choices for hot-weather clothing and active sportswear because they help release body heat and cool the wearer. Fabrics with low air permeability and thermal conductivity are desirable for cold-weather clothing because they help retain body heat. Clothing that retains body heat is especially important for infants and the elderly, whose bodies are inefficient at temperature regulation.

Researchers measure the thermal or insulative value of clothing (encompassing not only the fabric but the design, materials, and construction of the garment) according to its clo value. **Clo** is a unit of measurement approximately equal to the insulation required to keep a resting person comfortable at room temperature, or roughly the insulation value of typical indoor clothing. Thus, a garment with a high clo value would keep a person warmer than one with a low clo value.

Moisture Transfer. *Absorbency* is the ability of a fabric to take in moisture. **Wicking ability** is the rate at which a fabric diffuses moisture; and *moisture retention* is the rate at which a fabric dries. All three factors contribute to comfort in both hot-weather and cold-weather clothing. High absorbency allows the fabric to absorb perspiration and other body moisture. It also makes the fabric easy to dye, easy to launder, and resistant to static cling. Low moisture retention allows the fabric to dry quickly. However, the most important factor is wicking ability. Good wicking ability helps the fabric carry moisture along its surface and away from the body. Wicking cools the body in hot conditions by aiding in the evaporation of perspiration and, in cold conditions, carries perspiration away so that the wearer does not get wet and chilled. For example, ski socks need good wicking characteristics so that, as the feet perspire, the fabric carries away the moisture to keep the feet dry and therefore warm. Conversely, rainwear fabrics require low water permeability to keep the rain from reaching the body. They are usually worn over other fabrics (apparel) and therefore do not need absorbency for skin comfort.

Static cling is caused by low electrical conductivity. Electrical conductivity is the ability of the fabric to conduct electrical charges. Fabrics with good electrical conductivity avoid the buildup of static electricity. Garments with excess static tend to cling or billow, affecting comfort and also the garment's appearance. Generally, absorbent fibers have little problem with static buildup.

Ease of Care. For many consumers, the *ease of care* of a fabric is an important utility feature because of its effect on the care of the garment. All the fabrics used in the garment should have the same launderability or dry-cleanability so the finished garment retains its appearance and ability to function after refurbishing.

Ease of care also refers to the garment's tendency to resist soiling and wrinkling. For example, the ability of a fabric to resist perspiration staining is very important for men's dress shirts. Fabrics are generally easy to care for if they are soil resistant, absorbent, resilient, strong, abrasion resistant, dimensionally stable, colorfast, and resistant to heat and chemicals. Washable garments typically cost less to care for than do dry-cleanable garments. Garments that require special treatment, such as hand washing, drying, or ironing take extra time to care for properly.

Safety. One of the main issues in clothing *safety* for the general public is flame resistance. *Flame resistance* does not imply that a garment is fireproof. It means that the fabric resists catching fire, burns relatively slowly, and self-extinguishes or easily extinguishes after the flame is removed. However, flame-resistant fabrics *do* burn. For information on the Flammable Fabrics Act, see Chapter 2.

Some of the fabric characteristics to consider when discussing flame-resistant, safe clothing are fiber, construction, and finish. Natural fibers such as cotton and wool are slower to ignite and burn than synthetic fibers. Natural fibers also burn and leave an ash while synthetics burn and melt, thus depositing hot, molten material that can do more damage to skin than flames. Open and loose weaves are more likely to burn than tight, close weaves. In terms of fabric finish, napped and pile fabrics burn more readily than smooth fabrics. In general, the more air-permeable the fabric, the more readily it can ignite and burn.

Another safety consideration for some clothing is its ability to reflect light. Special, highly *light-reflective* fabrics are useful for biking and jogging clothing and for some occupational clothing, such as fire fighters' coats.

Related to safety are fabrics which offer *UV protection.* Clothing made from such fabrics blocks harmful ultraviolet rays from the sun. In recent years there has been an increased interest in UV-protective fabrics, especially for children and adults who spend a lot of time in the sun. ASTM recently formed a new committee on UV-protective clothing to establish appropriate standards.

Strength. The strength of a fabric is a measure of how well it resists deformation by external forces. **Tensile strength** or **tenacity** refers to the ability of the fabric to resist a pulling force. Strength may also be measured in *tear strength* (ability to resist tearing) or *bursting strength* (ability to withstand pressure without rupturing). Obviously, all three are closely related to garment durability. Garments with the highest strength tend to be work and athletic clothing, for example, jeans, overalls and dungarees. Garments needing the least strength are generally fashion items used more for appearance than function. Examples of items with low strength are scarves, women's gauze blouses, and chiffon evening gowns.

Abrasion Resistance.   **Abrasion resistance** refers to the amount of rubbing action a fabric can withstand without being destroyed. One type of abrasion is caused by the laundering or refurbishing process. This produces an overall loss of fiber, as seen when emptying the lint filters on washing machines, thus slightly weakening the garment during every refurbishing cycle. More severe abrasion in refurbishing occurs on any folded edge of the garment, including hems, cuffs, collars, and any squared or pointed edge. This is why holes often form first at these locations. The second type of abrasion happens in the normal wearing process. Each time the cloth is rubbed against a hard surface, a small loss of fiber occurs in this limited area of the garment. Normal points of wear include knee, elbow, and seat locations. Abrasion-resistant fabrics are important for durability; they are especially critical in apparel categories such as children's play clothing or occupational clothing that is subjected to intense abrasion.

Yarn slippage is the tendency of the yarns in a fabric to shift under stress, usually causing a raw edge in the seam. Yarn slippage often occurs near the seams of snug-fitting garments in areas that receive stress such as armscye seams on shirts and side seams on pants at the hip level. (Examples are shown in Chapter 10, Figure 10–3.) Yarn slippage reduces durability and is unattractive.

Resistance to Degradation.   Fabrics must withstand degradation from the environment. To be considered durable, a garment is made of fabric with the following characteristics:

1. *chemical resistance*, the ability to withstand degradation by chemicals. For example, active sportswear should withstand perspiration, and swimwear should withstand salt water and chlorine. Fabrics should withstand the cleansing agents required to care for the garment, for example, bleaches, detergents, and/or dry-cleaning solvents.
2. *launderability*, the ability to withstand the mechanical, thermal, and chemical actions of laundering (Figure 7–8)

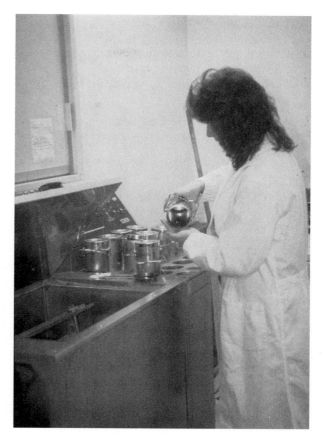

Figure 7–8   Technician using launderometer. (Courtesy of The Lee Company.)

3. *dry-cleanability*, the ability to withstand the mechanical and chemical action of the dry-cleaning process
4. *insect resistance*, the ability to repel moths, silverfish, and other insects which destroy the fabric by eating it
5. *mildew resistance*, the degree to which a fabric can resist the growth of fungi which may stain or weaken the fabric
6. *sunlight resistance*, the ability of a fabric to absorb sunlight without being damaged or destroyed. Fading is a common problem in retail stores, where garments are degraded by sunlight in display windows. Clothing worn by people who spend a lot of time outdoors also requires sunlight resistance.
7. *fume fading resistance*, the ability of a fabric to absorb normal gasses in the air (oxides of nitrogen, ozone, etc.) without being damaged. Fume fading is common to selected types of dyestuff.

It is possible that a garment may be considered practical and durable and not have all the characteristics discussed. If the garment has the majority of these characteristics, it will still be considered practical for normal use.

Storage conditions play as important a part as the fabric itself in factors 4 through 6. Clothing should be cleaned and stored in a well ventilated, dark place with relatively low temperature and humidity to avoid degradation by insects, mildew, and sunlight.

Fabric Performance Testing

Most mills and apparel manufacturers use standardized tests to check samples of fabric to see if they conform to specifications. Most manufacturers and many retailers also perform tests on the finished garments to ensure the garments meet specifications. The use of ASTM and AATCC standardized test methods enable suppliers and manufacturers to clearly communicate in the same "language" about performance requirements for fabrics.

Sometimes standardized test methods are adapted for practical use. For example, the AATCC fabric shrinkage test method calls for five cycles of washing and drying. The apparel industry has discovered that the majority of fabric or garment shrinkage is removed after three cycles. Due to the time involved in completing five cycles and the lack of dimensional stability change occurring in the last two cycles, the apparel industry commonly practices the test method using only three cycles. The home furnishings industry, however, retains the full five cycles for bedding products, as these products still show significant change in shrinkage during the last two cycles. If no method is available, the industry adopts a test method developed by a well respected company. One example of this is the test for elongation (stretch). The one used most commonly in industry was originally developed by the Blue Bell Corporation (Wrangler).

Most standardized textile tests are designed primarily to evaluate functional performance, while some tests have been designed to evaluate aesthetic characteristics. When aesthetic characteristics are evaluated, great efforts are made to turn subjective data into objective data. However, no matter how great the effort, the results are relatively inconsistent when compared to tests measuring functional performance.

While there are hundreds of fabric and fiber test methods, there are a few critical tests that apply to the majority of mass-produced apparel. These include: (1) count, (2) weight, (3) shrinkage, (4) tensile or bursting strength, (5) crocking, (6) lightfastness and (7) garment washability. A company can account for a majority of fabric performance considerations by performing only these seven basic tests.

Note: The first five test methods are conducted in rooms with controlled conditions. This means that the temperature and relative humidity are controlled. The temperature is 70° F ± 2°. The relative humidity is 65° F ± 5°. This allows for consistency of results from lab to lab and aids in the communication process.

Count or Gauge. The count or gauge of a fabric confirms the density and compactness of the fabrication and is specified in the purchase contract. **Count, thread count,** or **yarn count** refers to the number of *ends* (warp yarns) and *picks* (filling yarns), or the total *number of yarns per square inch* of woven fabric; **cut** or **gauge** refers to the number of loops per square inch of knit fabric. Count is performed according to its name; all ends and picks or courses and wales in a one-square-inch area are individually counted with the aid of a pick (magnifying) glass or stitch counter. (This process is shown in Chapter 3, Figure 3–9.) For example, a thread count of 180 means there is a total of 180 warp and filling yarns in one square inch of fabric. Sometimes more detail is provided by expressing the thread count of the warp and filling yarns separately, for example, 100 x 80 (100 warp yarns and 80 filling yarns per inch). Count can vary from as low as 20 to as high as 500. An average count for heavy-weight jeans might be 60 x 48. Fabrics with high thread counts cost more than comparable fabrics with low thread counts because they contain more fiber. In general, the higher the thread count or gauge, the higher the quality of the fabric. An exception to this is a fabric intentionally woven or knitted loosely for design effect, for example, gauze.

Fabrics with low thread count are subject to raveling, fraying, and yarn slippage. The yarns shift if they are not held firmly in place, as are the yarns of tightly woven fabrics. Fabrics with high thread counts generally contain fine yarns and are durable, dimensionally stable, and abrasion resistant and resist snagging, pilling, and raveling. High-thread-count fabrics have body and they press flat, making them suitable for tailored garments. Because so many yarns are packed into each square inch, they allow little air to penetrate, so they tend to be warm to wear. They are generally more opaque than fabrics with low thread counts. Fabrics with high thread counts may be initially water repellent but, once wet, they dry slowly. Because the yarns are packed so tightly together, they resist easing and have a tendency toward seam pucker. (An example appers in Chapter 10, Figure 10–2.) They are also stiffer and wrinkle more than low-count fabrics. The density of the fabric structure affects ease of garment production; dense fabrics are difficult for knives and needles to penetrate. Fabrics with low thread counts tend to be drapable; however, if the fabric does not have the desired amount of body, its hand is described negatively as limp or sleazy. The ratio of lengthwise and crosswise yarns in a fabric affects its durability. *Balanced fabrics,* with about the same size and number of lengthwise and crosswise yarns, are stronger and more durable, with less yarn slippage, than *unbalanced fabrics.* However, unbalanced weave structures provide ribbed and other special effects.

Weight. Weight is taken on a balance or scale in grams. The grams are converted to *ounces per square yard.* Like count, weight confirms the density or compactness of the cloth. Most purchase contracts are based on fabric weight. The *weight* of a fabric should be appropriate for the garment design. Lightweight fabrics are suitable for styles with gathering or delicate details. Tailored styles or bold details require slightly heavier fabrics with more body. The weight of a fabric depends on fiber type, yarn size, and the fabric's count or gauge.

1. *Top weights* include light-weight fabrics suitable for making shirts, blouses, and dresses. They are sometimes referred to as shirt weight, blouse weight, or dress weight. Top weights generally weigh between 2 and 5 ounces per square yard of fabric.
2. *Bottom weights* include somewhat heavier fabrics suitable for making pants, skirts, jackets, and coats. They are sometimes referred to as pant weight, skirt weight, suit weight, or coat weight. Bottom-weight fabrics range from 7 to 15 ounces per square yard. The average denim jean is made in cloth weighing 12 to 14 ounces per square yard, while a dress pant might average 6 to 8 ounces per square yard. Heavy coating fabrics can weigh over 20 ounces per square yard (Hudson, 1988).
3. Heavy top weights and light bottom weights are sometimes referred to as *mid weights.*

Fabric weight offers an excellent clue to garment cost and quality when comparing similar garments. Heavy fabrics generally cost more than light fabrics because they contain more yarn and fiber; an expensive fabric often indicates an expensive garment. For instance, jeans made of heavyweight denim cost more than those made of lightweight denim. A sweatshirt made of heavyweight fleece costs more than one made of lightweight fleece. Mail-order catalogs often call attention to the heavy weight of the fabric in a garment as a sign of quality. There are exceptions to these generalizations. For example, when considering fabrics intended to be very fine and lightweight, a light fabric may cost more than a heavy one. This is true if fine yarns and additional labor are required to create the lightweight fabric that is used, for example, to make a fine silk scarf.

Related to weight is fabric *thickness.* Thickness affects drape, hand, and comfort. The thicker the fabric, the warmer it is, up to about 1/4 inch (Solinger,

1988). Thick fabrics allow less air to penetrate and help the wearer retain body heat; conversely, thin fabrics help the wearer stay cool. The thickness of a fabric depends on yarn size and fabric structure.

For the manufacturer, fabric thickness affects ease of production. Very thin and very thick fabrics are difficult to handle and require special techniques for cutting and sewing. Designers, patternmakers, and sewing engineers may need to develop methods to reduce bulk in seams and hems for heavy fabrics.

Shrinkage. Shrinkage testing is performed in home laundering machines to simulate normal consumer home laundering conditions. Three complete cycles of washing and drying are performed using a standard 4-pound load size without any bleach or fabric softener. Some companies use a standardized test detergent and some use commercial home laundering detergent. After laundering and conditioning, the amount of shrinkage is measured and reported as a percentage. This information is used for planning the correct garment size so the garment fits both before and after the consumer washes it. A typical standard for both length and width is 4% or less shrinkage in most woven fabrics and 6% or less shrinkage in most knit fabrics.

Strength. Strength tests are important in determining if the garment will hold up to its intended use. *Tensile strength* tests are performed on woven cloth, and *bursting strength* tests are performed on knitted cloth (Figures 7–9 and 7–10). Both tests measure the amount of force in pounds required to rupture the cloth. A pair of heavyweight jeans might have up to 160 pounds strength in the warp and 90 pounds in the fill. A pair of dress pants averages about 40 to 50 pounds in both the warp and fill. Shirts typically have about 25 to 30 pounds strength.

Crocking. **Crocking** is one of the least expensive, quickest, and most important tests conducted on fabric. It determines the likelihood that dyestuff will rub off and transfer to other surfaces, under both dry and wet (moist) conditions. It is performed on both knits and wovens, solids and prints. The test is performed on a *crockmeter,* an apparatus with a stiff finger that rubs the cloth a specific number of times. (A crockmeter is shown in Chapter 3, Figure 3–11.) Any color that is rubbed off is rated to determine acceptability using the AATCC Chromatic Transference Scale. Dry ratings of 4 and above and wet ratings of 3 and above are considered acceptable for most fabrics. Fabric that successfully passes crocking tests will not experience color rub-off in the sewing plant, retail store, or in normal consumer use.

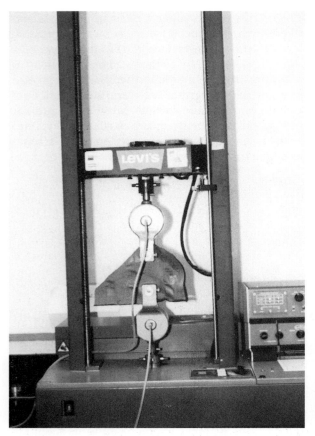

Figure 7–9 Instron® tester measuring fabric tensile strength. (Courtesy of Levi Strauss & Company.)

Lightfastness. Lightfastness is measured by simulating fading in a large machine commonly called a *weatherometer* or *fadeometer* (Figure 3–10). The newest models have a Xenon light source that reproduces the light generated by the sun. Samples of cloth are exposed to this light source for specified lengths of time and the amount of color loss is then evaluated. Lightfastness ratings are made by comparing the faded cloth with a sample of the original (unfaded) cloth. This difference is then compared to the AATCC Gray Scale for Color Change chart. This chart serves as a guide to associate the amount of color change with a number between 1 and 5. Fabrics with ratings of 4 and higher will not present noticeable problems during selling or wearing.

Washability. Washability testing is mainly performed on garments, not on fabric. It is conducted on both prototype garments and production garments to provide a complete picture of product performance. In the washability test, a fabric sample or completed garment is washed in home laundering equipment according to the care label instructions. If the fabric, garment, or any of the findings items falls apart,

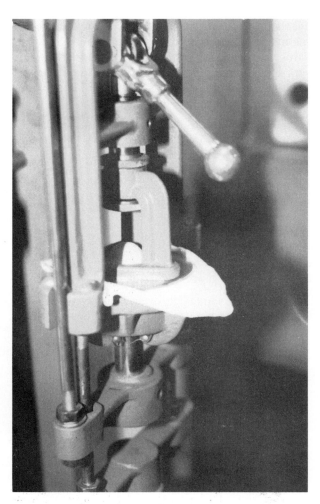

Figure 7–10 Close-up of bursting strength test. (Courtesy of Levi Strauss & Company.)

fades, stains, or has any other problem, the result is considered a failure and corrections are made as soon as possible. Some manufacturers and retailers launder garments up to 25 times to determine how well they will hold up in use. There is only pass-fail evaluation in garment washability testing, as preliminary testing of the component parts should have already determined any potential problems. The main purpose of this test is to confirm that all earlier quality evaluations were successful. This is the ultimate garment test. It evaluates fabric, findings, and how they interact together.

PHYSICAL FEATURES OF FABRIC

The physical features of a fabric determine its performance. No single physical feature is solely responsible for the performance of the fabric. Instead, the interplay among all the physical dimensions of fabric determines its performance. Understanding how the physical properties of a fabric influence its aesthetics, utility, durability, and cost is important for evaluating component and garment quality. The physical features of a fabric include its fibers and yarns, the structure of the fabric, and how it is dyed, printed, and finished.

The quality of the fabric is not the sole determinant of a garment's quality, but it is a critical ingredient. On the following pages, note the relationship between the physical features of the fabric and the resulting performance features, discussed earlier in this chapter.

Fibers

Fibers are the raw materials from which fabrics are made; they are the basic building blocks of a fabric. An individual fiber is a fine, hairlike structure. Knowing the fiber content of a fabric helps predict the aesthetic and functional performance of the fabric and the garment. The type of fiber or fibers from which a fabric is produced strongly influences the fabric's characteristics. Fiber content affects the aesthetics, comfort, durability, shape and appearance retention, ease of care, and other performance characteristics as well as the cost of the fabric. For example, fibers affect the hand of the fabric, including its texture and drape, because some fibers are inherently soft and others are stiff. Fiber content also affects the dimensional stability of the fabric. For example, wool fibers have a tendency to stretch and to shrink under warm, wet conditions. Other fibers, such as nylon, have the ability to return to their original length after being stretched, which improves the dimensional stability of nylon fabrics. A fiber with high abrasion resistance contributes to the durability of the fabric. Comfort factors such as the absorbency, moisture transmission and retention, water repellency, air and thermal conductivity, and electrical conductivity of a fabric are greatly affected by the properties of the fibers used to make the fabric. The luster of the fiber influences the luster of the fabric. Some fibers are fuzzy, making them likely to hide soil and to retain trapped soil, affecting the appearance and ease of care of the fabric. In addition to influencing fabric performance, fiber content is listed on the label of the garment and therefore affects the consumer's perception of quality.

Natural Fibers. Fibers fall into two broad categories: natural fibers, which occur naturally in the environment, and manufactured fibers. (For a complete list, see *ASTM Standard Terminology Relating to Textiles D123*.) The **natural fibers** used in apparel include

1. *protein fibers*—silk, wool, and other fibers from animal sources
2. *cellulosic fibers*—cotton, linen and its close relative ramie, and other fibers from plant sources.

In general, natural fibers are more costly and considered to be more luxurious than manufactured fibers. Consumers typically associate natural fibers with comfort, durability, and beauty.

Manufactured Fibers. **Manufactured fibers** or **man-made fibers** are formed through human effort. The manufactured fibers used in apparel include

1. *regenerated cellulosics* made from plant fibers—rayon, lyocell, acetate, and triacetate
2. *synthetics* made from petroleum products—nylon, polyester, acrylic, modacrylic, olefin, and spandex
3. *miscellaneous*—rubber and metallic.

In addition to their generic names, manufactured fibers have registered trade names, or brand names that identify the fiber producer. For example, *Lycra* is a brand of spandex made by DuPont (Table 7–2). For more information, contact the **American Fiber Manufacturers Association, Inc.**, 1150 17th Street N.W., Washington, D.C. 20036.

The characteristics of manufactured fibers vary widely. Synthetics, such as nylon and polyester, are associated with low to moderate absorbency, making them uncomfortable in hot, humid weather. But regenerated cellulosic fibers, especially rayon and lyocell, are typically more absorbent and more comfortable than synthetics. The strength and resilience of manufactured fibers range from very low to very high depending on the type of fiber and particular variation. Synthetic fibers tend to be stronger and more durable than regenerated cellulosics. The strength of synthetic fibers makes fabrics likely to pill because the strong fibers cling to fuzz balls that form on the fabric surface and do not let them fall off. Synthetic fibers are generally more resilient than regenerated cellulosics and natural fibers, so they are less apt to wrinkle and to require ironing. Unlike natural fibers and some regenerated cellulosics, synthetics can usually be heat set. This gives synthetic fabrics the ability to resist or retain creases and pleats as desired. Synthetics are generally more resistant to mildew, insects, fire, and chemicals than regenerated cellulosics and natural fibers.

Fiber Length. **Staple** fibers are short fibers measured in inches. All natural fibers, except silk, are staples. **Filament** fibers are fibers measured in yards.

Table 7–2 Generalizations About Usage, Cost, and Performance Characteristics of Common Apparel Fibers

---

Generic Fiber: cotton, the most widely used apparel fiber in the United States

-from seed pod of cotton plant

-*Pima* or *Supima, Sea Island,* and *Egyptian* varieties are high quality

-*Fox Fibre®* grows in colors

-*green cotton* is organically grown and processed using environmentally friendly methods

Chief apparel uses: warm weather apparel, underwear, sleepwear

Cost: moderate, slightly more expensive than manufactured fibers

Performance: appears dull; wrinkles easily unless specially finished; absorbent; draws heat from body; feels cool in hot, humid weather; moderate strength; colorfastness often a problem; deteriorated by mildew and sunlight; drapes well; easy to cut and sew; dyes readily; most rigorous care is machine wash and dry; exhibits relaxation shrinkage when laundered, especially in knitted fabrications, unless preshrunk; iron at high temperature

Generic Fiber: flax (linen)

-from stem of flax plant

-*Belgian* and *Irish* linen are finest

Chief apparel uses: warm-weather apparel

Cost: expensive luxury fiber, constitutes less than 1% of apparel fibers used

Performance: crisp, lustrous, wrinkles easily; absorbent; draws heat from body; cool in hot, humid weather; strong; tends to crack at creases or folds; does not shed lint; easy to cut and sew; most rigorous care is dry-clean; if machine washed and dried, may wrinkle, lose crispness, and exhibit relaxation shrinkage; iron at high temperature

Generic Fiber: ramie

-from stem of ramie plant

-frequently used in imported garments to extend cotton quotas

Chief apparel uses: warm weather apparel, especially sweaters, blends with polyester, cotton, linen, and acrylic are common

Cost: much less expensive than linen

Performance: aesthetics similar to linen; wrinkles easily; somewhat stiffer than linen; absorbent; draws heat from body; cool in hot, humid weather; stronger than linen; colorfast; brittle and difficult to twist into yarns and to weave; easy to cut and sew; dyes readily; most rigorous care is same as linen

Generic Fiber: hemp

-from stem of industrial/fiber hemp plant

-ancient fiber, but recently popular for apparel

-environmentally friendly to grow

Chief apparel uses: jeans, sneakers, hats, bags, backpacks

Cost: currently high because it is imported

Performance: appears natural; more absorbent than cotton; easy to dye; comfortable hand; stronger and more durable than cotton; most rigorous care is machine wash and dry, requires little ironing

Generic Fiber: silk

-from silkworm cocoons

-*raw silk* has not been de-gummed; *tussah silk* is coarse, uneven staple fibers from wild silkworms

-*noil silk* is staple-fiber silk

Table 7–2 Continued

Chief apparel uses: elegant suits, dresses, blouses, neckties, scarves

Cost: expensive luxury fiber, constitutes less than 1% of apparel fibers

Performance: dry hand; lustrous; wrinkles easily; luxurious hand; absorbent; lightweight; retains body heat; cool in summer, warm in winter; strong but not especially durable; deteriorated by sun and perspiration; does not stretch or shrink; dyes may bleed; drapes well; in filament form is slippery to cut and sew and may show needle holes; in spun form is easy to cut and sew; dyes readily; most rigorous care is dry-clean or hand wash, cool, gentle, soap, line dry; no harsh detergents; no chlorine bleach; iron at low temperature

Generic Fiber: wool

-from the fleece of sheep

-some of the highest quality comes from *Merino* breed

-*lambswool* is soft first shearing from lambs

Chief apparel uses: cool-weather apparel, especially sweaters; tailored suits and coats

Cost: relatively expensive; finer wool is more expensive than coarser wool

Performance: varies from dull/fuzzy to smoother/somewhat lustrous; resists wrinkling; wrinkles fall out; absorbent; some wool is scratchy; retains body heat; stretches but can recover; shrinks; relatively weak fiber, but fabric can be fairly durable depending on structure; finer wool is less durable; moths can destroy unless mothproof finish is added; malleable so tailors well; does not ravel easily; dyes readily; colorfast; most rigorous care is dry-clean or hand wash, cool, gentle, soap, dry flat; shrinks when machine washed and dried unless specially finished; no harsh detergents; no chlorine bleach; iron at low temperature

Generic Fiber: specialty hair fibers

-from the fleece of animals other than sheep, for example, *mohair, cashmere, alpaca, angora, camel, vicuña*

Chief apparel uses: same as wool

Cost: vicuña is most expensive; cashmere and camel are also expensive luxury fibers; others are generally more expensive than wool

Performance: aesthetics similar to wool; slightly more lustrous; retain body heat; most are softer, fluffier, smoother, and less scratchy than wool; most are slightly less durable than wool; ease of production similar to wool; most have somewhat less body than wool; most rigorous care is same as wool

Generic Fiber: rayon

-regenerated cellulose

-most rayon is *viscose* or *high wet modulus (HWM)/high performance (HP)*; HWM rayon is much more durable than viscose rayon

-*cuprammonium/cupra* rayon is imported

Trade name examples: Enkrome, Enkaire, Fibra, Narco, Polynosic (HWM), 2001 (microfiber), Zantrel (HWM microfiber)

Chief apparel uses: imitates natural fibers in light- and medium-weight apparel

Cost: varies widely, low to moderate

Performance: dull to lustrous; wrinkles easily unless HWM; absorbent; low strength unless HWM; tends to stretch and not recover well unless HWM; exhibits some relaxation shrinkage; deteriorated by mildew; drapes well; in filament form, difficult to cut and sew; prone to seam slippage; dyes readily; most rigorous care is dry-clean; iron at low temperature; HWM rayons may suggest machine wash and dry and iron at slightly higher temperatures

Generic Fiber: lyocell

-regenerated cellulose

-the newest generic fiber

-similar to rayon but more durable and more environmentally friendly to produce

(Continued)

Table 7–2 Continued

Trade name examples: Tencel

Chief apparel uses: top, mid, and bottom weights

Cost: low to moderate

Performance: similar to rayon but less apt to wrinkle or shrink; higher wet and dry strength; most rigorous care is machine wash and dry, iron at low temperature

Generic Fiber: acetate and triacetate

-regenerated cellulosics

Trade name examples of acetate: Celaperm, Celebrate, Celco, Chromspun, Estron, Loftura

Trade name examples of triacetate: no longer produced in United States

Chief apparel uses of acetate: light- and medium-weight apparel, especially linings, silklike bridal and formal wear and lingerie

Chief apparel uses of triacetate: apparel that needs to be heat set

Cost: relatively low

Performance: lustrous; acetate wrinkles easily, triacetate does not wrinkle easily; acetate moderately absorbent, more absorbent than triacetate; retains body heat; relatively weak; acetate prone to shrinking and stretching unless treated, triacetate resists shrinking and stretching; acetate may fade or change color from exposure to atmosphere; drapes well; ravels; stitching holes show; seams often pucker; slippery to cut and sew; can be difficult to dye; no chlorine bleach; most rigorous care for acetate is dry-clean, iron at low temperature; most rigorous care for triacetate is hand or machine wash and dry, iron at low temperature

Generic Fiber: nylon

-petroleum derivative, polyamide

Trade name examples: Anso-Tex, Antron, Cantrece, Caprolan, Cordura, Hydrofil (absorbent), Natural Touch, Shareen, Supplex, Tactel, Thermaloft (insulating), Ultron, Wear-Dated, Zefran, Zefsport, Zeftron

Chief apparel uses: hosiery, lingerie, blended with other fibers to add strength, wind-resistant garments

Cost: varies widely, low to moderate

Performance: dull to lustrous; does not wrinkle easily; moderately absorbent; lightweight; does not carry heat from body; may build up static; very strong and durable; tends to pill; resists abrasion; excellent elasticity; in filament form, difficult to cut and sew; may be difficult to dye; prone to oily stains; most rigorous care is machine wash and dry, iron at low temperature; light colors may scavenge/pick up other colors when laundered

Generic Fiber: polyester, second most widely used apparel fiber in the United States

-petroleum derivative

Trade name examples: BTU, Comfort Fiber, Dacron, Dyersburg E.C.O. (recycled from plastic bottles), Fortrel, Fortrel Microspun (microfiber), Kodel, Micromattique (microfiber), Micronesse (microfiber), Trevira, Trevira Finesse (microfiber)

Chief apparel uses: used to imitate other fibers or blended to improve characteristics of other fibers; cotton/polyester blends are common

Cost: varies widely, from low to moderate, but lower than most natural fibers; often added to blends to reduce cost and/or improve some dimensions of performance

Performance: can imitate most other fibers; dull to lustrous; does not wrinkle easily; low absorbency, but wicks moisture; retains body heat; tends to pill; strong and durable; dimensionally stable; in filament form, difficult to cut and sew; details may be heat set; dyes readily; prone to oily stains; known for easy care; most rigorous care is usually machine wash and dry, iron at low temperature; usually can be dry-cleaned

Generic Fiber: acrylic and modacrylic

-petroleum derivatives, polyacrylonitrile

Trade name examples of acrylic: Acrilan, Bi-Loft, Creslan, Du-Rel, Fi-lana, Orlon, Pa-Qel, Piltrol, So-Lara, Zefran

Trade name examples of modacrylic: SEF

Table 7–2 Continued

Chief apparel uses of acrylic: fleece and pile fabrics, sweaters, socks, to imitate wool

Chief apparel uses of modacrylic: fake fur, pile fabrics

Cost: varies widely, low to moderate

Performance: aesthetics similar to wool, does not wrinkle easily; low absorbency; fairly comfortable; some acrylics prone to stretching and shrinking, especially knits; details can be heat set; acrylic fair to good strength, modacrylic weaker; modacrylic inherently flame retardant; easy to cut and sew; resists dyeing; prone to oily stains; most rigorous care is machine wash and dry; acrylic iron at medium temperature, modacrylic iron at very low temperature; dry-clean deep pile/fur fabrics

Generic Fiber: olefin

-petroleum derivative, polypropylene or polyethylene

Trade name examples: Herculon, Marquessa Lane, Marvess, Spectra, Thinsulate (microfiber)

Chief apparel uses: thermal socks and underwear, active sportswear such as skiwear, glove linings

Cost: fairly low

Performance: waxy; nonabsorbent but wicks moisture away from the body; extremely lightweight; strong; fairly easy to cut and sew; very difficult to dye; very heat sensitive; most rigorous care is machine wash and line dry, iron at cool temperatures

Generic Fiber: spandex

-petroleum derivative, polyurethane

Trade name examples: Byrene, Cleerspan, Glospan, Lycra, Spandelle

Chief apparel uses: blended with other fibers to add stretch to foundation garments, swimwear and active sportswear, support hose

Cost: high, but only a small percentage is needed to achieve stretch—as low as 3% of total fiber weight

Performance: shiny; stretches more than 500%; recovery from stretch almost as good as rubber; such a small percentage is used in a blend that it usually does not affect garment comfort except for adding stretch; weak, but twice as strong as rubber; resistant to sun and chemicals such as perspiration, suntan oil, chlorine, and sea water; slippery to cut and sew; details can be heat set; dyes readily; most rigorous care is machine wash and dry, no chlorine bleach, iron at low temperature

Generic Fiber: rubber

-natural or manufactured (petroleum derivative)

Chief apparel uses: elastic thread, narrow elastic, to introduce stretch into garments

Cost: lower than spandex

Performance: rubber yarns are covered with other fibers that determine aesthetics; stretches more than 700%; excellent elasticity; becomes brittle over time; needles can pierce and damage rubber yarns; very low strength compared to spandex; deteriorates with age and exposure to heat, sun, and chemicals such as perspiration, suntan oil, and salt water; most rigorous care is machine wash; heat destroys rubber; chlorine bleaches and dry-cleaning solvents degrade and harden rubber

Generic Fiber: metal

-aluminum (usually) metal, plastic-coated metal, metal-coated plastic, or core covered with metal

Trade name example: Lurex

Chief apparel uses: decorative threads or yarns

Cost: varies from inexpensive to expensive

Performance: shiny if visible; excellent conductor of electricity; little or no drapability and resiliency; heavy; cannot be dyed, must be coated for color; most rigorous care is machine wash and dry, do not iron if plastic is used in combination with the metal

Manufactured fibers are produced as filaments but may be cut into staples. Staple-fiber fabrics tend to be comfortable to wear and dull or fuzzy in appearance. Filament-fiber fabrics are smooth, lustrous, and strong. (See section on Yarns later in this chapter for more information.)

Fiber Shape. The *shape* of the fibers influences the hand and luster of the fabric. The shape of natural fibers is predetermined. However, manufactured fibers can be engineered to possess a variety of shapes. For example, perfectly round fibers feel slippery and are shiny. Trilobal fibers have a soft luster and a silky hand. Other irregular shapes lend a cottony hand and less luster to the fabric.

Fiber Size. The *size* of the fibers greatly affects the hand of the fabric. Fine fibers make fabrics that are soft and drapable and generally are considered of high quality. Coarse fibers result in fabrics with body, crispness, or stiffness, which are desirable for certain end uses.

The size of fibers is measured in **denier,** the weight in grams of 9,000 meters of fiber or yarn. Denier is a direct system; the larger the number, the larger the fiber. Apparel fibers generally range from less than 1 to 7 denier. One to 3 denier represents fine cotton and wool, 5 to 8 denier average cotton and wool (Kadolph, Langford, Hollen, & Saddler, 1995). The denier of manufactured fibers can be engineered to suit end use.

For international use, the International Organization for Standardization (ISO) has adopted the tex system. **Tex** is the weight in grams of 1,000 meters of fiber or yarn. Tex is well suited to international use because it is a direct system, based on the metric system, and has the unique ability to designate the diameter of any type of fiber and of yarn made of any type of fiber. (See Chapter 8, Table 8–1 for suggested thread sizes by tex.) To convert from tex to denier, multiply tex by 9. To convert from denier to tex, divide denier by 9.

Fiber Content of Fabric. People often make assumptions about the performance of a fabric based on fiber content. However, the particular fabric in which a fiber is found may perform quite differently than one might guess from knowing the fiber content. For example, nylon is a very strong fiber. But nylon hosiery runs easily if the yarns are very fine and the structure of the fabric is delicate.

The relationship of the fabric to other components of the garment also affects performance. For example, a consumer might assume that a garment made of polyester is durable because polyester fibers are generally durable. But if the thread securing the seams is weak, the garment is not very durable.

Fibers that look and feel alike may perform quite differently in use. High-quality and low-quality fibers exist within each fiber type. Manufactured fibers in particular have limitless variations; they can be engineered to possess any number of characteristics. Therefore, it is impossible to accurately generalize about their performance. For example, different rayons vary widely in their durability. If a label reads *100% Rayon,* the consumer may assume a level of durability higher or lower than that particular variation of rayon possesses. The fiber properties of the fabric in a garment cannot be determined visually. Therefore, manufacturers should describe any special qualities of the fabric in writing on labels or hang tags if they want consumers to be informed. For example, fibers may contain flame retardants that make them suitable for use in children's sleepwear.

Blends of more than one fiber type increase or decrease the characteristics contributed by each fiber to the fabric. In a good blend, the qualities of all fibers in the blend are evident. The characteristics of the fiber present in the highest percentage generally dominate. Usually the fabric must have at least 15% of a fiber for that fiber to have an important impact on performance; exceptions are spandex and other elastomers. Care for blends must take into consideration the most delicate component of the blend.

Although generalizations about the properties of fibers may lead to erroneous conclusions about garment performance, fiber content is strongly related to fabric performance and provides a valuable clue to predict garment performance. The aesthetic and functional performance generally associated with each generic fiber are summarized in Table 7–2. Cost, chief apparel uses, and the most rigorous care suggested for the generic raw fiber are included. *Note:* It is not certain that a garment with a particular fiber content will withstand the care methods discussed in Table 7–2.

The manufacturer must determine the proper care instructions for a garment by testing all the garment components and their interaction in the finished garment. Care instructions cannot be based on fiber content. Therefore, the care methods listed in Table 7–2 do not directly relate to the care labels in most garments. In addition to the raw fiber, garment care labels also take into account fiber variants; the yarn and fabric structure; dyes and finishes used; and other components of the garment, such as the trim, which may require more delicate care than the raw fiber. Therefore, the care methods listed in Table 7–2 are merely examples of the most rigorous care the generic fiber can withstand in its raw state, before being restricted by additional yarn, fabrication, dye, print, finish, and other garment component and construction considerations.

Yarns

A group of fibers is twisted or *spun* into a continuous strand called a **yarn,** used to make fabric. A fabric's yarns affect functional and aesthetic performance, for example, hand, including drapability and texture; luster; durability, including strength and abrasion resistance; and comfort. The two main types of yarns are (1) spun and (2) filament. Several individual or single yarns of either type may be twisted together to create larger, stronger, ply yarns.

Spun Yarns. Spun yarns are composed of short fibers called *staple fibers.* As noted earlier all natural fibers except silk are staples. Manufactured fibers occur as filaments but may be cut into staples, if desired. When staple fibers are spun into yarns, the many fiber ends sticking out from spun yarns give them a dull appearance and a slight texture. Fabrics made from spun yarns are comfortable because they do not lie flush against the body. They ravel and shift less, press flatter, pucker less, and show wrinkles and construction errors less than do filament yarns.

Carded or Combed. As one of the steps in creating a yarn, the staple fibers are *carded* to semi-orient them in a parallel manner. The mill may also *comb* the yarn if it contains long staple fibers. Combing removes short fibers and further orients the remaining fibers in a parallel manner. **Carded** yarns are fuzzy and soft. **Combed** yarns are smoother and more lustrous than carded yarns, partly because of the longer fibers and partly because they are more tightly twisted. Combed yarns retain their appearance longer and are less likely to pill than carded yarns. Combed yarns cost more than carded yarns and are a sign of quality. Carded and combed are terms usually applied to cotton yarns.

Woolen or Worsted. **Woolen** refers to carded wool yarns; **worsted** indicates combed wool yarns. Worsted yarns cost more than woolen yarns. Worsted yarns are used in menswear and hard-finish suitings. Worsted fabrics wear well but have a tendency to become shiny in areas of hard wear, for example, the elbows of a jacket. Woolen fabrics are generally loosely woven and bulky. They tend to lose their shape more easily than worsteds. Woolen yarns are used in sweaters and soft, cold-weather suitings. Woolen yarns are good insulators.

Filament Yarns. Filament yarns are composed of long fibers called *filaments.* All manufactured fibers start out as filaments. Some get cut into short lengths called staple. The only natural fiber occurring in filament form is silk.

Because they contain long, continuous fibers, filament yarns are very smooth. Fabrics made from filament yarns have a lustrous appearance (unless they are delustered) and resist wrinkling. Filament yarns are usually stronger than staple yarns of comparable size and fiber content. They are also less absorbent than staple yarns and less comfortable to wear because they tend to stick to the skin when wet. Filament yarns involve fewer production steps, so they cost less to make than staple yarns. Filament-yarn fabrics ravel and shift during cutting and sewing because they are slippery. Thus, they cost more to cut and sew than comparable fabrics made from spun yarns, and it is more difficult to achieve smooth, attractive seams. Therefore, garments of filament-yarn fabric generally cost more than comparable garments of staple-yarn fabric. They tend to have more puckers and show more wrinkles and construction errors.

Many filament yarns are *texturized,* adding crimp and dimension. Texturized filament yarns are known as **bulk continuous filament,** or **BCF, yarns.** Although filament yarns are still economical, texturizing them makes them more comfortable to wear, less apt to wrinkle, and easier to cut and sew. Texturizing helps the yarn stretch and recover from stretch. It makes the yarn somewhat dull and increases the tendency of the yarn to snag or pill.

Compound and Novelty Yarns. While most fabrics contain simple, single yarns, more than one yarn may be twisted together to form *compound* yarns known as **plied** yarns (e.g., 2-ply, 3-ply, or 4-ply). Many knitting yarns and yarns in better shirtings and denims are plied. *Covered* yarns consist of a core yarn such as rubber or spandex wrapped with another, usually softer, yarn. *Core-spun* yarns consist of a core yarn covered with usually softer fibers.

Novelty yarns or *fancy* yarns are used to achieve special effects in fabrics. For example, *tweed* yarns have bits of contrasting colored fiber added to the plain yarn; *bouclé* yarns have regular, decorative loops; *slub* yarns are thick and thin; *chenille* yarns are fuzzy like a caterpillar; *ratiné* yarns have irregular kinked loops; *spiral* yarns consist of two different-looking yarns twisted together; *knot* or *spot* yarns have what appear to be knots along the length of the yarns; *spike* or *snarl* yarns have alternating unclosed loops on both sides of the yarn. Novelty yarns add to the design effect of the fabric and to its cost. Novelty yarns tend to decrease abrasion resistance because the uneven surface of the yarns wears unevenly and is prone to snagging. They require a looser fabric structure than plain yarns, making the fabric prone to stretching out of shape, snagging, and yarn slippage. The uneven surface of novelty yarns traps and hides soil. Although it does not show soil readily, it is difficult to clean.

Yarn Twist.   The amount of **twist,** measured in the number of turns per inch, is an important property of yarn. Tightly twisted yarns are stronger, finer, less apt to snag and pill, and generally retain their appearance longer than loosely twisted yarns. Tightly twisted yarns can be packed closely together, creating durable fabrics that are wrinkle resistant. These yarns are generally associated with increased cost and quality. In some applications, loosely twisted yarns are desirable because they create a soft, lofty, drapable fabric with a surface suitable for brushing or *napping.* But the fabric is also subject to pilling, snagging, and abrasion.

High twist generally adds luster to staple fibers but decreases the luster of filament fibers. Extremely high levels of twist create pebbly-looking crepe yarns which add texture to the fabric. High twist yarns are prone to shrinkage, some of which is released during wear due to the normal stress of body movement.

Yarn Size.   Yarn size, or diameter, affects the performance of the fabric. Large, coarse yarns tend to be stronger and more durable than small, fine yarns with the same amount of twist. The large yarns create fabrics with a rougher texture and stiffer hand which are less drapable than fabric made with fine yarns. The thick, warm, opaque fabrics made with large yarns do not wrinkle easily. Because large yarns cannot be packed as closely together as small yarns, the fabric is more prone to yarn slippage.

Yarn size is designated in various ways, depending on the type of fiber used in the yarn. The size of spun yarns is designated by **yarn number.** There are different yarn numbering systems for cotton, woolen, and worsted yarns, plus general systems such as metric yarn numbering. For a complete listing, see *ASTM Method D2260-89 Standard Tables of Conversion Factors and Equivalent Yarn Numbers Measured in Various Numbering Systems.* Yarn numbering is an indirect system; the larger the number, the smaller the yarn. Most of the numbers are based on pounds and yards, so they are not well suited for international use.

Filament yarn sizes are designated by denier or tex (see section on Fiber Size earlier in this chapter). Both denier and tex are direct systems; the larger the number, the larger the yarn. Tex has the added advantage of being able to describe the diameter of yarns made of any type of fiber; its use is endorsed internationally. Sometimes the term **decitex (dtex)** is used to describe fine yarns. Dtex is tex multiplied by 10, making dtex roughly equivalent to denier.

Because same-denier yarns may contain a few large fibers or many small ones, when describing filament yarns, the **denier per filament (dpf)** also provides useful information. For example, the description 100/30 dtex means that the yarn is 100 dtex and contains 30 filaments. Thus, the denier per filament is 3.3 decitex.

Fabric Structure

The structure of a fabric, or how it is fabricated, affects its aesthetic and functional performance. Fabric structure affects the hand of the fabric, including its drapability and texture. The structure of the fabric also affects luster, ability to stretch and breathe, and strength and abrasion resistance. Fabrics can be formed in a number of ways. The two most common methods of forming a fabric are weaving and knitting.

Wovens.   *Weaving* is the most common method of creating fabrics. *Warp* yarns are interlaced with *filling* or *weft* yarns at right angles to make the fabric. Closely *woven* fabrics are firm and strong. They can be easily tucked, pleated, dyed, and printed. They are better at blocking wind than knits. Because of their interlaced structure, woven fabrics have low stretch, ravel at cut edges, and can be prone to seam pucker (although pucker is more related to fiber and finish than to weave).

Woven fabrics vary from simple to complex weaves. All weaves are a variation of the plain weave, twill weave, or satin weave (Figure 7–11). These weaves refer to different arrangements of the yarns within the fabric.

1. In **plain weave** fabrics, the filling yarns pass alternately over and under the warp yarn. Plain weave fabrics are the simplest and the most common. They can be woven more compactly than other types of weaves and, because of their simplicity, lend themselves to being printed. These fabrics are more prone to wrinkling than other fabric constructions. Examples of plain weaves include broadcloth, calico, challis, muslin, percale, chambray, gingham, and poplin. Variations include cords and oxford cloth.
2. In **twill weave** fabrics, the filling yarns float or pass over or under two or more warp yarns in a staggered progression, producing a characteristic diagonal rib on the surface of the fabric. Twill weave fabrics are very durable. The floats allow the yarns to move, helping them resist abrasion. If the ribs of a twill weave fabric are flattened, the fabric develops shiny spots. Common twill weaves include denim, gabardine, chino, herringbone, houndstooth, and glen plaid.
3. In **satin weave** fabrics, the filling yarns pass over or under several warp yarns at one time. This

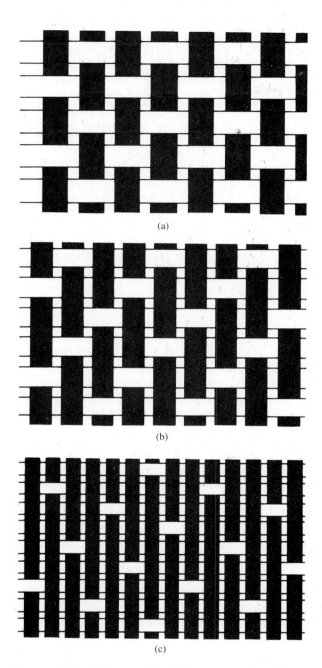

Figure 7–11 Weaves: (a) plain weave, (b) twill weave, and (c) satin weave.

Variations of the three simple weave types include:

1. *dobby* weaves, with small, regular designs woven into the fabric
2. *jacquard* weaves, which have complex designs woven into the fabric
3. *crepe* fabrics with crinkly, pebbly surfaces
4. *piqué* fabrics with a three-dimensional quilted-look surface created by the weave
5. *pile* fabrics with plush surfaces, such as corduroy, velveteen, velvet, and terry cloth.

Knits. *Knitting* is the other major method of creating fabric used in apparel. The yarns in a knit fabric are a series of connected loops. The interlooped structure of knits allows them to stretch significantly, making them more comfortable to wear than wovens. The amount of stretch depends on variations in the knitting process. Because they stretch so easily, knits can lose their original shape unless finished properly at the mill. Knit fabrics pose more challenges for apparel manufacturers than woven fabrics. Manufacturers take precautions not to stretch knit fabrics during apparel production; if the fabric is stretched during cutting and sewing, it later relaxes to its original size. This results in relaxation on the shelf or relaxation shrinkage during laundering of the finished garment. This causes knit garments to demonstrate lengthwise relaxation shrinkage, causing them to become shorter and sometimes wider.

Knitting is faster than weaving but not necessarily less costly because it may require finer, more even yarns. Knit fabrics wrinkle less than wovens. They are more subject to pilling and snagging because they do not hold the yarns and fibers in place as rigidly as do wovens. Knits are generally good insulators in still air, but are cool to wear if there is a breeze. They are less opaque than comparable-weight wovens. Knit fabrics have a tendency to curl at the edges. They have fewer problems with seam pucker than wovens, but seam grin is a problem. (For an example, see Chapter 10, Figure 10–3.) If a loop snags and breaks, the knit structure comes undone in most knits, for example, a run in a sweater, turtleneck, or hosiery.

Filling Knits. In **filling knits** or **weft knits**, the yarns run horizontally across the fabric (Figure 7–12). Hand knits are an example of filling knits. Fillings knits tend to run or ladder if a loop is severed; a whole row of loops may disconnect, especially if the yarn or fiber type is smooth. If a sewing needle cuts a single yarn of the fabric during construction of the garment, the fabric runs when stress is applied. Therefore, needle cutting is a major concern to manufacturers sewing these knits. The majority of knits used in apparel are

produces a long float, which gives satin weave fabrics their characteristic smooth, lustrous surface. More floats and fewer interlacings yield a strong, full-body, drapable fabric. The floats are prone to snagging, yarn slippage, and abrasion, making satin weave fabrics the least durable type of woven fabric. Fabrics with long floats should be handled carefully to avoid marring their surfaces. Most fabrics made with a satin weave are called, simply, satin. Staple-fiber versions are sateen.

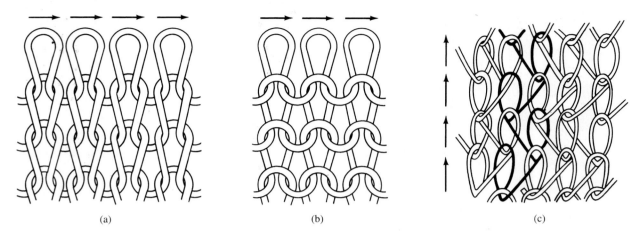

Figure 7–12 Knits: (a) wales on face of weft knits, (b) courses on back of weft knits, and (c) warp knit.

filling knits, including those used to make T-shirts, sweaters, and sweatshirts/sweatpants.

Most filling knits are knitted on circular machines that produce a tubular fabric. Producers split the tube of fabric and flatten it so that it can then be cut and sewn. In the case of T-shirts and sweatshirts, producers knit a narrow tube the desired circumference of the finished garment and leave it in tube form, eliminating the need for side seams. Unfortunately, the construction of circular knits gives them a tendency to twist in the finished garment, a condition called torque (Figure 7–5).

Single Knits. **Single knit** fabrics consist of one layer of loops. Filling single knits include jersey, rib knits, and purl knits. The simplest example of a single filling knit is *jersey,* the plain knit used to make T-shirts. You can distinguish jersey by the rows of vertical loops that run up and down the face or front of the fabric (called **wales**) and the horizontal loops that run across the back of the fabric (called **courses**). Jersey knits have good crosswise and lengthwise stretch and are the most drapable of the filling knits. The edges of jersey fabrics curl, which causes problems during cutting and garment assembly. Fibers or yarns inserted into the jersey knit structure create knitted terry cloth, velour, velvet, fleece, and fake fur.

Alternate wales and courses on the face of *rib knits* create rows of vertical stripes or ribs. They are referenced according to the number of rows of wales and courses. For example, a 1 x 1 rib knit has 1 wale row alternating with 1 course row; a 2 x 3 rib knit has 2 wale rows alternating with 3 course rows. (If the same number of rows of wales and courses are used, the fabric is reversible.) Rib knits are the stretchiest and most elastic knit fabric. This makes them desirable for close-fitting garments. Rib knit or ribbing is used at the neck, wrist, and hem of sweaters, T-shirts, and sweatshirts to allow the openings to stretch for

dressing and undressing. A 2-inch-wide piece of rib knit in a sweater can stretch to 20 inches (Hudson, 1988), so rib knits require a large quantity of yarn in their structure to permit such a high degree of stretch. When relaxed, rib knits are loftier than other knits because of the construction pattern.

A *purl knit* is reversible, with rows of courses resembling the back of a jersey fabric on both sides. Purl knits are bulkier than plain single knits, they have low crosswise stretch, and they do not curl. They are used mainly in infants' and children's wear, especially sweaters.

Double Knits. **Double knit** fabrics consist of two inseparable layers of loops. Double knits are heavier, stretch less, and retain their shape better than single knits. Their edges do not curl, making them the easiest knits to cut and sew. They cost more than single knits. Filling double knits include rib double knits and interlock double knits.

In *rib double knits,* the two layers of loops are staggered. Complex *Jacquard* patterns are often produced. Rib double knits come in a variety of looks. They snag but do not run. Their weight and hand make them especially suitable for tailored garments.

In *interlock double knits,* the two layers of loops are directly on top of one another. Interlock knits are reversible; the front and back look like the front of a plain single knit jersey. While at a glance garments made of jersey and interlock look similar, interlock knits are thicker, heavier, and firmer than jersey knits and less apt to stretch during production or when worn or cared for. They are also less apt to run. However, they are softer, lighter, and more drapable than rib double knits. Interlock knits are used to produce high-quality knit shirts and dresses.

Variations of the basic plain knit constructions produce patterned single- or double-knit fabrics. The main stitch variations are the *tuck stitch,* which combines multiple loops on the same course, and the *float* or *miss stitch,* which connects two loops that are not from adjacent wales.

Warp Knits.

In **warp knits**, the yarns run parallel to the length of the fabric (Figure 7–12c). Warp knitting machines interloop many yarns simultaneously across the width of the fabric; the loops interlock diagonally.

Warp knits are usually produced as flat goods. They do not run or ravel and have greater dimensional stability than filling knits. Warp knits are generally lightweight and not particularly lofty or resilient. The main types of warp knits used to make apparel fabrics are tricot and Raschel. Basic *tricot* jersey is a flat single knit, often made of nylon filament yarn, used in the production of panties, slips, and other lingerie. The wales and courses of tricot jersey knits are similar in appearance to those of filling jersey knits, except the courses of warp knits lie more diagonally than horizontally. Tricot accounts for the majority of warp knits. *Raschel* knits are constructed with a laid-in yarn that connects loops from one column to another column diagonally up the fabric. Most basic Raschel knits are open, lacy-looking fabrics. Tricot and Raschel knits include most low-cost net and lace; elastic fabrics for swimwear, lingerie, foundation garments, active sportswear, and elastic bands; and pile fabrics such as fake fur.

Other Fabric Structures.

A variety of other fabric structures, including fiberweb, bonded, film, lace, quilted, and flocked fabrics, are significant for use in the apparel industry.

Fiberweb or Nonwoven Fabrics.

Fiberweb or *nonwoven* fabrics are created by matting loose fibers together using a variety of techniques, including heat, adhesives, and mechanical interlocking. Fiberwebs are mainly used inside garments as interfacings to provide shape and stability because they are the least costly of all fabrics. Many of these nonwovens are backed with fusible adhesive for easy application.

The durability of nonwovens varies widely. A nonwoven inside the garment needs to endure wear and care as well as the body fabric and other components of the garments. Felt is a familiar example of a nonwoven fabric.

Bonded Fabrics.

Bonded fabrics are two distinct fabrics glued together as one. *Laminated* fabrics consist of a layer of fabric adhered to a layer of foam. Bonding and laminating may be used to add body to low-yarn-count fabrics. The main problems with low-quality bonded and laminated fabrics are uneven shrinking and separation of the two layers. Some film fabrics are bonded or laminated; few other apparel fabrics are bonded or laminated today.

Film Fabrics.

Film fabrics are continuous sheets of fabric made directly from a polymer solution, for example, plastic. Film fabrics are strong, durable, and difficult to sew unless they are bonded or laminated.

The most common plastic used in apparel applications is *vinyl.* Like many other synthetic materials, vinyl is a petroleum derivative. The most common vinyl material is *polyvinyl chloride (PVC)*. Vinyl is widely used in raincoats and to imitate leather in jackets and other apparel, as well as in belts, shoes, and other accessories. It costs considerably less than leather, and garments are cut from large sheets of vinyl more efficiently than from irregularly shaped leather hides.

Vinyl is generally considered to be of lower quality than leather because it tends to stiffen and crack with age. Also, vinyl melts if exposed to high temperatures. Vinyl is uncomfortable to wear next to the skin because it is not absorbent and does not breathe. The hand of vinyl depends on how much plasticizer the producer adds; more plasticizer results in a more flexible product. The producer adds air bubbles during the manufacturing process to create *expanded vinyls;* the air bubbles make these vinyls good insulators for cold-weather clothing. They closely imitate leather. Most vinyls may be wiped clean with a damp cloth or machine washed, but not machine dried.

Polyurethane plastics are also used in apparel applications. For example, a synthetic, leather-like fabric is *Ultrasuede®,* a blend of polyester fibers and polyurethane plastic. *Gore-Tex®* fabrics have a thin microporous film of polytetrafluoroethylene (PTFE) that allows water vapor but not water droplets to pass through. These fabrics are ideal for active sportswear, rainwear, skiwear, hunting clothes, etc. This makes Gore-Tex® fabrics ideal for all-weather outerwear that is waterproof but allows the wearer's perspiration to evaporate for comfort.

Lace.

Lace is a fabric structure resulting from twisting and knotting the yarns around one another (Various laces are pictured in Chapter 8, Figure 8–3.) Although lace originated as a handcraft, almost all lace today is machine made. For example, machine-made laces imitate crocheted and tatted laces so well that they are difficult to tell from handmade. There are many, many different types of lace, fabricated in various ways. The cost of lace is related to its fiber content and the complexity of its production. High-cost laces are made mainly on Leavers machines; low-cost laces are made mainly on Raschel knitting machines. Schiffli embroidery machines make eyelet (an embroidered fabric that is generally referred to as a lace).

Quilted Fabrics.

Quilted fabrics consist of two fabric layers joined to a nonwoven interlining such as *batting* (filler), foam, or down. Most quilted fabrics are stitched together. The quilting stitches form a puffy, raised design, often in a geometric or other decorative pattern. Some quilting in low-price garments is joined by ultrasonic fusing instead of stitches, if the fabric is made of thermoplastic fibers. Ultrasonic quilting is as durable as or more durable than stitched quilting, but its appearance is different, thus generating lower consumer acceptance than stitching. Stitched quilting costs more than fused quilting. Fabric is usually quilted by a quilting contractor before the garments are cut and sewn. Quilting is popular in coats, jackets, and vests.

Flocked Fabrics. *Flocked* fabrics have short, decorative fibers held on to the base fabric with an adhesive. Durability of the adhesive is a key factor in the durability of flocked fabrics. An example of a flocked fabric is dotted swiss.

Dyes

Dyeing adds color to undyed fabrics, called **greige goods** (pronounced "gray goods"). Dyeing is a merchandising decision as much as a technical decision because color is critical to consumers when considering which garment to purchase.

Dyestuffs. **Dyestuffs** or **dyes** are the liquid colorants used to color fabrics. Most dyes are water-soluble chemicals that bond with the fibers or build up on or within the fibers. Dyestuffs are carefully chosen based on price, fiber content, color range, and brightness (see Table 7–3).

The type of dye used influences the aesthetic and functional performance of the fabric. Dyestuffs need to be applied in a manner that achieves the best overall aesthetic performance possible without excessively changing other properties of the cloth. Dyes affect the fabric's strength, abrasion resistance, luster, absorbency, and dimensional stability. For example, different dyes alter the amount of stretch in a knit fabric. Dyes also influence the hand of the fabric, including its drape, texture, and ease of production. However, most undesirable qualities brought on by dyeing can be offset with appropriate fabric finishing (see section on Finishes later in this chapter). The type of dye used helps determine how the garment should be laundered or dry-cleaned, because dyeing affects a garment's washfastness and lightfastness. Some types and colors of dyes are more colorfast than others; some fade more than others in reaction to light, water, detergents, or bleaches. Colorfastness must be balanced with the desire for a particular color because, in some cases, the desired color is not available in the most colorfast dye. The color of the dye affects the fabric's opacity; dark colors are typically

more opaque, or have more *covering power,* than light colors. These problems are the concerns of dye chemists, who formulate the best dye type for the fiber, type of garment if known in advance (for example, swimwear should be colorfast to sunlight and chlorine), stage of application, and desired color. However, the cost to buy and then to apply dyestuffs varies considerably, so sometimes the dye chemist makes compromises. The formulas for producing dark colors generally cost more than the formulas for light colors.

Pigment dye, not a true dyestuff, is contained in a paste that is spread over the cloth and adheres to the cloth through the use of binders. It adds a special look not achieved by other dyeing methods. However, it can adversely stiffen the cloth if not carefully monitored.

Dye Application. Fabrics can be dyed in the fiber, yarn, fabric, or garment stage. The main methods of dye application include the following:

1. **Solution dyeing,** or **dope dyeing,** is the dyeing of manufactured fibers before the fibers are formed, while they are still in a liquid stage. Fabrics made from solution-dyed fibers have the best colorfastness because the dye penetrates and becomes part of the fiber. Solution dyeing, as well as the occasional dyeing of natural fibers in the fiber stage, is also called **fiber dyeing.** Fiber dyeing produces the most even dyeing results in the finished fabric. The main disadvantage of fiber dyeing is that mills have to commit to color decisions far in advance of the selling season, as much as two years before. To reduce the risk of making the wrong color decision, manufacturers fiber dye only basic colors. They make fashion-color decisions closer to the selling season to reduce the risk of making an incorrect prediction about what color will be most popular.

2. **Yarn-dyed** fabrics receive their dyes in the yarn stage. Yarn is wound on cones. The cones are processed in a dye liquor with high heat and pressure in order to penetrate the whole dye package evenly. This is the last chance to add color for stripes, plaids, and other designs that are to be woven in, not printed on. Yarn-dyed fabrics tend to be more evenly colored and colorfast than piece-dyed fabrics.

3. **Piece-dyed** fabrics are dyed in the fabric stage. This is the easiest and least expensive stage for adding color and probably the most common. Traditionally, the fabric is dyed using heat but no pressure and the garment is cut and sewn from the already colored fabric.

4. There is an increasing trend toward **garment dyeing.** The apparel manufacturer produces the

Table 7-3 Dyestuff Characteristics

Dyestuff	Appropriate Fibers	Wash-Fast	Dry-Cleaning	Crock-Fast	Light-Fast	Perspiration Resistant	Ease of Application	Cost	Comments
Acid	Protein Nylon Silk	Poor	Excellent	Fair	Poor to Good	Poor to Good	Easy	Low	Bright colors
Basic (Cationic)	Acrylic Modacrylic	Excellent	Good	Excellent	Excellent	Excellent	Moderate	Average	Bright colors / Designed for acrylic fibers
Chrome (Mordant)	Protein (Wool) Nylon, Silk	Excellent	Good	Good	Excellent	Excellent	Difficult	Moderate	Dull colors / Often used on floor coverings
Direct	Cellulose Silk	Poor	Good	Good	Poor to Good	Good	Easy	Low	Wide color range
Developed Direct	Cellulose Silk	Good to Excellent	Good	Good	Poor to Good	Good	Easy	Low	Wide color range
Disperse	Polyester Nylon, Olefin Acrylic Modacrylic	Excellent	Good	Good	Fair to Good	Good	Easy	Moderate	Wide color range
	Acetate	Poor	Good	Good	Fair to Good	Good	Easy	Moderate	Blue and violet on acetate fume fade
Indigo	Cellulose	Fair	Good	Fair	Fair	Good	Difficult	Moderate	Unique blue color / Desirable fading qualities
Napthol (Azoic)	Cellulose	Good	Good	Fair	Poor To Good	Good	Difficult	Moderate	Bright colors / Primarily red to orange color range / Possibly carcinogenic
Pigment	All, when applied as single color	Fair	Poor	Poor	Good	Fair	Moderate	Low	Not a true dyestuff / Wide color range / Mechanically adhered to surface / Heavy shades can stiffen fabric / Performance depends on binder
Reactive	Cellulose Protein, Nylon	Good	Good	Good	Good	Good	Moderate	High	Wide color range / Bright colors / Hard to match shades / Poor fastness to chlorine bleach
Sulfur	Cellulose	Good	Good	Poor	Good	Good	Difficult	Low	Dark color range, dull colors / Can cause tender goods over time / Poor fastness to chlorine bleach
Vat	Cellulose	Excellent	Good	Good	Excellent	Excellent	Difficult	Moderate	Dark color range / Good chlorine bleach fastness / Will crock if improperly applied

Note. The information presented in the dyestuff chart is vastly simplified. Specific information about each color produced by a particular dyestuff should be carefully researched. Cost information is intentionally general and applies only to the average cost of dyestuffs, not to other aspects of the dyeing process garment from PFD (prepared for dye) cloth and then has the finished garment dyed by a garment wet processor. The big advantage of garment dyeing is that the apparel manufacturer can make color decisions with short lead times, dyeing garments in the proven best-selling colors and avoiding a large inventory of colors that are not popular. For example, The Gap contracts the production of thousands of basic white T-shirts and then has them dyed them according to the best-selling colors as needed. For more information on garment dyeing, see Chapter 4.

Prints

Printing is the application of designs to the fabric using dyes or pigments in limited areas. Patterns, for example flowers or geometric designs, can be printed on or woven into fabrics. Generally, printed-on patterns are less costly than woven-in designs because of the complexity of weaving a patterned fabric.

A good-quality printed design is clear, focused, and sharp, not smudged. Each color should be precisely lined up or **in registration.** A print that is *out of registration* has white areas in the design or places where the colors overlap. Patterns containing numerous colors and details are generally costly to produce. Patterned fabrics, whether printed on or woven in, tend to mask wrinkling, puckering, soiling, and construction errors in the garment better than solid fabrics, improving ease of production.

Designs should be printed onto the fabric on the straight-of-grain. When plaids, checks, stripes, or other obviously directional designs are printed onto a fabric that is skewed or bowed, the design will appear crooked on the finished garment. If the design is printed on fabric only slightly off-grain, the cutter can cut the garment straight with the directional pattern rather than on the straight-of-grain. Although the garment may not hang perfectly straight, it will look straighter than a garment that hangs straight but has a crooked stripe or plaid. If the design is printed on drastically off-grain fabric, the fabric should not be used and should be returned to the mill.

For durability of a printed design, the dyes or pigments used to create the design must be absorbed by the fabric. A heavy application of color is generally more durable than a light application but can make the fabric stiff, affecting its drape. For this reason, chemicals are used to bond the dyestuff to the fiber or be a catalyst for the absorbtion of the color. Fabrics do not always absorb printed dyes, but merely hold them on the surface of the fabric. When knitted garments are stretched during wear, separation of the wales distorts the printed design, causing consumer dissatisfaction. This is less of a problem in woven apparel.

Figure 7–13 Screen printing. (Courtesy of Winning Ways.)

Manufacturers use several methods to apply prints to fabrics, including screen printing, direct roller printing, and heat-transfer printing.

Screen Printing. **Screen printing** applies colored ink, using a squeegee, through a screen that has some areas blocked off to create a stencil (Figure 7–13). A series of screens is used to apply different colors to achieve multicolored designs. The ink is then heat cured. High-speed rotary (roller) screen printers print entire fabrics; flat-bed screen printers apply designs either to fabrics or to finished garments like T-shirts and sweatshirts. Screen print ink is best absorbed by fabrics that are made entirely or mostly of cotton. Screen printing's affinity for cotton and its speed make it the most common fabric printing method today.

The more ink deposited on the fabric, the more durable the screen-printed design. The formulation of the ink and how it is cured also affect durability. Poorly cured screen prints crack or peel readily in use. High-quality screen prints are in registration and can withstand home laundering without cracking or losing color. Overall, screen prints cost less per garment than heat-transfer printing when large quantities are involved.

Direct Roller Printing. **Direct roller printing** involves applying a pattern by directly rolling it onto the fabric using a series of cylinders containing different colors of ink. The cost of preparing the rollers makes direct roller printing suitable only for large runs. Direct roller printing is still used widely for printing cotton and cotton-blend woven fabrics.

Table 7–4   Mechanical finishes for fabrics

Compressed: compressing the fabric to return it to its original dimensions to control relaxation shrinkage; sometimes combined with chemical shrinkage control finishes. Examples include the *Sanforized*® trademark on cotton and cotton blend fabrics, and its related labels, Sanfor Knit® and Sanfor Set®. All guarantee residual shrinkage of less than 1%.

Heat-set: used to control shrinkage of fabrics made from thermoplastic fibers. The amount of heat that will soften the fiber without melting is applied; then the fabric is cooled. After heat setting, the fabric will not shrink or wrinkle unless the heat-set temperature is exceeded. Heat setting is also used to permanently set details, such as creases or pleats, into a garment. Details that have been heat set maintain their shape throughout the life of the garment unless the heat setting temperature is exceeded.

Napped: fibers pulled up from the yarns to make the surface soft, thick, and warm

Brushed: nap or pile of the fabric raised by brushing

Embossed: decorative textures pressed into the fabric

Glazed: polished finish combining resins/wax/starch and heavy pressing; some glazes are more permanent than others.

Sanded/sueded/emerized: abrading the fabric surface to give it the look and feel of natural suede or chamois

Sheared: cutting the napped or pile surface to a uniform length, or carving in a design

Moiré: adding a wavy, watermark design to the surface of the fabric

Singed: flame passed along fabric surface to prevent pilling

Heat-Transfer Printing.   Heat-transfer printing involves transferring a design from a specially printed paper to the fabric using heat and pressure. Heat-transfer printing is performed on a small scale at the consumer level. Prints can be chosen by the consumer and applied to T-shirts and sweatshirts at the point of sale because the process requires a minimum of equipment. This process is also used on a large scale by mills to apply designs to fabric before it is sewn. Heat-transfer prints adhere best to fabric that is made entirely or mostly of synthetic fibers; thus, it accounts for a small portion of fabric printing today. The durability of heat transfer prints depends on the amount of heat, pressure, and time used to transfer the design. For permanency, the design must deeply penetrate and bond with the fabric rather than adhere only to the surface.

If properly executed, heat-transfer printing allows greater design clarity, better penetration of the fibers, and therefore a more durable design and less pollution (the paper can be recycled) than screen printing. Heat-transfer printers achieve a variety of three-dimensional, foil, and other special effects, including sometimes combining transfer prints with screen prints. Some heat-transfer prints tend to crack and peel over time, especially when exposed to high washing and drying temperatures. Heat-transfer prints are more economical than screen prints for small runs.

Finishes

A myriad of finishes, including both mechanical and chemical fabric treatments, is available for imparting desirable performance characteristics to fabrics. For more information, see Tables 7–4 and 7–5 for a description of mechanical and chemical finishes used on apparel fabrics. Many performance aspects of a fabric can be improved through the application of the appropriate finish. However, most finishes enhance one aspect of performance while simultaneously detracting from another; therefore, they must be carefully monitored and balanced. For example, mechanically brushing or napping a fabric improves the hand of the cloth while simultaneously reducing its strength. See Chapter 4 for information on finishes applied to garments during wet processing.

Usually, consumers are not aware of fabric finishes since most of them cannot be seen, but most fabrics have finishes. Some finishes can affect whether or not garments are washable or dry-cleanable; some finishes are damaged by improper care. The manufacturer's recommended refurbishing procedures, as noted on the care label, are designed to preserve the finish and ensure the garment performs as expected. Many finishes gradually diminish over the life of the

Table 7–5 Chemical finishes for fabrics

Wrinkle-resistant: see discussion in Chapter 4

Other wet processes: see discussion in Chapter 4

Optically brightened: makes fabric appear whiter or brighter

Shrinkage controlled: used alone or in addition to compressive shrinkage techniques to maintain dimensional stability of fabrics; for example, allow wool fabrics to be machine washed without shrinking

Sized: starches or resins added to the fabric to improve the appearance of and add body to fabrics. Sizings add to the aesthetic value of the garment at the time of purchase by making the surface smooth and crisp. They are often used on low-quality fabrics to improve their appearance and hand. Although some sizings are semipermanent, most are temporary. Temporary sizings can mislead consumers into buying garments that they would not otherwise purchase. After laundering, if the sizing washes out, the garment may be limp and lifeless, have little luster, and require ironing, leaving the consumer dissatisfied

Mercerized: strengthens cotton and linen; makes the fabric lustrous and absorbent (and thus more dyeable)

Water-repellent: helps fabric repel light rain and resist wet spotting and staining; important for raingear and other outerwear; well-known trademarks are Zepel and Scotchgard; not durable to care processes, but can be reapplied by dry-cleaner or consumer

Waterproof: completely repels rain; most are uncomfortable to wear because the fabric cannot breathe

Moth repellent: repels moths in wool fabrics

Soil-release: increases the absorbency of fabrics; increased absorbency also improves the launderability of the fabric, helping it repel and release soil and stains and reduce static buildup; generally improves fabric hand; some reduce durable press characteristics and cause yellowing or dullness

Antistatic: increases fabric's ability to absorb water and therefore conduct electrical charges; important for lingerie and some work uniforms

Softened: softeners give fabrics a pleasant hand but generally decrease absorbency; consumer use of fabric softeners in the laundry helps maintain softness and anti-static characteristics. Restrict use of softeners on diapers, terry cloth robes, and other garments intended to be absorbent

Flame-retardant: makes fabrics flame resistant. By law, flame-retardant finishes used on children's sleepwear must withstand 50 machine washings. They also must be nontoxic and noncarcinogenic (not cancer causing). Garments with flame-retardant finishes require special care even though they look and feel like other garments; consumers must follow the manufacturer's suggested care instructions

Parchmentized: gives a crispness and translucence to fabrics

Washable wool: controls the felting shrinkage of wool so that it can be machine washed; may impair hand and durability

Washable silk: non-water soluble additives allow silk to be hand (or sometimes machine) washed; do not dry-clean. Fabric has dull, distressed look with niche in casual sportswear market

Antibacterial: controls odor generated by bacteria in perspiration; found in some socks; Sanitized® and Biogard® are trade names.

garment, regardless of care, but appropriate care will maintain the finish for as long as possible.

LEATHER AND FUR

Leather and fur are other important textile materials, but they are unique in that they are naturally occurring. However, special treatment is required to ready them for use.

Leather. *Leather* is the *tanned* or preserved skin or hide from an animal. Manufacturers use leather to make jackets, coats, and other apparel as well as shoes, belts, and accessories. Consumers prize leather for its beauty and durability. They find it comfortable to wear because of its ability to breathe.

Genuine leather or **top grain** is the top layer of the hide. It represents the highest quality leather and the most expensive. Other layers of the hide are referred to as **splits.** Manufacturers sometimes give splits an artificial grain that looks like top grain, but splits are slightly rougher, do not wear as well, and cost less than top grain. **Suede** results when a manufacturer naps the leather, giving it a fuzzy surface.

Fashion greatly affects the demand for various types of leathers from different animals. Unblemished hides yield the most attractive and costly leathers. The thickness of the split, the rarity of the animal from which it is taken, and the tanning and finishing processes chosen also affect the cost and quality of leather. Hides go through an extensive tanning process to become leather, which partly explains their expense. Placement of pattern pieces on individual, irregular hides is not as efficient as on wide, even-width stacks of manufactured fabrics, another factor contributing to the cost of leather garments.

Leather and imitation leathers require special construction techniques because regular methods may cause damage. Stitches weaken these fabrics, so long stitches are used. Seams and hems may be glued or fused instead of stitched. Fasteners other than buttons and buttonholes may be used. Because these fabrics retain needle puncture marks, alteration of garments made from these fabrics is limited. Large leather garments require pieced panels because of the limited size of the hides. For example, most leather pants for adults have a seam across the leg.

Fur. *Fur* is an animal skin or hide with the hair still attached; it is used to make luxurious coats and jackets and for trims and accessories. Consumers value fur for its warmth and beauty.

Fashion greatly affects the demand for various types of fur from different animals. The Fur Products Labeling Act regulates the labeling of fur garments. Most fur today is taken from ranch-raised animals rather than from animals trapped in the wild.

Responsible furriers use fur only from species that are not endangered. Nevertheless, animal rights activists oppose the wearing of fur because it requires killing the animal for its coat.

The cost of a fur depends on the rarity of the animal from which it came and upon its quality. Fur quality relates to the softness, fluffiness, and density of the fur, and its color and luster. Animals raised in cold climates and fed nutritious diets tend to have dense, lustrous fur. How well the pelts within a garment match one another in shade and texture affects aesthetic quality. Fur from female animals tends to be softer and more desirable than fur from males. Female pelts are smaller than male pelts, thus requiring a larger number of pelts per garment. This makes them more costly. All furs go through an extensive dressing process to preserve and soften the hide and maximize the luster of the fur, which helps explain the cost of fur garments.

Fur garments require special construction techniques. The methods chosen help determine cost. **Fully-let-out** fur garments are by far the most expensive. Letting out involves cutting the pelts into narrow diagonal strips. These strips are sewn back together so that each pelt becomes a long, narrow panel that covers the length of the wearer's body. Fully-let-out furs lend a slimming appearance to the wearer. Letting out requires hours of hand labor and must be done by a highly skilled furrier. **Skin-on-skin** garments contain whole pelts sewn together. They are much less costly to produce than fully-let-out furs.

SUMMARY

Quality fabric is a prerequisite for a quality garment, but fabric alone cannot predict garment quality. The fabric interacts with the design, other materials, construction, and any finishes of the garment to yield its overall performance. However, fabric is an essential quality indicator because it makes the greatest single contribution to the cost and quality of the garment.

The design of a garment, its end use and price line, fashion trends, and personal preferences determine the required performance characteristics of the fabric in a garment. Aesthetic performance specifications include standards for color and pattern, color consistency, luster, opacity, and hand (drapability, compressibility, extensibility, resilience, density, texture, thermal character). Most aesthetic performance standards are subjective and difficult to accurately measure and specify. Most functional performance standards can be objectively measured and specified. Functional performance specifications deal with utility dimensions of the fabric, for example, its shape retention (resistance to shrinkage and stretching, and torque and skewness), appearance retention (color-fastness and resistance to wrinkling, snagging, pilling, and heat), comfort (breathability, warmth, absorbency, and electrical conductivity), ease of care, safety, and the number and severity of flaws (often rated using the Four Point System). Functional performance specifications also relate to the durability of the fabric, including its tear and bursting strength, abrasion resistance, and ability to withstand degradation by mechanical and chemical means and natural elements. Seven basic tests can account for a majority of fabric performance considerations: count, weight, shrinkage, tensile or bursting strength, crocking, lightfastness, and garment washability.

The performance of the fabric is a result of the interaction among its physical dimensions, including the fibers, yarns, fabric structure, dyes, prints, and finishes. Fibers are the basic building blocks of a fabric and provide important clues to fabric performance. Though fibers have some characteristics in common with others of their same type, either natural or manufactured, individual fibers vary considerably in performance. They are spun into yarns, from which fabrics are made. Yarns may be simple or complex; yarn size is generally specified in denier or tex. Weaving, the interlacing of yarns, is the most common method for producing fabric. Knitting, the interlooping of yarns, is a more economical fabrication than weaving. Knits tend to be comfortable but dimensionally unstable because they stretch. Fabrics with a high thread count or gauge tend to be stable and of high quality. Heavyweight fabrics generally cost more and are of higher quality than lightweight fabrics. Dyes add color to fabrics. The later in the production cycle the color is added, the more flexibility the producer has in following fashion color trends. Prints should be clear, durable, on grain, and in registration. Chemical and mechanical finishes are applied to enhance garment performance. For example, they can reduce shrinkage and wrinkling and increase body and luster.

Fabric Quality Checklist

If you can answer yes to each of these questions regarding the garment you are evaluating, it contains high-quality fabric. The ability of the garment to meet many of these performance standards cannot be evaluated visually but must be determined through laboratory or wear testing.

✔ Is the fabric free of flaws? If not, are the flaws inconspicuous?
✔ Is the appearance of the fabric compatible with the design and end use of the garment?
✔ Is the color consistent within the garment or ensemble (no shading)?
✔ Is the hand (including drapability and texture) of the fabric suitable for the design of the garment?
✔ Does the fabric lend itself to the mass production process?
✔ Does the fabric retain its original shape and size (resist shrinking and stretching) after wearing and refurbishing?
✔ Is the fabric grain true, without excessive torque or skewness?
✔ Is the fabric colorfast?
✔ Does the fabric retain desirable creases?
✔ Does the fabric resist wrinkling?
✔ Does the fabric resist snagging and pilling?
✔ Does the fabric resist heat damage?
✔ Is the fabric comfortable?
✔ Does the fabric stretch, if stretch is necessary for comfort and good fit?
✔ Does the fabric breathe?
✔ Is the fabric warm or cool, as called for by the end use of the garment?
✔ Is the fabric absorbent?
✔ Does the fabric have good wicking ability?
✔ Does the fabric resist static cling?
✔ Is the fabric easy to care for?
✔ Is the fabric safe (for example, fire resistant)?
✔ Is the fabric durable?
✔ Does the fabric resist tearing and bursting?
✔ Does the fabric withstand abrasion?
✔ Do the yarns resist shifting?
✔ Does the fabric resist chemical and mechanical degradation?
✔ Can the fabric withstand insects, mildew, and sunlight?
✔ Are the yarns tightly twisted?
✔ Is the thread count or gauge high?
✔ Are prints durable, clear, on grain, and in registration?
✔ Are finishes permanent or semipermanent?
✔ Is leather top grain and free of blemishes?
✔ Are furs soft and lustrous? Are fur garments made using fully-let-out versus skin-on-skin construction?

New Terms

If you can define these terms and differentiate between related terms, you have gained a good working vocabulary for discussing the topics in this chapter. The terms are listed in the order in which they appear in the chapter.

fabric
American Textile Manufacturers Institute (ATMI)

Kawabata Evaluation System for Fabrics (KES)
Fabric Assessment by Simple Testing (FAST)
mill flaw
put-up
major defect
flagging system
Four Point System
dye lot
shade lot
shading
metamerism
luster
opacity
hand
dimensional stability
elongation
elasticity/memory
shrinkage
relaxation shrinkage
felting shrinkage
residual shrinkage
torque
skew
bowed
colorfastness
snag
pill
heat resistance
thermoplastic
heat set
Clo
wicking ability
tensile strength/tenacity
abrasion resistance
yarn slippage
count/thread count/yarn count
cut/gauge
crocking
fiber
natural fibers
manufactured/man-made fibers
American Fiber Manufacturers Association
staple
filament
denier
tex
blend
yarn
spun yarn
carded
combed
woolen
worsted
filament yarn

bulk continuous filament (BCF)
plied
twist
yarn number
decitex (dtex)
denier per filament (dpf)
plain weave
twill weave
satin weave
filling/weft knit
single knit
wales
courses
double knit
warp knit
greige goods
dyestuffs/dyes
solution/dope dyeing
fiber dyeing
yarn dyeing
piece dyeing
garment dyeing
dyestuff/dye
in registration
screen printing
direct roller printing
heat-transfer printing
genuine leather/top grain
split
suede
fully-let-out
skin-on-skin

Review Questions

1. Explain the relationship of fabric quality to garment quality.
2. What percentage of shrinkage represents an approximate full size in a garment of woven fabric? of knit fabric?
3. What steps do manufacturers take to reduce garment shrinkage?
4. How does fiber content affect fabric performance?
5. Summarize the general characteristics of natural fibers versus manufactured fibers.
6. How does fiber content impact the care of the finished garment?
7. Discuss the effect of yarn type, twist, and size on fabric performance.
8. Compare and contrast the characteristics of woven fabrics and knit fabrics.
9. List and describe the three main types of weaves. Repeat for the two main types of knits.
10. What is the significance of count or gauge?

11. What are the advantages and disadvantages of garment dyeing?
12. List the criteria for a high-quality printed design.
13. Discuss how finishes can improve fabric and garment performance.

Activities

1. Visit an apparel manufacturer. Ask to see their fabric and garment testing facilities. Find out
   a. what instrumental and other tests they perform
   b. how they establish performance criteria for the fabrics they use.

2. Visit an apparel plant. Ask to see the fabric quality manager. Have the manager review
   a. how they inspect for flaws
   b. the number and type of acceptable flaws
   c. how they deal with flaws through the manufacturing process
   d. how they inspect for color consistency
   e. steps they take to avoid shading in the finished garment

3. Purchase three 1/2-yard pieces of fabric. Describe the fabric's physical and performance features, including the hand of the fabric. For each piece of fabric, select a picture of a garment for which the fabric is suitable and another for which it is unsuitable.

4. Purchase a new garment. Measure it before and after laundering. How much did it shrink in length and in width (inches and percentage)? Why did it shrink (or not shrink)? Compare results with those of others in your class.

5. Purchase two new, identical, colored garments. Wash one ten times. Evaluate the garments' fading, frosting, crocking, bleeding/staining, and/or yellowing by comparing the two after each washing. Compare results with those of your classmates.

6. Examine a sweater or sweatshirt that you have worn several times. Has the fabric pilled? If not, why not? If so, why? Where is the pilling concentrated and why? Do you find it objectionable?

7. Using 1/2-inch strips of colored paper, with one color as the warp and one color as the filling, weave a sample of the plain weave, the twill weave, and the satin weave. Find an example of each weave in your wardrobe.

8. Pull and twist a cotton ball into a yarn. Note the impact of increased twist on yarn strength, fineness, and luster.

9. Compare two similarly styled garments, one low-price and one high-price. What differences, if any, do you see in the thread count, weight, and thickness of the fabric?

10. Squeeze the fabric of a durable-press garment in your fist for 15 seconds and release. Repeat on a garment of similar fabric without a durable-press finish. What differences do you see?

8

Findings and Trim: More Quality Indicators

Chapter Objectives

1. Present a vocabulary of findings and trim names.
2. Examine the impact of findings and trim on the performance and cost of the garment.

Findings consist of all components of a garment except the body fabric; they include trims, labels, threads, elastics, underlying fabrics, zippers, buttons, other closures, and other miscellaneous items. **Trims**, a subdivision of findings, are decorative materials that adorn the garment. The term *trim* usually refers to ribbons, braids, laces, and other narrow fabric trims but also includes appliqués, flowers, beads, sequins, and other decorative items. Other terms such as *sundries* and *notions* may be used for findings and trim; however, the domestic apparel industry usually uses the terms *findings* and *trim*.

Findings and trim are critical to garment quality. Consumers rarely purchase garments based on these items;

however, they often discard garments upon the failure of the trim or findings. Although a seemingly minor component of garments, decorative trim that fails to perform leads to nonfunctioning or unattractive garments that are no longer a joy to wear, and when findings such as zippers malfunction, garments become unwearable. Therefore, the dependable functioning of findings and trim is vital to ultimate consumer satisfaction.

FINDINGS AND TRIM PERFORMANCE

The evaluation of findings and trim is as important as the evaluation of fabric when assessing garment quality. The quality of the findings and trim must reflect the same quality level as the fabric. Too often findings and trim are overlooked, forgotten, or taken for granted. It is unfortunate to produce a fine-quality career dress and have the bow or appliqué ruin the dress when it is refurbished. If the bow fabric or the appliqué thread is not tested and does not meet standards, this is a likely situation. Thus, the performance of the finding or trim could negate the performance of the body fabric if the correct selection is not made. Findings and trim must withstand the same conditions as the fabric. The aesthetic and functional performance standards for findings and trim are based on the end use, care, design, and body fabric of the garment.

As discussed in previous chapters, fabric quality is assessed at all stages of apparel production; this constant assessment is key because of the important role fabric plays in maintaining quality. However, findings and trim, if checked at all, are usually tested only once early in the development stage. They are not tested again until they have become part of production garment checks. This is due to the fact that long lead times make them unavailable until after the body fabric is made. Nevertheless, the quality of findings must not be overlooked.

Establishing Findings and Trim Specifications

The merchandisers and designers purchase findings and trim from suppliers according to predetermined specifications and standards. In many cases the specs for findings and trim are those established by the suppliers themselves or in partnerships with the supplier. The items are then submitted for testing to confirm that the supplier's products meet their own specifications for quality consistency. The reason this approach is taken is that no one apparel designer, merchandiser, or quality engineer can acquire the knowledge and experience needed to develop and establish standards and specs for the vast number of trim and finding products available, especially at the rate fashion changes. Thus, the supplier knows the most about findings items. Most retailers and manufacturers will defer to supplier knowledge on findings items not used frequently.

ASTM has developed standardized test methods and performance specifications for a few findings items. These include zippers, elastic, buttons, snap fasteners, and thread. The test methods primarily measure functional performance; therefore, manufacturers often develop their own test methods for aesthetic performance of findings and for any functional aspects not covered by ASTM test methods.

Imperfect findings and trim items are commonly called defectives or defects. Defectives come in as large a variety as the findings and trim themselves. Examples of defective findings and trim include a zipper tab with the wrong name imprinted on it, a molded plastic button with rough edges, a thread with excessive lubricant (causing staining), an embroidered appliqué with a section of missing stitches, and a fusible interfacing without an adhesive. The variety of possible findings and trim defects is endless. A comprehensive testing and inspection system helps detect and reject defective findings and trims before they are applied to garments.

Aesthetic Performance of Findings and Trim

The aesthetic performance considerations that apply to fabrics also apply to trim and findings. The aesthetic performance or attractiveness of findings and trim refers to the appearance of the items as they complement the appearance of the garment. Both findings and trim play an important part in the aesthetic performance of the garment. However, they must be considered in concert with the design, construction, and finish of the garment because design, materials, construction, and finish interact to produce the total aesthetic effect. Findings and trim should aesthetically harmonize with the garment; the color, size, shape, texture, and application of the items should complement its design and fabric.

Attractive, fashionable, and functional findings and trim help sell the garment. A savvy merchandiser knows when to invest in better findings and trim, for example, adding expensive buttons to improve the appearance of an otherwise ordinary garment so it commands a higher selling price. Aesthetic performance considerations for trims and findings include color, pattern, color consistency, luster, opacity, and hand, as discussed in the previous chapter on fabric.

Closures such as buttons and buttonholes, hooks and eyes, snaps, zippers, frogs, buckles, and other functional findings may double as decorative details. However, they may also serve as decorative details only. For example, sometimes manufacturers sew nonfunctional buttons to garments strictly for decorative purposes, for example, at the wrists of tailored jacket sleeves. The buttonholes on the lapels of some tailored jackets, reminiscent of the days when men wore flowers in their lapels, are another detail more decorative than functional. (Such a buttonhole appears in Chapter 12, Figure 12–4.) Some decorative details, such as metal nailheads, studs, rivets, and burrs, may also serve a functional purpose as reinforcements for seams and points of stress.

Functional Performance of Findings and Trim

The same functional performance considerations apply for trim or findings as for fabrics. The functional performance of a trim or finding item refers to its utility and durability as a component of the garment. Utility includes the influence of the trim or finding on these garment characteristics: (1) dimensional stability, (2) appearance retention, (3) comfort, (4) ease of care, and (5) safety. Durability refers to the serviceability of the trim or finding regarding these characteristics of the garment: (1) strength, (2) abrasion resistance, and (3) degradation by chemicals and other elements of the environment.

As with aesthetic performance, the design, materials, and construction of a garment interact to determine utility and durability. For example, tiny buttons at the center back of the garment are unacceptable in clothing for young children or people with limited arm mobility if they are to dress independently. All findings and trim need to be comfortable, not bulky or irritating to the skin, and positioned so the garment fits as intended. As another example, a durable sweater made with a strong yarn in a high-gauge knit construction becomes fragile when trimmed with decorative beads. Findings definitely influence serviceability.

Findings and trim must be compatible with the garment body fabric in terms of wear and care. Quality-conscious designers and merchandisers submit findings and trim for testing of colorfastness; strength and durability; and resistance to heat, water, bleach, and other elements. Closures that rust, corrode, harden, break, crack, peel, melt, fade, or discolor during wear or when laundered or dry-cleaned detract from garment appearance and function. These problems with findings are especially prevalent in garment-washed apparel (see Chapter 4).

Sometimes the application of the finding is more likely to fail than the item itself; an example is the common occurrence of buttons falling off because of insecure attachment. The button is still serviceable but is no longer performing a function on a garment. Consumers can sew on new buttons, but the replacement of some closures—zippers, for instance—involves too much time and skill for the average consumer to justify. In both cases, consumers experience frustration and goodwill is lost. Also, in the latter case, the garment is discarded as unwearable.

Dimensional Stability. As discussed in Chapters 3 and 7, one of the most important performance characteristics of a garment is dimensional stability. Torque and skewness do not affect most trim items due to the small amount of surface area used. However, shrinkage, elongation, and elasticity of trim do play a major role in maintaining garment quality. Findings, because of their material composition, are not affected by dimensional-stability problems.

Shrinkage. Trim items can shrink the same amount as, less than, or more than the rest of the garment. Zipper tapes, appliqué cloth, laces, ribbons, thread, and elastic all need to be planned to have shrinkage consistent with the body fabric. An approximate 2% variance between trim and body fabric will not adversely affect most garments. When a difference in shrinkage in excess of 2% occurs, this is called **differential shrinkage,** the shrinkage of garment parts in varying amounts. Differential shrinkage can cause a puckered, rippled look. It is especially prevalent when woven trims are applied to knitted body fabrics.

Elongation and Elasticity. If a fabric is extensible, it elongates or stretches in use. Any trim used on extensible fabrics must either be extensible itself or be used in small amounts. For example, elastic used at the waistband of spandex stretch leggings needs to stretch with the body fabric, but a woven satin appliqué on the front of a sweat shirt does not need to stretch with the body fabric.

Appearance Retention. As with fabric, findings and trim must maintain the desired appearance for the garment to remain aesthetically pleasing. They need to age consistently with the body fabric. A case in point involves putting synthetic trim items on natural-fabric body parts. Natural fibers such as cotton experience a gradual loss of color as they are worn and refurbished. Synthetic trim such as polyester retains its color. This combination could be a unique fashion look or a fashion disaster; the decision must be carefully considered and planned.

Abrasion Resistance. Abrasion resistance is more of an appearance consideration for findings and trim than it is a durability consideration (as it was for fabric). Most fabrics are soft and flexible. They move easily in the washing and drying process and while worn. Many findings and trim products are less flexible or totally inflexible and are therefore more subject to surface abrasion. Surface abrasion dulls the finish on metal findings, scratches the finish on wood and plastic findings, and removes the color on painted findings.

Colorfastness. Colorfastness is the ability of the trim or finding item to retain its color. Some loss of color can occur in fabric or plastic findings and trim while no significant loss will occur in most findings made of metal and wood. White buttons that yellow and colored buttons that fade are examples of color loss in findings. Aspects of findings and trim colorfastness of particular interest are resistance to bleeding and crocking. If a trim or finding article bleeds or crocks, it may discolor the body fabric, ruining the garment.

Heat Resistance. When thermoplastic trim or findings are combined with natural-fiber fabrics, the variation in heat resistance affects the suggested care for the garment. For example, silk-screened emblems on sweatshirts cannot be ironed. This is not usually a problem as customers do not customarily iron sweatshirts. However, when that same silk-screened emblem is applied to the back of a casual cotton shirt, the consumer runs a risk of melting the decoration during ironing. Both garments require an ironing caution stated on the care label such as *Do not iron decoration* to alert the consumer.

Comfort. Many factors help determine comfort. The hand of findings and trim is an important influence. For example, a scratchy label or a stiff, scratchy trim at the neckline of a garment may cause the consumer to resist wearing the garment for comfort reasons. The size and shape of findings also influence comfort. Shank buttons on the back of a blouse or dress may cause discomfort by pressing into the wearer's back as he or she is sitting in a chair. Too-narrow or too-tight elastic may bite into the skin.

Ease of Care. The findings used in the garment should have the same launderability or dry-cleanability as the body fabric. It is particularly important to test all findings and trim using the suggested garment-care instructions to maintain refurbishing compatibility. Patchwork fabric blouses made with numerous different lace trims are an example of garments requiring careful examination of all components for care compatibility.

Safety. One of the main issues in clothing safety for the general public is flame resistance. While the CPSC rulings pertain mainly to the garment body fabric, care must be exercised to prevent the use of highly flammable findings and trim items. An example of a potentially dangerous garment is a flannel shirt trimmed with rayon fringe.

Other safety considerations concern infant's and children's clothing. The apparel industry has adopted the CPSC Regulations for Toys and Children's Articles. These regulations spell out the test method and related standards for sharpness and choking hazards (see Chapter 2).

Another safety consideration for some garments is their ability to reflect light. Special, highly light-reflective fabrics are useful as trim or decoration on biking and jogging clothing and for some occupational clothing. Due to the expense of this feature, it is usually used in small amounts on prominent locations of the garment.

Strength. Findings in the form of zippers, buttons, and snaps are exposed to considerable stress because they help hold a garment together at points of strain. For this reason, their strength needs to be specified, and they need to be securely attached with an amount of strength proportional to the end use of the garment. With the exception of the pull-strength characteristics necessary for attaching trim on infants and toddler's garments, strength is not a major need for trim. Usually the trim items are decorative and their main purpose is to stay on the garment for aesthetic reasons.

Resistance to Degradation. Findings and trim, like fabric, must withstand degradation from the environment. To be considered durable, a garment is made of trim, findings, and fabric with the following characteristics (definitions provided in Chapter 7):

1. *chemical resistance.* For example, chlorine bleaching will degrade rubber; therefore, swimsuit and underwear elastic is made from spandex.
2. *launderability* and *dry-cleanability* without coming off the garment or losing parts, such as glued-on sequins and rhinestones or petals on fabric flowers
3. *light resistance,* such as trims that do not fade and as screen prints on athletic wear or swimwear that stay bright
4. *fume fading resistance.* For example, ozone damage can cause the bleached denim trim used on tops and slacks coordinates to change color.

PHYSICAL FEATURES OF FINDINGS AND TRIM

The physical features of a trim or finding item determine its performance. The physical features of a trim or finding item include its base raw material, its structure, and how it is dyed, printed, and/or finished. Also important are size, placement, attachment, and reinforcement.

Cost limitations as well as lead times are factors when choosing findings and trim; high-price garments are more likely to contain costly items than low-price garments. Cost does not directly predict the quality of a trim or finding item, but the two are often related. Any addition adds to the cost of the garment, but the cost varies depending upon the particular item and the amount of labor required to apply it to the garment. Designers and stylists work with industrial engineers to select findings and trim and the best method of application. Many findings and trim items are purchased by the *gross* (12 dozen, or 144).

Labels

Most apparel contains several types of labels, including brand, size, care, and fiber-identification. Some of this information is required by law, some is part of marketing the apparel product (see Chapter 2).

Some makers of high-volume casual clothing buy label *stock* and print their own labels. *Printed* labels take the least time and allow flexibility. Other manufacturers buy *preprinted* labels from the label supplier. This takes longer than printing one's own labels but has a shorter lead time than using woven labels and offers some flexibility. Makers of high-price apparel or those wanting to create an impression of high quality often have cloth labels woven to specification. *Woven* labels are generally more expensive than printed labels, due to the cost of materials and lead times, but aid in creating an impression of high quality. Most woven labels are soft and comfortable to wear; however, those cut with a hot knife can have stiff, fused edges which may cause skin discomfort. Nonwoven, printed labels (called paper labels in the industry) are used on casual and low-price clothing. Like woven labels, printed labels can sometimes cause wearer discomfort due to excessive stiffness and rough, scratchy edges. Most quality-assurance personnel are aware of this and try to screen out stiff labels, so consumers do not remove labels because they are uncomfortable and therefore defeat the purpose of care labeling.

It is important that any label required by law be permanently attached to the garment and the wording be legible for the life of the garment. Meeting these standards often requires extensive research and development if the label is to be subjected to garment wet processing; the labels must withstand both garment wet processing and repeated home laundering. Often special label stock is designed to withstand the harsh chemical wet-process treatments used on some ready-to-wear. Labels, often taken for granted, can be responsible for a significant portion of the product cost.

Paper labels called *hangtags* and *billboards* are part of the apparel at point of sale. These are temporary labels that are designed primarily for marketing purposes. Because of this usage, these labels will not be discussed in this chapter. However, it is important to note that these labels must be designed, developed, and ordered at the same time as garment labels. They contribute to the cost of the garment and must be included in any costing estimates.

Thread

Thread is the yarn that forms the stitches that hold a garment together. Thread also may be used to create decorative effects such as topstitching and embroidery.

(For more information, see Chapter 11.) Thread is often the least costly component of a garment, but its failure must not be underestimated as it can cause the entire garment to fail. The strength, durability, appearance, and texture of the thread affect the performance of the stitches and the garment.

Thread Strength. The strength of thread is critical to the durability of stitches and seams. Repeated breakage of weak thread slows down the manufacturing process and results in ruptured stitches and weak seams. An important and easy-to-measure aspect of thread strength is *single end strength*, the strength required to break the thread. Another important aspect of thread strength is *loop strength*, or the force necessary to separate two stitches. Thread should be compatible in strength with the fabric, never stronger. (For further discussion, see Chapters 9 and 10.) Thread must withstand the same wear and care as the garment.

Threads need to be dimensionally stable but also extensible enough to withstand stress without breaking, especially in stretchy fabrics such as knits. However, if an extensible thread stretches during sewing, it puckers the surrounding fabric when it later relaxes to its original length. Cotton thread is prone to this problem.

Heavy fabrics require coarse, multiple threads, and lightweight fabrics demand fine threads. Large-diameter threads are strong but also are subject to abrasion and tend to cause seam distortion if chosen for the wrong applications. Threads exposed to heavy wear, like those used to make buttonholes, should be abrasion resistant. Threads with inadequate abrasion resistance fray and wear out quickly. To minimize puckering, the finest thread possible should be used, considering the weight of the fabric and the strength and durability requirements of the seam. A strong fiber type and high amount of twist improve the strength of a thread. For example, fine, tightly twisted threads are stronger and more abrasion resistant than large, loosely twisted threads. However, too much twist causes knotting and kinking that interferes with stitch formation.

Fiber Content of Thread. Sewing thread can be made from almost any textile fiber. Most threads are polyester, nylon, cotton, or rayon. *Polyester* and *nylon* lend strength and resistance to the chemicals used in wet processing. *Cotton* is weaker and less resistant to chemicals than the synthetics but has excellent sewability characteristics. *Mercerized cotton* threads are stronger than soft, unfinished cotton threads because the finishing process strengthens the cotton fibers. *Rayon* thread is rather weak, yet dyes beautifully and is lustrous; *silk* thread is rare, costly, and beautiful. Cotton, rayon, and silk threads are used when polyester or nylon threads are too strong for the fabric and for decorative stitches.

Thread Types. The main types of thread used in apparel manufacturing are spun and corespun. Filament thread, both monofilament and multifilament, is used in limited operations.

Spun Thread. **Spun thread** consists of staple fibers spun into single yarns; two to six of these yarns are twisted together to make a thread. The most common thread is spun polyester. Spun threads are strong, elastic, and abrasion resistant but subject to needle heating. They are also slick, increasing the tendency of stitches to ravel. Spun threads are generally less pleasant to the touch than corespun threads unless they are **texturized** for comfort. Texturizing provides soft, bulky, extensible underthreads for 400-, 500-, and 600-class stitches (see Chapter 9). These stitch types expose the skin to thread buildup and are comfortable only if a soft underthread is used. Infants, the very elderly, and bedridden people have a special need for comfortable threads and seams because their skin is thin and sensitive. Some thread and seam types are more comfortable than others. Spun thread costs significantly less than corespun thread.

Corespun Thread. Each ply of **corespun thread** consists of a spun core of polyester or nylon wrapped with cotton or other fibers. Several plies are usually twisted together to make one thread. A synthetic core makes the thread fine, strong, and elastic. Corespun threads generally have greater strength for their size than spun threads. Because of their fineness, they are less apt to cause puckering, and the imprint of the stitches is less apt to press through a thin fabric. A cotton wrapping lends the thread resistance to needle heating and allows for consistency of dye color when used in garment-dyed products. Corespun threads, with a soft outer layer of cotton, tend to be comfortable. Overall, corespun threads are superior in sewability to spun threads.

Filament Thread. **Monofilament** is the most common filament thread. It is a clear thread made of a single filament of nylon resembling a fishing line. Clear monofilament thread is inconspicuous in a garment of any color. Therefore, manufacturers that use monofilament thread reduce the amount of time spent changing thread cones and rethreading machines when they sew different colors of garments. The use of monofilament thread also eliminates the need for a costly inventory of thread in multiple colors. Thus, monofilament thread is cost effective.

Monofilament nylon thread is very strong and abrasion resistant. However, it is *too* strong for many fabrics. When a monofilament thread ruptures, it is so slippery that a number of stitches readily ravel. Monofilament thread can irritate the wearer's skin if a free end comes loose and contacts the skin. Because of these disadvantages, monofilament thread is used primarily in low-price lines and occasionally for hems in other price lines.

Multifilament threads consist of several filament yarns twisted together to make a very strong thread. These threads may be texturized, which reduces their high luster and gives them greater coverage, useful for cover stitches. Texturized threads also are more comfortable for stitches that contact the skin. They are less apt to ravel than slippery filament threads. They have increased stretch, making them suitable for sewing on knits and for seams in locations that need to "give," and they are low cost.

Thread Color. A well-coordinated thread color is a mark of quality. The hue, shade, and luster of the thread should match or complement the dominant color of the fabric. When matching thread to fabric, a thread color slightly darker than the fabric is usually selected for the best match. Attention to a minor detail such as matching thread color not only demonstrates the overall care in developing the garment but also increases cost. It is costly for the manufacturer to buy enough thread to match each fabric and to maintain the needed inventory of colored thread. For these reasons, many manufacturers of low-price apparel use whatever thread they have on hand to reduce costs.

Most manufacturers carefully balance thread and garment costs. Basic thread colors of black and white are usually less costly than basic fashion colors, which are less costly than having thread made in a "dyed to match" color. In parts of the garment that do not show, basic colors can be used if they blend well enough with the cloth color. Examples of this technique can readily be found in jeans. Most jean fabric has a white fill yarn. White thread is less costly than indigo; therefore, many jeans manufacturers use white thread on inside seams to blend with the white fill yarns. The more costly indigo thread is used on seams near openings (waist and hem) that will be seen frequently. This may sound like a minimal cost-reduction technique but when making hundreds of thousands of garments annually, a one or two cent cost savings is significant.

Thread should be colorfast. If a thread fades at a different rate than the rest of the garment, or if it changes color, it no longer coordinates with the garment. Although no thread or fabric is 100% colorfast, they should fade in unison. For example, natural-fiber threads fade like natural-fiber fabrics, while synthetic threads fade like synthetic fabrics. A thread should not bleed or crock onto the garment or accept color from the garment. White thread should not yellow.

Table 8–1 Apparel Sewing Thread Selection Guide by Tex Size for Major Seams.
(Courtesy of Coats American.)

End Use	Spun Polyester	Texturized Polyester	Locked-Filament Polyester	Polyester/ Cotton Core Spun	Polyester Core Spun	Cotton	Continuous-Filament Nylon	Continuous-Filament Polyester
Suits and coats	40 45	24 35	40	30 40	30 40	50 60	24 35	24 30
Work shirts	40 45	24 35	40	30 40	30 40	50 60	24 35	24 30
Dress shirts and blouses	21	18 24	27	18 24	18 24	30 35	16	16
T-shirts and briefs	21	18 24	27	24	18 24	30 35	16	16
Work pants	45 60	35 70	40 60	40 60	40 60	—	35 45	30 45
Slacks and skirts	40 45	24 35	40	30 40	30 40	50 60	24 35	24 30
Swimsuits	40 45	24 35	60 80H 100	30 40	30 40	—	24 35	24 30
Jeans - over 12 oz.	60 80 105	70 90	60 90	60 80H 100	60 80H 100	105 135	—	—
Jeans - under 12 oz.	40 45	35	40	40	40	60	35	30
Raincoats	40 45	24 35	40	30 40	30 40	50 60	24 35	24 30
Fleece goods	27 40	18 24	27 40	24 30 40	24 30 40	35 50 60	16 24	16 24
Dresses	27	18 24	27	24	24	35	16	12 16
Lingerie	21	18 24	—	24	18 24	30 35	16	16
Foundation garments	27 40 45	24 35	27 40	24 30 40	24 30 40	35 50 60	16 24 35	16 24 30
Uniforms	40 45	24 35	40	30 40	30 40	50 60	24 35	24 30
Children's tops, shirts	21 27	18 24	27	24	24	35	16	16
Children's sleepwear	21 27	18 24	27	—	—	—	16	16
Embroidery	27	—	—	24	24	—	—	27 30

Note. Since applications, sewn product exposures, and many other factors are so variable, Coats American cannot guarantee results using this guide. Suggested choices are intended as starting points from which a manufacturer can further refine choice of thread product to ideally suit all end use requirements including total thread cost.

Thread Size. Most thread suppliers are now citing thread sizes using the *tex* system (because threads are, technically, a yarn). Tex is well suited to international use because it is a direct system, based on the metric measurements, and designates the diameters of any type of fiber and yarn (in this case, threads) made of any type of fiber (see Chapter 7). Table 8–1 lists some commonly mass-produced products with the suggested thread sizes listed in tex.

Trim

Trims such as ribbons, braids, laces, and other narrow fabric trims are widely used to adorn childrenswear, lingerie, and bridal wear. Nonfabric trims are used to adorn a variety of casual and special occasion garments for women and children. The type and amount of trim used on womenswear depends upon current fashion trends; trims have limited use in menswear. Narrow fabric trims and nonfabric trims are discussed in this chapter. Decorative details made of the body fabric, such as tucks and pleats, are discussed in Chapter 11.

Although trims generally enhance garment appearance, a trim that ravels, falls off, shrinks, fades, bleeds, or discolors leaves the consumer dissatisfied. All trims should be compatible with the wear and care requirements of the garment. Manufacturers who have trims tested to verify wear properties and care requirements avoid trim problems in the finished garments.

The ability to recognize fine trims is important in apparel analysis. For example, complex trims generally cost more than simple ones, and wide trims cost more

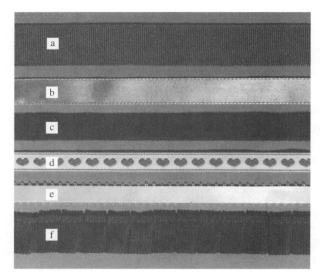

Figure 8–1 Ribbons: (a) grosgrain, (b) satin, (c) velvet, (d) novelty, (e) picot-edge satin, (f) grosgrain ruching.

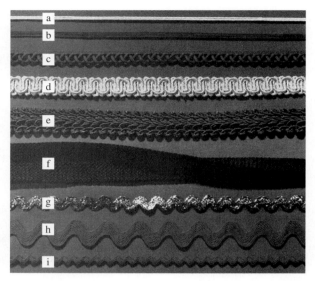

Figure 8–2 Braids: (a) soutache, (b) middy, (c) loop, (d) scrolling, (e) gimp, (f) foldover, (g) metallic rickrack, (h) jumbo rickrack, and (i) baby rickrack.

than narrow ones. The fiber from which a trim is made also affects its cost. Cotton trims generally cost more and are softer but have a greater tendency to shrink than polyester trims; a silk trim is usually lustrous, elegant, and costly. The amount of trim and the method used to attach it affect cost. Glued-on trims generally cost less than sewn-on trims. The most costly but secure tacking attachments involve double tacking and/or adding glue to the tack. Trims are occasionally sewn on by hand to achieve soft, invisible results or because the cost of automation cannot be justified, but hand sewing is not consistently durable and domestic hand sewing is costly.

Ribbon. **Ribbon** is a narrow, woven fabric used as a trim and to make ties and bows (Figure 8–1). Ribbon is available in a variety of widths ranging from 1/16 inch to several inches wide. Ribbons that feel papery (have too much sizing and leave creases when folded) are inexpensive and low quality. They generally do not hold up well to wear and care and need to be carefully selected and thoroughly tested. Types of ribbon include the following

1. *Grosgrain ribbon* (pronounced "grow´ grain") has a dull, ribbed appearance. Manufacturers use it for decoration, but it sometimes serves a functional purpose, for example, when it faces the button placket of a cardigan sweater.
2. *Satin ribbon* is shiny and smooth; it is made using a satin weave.
3. *Velvet ribbon* has a soft, three-dimensional pile surface.
4. *Novelty ribbons* feature unusual weaves and/or unusual designs.

5. *Picot-edge ribbons* or *feather-edge ribbons* have tiny decorative loops on one or both edges.
6. *Ruching* is a ribbon or other trim that has been gathered or pleated. Ruching requires extra material, especially if it is generously full, increasing costs.

Braid. **Braids** are formed by intertwining a set of yarns according to a definite pattern to form a narrow fabric (Figure 8–2). Braids appear in many styles, most of which are referred to simply as braid. However, the following are some types of braid:

1. *soutache braid*, a narrow braid used for decoratively trimming bolero-style jackets
2. *middy braid*, slightly wider than soutache braid; it is often used to trim sailor collars
3. *loop braid*, which consists of many loops
4. *scrolling*, a wavy braid
5. *gimp braid*, a complex, highly decorative braid made from gimp thread (a cord), sometimes used to trim high-price women's jackets
6. *rickrack*, zigzag-shaped trim used on children's, junior, and missy clothing. *Jumbo rickrack* is wide and *baby rickrack* is narrow
7. *foldover braid*, a general term for any braid used to bind edges. Foldover braid is available in many widths and qualities. As an edge finish binding, it is both decorative and functional

Lace. **Lace trim** is a narrow lace fabric (in contrast to *allover lace,* the lace fabric from which entire garments are constructed). Lace trim can vary greatly in cost, depending on its fiber content, intricacy and complexity, width, and, if gathered, fullness. Full,

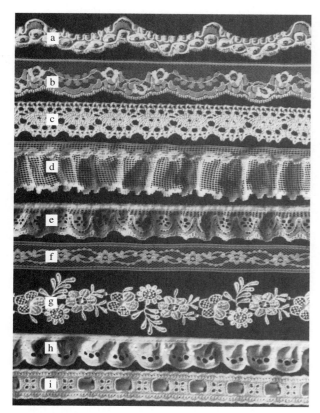

Figure 8–3 Laces: (a) Alençon galloon, (b) Chantilly edging, (c) Cluny edging, (d) filet gathered edging, (e) Raschel knit gathered edging, (f) Raschel knit insertion, (g) Venice galloon, (h) eyelet gathered edging, and (i) eyelet beading. *Note:* Technically, eyelet is not a lace, but it is often referred to as one.

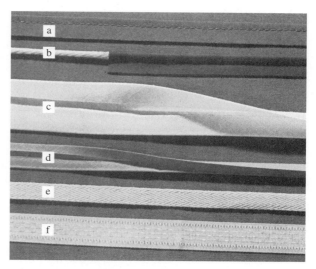

Figure 8–4 Miscellaneous trims: (a) piping, (b) corded piping, (c) and (d) bias tape, (e) twill tape, and (f) seam/hem tape.

gathered lace trim costs double or triple what a skimpily gathered or flat lace trim costs.

Lace making originated as a handcraft, but the vast majority of laces today are made by machine (see Chapter 7). Figure 8–3 shows a few popular lace trims. They include the following:

1. *insertion*, any flat lace trim with two straight edges. It is often inset between two pieces of fabric.
2. *galloon*, any flat lace trim with two scalloped edges
3. *edging*, any lace trim with one scalloped edge and one straight edge. Edging may be flat or gathered.
4. *beading*, lace trim through which ribbon is threaded
5. *medallion*, an individual lace motif applied, for example, as an appliqué, collar, or cuff.

Other Narrow Fabric Trims. A number of other narrow fabric trims are used on clothing (Figure 8–4). A few miscellaneous types of trim are listed here, but many miscellaneous trim styles have no particular names and are referred to simply as trim.

1. *piping*, a narrow, folded strip of fabric included in a seam that often contrasts with the color of the garment. Piping lends itself best to straight seams. It is difficult to apply around sharp curves or corners; a skilled operator is required to avoid bulky or puckered results. Manufacturers use piping to decorate the inside of some lined jackets and coats as well as the outsides of garments. Seams containing piping are referred to as *piped seams.*
2. *corded piping*, piping with a cord in it to create a round tube. Corded piping should be flexible enough that it does not distort the seam. Stiff piping is subject to abrasion, but does help reinforce the seam.
3. *bias tape*, bias-cut strips of fabric, which may be used as a decorative binding
4. *seam tape* or *hem tape*, a smooth ribbonlike fabric used to trim interior seam and hem edges. (A seam finished with hem tape appears in Chapter 10, Figure 10–7.)
5. *twill tape*, a twill-weave fabric used to trim casual garments; also reinforces and prevents stretch
6. *fringe*, trim with even dangling yarns
    a. *shimmy fringe*, shiny fringe that moves when the wearer moves
    b. *brush fringe*, thick, even fringe that resembles a brush
    c. *tassel fringe*, groups of fringe tied together into tassels at intervals
    d. *ball fringe*, fringe with round balls hanging from the trim at intervals

Appliqués. **Appliqués** are decorative fabric patches applied to the garment, generally die cut from fusible-backed fabric, ironed on, and then permanently attached with satin stitches (Figure 8–5). Examples of appliqués include the Greek letters sewn onto college

Figure 8–5 Appliqué secured with zigzag stitches.

sweatshirts and the whimsical fabric shapes stitched onto childrenswear. Emblems are pre-embroidered appliqués, also known as patches, badges, or insignia, such as those used on scouting and military uniforms. Many appliqués are embroidered. For information on evaluating the quality of embroidery, see Chapter 11.

Nonfabric Trims. **Nonfabric trims** include beads (e.g., cylindrical *bugle beads* and round *seed beads*), sequins (including large sequins called *paillettes* or *spangles*), rhinestones, flat metal nailheads, raised metal studs, rivets and burrs (as on jeans), plastic or silk flowers, feathers, jewels, and pearls. Real pearls and jewels are found on only the rarest and most costly couture garments; most jewels and pearls are plastic simulations. The trim and its method of application must both be able to withstand the care procedures recommended for the garment. Sequins, feathers, and rhinestones, for instance, may be ruined by laundering or dry-cleaning.

Closures

Closures refer to the fasteners that secure garment openings. Closures unfasten to enlarge the garment for dressing and undressing and then fasten to make the garment fit the body. Manufacturers use a wide variety of closures in ready-to-wear apparel. Closures include buttons and buttonholes or loops, zippers, hooks and eyes, snaps, and other fasteners. To some extent, tradition indicates whether to use buttons, a zipper, or some other type of closure in a garment. For example, dress shirts are usually buttoned and pants are usually zipped. Fashion also influences the choice of closure.

Buttons. Buttons have been widely used as garment closures since the Middle Ages. Most buttons are both a decorative feature of the garment and a functional closure. However, some buttons are strictly functional, for example, concealed button closures and buttons inside double-breasted garments to help them hang smoothly. And other buttons are strictly decorative, for example, the nonfunctional buttons at the wrists of most suit and sport-jacket sleeves. These buttons imitate the functional and decorative buttons on the sleeves of high-price jackets, which increase costs because they require functional buttonholes. A compromise that achieves the same look is nonfunctional buttons sewn on closed, nonfunctional buttonholes.

Composition of Buttons. The least costly buttons are molded of plastic *(nylon)*, or stamped out of a sheet of plastic *(polyester)*. Elaborate plastic buttons cost extra. Plastic buttons can be dyed any color. They often imitate buttons made of natural materials. Plastic buttons are more uniform than natural-material (shell or mother-of-pearl) buttons but often are considered less beautiful (Figure 8–6). Plastic buttons that fade or yellow are of low quality.

Natural-material buttons comprise only about 10% of all buttons (Frings, 1994). Buttons made of natural materials such as wood, metal, animal horn, leather, shell or mother-of-pearl, nuts, or seeds cost

Figure 8–6 Buttons: (a) wood, (b) leather, (c) mother-of-pearl, (d) horn, (e) bone, (f) metal, (g) self-covered, (h) cleated on, (i) rhinestone, (j) toggle for removable buttons, (k) plastic eyed, and (l) plastic shank.

more than plastic buttons. Natural-material buttons are confined to high-price lines.

Most *metal buttons* are made by stamping out a brass face and attaching it to a metal base. They are more durable and more expensive than *metalized buttons*, which consist of a gold- or silver-colored metal coating over a copper-covered plastic (acetate) base. Metalized buttons have a tendency to chip and peel. Some buttons made of pewter are cast in molds. Due to the shape of the mold, the attaching thread is easily abraded by molded metal buttons. It is important to test molded buttons for this characteristic and plan the attaching thread size accordingly.

Self-covered buttons are covered with fabric. Self-covered buttons are an excellent choice when the desired color of button is difficult to find or when the button needs to blend in with the garment. Self-covered buttons are made to order by contractors.

Typically, buttons made from leather or wood and some other buttons, such as those with rhinestones or iridescent coatings, are not washable. Buttons may be damaged by dry-cleaning solvents. If the buttons will not withstand the same care as the garment, they may be temporarily attached with small clips so the consumer can remove them each time the garment is cleaned. Removable buttons increase costs. *Studs* or *cuff links* are another alternative to permanent buttons; they are clasped through buttonholes in the layers being joined.

Button Size. The size of buttons is measured in **lignes** (pronounced lines), with 40 lignes equal to a diameter of 1 inch. For example, a 30-ligne button is three quarters of an inch in diameter. Large buttons cost more than small buttons. Aesthetically speaking, button size should be proportional to the size of the garment. Functionally speaking, buttons about 1/2 inch in diameter are easy for preschoolers to manipulate while people with arthritis may require larger buttons.

The optimum number of buttons on a garment depends upon the size of the button and the fit of the garment. In general, large buttons are placed farther apart than small buttons. Garments designed to fit the body loosely require fewer buttons than garments that conform to the body, since the latter require closely spaced buttons to prevent gaping. An example of this concept is that there are as many buttons on the 6-inch fly of a pair of close-fitting jeans as on the 18–inch front of a loose-fitting blouse. Buttons are purchased by the *gross* (144).

Button Types. Buttons are either of the eyed or shank variety. Eyed buttons are slightly more casual looking than shank buttons. Shank buttons cost more to buy. However, both eyed and shank buttons can be found on clothing of all types and in all price lines. Eyed buttons, also called holed or sew-through buttons, usually have two or four holes. Shank buttons have a stem of plastic, metal, or cloth built into the button. The button is sewn to the garment through the shank. Shank buttons tend to be bulkier than eyed buttons. Shank buttons also require more labor to attach. (Both eyed and shank buttons are pictured in Chapter 12, Figure 12–10.)

A flat, eyed button is best for the lower button of shirts and blouses, to avoid a lump showing on the outside of the outer garment when the shirt or blouse is tucked in. Concealed button closures call for flat, eyed buttons so the buttons do not make the fabric over the buttons appear lumpy. On garments that button in back, flat, eyed buttons offer greater comfort when sitting or leaning back than do shank buttons. Cloth shanks offer greater comfort in such cases than do plastic or metal shanks.

Button Loops. **Button loops** are used in some garments instead of buttonholes to fasten buttons. (*Buttonholes* are discussed in Chapter 12.) Loops are made of narrow tubes of bias fabric; strips of cording, braid, or elastic; or thread chains. They must have adequate size or elasticity to slip over the buttons. Sometimes *button looping*, a fabric strip with presized, prespaced loops, is used to ensure loops that are evenly spaced and identical in size. This is used, for example, on the backs of wedding gowns that require closely spaced button loops.

A **frog** is a highly decorative button-and-loop closure. Frogs are made of elaborately coiled cord or braid (Figure 8–7). They are commonly used in combination with a Chinese ball button, which is cord or braid knotted into a ball.

A **toggle** is a decorative button-and-loop closure sewn to the face of coats, jackets, and other garments,

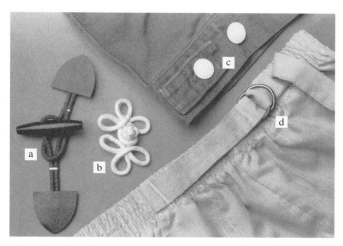

Figure 8–7 Closures: (a) toggle, (b) frog, (c) tab with button, and (d) d-ring.

especially those of heavy fabrics (Figure 8–7). Toggles consist of two loops; one has a rod-shaped button attached to it. When closed, a toggle looks like two symmetrical loops over the same button.

Zippers. Zippers are a fast, easy means of getting in and out of garments. They have been widely used in ready-to-wear apparel since the 1930s; they have continued to grow lighter, more supple, and less obvious since their invention around 1900. For definitions of zipper terms, refer to *ASTM Standard Terminology Relating to Zippers D-2050.*

Because of their somewhat stiff nature, zippers are more appropriate than buttons for flat areas within garments. Zippers are not well suited to bloused areas because the stiffness interferes with the intended drape of the fabric and results in zipper hump. **Zipper hump** is the term for a wavy zipper chain (Figure 7–7). It detracts from the appearance of the garment and stresses the zipper. Although zipper hump may be due to installation in a bias seam, stretching the fabric during application, zipper tape shrinkage, or garment shrinkage, it also results from using a zipper in a fabric that is too soft to support a zipper, for example, a lightweight knit. In such situations, buttons or other closures are preferable to zippers.

Designers and merchandisers usually choose zippers over buttons for close-fitting garments. Zippers are the better choice because unless buttons are very closely spaced on such garments, the opening tends to gape. For example, the fitted bodices of some wedding gowns are buttoned all the way down the back with closely spaced buttons. Others combine a zipper for smooth, nongaping closure with nonfunctional buttons sewn on for a traditional, decorative look. The choice of closure depends on whether the opening is in the front or back of the garment. Zippers are usually more smooth and comfortable to lean against than buttons, so they are often better for back closures. Buttons are decorative and thus are often the choice for front closures. Very plain buttons may cost less than a zipper, but elaborate buttons usually cost more than a zipper. Also, extra fabric and labor are required to produce button closures. Therefore, zipper closures are usually less costly than button closures.

Zipper Parts. The main parts of a zipper include the tape (fabric portion), chain, slider, pull, and top and bottom stops (Figure 8–8). The zipper chain is composed of either continuous elements or separate elements.

Zipper Tape. The **zipper tape** is the fabric portion of the zipper that is sewn to the garment. The strength of the tape affects the overall strength of the zipper. Woven tapes, usually made of a strong twill weave, come in varying weights and amounts of stiffness.

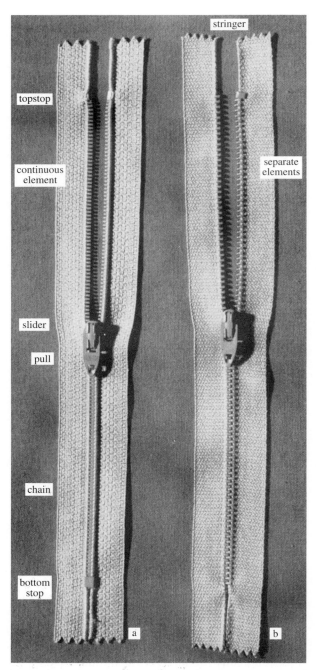

Figure 8–8 Parts of a zipper: (a) continuous element zipper, and (b) separate element zipper.

They are used primarily for metal zippers in applications requiring strength and durability. Woven zipper tapes are usually made of cotton fibers or a blend of cotton and synthetic fibers. Most zippers of average or better quality are made with shrinkage-controlled tape. Low-price zippers might have tape that will shrink when laundered thus causing unsightly puckering. Knitted zipper tapes are light and flexible; they are used primarily for plastic zippers in applications subject to low stress. Knitted tapes are made of synthetic fibers, usually polyester. Because synthetics are easily stabilized, knitted tapes do not have the same tendency to shrink as much as low-price cotton tapes. Knitted tapes, however, are prone to yarn slippage, especially if low gauge and made of filament yarns. Thus, tapes with a sleazy hand should be avoided because the zipper elements may become detached if yarn slippage occurs.

Zipper Chain.   The **zipper chain** is part of the zipper that interlocks when the zipper is closed. A common problem associated with low-quality zippers or broken zippers is ratcheting of the zipper chain. *Ratcheting* refers to a zipper coming unzipped when stress is applied to the two sides. A zipper chain that ratchets will not stay zipped when the garment is worn. Ratcheting cannot be repaired once it occurs.

Separate-element zippers are made up of separate **elements,** the industry term for the *teeth* of a zipper. Separate-element zippers are made by attaching the metal or plastic scoops to the zipper tape. The zipper elements are interlocked by the slider, which meshes them together to create the zipper chain. If a zipper element breaks off or pulls away from the tape, or if the elements somehow become unmeshed below the slider, the zipper no longer functions.

Continuous-element zippers or **coil zippers** are made by twisting a continuous strand of monofilament nylon into a spiral. A continuous element is attached to the zipper tape and enmeshed by the slider to create the zipper chain. Continuous-element zippers do not have sharp edges, so they do not snag fabric or scratch the skin as single element zippers sometimes do. Continuous-element zippers are lighter and more flexible than separate-element zippers, so they are ideal for light- and medium-weight fabrics. Although continuous-element zippers are strong, they cannot withstand as much stress as separate-element zippers. Continuous-element zippers tend to split apart when too much steady, transverse stress is applied. They are not suitable for heavy duty applications. However, because of their flexibility, they sometimes absorb sudden stress that would damage a separate-element zipper. They also have the unique property of *self-healing*, by which they can be enmeshed again after splitting, unlike a separate-element zipper, which is useless after it loses an element. However, this healing may be only temporary.

Zipper Slider.   The **slider** is the portion of the zipper that glides up and down the chain, engaging and disengaging the two halves of the chain. The slider of the zipper has a **pull** or **tab** for easy grasping. This pull is usually unobtrusive, but occasionally it is large and decorative. The slider should glide easily up and down the zipper chain. Sliders that have been crushed

or spread in the manufacturing process may not glide easily. Loose, dangling threads also interfere with the slider action. The slider movement must adequately clear the fabric of the garment, of special concern if the zipper crosses a heavy or bulky seam.

Most zippers contain some sort of locking mechanism within the slider, which prevents the zipper from unzipping by itself. The locking mechanism may be automatic, or the wearer may need to manually engage it by pressing the pull tab flat. Locking zippers withstand stress and stay zipped better than zippers without locking mechanisms. If the locking mechanism fails in a critical location, the zipper tends to ratchet open during wear and could possibly damage the zipper chain.

Top and Bottom Stops.   **Stops** prevent the slider from leaving the chain at either end of the zipper. Most zippers have both a top and bottom stop. A bottom stop applied directly over and enmeshing the lower scoops or coils is more durable than one with the stop placed below the zipper chain. A strong bottom stop, appropriately placed, may be the most important prevention of zipper failure. For applications that are open at the top, for example, waistline or neckline applications, a bottom stop holds the two tracks together at the base, and a top stop prevents the slider of the zipper from going beyond the track at the upper edge. If no top stop is present, the zipper elements should be caught in the seam (e.g., at the waistband) to form a stop so the slider cannot come off. When including zippers in a seam, with the seam serving as the stop, most nylon chains can be sewn across. For metal and plastic chains, however, a few of the elements at the seam must be removed. This must be done accurately, because if a gap (commonly called a "gate" in the industry) is left between the separate elements and the seam, the zipper slider may come off.

Zipper Size.   The size of a zipper is denoted by the width of the zipper chain in millimeters. For example, a size 7 zipper has a chain 7 millimeters wide. The larger the size of the zipper chain, the larger the number of the zipper. Sizes range from size 1 to 9, with size 1 being the finest zipper and size 9 the bulkiest zipper.

Large zippers are stronger than small ones of the same type and material. The larger the zipper, the higher its cost. A zipper must be chosen with a large enough chain to withstand the stress of the intended use, but large zipper chains may detract from the appearance of the garment. Manufacturers balance size with desired aesthetics and cost limitations.

Zipper Length.   A zipper chain is more expensive than a plain seam of comparable length, so most designers and patternmakers plan the shortest zipper practical for the opening. Zippers must be long enough so the opening created is large enough for dressing and undressing. If the opening is too small, the stress from dressing and undressing damages the lower portion of the zipper and the seam at its base. Aesthetically, the length of the zipper should relate to the garment design and not be so long that it is out of proportion with the garment. The most common zipper lengths used in adult clothing are 7-inch in women's skirts and slacks, 9-inch in men's slacks, and 22-inch in dresses.

Zipper Chain Composition. The material of which the zipper chain is made affects the strength of the zipper. *Metal* elements generally yield the strongest zipper, making them suitable for applications that receive heavy use and strain, such as jeans. *Brass* is commonly used to make high-quality zipper chains because it is durable and does not tarnish or corrode readily; brass zippers are traditionally used in better pants and jeans. *Nickel* zippers are moderate in cost and durability. *Zinc* zippers have high strength and are often used in heavy-duty work clothing. The disadvantages of zinc zippers are that they corrode readily, are prone to slider difficulties, and sometimes fail in extremely cold weather. *Aluminum* zippers are the least costly and the least durable choice. Aluminum zippers discolor quickly and wear down and corrode readily so the slider becomes difficult to move. They are sometimes found in low-price lines. They are suitable only for low-stress applications. *Alloys,* or combinations of metals, are often used to obtain the desired balance between strength, durability, and cost.

Because of their natural color, metal zippers are often less attractive than plastic zippers in positions where the zipper chain shows on the outside of the garment. Metal can be painted, but the enamel tends to wear off during use. Sometimes, a less costly metal is painted to resemble a more desirable metal, for example, brass.

Plastic zipper elements cost more than most metal elements. Plastic elements are stronger than aluminum but not as strong as other metal elements. They are more flexible and lighter weight than metal elements. Plastic elements are not as cold to the skin as metal elements when worn in cold weather. They do not corrode and they slide easily in all types of weather. Therefore, plastic elements are superior in some applications, such as ski wear and other outerwear, where they also mesh more closely and block out wind and water better than metal elements. Also, plastic elements come in a variety of colors and can be dyed to match the garment.

Continuous elements are usually made of *nylon.* They are more costly than nickel zippers but less costly than brass. Continuous-element zippers are strong but not as strong as most separate-element

zippers. However, they are adequate for most light- and mediumweight uses. They can be dyed to match the color of the garment. Continuous-element zippers are the most lightweight and flexible type of zipper. For this reason, they are the best choice for most garments of knit fabrics. However, in very lightweight knits, they still may be too stiff and cause zipper hump. Continuous elements melt if they contact a hot iron.

Zipper Types. The three main types of zippers are (1) conventional or regulation, (2) separating, and (3) invisible. The cost of these zippers varies depending upon the materials and construction of the zippers and the amount of labor required to install them.

Conventional Zippers. A **conventional zipper** is by far the most common in ready-to-wear apparel (Figure 8–9a). A conventional zipper has a visible chain; one end, or sometimes both ends, of the zipper remain attached when it is unzipped. It is the zipper type generally used in neckline, waistline, side seam, and pocket applications.

Separating Zippers. A **separating zipper** is constructed so the two sides of the zipper separate into two unattached halves when unzipped (Figure 8–9b). Only separate-element zippers can separate. Separating zippers are found on coats and jackets with center front openings, on detachable hoods, zip-out linings, and garments with adjustable, zip-off lengths. To avoid malfunctioning, separating zippers should not be zipped until the parts are fully aligned and seated at the base.

Invisible Zippers. An **invisible zipper** is constructed so the chain of the zipper is concealed beneath the tape when the zipper is closed (Figure 8–9c). The only portion of the zipper that is visible on the outside of the garment is the zipper tab. Invisible zippers are mainly used when a conventional zipper would interfere with the appearance of the garment. Although containing continuous elements, invisible zippers add considerable bulk and are therefore inappropriate for garments made of very lightweight fabrics. They lack flexibility and should not be used in blouson-style garments. Because invisible zippers are more costly to purchase and to apply than conventional zippers, they are rarely used except in high-price lines and evening wear, in which the cost is justified. (Figure 11–11 in Chapter 11 shows an invisible zipper in a garment.)

Miscellaneous Zipper Types. Some other types of zippers are

1. *novelty zippers,* zippers of any of the previously mentioned types with unusual decorative tapes, large or contrasting-color elements and/or decorative pulls. Although in most cases zippers are concealed,

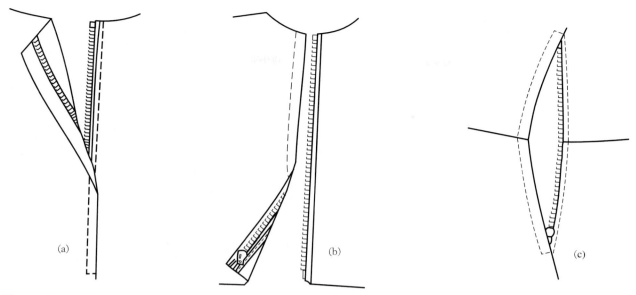

Figure 8–9 Zipper applications: (a) one end open, conventional zipper, (b) both ends open, separating zipper, and (c) both ends closed, dress zipper.

occasionally the zipper is the focus of the garment; novelty zippers are used in these situations. The use of novelty zippers is greatly affected by fashion trends. However, novelty pulls serve an important function on clothing for children and the handicapped, and on active wear such as ski wear because they are easy to grasp.

2. *trouser zippers,* conventional zippers with wide tapes to support double stitching. They have a durable tape, strong scoops, and a reinforced slider to withstand heavy use and frequent laundering.

3. *dress zippers,* zippers that feature metal bars spanning the chain at both ends of the zipper to absorb stress. Dress zippers are used in side seam applications (Figure 8–9a).

4. *reversible zippers,* zippers with tabs on both sides of the slider, used in reversible garments

5. *two-way zippers,* which have a slider attached to each end so the zipper can be zipped or unzipped from either end. These zippers are used in ski wear, sportswear, and clothing for physically challenged people.

Snap Fasteners.   **Snap fasteners** of two types are used in the production of apparel. One type, called *sewn on,* is sewn on by hand or machine sewing. It is used primarily on garments made in lightweight, dressy fabrics. The other type, called *mechanically attached,* is used on garments made of medium- and heavyweight casual fabrics and is attached by *pneumatic* (compressed air) machines or kick presses.

Sewn-on snap fasteners consist of two parts, a ball or *stud* and a *socket,* that interlock when pressed together.

Covered snaps are sewn-on snaps in which both the stud and socket are covered with matching fabric; these are used strictly in high-price lines.

Mechanically attached snap fasteners consist of four parts. Both studs and sockets have a top and bottom part with fabric plies sandwiched in between. This is the strongest and most durable snap fastener style. They come in several variations, including ring or open-prong, closed or capped-prong, and specialized fasteners (Figure 8–10). Snaps may be concealed or visible and decorative.

Snap closures cannot withstand as much stress as buttons, zippers, or hooks and eyes; therefore, most snap closures are located in areas where there is relatively little strain. Snaps, alone or in conjunction with

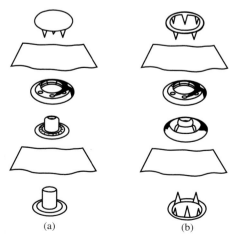

Figure 8–10   Mechanically attached snap fasteners: (a) capped, or closed, and (b) ring, or open.

button or zipper closures, prevent garment openings from gaping. Snaps are used to hold temporary garment pieces such as detachable collars and cuffs or dress shields in place. Snaps may also serve as a functional closure when placed under nonfunctional, decorative buttons. Securely attached, carefully positioned snaps are a mark of quality.

Snap Size. Small snaps have less gripping power than large snaps. The appropriate-size snap depends upon the weight of the fabric and the location and intended job of the snap. Small snaps are best at holding garment parts in desired position, while large snaps serve as actual closures. For example, a large snap used at the neckline of a lightweight dress is unnecessary, uncomfortable, and unsightly. However, the same snap used as the closure at the cuff of a mediumweight shirt is appropriate. Sewn-on snap sizes range from size 4/0 (small) to size 4 (large), while mechanically attached snap sizes range from 12 ligne to 30 ligne (40 lignes = 1 inch). Snaps of the same size but different types and materials vary in durability when measured according to the number of times they need to withstand repeated snapping and unsnapping. Mechanically attached snaps are used on infants' and toddlers' clothing (inseams), and on jeans, casual sportswear, and western wear due to superior strength (Figure 4–12).

Snap Composition. Most ordinary snaps of either steel, brass, or nickel are coated with nickel, zinc, or enamel paint (Figure 8–11). A steel base is strongest but must be properly finished to prevent rusting. The portion of mechanically attached snaps visible on the outside of the garment is a plain or enameled metal ring or a plastic, colored glass, decorative metal (often specially designed with company logo or trademark), or mother-of-pearl cap; cost varies widely. *Plastic* snaps are an alternative to *metal* snaps and come in both sewn-on and mechanically attached styles. Clear plastic snaps are inexpensive, unobtrusive, and blend with any fabric. Colored plastic snaps can be selected to either match or contrast with the body fabric. The main drawback of plastic snaps is that they are not as durable as metal snaps. Plastic snaps melt in contact with a hot iron and distort when dried in excessive heat.

Snap Tape. Snap tape is often used to apply a series of snaps. **Snap tape** is a strip of fabric, often twill tape, onto which the snaps are mechanically attached by the supplier (Figure 8–11) or a thermoplastic tape into which plastic snaps are fused. The snap tape is then sewn to the garment. Advantages of snap tape include that the snaps are evenly spaced, securely attached to the tape (a safety advantage), and easier to

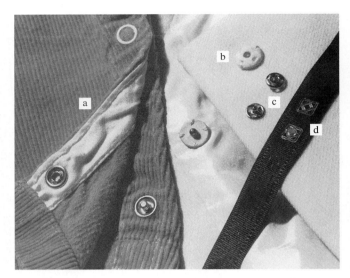

Figure 8–11 Snaps: (a) snap tape on inseam of child's overalls, (b) covered snap on designer jacket, (c) metal snap, and (d) plastic snap.

apply than attaching many snaps individually. Snaps are commonly used in the crotch of infantswear to allow for convenient diapering. Snap crotches are costly to manufacture but appreciated by parents; they are preferred to zippers in infant sleepers. Snap tape is also used in some casual garments. However, it adds considerable bulk so is not suited to many garment styles.

Snap tape has a few disadvantages—color choices are limited and the set distance between the snaps on the tape limits design flexibility in snap placement. Another problem with snap tape and with tape used to reinforce snaps is that it may shrink during laundering. It frequently shrinks more than the fabric to which it is attached, distorting the fabric and causing "snap hump." This is another example of the need for testing to determine the compatibility of garment component performance. Preshrinking by the supplier might be necessary before sewing the snap tape into the garment, thus eliminating problems for the consumer.

Hooks and Eyes. **Hook-and-eye** closures consist of two interlocking parts, a hook and an eye, a receptacle for the hook. Hooks and eyes offer the advantage of being small and easy to conceal but can carry a heavy stress load. A hook-and-eye closure is stronger than a snap closure of similar size. Hooks and eyes should be used instead of snaps in areas where there is heavy strain. The majority of hooks and eyes are concealed closures, but visible hooks and eyes are used in bras and some sportswear.

Hook and Eye Size. Hooks and eyes vary in size; small ones are unable to withstand great stress, and large ones are quite strong. Most general-purpose

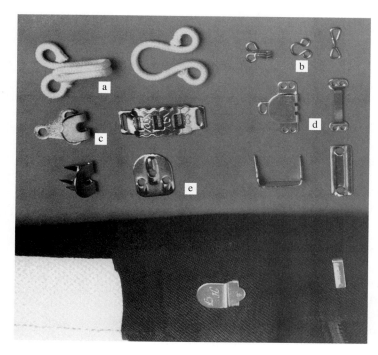

Figure 8–12 Hooks and eyes: (a) gimp-covered, (b) metal, (c) adjustable, (d) large sewn-on, and (e) mechanically attached (shown attached on waistband).

hooks and eyes range from small sizes for light- to mediumweight fabrics to large sizes for heavy fabrics. Hooks and eyes are numbered from size 0 to size 3, with small sizes representing small hooks and eyes. Large, special-purpose hooks and eyes for jackets and coats are available. Heavy-duty waistband hook-and-eye closures fasten pants and skirt waistbands; they are sets of metal plates consisting of a raised bar for the eye and a strong, flat hook that does not slide off the eye easily (Figure 8–12).

A hook and eye should be compatible with the fabric weight and the position and intended job of the hook and eye. For instance, a small hook and eye are appropriate for neckline closures while a large, special-purpose hook and eye is necessary for securing a waistband. The hook and eye should withstand the wear and care of the garment without bending.

Hook and Eye Composition. Hooks and eyes are usually made of the same metals as snaps. *Bra hooks* for bra backs have two or more sets of eyes for each hook so the wearer can adjust the bra to different circumferences. *Gimp-covered* or other *thread-covered* hooks and eyes, covered with thread to be inconspicuous, are considerably more costly than plain hooks and eyes (Figure 8–12a). They are found in high-price suits and coats and in fur coats.

Eye Types. The type of eye used with a hook varies. A *round* (curved) metal eye is intended for edges that abut; a *straight* or bar eye is intended for edges that overlap. Adjustable metal eyes offer more than one

position for the hook (Figure 8–12c). Adjustable eyes are bulky but provide for slight fluctuations in size, especially helpful at the waistline. A fabric loop, a group of threads, or a thread chain may serve as an eye for the hook. These are useful when a soft, color-matching eye is desired and when durability is not especially important.

Most hooks and eyes are applied at the stress point of the garment opening, such as at the waistline or neckline. However, hooks and eyes can be used to close an entire garment opening. When a number of hooks and eyes are sewn on, they may be prespaced and attached to a fabric strip, often twill tape. The tape is then sewn to the garment like snap tape.

Hook and Loop Tape (Velcro®). A finding that has gained popularity in recent years is pressure sensitive **hook-and-loop tape;** the best-known brand is **Velcro®.** Hook-and-loop tape operates on the same principle as a cockle burr that clings to clothing after a walk in the woods. The complete tape consists of two separate tapes that interlock to create closure when pressed together. To open, the two parts are pulled apart. The hook portion, which feels scratchy, consists of many tiny, flexible hooks embedded in a nylon fabric strip. The loop portion, which feels soft, consists of many tiny loops embedded in a nylon fabric strip. Hook-and-loop tape is available in various widths and gripping strengths for various uses. Generally, the coarser the hooks and loops, the greater the gripping strength and holding power of the tape. Other factors that affect the strength of the hook and loop tape include the number of hooks per square inch and the amount of pressure applied to join the two portions.

Hook-and-loop tape is a convenient closure. It is ideal as a button, snap, or hook and eye substitute on garments for small children or people who have difficulty with closures requiring finger dexterity and is useful for attaching detachable items, such as shoulder pads, to garments. A disadvantage of hook-and-loop tape is that it adds considerable stiffness and bulk to the garment; it is incompatible with soft fabrics because its stiffness interferes with the drape of the garment. Hook-and-loop tape is costly but requires little labor to attach.

The larger the piece of hook-and-loop tape used, the greater the holding power. Long strips of hook-and-loop tape are effective in maintaining closure and yet are easily unlocked if pulled apart. Small circles and squares of hook and loop tape substituted for a long strip are much less effective in gripping but are effective substitutes for buttons and buttonholes for arthritics.

Hook-and-loop tape is a concealed closure and can be used only in areas that lap. For comfort, manufacturers usually attach the hook portion of the tape to the underlap and the loop portion to the overlap. Machine stitches surrounding the tape and penetrating all plies of the garment are required for durable application, but the stitches show on the outside of the garment. Hook-and-loop tape is occasionally applied with adhesives, by heat or ultrasonically.

The two sides of hook-and-loop tape should be locked together during laundering. If not, the hook portion of the tape damages other fabrics in the load and collects thread and lint. Hook-and-loop tape melts in contact with a hot iron.

Miscellaneous Closures. Although used in fewer garments than buttons, zippers, snaps, and hooks and eyes, there are other types of findings that serve aesthetic as well as fastening purposes. D-rings, buckles, eyelets, grommets, and cords or ties are examples of these closures.

D-Rings. **D-rings** are an effective, adjustable closure named for the characteristic *D* shape (Figure 8–7d). Usually two d-rings of the same size are required to complete the closure. The two metal or plastic rings work together to adjust the length of a fabric strip, for example, a belt or a coat sleeve tab. D-rings come in a variety of sizes to accommodate fabric strips of varying widths.

Buckles. Buckles of various types, materials, shapes, and sizes are used as functional fasteners and as decorative details. Although typically a closure for belts,

buckles may also be used on straps and tabs at the ankle, and wrist, shoulder, and on pockets. A buckle with a center bar usually has a prong that engages with eyelets to adjust the belt to various circumferences.

Buckles typically are made of plastic, wood, metal, or shell. Solid buckles are more durable than hollow ones, which break easily. Buckles may be fabric covered to complement the fabric of the garment. The cost and quality of buckles vary widely.

Eyelets and Grommets. **Eyelets** and **grommets** are reinforced holes in a garment. Eyelets and grommets are used to accept laces for lacing, to accept the prongs of belt buckles, and to accommodate cuff links. Eyelets are usually 1/4 inch in diameter, while grommets are larger. Typically, grommets and eyelets are reinforced with plastic or metal to form rimmed openings. Metals that have been painted tend to peel after wear and care. Occasionally, eyelets are made with thread, like a stitched buttonhole, instead of metal. The more densely the edge is covered with thread, the more durable. Thread eyelets are soft and not particularly durable but are the best choice for delicate fabrics because a metal eyelet would tear away from the garment in use.

Cords or Ties. A garment opening may be closed by tying it shut using **cords** (strings or ropes) or **ties** (fabric strips or tubes). Cords and ties are probably the oldest forms of closure. Common locations for cords or ties are at the waist, neck, ankles, and bottoms of sleeves. Cords or ties may be used to tie an opening shut, as drawstrings, or for lacing. A pair of ties may be an extension of the garment for example, the neckline of a halter top. Cords are attached to the garment. If included in a seam, cords and ties must be securely attached so they do not pull out of the seam when stressed. Most cords and ties are more decorative than functional.

Underlying Fabrics

Underlying fabrics—interfacings, linings, underlinings, and interlinings—lend shape and support to garments. In the industry, narrow (less than 12 inches wide) underlying fabrics are considered findings while full-width (greater than 12 inches wide) are considered fabrics. All underlying fabrics are discussed in this chapter, but the performance features and physical features of fabric discussed in Chapter 7 apply.

Interfacing Fabrics. Interfacing fabrics range from extremely lightweight fabrics (0.4 ounces per square yard), which lend soft or light support to very heavy fabrics (4 ounces per square yard), which give crisp or heavy support (Glock and Kunz, 1995). Interfacing should be the same weight as or lighter in weight than the fabric of the garment. A too-heavy or too-stiff interfacing overpowers the fashion fabric and makes the shaping look and feel artificial. The appropriate hand of the interfacing is determined by the amount of shaping desired; the interfacing should not be too limp or too stiff to achieve the desired appearance and hand. For example, men's dress shirt collars require a crisp interfacing; a softer interfacing is usually used in women's blouse collars; waistband interfacings require enough body to prevent the waistband from rolling. Dress pants, especially menswear, often feature a *waistband curtain,* incorporating a stabilizing interfacing with a facing for the waistband. (For more information, see Chapter 12.)

Interfacings should withstand the same wear and care as the garment; interfacings that tear, roll, or shrink detract from quality. For this reason, some manufacturers use self-fabric interfacings, made from the shell fabric, because they are perfectly compatible with the garment in durability, care, color, weight, and hand. However, self-fabric interfacings usually cost more than other types of interfacing.

Structure of Interfacings. Interfacings are woven, knitted, or nonwoven. Each fabrication has advantages and disadvantages.

Woven Interfacing. The important features of **woven interfacings** are that they

1. are strong.
2. add shape without looking boardy (if not too heavy for shell fabric); this makes them effective for use in tailored garments. For example, *hair canvas* and *wigan* (lighter than hair canvas) are resilient, woven interfacings made of hair fibers or blends; they are used in the traditional tailoring of better garments.
3. do not stretch, thus adding stability to the area. Woven interfacings are used in knit garments only if the designer wants to inhibit the natural stretch of the knit for example, in button and buttonhole areas.
4. must be cut on grain for stability or be cut on the bias in areas that must roll, fold, or drape smoothly, such as under collars, hems, and men's neckties, because fewer yarn interlacings on the bias allow the fabric more flexibility.
5. tend to ravel.
6. are more costly than other types of interfacing.

Knit Interfacing. **Knit interfacings** have become popular in recent years. Their important characteristics are that they

1. stretch, making them well-suited for knit garments. At the same time, knit interfacings lend some stability because adding any fabric layer to an area makes it harder to stretch.
2. add softer shape and drape than woven interfacings.
3. do not ravel, but the edges may curl.
4. must be cut "on grain." Remember, knits do not have a grain as do woven fabrics (see Chapter 7) but must be cut as if they did have one.
5. cost less than woven interfacings.
6. feature an extra filling yarn inserted through the knit structure in *weft-insertion knit* interfacings. These knit interfacings have become very popular in tailoring because they add shape and stability without sacrificing drape and flexibility.

Fiberweb Interfacing. **Fiberweb** or **nonwoven interfacings** are the most common type. They are neither woven nor knitted but made of fibers (usually polyester or nylon) that have been entangled, glued, or fused together into a sheet of fabric. The main characteristics of fiberweb interfacings are they

1. generally lend good stability.
2. are not very drapable and may interfere with the fold, roll, or drape of some face fabrics. Heavyweight fiberwebs are especially stiff.
3. have no grain if the fibers are randomly oriented. They may be cut with the pattern pieces placed in any direction, making the tightest possible marker arrangement and achieving maximum material utilization. A few fiberwebs have directionally oriented fibers; they must be cut on-grain, lowering material utilization but providing greater stability than random orientations.
4. do not ravel, but the edges of lightweight fiberwebs may curl.
5. are often less durable than knit or woven interfacings if exposed to heavy wear and care
6. have a propensity to pill.
7. are usually the least costly type of interfacing.

Fusible versus Sew-In Interfacing. Interfacing can be fused or sewn to the back of the garment body fabric. Fusible and sew-in interfacings are available in woven, knitted, and fiberweb varieties.

Fusible Interfacing. The most common type, **fusible interfacings** have a heat-sensitive adhesive on the back; a hot press is used to melt the adhesive and laminate the interfacing to the back of the fashion fabric. When fusible interfacings were developed in the 1960s, quality problems associated with them were common. Fusible interfacings tended to shrink and delaminate, distorting the fashion fabric of the garment. Improved adhesives have been developed and, when properly applied, most modern fusible interfacings perform well.

The important characteristics of fusibles are that they

1. are slightly stiffer (after the melted adhesive cools and solidifies) than sew-in interfacings; fusible interfacing should barely extend into the seam allowance to avoid unwanted bulk.

2. make the face fabric very stable. This is usually desirable except in knit garments, where the stability of fusibles restricts the stretch of the knit.

3. provide a slightly flatter shaping than sew-in interfacings. However, high-quality fusibles are fairly pliable and supple.

4. bond to the fibers of the shell fabric and prevent them from migrating to the surface; fusibles retard pilling, very important in shirt collars and cuffs.

5. do not tear or roll as easily as sew-in interfacings because of being laminated to the fabric. Therefore, some fusible interfacings are more durable than sew-ins.

6. must be tested for ease of production and compatibility with the care of the body fabric. Fusibles may blister, bubble, or delaminate if they are not applied correctly, if the adhesive is uneven, or if the garment receives improper care. Incorrect application of fusibles can cause **strike-through** if adhesive leaks through the fashion fabric. It shows up either as spots or as a discoloration of the fashion fabric and may make the garment unwearable. (An example of strike-through appears in Chapter 11, Figure 11–14.) Fusibles can cause a puckering effect if the interfacing shrinks differently from the fashion fabric.

Sew-In Interfacing. **Sew-in interfacings** are stitched into the garment. The main features of sew-in interfacings are that they

1. provide body without the stiffness of fusible interfacings

2. can hide seam allowances that might otherwise show through, if sewn to the garment rather than the facing. This is desirable in translucent or sheer fabrics.

3. can cause slight puckering if they shrink differently from the fashion fabric; however, bubbling, blistering, delamination and strike-through are not problems with sew-in interfacings.

4. are often preferred in knit garments; they maintain the fabric's extensibility by leaving the loops of the knit free rather than fusing them in place.

5. are used extensively in finely tailored and couture apparel because of soft shaping capabilities. The skillful selection and application of interfacing are especially important in tailored garments. High-quality tailored garments possess a permanent,

Table 8–2 Fibers Used in Lining Fabrics

Acetate linings: often used because they are smooth and pretty, but they require dry-cleaning and are not as durable as polyester, nylon, or silk; acetate linings often wear out before the fashion fabric.

Polyester and nylon linings: extremely durable. They are smooth but not as absorbent and comfortable as acetate and silk.

Silk linings: luxurious and comfortable but very costly and not as durable as synthetics.

Cotton linings: comfortable, but do not help the garment slide on and off easily.

Rayon linings: comfortable but not very durable.

Wool linings: rare, but provide great warmth.

molded shape that has been imparted through the use of the proper interfacing, pad stitching, and careful pressing.

Lining Fabrics. The choice of lining fabric depends upon the fashion fabric and the end use and price line of the garment. Various fibers offer different advantages and disadvantages in lining fabrics, as summarized in Table 8–2. Most lining fabrics are woven rather than knit, for greater stability. Satin weaves are common because they help the garment slide on and off easily.

A high-quality lining fabric

1. is smooth, to help the garment slip on and off easily

2. is lightweight and nonbulky

3. is resistant to staining from perspiration and body oils

4. is able to withstand the same wear as the garment. A lining fabric that rips, fades or wears out before the face fabric makes the garment unwearable.

5. has the same care requirements as the garment. For example, a dry-clean-only lining sewn into a washable garment increases maintenance costs unnecessarily.

6. adds warmth to cool-weather garments and adds as little warmth as possible to warm-weather garments

7. is absorbent, for comfort

8. is static-free so the lining does not cling to the garment or to anything worn under it

9. is opaque to keep the seam allowances and other construction details from showing through inside the garment

10. is of a color and pattern that complement the fashion fabric of the garment.

Underlining Fabrics. Many of the same types of fabrics used for lining are used for underlining. However, fabrics that are crisper or more fluid (including knits) than traditional lining fabrics are most appropriate for producing the desired shape in the finished garment. Slippery fabrics that might make good lining fabrics are not usually used as underlinings.

Interlining Fabrics. Interlining fabrics should be lightweight and nonbulky, and should withstand the same care as the garment. Recently developed fabrics such as the Thinsulate® and Thermaloft® brands are ideal interlinings because they are designed to be extremely warm but thin, lightweight, and easy care. They are used in ski pants, jackets, and gloves. Polyester fleece is a popular, low-cost interlining in many quilted fabrics. Down and lambswool are traditional interlinings in coats and other cold-weather outerwear. Interlining is one place where used wool is sometimes found in apparel because used wool may not look or feel as good as new wool but remains a good insulator.

Other Shaping and Supporting Devices

Other findings items used in ready-to-wear that come under the classification of shaping and supporting devices include elastic, collar stays, seam stays and bridles, horsehair braid, boning, and weights. All these items can be ordered from suppliers. Shoulder pads, chest pieces, sleeve pads, bra cups, and hoops and bustles can be purchased already made or can be made in the factory as part of the assembly process. Either way, the assembled items or raw materials to make them must be ordered early in the production cycle with other findings and figured into the total garment cost.

Elastic. Elastic is a fabric with a high degree of stretch and recovery. Numerous types of narrow elastic are available to meet various design and end-use requirements (Figure 8–13). For example:

1. *Swimwear elastic* must withstand water, chlorine, sunshine, perspiration, and suntan lotions.
2. *Plush-back elastic* has a soft surface for applications worn next to the skin.
3. *Lingerie elastic* is a plush-back elastic with a decorative edge or edges used on bras and feminine underwear.
4. *Stretch lace*, an elastic lace, is another popular choice for lingerie.
5. *Pajama elastic* is a wide, soft elastic used inside the waistlines of boxer shorts and pajama bottoms.
6. *Nonroll elastic* is a ribbed elastic used at the waist and in other locations where rolling elastic is uncomfort-

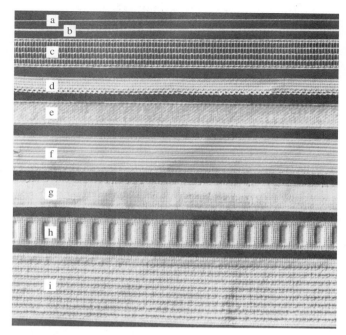

Figure 8–13 Elastic: (a) thread, (b) cord, (c) mesh, (d) knitted lingerie, (e) plush-back, (f) braided, (g) knitted, (h) woven nonroll, (i) webbing with grooves for stitching.

able and unsightly. However, nonroll elastic is more costly and it is bulkier and stiffer than other types.

The amount of stretch required in an elastic product depends upon the end use of the garment. Spandex or rubber elastic comes in different gauges, each with varying amounts of stretch and power. The elastic's construction and method of application also affect the amount of stretch and power. Designers and patternmakers must work closely with elastic suppliers and production engineers to select the correct elastic product and plan the appropriate amount of elastic and method of application to achieve the needed dimensions.

Fiber Content of Elastic. Elastic is made of extensible fibers, either rubber or spandex. The rubber or spandex is covered with polyester, cotton, or some other fiber to add comfort and aesthetic appeal. The amount of rubber or spandex used and the structure of the elastic determine extensibility. Both rubber and spandex have excellent stretch and recovery. Spandex elastic is stronger and generally lasts longer than rubber elastic because it is more resistant to deterioration from aging, sunlight, perspiration, salt water, suntan and body oils, heat, chlorine bleach, and dry-cleaning solvents. However, some synthetic rubbers also have good resistance to degradation from the elements listed, and rubber generally costs less than spandex.

Elastic Structure. High-quality elastic may be woven, knitted, or braided. *Braided elastic* has excellent stretch. However, it is bulky and stays narrow after being stretched, so it should not be stitched directly to cloth (which prevents its recovery); it should be attached within a casing. *Woven elastic* is heavier and more stable than other elastics. Designers use woven elastics where firm control is needed, although it is generally the most costly type of elastic. *Knitted elastic* is usually soft and lightweight; it generally costs less than other types of elastic. Both woven and knitted elastics may be stitched directly to the garment or attached within a casing. Some knitted elastics have channels or grooves knitted into them so they can be stitched to the garment (in the grooves) without piercing the elastic fibers. However, the spacing of the sewing machine needles must match the spacing of the channels in this type of application.

Width of Elastic. Elastic should be of a width that is comfortable and gives the desired look. The wider the elastic, the higher the price. The narrowest elastic is *elastic thread*. Manufacturers use elastic thread to create single or multiple rows of elasticized gathering that shape the garment and stretch with the wearer's movements. For example, elastic thread is found in tube tops, in the waist and bodice areas of shirred sundresses, and at the lower edge of ruffled blouse and dress sleeves. Round, narrow elastic is called *elastic cording*. Other elastics are 1/8 inch or wider. Wide elastics are less apt to cut or dig into the wearer's skin but may cause discomfort if they twist or roll. Multiple rows of stitches may be necessary to prevent this; another solution to this problem is *nonroll elastic*.

Belts. **Belts** help hold the garment in position and shape it to the body at the waist, but they are also decorative. Belts buckle, tie, or otherwise fasten around the body. *Self-belts* are made of the same fabric as the garment. Other belts may be made of a different fabric, vinyl, metal, leather, or other materials. Belts are made by the manufacturer or by a contractor. The cost of soft fabric belts is relatively low. Stiff fabric belts are made by stitching or gluing the fabric around *belting,* a stiff interfacing; stitched belts cost more and are more durable than glued belts.

A belt often increases the *hanger appeal* of the garment, or its ability to attract the consumer when hanging on the sales rack. The addition of even a low-quality belt can significantly increase the garment's salability. Therefore, many manufacturers purchase belts to add to the garments they produce. Color selection is important when purchasing belts. The belts purchased by manufacturers to be used on dresses, skirts, and pants and sold on garments (called the *cut-up trade*) are generally of lower quality than the average belt bought by retailers to be sold separately (called the *rack trade*). High-quality belts on garments are found only in high-price lines.

Shoulder Pads. **Shoulder pads** are another important shaping device in tailored jackets and coats. (A shoulder pad in a man's jacket is shown in Chapter 11, Figure 11–15.) They are also used in shirts, blouses, and dresses as fashion demands. Shoulder pads vary from a 1/4 inch to an inch or more in thickness, depending on the desired look. They vary in style, with some creating a square-shoulder look and others creating a soft look. (For more information, see Chapter 5.)

Shoulder pads are made of a single layer of molded foam or multiple layers of foam or *batting* (fibers fused, stitched, or tangled together). The pad should withstand the same wear and care as the garment without lumping, rolling, or shrinking. The edges of the pad are graduated so they do not create a ridge on the outside of the garment. Shoulder pads in unlined garments should be covered with the garment fabric or a fabric that does not show through the garment. Removable shoulder pads are a good selling point because they can be taken out to help avoid the stacked look of multiple pads when wearing a blouse, jacket, and/or coat.

Chest Pieces. **Chest pieces** are an important shaping device in tailored jackets and coats, mainly in menswear. (An illustration appears in Chapter 11, Figure 11–15.) The chest piece is a pad consisting of several layers of supporting fabrics. Chest pieces fill out and smooth the hollow area below the shoulder near the armhole. A high-quality chest piece creates a smooth front on the garment without hollows, ridges, or lumps.

Low-price jackets usually feature *fully fused fronts*, which means that the chest piece is fused to the jacket along with the front interfacing. Some high-price jackets feature *floating chest pieces*. Floating chest pieces are attached with loose stitches around the sides and edges. They are preferable because they float, allowing the jacket to conform naturally to the wearer's movements rather than remaining in a fixed, fused position.

Sleeve Heads. **Sleeve heads** or **sleeve headers** are used in some tailored jackets and coats and occasionally in other types of garments. Sleeve heads consist of two or three narrow layers of shaping fabric sewn into the upper portion of the armhole and extending out into the sleeve. The purpose of sleeve heads in tailored garments is to create a soft, smooth roll in the cap of the sleeve without creating a hollow, ridge, or lump across the top of the sleeve. Without a sleeve head, the sleeve cap may be wrinkled and slightly hollow where it drops at a sharp angle from the shoulder seam. Sometimes manufacturers use crisp sleeve heads in garments with full, gathered sleeves to support the puff of the sleeve cap.

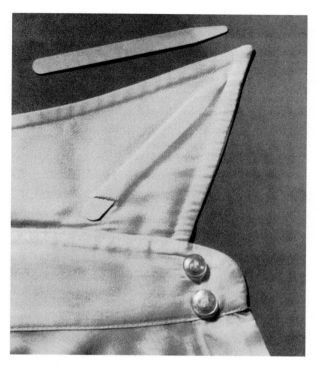

Figure 8–14   Removable collar stays.

Seam Stays and Bridles.   As discussed in Chapter 10, seams may require stay tapes to stabilize them. Lapels in better-quality jackets and coats contain a **bridle**, a stay tape sewn at the roll line (the fold) of the lapel. (This is also shown in Chapter 11, Figure 11–15.) The operator eases the lapel to the bridle, which is slightly shorter than the lapel, shaping the roll line to the body. The bridle holds the lapel in shape, helping it hug the body for a smooth fit. Additional fabric can be eased to the bridle in garments for women with large busts or men with highly developed chests to prevent the lapels from gaping. Usually twill tape or some other nonstretchy, narrow fabric is used for stays.

Collar Stays.   **Collar stays** are thin plastic strips inserted in collars to make them "stay" flat and prevent the collar points from curling. Collar stays are used in men's dress shirts and some sport shirts. Most shirts either do not have collar stays, or the collar stays are sewn permanently inside the collar. Some high-price shirts have *removable stays*. Removable stays can be taken out when the shirt is laundered. This prevents the stays from bending or breaking and avoids pressing the imprint of the stays through to the outside of the collar. Extra labor costs are involved in making a collar with removable stays (Figure 8–14). Shirts with button-down collars do not require collar stays.

Bra Cups.   *Bra cups* provide support, shape, and smoothness to the bustline of swimsuits, strapless

Figure 8–15   Boning in a bra.

evening gowns, and other garments. They often contain fiberfill or foam to enhance the bust size and shape. Such padding should withstand care procedures without lumping or disintegrating.

Boning.   **Boning** gives support to a garment through the use of stiff plastic (at one time whalebone) strips. Boning comes and goes in popularity as fashion demands. It was very important in womenswear in the late 1800s but today is mainly confined to formal, fitted dresses and some supportive bras, girdles, and women's swimsuits. Strapless bodices usually require boning in the side seams (and other seams in the midriff area) to shape the garment to the body and help it stay up. Heavily boned garments do not move with the wearer but mold the wearer to the shape of the garment, so boning can be quite uncomfortable. The boning is encased in fabric and sewn, on the inside of the garment, over the vertical seam allowances (Figure 8–15). Careful positioning and suitable lengths of boning for the size and design of the garment are important for appearance and wearing comfort.

Hoops and Bustles.   Large plastic or metal rings or **hoops** may be sewn into the lower portion of a slip or underskirt to support a full skirt. Rows of stiff netting or *crinoline*, a stiff fabric, create a similar but less rigid

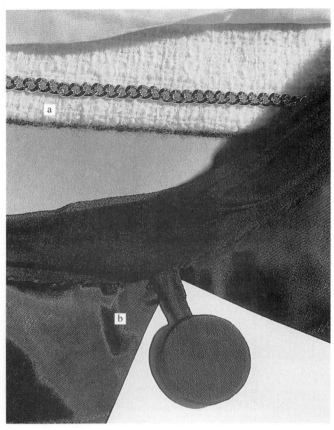

Figure 8–16   (a) Chain weight in hem of Chanel® jacket, and (b) weight in neckline of evening gown.

effect. A **bustle** is a basket-like device used to expand and support the fullness and draping of the material in the back of a skirt. The popularity of hoops and bustles depends upon fashion. In this century, their use has mainly been confined to wedding and formal gowns.

Horsehair Braid.   **Horsehair braid** is used to face and stiffen hems in wedding and formal gowns with full skirts. It is a stiff, narrow braid once made of horsehair but today made of sheer nylon. Operators sew the braid to the hem using a narrow seam allowance and stretching the braid slightly as it is applied. Because the horsehair braid has been stretched slightly, it naturally pulls to the inside of the garment, keeping the hem edge turned under and in place. It is tacked to the seam allowances, so no stitches show on the outside of the garment. The horsehair braid stiffens the hem edge, making the hem stand out gracefully from the body.

Weights.   Designers may plan for **weights** in high-quality garments to perfect drape; small, thin lead weights are encased in fabric and tacked into position (Figure 8–16). Weights increase costs but add to quality. The following are some uses of weights:

1. most frequently, to help hems hang evenly; for example, at center front edges of heavyweight coats to help corners hang flat. Sometimes lightweight chains serve as weights; for example, a chain at the hem is one of the signatures of a true Chanel jacket.
2. to achieve desired drape in cowl necklines of evening gowns.
3. to prevent lightweight skirts from catching a breeze and blowing up immodestly.

Weights should be carefully positioned to achieve the desired effect. They should be made of a *nonferrous* (nonrust) material, and care should be taken when pressing so an imprint of the weight does not show through to the outside of the garment; weights may need to be removed when the garment is cleaned and pressed.

Dress Shields.   **Dress shields** or **underarm shields** absorb perspiration and prevent the formation of perspiration stains on the outside of the garment. Underarm shields should be carefully positioned inside the garment in the underarm area for maximum absorbency. They may be tacked in place for easy removal for laundering. Underarm shields extend the life of the garment by preventing perspiration damage. They are a mark of quality found in high-price bridal and evening gowns and in suits for men and women.

SUMMARY

Findings and trim items are subject to most of the same aesthetic and functional performance considerations as fabric. Findings and trim should be chosen for compatibility with the garment. They should complement the appearance of the garment and be able to withstand the same use and care as the garment. Labels must be permanently attached, comfortable to wear, and remain legible for the life of the garment. High-quality thread has appropriate size, strength, dimensional stability, skin-contact comfort, and color.

The fiber content, complexity, width, and fullness affect the cost of narrow fabric trims. Ribbon is a narrow, woven trim; braid, a narrow, braided trim; lace, a narrow lace fabric; piping, a narrow, folded fabric in a seam; corded piping has a cord in it. Other narrow fabric trims include bias tape, seam or hem tape, twill tape, and fringe. Appliqués are decorative fabric patches. Nonfabric trims include beads, sequins, rhinestones, flat metal nailheads, raised metal studs, rivets and burrs, plastic or silk flowers, feathers, jewels, and pearls.

Closures are vital to the functional performance of a garment. When a closure malfunctions, the garment is unwearable. Buttons of natural materials are usually more costly than the more common plastic buttons. Button size is measured in lignes. Zipper tape should be stable. The zipper chain may be composed of elements, which are stronger, or coils, which can withstand sudden stress better. The slider of the zipper is moved up and down the zipper by holding onto the zipper tab. The zipper needs a top and bottom stop to prevent the slider from leaving the track. Zipper strength is related to the size (measured in mm) and composition of the zipper element. Most metal zippers are stronger than plastic zippers, but plastic zippers are more appropriate in lightweight fabrics. Zippers may be of the conventional, separating, or invisible type. Novelty zippers, trouser zippers, dress zippers, reversible zippers, and two-way zippers are useful for special purposes. Large snaps and hooks and eyes are stronger than small ones. Hook-and-loop tape is easy for the wearer to manipulate but adds bulk to the garment. D-rings, buckles, eyelets and grommets, and cords or ties are other ways garment openings are fastened.

Interfacing should add the desired amount of body or crispness to the garment without overpowering it. Interfacings are woven, knitted, or fiberweb. Linings and underlinings should be made of a smooth, absorbent, opaque fabric. Interlinings should provide warmth without excessive weight. Other shaping and supporting findings include elastic, belts, shoulder pads, chest pieces, sleeve heads, bridles and seam stays, collar stays, bra cups, boning, hoops and bustles, horsehair braid, and weights.

Findings and Trim Quality Checklist

If you can answer yes to the following questions regarding the garment you are evaluating, it has high-quality findings and trim.

✔ Are the size and type of finding or trim compatible with the garment? Do they enhance the appearance of the garment?
✔ Will the findings and trims perform as well as the garment, withstanding the same wear and care as the garment?
✔ Is the finding or trim comfortable?
✔ Does the color of the finding or trim match or complement the garment and retain its color?
✔ Are the labels comfortable for the wearer?
✔ Will the care label remain legible for the life of the garment?
✔ Is the thread as strong as the fabric, but not stronger?
✔ Are gathered trims fully and evenly gathered?

✔ Are enough buttons used to prevent gaping?
✔ Are buttons that cannot withstand the same care as the garment attached with small clips so consumers can remove them?
✔ Are large, metal, separate-element zippers used for heavy-duty applications?
✔ Are small, nylon, continuous-element zippers used for lightweight applications?
✔ Does the zipper have a locking slider and secure top and bottom stops?
✔ Are the durability, weight, hand, and color of supporting fabrics compatible with the garment?
✔ Does elastic provide appropriate stretch and recovery for end use?
✔ Is elastic a comfortable width? Comfortable length?
✔ Are belts stitched, not glued?
✔ Do lining and underlining provide desired body and/or opacity?
✔ Does interlining provide warmth without weight?
✔ Do chest pieces, shoulder pads, and sleeve heads follow the lines of the body with no visible ridges? As a quality extra, are chest pieces floating?
✔ Do shoulder pads and sleeve heads not draw attention to themselves by creating a ridge on the outside of the garment? As a quality extra, are shoulder pads removable?
✔ Does a shirt collar have collar stays? As a quality extra, are collar stays removable?

New Terms

If you can define each of these terms and differentiate between related terms, you have gained a good working vocabulary for discussing the topics in this chapter. The terms are listed in the order in which they appear in this chapter.

findings
trim
differential shrinkage
thread
spun thread
texturized thread
corespun thread
monofilament thread
multifilament thread
ribbon
braid
lace trim
appliqué
nonfabric trim
lignes
button loop
frog

toggle
zipper hump
zipper tape
zipper chain
elements
coil zipper
slider
pull/tab
stop
conventional zipper
separating zipper
invisible zipper
snap fastener/snap
snap tape
hook and eye
hook-and-loop tape/Velcro®
d-ring
eyelet
grommet
cord
tie
woven interfacing
knit interfacing
fiberweb/nonwoven interfacing
fusible interfacing
strike-through
sew-in interfacing
elastic
belt
shoulder pad
chest piece
sleeve head/header
bridle
collar stay
boning
hoop
bustle
horsehair braid
weight
underarm/dress shield

Review Questions

1. Discuss the considerations in choosing sewing thread for the following garments:
   a. silk satin wedding gown
   b. nylon jogging shorts
   c. cotton casual shirt
   d. wool dress pants

2. List the aesthetic and functional performance criteria that garment trims should meet.

3. Differentiate between insertion lace, galloon lace, lace edging, beading, and medallion lace.

4. How is piping different from corded piping?
5. How are buttons sized? Zippers? Snap fasteners? Hooks and eyes?
6. What are the advantages of buttons versus zippers?
7. List and describe the parts of a zipper.
8. What are the advantages and disadvantages of continuous-element zippers versus separate-element zippers?
9. Which withstand greater amounts of stress, snap fasteners or hook and eyes?
10. What are the advantages and disadvantages of metal snaps? covered snaps? plastic snaps?
11. What are the advantages and disadvantages of hook-and-loop tape?
12. Differentiate between interfacing, lining, underlining, and interlining.
13. Which closures lend themselves to easier manipulation by children and adults with limited finger dexterity?
14. Compare and contrast braided elastic, woven elastic, and knitted elastic.
15. What are the advantages and disadvantages of clear monofilament thread?

Activities

1. Attend the Bobbin Show™ in Atlanta, GA. Collect literature and talk to findings and trim producers about the cost and quality of their products.
2. Find garments containing the following trims, and evaluate the quality and application of the trim:
   a. grosgrain ribbon
   b. satin ribbon
   c. velvet ribbon
   d. novelty ribbon
   e. picot-edge ribbon
   f. soutache braid
   g. middy braid
   h. loop braid
   i. scrolling
   j. gimp

3. Examine low-price and high-price women's blouses. Do the buttons appear to differ in cost?
4. Survey five friends. Do they ever cut labels out of garments? If so, why? If not, why not?
5. Examine garments with seam failure. Can any of these failures be traced to the use of improper thread? Support your answer.
6. Find a buttoned garment that gapes. Compare it to a garment that does not gape. Which garment

has more buttons? How does button placement vary?

7. Find examples of the following types of zippers:
   a. conventional zipper
   b. separating zipper
   c. invisible zipper

   In what types of garments is each type of zipper used?

8. Examine low-price and high-price infantswear. Examine the quality of the inseam and crotch area closures. Can any differences found be related to price line?

9. Examine low-price and high-price evening gowns. Are there any differences between price lines in the amount or quality of findings used? If so, are these differences aesthetic? Functional? Both?

10. Go to a thrift shop and purchase two men's suit jackets of different qualities. Remove half the lining in each. Purchase two men's dress shirts of different qualities.

   a. Examine the suit jackets for quality and quantity of shaping and supporting features. For example, look for fusible interfacing versus sew-in interfacing, fully fused fronts versus floating chest pieces, machine pad stitching versus hand pad stitching, full linings versus partial linings, sleeve heads, bridles, ease at back shoulder seams, lining attached at armscyes or not attached.
   b. Examine the dress shirts. Look for evidence of quality shape and support, for example, removable collar stays; crisp, smooth interfacing; and split yokes.

11. Survey five male and five female friends about shoulder pads in their clothing. What do they like and dislike about shoulder pads from the standpoint of attractiveness? Comfort? Durability? From your results, what do you predict to be the future of the shoulder pad in menswear and womenswear?

Stitches: Holding the Garment Together

Chapter Objectives

1. Differentiate between stitch types.
2. Evaluate the advantages and disadvantages of various stitch types.
3. Discuss the influence of stitch length and tension and other features on stitch performance.

Stitches hold a garment together; therefore, stitch quality is a critical gauge of apparel quality. The care the spec technician uses in establishing stitch specifications often represents the overall quality standards used in producing the garment. The thoughtful selection of stitch types and the appropriate choice of stitch length, needle size, and thread type and size positively influence stitch, and thus garment, performance. The evaluation of the stitches used in a garment is important information involved in judging its overall quality. (For more information, see Related Resources: Stitches and Seams).

STITCH PERFORMANCE

The term **stitches** refers both to the thread interloopings or interlockings used to make seams—the joints between two pieces of fabric that are sewn together (discussed more fully in Chapter 10)—and to stitchings, which perform functions other than joining pieces of fabric together. Edge finish stitchings (EF) finish garment edges, and ornamental stitchings (OS) add decoration (see Chapter 10). Stitches are by far the most widely used technique for assembling apparel. Stitches help determine the functional and aesthetic performance of a garment. Their durability, comfort, and attractiveness are important performance considerations determined by the end use and design of the garment, the type of fabric used, and the location and purpose of the stitches. Cost considerations also affect the choice of stitches.

Strong, durable stitches directly affect seam strength and garment durability. Weak, nondurable stitches lead to premature seam failure. Garments that receive hard wear and heavy laundering require more durable stitches than those worn for special occasions. Locations subject to stress require stronger stitches than low-stress locations. Highly stressed seams also require extensible stitches. For example, one of the most common places for seam rupture is the seam joining the sleeve to the body of the garment. Another common place for seam failure is the seat seam (center back seam) of pants. These highly stressed seams are cut on the bias of the fabric, which provides stretch and comfort to the wearer. However, if the stitches used to sew the seams do not stretch with the fabric, the stitches can rupture.

Garments made of knit fabrics, such as swimsuits and sweaters, require more extensible stitches than those made of woven fabrics. The stitches must withstand without rupturing the amount of stretch to which the fabric is subjected. To test for adequate stitch extensibility, moderately stretch a garment seam in a high-stress area. Adequately extensible stitches do not rupture under moderate stretch.

Uniform stitches placed in a straight line (or a smoothly curved line on curved seams) contribute to the attractiveness of the garment. Stitches that cause puckers, holes, snags, or runs, or that allow the seams to spread open or fail detract from the garment's appearance. Some stitches are attractive for decorative stitching; others are appropriate only for use inside the garment.

Consumers accept stitches more readily than they accept stitchless techniques such as adhesives and ultrasonic welding. Adhesives are mainly useful in leather and leatherlike garments. Sometimes they are used to attach emblems to shirts and caps, beads and appliqués to casual clothing, or as a temporary tack during assembly. *Ultrasonic welding* melts and fuses together fabrics with at least 65% synthetic (thermoplastic) fibers, and costs about one tenth as much as stitches. However, fusing is well accepted only in raingear, to seal the seams and make them waterproof. For other fabrics and other end uses, these methods, although less costly, are perceived as less durable (and if all variables are not carefully controlled, they are less durable), less comfortable (stiffer), and less attractive than stitches. However, recent progress in this area resulted in adhesive seams that are stronger than sewn seams. Seam pucker is avoided and needles, thread, and skipped stitches are eliminated, thus enhancing automation. New *laser-enhanced bonding (LEB)* technology uses laser energy to drive a polymer into the fabric panels. The polymer becomes part of the fabric, creating a seam many times stronger than traditional sewn seams. The resulting seam is not only durable but flexible and attractive and can be made as many as 8 times faster than sewing. Alternative methods of joining fabrics will likely be further developed to improve their performance; meanwhile, stitches are the basis of most garment construction.

PHYSICAL FEATURES OF STITCHES

The desired aesthetic and functional performance of stitches is achieved by controlling the following physical features of stitches: stitch type; stitch length and width; needle type, size and condition; thread type and size; tension and other sewing machine adjustments; and operator accuracy. Spec technicians in consultation with costing engineers choose the physical features of stitches based on desired stitch performance balanced against cost. Manipulating the physical features results in various levels of performance and cost.

Industrial sewing machines, unlike home sewing machines that can perform many stitch types, perform only one stitch type per machine. Most manufacturers maintain an inventory of machines that can perform the most frequently used stitch types. When a new garment style is about to be assembled, the sewing equipment for that line must be planned. Machines already in use on the line do not normally need any special attention. Machines that are held in inventory must be **sewed out** (cleaned, oiled, and adjusted for sewing) and set up. Machines that are not currently owned by the company must be ordered, assembled, sewed out and set up. Depending upon the new garment style being produced, setting up a new line can take anywhere from a few hours to a few days.

Stitch Type

Stitch type imparts functional and aesthetic performance. Several different stitch types may be used in constructing a single garment (Figure 9–1 on pp. 224–225). Each stitch type has performance advantages and disadvantages and purposes for which it is best suited. Spec technicians and patternmakers consider the fabric of the garment; the location and purpose of the stitches; the style, fit, and end use; and the equipment available to determine which types of stitches to use. The cost of stitches depends on the amount of labor, thread, and fabric required and the sewing machine used.

Lockstitch and Chainstitch Sewing Machines. Most machine-made stitches are formed by either a **lockstitch** sewing machine or a **chainstitch** sewing machine. Lockstitch machines rely on *interlocking* threads; chainstitch machines rely on *interlooping* threads. Lockstitch and chainstitch machines both feature a *needle thread.* The needle thread enters the fabric from above, carried by the sewing machine needle. The needle thread feeds from a large cone or other type of thread package. The difference between lockstitch and chainstitch machines lies in the delivery of the *underthread*, which enters the fabric from below.

Lockstitch Machines. Lockstitch machines feature an underthread called a *bobbin thread.* The bobbin thread feeds from a small, round *bobbin,* a cylinder of thread located beneath the needle. As the machine sews, a rotary hook, or shuttle hook, revolves around the bobbin. The rotary hook catches the needle thread when the needle brings it down through the fabric. The rotary hook carries the needle thread all the way around the bobbin; then the needle pulls the needle thread back up to the top of the fabric again. The needle thread and bobbin thread become interlocked, forming a lockstitch.

To achieve high sewing speeds, the size of the bobbin around which the rotary hook must revolve is limited. Because of its limited size, a bobbin can hold only about 100 yards of thread. Operators must remove and replace the bobbin frequently during sewing, interrupting productivity and increasing labor costs. Depending upon the complexity of the operation, a single operator might make over 100 bobbin changes in an 8-hour shift. Each time, the operator must stop sewing to insert a new bobbin. Some bobbins are automatically wound during sewing while others are purchased prewound from a thread company. Sewing engineers study jobs requiring frequent bobbin changes and try to design the method using prewound bobbins and other techniques for cost effectiveness.

Chainstitch Machines. Most chainstitch machines feature one or more underthreads, called *looper threads,* instead of a bobbin thread. (Some chainstitch machines have no underthreads.) Each looper thread is carried back and forth by a moving arm, either a *looper* or a *spreader.* The looper or spreader holds the underthreads in position to interloop with the needle thread every time the needle brings it down. This repeated action forms a chain of thread on the underside of the fabric, creating the chainstitch.

Looper threads feed from large cones of thread; no bobbin is required. This allows the operator to sew without the interruption of changing the bobbin, making chainstitches less costly in labor than lockstitches.

U.S. Fed. Std. No. 751a. U.S. Fed. Std. No. 751a: *Stitches, Seams, and Stitchings* schematically diagrams the conformation of each stitch type and defines it. The original purpose of the federal standard was to achieve greater uniformity in sewn products such as military uniforms that the government contracts out. Because of its usefulness, the federal standard has been adopted by the apparel industry for general use. It enables manufacturers, contractors, and retailers to differentiate between stitch types and communicate about them more accurately, eliminating misunderstandings about specifications. The stitch types are illustrated, which makes the federal standard well suited to international communication. The federal standard includes most, but not all, stitch types used in ready-to-wear. This chapter discusses the most widely used stitch types within each class. Refer to a copy of U.S. Fed. Std. 751a for a complete listing. U.S. Fed. Std. No. 751a can be obtained for about $25 from the U.S. **General Services Administration (GSA)**, Specifications Section, Room 6654, 7th and D Streets, Washington, D.C. 20407.

At the time of this writing, the American Society for Testing and Materials (ASTM) is beginning to convert Fed. Std. no. 751a from a government document to a consensus civilian standard. It will be known as *Standard Practice for Seams and Stitches.* Although it is expected that initially this document will be essentially the same standard in ASTM format, expect new items such as bar tacks to be incorporated into future revisions of this standard.

Stitch Classes. U.S. Fed Std. No. 751a established six classes of stitches. The general performance of stitches in the six classes is summarized in Table 9–1. The classes used to categorize stitches are as follows:

Stitch class 100 Simple chainstitches
Stitch class 200 Hand stitches and their machine simulations
Stitch class 300 Lockstitches
Stitch class 400 Multithread chainstitches
Stitch class 500 Overedge stitches and safety stitches
Stitch class 600 Cover stitches

The first digit of a three-digit number identifies each stitch class. The second and third digits of the number identify the stitch type within the class. (An example of such a number is shown in Chapter 10,

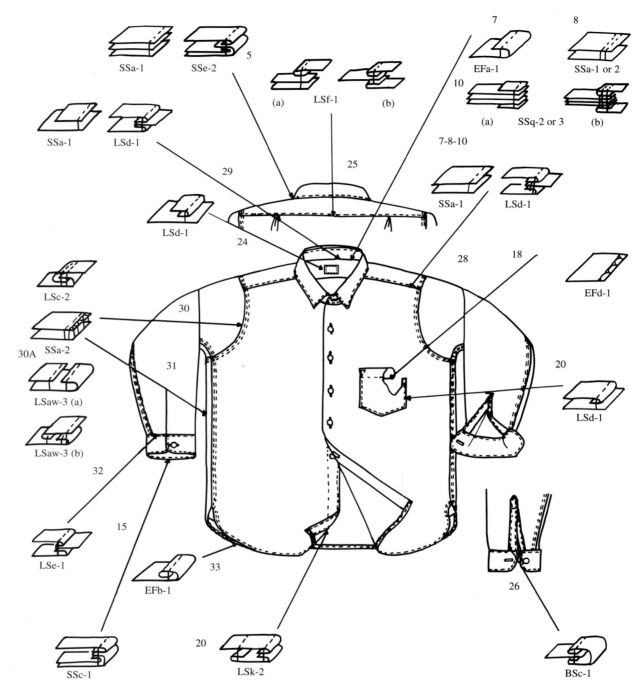

Figure 9–1   Stitches, seams, and stitchings used to make a dress shirt. *(Courtesy of Union Special Corporation Technical Training Center.)*

Figure 10–4.) For example, 503 and 521 are stitch types within the 500 class. Stitch types within a class are similar but vary in the number and exact arrangement of threads. The federal standard is the best available tool for identifying stitches and is used widely in the industry to designate stitch types. Appendix B lists the stitch types used for various garment construction operations. To make multiple rows of the same stitch type, each row may be sewn separately. More commonly, however, independent, parallel rows of stitches are sewn simultaneously using a multineedle machine. Special machines allow multiple needles to negotiate sharp corners so that the rows of stitches stay parallel at collar and lapel points and other corners.

OPERATIONS DESCRIPTION	SEQUENCE OF OPERATIONS	
	Stitch/Seam	Est. Doz./Hr.
Collars		
1. Fuse collar & band		50
2. Attach plastic stays	301 SSa-1	30
3. Runstitch collar	301 SSa-1	15
4. Trim, turn, & press collar points		
5. Topstitch collar	301 SSe-2(b)	16
6. Trim collar edge		
7. Hem collar band	301 EFa-1	20
8. Attach collar band to collar	301 SSa-1	15
9. Turn & press collar band		
10. Sew-down collar band	301 SSq-2(b)	18
11. Buttonhole collar band		
12. Button sew collar band	101	37
13. Trim & notch collar band	Hand	
Cuffs		
14. Precrease cuffs		
15. Topstitch cuffs	301 SSc-1	7-1/2
16. Buttonhole cuffs		25
17. Button sew cuffs	101	24
Pockets		
18. Serge pocket tops	504 EFd-1	40
19. Precrease pockets		
Fronts & Backs		
20. Hem button stay (Rt side)	401 EFb-1(inv)	30
21. Buttonhole front (Rt)		10
22. Set center plait	401 LSm-2	25
23. Button sew front	101	10
23a. Set pocket to Lt front	301 LSd-1	18
24. Attach label to yoke	401 LSd-1	16
25. Set back to yoke	401 SSa-1	20
Sleeves		
26. Attach sleeve facing	301 BSc-1	12-1/2
27. Tack sleeve facing	301	10
Assembly		
28. Join shoulder seam	401 SSa-1	15
29. Attach & sew down collar	301 LSf-2(b)mod	4
30. Set sleeves	401 LSc-2	8
ALT. (French sleeving)	301 LSaw-3(b)	8
31. Side seam & close sleeves	401 LSc-2	8
32. Set cuffs	301 LSe-1	7-1/2
33. Hem bottom	301 EFb-1	7-1/2
34. Trim & inspect	Hand	

Figure 9–1 (Continued)

100-Class Stitches. Stitches in the **100 class** are **single-thread chainstitches** (Figure 9–2). These chainstitches are categorized separately from their nearest relatives, 400-class chainstitches because they usually are made using only a needle thread with no underthread. The needle thread interloops with itself on the back of the fabric to form a simple chain.

Advantages. The loops of their chainlike structure give 100-class stitches extensibility. The use of only one thread for most 100-class stitches makes them economical.

Disadvantages. Simple chainstitches can give an impression of low quality when used in inappropriate locations because they lack durability. The last stitch must be secured or the stitches may ravel ("ravel back") or come undone ("run back").

Variations. Variations of 100-class stitches secure hems, sew on buttons, and make buttonholes and tacks at high speeds. However, 100-class stitches are not the most durable choice in any of these cases.

The most common stitch type of the 100 class is the *101*. It is a continuous row of straight stitches on the face of the fabric and a continuous chain of interlooped stitches on the back side. The 101 stitches are useful for **basting,** or temporary stitches, because they are easily unraveled. They are also used to close bags of pet food. The *103* is a blindstitch. A **blindstitch** joins layers of fabric without the needle thread fully penetrating the top layer and it should be imperceptible, or nearly so, from the outside of the garment (Figure 10–21 in Chapter 10 shows a blindstitched hem.) The depth of the stitches must be adjusted so that each one barely catches a few yarns of the outermost layer of fabric, securing the other layers to it but remaining as inconspicuous as possible. Although they are used for hemming (see Chapter 10), 100-class blindstitches lack durability, but they are easily removed for hem alteration. The 104 stitches are decorative saddle stitches.

200-Class Stitches. Stitches in the **200 class** originated as **hand stitches.** Manufacturers use **machine-made versions** of 200-class stitches for decorative and other special purposes. The stitches are created on machines that pass a single thread through one side of the material and then the other. These machine imitations are produced much faster than actual hand-made stitches, which are found only occasionally in ready-to-wear. The 200 class does not include all the hand stitches and machine imitations of hand stitches used in ready-to-wear, only those classified for use in government procurement.

Advantages. Machine imitations of hand stitches are similar in durability, uniformity, and cost to other types of machine stitches. Though hand stitches are rarely found in ready-to-wear apparel, they are desirable in some cases because they provide shape, control, flexibility, and softness. They are used only where their cost is justified by the price of the garment. For example, high-quality men's neckties are hand slipstitched and hand tacked for soft drape and

Table 9–1   Summary of Stitch Class Performance

Class 100

Description	Simple chainstitches, interlooped
Cost	Very inexpensive
Durability	Flexible but unravels easily
Appearance	Plain on face, single chain on back
Comfort	Less comfortable than 300
Limitations	Unravels too easily for use in quality apparel
Special features	Uses only one thread

Class 200

Description	Hand stitches/machine simulations, one thread up and down through fabric
Cost	Extremely high if by hand, by machine varies
Durability	Machine is more durable
Appearance	Machine is more uniform, hand may be less noticeable
Comfort	Hand is softer
Limitations	Decorative and specialty uses, not used for structural seams
Special features	Most are made on specialty machines

Class 300

Description	Lockstitches, interlocked
Cost	Labor costs higher than 400 but requires less thread
Durability	Strong, not very extensible
Appearance	Seams do not grin but tend to pucker, reversible
Comfort	Very comfortable, flat, nonbulky
Limitations	Bobbin must be changed, slowing production, not very extensible
Special features	Hard to unravel, 301 is most widely used stitch in industry

---

Class 400

Description	Multithread chainstitches, interlooped
Cost	Labor costs less than 300 but requires more thread
Durability	Strong, more extensible than 300
Appearance	Seam grin, less likely to pucker than 300
Comfort	Slightly less comfortable than 300 unless soft thread is used, bulkier than 300
Limitations	Can abrade, catch, and unravel easily
Special features	Main competition of 300, combines with 500 in most safety stitches, can cover bottom of seam

---

Class 500

Description	Overedge stitches, interlooped
Cost	Labor costs less than 300 but requires more thread

Table 9–1 Continued

Durability	Very extensible, strong, safety stitches very durable
Appearance	Seam grin a problem, not likely to pucker
Comfort	Less comfortable than 300 unless soft thread is used, somewhat bulky
Limitations	Can be used only on edges
Special features	Stitches seam, trims, and finishes edge simultaneously, most widely used in knitwear industry

Class 600

Description	Cover stitches, interlooped
Cost	Labor costs less than 300 but requires more thread
Durability	Very extensible, strong
Appearance	Several threads show face and back, not likely to pucker
Comfort	Less comfortable than 300 unless soft thread is used, stitch somewhat bulky but seam often not
Limitations	Stitches flat seams
Special features	Joins abutted or overlapped edges, covers top and bottom of seam simultaneously

attractive knotting. Finely tailored and couture clothing often feature hand stitches, lending the connotation of craftsmanship and quality. Some handwork is used in moderate-price apparel when relatively low production numbers do not justify mechanization of certain processes. Examples include sewing on closures, such as hooks and eyes, or decorative features, such as feathers. This occurs more often in womenswear than menswear because of frequent fashion changes which defy the cost-effective mechanization of some production processes.

Disadvantages. Machine imitations of hand stitches are similar in performance to other types of machine stitches. However, hand stitches are generally less durable and less uniform than machine stitches. Hand stitches drastically lower production speeds and increase costs compared to machine stitches. For these reasons, almost all ready-to-wear apparel is sewn entirely by machine.

Variations. Figure 9–3 illustrates variations of the 200-class stitch. Stitch type *202* is a **backstitch.** Backstitching is a secure form of stitching in which one small stitch is taken backward (on the outside of the garment) for every large stitch taken forward (on the inside of the garment). A variation of the 202 is the **pickstitch,** or **prickstitch.** Pickstitches are tiny, decorative backstitches used to flatten and define lapel edges on jackets. They are also used to insert zippers by hand in couture clothing. Stitch type *203* is a **decorative chainstitch.** It is identical to the 101 stitch except the chain appears on the face side of the fabric rather than the back side. Stitch type *204* is a

catchstitch. The catchstitch looks like a series of uneven Xs. It is a flexible, extensible stitch as well as a decorative one. Catchstitches are used to attach labels in high-price clothing and to perform other tacking jobs.

The simplest 200-class stitch is the *205,* the **running stitch.** The running stitch is created as the needle passes up and down through the fabric, always moving forward, creating a space between stitches. Long running stitches are used to *baste,* or temporarily join, garment pieces. **Saddle stitches** are decorative running stitches, 1/4 inch to 1/2 inch long, used to accent the edges of lapels, pockets, and yokes, particularly of men's western wear. The **slipstitch** is an "invisible" form of the running stitch. Slipstitches join a folded edge to another ply of fabric. The stitches are hidden in the fold. Slipstitches are used to attach linings at the armscyes of high-quality tailored jackets and to close men's neckties.

300-Class Stitches. Stitches in the **300 class** are **lockstitches.** Lockstitches are composed of a needle thread interlocked with a bobbin thread. The threads interlock between the plies of fabric (Figure 9–4).

Advantages. Because the stitches are interlocked between the fabric plies, lockstitches appear identical on both sides; they are reversible. The stitches are flat and smooth on both sides, making them comfortable and protecting the thread from abrasion. The 300-class stitches are very tight and secure. Each stitch interlocks with the stitch on either side of it, so 300-class stitches resist unraveling. They require less thread than other stitch types; they cause little bulk.

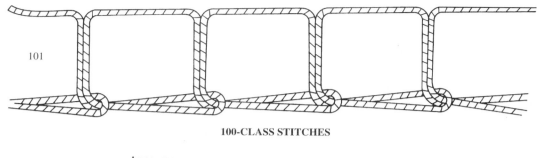

100-CLASS STITCHES

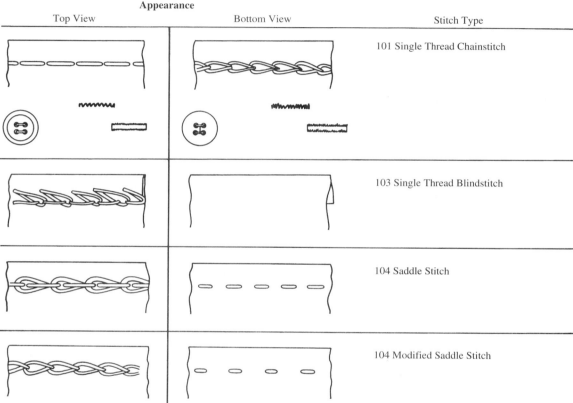

| | Appearance | |
Top View	Bottom View	Stitch Type
		101 Single Thread Chainstitch
		103 Single Thread Blindstitch
		104 Saddle Stitch
		104 Modified Saddle Stitch

Figure 9–2   100-class stitches. *(Courtesy of Union Special Corporation Technical Training Center.)*

Disadvantages.   Lockstitches are not very extensible however; they rupture easily if stretched or strained. They cause more seam pucker than other stitch types because most of the thread lies between the plies of the seam, crowding the area. The 300-class stitches require the operator to frequently interrupt the sewing process to replace the bobbin, making lockstitches more costly than chainstitches in terms of labor. Also, lockstitch machines stitch 3,000 to 5,000 **stitches per minute (SPM)**, slower than most other types of industrial sewing machines.

Variations.   The *301* stitch is the most popular stitch in the 300 class and the *most frequently used stitch in the production of apparel*. The 301, also called the **plain** stitch or **straight stitch,** is the same stitch made by conventional, home sewing machines. The 301 results in a single, straight, continuous row of stitches on both sides of the fabric (Figure 9–5). It is widely used to sew seams in woven-fabric garments and to construct garment details. The 301 is popular for several reasons. It offers a flat, uniform, reversible appearance plus comfort and durability. And it is the tightest of all stitch formations, minimizing seam grin.

The *304* is a **zigzag stitch.** The needle moves from side to side to produce a symmetrical zigzag pattern. The chief advantage of zigzag stitches is their elasticity; they stretch when the seam is stretched so that the stitches do not rupture. Spec technicians specify

200-CLASS STITCHES

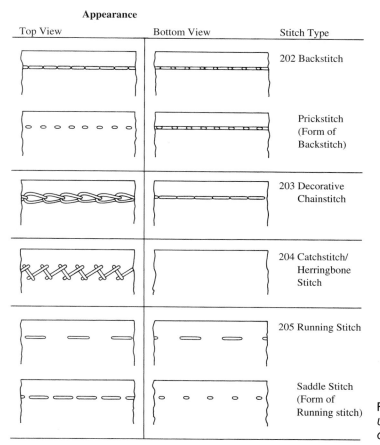

Figure 9–3   200-class stitches. *(Courtesy of Union Special Corporation Technical Training Center.)*

zigzag stitches to attach lace and elastic and to sew underwear, foundation garments, and swimwear. Closely spaced zigzag stitches create buttonholes and tacks. Lockstitched buttonholes and tacks are more costly but more durable than if chainstitched. The *308* and *315* are **multiple-stitch zigzag stitches.** The stitches resemble a 304 zigzag and are made in much the same way except that each diagonal portion of the zigzag is made up of more than one stitch.

Stitch types *306, 313,* and *314* are **lockstitch blindstitches.** Like blindstitches in the 100 class, they join plies of fabric with stitches that are imperceptible, or nearly so, from the outside of the garment. Lockstitch blindstitches are the most durable type of blindstitch. They are used to secure hems in high-quality garments.

400-Class Stitches. Stitches in the **400 class** are **multithread chainstitches** or **double-locked chainstitches** (Figure 9–6). The term "chainstitch" usually

refers to the 400-class multithread chainstitch rather than to chainstitches in the 100 class. Multithread chainstitches are formed by one or more needle threads passing through the fabric and interlooping with a looper thread. The 400-class stitches are widely used in the apparel industry.

Advantages. The 400-class chainstitches have some advantages over their closest competition, 300-class lockstitches. Because they do not require bobbins, chainstitches help achieve high production speeds. Chainstitch machines can achieve speeds up to 9,000 SPM. Chainstitches are more extensible than lockstitches because of their looped structure, which stretches somewhat when stressed. This prevents the chainstitch from rupturing as easily as the lockstitch. Chainstitches are less likely than lockstitches to cause seam pucker because most of the thread is outside the fabric plies. They do not require bobbins, making

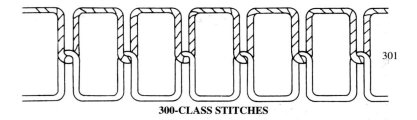

300-CLASS STITCHES

301

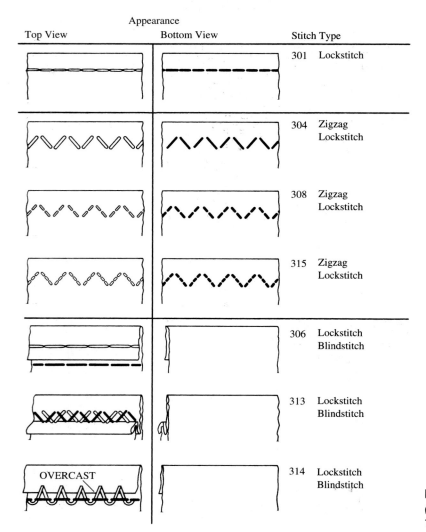

Appearance		
Top View	Bottom View	Stitch Type
		301 Lockstitch
		304 Zigzag Lockstitch
		308 Zigzag Lockstitch
		315 Zigzag Lockstitch
		306 Lockstitch Blindstitch
		313 Lockstitch Blindstitch
OVERCAST		314 Lockstitch Blindstitch

Figure 9–4 300-class stitches.
(Courtesy of Union Special Corporation Technical Training Center.)

them relatively less costly to produce than lockstitches. Chainstitches are quick and easy to unravel if the garment needs repair or alteration.

Disadvantages. Chainstitches have several disadvantages when compared to lockstitches. Chainstitches create a looser seam than do lockstitches and are more prone to seam grin. They also require more thread and thus create a bulkier seam than do lockstitches. Because chainstitches are formed outside the fabric layers rather than embedded between the

layers like lockstitches, they may be less comfortable unless a soft thread is used. Because the thread is built up on the fabric, it abrades away more easily than that of lockstitches, which hug the fabric surface. The raised loops of some chainstitches are easy to rupture on rings or jewelry, and the chainstitch is less durable than the lockstitch after rupturing. Pulling on a loose looper thread from a broken or unsecured stitch in the direction of the stitching can unravel many of the stitches. The double-locked structure of 400-class chainstitches makes them

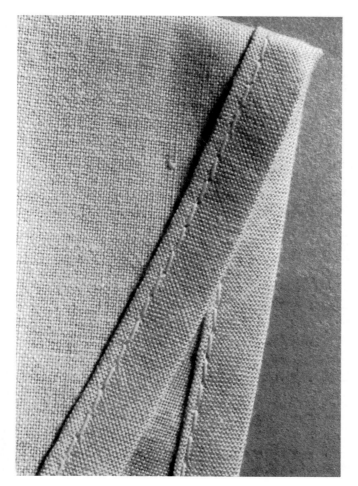

Figure 9–5   Face and back of 301 stitch.

more immune to unraveling than 100-class chainstitches but not nearly as resistant as lockstitches.

Variations.   The most common of the 400 stitches is the *401*, the **two-thread chainstitch.** It consists of a needle thread interlooping with a looper thread. Because of their strength and extensibility, 401 chainstitches are more suitable than 301 lockstitches for sewing elastics, knit-fabric garments, or seams in woven-fabric garments subject to stretch and stress, for example, crotch seams, armscye/ seams, and elastic applications. The 401 looks like a 301 lockstitch on the face of the fabric, but you can distinguish it by the double loops visible on the back (Figure 9–7). One must examine closely to differentiate the double loops of the desirable two-thread chainstitch from the single loops of the undesirable 101 single-thread chainstitch. 401 stitches are significantly stronger and more durable than 101 stitches.

The *402* is a **cording stitch.** It secures creases, such as those on the fronts of pant legs or the backs of gloves. Two rows of straight stitches appear on the face side with a looper thread on the back. The *404* and *405* are **bobbinless zigzag stitches.** They resemble a plain, lockstitch zigzag on the face side, but interloopings are visible on the back side. They serve the same purposes as lockstitch zigzags but are more elastic.

The *406* and *407* are **bottom cover stitches** or **bottom-covering chainstitches.** They feature two or three parallel rows of straight stitches visible on the face side. The many thread interloopings on the back side of these bottom cover stitches flatten the area and conceal raw edges by covering them with thread (Figure 9–8). Bottom cover stitches are used to make belt loops, to attach elastics and bindings to underwear, to hem T-shirts, and to flatten seam allowances of seams after they are sewn. For example, T-shirt and sweatshirt neckline seams (sometimes only the back half) are improved with the addition of a bottom cover stitch. Although requiring two passes through the machine, one to sew the seam and one to flatten it with the bottom cover stitch, the finished seam is comfortable and attractive.

500-Class Stitches.   The term **overedge** is probably the best descriptive term for the **500-class stitches** (Figure 9–9); these are formed, as the description implies, over the edge of the fabric, encasing the edge in thread interloopings. Overedge stitches, an advanced form of chainstitch, sew a seam and simultaneously finish its raw edges to prevent raveling. **Overlock, serge, overseam, overcast,** and **merrow** also refer to 500-class stitches. Serging and merrowing generally refer to sewing on the edge of a single ply of material rather than to sewing a seam. Merrow is actually a brand of machines that make this stitch type.

Overedge stitches are made on small, unconventional sewing machines called *overedgers* or *sergers.* Sergers stitch *only* at the edge of a fabric, unlike conventional sewing machines used to make other classes of stitches, which can sew anywhere. Sergers often have a knife attachment that evenly trims the edge of the fabric just before the stitches are made, finishing the raw edge and preventing it from raveling. The stitches are formed over the trimmed edge by looper and/or spreader mechanisms that carry threads to the fabric edge where they interloop. Sergers are well suited to stitching and finishing narrow seams at garment edges. They cannot stitch within the body of a garment. They cannot stitch wide seams; their width is limited to about 3/8 inch. They can stitch straight or gently curved seams but have difficulty stitching around intricate curves or sharp angles.

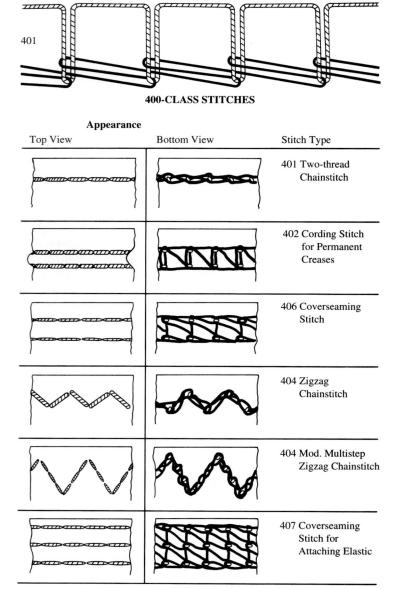

Figure 9–6 400-class stitches. *(Courtesy of Union Special Corporation Technical Training Center.)*

Advantages.   Overedge stitches are the most extensible of all the stitch classes because of their many interloopings. The ability to stretch without breaking has made them the workhorse of the knitwear industry. They are also popular in garments made of woven fabrics. Because they cover the raw edge of the material, overedge stitches neaten and prevent fabric edges from raveling better than any other stitch class. Overedge stitches are sometimes used to finish the raw edges of individual garment pieces before the garment is assembled. Overedge stitches cause little seam pucker because most of the thread bulk is outside the seamline. Seams sewn with overedge stitches require narrow seam allowances, conserving fabric. Sometimes the stitches compress the plies of thick fabric to lessen bulk. Overedge stitches require a lot of thread, but they reduce labor when used instead of separate seaming and seam finishing operations because they perform both steps simultaneously. And they sew fast—up to 9,000 SPM.

Disadvantages.   Because overedge stitches have a fairly loose stitch formation, they are prone to seam grin. Most overedged seams cannot be pressed open to reduce bulk because the plies are sewn together at the edges. This is unacceptable for some garments and fabrics. Overedge stitches require more thread than most other stitch types. The presence of all that thread can make overedge stitches uncomfortable, but if the interloopings are flat and a soft thread is used, the

Figure 9–7   Face and back of 401 stitch.

Figure 9–8   Face and back of bottom cover stitch. Also note illegible printed label.

stitches are adequately comfortable. Although overedge stitches rarely rupture as a result of stress, they do rupture if one of their interloopings catches on a sharp object. Once broken, the effort required to unravel an overedge stitch depends on the stitch; some forms of the stitch unravel easily while others are resistant. Overedge stitches tend to unravel more easily than lockstitches but not as readily as 100- or 400-class chainstitches.

Variations.   The *504* is the most popular stitch type in the 500 class. It features a needle thread and two looper threads. It simultaneously sews the seam and neatens the edge by trimming and finishing it, making it a very useful stitch (Figure 9–10). Its extensibility makes it ideal for sewing knitwear, in which narrow seams are acceptable. The 504 has a **purled edge,** a series of raised loops formed by the interloopings of the looper threads at the edge. The purled edge covers the raw edge of the fabric, preventing it from raveling. The tight needle thread of

the 504 creates a tighter seam than most other overedge stitches. The other even-numbered stitches, *502, 512, 514,* and *516,* also have fairly tight stitch formations for seaming. But they are not particularly strong or durable choices for seaming woven fabrics.

The *501, 503, 505,* and *521* stitches, because of their loose stitch formations, hinge open flat like a notebook; thus, they are sometimes called **break-open stitches.** None are well-suited for sewing structural garment seams; they are prone to seam grin. The 501, made with a single thread, does not make a strong, tight seam, but its break-open characteristics make it useful for joining pelts in fur coats and for joining lengths of fabric together for dyeing. The 503 stitch, made with two threads, is commonly used to hem T-shirts and other knit garments. The resulting hinged-open hem closely resembles a blindstitched hem, and the purled edge helps prevent raveling of the fabric. The 503 is also used to overedge seams. The 505, made with three threads, is similar to the 503; it is sometimes called the **square edge** or **box edge stitch.** Stitch type 521 is a three-thread overedge stitch for seaming hosiery. The arrangement of the threads in the stitch makes it strong and extremely elastic.

The 503, 504, and 505 are the most frequent choices for overedging raw edges. Some manufacturers

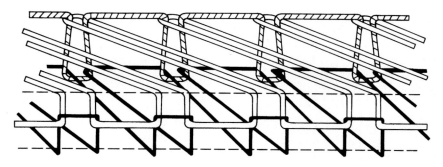

Appearance			
Top View	Bottom View	Stitch Type	Application
1 Thread	Ndl. Thd.	501	Break-open Seaming (easily unraveled) Note: No purl
2 Threads	Ndl. Thd.	502	Seaming Bags, etc. Note: No purl
2 Threads	Ndl. Thd.	503	Serging Blindhemming Break-open Seaming Note: Purl on edge
3 Threads	Ndl. Thd.	504	Seaming Knit Goods, etc. Serging Note: Purl on edge
3 Threads	Ndl. Thd.	505	Serging Break-open Seaming Note: Double purl
4 Threads	Ndl. Thd.	512	Seaming Switch Mock Saftey (simulated saftey stitch) Note: Purl on edge
4 Threads	Ndl. Thd.	514	Seaming Switch (produces strong seams on wovens or knits) Note: same as 512 but with long upper looper
4 Threads		515 (401 & 503)	Safety Stitch Seaming
5 Threads		516 (401 & 504)	Safety Stitch Seaming
6 Threads		519 (401 & 602)	Safety Stitch Seaming
3 Threads	Ndl. Thd.	521	Hosiery Stitch Note: Break-open stitch

Figure 9–9 500-class stitches. *(Courtesy of Union Special Corporation Technical Training Center.)*

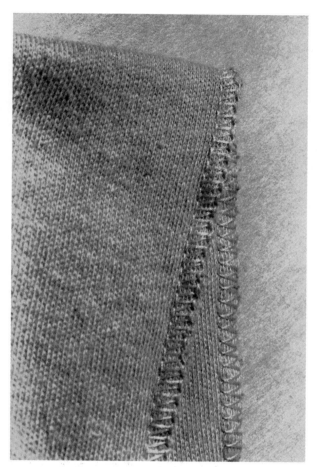

Figure 9–10   Face and back of 504 stitch.

overedge individual garment pieces before the garment is assembled. This process may be automated, with the machine serging one edge of a single garment part, pivoting at the corner, serging the next edge, and so on until all the edges are overedged.

Safety Stitches.   Perhaps the best overedge stitches for general seaming purposes are those classified as **safety stitches.** Safety stitches combine a row of overedge stitches with a row of straight lockstitches or chainstitches. The two independent rows of stitches simultaneously neaten and finish the raw edges of the seam. Safety stitches make a more durable seam than a single row of stitches. Two rows of stitches must rupture before the seam ruptures, providing a "safety" factor, thus the name. Safety stitches also create wider seam allowances than ordinary overedging, contributing to seam strength.

Safety stitches can be identified by the two independent rows of stitches on the face *and* back of the fabric. The row of straight stitches is parallel to the overedge stitches. A safety stitch requires more thread than stitch types consisting of a single row of stitches.

Safety stitches are used in the manufacture of shirts, blouses, jackets, pants, jeans, and skirts from both knit and woven fabrics of all weights. They are the most common stitch type used for sewing structural seams in unlined garments.

The three most common safety stitches are the *515, 516,* and *519.* They combine a row of overedge stitches with a row of 401 multithread chainstitches (Figure 9–11). These safety stitches simultaneously sew the seam twice, trimming and finishing the raw edge in just one pass through the machine. Safety stitches have the same advantages and disadvantages as the stitch types used to make them.

The *517* and *518* safety stitches combine a row of stitches with a row of 301 lockstitches (Figure 9–11). These safety stitches are made by running the fabric through two different machines; a conventional sewing machine produces the lockstitch, and a serger produces the overedging. The two runs require more labor and make these safety stitches more expensive to produce than those that are chainstitched. But safety stitches featuring the lockstitch have the advantages of resistance to unraveling, low bulk, minimal seam grin, and lower thread requirements. The disadvantages, besides higher labor cost, are low extensibility and a tendency to pucker.

Mock Safety Stitch.   Stitch type *512* is the **mock safety stitch** or **simulated safety stitch.** It resembles the safety stitches. Distinguish between mock safety stitches and true safety stitches by looking at the back of the stitch. On the face side they resemble true safety stitches, with what appears as two independent rows of stitching, but on the back side the rows of stitches interloop (Figure 9–11c). Mock safety stitches are strong and extensible but once ruptured, they unravel more easily than true safety stitches. Only one row of stitches prevents a total seam rupture, as opposed to two in a true safety stitch. Mock safety stitches have a greater tendency to grin than true safety stitches. Mock safety stitches are less costly than true safety stitches because they can be produced at higher speeds. The *514* is similar in function to the *512,* but does not resemble the safety stitches. The *514* is the main stitch used to sew spandex fabrics.

600-Class Stitches.   Stitches in the **600 class** are **cover stitches,** also sometimes called *flat seam stitches, interlock stitches,* or *flatlock stitches* (Figure 9–12). Cover stitches sew flat seams in which the fabric plies abut or overlap slightly and are interlocked by the stitches. Occasionally, they are used to flatten the seam allowances of plain seams. Cover stitches, an advanced form of chainstitch, are characterized by their many ornamental interloopings. These interloopings appear on both the face and back side of the flat seam.

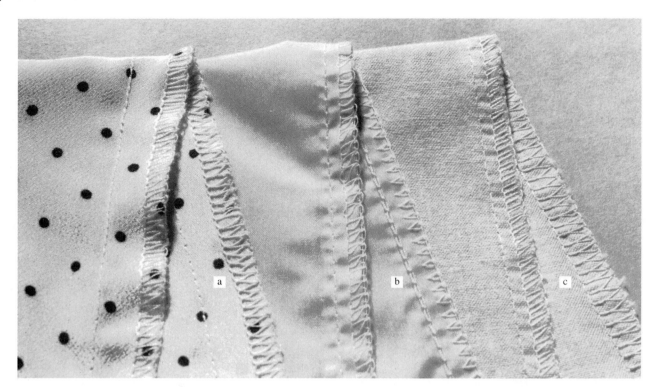

Figure 9–11   Face and back of safety stitches made with (a) lockstitch, (b) chainstitch, and (c) mock safety stitch.

Advantages. The 600-class stitches join two fabric plies and cover the face *and* back of the seam with stitches in a single run through the machine. Thus, 600-class stitches are sometimes called **top-and-bottom-covering chainstitches.** The top-and-bottom-covering capability of 600-class stitches is accomplished with the addition of *cover threads* interlooping with the needle and looper threads. The many interloopings of cover stitches yield strong and extremely extensible seams. The loops of 600-class stitches do not rupture when stretched. If torn on a sharp object, 600-class stitches do not unravel easily because of the many interloopings, although some unravel more readily than others. The 600-class stitches are not apt to pucker because most of the thread is not between fabric plies or on the seamline. The many interloopings of the stitch finish the raw edges of the fabric.

Cover stitches require little or no seam allowances which conserves fabric. They are also more economical in terms of labor than the combination of a plain seam and a bottom-covering chainstitch, which requires two runs to produce a flat, comfortable seam. Machines making cover stitches run at high speeds— 7,000 to 8,000 SPM.

Disadvantages. Cover stitches use a lot of thread. The many interloopings of 600-class stitches, although fairly flat, can make seams uncomfortable unless a soft underthread is used. Manufacturers primarily use cover stitches on fabrics resistant to fraying and raveling, for example, knits. Cover stitches are unsuitable for joining abutted edges of woven fabrics but are used to sew one ply on top of another.

Variations. The most common stitch in the 600 class is the *605* (Figure 9–13). It yields flat, strong, elastic seams for knit underwear, infantswear, swimwear, and active sportswear. The *602*, similar to the 605, is also widely used. The most complex cover stitch is the *607*, which requires six threads: four needle threads, a looper thread, and a cover thread. The 607 stitch provides the best stretch, security, and smoothness of the 600-class stitches but is more costly than those requiring less thread.

Stitch Length

Stitch length is an important determinant of the aesthetics and function of stitches. Stitch length is measured in terms of the number of **stitches per inch (SPI).** A standard stitch length for mediumweight fabric is approximately 12–14 SPI; heavyweight and densely woven fabric requires long stitches, usually 6–10 SPI; lightweight and loosely woven fabric requires short stitches, usually 15-18 SPI or higher.

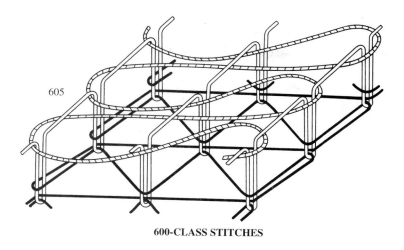

605

600-CLASS STITCHES

Appearance

Top View	Bottom View	Stitch Type
		602 Coverstitch
		605 Coverstitch
		607 Flat Seaming Stitch

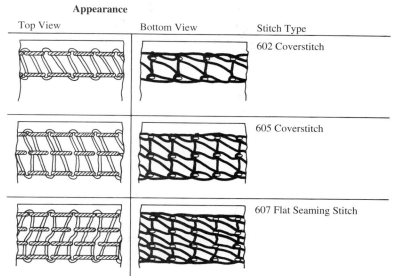

Figure 9–12   600-class stitches.
(Courtesy of Union Special Corporation Technical Training Center.)

Appropriate stitch length depends upon the type of fabric and its weight and density and also upon the stitch type and purpose. Different seams within the same garment may have different but appropriate stitch lengths. For example, structural seams on a pair of jeans might be spec'ed at 8 SPI. The serged edge on the seams might be spec'ed at 14 SPI. And the buttonhole may be spec'ed at 22 SPI. In evaluating apparel, it is useful to be able to roughly estimate SPI at a glance (Figure 9–14). In many cases, stitch length is the best single criterion to use in quickly evaluating the overall construction quality of a garment.

Stitches too long or too short for the fabric may lead to puckering. (A puckered seam is shown in Chapter 10, Figure 10–2.) Pucker occurs when short stitches are used in densely woven or knit fabrics because the yarns of such fabrics are closely packed together. The addition of the thread from many short stitches to a densely packed yarn structure crowds the yarns of the fabric and causes the fabric to pucker. If extremely long stitches are used on lightweight or loosely woven fabrics, puckering also occurs. When the thread relaxes to its original length after being stretched during sewing, it tends to pull up or pucker the surrounding material. The puckering intensifies if there are fewer stitches and therefore less thread length to relax. The problem shows up most in lightweight and unstable fabrics because they succumb readily to the pulling.

Leather, as well as vinyl and other film fabrics, requires long stitches, 6–8 SPI. Short stitches make too many perforations in these materials and weaken the fabric. Therefore, stitches used to sew such fabrics are exceptions to the general rule that short stitches withstand more stress than long stitches.

The purpose of stitches helps determine their ideal length. For most seams, the previously discussed

Figure 9–13   Face and back of 605 stitch.

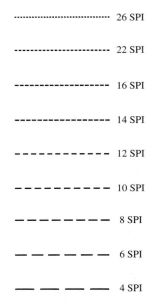

Figure 9–14   Stitches per inch.

guidelines apply. To reinforce points of particular strain, small **reinforcement stitches** are used to help bear the stress. Reinforcement stitches, generally 18–20 SPI, reinforce areas that have narrow seam allowances and would otherwise rupture or ravel.

Topstitching is the use of stitches for decorative purposes (see Chapter 11). Slightly longer stitches than those used to construct the garment are appropriate for topstitching. Long stitches are more visible and therefore more attractive than short stitches for decorative topstitching. Because topstitching does not hold the structure of the garment together, long stitches do not detract from the durability of the garment.

Although topstitching is most commonly used for decorative purposes, it can also serve as reinforcement or to hold a seam allowance in a certain direction. An example of using topstitching for nondecorative purposes is the side seam in some brands of blue jeans. Some jeans have an approximate 6–8-inch length of the side seam topstitched from the waistband to the hips. The purpose is to hold the thick bulky seam flat in an area of stress, thus making the jeans more comfortable to wear.

Basting holds two or more layers of fabric in place temporarily. Because durability is not wanted, basting stitches are very long so they can be removed quickly. They hold fabric plies in position until these are permanently stitched, or hold welt pockets and skirt pleats in place until the garment is sold.

Short stitches generally contribute to increased stitch strength and durability. The advantages of short stitches include:

1. They withstand stress better than long stitches.
2. If they fail, short stitches make a smaller rupture in the row of stitches than when longer stitches break.
3. They are less apt to cause seam grin than long stitches because they make a tighter seam.
4. They deposit more thread in the seamline than long stitches, allowing the seam to be more extensible.

The general rule associating short stitches and durability is true only to a point; extremely short stitches perforate the fabric and its yarns so frequently that they may damage the fabric and actually weaken the seam.

In general, short stitches contribute to manufacturing costs. Because stitch length relates directly to the amount of labor required to sew a garment, it offers a good clue to the overall cost of manufacturing the garment. The longer the stitch, the farther a sewing machine can sew in the same amount of time. For example, if a sewing machine stitches 3,000 stitches per minute, at 10 SPI it sews 300 inches in one minute. But at 15 SPI, that same machine sews only 200 inches in one minute. Shortening the stitch length directly increases the amount of time required to sew a row of stitches and requires slightly more thread as well. Therefore, lengthening stitches is an easy way for manufacturers to cut costs. Stitch length has little effect on cost if the garment is manufactured in a very low-wage country. In such a case, short stitches can be put into a garment at little additional cost.

The quality assurance personnel in most manufacturing plants continually monitor stitch length. Most industrial sewing machines are preset with a device that limits the variation in stitch length. This prevents the operators from varying the length of the stitch more than a few stitches per inch. The piece rate system, however, tends to contradict the message to sew at a specified stitch length. Some operators, trying to maximize their earnings by sewing a large daily volume, learn how to override these devices and sew their products with a longer-than-specified stitch length.

Stitch Tension

Stitch *tension* refers to how loosely or how tautly the threads are held by the sewing machine as it sews. If the machine's tension is balanced, each stitch is formed correctly. However, if the machine holds the thread or threads too loosely or too tautly, the conformation of the stitches is altered, adversely affecting stitch appearance and lowering stitch strength. For example, tight tension stretches the thread more than usual as it is sewn. The thread then draws up or puckers the fabric when it eventually relaxes to its original length. Loose tension causes a loose stitch formation. To achieve consistently high-quality stitches, a trained mechanic varies the tension and other sewing machine adjustments to suit the fabric.

Lockstitch Tension. Lockstitches are affected by unbalanced tension more than other stitch types. With unbalanced tension, lockstitches especially tend to pucker the fabric. Lockstitches with balanced tension contain a one-to-one ratio of needle thread to bobbin thread, where these interlock in the middle of the fabric. When tension is unbalanced, the tension on either the needle thread or bobbin thread is tighter than the other, upsetting the one-to-one ratio. As a result, the threads do not interlock exactly in the middle of the fabric and are not equal in length to one another. The shorter thread, with the tighter tension, draws up the stitches and causes them to pucker the fabric.

Unbalanced tension can be visually identified. If the needle thread is tighter than the bobbin thread, the needle thread floats on the surface of the fabric and interlocks with the bobbin thread on top of the fabric instead of between the plies. Conversely, if the bobbin thread is tighter than the needle thread, the bobbin thread floats on the surface of the fabric and

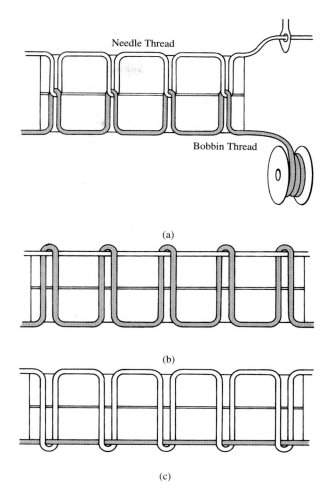

Figure 9–15   Lockstitch tension: (a) balanced, (b) needle thread too tight/bobbin thread too loose, and (c) needle thread too loose/bobbin thread too tight. *(Courtesy of Union Special Corporation Technical Training Center.)*

interlocks with the needle thread underneath the fabric instead of between the plies (Figure 9–15). Lockstitches with balanced tension appear identical on both sides of the fabric.

Balanced tension is crucial to the durability of lockstitches. Lockstitches with unbalanced tension rupture easily under stress. Evaluate lockstitch tension by pulling very firmly on each end of the row of stitches. If the tension is properly balanced, there is an equal amount of needle thread and bobbin thread in a row of stitches. Therefore, they extend to the same point and do not rupture easily. If the tension is unbalanced, there is more (or less) needle thread than bobbin thread. The longer of the two threads extends under stress, but the shorter thread breaks (Figure 9–16).

Chainstitch Tension. Perfectly balanced tension is not as important to the durability of chainstitches

Figure 9–16   Stitches with unbalanced tension ruptured under stress.

as it is for lockstitches, but it still is important. Chainstitches have more inherent extensibility in their stitch structure than do lockstitches. Therefore, the chainstitches do not rely on an equal ratio of needle thread to underthread for the ability to "give." Balanced tension is even less important to the durability of overedge and cover stitches because of their great extensibility. However, the integrity and appearance of any stitch type is adversely affected if tension problems are severe and especially so if the garments are to be wet processed. The agitation and abrasion created by garment dyeing and wet processing machines will greatly stress any seam sewn with unbalanced tension. (Figure 9–17).

Skipped Stitches

Skipped stitches occur when a machine fails to sew an uninterrupted row of two or more stitches; the stitches fail to interlock or interloop. Skipped stitches show up as a long float of thread instead of individual stitches. The result is unattractive and creates a weak spot in the seam. Skipped stitches result from use of the wrong needle or a defective needle; the incorrect thread for the fabric; improper sewing speed, feeding, or operator handling; or maladjusted tension and other machine problems. A new device that can be attached to some sewing machines is a skipped stitch detector so the defective row of stitches can be repaired before the garment is passed to the next operator.

Stitch Width

Zigzag, overedge, and cover stitches have width as well as length. Most stitch widths or bites are 1/8 to 3/16 inch; more than 1/4 inch is unusual. Wide overedge stitches and cover stitches generally represent high quality when used to sew seams because wide stitches yield wide and thus strong seams.

Wide zigzags and overedge stitches are not suitable for lightweight fabrics. Wide bites distort lightweight fabrics because the fabric does not have the body to support wide stitches.

Needles

Sewing machine needles of the correct size, type and condition yield high-quality stitches. Heavy fabrics and loose weaves call for large, coarse needles. Light fabrics and tight weaves require small, fine needles. Needles that are bent, blunt, or *burred* (damaged) and needles of the wrong size or type for the fabric lead to skipped stitches, needle cutting, needle heating, and needle chewing.

Needle Cutting.   **Needle cutting** results when the needle cuts, or severs, the yarns of the fabric rather than slipping between the yarns. The needle damages the fabric, leaving unsightly holes, pulls, or snags. Needle cutting is a big problem in sewing knit fabrics. It is caused by a needle that is too large for the fabric, is blunt or burred, or has the wrong type of tip. Most woven fabrics are sewn with round point, *sharp tip* needles. *Ball tip* needles with slightly rounded tips should be used for sewing knits and very delicate wovens, which are prone to needle cutting. The rounded tips slide more readily between yarns of the fabric rather than severing them. Needles with flat-shaped tips are used on leathers and leather-like fabrics to minimize needle cutting, which weakens the fabric.

Needle Heating.   **Needle heating** occurs when sewing friction heats the needle, which *fuses* or melts the finishes or fibers of the thread or fabric. Needle heating results in a loss of thread strength and therefore stitch strength. Also, buildup of the melted fibers on the needle causes it to skip stitches. Needle heating is a problem with synthetic threads and fibers that are *thermoplastic*, or heat sensitive. Large-diameter needles are prone to needle heating. Using the smallest needle possible without its breaking or cutting the thread reduces needle heating. A lubricant or special finish applied to the needle, thread, or fabric

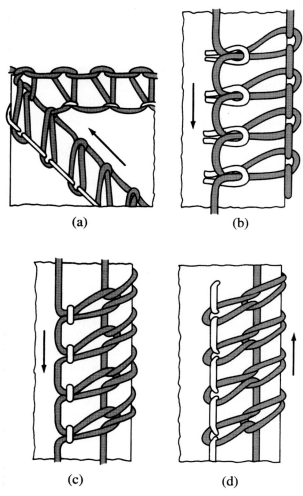

(a)   **(b)**

(c)   **(d)**

Figure 9–17 Overedge tension: (a) balanced, (b) lower looper thread too tight/needle thread too loose, (c) lower looper thread too tight/upper looper thread too loose, and (d) upper looper thread too tight/lower looper thread too loose. *(Courtesy of Union Special Corporation Technical Training Center.)*

also reduces friction and needle heating. Sometimes manufacturers blow compressed air on the needle to keep it cool. However, fast sewing speeds are the main cause of needle heating, so in theory the simplest solution to the problem is for the operator to slow down. For example, lowering the sewing speed by 2,000 SPM drops the needle temperature 160° F (Glock and Kunz, 1995). This solution is noted as theoretical only, as slowing down operator speed causes reduced wages for the operator and loss of production for the company. Neither situation is desirable, so a careful balance of all factors must be considered when taking any corrective action.

Needle Chewing. Needle chewing results in jagged, enlarged needle holes in the fabric. These are caused most frequently when an operator rips out inaccurate sewing and resews the same seam. It also is caused when the fabric does not move forward properly and the needle repeatedly enters the same area. The machine appears to "eat" the fabric as the operator and/or machine tries to force the fabric forward. Needle chews often do not show until a garment has been wet processed or laundered at home. They detract from the attractiveness and durability of the garment.

Sewing Accuracy

The accuracy of the sewing operator plays an important role in the neatness, straightness, consistency, and uniformity of stitches. Sewing machines commonly sew at 3,000 to 9,000 stitches per minute, challenging operators to do accurate work. Considering that they are usually paid by the piece, not by the hour, operators must develop great skill to achieve both accuracy and the speed required. A skilled operator sews stitches that enhance the appearance of the garment and the durability, comfort, and fit of seams and stitchings. Crooked stitches, stitches that sew past the intended stopping point, sloppily stitched corners and curves, stitches that are an uneven distance from the edge, and misplaced reinforcement tacks are examples of substandard sewing. A close examination of stitches makes sewing inaccuracies readily apparent, even to the untrained eye.

Back Tacking and Latch Tacking

Back tacking is restitching at the beginning and end of the row of stitches. Back tacking secures the stitches and prevents unraveling; it is a sign of high quality. Industrial sewing machines can be fitted with devices that automatically back tack at the beginning and end of each seam. Because it takes extra time, back tacking is used primarily on seams that will not be crossed by another seam. It greatly contributes to the durability of seams, especially those made with stitch types prone to unraveling. Machines that make 500- and 600-class stitch types are not capable of back tacking. To secure these stitches, **latch tacking** draws the excess thread chain at the beginning of each row of stitches into the stitches to secure them. For rows of stitches that are not latch tacked, a short chain of thread (more than 1/2 inch but less than 1 inch long) left at each end prevents the unraveling of the stitches. (This chain is seen in Chapter 12, Figure 12–7.)

Long Threads

Consumer perception of garment quality is negatively affected by the presence of excessively long, dangling threads. Dangling threads not only detract from the garment's appearance but, if pulled, may un-ravel the stitches. They also interfere with the func-tioning of zippers and other closures. However, clip-ping threads too short at the beginning or end of an unsecured row of stitches may lead to the unraveling of the stitches. Some sewing machines have thread trimmers that clip threads automatically and remove them via suction. Operators are responsible for long thread removal, and the trim and inspect inspectors at the end of the line are responsible for removing any that the operators miss.

SUMMARY

Stitches are the thread arrangements in fabrics that make stitchings and seams. Most stitches are formed by either a lockstitch machine, which interlocks threads and requires both a needle thread and a bobbin thread, or a chainstitch machine, which inter-loops the thread or threads. U.S. Fed. Std. No. 751a: Stitches, Seams, and Stitchings identifies six classes of stitches. The classes include the 100-class simple chainstitches, 200-class handstitches and their ma-chine simulations, 300-class lockstitches, 400-class multithread chainstitches, 500-class overedge stitches, and 600-class cover stitches. Simple chain-stitches are not durable. Handstitches are usually simulated by machine except in high-price apparel. Lockstitches are the main stitches used for woven-fabric garment construction. They are abrasion resis-tant, reversible, and nonbulky. Multithread chain-stitches are extensible, pucker resistant, and economical. They include bottom cover stitches. Overedge stitches are made only at edges. They are the main stitches used on knitwear because they are very extensible. Safety stitches feature two rows of parallel stitches for security, consisting of a row of overedge stitches and a row of either chainstitches or lockstitches. Mock safety stitches, when viewed from the top, visually imitate true safety stitches. Cover stitches make flat seams. They cover both the top and bottom of the seam with the thread.

In general, short stitches are more durable but cost more than long stitches. However, stitch length should be appropriate to the type, weight, and den-sity of the fabric, and the purpose of the stitches. Stitch length is measured in stitches per inch (SPI). Balanced stitch tension, especially for lockstitches, avoids ruptured and puckered stitches. Needle type, size, and condition should be compatible with the fabric of the garment. Operator accuracy is important in producing stitches that are neat and attractive. Back tacking or latch tacking and removal of exces-sively long threads are signs of quality.

Stitch Quality Checklist

If you can answer yes to each of these questions re-garding the garment you are evaluating, it contains high-quality stitches.

✓ Is the stitch type appropriate for the fabric, the de-sign, and the end use of the garment and its loca-tion and purpose?
✓ Are the stitches reversible if they will be seen from both sides?
✓ Do the stitches avoid puckering the fabric?
✓ Do the stitches create seams that resist grinning?
✓ Are the stitches adequately extensible?
✓ Do the stitches resist abrasion?
✓ Do the stitches resist unraveling?
✓ Are the stitches comfortable when the garment is worn?
✓ Are the stitches flat and nonbulky?
✓ Is the stitch length appropriate for the fabric type, weight, and density, and for the purpose of the stitches?
✓ Is stitch tension balanced, especially for lockstitches?
✓ Was the appropriate size of needle used to sew the garment, to avoid needle chews, needle heating, and needle cutting?
✓ Are the stitches neat, accurately placed, continuous lines?
✓ Are rows of stitches back tacked or latch tacked?
✓ Are excessively long threads trimmed and removed?

New Terms

If you can define each of these terms and differentiate between related terms, you have gained a good working vocabulary for discussing the topics in this chapter. The terms are listed in the order in which they appear in the chapter.

stitch
sewed out
lockstitch
chainstitch
U.S. Fed. Std. No. 751a: Stitches, Seams, and Stitchings
General Services Administration (GSA)
100-class single-thread chainstitches
basting
blindstitch
200-class hand stitches/machine-made versions
backstitch
pickstitch/prickstitch
decorative chainstitch
catchstitch

running stitch
saddle stitch
slipstitch
300-class lockstitches
stitches per minute (SPM)
plain/straight stitch
zigzag stitch
multiple-stitch zigzag stitch
lockstitch blindstitch
400-class multithread/double-locked chainstitches
two-thread chainstitch
cording stitch
bobbinless zigzag stitch
bottom cover/bottom-covering stitch
500-class overedge stitches
overlock/serge/overseam/overcast/merrow
purled edge
break-open stitch
square edge/box edge stitch
safety stitch
mock/simulated safety stitch
600-class cover stitches/top-and-bottom-covering
   chainstitches
stitches per inch (SPI)
reinforcement stitches
balanced tension
needle cutting
needle heating
needle chewing
back tacking
latch tacking

Review Questions

1. What are the main differences between lock-stitches and chainstitches?
2. How is the U.S. Fed. Std. No. 751a: Stitches, Seams, and Stitchings useful to apparel manufacturers?
3. List the six main stitch classes in U.S. Fed. Std. No. 751a and summarize the performance advantages and disadvantages of each.
4. What stitch type is the most frequently used in the apparel industry? What stitch class is the most frequently used to produce knitwear?
5. How is a safety stitch different from a mock safety stitch?
6. What is the blindstitch and where is it commonly used?
7. What are the quality advantages of short stitch lengths? When are long stitches appropriate?

8. For which stitch type is balanced tension most critical? Why?
9. What are the problems that arise from using damaged needles or needles that are too large for the fabric?
10. Define back tacking and latch tacking.

Activities

1. Find garments containing an example of each of the major stitch classes.
2. Compare the stitch length of major seams of low-price and high-price garments in the following classifications:
   a. jeans
   b. men's dress shirts
   c. women's blouses
   What differences, if any, did you find and why?
3. Unravel the stitches in a seam or hem sewn with lockstitches and another sewn with chainstitches. Which one unraveled more easily and why? Compare the amount of thread used.
4. Visit an apparel manufacturer. Find out
   a. what types of machines they have
   b. how they decide what stitch type to use for each operation.
5. Stretch a seam sewn with a lockstitch/balanced tension and another sewn with a lockstitch/unbalanced tension. Which one is stronger?
6. Sew a row of long stitches and a row (the same length) of short stitches. Which stitch length is most time-efficient for sewing the same distance?
7. Examine ready-to-wear in various price lines. How are lines of stitches secured at their beginnings and ends?
8. Study the Union Special Corporation Technical Training Center's *Garment Construction Guide* (see examples in Figures 9–1, 11–1, 11–2, 11–16, and 12–1). Tell how many stitch types are used in constructing each of the following:
   a. dress shirt
   b. children's underwear
   c. bib overalls
   d. wool skirt
   e. trench coat
9. Examine garments in various price lines. Is price related to neatness of the stitches? Why or why not?
10. Choose a garment from your wardrobe and write stitch specifications to duplicate it.

Seams and Edge Treatments: Providing Structure

Chapter Objectives

1. Differentiate between seam types, and evaluate the advantages and disadvantages of each type.
2. Recognize hems and other edge treatments of various types and understand the appropriate applications of each.

Seams are used to assemble fabric panels, to create the structure and details of a garment. Most garment edges require some form of treatment to make them attractive and durable. An examination of the seaming and edge treatments of garments is important in evaluating the quality of ready-to-wear because the performance of the seams and edge treatments is critical to the aesthetic and functional performance of the garment. Appropriateness of seam type and seam allowance width are especially important to garment quality.

(For more information, see Related Resources: Stitches and Seams.)

SEAM PERFORMANCE

Seams are the joints resulting when two or more fabric pieces are sewn together. The **seam line** is the stitched line of a seam; it is usually parallel to and always a specified distance from the raw edge of the fabric. The **seam allowance** or **seam margin** is the

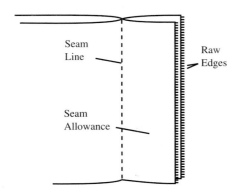

Figure 10–1   Parts of a seam.

narrow width of fabric between the seam line and the cut edge of the fabric (Figure 10–1).

Seam Pucker

The appearance of the seams affects overall attractiveness of a garment. Straight, neat, smooth, even seams that are not twisted, ropey, or rippled contribute to aesthetics. Perhaps the main factor detracting from seam appearance is puckering. **Seam pucker** is the lack of seam smoothness, or buckling of the fabric along a row of stitches (see Figure 10–2a; also Figure 10–13b later in this chapter). Seam puckering can occur in all price lines; it seriously mars the otherwise pleasing appearance of a garment. In severe cases, puckered seams and stitchings also reduce durability.

Most seam puckering is categorized as either shrinkage pucker, feed pucker, structural jamming pucker, or tension pucker. Many of the causes of puckering are related to characteristics of the fabric and the stitches (see Chapter 7 and Chapter 9). For example, densely woven fabrics and lockstitch seams are prone to puckering.

Differential shrinkage, or different rates of shrinkage between the fabric and another component such as thread or a decorative fabric, can result in puckering. *Differential feeding,* or feeding the layers of fabric through the sewing machine unevenly, can result in puckering. Differential feeding and the resulting material distortion may be due to uneven feeding by the sewing machine or mishandling by the sewing machine operator. Unbalanced thread tension or a stitch length that is inappropriate for the fabric weight also leads to puckering. It may be caused as well by the sewing together of fabric plies cut on different grains, sewing speeds that are too fast, and sewing machine pressure maladjustment. *Structural jamming* occurs when needles and/or threads that are too large crowd the yarns of the fabric and cause puckering. In quality-conscious apparel manufacturing companies, industrial sewing machines are continuously being

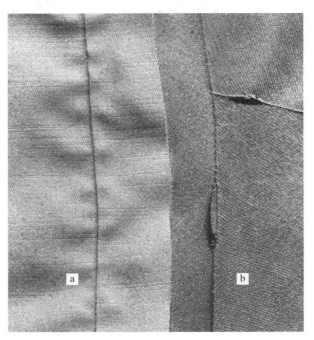

Figure 10–2   Seam defects: (a) seam pucker, and (b) broken seam.

adjusted by the plant mechanics. This is necessary as the high speeds, long hours of use, and use by different people on different shifts all contribute to parts slipping out of adjustment. Most plants have several mechanics on permanent staff just for this purpose.

Joining multiple plies of fabric compounds puckering problems. For this reason, some seam types are more prone to pucker than others. In general, the least amount of pucker occurs when the seam is on the bias (unless the fabric is stretched too much as it is sewn). The most pucker occurs where stitches are made parallel to the lengthwise grain of the fabric. This is apparent in the topstitching of fly front zippers on slacks. The upper part of the stitching often puckers where it is parallel to the lengthwise grain. Where the stitches curve near the bottom of the zipper placket and follow the bias, there is usually no puckering.

Although pucker cannot be completely eliminated in some cases (because of the displacement of the fabric yarns by the sewing threads), it can be reduced to an acceptable level. To produce smooth seams, many factors must be controlled; pucker-free seams are a mark of quality.

Bulk

Bulky seams detract from a garment's smooth appearance. Although some bulk is unavoidable, construction steps that eliminate excess bulk indicate quality. Bulky seams are lumpy, unsightly, and uncomfortable.

Multiple layers of fabric—especially a heavy or thick fabric—stacked up in the same area create bulk. For example, a flat-felled seam containing several fabric plies produces a strong but bulky seam. Many seam finishes that prevent raveling also add bulk.

Bulk reduces seam flexibility. Flexible seams contribute to the wearer's comfort because they allow freedom of movement. Bulky, rigid seams can make the wearer uncomfortable and prevent the fabric from draping naturally, interfering with the garment's appearance. In knit garments, for example, rigid seams tend to ripple. Also, because of their inflexibility, rigid seams are subject to abrasion. Notice that the bulkiest seams in a pair of jeans, although often the strongest, also exhibit the most frosting and abrasion.

In industrial sewing, bulk is handled differently than it is in home sewing. In home sewing, seams are stitched and the bulk is then trimmed by hand. In industrial sewing any unnecessary motion is an added expense. Picking up a pair of scissors and trimming a seam is motion that is not cost effective. Instead of this expensive manner of trimming, patterns are created with as little bulk as possible; when the panels are cut, the bulk is also removed. This, combined with automatic trimming during the sewing operation, leaves a minimal amount of manual bulk reduction by the operator.

Seam Strength

If the seams split, the garment falls apart, so obviously the strength and durability of its seams affect overall garment durability. Seam strength and durability should be commensurate with the intended use of the garment and the wear and care it will receive. Good-quality seams are as strong as the fabric of the garment; they withstand the same amount of stress as the rest of the garment. Seams in some locations, such as the crotch and underarm, must withstand the extra stress that the wearer's movements cause in those areas. However, seams stronger than the fabric are unnecessary; in fact, under stress, they cause the fabric to tear near the seam.

Seam strength and durability are a result of the type and width of the seam, the strength and tendency to ravel of the fabric, and the characteristics of the stitches. The integrity of a seam may fail in one of four ways: (1) raw edge, (2) broken seam, (3) seam slippage, and (4) seam grin. All lead to unaesthetic and/or nonfunctional seams.

Raw Edge. A **raw edge** is a hole in the seam not caused by broken stitches but by not stitching *both* seam allowances deeply enough (see Figure 10–13b later in this chapter). This causes one or both seam allowances to pull away from the seam stitching. A hole is created and the raw edge of the fabric shows on the outside of the garment. Narrow seam allowances and raveling fabrics contribute to the creation of raw edges. Raw edges are usually detected and repaired in wet processed products because the wet processing accelerates the raveling of raw edges and makes them readily apparent before the garment is shipped. Raw edges in other garments usually remain latent until they are discovered by the consumer after the first laundering.

Broken Seam. A **broken seam**, also called **broken stitches,** occurs when the stitches break and the seam splits apart or *bursts* (Figure 10–2b). Most consumers refer to this as a ripped or split seam. Broken seams are unattractive and may make the garment unwearable, depending on the size and location of the break. Many consumers discard a garment when its seams rupture unless the value of the garment justifies the cost of repair.

Seam break, also called *seam crack,* is usually due to using the wrong thread size, wrong stitch type, wrong seam type, unbalanced stitch tension, long stitch length, or incorrect needle. Weak fabrics also lead to seam break.

Seam Slippage. **Seam slippage** is most often found in garments of coarsely woven fabrics. It occurs when the fabric pulls away from the stitches at the seamline (Figure 10–3a), eventually producing a raw edge. Seam slippage is unsightly and can weaken the seam to the point of a raw edge; however, a garment with severe seam slippage is usually declared unwearable for aesthetic reasons before a raw edge develops.

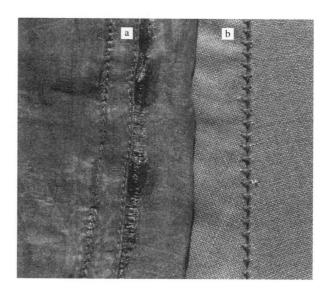

Figure 10–3 Seam defects: (a) seam slippage, and (b) seam grin.

Slippage occurs when the thread, stitch, or seam type is stronger or more stable than the fabric. The stitches remain stable, but the fabric pulls away. For example, nylon thread used to sew seams in silk garments can lead to seam slippage. Fabrics subject to yarn slippage are those with slick fibers and yarns and loose weaves. The slippage is most evident in seams exposed to high stress and in areas that fit close to the body. Seams on the straight-of-grain slip more than seams on the bias because the same yarn is stressed along the entire row of stitches. Slippage is prevented in fabric with slick fibers by using enclosed or lapped seam types that require one or two folds in the seam, for example, flat-felled or French seams (discussed later in this chapter).

Seam Grin. Seam grin occurs when the seamline spreads open, exposing the stitches so they appear similar to the teeth in a grin or smile (Figure 10–3b). Grinning seams are unattractive and in extreme cases affect durability. Seam grin is especially a problem in garments of stretch fabrics, knit and woven. Garments with a snug fit have a greater tendency to grin than loose-fitting garments. Some stitch types are more prone to grinning than others (see Chapter 9). Long stitches and unbalanced tension also increase the tendency for a seam to grin. Some seam types, such as plain seams, are more apt to grin than others.

PHYSICAL FEATURES OF SEAMS

The performance of seams is determined by the physical features of the seam—the type and width of the seam and how it is stitched, pressed, and finished. In apparel production, the physical features of seams are balanced by desired performance and cost.

Seam Type

The types of seams used to assemble a garment influence its appearance, durability, comfort, and ease of alteration. A single garment may contain several different seam types (See garment construction diagrams in Figures 9–1, 11–1, 11–2, 11–16, and 12–1.) The choice of seam type is based on the location of the seam within the garment; the end use, design, fit, fabric, and care of the garment; and current fashion trends, all balanced with cost limitations. The cost of a seam depends on the amount of fabric, thread, and labor it requires. Additional cost is incurred if special sewing machines or attachments are needed.

Complex seams, with multiple rows of stitches, are generally strong. Multiple rows of stitching absorb more stress without rupturing than a single row of stitches; seams subjected to high stress require stitch types containing two or more rows of stitches. Topstitching also contributes strength to seams and serves as decoration. However, seam complexity increases costs. Some seam types involve multiple plies of fabric, which add strength but create unwanted bulk.

Some seam types leave unfinished edges on the cloth; these types of seam allowances usually require edge finishes. Finishing the edges of seam allowances improves their strength and appearance. It prevents raveling of woven fabrics and some curling of knit fabrics. However, seam finishes generally add bulk and increase costs. Edge finishes used to finish seams are discussed later in this chapter.

Seam types, like stitches, are defined, diagrammed, and categorized in U.S. Fed. Std. No. 751a: Stitches, Seams, and Stitchings. The four seam classes established by the federal Standard are (1) *superimposed seams (SS)*, (2) *bound seams (BS)*, (3) *lapped seams (LS)*, (4) *flat seams (FS)*.

Spec technicians use many variations of these basic seam types as they plan the construction of ready-to-wear apparel. The federal standard categorizes seams according to the fabric ply arrangement. A close examination of the arrangement of the fabric plies within a seam and a comparison to the federal standard are required to identify the seam classification because different seam types are quite similar. This chapter contains generalities about the seam classes and discusses the most widely used seam types within each class. For a complete listing, see Appendix A, which contains schematic illustrations of the fabric ply arrangement of each seam type.

The federal standard identifies each seam class by two uppercase letters, which abbreviate the name of the class (Figure 10–4). Seam types within the class are further identified with a lowercase letter or letters.

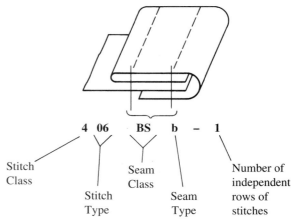

Figure 10–4 Example of a U.S. Fed. Std. No. 751a stitch and seam designation. *(Courtesy of Union Special Corporation Technical Training Center.)*

Lowercase letters early in the alphabet usually represent simple variations. The letters are followed by a numeral designating the total number of rows of stitches used to make the seam. For example, SSa-1 is a superimposed seam of the simplest type, made with one row of stitches; some stitch types require more. If additional rows of stitching are added for decorative or reinforcement purposes, the number at the end of the seam type designation is higher. Combined with the stitch number, the federal standard seam designation accurately communicates the method of construction for any apparel production operation. As mentioned in Chapter 9, Fed. Std. No. 751a is currently in the process of being converted to an ASTM standard to be known as *Standard Practice for Seams and Stitches.*

A seam type remains the same regardless of the stitch type used to sew it. For example, Figure 10–5 shows eight variations of an SS seam made with different stitch types and various edge finishes and the labor costs associated with each. Note that one of the least costly seams (B) and the most costly seam (H) produce garments with the same outer appearance but at a cost difference of $4.26 for just six seams. However, seam types generally lend themselves better to some stitch types than to others. Appendix B contains the Guide for the Use of Stitches, Seams, and Stitchings from the federal standard, which suggests the stitch types suited to each seam type. It also lists the typical operation performed using each seam type.

Superimposed Seams. The majority of seams are superimposed (Figure 10–6). Most **superimposed seams (SS)** are created by superimposing fabric plies, or stacking them on top of one another with edges even and sewing them together near the edge. Most major structural seams and many minor detail seams are superimposed. There are 54 variations of the SS in the federal standard (see Appendix A).

Plain Seams. The plain seam is by far the most common seam for joining major garment pieces. A **plain seam** (SSa) is a simple superimposed seam. For major structural seams such as side, waist, and sleeve seams, the fabric plies are sewn, face sides together, near the edge and then opened (Figure 10–7). For other plain seams, such as those joining elastic to the garment at the waist (SSt) and those closing pocket bags, the plies are not opened after sewing but are left superimposed.

A plain seam appears as a line with no visible stitches on the outside of the garment, but the seam allowances are visible inside the garment. Plain seams may be topstitched on one or both sides of the seamline to provide decorative effect or reinforcement or to imitate other seam types, or they may be flattened with a bottom cover stitch (SSh).

Plain seams are not especially strong. They have a greater tendency to grin than other seam types. However, they are inconspicuous, nonbulky, easy to alter, and inexpensive to produce.

Ideally, each seam is pressed before another seam or stitching crosses it. The seam allowances of plain seams may be pressed to one side, or they may be pressed open, which is called **butterflied** or **busted** (Figure 10–7). Busting reduces bulk by distributing the seam allowances to each side of the seam line. The reduction of bulk contributes to attractiveness and comfort. Busted seams are found in high-quality garments, especially tailored ones. However, they increase costs because they require an extra pressing operation. When a seam crosses a previously made seam, bulk resulting from the several plies of fabric can be uncomfortable and unsightly. To reduce bulk, the first seam may be busted before the second seam crosses it. Bulk is further reduced if the seam allowances of the second seam are also pressed open. Such underpressing improves the comfort, appearance, and sometimes the fit of the finished garment. For instance, in high-quality pants, the inseams are pressed open before the seat seam is sewn, to reduce bulk where the seams intersect at the crotch; the seat seam and outseams are pressed open before the waistband is attached, for the same reason.

The seams in some garments, both low and high quality, may be pressed only at the end of construction or not at all depending upon the seam types used. Sometimes seams are finger pressed by an operator. Of course, seams that are overedged cannot be pressed open because the seam allowances are held together by stitch interloopings.

A few plain seams, such as armscye seams and seat seams in the crotch area, are never pressed open. The seam allowances are left standing together to provide for comfort and durability and to avoid distortion of the seam.

Enclosed Seams. To make an **enclosed seam,** the operator sews the fabric plies face sides together near the edge, opens out the plies, and turns them back sides together to encase the seam allowances (Figure 10–8). Enclosed seams occur only at edges, where they appear as a line with no visible stitches along the edge. The stitches and seam allowances are not readily visible inside the garment, either, because they are sandwiched between the fabric plies. The seams at most garment and detail edges are enclosed seams, for example, at the outer edges of necklines, collars, and cuffs. Enclosed seams are the second most common seam type after plain seams.

Bulk is a problem in enclosed seams because multiple layers of the garment and its seam allowances lie in the same direction, on top of one another, in the

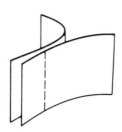

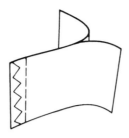

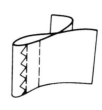

Type "A"
Plain Lockstitch
Seam
This type of seam uses
two threads, utilizing
a lock-type stitch.
Taking about 30 seconds
to sew approximately
12" = $.035 seam.

Type "B"
Sew Pink Seam
This type of seam uses
two threads, utilizing
a chain lock stitch
costing about $.0175
per seam.

Type "C"
Overlock Seam
This type of seam uses
three threads, utilizing
a stretch stitch costing
$.0175 per seam.

Type "D"
Safety Overlock
This type of seam
uses five threads, giving
the clean finish of an
overlock, plus the
strength and safety of
a lock stitch, costing
about $.0232 per seam,
plus extra thread.

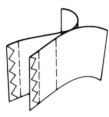

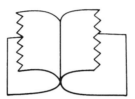

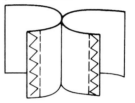

Type "E"
Double Overlock/
Lock Stitch Seam
This type of seam uses
eight threads, giving
a clean finish on each ply
and seamed with a
lock stitch costing $.07
per seam, plus extra thread.

Type "F"
Plain Seam
Pressed Open
The cost of seaming is
$.035 plus the cost of pressing
$.028 = $.063 per seam.

Type "G"
Pinked Seam
Pressed Open
The cost of seaming
$.0175 plus the cost of pressing
$.035 = $.0525 for seam.

Type "H"
Double Overlock
Pressed Open
The cost of seaming
$.07 plus pressing
$.028 = $.098 per seam.

Type "B" Seam Construction

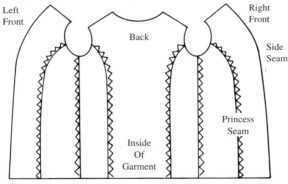

CONSTRUCTION	"B"	"H"	Note:
A. Cost To Contractor	$.0175	$.07 +.028 (Press) = .098	A = Cost Of Type Of Seam
B. Cost To Manufacturer	$.0525	$.21 + .02 = .23	B = 3A Or 3 Times Needle Time
C. Cost To Buyer	$.105	$.46	C = B + 100%
D. Cost To Consumer	$.21	.$.92	D = C + 100%

Type "B" & "H" Construction

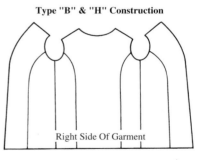

Type "H" Seam Construction

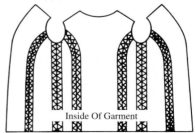

Figure 10–5 The labor costs of sewing 12 inch-seams of the same seam type but using various stitch types. The associated labor costs are calculated on a base pay of $4.20 per hour. Also shown, cost comparison and the inside and outside of garments sewn using the least costly and most costly methods.
(Reprinted with permission from Bobbin® Magazine, *April 1985. Copyright 1985 by Bobbin Blenheim Media. All rights reserved.)*

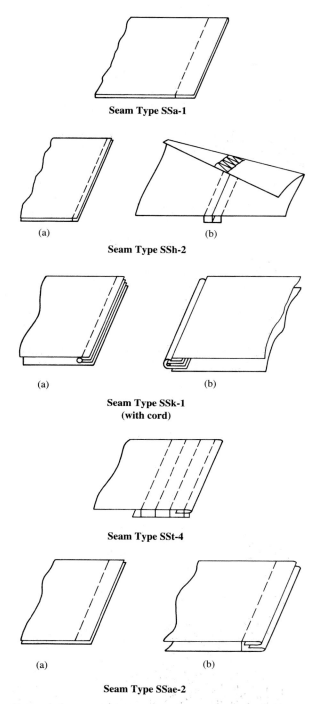

Seam Type SSa-1

(a)   (b)

Seam Type SSh-2

(a)   (b)

Seam Type SSk-1
(with cord)

Seam Type SSt-4

(a)   (b)

Seam Type SSae-2

Figure 10–6   Superimposed seams: (SSa) plain seam, (SSh) plain seam flattened with bottom cover stitch, (SSk) enclosed seam with piping, (SSt) for attaching elastic, and (SSae) French seam.

Figure 10–7   Plain seams: (a) butterflied, with wide seam allowances, and (b) finished together, with narrow seam allowances. Also note (a) wide, blindstitched hem (finished with hem tape), and (b) narrow, topstitched hem.

finished seam. If the seam allowances of an enclosed seam are not narrowly trimmed, the seam may be bulky and may not turn smoothly, especially at sharp curves and corners. The seam allowances of enclosed seams are often trimmed extremely narrow at corners to eliminate bulk for example, in collar points.

However, if seam allowances are too narrow, they fray and raw edges develop. High-quality enclosed seams are durable and nonbulky and have sharp, flat points and smooth, flat curves. A technique used to help enclosed seams lie smooth is to clip the seam allowances on concave curves and notch the seam allowances on convex curves. The seam allowances are also **graded, blended, layered,** or **beveled,** trimming each ply to a slightly different length. Blending the seam allowances prevents them from making a visible imprint on the outside of the finished garment when pressed. Blending is done by hand in couture garments, and the same effect is achieved in ready-to-wear by machine blades that trim the seam allowances at an angle.

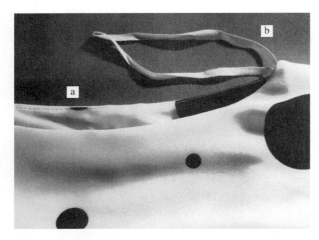

Figure 10–8   Enclosed seam at neckline with (a) control stitching. Also note (b) hanger strap.

Enclosed seams require more careful pressing than other seam types to produce the full size and intended shape of the garment piece. The lower ply of an enclosed seam has a tendency to slip out and show on the outside of the garment. The seamline of an enclosed seam is pressed about 1/16 inch toward the underneath side to help prevent this. A *channel* is an undesirable groove that appears in an enclosed seam when the seamline is not fully pressed out toward the edge (Figure 10–9a). In high-price garments, collars, cuffs, and other details may be *slipped* or *bubbled* to keep the lower ply of enclosed seams from showing at the outer edge (see Chapter 11).

A quality feature on enclosed seams is **control stitching** or **understitching** (Figure 10–8). It attaches the seam allowances to the lower ply. Control stitching keeps an enclosed seam flat and prevents its lower ply from slipping out and showing. Most collars and cuffs and faced necklines, waistlines, and armholes require control stitching for quality results, but it is found mainly in high-price lines. Control stitching is unnecessary if topstitching is used to keep the seam flat.

French Seams.   The **French seam** (SSae-2) is a "seam within a seam" (Figure 10–10a). Operators make French seams by sewing a narrow plain seam with the back sides of the fabric plies together. Then a slightly wider second plain seam is sewn, with the face sides of the fabric plies together, to encase the seam allowances of the first seam.

On the outside of the garment, the French seam looks like a plain seam. The main appeal of French seams is the attractive, finished appearance inside the garment; a single row of stitches is visible, but all raw seam allowance edges are hidden in the first,

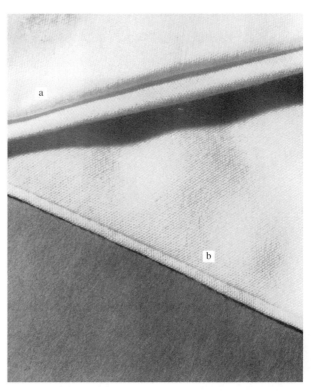

Figure 10–9   Enclosed seam on collar with (a) channel from poor pressing and (b) facing that slips out and shows at edge. (It needs control stitching.)

enclosed seam. To sum up its advantages and disadvantages, the French seam

1. prevents raveling by enclosing the raw seam allowances of the first seam within the second seam
2. is no stronger than a plain seam but, in slick fabrics, does prevent seam slippage better than a plain seam
3. adds elegance, especially for sheer, thin fabrics with a tendency to ravel
4. is suitable for short, fairly straight seams, but not well suited for long seams or extremely curved seams
5. is difficult to alter; it cannot be let out to make the garment larger
6. is costly to make, being found mainly in high-price womenswear and lingerie.

Mock French Seams.   The **mock French seam** or **false French seam** is used to create the appearance of the true French seam at more cost-effective rates. The mock French seam is an adaptation of the plain seam. In one version, operators fold under the raw edges of the seam allowances of a plain seam and stitch them together. In the version pictured in

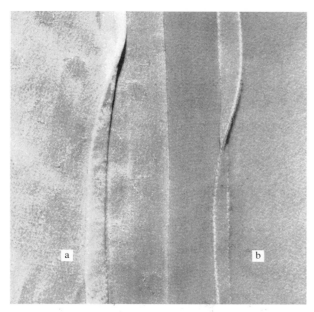

Figure 10–10 Both sides of (a) French seam and (b) mock French seam. They appear as plain seams on the outside of the garment.

Figure 10–10b, the plain seam is merely stitched twice and trimmed close to the second stitching to resemble a true French seam. Mock French seams, like French seams, look like plain seams on the outside of the garment. However, the mock French seam can be distinguished from the true French seam because the mock French features two rows of stitching visible inside the garment rather than one.

Mock French seams are simpler and less costly to construct and can be altered more easily than true French seams, and they are strong and ravel-resistant. They can be used on long seams or curved seams, for which true French seams are unsuitable.

Lapped Seams. **Lapped seams (LS)** are made by overlapping the seam allowances of two or more fabric plies and sewing them together, with the fabric plies extending in opposite directions (Figure 10–11). Lapped seams are usually more casual looking than superimposed seams because they always have some form of topstitching. The federal standard contains 102 versions of the LS, making it the largest seam class (see Appendix A).

Many special-purpose seams are lapped seams. Raingear, for example, often features lapped seams because they are more waterproof than other seam types. Lapped seams attach elastic at the waistline of underwear and sportswear because they are less bulky than superimposed seams.

Patternmakers lap front panels over back panels when planning lapped side seams for the smoothest,

most slimming look. If a lapped seam contains gathering, easing, pleating, or tucking, the less-full panel is lapped over the fuller panel.

The simplest type of lapped seam (LSa) is produced by lapping the seam allowances without folding them under. The raw edges of the seam allowances are visible inside and outside the garment, but if a nonraveling fabric is used, the exposed raw edges are acceptable. Because lapped seams are less bulky than other seam types, they are useful for constructing garments of nonraveling materials like leather and vinyl. They may also be used to sew lace fabrics together for an uninterrupted flow of the lace motifs at seamlines.

Most lapped seam types involve folding under the seam allowances of the upper fabric ply before lapping and stitching it over the lower ply (LSb). Lapped seams of this type appear almost identical to topstitched, superimposed seams from both the face and the back of the seam. Examine the seams closely; the topstitching holds a lapped seam together, whereas the topstitching on a superimposed seam is merely decorative. Lapped seams of this type are used, for example, to attach the waistband curtain to pants and to sew on patch pockets.

Lapped seams with the upper ply folded under are useful for joining unusually shaped fabric panels. For example, patternmakers planning Western-style shirts with curved or pointed yokes would find it difficult and costly to accurately join the yoke pieces to the shirt using superimposed seams. To solve this problem, they may specify pressing under the seam allowances of the shaped yoke, lapping it over the shirt body, and topstitching it to make the joining easier and less costly; this also is more likely to yield smooth, durable results.

Both seam allowances of a lapped seam may be turned under. This results in a strong but somewhat bulky seam. The most common seam of this type is the flat-felled seam.

Flat-Felled Seams. **Flat-felled seams** (LSc) are the most common type of lapped seam (Figure 10–12a). Operators make flat-felled seams by folding under or *felling* the raw edges of both seam allowances as the seam is stitched. A skilled operator is required to feed the fabric plies accurately to the folding attachment on the sewing machine because much of the operation is executed by feel instead of sight. A new development is a fell seamer that automatically forms the seam and allows even an unskilled operator to achieve excellent results. In either case, at least one but usually two or more rows of stitches are used to sew the seam, keeping both seam allowances turned under. Thus, the seam exposes no raw edges inside or

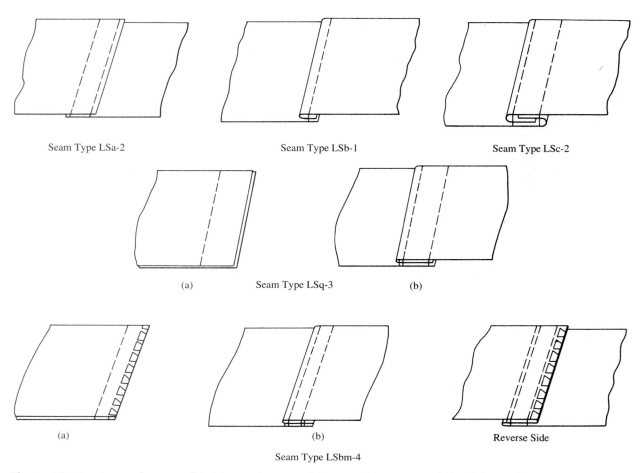

Seam Type LSa-2   Seam Type LSb-1   Seam Type LSc-2

(a)   Seam Type LSq-3   (b)

(a)   (b)   Reverse Side

Seam Type LSbm-4

Figure 10–11   Lapped seams: (LSa) lapped seam with raw edges exposed, (LSb) lapped seam with raw edge of top ply turned under, (LSc) flat-felled seam, (LSq) welt seam (actually a modification of LSq because encased seam allowance is trimmed to pad the seam), and (LSbm) mock flat-felled seam.

outside the garment, and the seam appears identical inside and outside the garment. To summarize their characteristics, flat-felled seams

1. are strong and durable; they are used in jeans, shirts, work clothing, and pajamas.
2. prevent raveling because all the raw edges are enclosed
3. are bulky and rigid in heavy fabrics
4. are difficult to alter
5. can be used only on straight or fairly straight edges.

Mock Flat-Felled Seams.   The **mock flat-felled seam** (LSbm), commonly called a **mock fell**, imitates the flat-felled seam (Figure 10–12b). Operators produce mock flat-felled seams by sewing a plain seam using a safety stitch; then the seam allowances are pressed to one side and topstitched. Using this method, the resulting seam looks like a flat-felled seam on the outside of the garment. Inside, the seam allowances can be seen, unlike a flat-felled seam (Figure 10–13).

Mock flat-felled seams cost less to produce than true flat-felled seams; they require less-skilled labor. They generally are not as strong or as durable as true flat-felled seams. However, if a garment does not receive heavy wear, true flat-felled seams are unnecessarily bulky, and mock flatfelled seams provide the same look and more flexibility at a lower cost, plus more strength than a plain seam.

Tuck and Slot Seams.   Most lapped seams are stitched close to the edge of the upper ply. If stitched farther back to create a small flap, the lapped seam is called a **tuck seam** because the seam resembles a tuck. **Slot seams** are a decorative variation of the lapped seam. The edges of two fabric plies are turned under and nearly abutted. They are lapped over and stitched to a narrow fabric underlay, usually of a contrasting color. The contrasting color shows through the narrow slot where the fabric panels almost touch (Figure 10–14a). Slot seams are costly in both fabric and labor; they are extra costly if the seam is curved, requiring an identically shaped fabric underlay.

Figure 10–12 Top and bottom of (a) flat-felled seam, and (b) mock flat-felled seam.

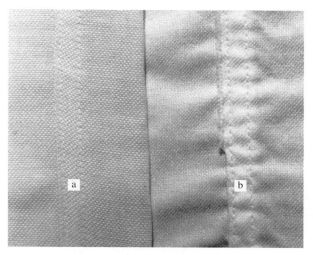

Figure 10–13 Flat-felled seams on shirts: (a) smooth, well-made seam, and (b) puckered seam with too-narrow seam allowances that were inadequately caught in the seam, resulting in a raw edge.

Welt Seams. **Welt seams** (modified LSq) are made by superimposing two plies with the raw edges uneven and sewing a plain seam; both seam allowances are pressed in one direction and topstitched to catch the wider seam allowance. Dimension is provided by the narrower seam allowance which pads the area; the finished seam appears somewhat puffy, creating a decorative welt (Figure 10–14b). Welt seams emphasize style lines in garments of heavy fabrics. A welt seam cannot be let out to make the garment larger.

Bound Seams. **Bound seams (BS)** are made by using fabric binding strips to encase raw edges; bound seams are found only at edges (Figure 10–15). A folder on the sewing machine folds the binding and holds it in position as it is stitched. Bound seams are not used to create structural seams of the garment but to cover and finish raw edges, for example, necklines, armholes, waistlines, hems, and hem and seam allowances. This chapter discusses bound seams as an edge finish, but the federal standard classifies bindings as seams because they fulfill the definition of joining two or more fabric plies. Eighteen variations of the BS are included in the federal standard (see Appendix A).

Bindings eliminate the need for additional edge finishes. Bindings produce a neat finish for edges exposed to view, prevent raveling of edges exposed to wear, and cover the raw edge to make the wearer comfortable (unless the binding adds too much bulk). Many bindings are visible from both inside and outside the garment. Therefore, they may be decorative as well as functional.

Any narrow, nonbulky, flexible strip of fabric makes a suitable binding. Thin fabrics make good bindings because of their flexibility and light weight. Foldover braids make good bindings because of their flexibility and varied, decorative style; however, some are bulky. Woven fabrics used as bindings are usually cut on the bias to lend flexibility, especially for use on curved edges. *Bias tape* is a woven fabric strip cut on the bias with both raw edges folded under; it is commonly used to bind garment edges. (Bias tape is pictured in Chapter 8, Figure 8–4c and d.)

Most bindings are attached by folding the binding over the raw edge of the garment, usually with the aid of a folder on the sewing machine, and by topstitching the binding to the garment (Figure 10–16). The simplest form of binding (BSa) involves folding a strip of fabric around the raw edge and topstitching it to the garment (Figure 10–15). This method of binding is the least bulky. However, on bound garment edges it exposes the raw edges of the binding both inside and outside the garment. Therefore, this method is more often used to bind the edges of seam allowances than to bind garment edges. It requires the use of a nonraveling binding strip such as a knit or a woven tape, or the raw edges of the binding strip must be finished to prevent raveling.

A common method of binding garment edges and seam allowances is to fold under the upper edge of the binding strip (BSb). This gives a finished appearance from the top side. It adds less bulk than folding under both edges of the binding. The lower edge of the binding must be finished to prevent raveling unless the binding is a nonraveling material.

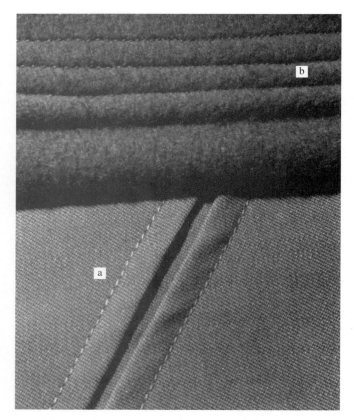

Figure 10–14   Decorative seams: (a) tuck/slot seam, and (b) welt seam with multiple rows of topstitching.

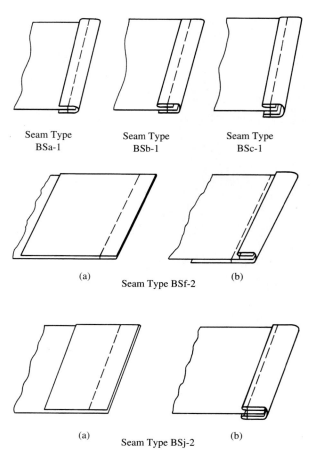

Figure 10–15   Bound seams: (BSa) bound seam with raw edges of binding exposed, (BSb) bound seam with one raw edge of binding turned under, (BSc) bound seam with both raw edges of binding turned under, (BSf) binding seamed on and then stitched in the ditch, and (BSj) binding seamed on and then topstitched.

Some seams are bound with both edges of the binding turned under before folding it around the edge (BSc). However, turning under both edges of the binding creates bulk. Therefore, this method should not be used if the binding or garment is made of a heavy fabric. A binding with both edges turned under looks equally neat and attractive from either side, so it is useful when the binding is viewed on both sides, for example, on a reversible garment and at opening edges. Seam allowances bound this way tend to press through to the outside of the garment because of the excess bulk.

Occasionally, one edge of the binding is sewn with a plain seam to the garment; the binding is then folded around the edge and caught by topstitching (BSj). The topstitching may be **stitched in the ditch** or **crack stitched**, with straight stitches placed in the crevice between the garment and the binding (BSf). Seams bound this way require considerable time and skill, but if done well the topstitches are inconspicuous.

High-quality bindings bite the fabric edge as deeply as possible. If a binding barely hangs on the edge, it is not secure and a raw edge will develop. Sewing on a binding with straight stitches requires a skilled oper-ator; the stitches must be accurately placed to catch both edges of the binding. If only one edge of the binding is caught in the stitches, the binding is not secure. Zigzag stitches, bottom-covering chainstitches, or top-and-bottom covering chainstitches increase the likelihood of catching both edges of the binding. They also serve as a finish for raw edges on the binding, if any.

Corners are difficult to bind; ideally, bindings should be mitered around corners (Figure 10–16a). **Mitering** involves seaming or folding the binding diagonally to conform to corners. Mitered corners are less bulky and more attractive than unmitered corners. Mitering requires a skilled operator and is mainly found in high-price garments.

At most necklines, armholes, and garment and sleeve hems, the binding is attached to the flat edge and then the garment is seamed into a circle. A more costly method is to sew the garment into a circle, sew

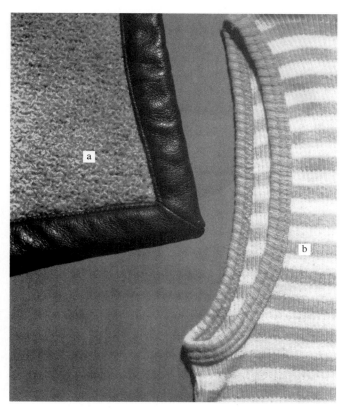

Figure 10–16 Binding: (a) with mitered corner, and (b) on curved armhole.

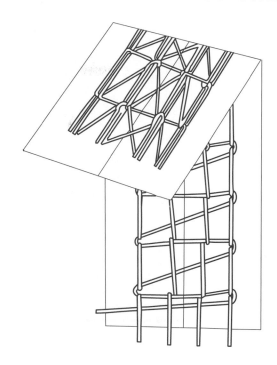

Seam Type FSa-1

Figure 10–17 Flat seam: (FSa) ordinary flat seam.

the binding into a circle, and then join the two together in the round. This requires considerable skill and great accuracy to ensure that the two circles are the same circumference so they can be sewn together smoothly. The end of the seam joining the garment into a circle is concealed within the binding, making this method more attractive and more comfortable than bindings attached flat. High-quality garments feature bindings applied in the round.

Flat Seams. **Flat seams (FS)** join fabric plies whose raw (or sometimes folded) edges are abutted (or sometimes slightly lapped) and sewn together (Figure 10–17). Flat seams are sometimes called **butt seams** or **exposed seams**. The joining stitches are typically 600-class cover stitches, although zigzag or bottom-cover stitches may be used. Flat seams appear similar on both sides; the stitches cover the raw edges and are visible on the face and back of the seam. The federal standard contains only six variations of the FS (see Appendix A).

Because flat seams have little or usually no seam allowances, they are economical in fabric usage and are the least bulky of all seams. However, because they have no excess seam allowances, most flat seams cannot be let out to enlarge the garment. Having no

excess seam allowances leaves little room for error; flat seams that are not completely abutted or that are joined with too-narrow cover stitches are likely to separate and develop holes.

Flat seams are used in knit garments where thick seams are intolerable, for example, underwear, foundation garments, sweatshirts, sweatpants, and some childrenswear. Flat seams are inappropriate in garments of woven fabric because the fabric ravels and the garment splits apart at the seams.

Seam Allowance Width

The width of the seam allowances affects the strength, durability, appearance, comfort, and cost of a garment. Wide seam allowances are a construction feature worth pointing out to the consumer because they have many advantages. In general, for seams subject to stress, such as the main structural seams of a garment, wide seam allowances are a mark of quality (Figure 10–7a). Their main advantages are that seams with wide seam allowances generally

1. are stronger and more durable; they help absorb stress so the stitches are not strained, and they are less prone to seam slippage.
2. help to slow raveling of the fabric to the seamline.
3. help the garment hang smoothly because of their weight.

Mass-production apparel makes up the majority of garments made and sold in America. This type of apparel consists of low-quality expendable apparel as well as high-quality timeless classics. In high-quality garments, seam allowances as wide as one inch or more may be used in areas subject to frequent alteration. For example, the seat in men's pants is a common area for alteration. (A wide seam in this location is shown in Chapter 12, Figure 12–8.) Side seams in skirts and inseams in pants are other seams whose seam allowances are cut wide in high-quality garments to accommodate alterations.

However, wide seam allowances require extra fabric and therefore are costly; seam allowances account for over 5% of total apparel fabric (Hudson, 1988). High-quality ready-to-wear generally features seam allowances on major structural seams of 1/2 inch or wider. Low-quality garments often have very narrow seam allowances to conserve fabric. However, to some extent, short stitches and stitch and seam types that are strong and prevent raveling may substitute for wide seam allowances.

Narrow seam allowances are preferable on seams where bulk is unacceptable. For example, enclosed seams such as those in collars and cuffs are usually little more than 1/8 inch wide to reduce bulk and yield a smooth, flat edge. Wide seam allowances in these areas actually detract from quality. However, if the seam allowances are too narrow, the fabric ravels out past the stitches, creating a hole. It is difficult for operators to evenly catch all the fabric plies when sewing seams with narrow seam allowances. Therefore, the seam is usually stitched and the seam allowances are simultaneously trimmed to a uniform, narrow width in detail areas where reducing bulk is important. Enclosed seams subjected to stress, such as in waistbands, call for medium-width seam allowances. A medium width is a compromise between the durability of wide seam allowances and the low bulk of narrow ones.

Wide seam allowances are unsuitable for seams in the crotch and underarm areas; they interfere with comfort and fit in these areas because they cause pulling and chafing. And wide seam allowances are unsuitable for sharp curves because they interfere with the flatness and smoothness of the curve.

Most stitch types can be used to sew seams with seam allowances of unlimited width. An exception is seams made using overedge stitches and cover stitches; they are confined to a maximum width of about 3/8 inch. Most seam types can be made in varying widths but some, such as flat seams, are always narrow.

Seam Stays

The term **stay** is a general one. It refers to any stable, narrow, nonbulky tape, ribbon, fabric strip, or other device used to stabilize a seam. A stay makes the seam "stay" the same size or shape without stretching or distorting. Stays strengthen and stabilize seams and preserve and enhance the shape of the garment. A seam with a stay is more costly than one without, but it maintains its shape and size better. Stayed seams are unlikely to rupture because the stay absorbs the stress of use. However, stays add bulk to the seam. Stays that shrink at a different rate than the garment can cause puckering.

Seams subject to stress may stretch or distort if they are not stayed. Seams are often stayed at shoulder, neckline, waistline, underarm, and crotch seams, and pocket edges. In high-quality tailored garments, the armscyes, lapels, collars, and other areas may be stayed. Crotch seams and inseams of better pants are often stayed with a narrow triangle of lining fabric. Any area cut on the bias is especially subject to stretching, and if it receives stress, it requires a stay to maintain its shape. Stays can be eased to the garment to pull up the fabric and make them hug the body. This technique, although costly in labor, is useful in preventing lapels, low necklines, and large armholes and pockets from gaping. Although stays add to both material and labor costs, they help the garment look better and last longer.

Taped seams (SSab) are created by staying them with narrow strips of twill tape or fabric (Figure 10–18). Superimposing the tape on the fabric plies and sewing it in as part of the seam is a common method of taping shoulder seams in better knit shirts and sweaters and waistline seams of fitted garments. Or a strip of fabric is sewn over the completed seam

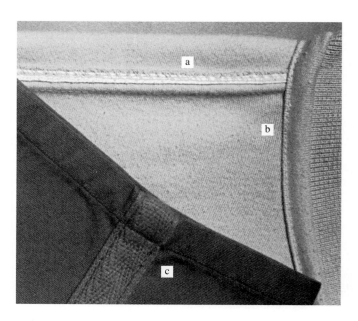

Figure 10–18 Stayed seams: (a) taped, (b) stripped, and (c) strapped.

inside the garment, creating what are sometimes called **stripped seams** (SSf). Some T-shirt neckline and shoulder seams are taped in this manner. Such taping increases the wearer's comfort by preventing the seam allowances from chafing the skin and increases the attractiveness of neckline seams visible at the point of sale or when being worn. Continuous tape across the neck and shoulders gives the most support. Seams that feature a strip of fabric sewn over the seam on the outside of the garment are sometimes called **strapped seams** (SSag). The strapping decorates as well as reinforces, for example, the satin stripes on the side seams of tuxedo pants. Strapped seams are also found on men's and boys' briefs.

Sewing Accuracy

Seam and stitch quality are impacted by many factors including choice of raw materials, spreading accuracy, cutting accuracy, bundling accuracy, stitch and seam type chosen, and functionality of the machine. The skill of the sewing operator is another factor that impacts seam and stitching quality. Seams that are sewn evenly, with adequate seam allowances and no raw edges, are attractive, comfortable, and durable. They allow the garment to fit properly. Inaccurately sewn seams with stitches that miss the intended seamline reduce the durability, comfort, and fit of the garment. Crookedly sewn seams are unattractive and do not withstand stress well. Seams should not have accidental tucks, pleats, or gathers. Seams with these defects do not lie smoothly. Seams that cross other seams should be aligned on both sides of the intersecting seam within tolerance, especially if the intersection is in a highly visible location.

Sewing operators contribute to seam pucker and twisting of garment panels if they feed seam plies at uneven rates. However, sometimes panels of two different lengths must be sewn together, and the operator is expected to ease one to the other until they come out even. Sometimes cutting inaccuracies cause two panels of uneven lengths to be given to an operator, and the operator is expected to know they are inaccurate and not sew them until a sewing engineer or line supervisor has corrected them. Both situations affect the fit of the garment. An experienced, skilled operator knows these different situations and makes the right decision.

Sewing panels together which are cut on different grains can cause puckering. Bias-to-straight and lengthwise-to-crosswise panel joins are particularly difficult to handle and are avoided if possible. When panels cut on different grains must be joined, care is taken to evenly feed the layers and avoid easing or stretching them. Stretching a bias-cut or knit seam as it is sewn also leads to puckering.

Seams and stitchings sewn on the bias of the fabric have a tendency to ripple and pucker. The ripple and pucker worsens if the fabric is stretched when sewn. Therefore, it is important that seams on the bias have directional stitching in the direction of the grain to minimize stretching. **Directional stitching** calls for sewing from the wide end to the narrow end of the fabric panels on vertical seams and from high side to low side of the fabric panels on horizontal seams. The vertical side seams of a flared shirt are stitched from wide to narrow, in other words, hem to waist. The horizontal shoulder seams of a shirt are stitched high to low, from neckline to armhole. Operators are trained to sew each seam and stitching in the appropriate direction.

Directional stitching makes a difference in the appearance of some finished garments. For example, pockets on the fronts of jeans often ripple and pucker along the upper edge if they are stitched in the wrong direction. Long seams, such as skirt side seams, and seams close to true bias, like very flared skirt side seams, ripple and pucker from nondirectional stitching.

PERFORMANCE OF EDGE TREATMENTS

Edge treatments or **edge finishes** finish the raw or cut edges of a garment. Generally, consumers think of garments with neatly finished edges as being of higher quality than garments with untreated edges. Indeed, sometimes edges are poorly finished or not finished at all due to fashion looks (fads) or cost limitations. However, in certain situations, edges left untreated do not sacrifice quality; for example, garments made of leather or leather-like fabrics often have untreated, raw edges in order to avoid bulk. And producers of lined garments avoid finishing seam-allowance edges because the lining hides the raw edges and helps prevent raveling. On garments made from knit fabrics with no tendency to roll or woven fabrics with no tendency to ravel, patternmakers also may leave seam allowances, and sometimes other raw edges, untreated without detracting from the garment's performance. (An unfinished edge is shown in Figure 10–27b, later in this chapter.)

Edge treatments affect garment quality, whether they are on the outside of the garment (for example, necklines, waistlines, and sleeveless armholes) or on seam- and-hem allowance edges inside the garment. The evaluation of the treatment of a particular edge depends on the location and purpose of the edge, the fabric from which the garment is made, and the style and end use of the garment.

The aesthetic and functional performance of an edge finish includes its attractiveness, durability, and comfort. Performance results from the interaction between the fabric, the stitches, and the seam. Edge finish performance affects consumer satisfaction with the garment both at the point of sale and in use. Performance considerations for edge finishes include smoothness, strength, and resistance to failure, balanced with cost limitations.

Covering raw edges makes them more attractive, which is especially important for edges visible on the outside of the garment. Edge treatments should complement the garment's fabric and style. A high-quality edge treatment is even throughout its length. It does not ripple or distort the shape or size of the edge. Curves are smooth and corners are mitered or otherwise handled to create a sharp angle. Edge finishes inside the garment do not show through to the outside. Most edge finishes add bulk to the edge, but bulk should be kept to a minimum because bulky edges detract from the appearance and comfort of the garment.

A major function of most edge finishes is to prevent raveling of woven fabrics. They also prevent the edges of light- and mediumweight knit fabrics from rolling or curling. Edge finishes contribute to the strength, abrasion resistance, and stability of edges. And finished edges usually improve the wearer's comfort, especially in locations such as armholes. Edge finish performance requirements are based on several factors, including the location and purpose of the edge, the shape of the edge, the style of the garment, and the weight and type of the fabric. Edge finishes should withstand the same wear and care as the garment. For example, edge finishes on seam allowances in the crotch and underarm areas require abrasion resistance; edges prone to distortion need stable edge finishes; heavy fabrics require nonbulky finishes; and fabrics that ravel readily demand edge finishes that prevent raveling.

Many edge finishes add unwanted bulk, some types more than others. The bulk of an edge treatment depends on the type of edge finish, the bulk of the fabric, the number of plies of fabric, and the amount of thread and other materials at the edge. Bulk can be reduced in edge finishes by pressing open seam allowances that intersect the edge, and trimming wide seam and hem allowances that intersect the edge. However, because of the cost, these techniques are used only in high-price lines.

Some seam types have raw edges inside the garment that require finishing. Producers of most low- and moderate-price garments finish the raw edges of a seam's allowances together. However, producers of high-quality garments may finish the seam allowances of major structural seams separately. For example, butterflying the seam allowances of plain seams and finishing each one separately results in a smooth, nonbulky seam. However, this method costs at least twice as much as finishing the seam allowances together (Figure 10–7).

PHYSICAL FEATURES OF EDGE TREATMENTS

The physical features of edge treatments include the type of edge treatment and how well the edge treatment is executed. These factors determine the aesthetic and functional performance of the edge treatment. The main types of edge treatments are (1) edge finish stitchings, including hems; (2) unstitched finishes; (3) facings; (4) bindings; (5) bands; and (6) plackets.

Edge Finish Stitchings

Stitchings are stitches applied to finish an edge or for ornamental purposes; they do not join fabric pieces together as do seams. Stitchings are classified in U.S. Fed. Std. No. 751a: Stitches, Seams, and Stitchings as either *edge finish stitchings (EF) or ornamental stitchings (OS)*.

Edge-finish stitchings (EF) are a series of stitches that finish an edge (Figure 10–19). They include hems, most seam finishes, and other sewn finishes for raw edges, such as those used to finish the raw edges of belt loops and shoulder straps. Any stitching that finishes a raw edge without attaching a separate piece of fabric qualifies as an edge-finish stitching. The federal standard contains 32 variations of EF stitchings. Only the most common edge-finish stitchings are discussed in this chapter, but Appendix A diagrams all the EF stitchings. EF stitchings can be made using any suitable stitch type. For example, a blindstitched hem (EFc) can be made using any blindstitch, from class 100, 300, 400, or 500. Appendix B lists the apparel production operation performed by each EF stitching and the suitable stitch types.

Hems. *In general, a hem refers to any finish at the edge of a garment.* For example, terms such as *banded hem, bound hem,* or *faced hem* refer to edges finished by bands, bindings, or facings. The edge treatment used to finish the lower edge of the garment affects the overall quality impression the garment makes. *Note:* Various lengths of the lower edge of garments are illustrated in Figure 5–20.

As an edge-finish stitching, a hem refers to turning under a raw edge and securing it to the garment. Any raw edge, not just the lower edge of the garment, may be finished

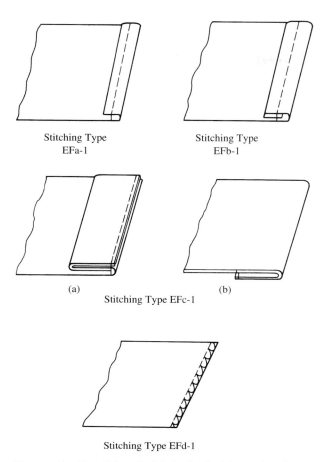

Stitching Type
EFa-1

Stitching Type
EFb-1

(a)

Stitching Type EFc-1

(b)

Stitching Type EFd-1

Figure 10–19   Edge finish (EF) stitchings: (EFa) single-fold hem, (EFb) double-fold hem, (EFc) blindstitched hem, and (EFd) overedged.

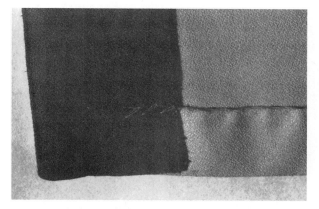

Figure 10–20   Garment should be hemmed before facing is turned in, as shown here.

with a hem, which leaves a folded edge in place of the raw one. Hems are the most common EF stitchings.

When a hem is combined with an opening, such as on jacket sleeve or back vents, producers of high-quality garments hem the garment first and then finish the opening edge (Figure 10–20). If the garment is hemmed after the opening edge is finished, the hem tends to show at the opening edge. However, because of the construction sequence, garments are often hemmed last.

Sometimes, a *hem tape* or *seam tape* is lapped over and sewn onto a raw hem allowance to cover and finish the edge (Figure 10–7). Taped edges attractively finish the hems in moderate- and high-quality dresses, skirts, and pants.

Secure hem attachment is important. In high-quality garments, spec technicians specify hems with stitch types that do not unravel at the pull of a thread. The stitches (SPI) in quality hems are small and close so that the heel of the wearer's shoe or a piece of jewelry cannot catch in the hem stitches and cause them to rupture.

Folded Hems.   The **folded hem** is a simple hem finish in which the raw edge is turned under and stitched to the garment. The edge may be folded under once (EFa), as shown in Figures 10–19, 10–20, and 10–21, or there may be a double fold (EFb), shown in Figures 10–19 and 10–22. Folded hems are the most frequently used method of finishing the lower edge of garments, and they are a popular finish for the raw edges of details such as pockets and ruffles and the lower edges of sleeves without cuffs.

Designers of better-tailored garments interface the folded hems at the lower edge of the garment and sleeves for body and durability. They specify strips of woven interfacing on the bias to use in these hems because it lends support without rigidity. The interfacing ends at the fold of the hem for a flat, crisp look or extends slightly beyond the fold for a soft, rolled look.

Hem Attachment.   Topstitched hems are specified, especially in casual garments and shirts that are worn tucked in, due to the appearance, cost effectiveness, and ease of the operation. (Topstitched hems are shown in Figures 10–7b and 10–22.) Topstitched hems are secure. Good-quality topstitched hems are smooth and flat. Because they are more noticeable than blindstitched hems, they serve as a decorative feature of the garment.

Most hem allowances in tailored and dress garments are attached to the garments with blindstitches (EFc). For durability, each blindstitch should fully catch a few yarns of the fabric but not take such a large bite that the stitches are highly visible on the outside of the garment (Figure 10–21); for this reason they are called **blind hems**. Some blindhemmers simultaneously finish the raw edge of the hem allowance with overedging (EFl). Good-quality blind hems are smooth and sewn in an inconspicuous thread color.

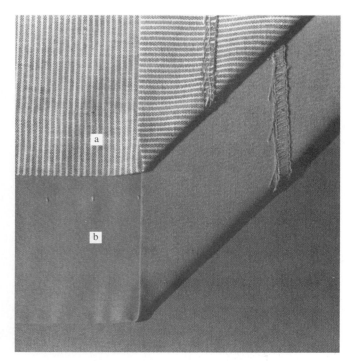

Figure 10–21 Blindstitched hems: (a) is less visible than (b).

Glued hems are common in expensive garments made of leather or leatherlike fabrics that could be weakened by the needle holes made when hems are stitched. Glued or fused hems also appear in some low-price garments, where they usually represent low quality because of poor durability and aesthetics.

Hem Width. **Hem allowances** (the amount turned under) in high-quality garments are wider than those in low-quality garments (Figure 10–7). Wide hem allowances require more fabric than narrow hem allowances, so they cost more. Patternmakers often reduce hem width in low-price garments when challenged to cut costs.

Wide folded hem allowances are desirable for several reasons that should be pointed out as benefits to consumers:

1. The garment tends to hang smoothly when weighted by a wide hem allowance.
2. A wide hem allowance can be let down to lengthen the garment to suit different people's personal preferences regarding garment length.
3. Wide hem allowances can be let down to conform to changing fashions.

Designers and patternmakers ultimately determine hem width based on three main factors: (1) the flare of the garment, (2) the weight of the fabric, and (3) the end use of the garment, balanced with cost limitations.

Garment Flare. Straight garments lend themselves to medium to wide hem allowances. Narrow hems in straight garments other than slacks usually appear skimpy and are often a mark of low quality. Consider a 2-inch hem as a quality standard in fairly straight skirts, dresses, pants, coats, and jackets; full-length coats may feature even wider hems. High-price or couture garments may feature hems slightly wider than 2 inches, denoting generous use of fabric. However, hems much wider than 3 inches are not usually recommended for aesthetic reasons.

Garments that flare require narrow hems; the more flare, the narrower the hem. Circular skirts may have hems as narrow as 1/8 inch or, instead of hems, have decorative stitches finishing their edges.

Medium and wide hem allowances on flared garments require special handling. The raw edge of the hem has a greater circumference than the garment at the level at which the hem is attached; thus, the excess circumference of the hem allowance must be eased or otherwise shaped to the garment. To ease the edge, it is easestitched, and the easestitching is pulled (see Chapter 5). The grainlines of the hem and the garment must be aligned so the hem edge lies smoothly, without pleats or tucks, against the garment. Eased hems are costly; they are used in high-price garments. If its edge is only slightly too full to fit the garment smoothly, a hem may be **wedged.** Tiny wedges of fabric are cut out and the hem edges lapped at the wedge to remove the fullness. This is common in men's pants when flared bottoms are popular. It contributes to quality if done neatly and if the cut edges do not ravel. As another alternative to easing, the hem may be **flanged.** Hem-allowance flanges, or projections below the hemline, are cut as a mirror image of the garment above the hemline. They enable the hem allowance edge to lie flat and smooth against the garment when folded up. Flanges also help create smooth hems in tapered areas, such as close-fitting sleeves or pant legs, when the hem allowance is too small to fit the garment without flanges.

Weight of Fabric. Garments of heavy fabrics do not require hem allowances as wide as those using lightweight fabrics. Heavyweight fabrics hang nicely with minimal hem widths, whereas thinner and less dense materials require the weight of wide hem allowances to hang gracefully. If the fabric is sheer and lightweight and the garment is fairly long, full, and straight, a hem width of up to 6 or 8 inches may be required On a long, gathered organza skirt, for example, a wide hem is needed to give the proper hang and to balance visually with the length of the garment.

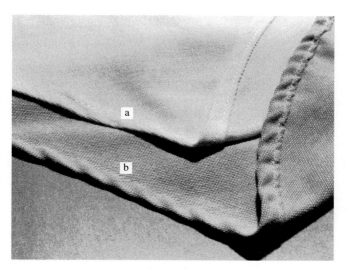

Figure 10–22   Shirttail hems: (a) is smoother than (b).

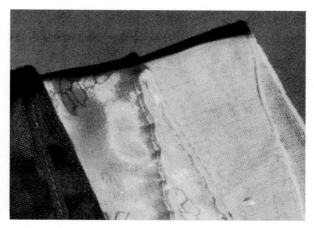

Figure 10–23   Rolled hems on scarves and a handkerchief.

End Use. Wide hems at the lower edge of garments are not always representative of high quality. Sometimes narrow hems are the preferred quality choice. For example, a wide hem on a shirttail that is tucked in is bulky and unnecessary. Hems on accessories like ruffles, scarves, or handkerchiefs also need not be wide; narrow hems are adequate to finish the edge without adding unwanted bulk. Although they reduce costs, narrow hems are a negative feature only if they sacrifice quality.

Shirttail Hems. A **shirttail hem** (EFb) is a narrow hem that is folded under twice and topstitched in place. Most shirttail hems on shirts are about 1/4 inch wide and feature a single row of stitches. Shirttail-style hems on dresses may be slightly wider than on shirts and, for decoration, sometimes feature two or more rows of stitching. Designers use shirttail hems on garments that have a lot of flare or an unusual shape, on garments worn tucked in such as shirts, and to give a casual look to clothing. A shirttail hem is durable and lower in cost than a wide hem because it requires little fabric. High-quality shirttail hems completely enclose the raw edge and are smooth and flat (Figure 10–22). However, bias edges on shaped shirttails often feed unevenly and stretch as they are sewn, distorting the finished shirttail hem. This detracts from the hem's appearance but is not critical if the garment is worn tucked in.

Rolled Hems. A **rolled hem** is a very narrow hem that is rolled up to enclose the raw edge of the hem (EFw), as shown in Figure 10–23. The roll of fabric, only about 1/8 inch wide, is secured to the garment with topstitching, blindstitching, or overedging. Designers select rolled hems to finish the edges of garments; ruffles and other garment details; and

scarves, handkerchiefs, and other accessories made of sheer or lightweight fabrics. Hand-rolled hems, secured with hand slipstitches, may be found in couture clothing.

Clean Finish. The **clean finish** is used occasionally in moderate- and high-quality garments to neatly and attractively finish edges inside the garment (Figure 10–24a). To create this finish, also called **turned and stitched,** the raw edge of the seam or hem allowance is folded under once and stitched (EFa). Essentially, a clean finish is a narrow hem on the edge. Clean finishes add bulk, so they are limited to light- and mediumweight fabrics. Nevertheless, when the garment is pressed, a ridge from the clean finish may make an impression on the outside of the garment. The clean finish impedes the progress of raveling. Clean finishing is costly in labor because it requires four passes through a sewing machine— (1) sewing the seam, (2) butterflying the seam allowances, and (3) and (4) stitching through the folded edge of each of the two seam allowances.

Booked Seams. **Booked seams** or **tailored seams** (SSba) are plain seams, butterflied, with the raw edges of the seam allowances folded under and blindstitched. Essentially, the seam allowances are narrowly hemmed (Figure 10–24b). Booked seams are common in unlined men's jackets. They are durable but costly in terms of labor because each seam requires four operations—(1) sewing the seam, (2) butterflying the seam, and (3) and (4) blindstitching the edges of each of the two seam allowances. Booked seams are somewhat bulky.

Miscellaneous EF Stitchings. *Overedging* (EFd) is the simplest and most common edge-finish stitching for seam allowances, hem allowances, and other raw edges inside the garment, for example, pocket bags

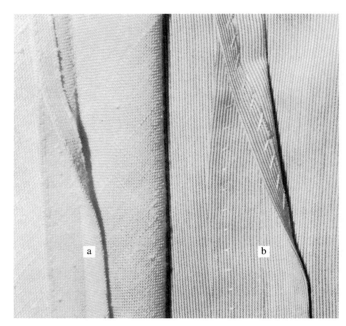

Figure 10–24   Seam-allowance finishes: (a) clean finish, and (b) booked seam.

Figure 10–25   Overedging used to finish raw edges of lapels and raw edges of center back seam allowances in designer-label wool jacket.

and facing edges. Overedging is used occasionally to finish and decorate edges visible on the outside of garments (Figure 10–25), but it is not generally considered as attractive as other edge treatments in such locations. Overedging, using 500-class stitches, trims the raw edge while simultaneously overcasting it with thread. It is an effective finish because it prevents raveling by covering the raw edge with thread interloopings but does not add much bulk. For example, the lower edges of infants' undershirts are sometimes overedged because they are softer and less bulky for babies to wear next to their skin than a bulky folded hem. Overedging is flexible and extensible. The handmade version of machine overedging, found in some couture garments, is **hand overcasting**; a series of evenly spaced, diagonal stitches cover the seam- or hem-allowance edges to retard raveling.

Decorative stitchings may substitute for overedging if an ornamental finish for the raw edge is desired. Figure 10–26 illustrates a few popular decorative stitchings used to finish garment edges. A series of stitches shaped, for example, as hearts, ducks, waves, or scallops can finish the edge. The **shell hem** features a scalloped effect created by a decorative shell stitch that attaches the narrow, folded hem allowance to the garment. It is used on lingerie and feminine clothing. A **lettuce-edge hem** is created by the operator, who stretches the edge as it is stitched so that it ripples attractively; the edge must be stretched consistently for even ripples. The lettuce edge is used on ruffles and hems of feminine-looking apparel. This type of edge styling happens also to demonstrate clearly *why*, under ordinary circumstances, fabrics should not be stretched as they are sewn, to avoid unwanted rippling.

Occasionally a spec technician selects *zigzag stitches* for raw edges. This can be effective but if used on lightweight fabrics, zigzagging tends to pucker the edge. A row of *straight stitches* may be sufficient to prevent the seam allowances of knit garments from curling. However, it impedes raveling to a very limited extent.

Other Edge Treatments

U.S. Fed. Std. No. 751a: Stitches, Seams, and Stitchings limits its discussion of edge finishes to stitchings (EF stitchings). This chapter goes beyond that narrow definition to encompass other edge treatments, including facings, bindings, bands, and plackets that are seamed to the garment to finish an edge.

Unstitched Finishes.   A simple method for finishing edges inside garments is to **pink** them; the edge is cut with a serrated blade (Figure 10–27a). Generally, only opaque fabrics are pinked because the serrations show through sheer or translucent fabrics. Pinking retards raveling but does not prevent it. It is an inexpensive, nonbulky edge finish, but it is rarely used now to finish seam allowances because overedging has been found to be more effective. A common place to see pinking is at the lower edge of men's pants that are unhemmed at the point of sale.

Production personnel *glue* seam and hem allowances flat in garments made of leather and

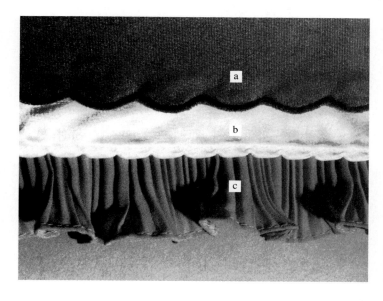

Figure 10–26 Decorative hem finishes: (a) scalloped hem, (b) shell hem, and (c) lettuce-edge hem.

leatherlike fabrics. In these cases, gluing is not considered a low-quality finish, as it would be on conventional fabrics. Because leather and leatherlike fabrics are bulky and cannot be pressed, gluing down and pounding the seam allowances flattens them in a desirable manner.

An edge finish used to a limited extent involves coating the raw edges with a heat-sensitive material that is *fused* to the edges with heat. This method is effective for preventing raveling but causes discomfort when the edges contact the wearer's skin. A *liquid plastic* applied to raw edges, which dries to prevent raveling, yields similar results.

Facings. A **facing** is any piece of fabric used to finish raw edges of the garment, for example, at the neckline, armscye, and front and back openings. The facing is turned to the inside of the garment so it backs the garment at the edge, facing the wearer. Facings are folded, or sewn to the garment using an enclosed seam. The three main types of facings are (1) extended facings, (2) shaped facings, and (3) bias facings.

Facings are the least conspicuous edge finish, because they are typically visible only inside the garment (except at folded-back edges, such as lapels). Occasionally a designer designs a facing to show on the outside of the garment for a novelty effect, but facings are usually designed to be seen only from inside the garment. For example, a man's shirt with a **French front** is faced at center front. The smooth French front draws less attention than a **button band** (also called a placket), the band of fabric at the center front of many men's shirts. (Button band and French front are shown in Chapter 12, Figure 12–17.)

Most facings are 2 to 3 inches wide. In low-price lines, facings may be cut narrower than 2 inches to conserve fabric. A common example is a neckline

facing in a blouse cut so narrow it slips out and shows when the garment is worn (Figure 10–28). In high-price lines, some facings may be cut considerably wider than 2 inches. For example, a facing at the center back neckline is sometimes cut several inches wide. The main advantage of a wide back neckline facing is that it looks attractive at the point of sale because it covers the inner construction otherwise visible when the garment is on a hanger. A wide facing also protects the fashion fabric of the garment from perspiration and body oils during wear. However, a wide facing requires extra fabric and does not necessarily provide greater quality; it may add unwanted bulk and create a visible line within the body of the garment. It can be difficult to keep in place if it shifts

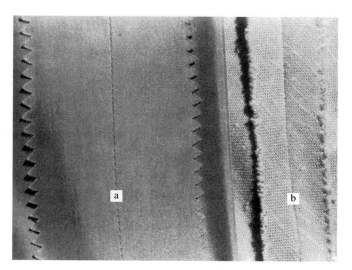

Figure 10–27 Seam allowance finishes: (a) pinked, and (b) no finish, because bias-cut edges do not ravel readily.

Figure 10–28   Too-narrow facing slips out and shows on outside of blouse.

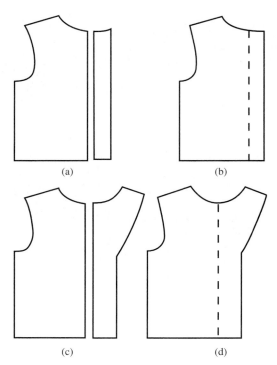

Figure 10–29   Center front facings: (a) shaped, and (b) extended. Combination center front and neckline facing: (c) shaped, and (d) extended.

during wear and may slip out and show on the out-side of the garment.

Facings in high-quality garments are tacked in place at seam allowances. Otherwise, the facing shifts position during wear and slips to show on the outside of the garment. If not topstitched, facings with enclosed seams require understitching or con-trol stitching (Figure 10–8). Either keeps the facing from slipping and showing on the outside of the garment. However, control stitching is generally confined to high-price garments. On some better garments, facings with enclosed seams also may be *slipped* or *bubbled*. (See discussion earlier in this chapter.)

Facings add to the cost of the garment because they require additional fabric and labor. However, the cost of facings varies depending on the type used.

Extended Facings.   The simplest type of facing is the **extended facing.** The fabric at the edge to be faced is extended and folded under (Figure 10–29b). An extended facing can be identified by the fold at the edge. The important characteristics are that ex-tended facings

1. require the least labor and add the least bulk of the facing types
2. are used less than shaped facings because they re-quire more fabric. As an extension of the garment piece, the addition of an extended facing often cre-ates a large and awkwardly shaped piece that

lowers material utilization. Low-price garments sometimes have extended facings that are nar-rowly cut in an effort to compact the layout and provide efficient material utilization.

3. can only be used to face straight edges—to finish front and back openings, and collars, cuffs, waist-bands, and other details with straight edges. The folded edge cannot conform to other shapes without pulling or buckling the garment.

Shaped Facings.   **Shaped facings** are fabric pieces shaped identically to the garment edges they face (Figure 10–29a). Shaped facings should be cut on the same grain as the garment piece they face so garment and facing conform to one another smoothly. The garment and facing are joined using an enclosed seam. Ideally, operators attach shaped facings in the round rather than flat. Shaped facings can be distin-guished from extended facings by the enclosed seam instead of a fold at the finished outer edge of shaped facings (Figure 10–30b).

Shaped facings are usually cut from the same fabric as the garment unless the garment is made from a very heavy or bulky fabric. In such cases, the facing is cut from a fabric lighter in weight than the garment but of a matching color. Shaped facings in high-quality garments are usually interfaced for body and support. Shaped facings

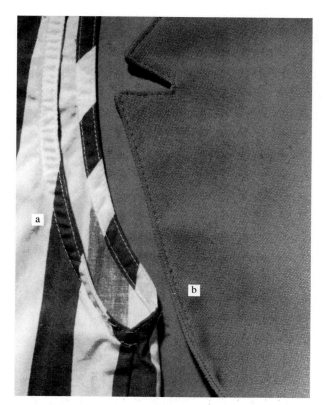

Figure 10–30 Facings: (a) bias facing at armhole, and (b) shaped facing (note enclosed seam at edge).

1. are ideal for finishing unusually shaped necklines or hems and sleeveless armholes because they conform to any shape, including sharp corners and curves
2. require less fabric than extended facings because the separate pieces are laid out to better advantage
3. allow collar or trim to be sewn to the edge before it is faced because shaped facings are sewn on, not folded back
4. require more fabric for curved than for straight pieces. For example, shaped facings at the waistline cost more than straight waistbands but about the same as contour waistbands.
5. do not absorb stress well when curved because they are cut on the bias rather than on the straight-of-grain. The stretch introduced by the bias areas of the facing should be reinforced to prevent loss of shape in those areas. For example, manufacturers stay bias-faced waistbands with a strong, nonstretch tape to prevent it from stretching out of shape during wear.

Sometimes patternmakers combine a shaped facing with an extended facing to create a **combination facing.** For example, they combine the extended facing at the center front of a blouse with the shaped facing that fits the neckline (Figure 10–29c and d).

Combination facings reduce bulk and lower labor costs but require more fabric than shaped facings.

Bias Facings. **Bias facings** are narrow, bias strips of fabric used to face raw edges (Figure 10–30a). The narrow bias strips are sewn to the raw edges to be faced and turned to the inside of the garment. The lower edge of the bias strip is turned under (usually) and then topstitched, blindstitched, or tacked to the garment to form a neat, inconspicuous facing, usually no more than about half an inch wide. Bias facings

1. require little fabric; bias facings are economically cut from the fashion fabric or purchased as a precut notion.
2. require no patternmaking and no interfacing, thus being more cost efficient than other facing types
3. are useful for sheer fabrics; if they show through, they do not interfere with the appearance of the garment because they are so narrow.
4. are low in bulk and thus suitable for garments made of heavy or bulky fabrics
5. are not well-suited for use on intricately shaped edges with sharp corners or curves because of the difficulty and cost in applying them to such edges; patternmakers face these with shaped facings.

Bindings. A **binding** covers the raw edge of the garment with a strip of fabric that is visible from both inside and outside the garment (Figures 10–15 and 10–16). The federal standard categorizes bindings as seams (BS) because they join together two or more pieces of fabric; thus bindings were discussed earlier in this chapter in the discussion of seam types. However, bindings are often used as an edge finish, so they are discussed again briefly in this section. Edges may be *bound* by any of the methods discussed earlier in this chapter. The best bindings are nonraveling, nonbulky, and comfortable, and match or coordinate with color of the fabric. Bindings may be decorative as well as functional, especially if they contrast with the color of the garment. Bindings can be distinguished from bands because *bindings cover but do not extend garment edges.*

Designers use bindings to decoratively finish outer garment edges such as necklines, armholes, front and back opening edges, and the lower edges of the garment and sleeves. Because bindings look the same from both sides, they are a common choice for finishing the outer edges of reversible garments. Bound seams cannot be let out if the garment requires altering.

Bound seam allowances (SSbh) and hem allowances look attractive inside a garment, add strength to the edges, and prevent raveling and abrasion. However, seams and hems with bound allowances are often quite stiff and bulky, and their

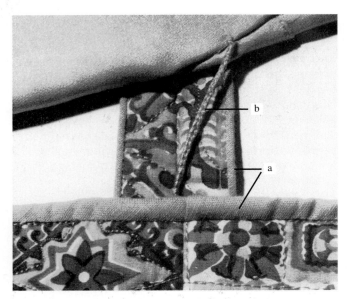

Figure 10–31 (a) Hong Kong bindings on seam and hem allowances, and (b) swing tack between garment and free-hanging lining.

impression sometimes presses through to the outside of the garment. Bound seam and hem allowances are costly in terms of both materials and labor; they are only found in expensive garments. An unlined garment with bound seam allowances costs more and represents higher quality than a fully lined garment in which narrow seam allowances and poor construction are covered by the lining.

A **Hong Kong binding** is a very narrow bias strip, often color-contrasting or shiny, used to decoratively bind seam and hem allowances and other edges inside high-price tailored and couture garments (Figure 10–31a). The binding strip is seamed to the edge, folded around, and stitched in the ditch (BSf). Hong Kong binding is an elegant, costly finish that is valued for its ornamental appearance.

Edges are occasionally *self-bound*. One seam allowance is extended, wrapped around the shorter seam allowance, and stitched in place.

Bands. **Bands** are pieces of fabric seamed usually to the straight raw edges of garments to extend and finish the edge. Bands are used mostly on outer garment edges. Bands can be differentiated from bindings because (1) bands extend beyond the edge they finish, and (2) bands are generally wider than bindings.

A band consists of a single piece of fabric folded lengthwise or of two pieces, the band and its facing. Collars, cuffs, and waistbands are all examples of bands (see Chapter 5). Other examples are the rib-knit bands at sweatshirt hems, necklines, and wrists. For these bands, a strip of rib-knit fabric is folded in half and sewn to the garment. The crosswise direction

of the knit fabric, the most stretchy direction, runs around the body, neck, or wrist so it can stretch when the garment is put on and taken off but return to original size and smoothness when the garment is worn. In some garments, single-layer knit bands are used instead of folded bands; the bands are knitted with a finished outer edge.

A useful technique for applying bands is to seam the garment, seam the band, and then join the two together in the round. However, in lower-price garments the band is usually joined to the garment while the two are in flat form and then both are joined into a circle. (Both techniques are shown in Chapter 12, Figure 12–7.) This finish is inexpensive, but the final seam shows at the edge, detracting from the garment's appearance; the seam is also subject to unraveling. Circular bands may be cut from tubular fabrics or knit into the correct circumference to fit the garment. This eliminates the need for seaming the band to fit, but different-size bands must be knit for each size garment produced. Such bands at the necklines of T-shirts, sweatshirts, and sweaters are sometimes called *collarettes*.

A band should be uniform in width throughout and of the correct length for the edge to which it is attached. Sewing operators stretch bands applied to concave curves to prevent ripples at the outer edge; for example, T-shirt necklines gape if they are not stretched slightly as they are sewn. Operators ease bands applied to convex curves to prevent pulling at the outer edge. The wider the band and the sharper the curve of the garment edge, the more need for stretching or easing the band to fit. If the band is made from a firm material that does not lend itself to stretching or easing, a shaped band with facing is required for curved applications. Bands applied to corners or points require mitering or seaming to remove excess fullness at the angles and to shape the band to the corner or point (Figure 10–32).

Figure 10–32 Mitered band.

Figure 10–33 (a) true band, and (b) topstitching imitating band.

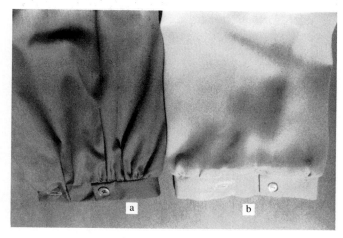

Figure 10–34 Horizontal plackets: (a) better if invisibly stitched and with pleat, than (b) topstitched and without pleat.

Sometimes designers simulate the look of a band by topstitching the garment at approximately the width of a band (Figure 10–33b) or by turning a facing to the outside of the garment rather than the inside and topstitching it in place.

Plackets. A **placket** is a finished garment opening that allows a body part to pass through for dressing and undressing. Plackets are required when the garment opening is closely fitted and does not stretch. They open necklines, waistlines, and sleeves, for example, so that garments can be put on and taken off easily. A fitted cuff with an opening to fit over the hand requires a coordinating placket opening in the sleeve. A shirt with a fitted collar requires a placket at the neckline to pull the garment over the head. A pair of fitted pants requires a placket opening at the waistline to pull the garment on and off over the hips. The fly front zipper placket common to jeans and men's pants is discussed in Chapter 11.

Placket edges may be hemmed, faced, bound, or banded. The resulting opening edges are closed by lapping, abutting, or superimposing the finished edges and fastening them with a closure.

Slashed Plackets. Manufacturers sometimes cut a slash in a garment and turn under the raw edges of the slash to form a placket. This method is suitable only when the fabric does not ravel readily. It is not durable unless the point of the placket has been reinforced.

Horizontal Plackets. A **horizontal placket** is so named because it is constructed in a horizontal direction, parallel to the opening. Horizontal plackets are used almost exclusively on sleeves, where they provide a simple, low-cost opening. Two clips are made, 1 or 2 inches apart, in the lower edge of the sleeve and then the area is narrowly hemmed to create a finished opening (Figure 10–34). If the area has reinforcement stitching, and if the raw edge is overcast and blindstitched in place, the horizontal placket is quite inconspicuous and secure. If the raw edge is merely topstitched in place, the horizontal placket is conspicuous and possibly not secure.

Horizontal plackets are suitable for sheer fabrics and informal wear where a narrow, discreet placket is desired. They are not desirable if the wearer wants to roll or push the sleeves up on the arms, because the horizontal placket provides less roominess than longer, vertical plackets. Also, the horizontal placket tends to slip out and show on the outside of the garment unless a small pleat is stitched in, a detail found in high-quality garments (Figure 10–34a). Horizontal plackets are found in garments in all price lines, in budget apparel because of the low cost and in other apparel when a nearly invisible placket is required.

Faced Plackets. **Faced plackets** are made by cutting a straight or shaped slash in the fabric perpendicular to the edge of the garment; the slash is faced with a rectangle of fabric sewn on with an enclosed seam (Figure 10–35a). If the slash is pointed, the point should be reinforced to prevent a hole from forming. Excess seam allowances at the point prevent the placket from turning smoothly and cause puckering

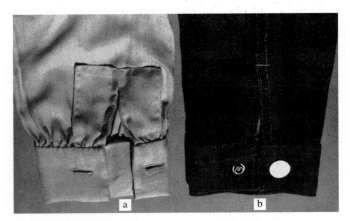

Figure 10–35   Plackets: (a) faced, and (b) in-seam.

Figure 10–36   Continuous-bound plackets: (a) with diagonal row of stitches at upper end, and (b) without a row of diagonal stitches at upper end, allowing placket to slip out and show on outside of garment.

at the point. A faced placket is fairly simple to produce, but the facing creates unwanted bulk in heavy fabrics and shows through sheer fabrics. The facing tends to slip out and show on the outside of the garment; topstitching, control stitching, or tacking prevents this.

Faced plackets are most often found at necklines that close with a single button at the top of the placket. They are occasionally used on sleeves.

Continuous Bound Plackets. The **continuous-bound placket** is one of the most widely used sleeve plackets (Figure 10–36); it is rarely used in other locations. The operator binds a vertical slash in the lower edge of the sleeve with a narrow strip of fabric. To avoid puckers or a hole at the point of the placket (two common defects), the point of the slash should be reinforced with stitching, and the binding must be stitched on accurately. A well-made continuous-bound placket is attractive and durable. This type of placket is somewhat bulky and should not be used in heavy fabrics.

The continuous-bound placket has a tendency to slip out and show on the outside of the garment. A diagonal row of stitches or a bar tack through the upper end of the finished placket prevents this. These stitches should be placed through all layers of the binding to keep it inside the garment (Figure 10–36a). The absence of a row of diagonal stitches or a bar tack inside a continuous-bound placket detracts from quality.

The side of the placket connected to the overlap side of the cuff should be turned under. The side of the placket connected to the underlap side of the cuff should lie flat.

In-Seam Plackets.   The **in-seam placket** is the simplest and least expensive placket to construct (Figure 10–35b). It is mainly used on sleeves and occasionally

at necklines and on pant legs. A seam entering the opening at the desired position for a placket is left unsewn for the last 3 inches or so. The operator finishes the seam allowance edges by clean finishing or overedging and then blindstitches or topstitches them in place. The placket should be bar tacked or otherwise reinforced at the seamed end for durability.

The chief disadvantage of in-seam plackets for most sleeves is that the cuff buttons are underneath the wrist, rather than on the outside of the wrist as required. This makes them inconvenient to button, unattractive, and uncomfortable when the arm is rested on a hard surface. However, when an in-seam placket is used in garments with two-piece sleeves, the placket is positioned correctly. Although they represent low quality when used on garments with one-piece sleeves, in-seam plackets are often used in high-quality leather and denim jackets with two-piece sleeves. In fact, the **sleeve vents** at the wrist of high-quality tailored suit and sport jacket sleeves are a form of hemmed in-seam placket.

Tailored Plackets.   The **tailored placket** consists of a bound slash (Figure 10–37). The overlap portion of the slash is bound with a topstitched strip of fabric. The overlap hides the underlap, which is bound with a narrower strip of fabric. The placket is

Figure 10–37 Tailored plackets: (a) with gauntlet button, and (b) without gauntlet button. Note that cuff on (a) has a single button, and (b) has two buttons so cuff can be loosened or tightened to alter sleeve length slightly.

usually interfaced and the end is topstitched for re-inforcement. Designers use the tailored placket on men's dress shirts (it is sometimes called the **shirt sleeve placket**) and on some casual women's blouse and dress sleeves. Variations of the tailored placket are used at the necklines of polo-style knit shirts.

The tailored placket is the most complex and costly placket to manufacture. It requires more fabric pieces and more labor than other placket types. In most cases, the production of tailored plackets on shirt sleeves is automated; automation reduces costs and produces more consistent results than manually made plackets. Poorly made plackets have holes, tucks, or puckers.

Tailored plackets draw more attention than other placket types and are an important style detail of a garment. They provide the longest opening of all placket types, allowing sleeves to be rolled up on the arm easily.

An extra button and buttonhole, the **gauntlet button,** placed on the tailored placket prevents it from gaping (Figure 10–37a). Gauntlet buttons also aid in keeping sleeves in place if they are rolled up.

The gauntlet button adds a touch of quality as well as extra cost to a placket.

SUMMARY

Seams are the joints between fabric pieces. The most common seam defects are puckering (lack of smooth-ness), raw edges, breaking (rupturing), slippage, and grinning. U.S. Fed. Std. No. 751a: Stitches, Seams, and Stitchings contains four classes of seams: SS su-perimposed seams, LS lapped seams, BS bound seams, and FS flat seams. Superimposed seams, the most common type, are layers of fabric plies stacked on top of one another and sewn together. They in-clude plain seams, used for most major garment seams. Butterflied plain seams, with seam allowances pressed open, cost more but are less bulky than seams which are not butterflied. Enclosed seams, su-perimposed seams used at garment edges, should be pressed and possibly control stitched so the lower ply does not slip out and show. The French seam, a seam within a seam, and the mock French seam, which looks similar, are other superimposed seams. Lapped seams are made by lapping the fabric ply edges; there are more different types of lapped seams than of any other seam class. Besides simple lapped seams, they include flat-felled seams, which enclose all the raw edges, and mock flat-felled seams, which look sim-ilar. Other lapped seams include tuck seams, slot seams, and welt seams. Bound seams are made by binding the edge of a fabric with a fabric strip; they are used only at raw edges. Flat seams are usually made by abutting the edges of the fabric ply and joining them with cover stitches. They are appro-priate for use only on nonraveling fabrics.

In general, complex seams are durable but create unwanted bulk and increase costs. Seams with raw edges may have edge finishes to prevent raveling and improve appearance; edge finishes often add strength to the seam but increase costs and add unwanted bulk. Wide seam allowances also make seams durable and provide ease of alteration but increase costs; narrow seam allowances are appropriate in enclosed seams. Some seams have stays, nonstretch fabric strips, that reinforce the seam and prevent stretch and distortion.

The main purpose of edge treatments is to finish raw edges both inside and outside the garment. Edge treatments should complement the appearance of the garment and prevent raveling without adding unnec-essary bulk.

Hems, the most common edge treatment, are cate-gorized as an edge-finish stitching by the U.S. Fed. Std. No. 751a. The edge is turned under and stitched to the garment. Wide hem allowances generally indicate high quality. Appropriate hem width, however, depends on the flare of the garment, the weight of the fabric, and the end use of the garment. Other edge-finish stitchings include overedging and other stitches, sometimes decorative.

Facings are visible only inside the garment. They are either extended, shaped, or bias. Extended facings are a folded-under extension of the garment edge. Shaped facings are the same shape as the garment edge being faced. Bias facings are narrow, inconspicuous, and low cost. Bindings enclose raw edges with a strip of fabric; they are classified as seams by U.S. Fed. Std. No. 751a. Bands are strips of fabric that cover and extend garment edges. Bands are generally wider than bindings.

Plackets are finished garment-opening edges; for example, in sleeves, necklines, and waistlines. Plackets may be hemmed, faced, bound, or banded. Horizontal plackets are inconspicuous. The facing of faced plackets tends to slip out and show. Continuous-bound plackets should be diagonally stitched at the upper end to keep the placket inside the garment. In-seam plackets are appropriate on necklines and two-piece sleeves where a seam occurs at the desired position for the placket. Tailored plackets are the most complex and costly placket to construct. A gauntlet button on a tailored placket prevents it from gaping.

Seam and Edge Treatment Quality Checklist

If you can answer yes to each of these questions regarding the garment you are evaluating, it contains high-quality seams and edge treatments.

✔ Are the seams and edge treatments appropriate to the fabric, end use, and price line of the garment?

✔ Is the seam type resistant to raw edge, broken seam, seam slippage, and seam grin?

✔ Are the seams nonbulky and free of puckers?

✔ Are stitches accurately placed on the seamline?

✔ Are plain seams pressed flat and enclosed seams pressed to their full dimension to avoid channels? As an extra quality feature, are the seam allowances of plain seams pressed open (butterflied)?

✔ Are the facings of enclosed seams concealed by pressing and topstitching or control stitching?

✔ Are seams that are subjected to high stress or stretch reinforced?

✔ Are seam allowances wide enough to withstand the wear and care of the garment without adding excessive bulk?

✔ Do the seam allowances and other edges have edge finishes, if needed? Do edge finishes prevent raveling of woven fabrics and curling of knit fabrics without adding excessive bulk?

✔ Are all edge finishes even, flat, and nonbulky? Are curves smooth and points sharp?

✔ Is the hem width appropriate to the amount of garment taper or flare, fabric weight, and garment style?

✔ If the garment is tapered or flared and the hem is wide, is the hem allowance eased, flanged, or wedged to help it lie smoothly?

✔ Is the hem attached with close, secure, inconspicuous stitches?

✔ If the garment is tailored, are hems interfaced?

✔ Are shaped and extended facings about 2 inches in width?

✔ Are facing edges invisible from the outside of the garment? Are they tacked in position at seams and other anchor points? In high-price garments, are facings slipped or bubbled?

✔ Do bindings completely cover raw edges? Are bands and bindings stretched slightly around concave curves and eased around convex curves? Are they mitered at corners?

✔ Is control stitching used on facings with a tendency to slip out and show on the outside of the garment?

✔ Are horizontal plackets and continuous-bound plackets tacked to prevent them from slipping out and showing on the outside of the garment?

✔ Do tailored plackets have a gauntlet button?

New Terms

If you can define each of these terms and differentiate between related terms, you have gained a good working vocabulary for discussing the topics in this chapter. The terms are listed in the order in which they appeared in the chapter.

seam
seam line
seam allowance/margin
seam pucker
raw edge
broken seam/broken stitches
seam slippage
seam grin
superimposed seam (SS)
plain seam
butterflied/busted
enclosed seam
grade/blend/layer/bevel
control stitching/understitching
French seam
mock French/false French seam

lapped seam (LS)
flat-felled seam
mock flat-felled/mock fell seam
tuck seam
slot seam
welt seam
bound seam (BS)
stitched in the ditch/crack stitched
mitering
flat seam (FS)/butt seam/exposed seam
stay
taped seam
stripped seam
strapped seam
directional stitching
edge treatment/finish
stitching
edge-finish stitching (EF)
folded hem
blind hem
hem allowance
wedged hem
flanged hem
shirttail hem
rolled hem
clean finish/turned and stitched
booked/tailored seam
hand overcasting
shell hem
lettuce-edge hem
pink
facing
French front
button band
extended facing
shaped facing
combination facing
bias facing
binding
Hong Kong binding
band
placket
horizontal placket
faced placket
continuous-bound placket
in-seam placket
sleeve vent
tailored placket/shirt sleeve placket
gauntlet button

Review Questions

1. What are the main causes of seam pucker?
2. List the four main seam classes in U.S. Fed. Std.

No. 751a and summarize the performance advantages and disadvantages of each.
3. What are the advantages of butterflied seams? Why are butterflied seams more costly than those that are not pressed open?
4. When are French seams desirable?
5. What are the four main types of seam failure?
6. List three seam locations that are frequently stayed.
7. Why are wide hems generally desirable? In what circumstances are narrow hems appropriate?
8. How is a shirttail hem different from a rolled hem? In what types of garments is each type of hem appropriate?
9. What might be responsible for a band rippling or pulling at its outer edge?
10. How does a row of diagonal stitches or a bar tack at the end of a continuous-bound placket contribute to quality?

Activities

1. Find examples of the following seam failures:
   a. raw edge
   b. seam grin
   c. seam slippage
   d. seam pucker

   What would you recommend to avoid these problems?
2. Find garments containing examples of each major seam class and the main types within each class. Explain how the configuration of each type is different from the others.
3. Visit an apparel manufacturer. Find out
   a. what types of seams they use
   b. how they decide which seam types to use
   c. what machines are required to make each seam type
   d. whether any seams are butterflied. Why or why not?
4. Examine the seam types in low-price and high-price garments in the following classifications:
   a. women's suits
   b. men's sport coats
   c. men's pants
   d. T-shirts
   e. jeans
   f. formal dresses
   g. children's play clothes
   h. lingerie

   What differences, if any, did you find? Is seam type determined by price? By classification of merchandise? By location within the garment? By fabric type?

5. Compare a flat-felled seam with a mock flat-felled seam. Which is more durable?

6. Miter the corner of a piece of paper. Turn under both edges of another corner. Compare the appropriateness and bulkiness of the two methods.

7. Study the Union Special Corporation Technical Training Center's *Garment Construction Guide* (see examples in Figures 9–1, 11–1, 11–2, 11–16, and 12–1.) How many different seam types are used in constructing
   a. a dress shirt
   b. children's underwear
   c. bib overalls
   d. a wool skirt
   e. a trench coat

8. Choose a garment from your wardrobe and write seam specifications to duplicate it.

9. Examine the hems in low-end and high-end garments in the following classifications:
   a. dresses
   b. men's dress shirts
   c. wool coats
   d. T-shirts
   e. men's pants
   f. women's pants

What differences, if any, did you find in hem width? Is hem width determined by price line? Fabric weight? Garment style? What differences, if any, did you find in hem attachment? Is method of hem attachment (i.e., topstitched vs. blindstitched) determined by price line? Fabric weight? Garment style?

10. Find a garment with an example of a binding and another with an example of a band. How are the two edge treatments the same? How are they different?

11. Find garments with examples of an extended facing, a shaped facing, and a bias facing. What are the advantages and disadvantages of each?

12. Find examples of the following placket types:
    a. horizontal
    b. continuous-bound
    c. in-seam
    d. tailored, on sleeve
    e. tailored, at neckline

Which type required the most fabric and labor? The least? What is the most appropriate application for each? Evaluate the quality of each.

Preliminary Garment Assembly: Parts and Panels

Chapter Objectives

1. Identify industry production flow process for preliminary garment assembly.
2. Evaluate cost and quality of various assembly procedures.

A review of the Production Cycle found in Chapter 4 illustrates that garment assembly is only one facet of the apparel production process. It is, however, critical in the production process because this is the stage where a product is created. Good design and fine-quality raw materials alone do not constitute a quality product. To support and enhance the design and raw materials, appropriate and properly executed production techniques are required. If this does not happen, the best design and highest-quality raw materials can be downgraded by inappropriate and improperly executed production methods. Lack of attention during the assembly process can make or break the most well intentioned company. (For more information, see Related Resources: Mass Production/ Assembly.)

As discussed in Chapter 4, apparel is mass produced in a sequence that can be summarized by the *four Ps, "Parts, Panels, Pieces, and Products"* or the equations **"Parts + Panels = Pieces"** and **"Pieces + Pieces = Products."** This concept provides the framework for this and the following chapter. Chapter 11 discusses the first part of the equation, "Parts + Panels = Pieces," and Chapter 12 covers the second part of the equation, "Pieces + Pieces = Products." Knowledge of apparel analysis is not complete without an understanding of the processes represented by both the equations.

The specific **construction sequence** for assembling a particular apparel product varies depending on the product and the manufacturer making it.

However, all garments are assembled according to this general scheme (see Table 11–1). For more information, see the Union Special Corporation Technical Training Center's *Garment Construction Guide*, which contains examples of many different types of garments and the suggested sequence of construction

Table 11-1   The Four Ps of Garment Construction: Parts, Panels, Pieces and Products

Parts Assembly

Edges serged

Labels attached

Decorative stitchings added

Trims added

Zippers applied

Pockets constructed

Belt loops added

Miscellaneous loops added

Interfacing applied

Underlining attached

Reinforcements applied

Panel Assembly

Darts

Pleats

Tucks

Ease

Gathers

Seams

Elastic

Hems

Other edge treatments

Piece Assembly

Collar set

Sleeves set

Cuffs set

Waistband set

Shoulder pads attached

Lining applied

Product Assembly and Finishing

Buttons attached

Buttonholes/Button loops made

Snap fasteners applied

Hooks and eyes attached

Miscellaneous closures applied

Finish pressing done

Note. The 4 Ps defined here convey the general idea of a typical sequence of operations used to construct a garment. However, the actual manufacturing sequence for a particular garment varies depending on the type of garment and the manufacturer.

for each. Some of these examples are included in this chapter and in Chapter 12. Note that some garments are so simple they require no preliminary assembly; this allows the panels to be constructed directly into products. An example is underwear as shown in Figure 11–1.

PARTS ASSEMBLY

Before garment assembly can take place, small parts must be prepared (Figure 11–2). These **preliminary assembly** operations include serging raw edges of parts or panels, attaching labels, applying decorative stitchings such as embroidery, attaching trims, partially making zippers, constructing pockets, making belt loops as well as other miscellaneous loops, and applying interfacing and underlining. Once garment parts are made and inspected, they are then ready to be attached to panels or incorporated directly into the garment.

Serging Raw Edges

As discussed in Chapter 10, most garment edges require some type of finish, and the most common type is serging. The edges of many pieces and panels can be serged most efficiently while still in flat form, before any assembly takes place, so this is often one of the first operations performed in the production of a garment. Operators feed pieces or panels into a serger, where the edges are overcast with thread to prevent raveling. Some manufacturers have automated this simple but important process.

Attaching Labels

Spec technicians specify label position and attachment method. These instructions are part of the garment specifications and are some of the first operations performed in most apparel assembly. The terms used to describe label type vary according to supplier and manufacturer; however, they refer to five basic types of labels. Ready-to-wear apparel usually contains one or more of (1) cut-and-fold labels, (2) loop labels, (3) single labels, (4) mitered labels, and (5) four-side sew labels (see Figure 11–3).

Cut-and-fold labels are most often used in the center back of a garment. They are attached on two ends directly to the facing or the back panel. Each of the two stitched ends has been folded about 3/8 inch and the folded end caught securely under the stitching. Back tacking two or three stitches on both rows of stitching is important for attaching a secure label.

Loop labels and *single labels* are used extensively on both tops and bottoms of garments. They are sewn into the seam as the seam is sewn. The loop label is folded (looped) in half, the top two edges inserted into the seam, and the seam and label are sewn as one. Single labels follow the same process without folding the label.

Mitered labels, used primarily on tops and outerwear, are also sewn in the seam. Both ends of the labels are folded with a mitered corner, slipped into the seam, and sewn as one with the seam.

Four-side-sew labels are used primarily on shirts and outerwear. They are applied as the name describes; labels are sewn on all four sides. Back tacking is not necessary on a four-side-sew label if an oversew is taken for two or three stitches. Some highly automated manufacturing plants have equipment to stitch four-side-sew labels automatically using either single-needle machines or tacking machines.

Care labels need to be securely attached for the life of the garment, according to federal regulations. Manufacturers want their brand identification and other labels to be attached equally securely. For these reasons, most labels are sewn into the apparel product. It costs less to sew a label into a seam than to sew a label flat to a section of the garment. In-seam labels sewn as a loop are less apt to roll but cost more to apply than single-layer labels. Glued labels generally indicate a low-price product. Labels attached with monofilament thread can irritate skin (as can some labels; see Chapter 8). Astute manufacturers monitor consumer comfort as part of the garment development process and avoid choices that could cause skin discomfort. Relocation of care and fiber identification labels within a garment to improve comfort is not an option because specific positioning of these labels is regulated by the FTC. However, positioning of brand and marketing labels is left up to the apparel designer and spec technician (see Chapter 2).

Adding Decorative Details

The right decorative details, properly executed, greatly enhance the attractiveness of the garment. While decorative details add to manufacturing costs, they also contribute to salability. However, a poorly chosen, sloppily executed, or unnecessary detail may destroy an otherwise attractive appearance. A decorative detail may also enhance garment function. For example, a fancy belt loop serves as both an aesthetic and a functional detail. Decorative details should be in character with the style and end use of the garment and with the weight and type of fabric. They should be able to withstand the wear and care to which the garment is subjected. The choice of decorative details is strongly influenced by fashion trends, balanced with cost limitations.

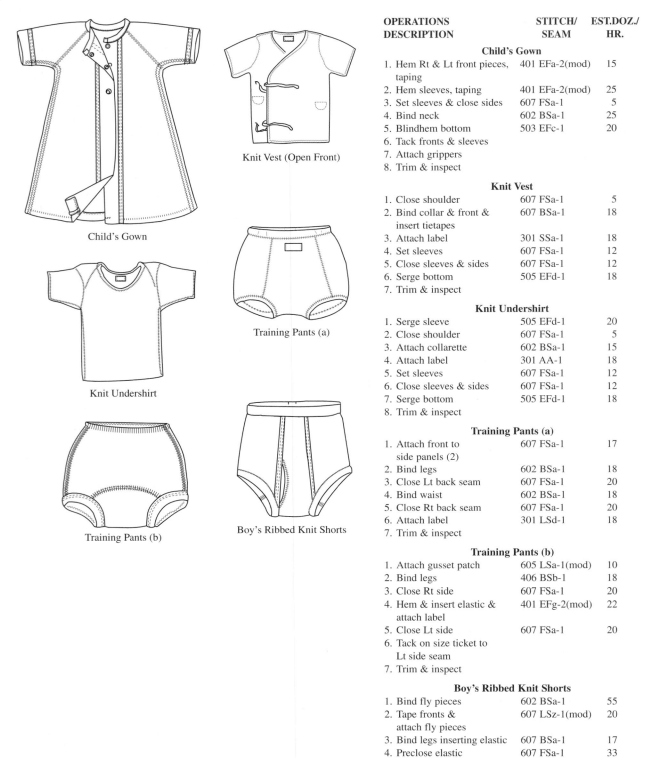

OPERATIONS DESCRIPTION	STITCH/ SEAM	EST.DOZ./ HR.
Child's Gown		
1. Hem Rt & Lt front pieces, taping	401 EFa-2(mod)	15
2. Hem sleeves, taping	401 EFa-2(mod)	25
3. Set sleeves & close sides	607 FSa-1	5
4. Bind neck	602 BSa-1	25
5. Blindhem bottom	503 EFc-1	20
6. Tack fronts & sleeves		
7. Attach grippers		
8. Trim & inspect		
Knit Vest		
1. Close shoulder	607 FSa-1	5
2. Bind collar & front & insert tietapes	607 BSa-1	18
3. Attach label	301 SSa-1	18
4. Set sleeves	607 FSa-1	12
5. Close sleeves & sides	607 FSa-1	12
6. Serge bottom	505 EFd-1	18
7. Trim & inspect		
Knit Undershirt		
1. Serge sleeve	505 EFd-1	20
2. Close shoulder	607 FSa-1	5
3. Attach collarette	602 BSa-1	15
4. Attach label	301 AA-1	18
5. Set sleeves	607 FSa-1	12
6. Close sleeves & sides	607 FSa-1	12
7. Serge bottom	505 EFd-1	18
8. Trim & inspect		
Training Pants (a)		
1. Attach front to side panels (2)	607 FSa-1	17
2. Bind legs	602 BSa-1	18
3. Close Lt back seam	607 FSa-1	20
4. Bind waist	602 BSa-1	18
5. Close Rt back seam	607 FSa-1	20
6. Attach label	301 LSd-1	18
7. Trim & inspect		
Training Pants (b)		
1. Attach gusset patch	605 LSa-1(mod)	10
2. Bind legs	406 BSb-1	18
3. Close Rt side	607 FSa-1	20
4. Hem & insert elastic & attach label	401 EFg-2(mod)	22
5. Close Lt side	607 FSa-1	20
6. Tack on size ticket to Lt side seam		
7. Trim & inspect		
Boy's Ribbed Knit Shorts		
1. Bind fly pieces	602 BSa-1	55
2. Tape fronts & attach fly pieces	607 LSz-1(mod)	20
3. Bind legs inserting elastic	607 BSa-1	17
4. Preclose elastic	607 FSa-1	33
5. Attach elastic to waist	407 LSa-1	17
6. Close inseam	607 FSa-1	28
7. Tack legs		
8. Trim & inspect		

Child's Gown · Knit Vest (Open Front) · Knit Undershirt · Training Pants (a) · Training Pants (b) · Boy's Ribbed Knit Shorts

Figure 11–1 Sequence of construction for children's underwear. *(Courtesy of Union Special Corporation Technical Training Center.)*

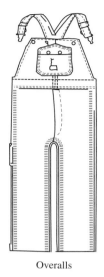

Overalls

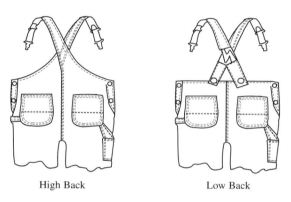

High Back   Low Back

OPERATIONS DESCRIPTION	STITCH/ SEAM	EST.DOZ./ HR.
Parts Assembly		
1. Make hammer loop	406 EFh-1	50
2. Hem pocket flap	301 EFa-2	20
3. Hem bib pocket piece	301 EFa-2	30
4. Join bib pocket pieces	301 LSa-1(mod)	30
5. Tack label to bib pocket		18
6. Attach lining to inner bib pocket	301 SSv-2	16
7. Hem bib pocket	301 EFa-2	16
8. Attach grippers to bib pocket & flap		35
9. Decorative stitch hip pockets	401 OSa-2	18
10. Hem hip & tool pockets	401 EFb-2(inv)	18
11. Hem Rt watch pocket facing	401 EFa-2(inv)	25
12. Sew facings to front pockets	602 (mod)LSa-1	13
13. Bag front pocket	515 SSa-2	18
14. Buttonhole Lt fly piece		12
Panel Assembly		
15. Join bib pieces	401 LSc-3	25
16. Attach bib facing	401 LSk-2	18
17. Set bib pocket, flap & stitch pencil pocket	301 SSv-2	12
18. Bartack pocket		12
19. Attach topstitch Lt fly & hem crotch	301 SSa,LSd,EFb-1	10
20. Attach Rt fly	301 SSa, LSd-1	12
21. Set front swing pocket	301 SSp-2	12
22. Stay pocket top & side	301 SSa-1	15
23. Crotch seam	301 LSas-2	15
24. Hem & make straps	401 EFp-2	12
25. Attach button facing to side	301 SSc-1	6
26. Set tool, rule & hip pockets & insert hammer loop	301 LSd-2	5
27. Sew seat seam	401 LSc-3	15
28. Make diamond	301 SSa-2	10
Pieces Assembly		
29. Join bib to front	401 LSl-3	12
30. Hem sides	301 EFb-1	5
31. Sew side seam & inseam, inserting hammer loop	401 LSc-3	4
32. Hem legs	401 EFb-1(inv)	12
33. Bartack fly & pockets		8
Product Assembly/Finishing		
34. Buttonhole sides & bib		7
35. Attach tack button		6
36. Attach hardware & trim & inspect		10

Figure 11–2   Sequence of construction for bib overalls, with parts sequence highlighted. *(Courtesy of Union Special Corporation Technical Training Center.)*

Decorative details include decorative stitchings, such as topstitching, edgestitching, and embroidery, including monograms, cutwork, and trapunto. Decorative details also include narrow fabric trims such as lace, ribbon, and braid; fabric appliqués; and nonfabric trims such as beads and sequins. Decorative details, as discussed in Chapter 4, may be applied at various stages in the production process. Some decorative stitchings (for example, most embroideries) are applied and most appliqués and trims are attached during preliminary assembly, while garment parts and panels are still flat and easy to handle. However, some stitchings (rows of topstitching that cross finished seams) and a few trims (beads that are glued on as a last step) are applied later, perhaps as one of the final finishing processes. Although decorative details are discussed here, remember that the point in the production process at which one is applied depends on the particular detail and the particular garment. For more information about evaluating the quality of trim and finding items, see Chapter 8.

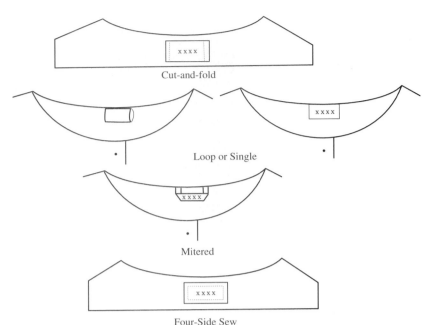

Cut-and-fold

Loop or Single

Mitered

Four-Side Sew

Figure 11–3   Types of label attachment.

Decorative Stitchings. Decorative stitchings include the **ornamental stitching (OS)** defined in U.S. Fed. Std. No. 751a (Figure 11–4). Ornamental stitchings are applied for decorative purposes. They include all forms of topstitching and other decorative stitchings that are aesthetic and have little or no functional purpose. All the ornamental stitchings included in the federal standard are diagrammed in Appendix A. Appendix B lists the apparel production operations performed by each OS stitching and the suitable stitch types.

Topstitching. **Topstitching** or **accent stitching** is visible, decorative stitching done on the outside of the garment. Topstitching may be placed anywhere within the body of the garment (OSa) (Figure 11–5) or near edges (OSf) (Figure 11–6). If placed very close to an edge (within 1/8 inch), topstitching may be called **edgestitching.** Besides being ornamental, topstitching near edges (OSf) provides body, flattens and reinforces the edge, and keeps facings from slipping out and showing on the outside of the garment. Reversible edges (e. g. , the front of a jacket with rolled lapels) should be stitched with lock stitches, which appear identical from both sides.

Topstitching, more than any other stitching, affects the appearance of the garment. It should be straight, uniform, and accurately placed on the intended line. It should not cause puckering. The thread color should match or complement the fabric. Because it is visible to the consumer, consumers use topstitching more than other stitchings to gauge quality. Manufacturers usually use straight stitches for topstitching, but decorative stitches may also be used.

High-quality topstitching contributes to the garment design. Too much topstitching is a poor substitute for quality fabric and design. Remember the design credo "Less is more" when evaluating topstitching.

Embroidery. **Embroidery** is decorative stitching used to form designs or patterns. Most machine embroidery is satin-stitch embroidery, which features long stitches sewn densely to create an embroidered design with a satiny look. Designs containing extensive detail and made with closely spaced stitches cost more than simple designs made with sparse stitches. Embroidery requires thread that is strong, fine, smooth and, usually, lustrous; rayon, polyester, and cotton are common choices. Embroidery found on ready-to-wear is almost always machine embroidery; one machine can embroider up to 20 garments simultaneously. A wide variety of hand embroidery stitches exists, but hand embroidery is found primarily in couture and other high-price apparel and occasionally in imports.

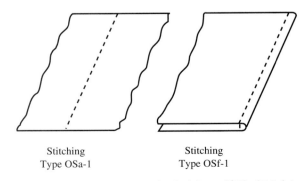

Stitching
Type OSa-1

Stitching
Type OSf-1

Figure 11–4   Ornamental stitchings (OS): (OSa) in body of garment, and (OSf) at edge.

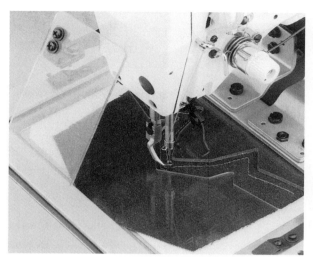

Figure 11–5   Automated decorative topstitching on jeans pocket. *(Courtesy of Union Special Corporation Technical Training Center.)*

Figure 11–6   Double-needle topstitching at garment edge. *(Courtesy of Union Special Corporation Technical Training Center.)*

Embroidery should be backed with a light interfacing to support the area. The interfacing strengthens the fabric to prevent tearing. Interfacing also prevents puckering and makes the stitches smooth and attractive. If tear-away interfacing is used, the excess interfacing should be removed after the area is embroidered. Pucker caused by embroidery, especially a problem on knits, can be reduced by using a woven backing, slowing down sewing speeds and production, and reducing the density of stitches (but continuing to provide complete coverage). High-quality embroidery has a high stitch count so that the embroidery covers the fabric with thread.

Appliqués are sometimes embroidered (for example, emblems); to distinguish between machine embroidery and appliqué, look for the stitches of the entire design, which are visible inside a machine-embroidered garment. If the design is appliquéed, only the outline stitches can be seen inside the garment. The Izod alligator is an appliqué, whereas Ralph Lauren's polo player is machine embroidered (Figure 11–7).

Embroidery that forms the initials of the wearer's name is a **monogram** (Figure 5–26). Besides denoting ownership, monograms give an impression that the garment is custom made, although they can be purchased ready made and even acquired by mail order.

The monogram on a man's shirt is usually placed on the pocket, cuff, collar, or occasionally on the body of the garment three to five inches above the waist. Tasteful shirt monograms are discreet, often white on white, and no more than 1/4 inch high. Manufacturers usually place sweater monograms on the chest, centered or to one side. Handmade monograms are raised

and denote more prestige than the more common machine-made monograms, which are flat.

Cutwork consists of holes in the fabric surrounded by embroidery. Cutwork was originally a handicraft, but today it is done by machine. Cutwork decorates collars and other details on feminine garments and is the process used to make eyelet, a lace substitute. (See Figure 11–9b later in this chapter.)

Trapunto is a form of embroidery that resembles quilting. In better garments, trapunto involves padding the stitched areas of the garment so they stand out in relief, producing a three-dimensional effect. Twin needles stitching on both sides of cording provide this raised, decorative effect in most ready-to-wear (Figure 11–8). Another method utilizes jets of air to force thread into the areas to be padded.

Hemstitching and Fagoting. Hemstitching and fagoting are ornamental stitchings that come and go in popularity, depending on fashion trends. The art of

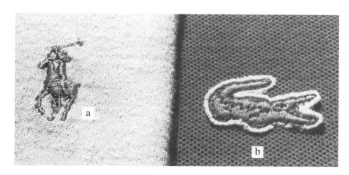

Figure 11–7   Ralph Lauren's Polo® trademark (a) is machine embroidered, and Izod's alligator trademark (b) is an embroidered appliqué.

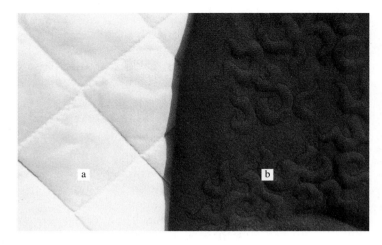

Figure 11–8   (a) Quilting and (b) trapunto.

hand **hemstitching** involves removing a group of parallel yarns from a fabric and tying the remaining perpendicular yarns together with decorative stitches (Figure 11–9a). Machine hemstitching pierces the fabric and stitches the edges with a vibrating needle to achieve the same look. By cutting machine hemstitching, a picot edge finish is produced. Hemstitching is used to secure hems and for a decorative effect.

Fagoting is a decorative stitching that holds two closely spaced folded edges of fabric together with ornamental stitches (Figure 11–9c). Hemstitching and fagoting appear similar at a glance, like a piece of lace inset between two pieces of fabric. Both expose the area beneath the decorative stitches. However, hemstitching is an integral part of the fabric while fagoting joins two separate plies of fabric, with their seam allowances visible inside the garment. Besides being decorative, fagoting is sometimes used on "clip-to-fit" slips; the customer clips through one of several rows of fagoting at different levels to shorten the slip to the desired length.

Trims.   Trims include narrow fabric trims, fabric trims such as appliqués, and a wide variety of non-fabric trims.

Narrow Fabric Trims.   Narrow fabric trims (ribbon, braid, lace, and so forth) may be (1) applied directly to the body of the garment, (2) applied directly to a garment edge, (3) included in a seam, or (4) inset between two fabric panels. Trims should be stretched slightly around concave curves and eased slightly around convex curves to avoid distortion. The wider the trim and the more extreme the curve, the greater the amount of stretching and easing required. Trims generally add strength and stability but also bulk. For more information on trims, see Chapter 8.

Ribbons, flat laces, and other flat, nonflexible trims are confined to use on straight edges because they are not flexible enough to fit smoothly around curved edges. Braids and gathered laces are generally flexible and can be applied on straight edges or curves. Trim is used most effectively around corners if it is mitered (Figure 10–16a). Mitering adds to labor cost, but trim that is not mitered at corners may appear sloppy and bulky. The application of the trim should be neat, smooth, and attractive.

Glued-on trims generally cost less than sewn-on trims. The most costly but secure tacking attachments involve double tacking and/or adding glue to the tack. Trims are occasionally sewn on by hand because of the soft, invisible results or because the cost of automation cannot be justified, but hand sewing is not especially durable and domestic hand sewing is costly.

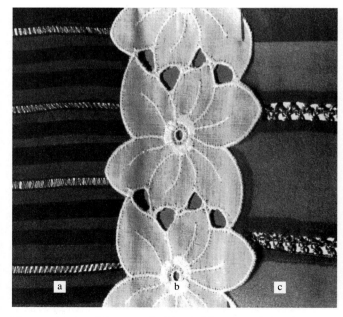

Figure 11–9   (a) Hemstitching, (b) cutwork, and (c) fagoting.

Ribbon ends ravel readily, especially if exposed. A ravel-proof finish on the raw ends of ribbon bows is a sign of quality that most manufacturers neglect. The raveling problem usually surfaces after the purchase when the garment is worn and laundered, but garments that have been on the rack for some time may show evidence of raveling ribbons even before they are sold.

Appliqués. Stitched-on appliqués are generally more durable than glued-on or heat-sealed appliqués. A smooth, dense zigzag stitch, called a **satin stitch,** is the most costly and durable method of attachment for most appliqués; however, the stitches should not be so close that they damage the fabric of the garment or build up at the corners of the appliqué. Emblems are best applied using a straight lockstitch. Changing thread colors to sew on multicolored appliqués is a sign of quality. High-quality appliqués have interfacing behind the stitches for reinforcement. Interfacing gives the area the body it needs to yield smooth, pucker-free stitches around the appliqué. Coating the back of the appliqué itself with plastic or fusible interfacing gives it body. Sometimes appliqués are padded for a three-dimensional effect.

Nonfabric Trims. Most nonfabric trims (beads, sequins, and so forth) are applied individually. Some may be applied in strings, which reduces cost. Gluing is the least costly method of application but is not always durable, especially when the garment is laundered. Many metal trims are mechanically attached to the fabric; they should be adequately interfaced for durability. Stitching or mechanically attaching the trim onto the fabric costs more but is more durable than gluing. Most trim is stitched on by machine, but hand stitching is used when the volume being produced does not justify mechanizing the process, for example, when feathers are applied to a small production run of dresses. For more information on nonfabric trims, see Chapter 8.

Applying Zippers

Zippers can be applied to garment panels in a variety of ways. Some garments lend themselves to partial zipper application in stages while other garments lend themselves to the application of a complete zipper. The decision about which method to use depends upon the volume being produced and the degree of automation available in the manufacturing plant.

Operators apply continuous-element zippers fully assembled, with the slider, pull, and stops attached to the chain and tape by the zipper supplier (see Figure 8–8). However, separate-element zippers are often assembled during the assembly process using rolls of *stringer*, zipper tape with elements attached, from which lengths are cut for each zipper. The operator sews the stringer to the garment part or panel and then attaches the slider, pull, and stops. Using stringers is cost effective because it eliminates the need for an inventory of zippers of various lengths. Zippers are easy to install this way because small pieces or panels of the garment are being handled rather than the entire garment.

Inserting stringers requires skill because the operator must set the slider on evenly and place the stops accurately, important for the smooth functioning of the zipper. In addition, the top stop of the zipper must fall approximately 1/4 inch below the seam line that will cross the tape. Because of the complexity of this operation and the shortage of skilled operators, automated equipment has been developed in the jean industry for this production technique. This equipment completely assembles the zipper after the operator has fed in the facing pieces.

Zippers are applied using a straight lockstitch (301). Topstitching should be smooth, straight, and parallel to the zipper opening. Crooked stitching causes uneven stress on the zipper chain, tape, and slider. The topstitching should end approximately 1/8 to 1/4 inch below the bottom stop. Stitches placed too close to the zipper chain prevent the slider from gliding smoothly when operated.

Frequent problem spots in lapped zipper applications occur when the topstitches are too near or too far from the zipper slider. The bulk of the slider sometimes prevents stitching close enough to the scoops under it, causing the topstitching to curve out around it. This problem is resolved when an extra motion is planned into the operation to allow the operator to reposition the slider. This extra motion, however, increases the pay rate of the operation, which in turn increases the cost of the garment.

Seam allowances in zipper applications must be wide enough so they are caught when the zipper is stitched to the garment panel. Wide seam allowances help to stabilize the zipper.

Zippers are usually applied with one end open and the other end closed, as in a pair of pants. Zippers can also be applied with both ends caught in a seam, for instance, at pocket openings or in the side seam of a dress. Separating zippers are applied so both ends are open. This allows the zipper to be completely disconnected into halves, as at the center front of a jacket or parka (Figure 8–9).

In a correctly applied zipper, the zipper opening in the garment is as long as the zipper chain. If the opening is too short, the seam or the reinforcement will undergo excessive stress and can rupture. If the opening is too long, the bottom stop of the zipper and/or the unzipped tape edges can be unsightly. Nylon zipper tapes such as those at the waist, may be crossed by seams, but due to their greater bulk and sewing difficulties, metal zippers cannot be crossed by seams. Therefore, a few elements must be removed from metal zippers whenever they are crossed by seams. In addition, a top stop must be carefully placed at the point where elements have been removed to prevent the slider from coming off.

Occasionally, hand pickstitches are used in place of machine topstitching. A zipper applied this way is referred to as **hand picked**. If done well, the pickstitches are straight, even, and very tiny so they are barely visible on the face of the garment. Manufacturers of better and couture garments specify hand stitches when machine stitches would detract from the appearance of the garment. The advantage of a hand-picked zipper is aesthetic, as it is not as durable as a machine-stitched zipper. Because of the labor expense, hand-picked zippers are found only in very high-price lines.

Slot Zippers. A **slot zipper,** or centered application, is characterized by two visible rows of topstitching on the outside of a garment, one on either side of the zipper chain. The lines of stitching are about 1/4 inch from and parallel to the seam line (Figure 11–10a). The folded seam edges of the garment abut to cover the zipper chain. The slot application is used in center front and center back openings and for some side openings. In all price lines, both conventional and separating zippers are applied by the centered method. But the slot zipper exposes the zipper chain more than do other zipper applications.

Occasionally, designers plan the installation of slot zippers so that the zipper chain intentionally shows. This is known as an **exposed** zipper application, a type of slot application (Figure 11–11a). Exposed

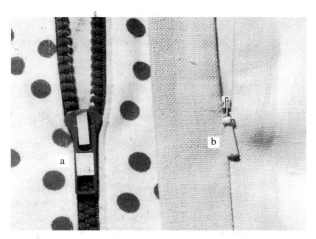

Figure 11–11 Zipper applications: (a) exposed (note plastic separate elements), and (b) invisible, using invisible zipper.

applications are decorative, especially for novelty zippers. Exposed applications are required when a zipper must be inserted in a slash in the fabric rather than in a seam or placket as most zippers are. This is because the slashed edges of the fabric are turned under and sewn to the zipper tape, exposing the zipper chain.

Zippers in jackets or coats, especially ski wear, may feature **wind flaps** over and/or under the zipper chain. These extra fabric pieces help prevent skin irritation from a cold or scratchy zipper and help to keep the wind and water away from the zipper and the wearer's skin. Such extra features add to the cost as well as comfort of a garment.

Lingerie guards are ribbon or fabric strips attached behind the zipper chain so that it cannot irritate the wearer's skin or undergarments. This feature is rarely used, and if used, is found only in high-price lines.

Lapped Zippers. A **lapped zipper** is characterized by only one line of visible stitching on the outside of a garment. The topstitching is on one side of the opening and is about 1/2 inch away from the folded seam line (Figure 11–10b). It causes one folded seam edge to form a tuck that conceals the zipper closure. Lapped zipper applications are used at center front and center back garment openings and for most side openings.

The average lapped zipper application probably does a better job of concealing the zipper teeth than the average slot application. But because the lapped zipper insertion involves several steps, it is usually confined to moderate- and high-price lines.

Fly Zippers. The **fly zipper** or **fly-front zipper** is a form of the lapped zipper application. The fly zipper is characterized by topstitching on one side of

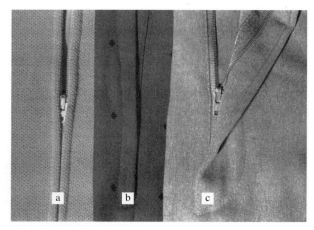

Figure 11–10 Zipper applications: (a) slot, (b) lapped, and (c) fly front.

the opening, about 1½ inches from the folded seam line (Figure 11–10c). A fly zipper differs from a regular lapped zipper in that one side of the zipper is stitched to a facing, and the facing is topstitched to the garment. This allows for the wide topstitching characteristic of the fly-front application. The width of the facing lends support and helps the fly-front zipper to withstand greater stress than a regular lapped application. If done properly, the fly-front application conceals the zipper chain better than other applications. However, if the zipper is not stitched to all the fabric plies in the fly-front application or if the stitches are crooked, the zipper chain may show.

Fly-front applications are used in jeans, most men's and boy's pants, many women's and girl's pants, and some casual skirts. They are also used in jackets and sportswear where an exposed zipper would interfere with the design. Because fly-front zippers involve more fabric and are more labor intensive, they cost more than regular lapped zipper applications.

Overlap. Most fly fronts look fairly similar on the outside of a garment, but they are constructed in a variety of ways. The overlap portion conceals the zipper. The simplest overlap, often used on women's and children's garments, has an extended facing to which the zipper is stitched. This overlap is non-bulky, comfortable, and low cost. Or the overlap may be faced with a shaped facing; this method is slightly bulky. Because men's flies are longer, extending into the curved crotch area, they usually require a separate, shaped facing.

Underlap/Fly Shield. An underlap or **fly shield** beneath the zipper protects the skin and undergarments from irritation by the zipper chain. The absence of an underlap leaves the skin directly exposed to the zipper chain. A more acceptable technique is to form an underlap by extending the fashion fabric. Some fly fronts have no underlap, which reflects low quality standards.

In high-price garments, the underlap may consist of a separately constructed fly shield. The fly shield is faced or lined and attached behind the zipper. Although bulkier than ordinary underlaps, these fly shields are generally more comfortable and durable.

The overlap and underlap of fly-front zipper applications must be the same length. Both must be caught evenly in the waistband. Otherwise, the fly will buckle (Figure 11–12).

French Fly. A **French fly** is found on high-quality pants. A French fly has a tab or extension on the underlap, which buttons to the inside of the pants near the waist. (A French fly is shown in Chapter 12, Figure 12–8c.) This extension provides additional support to keep the front of the pants smooth and neat.

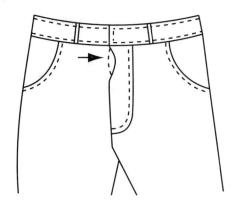

Figure 11–12   Underlap and overlap of different lengths cause overlap to bubble.

The fly front of high-quality men's pants usually features an overlap with a shaped facing and a lined, French fly shield. Sometimes, the lower portion of the fly shield is extended for a few inches into the crotch seam to further reinforce the area. Complex fly fronts involve more pieces of both fashion fabric and lining and more labor to construct than simple fly fronts. Complex fly fronts are usually comfortable and durable but may add bulk and definitely increase costs.

Reinforcements and Closures for Zippers. A bar tack or tacks or some other type of reinforcement is needed near the base of fly zipper applications to help absorb the stress of use. Reinforcements protect the bottom zipper stop from excessive strain, as well as protect the fabric and seam at the base of the zipper from stress. For example, when pants are slipped on and off over the hips, the base of the zipper is stressed and the seam below it may rip out unless a reinforcement is present. Reinforcements placed too low do not absorb adequate stress and can lead to zipper failure, seam failure, or fabric failure at the base of the zipper.

A closure at the top of the zipper is vital to absorb the stress on the chain and slider when the zipper is closed. If the closure is too small, too weak, or poorly attached or mislocated, stress may ratchet the zipper and damage it. Garments that are too small for the wearer and worn with the waist closure left open produce the same result.

Invisible Zipper. **Invisible zipper applications** require specially designed "invisible" zippers. No lines of stitching are visible on the outside of the garment (Figure 11–11b). When properly inserted, the finished zipper installation looks like a plain seam, with only part of the tab visible on the outside of the garment. Invisible zippers are applied with a specially designed machine attachment and are not common in low-price mass production products.

Constructing Pockets

Pockets are made and applied at different stages in production, depending on their type. The three main types of pockets are patch pockets, in-seam pockets, and slashed pockets (see Chapter 5). Any of these pocket types may have flaps attached.

Patch Pockets. Patch pockets are usually made and applied in preliminary assembly. The outer edges of patch pockets are turned under so no raw edges are exposed when the pocket is stitched to the garment. On high-quality garments, the pocket edges are turned under before the upper edge of the pocket is hemmed, thus eliminating exposed raw edges at the top of the pocket. If the upper edge of the pocket is hemmed before the sides are turned under, the exposed raw edges near the top of the pocket are turned or clipped at an angle and reinforced with tacks or topstitching so they do not show.

Automatic Pocket Setters. Pockets on basic garments, such as shirts and jeans, are made and applied in the same operation using automatic pocket-setting machines that turn under the raw edges, position the pocket, and sew it to the garment. The machine forms the prehemmed pockets around a **template**, a pocket-shaped piece of metal around which the pocket edges are pressed to ensure the desired shape and size. Automatic pocket setters achieve consistency from garment to garment. Therefore, the manual construction of pockets on fashion garments may be less consistent than the automated construction of pockets on high-volume basic garments.

Pocket Shape. A patch pocket with square corners is the easiest to make and should have sharp, even corners. Although it is more costly, mitering the corners when turning them under contributes to sharp points, eliminates bulk, and prevents raw edges from showing along the pocket edges.

Rounded pockets are harder to make than pockets with square corners. The raw edges of a rounded patch pocket must be turned under evenly to form a smooth, even curve. Designers of high-quality garments may line or face unusually shaped pockets to facilitate turning under the raw edges evenly, but this adds to production time and expense.

Underlying Fabrics for Patch Pockets. Patch pockets that are very large and those on tailored garments or those made in limp fabrics are usually lined and/or interfaced. Interfacing provides shape maintenance. A lining also reduces the raveling of raw edges inside the pocket and prevents raveling edges from showing, making the inside of the pocket smooth. However, the lining should not show at the pocket edges.

Patch pockets may be fully lined to the top but more commonly are lined up to the pocket hem so the lining does not show when the pocket is used. A small opening at the hem or a short slit in the lining is used to turn the pocket through after sewing the lining and pocket together. In high-quality garments, the slits and openings in pocket linings are closed after turning, while in low-quality garments they are often left open.

Stitching and Reinforcement of Patch Pockets. Patch pockets are usually topstitched to the garment. The topstitching should be placed near the edges of the pocket to keep the edges flat. Some patch pockets are fused to the garment at the edges to keep the edges flat and then topstitched for durability. On high-price garments, patch pockets may be stitched to the garment invisibly from inside the pocket, using a series of sewing operations on alternating sides of the pocket rather than one continuous line of stitches. This method is labor intensive and therefore costly but results in a secure and unobtrusive pocket.

The opening edges of pockets are reinforced so the pocket can withstand the stress of use. Rivets, bar tacks, backstitching, or stitches in the shape of a triangle or rectangle commonly secure the corner edges of patch pockets. Heavily used pockets in medium- and heavyweight fabrics should be bar tacked or riveted for maximum reinforcement.

In-Seam Pockets. The pocket opening of an in-seam pocket occurs where the garment seam is left partially unsewn. The ends of the pocket opening are reinforced with bar tacks or rivets so the pocket can withstand the stress of use. Sometimes patternmakers incorporate the garment opening with the in-seam pocket in the side seam of skirts or pants. When this is done, the upper edges of the pocket are sewn into the waistline's overlap and underlap. When the waistline's closure is fastened, the pocket assumes its proper position. In-seam pockets are made during panel assembly.

The opening edge of in-seam pockets should be directionally stitched with the grain to avoid stretching and rippling. A stay eased to the opening edge of the pocket helps the pocket hug the body, thus preventing it from stretching and standing away from the body when the garment is worn. This is especially important on wool, rayon, and other fabrics that may have the tendency to stretch.

Pocket Bag. The **pocket bag** (the pouch of fabric that forms the functional part of the pocket) hangs inside the garment. Some pocket bags are made in preliminary assembly, while others are made as the side seams of panels are sewn. On some zip-front, pleated pants and skirts, the bags of the side pockets are extended to the center front. This helps control the abdomen and keep the pleats flat, which results in a smooth front. A *pot holder* of lining or pocketing fabric attached between the pockets and center front can serve the same purpose.

The pocket bag should be large enough for its intended use. Work clothing and sportswear generally require larger pockets than formal clothing. Generous pocket bags indicate high quality. However, if pocket bags are too long, they cause excess bulk and, on shorts, may show below the hem.

The pocket bag must be double stitched and edge finished for security, to prevent raveling and holes from forming later. The seam around the pocket bag should be strong but nonbulky so a ridge does not show on the outside of the garment. Stitches must be short to help provide strength.

If the garment body fabric is lightweight, the spec technician may use it to make the pocket bag. However, if the garment body fabric is printed or white, a solid or neutral-colored fabric is used for the pocket bag to prevent it from showing through. (The color should be the same as or lighter than the garment fabric.) In-seam pockets are unsuitable in garments made of sheer or translucent fabrics because the pocket bags show through to the outside of the garments. If the fabric is medium- or heavyweight, a lightweight pocket bag fabric eliminates bulk.

For garments that receive heavy wear, spec technicians usually use special pocketing fabrics that are durable but lightweight and nonbulky; low-count, heavily starched pocketing fabrics such as muslin represent low quality and do not hold up well.

To reduce fabric requirements and eliminate bulk, some technicians specify a single layer of pocketing fabric, with the garment serving as the other half of the pocket bag. When this is done, the outer edges of the single ply of the pocket bag are stitched to the garment. Pockets made by this method can be recognized by the pocket-bag-shaped topstitching visible on the front of the garment. The downside of this method is that it puts stress on the fabric of the garment, especially if it is close fitting. Generally, single-layer pockets are typical of low-price garments, but when used for decorative effect they are found in other price lines.

Concealed Pocket. In-seam pockets are least conspicuous when the opening edges of the pocket are abutted; the seam containing the opening appears to be sewn closed, concealing the pocket (Figure 11–13a). The pocket bag of a **concealed in-seam pocket** is stitched to the seam allowances of the garment. In high-quality apparel, the patternmaker extends the seam allowances slightly so that the pocket

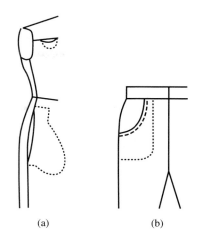

Figure 11–13 In-seam pockets: (a) concealed, and (b) exposed.

bag may be sewn to these extensions. This requires extra fabric but prevents the pocket bag from showing at the opening, which is especially important if it is not made of the fashion fabric. Occasionally, the entire pocket bag is an extension of the seam allowance. If the garment body fabric is lightweight enough to form a nonbulky pocket bag, this method yields good results because it eliminates the bulk of a seam as well as an extra production step. However, this method requires so much extra fabric that it is rarely done except to make very small pockets.

Exposed Pocket. An underlay of fashion fabric forms the exposed portion of an **exposed in-seam pocket** (Figure 11–13b). The underlay forms part of the pocket bag. If the fashion fabric is lightweight, the spec technician may use it to construct the pocket. However, if the fashion fabric is bulky or scratchy, the bag portion of the pocket should be made of pocketing fabric. In this case, the fashion fabric underlay should extend an inch or more below the opening edge, and the opening edge of the pocket should be faced with fashion fabric, so the pocket bag does not show when the pocket gapes open. (Gaping is especially likely when the wearer sits.) In some garments in low-price lines, the pocket facing is cut with emphasis on material utilization and not aesthetics. As a result of cost cutting, the pocketing fabric is visible when the garment is worn. Each extra piece used to construct a pocket adds to fabric and labor costs, which must be balanced with the comfort and appearance of the pocket as well as the price point of the garment.

Slashed Pockets. Slashed pockets are bound or faced slits within the body of a garment, with the pocket bag sewn behind the slit, inside the garment.

Slashed pockets are the most difficult pockets to construct. If made manually, precision is often low. Today, most slashed pockets are produced by full or partial automation during the preliminary stages of production. Since automation, the overall consistency and quality of slashed pockets have vastly improved and the labor cost has gone down. But because of the many pieces required to make them and the complexity of the operation, slashed pockets remain more costly to construct than most other pocket types. Inside men's suits, slashed pockets that extend beyond the lining into the facing of fashion fabric cost more to produce but are more accessible than those confined to the lining.

Criteria for Slashed Pockets. Marks of a high-quality slashed pocket include the following:

1. It is a perfect rectangle.
2. It has even lips.
3. It is cut on grain (unless intentionally angled for design purposes).
4. A single-welt pocket lip meets the upper edge of the slashed opening.
5. Double-welt pocket lips meet but do *not* overlap.
6. Lips do not sag or gape.
7. Pocket area is interfaced, and sometimes underlined, for reinforcement.
8. Pocket bag is made of a lining or pocketing fabric light enough in color and weight that it does not show through or press through to the face of the garment.
9. It is faced with fashion fabric so the pocket bag does not show when the pocket gapes.
10. Ends of the slashed pocket are reinforced with topstitching or bar tacks. (If the fabric is fraying or if there are tiny holes at the ends of the pocket, the pocket is low quality.)
11. It may be basted shut so pocket stays flat and closed until the garment is sold.

Types of Slashed Pockets. The simplest and least expensive type of slashed pocket is made by slitting the fabric and turning under the raw edges of the slash. This type of pocket is used in outerwear and active sportswear with a zipper set in the slash. It is suitable only for strong fabrics with little tendency to ravel. Quality is improved by sewing around the opening before slashing the fabric; these stitches reinforce the opening.

Most slashed pockets are bound slashes, called *welt* pockets, either single-welt or double-welt (Figures 5–27 and 5–28). A button or button tab may be used on welt pockets to secure the opening and prevent gaping. Bar tacks on the ends of welt pockets are used to help them withstand hard use; for example, the back hip pocket on men's pants must endure a wallet being put in and taken out several times a day.

Although at first glance they look like single-welt pockets, the flap of upturned flap pockets is not a binding for a slash but a flap that is attached to the bottom of a finished slash, extending up (not down like a regular flap). Because the flap extends up, it must be topstitched or slipstitched at the edges to keep it upturned (Figure 5–28). Another clue for telling the two pockets apart is that the flap on an upturned flap pocket is generally wider than a single welt.

Adding Belt Loops and Miscellaneous Loops

Designers add **belt loops** (narrow fabric strips or thread chains) at the waistline to keep belts in position. The space allowed for a belt should be wide enough to accommodate the currently popular belt width. A belt loop should always be located at center back to prevent the belt from riding up above the waistline. *Keystone belt loops* are intricately shaped loops used in western-style clothing. *Thread belt loops* made of interlooped thread chains are often used on womenswear. Thread loops hold the belt in place until the garment is sold. (The consumer may remove them before wearing the garment.)

In high-quality men's pants, the center back belt loop may be sewn off center on the waistband or placed in a pocket until the sale is made. After the center back seam is altered to fit the wearer, the belt loop is then sewn into its correct position on the waistband.

In low-price lines, designers often eliminate the center back belt loop to reduce costs. Generally five belt loops are placed on small sizes and seven loops on large sizes of high-quality pants and skirts.

Operators make most belt loops by seaming tubes of fabric, or feeding narrow strips of fabric through a folder and hemming them with straight topstitching (301), blindstitches (100 or 300 class), or bottom-covering chainstitches (500 class) in the preliminary process. Some have fusible interfacing inside the loop because belt loops with narrow seams or narrow folds can easily ravel. Belt loops made of lightweight fabrics are sewn into the seams of waistbands. The operator must catch the end of the belt loop securely in the seam, or the belt loop may pull out of the seam under stress (especially likely at the upper edge).

Some belt loops are bar tacked to the waistband for a more durable attachment. The ends of the belt loop should be turned under evenly for a neat appearance. In dressy and tailored garments, belt loops are often sewn in the waistline seam and bar tacked at the upper edge of the waistband.

Loops may be sewn inside garments and used to hang the garments up when they are not being worn. For example, a metal chain or fabric loop inside the neckline of a high-quality coat or jacket allows the wearer to hang the garment over a hook. A fabric *locker loop,* sewn into the yoke seam on the back of a shirt, was originally intended for hanging the garment but has become a decorative feature. (See Chapter 12, Figure 12–2.) Loops are usually applied during panel assembly.

On women's garments, manufacturers often include *hanger loops,* which are loops that help absorb the weight of the garment when hung on a hanger (Figure 10–8). Hanger loops take the strain off the seams, avoiding distortion of the garment. Hanger loops are found in moderate- and high-price lines, especially in slick garments with wide necklines, in heavy blouses and dresses with delicate shoulders (for example, sequined dresses), and in skirts.

Lingerie strap keepers are loops used inside moderate- and high-price evening gowns and other women's garments to hold bra and slip straps in place. They also keep garments with wide or low necklines properly positioned at the neckline and shoulders. Strap keepers should be nonbulky so an impression does not show on the outside of the garment.

Wrist loops are attached to the trains of bridal gowns. After the ceremony, when the wearer places the loop over her wrist, the train is lifted to allow freedom of movement for walking and dancing. (Alternatively, techniques may be used to remove or shorten the train to allow it to become a bustle during the reception.)

The *keeper* is the loop on the back of men's neckties. The short end of the tie is kept hidden behind the front of the tie when it is tucked into the keeper (Figure 1–2).

Applying Interfacing

Fusing is the most common method of interfacing application. Smooth, well-shaped jackets and stable waistbands are produced using fusible interfacings at great savings in labor. This is because fusibles are less time-consuming to attach than sew-in interfacings. Because the fusing process is so well adapted to mass production, most tailoring is done with fusible interfacings, except in high-price lines, where sew-in interfacings are sometimes used.

Fusibles can blister, bubble, or delaminate in sections or throughout the entire piece if applied to a part or panel using incorrect time, temperature, or pressure (Figure 11–14). The best test for checking the application of fusible interfacing is to use the fingernails to attempt to separate the two plies. Correctly adhered interfacing will not pull away from the panel more than 1/16 to 1/8 inch when cooled to room temperature. Fusibles not firmly attached may be sent through

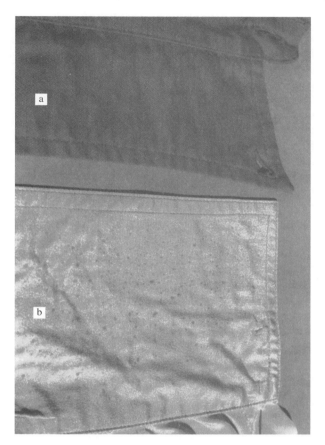

Figure 11–14   Interfacing problems: (a) bubbling, and (b) strike-through, which occurred after one dry-cleaning.

the fusing machine a second time without adverse effect after fusing conditions have been corrected.

Interfacing can be fused to the facing piece rather than to the garment panel, which may reduce the visibility of interfacing problems (bubbling, blistering, and strike-through). However, this method does not allow the interfacing to hide seam allowances as does interfacing applied to the garment panel itself.

Sew-in interfacings are held in place by the seams of the garment. The interfacing needs to extend just beyond the garment's seamlines; more than that adds unwanted bulk and cost. Sometimes sew-in interfacings are not secured around all edges (for example, at the fold of extended facings). If one or more edges are left loose, the interfacing can rumple, tear, or distort during wear and care. These problems may be prevented by securing the loose edge of the interfacing with a row of basting stitches. For example, interfacing in shirt cuffs is often sewn to the cuff at the upper edge to prevent the interfacing from rolling.

Pad stitching is a trademark of fine traditional tailoring. Hand pad stitches are many tiny hand stitches made through the sew-in interfacing, barely catching the fashion fabric. The collar and lapel are rolled slightly as the stitches are made to impart the desired rolled shape to the finished garment. Hand pad stitching is the softest and subtlest of shaping methods. However, hand pad stitching is an art found only in apparel of the highest price and quality because of the time and skill it requires. For example, men's suit brands such as Oxxford® and Hickey-Freeman® feature hand pad stitching in the collar and lapel areas of jackets.

Some custom tailoring still exists today but most tailoring has evolved into a combination of custom tailoring and mass production. As many mass-production techniques as possible have been adapted to tailored garments, making them more affordable for the general public that wants high-quality, structured clothing. Fusible interfacings had made pad stitching almost obsolete except in high-price lines, but recent innovations in automated machine pad stitching are again making pad stitches an important feature of some moderately priced tailored apparel (Figure 11–15). Machine pad stitching offers many of the subtle shaping characteristics of hand pad stitching but at a much lower cost.

Knee patches (patches of strong, abrasion-resistant fabric) are sometimes placed on the inside or outside of a pair of pants at the knee. Knee patches extend the life of the pants in the knee area, an area subject to hard wear. They are most common in children's pants. Similarly, *elbow patches* extend the life of the garment by protecting the elbow area. Most elbow patches are made of a contrasting fabric which can serve as decoration, as on the elbows of men's sport jackets. Operators usually fuse patches to the garment panels early in preliminary assembly. Any decorative or reinforcing stitching (topstitching) is also done at this time while the panel is flat and easy to handle.

A *heel guard* or *kick tape* is a layer of abrasion-resistant tape sewn at the back of a pant hem to reinforce that area. It is found in high-quality dress pants. Heel guards help pants to wear longer by protecting them from the abrasion of walking.

Attaching Underlining

Pieces cut of underlining fabric are exact duplicates of the major pieces of fashion fabric required to make the garment. Each piece of underlining is attached to the back of its coordinating piece of fashion fabric as part of preliminary operations. The two plies are then handled as one, as if the underlining were not there, as the garment is constructed. Each underlining piece must be cut on the same grain as its coordinating fashion fabric piece and should not pull, pucker, or distort the hang of the fashion fabric.

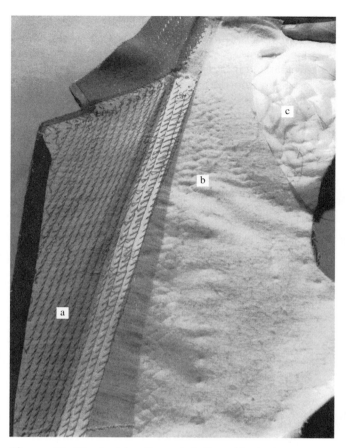

Figure 11–15   Inside of man's tailored jacket features (a) pad stitching on hair canvas interfacing, (b) floating chest piece, and (c) shoulder pad. Also note black stay tape at outer edge of lapel and white stay tape at roll line. *(Jacket courtesy of Jack Henry.)*

Underlining is attached to the garment at every seam, whereas lining is attached only around the outer edges of the garment. The only situation in which the underlining and fashion fabric layers are not treated as one is when details, such as darts, are constructed separately in the underlining and in the fashion fabric to reduce bulk. Underlining, like pad stitching, is used primarily in high-quality, high-price garments and is not seen in the majority of mass-produced apparel.

Applying Reinforcements

Reinforcements, such as rivets and tacks, lend strength to areas that experience hard wear or excessive strain. Some reinforcements are applied early in the production process while others are applied in finishing.

Rivets, made of copper, brass, or another nonrust metal, reinforce pocket corners (Figure 5–31) or seams. After the seams to be reinforced have been sewn, rivets are forced through the fabric into metal *burrs*, where they expand, securing the rivets to the burrs. Rivets are an example of a functional detail that possesses aesthetic appeal as well; they have become associated with the look of traditional jeans and leather jackets.

Tacks consist of several adjacent or overlapping zigzag stitches. They are used to sew on labels and secure facings and shoulder pads. Tacks, like other reinforcements, are applied either during preliminary assembly or to the completed garments, depending on the location and purpose of the tack.

Bar tacks consist of a short series of close zigzag stitches. Spec technicians use bar tacks to reinforce areas of high stress, for instance, at pocket corners, at the base of zippers, and in the attachment of belt loops (Figure 5–31). When stitched in contrasting thread, bar tacks also become a decorative feature.

Ticket tacks are a version of bar tacks used for attaching paper labels to apparel. Ticket tacks consist of fewer overlapping zigzag stitches than bar tacks and are easy to remove. For this reason, they are used for low-strength operations such as attaching paper size labels to the outside of apparel, as on men's slacks.

Arrowhead tacks are made of stitches in the shape of arrowheads and are used mainly as decorative reinforcements at pocket corners and yoke edges on western-style clothing. When used on custom tailored apparel, arrowhead tacks are usually made by hand, which is a sign of exceptional quality.

PANEL ASSEMBLY

After small parts are assembled as discussed in the previous sections, work then begins on the main panels of the garment (Figure 11–16). Operators shape and seam the two-dimensional panels into three-dimensional garment pieces. Waistbands (see Chapter 12) and elastic are applied and panels are hemmed.

Shaping

Shaping is often one of the first steps in panel assembly. Shape may be introduced into the garment in a variety of ways, including darts, pleats, tucks, ease, gathers, and seams. (For more information, see Chapter 5.)

Darts. Darts must be sewn and pressed accurately for smooth-fitting, eye-appealing results. (For more information on darts, see Chapter 5.)

Sewing Darts. The stitches used to sew a dart should be straight until they approach the tip and then gradually taper off the folded edge (Figure 5–6). If the stitches at the dart tip are not tapered gradually, the dart bubbles or *dimples* at the tip rather than fitting the body bulge smoothly. The tip of a dart may be marked with a tiny *drill hole* or other marking to guide the operator in constructing the dart. If drill holes are used, the stitching at the dart tip must go slightly beyond the drill hole (usually about 1/2 inch at the tip) so the hole does not show on the outside of the garment. If drill holes are used in fabrics that fray, they lower the wear life of the dart at the tip.

Darts with raveling stitches at the tips detract from garment appearance and are evidence of low quality standards. The stitches at the dart tip should be secured to prevent them from raveling. The usual method is to leave a short length of twisted threads at the tip of the dart. When these threads eventually untwist, the stitches at the dart tip begin to ravel, which often happens before the garment leaves the retail store. The longer and more twisted the threads, the more durable the dart tip.

Another method of securing the tip of a dart is by backstitching. However, because backstitching causes bulk at the tip, it is not a desirable dart-tip finish. Perhaps the ideal method for finishing dart tips is a knot. A knot prevents the stitches from raveling, but it is too labor intensive for garments in most price lines and as a result is rarely found in mass-produced ready-to-wear.

Pressing Darts. Darts should lie flat. Ideally, they are pressed after construction, with vertical darts pressed toward the center front or center back of the garment and horizontal darts pressed down. An imprint of the dart should not show through to the outside of the garment. Best results are achieved if darts are pressed over a slightly rounded surface, enhancing the shape built into the garment by the dart and preventing channels or creases at the dart tip. Darts made in thick or heavy fabrics may need to be trimmed and pressed open to reduce bulk. Double-pointed darts may require clipping at the widest point in order to lie flat.

Pleats and Tucks. Whether used for shaping the garment or strictly for decoration, accurately formed pleats and tucks have a big impact on the appearance of the finished garment. Each pleat and tuck should be evenly spaced, perfectly even along its whole length, on straight-of-grain, and crisply pressed, if applicable. Unstitched pleats should be caught in the seam at the proper angle or they will distort the fit of the finished garment. Pleats that slightly overlap the adjacent pleats should entirely cover the stitching of

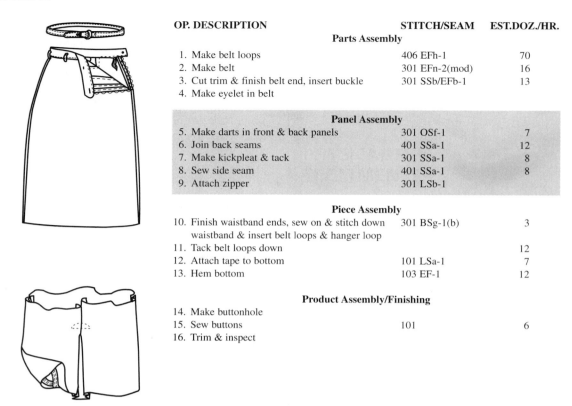

OP. DESCRIPTION	STITCH/SEAM	EST.DOZ./HR.
Parts Assembly		
1. Make belt loops	406 EFh-1	70
2. Make belt	301 EFn-2(mod)	16
3. Cut trim & finish belt end, insert buckle	301 SSb/EFb-1	13
4. Make eyelet in belt		
Panel Assembly		
5. Make darts in front & back panels	301 OSf-1	7
6. Join back seams	401 SSa-1	12
7. Make kickpleat & tack	301 SSa-1	8
8. Sew side seam	401 SSa-1	8
9. Attach zipper	301 LSb-1	
Piece Assembly		
10. Finish waistband ends, sew on & stitch down waistband & insert belt loops & hanger loop	301 BSg-1(b)	3
11. Tack belt loops down		12
12. Attach tape to bottom	101 LSa-1	7
13. Hem bottom	103 EF-1	12
Product Assembly/Finishing		
14. Make buttonhole		
15. Sew buttons	101	6
16. Trim & inspect		

Figure 11–16   Sequence of construction for wool skirt, with panels sequence highlighted. *(Courtesy of Union Special Corporation Technical Training Center.)*

the adjacent pleats. Pleats that gape and parallel pleats that are not parallel indicate low quality.

Ease.   Easing requires an operator to evenly sew a longer piece of fabric to a shorter piece. High-quality easing looks smooth and has no tucks, pleats, or gathers. It is relatively easy to accomplish on long, straight seams but requires skill on curved seams such as sleeve/armscye seams and some collar/neckline seams. Machines that ease one ply while simultaneously sewing it to another ply help ensure an even distribution of ease.

Gathers.   High-quality gathers are perfectly even and fall in parallel folds. For example, high-quality ruffles are gathered evenly, with no pleats or tucks. Accomplishing this requires either very skilled operators, special feeding attachments, or programmable sewing machines adjusted to evenly gather the fabric. Even gathers generally cost more to produce than uneven gathers, but this depends upon the degree of mechanization in the factory. Sometimes a row of stabilizing stitching is used to hold gathers in place until the gathered panel can be joined to the next panel. This stitching, a costly operation, must be completely inserted into the seam (as at a waistband) to hide it, another sign of quality gathering.

Gathering may also be accomplished through the use of elastic or a drawstring. Decorative forms of gathers, such as shirring or smocking, also can serve as dart substitutes (see Chapter 5).

Seaming

Operators seam panels of the garment together using specified stitch and seam types (see Chapters 9 and 10). Seaming causes the garment panels to take on the shape of recognizable garment pieces.

Matching Notches.   One of the keys to assembling fabric panels accurately is matching notches and ends of panels. **Notches** (small slits or wedges cut into the seam allowance) serve as key points for matching the panels. Most seams in garments have notches placed at distances equal to the approximate distance an operator can sew without having to reposition the panels. A tolerance of ±1/4 inch is usually allowed for matching notches as this small amount will not affect the overall performance of the panels when they become a garment. The ends of the panels serve the same purpose. Panels must be matched within a ±1/4-inch tolerance at start and finish of a seam for the garment to hang properly. Feeding mechanisms on the sewing machines must be kept

Table 11–2   Key Seams and Locations Where Pattern Matching is Expected in a High-Quality Garment

- Center front and center back
- Side seams
- Collar at center back (for collars that open in front); collar at center front (for collars that open in back)
- Armscye at bust/chest level
- Shaped facings
- Sleeve plackets
- Pockets/pocket flaps
- Two-piece outfits where they overlap, so that the pattern appears continuous from top to bottom.
- Shoulder seams

balanced to prevent stretching of one layer of cloth and thus uneven bottom edges. Pants and slacks having a side seam with a slightly eased back panel and a perfectly flat front panel exhibit evidence of unbalanced feeding or mismatched notches.

Matching Patterned Fabric.   Mass-producers using striped or plaid fabric with a pattern of approximately one inch or larger attempt to match the pattern at key seams and locations (see Tables 11–2 and 11–3). Usually there is a tolerance to the matched patterns of ±1/4 inch due to the flexible nature of *soft goods* (fabric). Manufacturers of high-quality apparel may match smaller patterns and apply a tighter tolerance than ±1/4 inch. Patterned fabrics that match at seamlines represent high quality. Matching linear patterns and planning the placement of large motifs requires more fabric and is more labor intensive than using solid-color fabrics or overall prints. Remember that the matching of a patterned fabric during construction is possible *only* if the marker is matched and the cutting is accurate. (For more information on matching, see Chapter 4.)

Sewing Seams and Edge Treatments—Flat versus In the Round.   It is less costly to sew seams with the

fabric pieces **flat** than **in the round.** Usually garments are constructed so that as many seams as possible are sewn with the fabric panels and pieces flat. The order in which an operator sews the seams of a garment determines whether the seams are sewn flat or in the round. As a general rule, garments are sewn together with most seams flat because it costs less. But, unfortunately, the finished product does not always fit as smoothly and comfortably as garments with seams sewn in the round. Also, seams sewn in the round are generally more attractive at garment edges than seams sewn flat.

Jeans are constructed with most seams sewn flat by sewing first the **seat seam** (center back seam), then the **outseams** (outer leg seams), and finally the **inseams** (inner leg seams). In contrast, dress pants usually have the seat seam sewn in the round, with the outseams and inseams sewn flat. This method costs more to construct but makes the crotch a free, upstanding seam that is more comfortable to wear, conforms better to the body's natural shape and movements, and is less apt to wrinkle or "smile" at the seat than jeans crotches. The concept of seams sewn flat versus in the round is discussed repeatedly throughout this chapter and Chapter 12.

Table 11–3   Places Where Matching Cannot be Expected at Any Quality Level Because of the Varying Angles of the Pattern Pieces

- Seams with darts (seams with horizontal darts can be matched below the darts.)
- Any area which contains ease or gathers (for example, shoulder seams)
- Yokes (if the yoke is a dart-substitute yoke)
- Armscye backs
- Armscye fronts above bust/chest level
- Raglan sleeves
- Cuffs
- Waistline seams and waistbands

Partial matching may be achieved in many of these areas and is more attractive than no attempt at matching. However, complete matching throughout a fitted garment is impossible if the garment pieces are properly shaped and constructed.

Ideally, operators hem garments in the round after all seams entering the hem line are sewn. This costs more than hemming the garment flat but represents quality construction. Low-price garments are usually hemmed flat and then seamed. The difference between these two techniques is seen in budget versus better T-shirt sleeve hems. An exception to this rule is some pleated skirts; the skirt sections are first hemmed and pleated and then sewn together at the side seams because it would be difficult to accurately hem a skirt after it has been pleated.

Single-Needle Tailoring. Single-needle tailoring indicates the use of single-needle sewing machines even though the seams have multiple rows of stitches; each row of stitches is made in a separate pass through the machine. The alternative is to use machines with two or more parallel needles to make multiple rows of parallel stitches simultaneously. Sewing seams with multiple passes is costly but produces a high-quality, smooth seam.

Single-needle seams are not significantly stronger than multiple-needle seams, but they are more attractive. Many shirt sleeves on men's dress shirts are set in using single-needle tailoring, as indicated by a single row of stitching visible around the armscye on the outside of the garment, but two rows inside the garment (Figure 11–17). Armscye seams constructed this way are stronger than plain safety-stitched seams. Men's shirts are commonly labeled *single-needle tailoring,* although at lower price lines single-needle seams may be found only at the armscye.

Attaching Elastic

Elastic operations are some of the most complicated in ready-to-wear apparel. Special care must be taken to ensure a smooth and accurate application. For most elastic attachments, at the edge or within the body of the garment, applied or within a casing, stitches show on the outside of the garment. The stitches used to apply elastic should be extensible (i.e., 400-, 500-, or 600-class stitches or 300-class zigzag stitches) so they can stretch with the elastic without rupturing. If overedge stitches are used, the knife may be removed from the serger to avoid cutting the elastic.

Sometimes elastic is used in a limited area, for example, across the back of a pair of pants or a jacket. This allows the front of the garment to fit smoothly but shapes the back and allows it to stretch to accommodate a variety of sizes. In such cases, the elastic is sewn flat to the back panel of the garment before the garment is assembled into a circle.

Elastic may encircle an entire body part, such as the waist, wrist, neck, or leg. When elastic encircles a

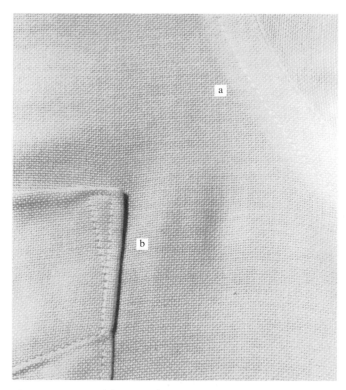

Figure 11–17 (a) Single-needle tailoring on armscye of men's dress shirt, and (b) triangular reinforcement on patch pocket.

body part, the construction sequence calls for sewing all of the garment seams except one. Then the elastic is attached to the garment while both are flat. Finally, the garment and the elastic are joined into a circle using a superimposed seam. This method is lower cost but rather bulky.

In an alternative method for attaching elastic that is found primarily in high-price garments, both the garment and the elastic are sewn into circles before the elastic is attached to the garment. Attaching elastic to the garment in the round results in a smooth, flat, and comfortable elastic application, especially if the elastic is seamed with a nonbulky, lapped seam (Figure 11–18). However, attaching elastic in the round is one of the more expensive variations of elastic application.

When sewing elastic into a circle or when joining two lengths of elastic, lapped seams are preferable to superimposed seams because they are less bulky. Ideally, a rectangle of stitches joins seams in elastic and is less apt than a bar tack to weaken the elastic. (The needle perforations of many stitches weaken the elastic.) In better garments, exposed elastic seams may be covered with a label or a small square of fabric or at the very least bar-tacked flat. These techniques prevent fraying and make the join flat and comfortable (Figure 11–18).

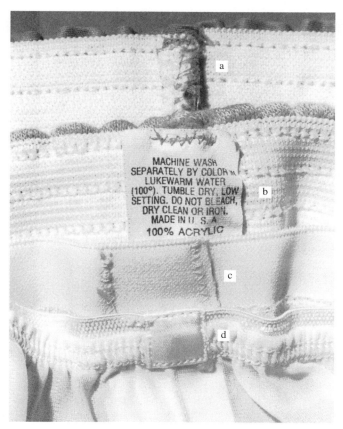

Figure 11–18 Seams in applied elastic: (a) superimposed seam tacked flat, (b) superimposed seam covered with label, (c) lapped seam, and (d) lapped seam covered with square of satin.

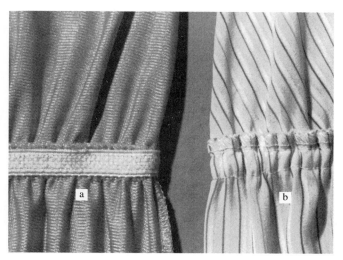

Figure 11–19 Elastic in body of garment: (a) applied, and (b) in casing made from seam allowances stitched to garment.

Applied Elastic. **Applied elastic** is stitched directly onto the garment (either on the inside or outside) to add shape where desired (see Figure 11–19a). At garment edges, the raw edge of the garment is usually folded under and caught between the fabric and the applied elastic during the set elastic operation. As it is applied, the elastic is stretched to fit the garment. This difficult operation is carried out in one of two ways. One involves the use of metering devices on the sewing machines. Metering devices are useful in medium- and lightweight fabrics but are less accurate when used on heavyweight fabrics. Their main advantage is the consistency and even distribution of fullness, but sizing accuracy can be lost if the correct amount of elastic is not fed into the machine.

The other method of applying elastic uses elastic cut to size and is dependent on the skill level of the operator. Cutting to size has the advantage of getting the correct length of elastic into the garment but does not guarantee that the fullness will be evenly distributed as the operator stretches the elastic manually during application.

Elastic Casings. **Elastic casings** (tunnels) must be large enough to accommodate the elastic without causing it to fold, but not so large as to allow the elastic to twist within them. Additional rows of stitching stabilize the casings and prevent the elastic from twisting. For elastic waistlines, multiple narrow elastic casings look trimmer and less bulky than a single wide casing.

Most set elastic operations call for stitching the elastic to the casing and the casing to the garment simultaneously. However, in some high-quality garments, the elastic is not stitched to the casing but floats freely within it.

If the elastic moves freely about within the casing and the fabric can be redistributed over the length of the elastic, the casing contains free-floating elastic. **Free-floating elastic casings** are less bulky and more comfortable to wear than other casings. However, because the elastic floats freely within the casing, it has a tendency to twist and roll, so nonroll elastic is recommended, especially if the casing is wide. Free-floating elastic casings cost more to produce than other casings.

Edge Casings. *Edge casings* are fast and economical to make, they do not allow the elastic to twist, and they reduce the tendency of the elastic to roll. However, this method is somewhat bulky and necessitates a stiff, bulky seam through all layers to close the garment into a circle. To alter or replace the elastic, all the stitches must be removed. To make a folded casing at an edge, the raw edge is usually overedged to the elastic; simultaneously, the edge is turned under (to enclose the elastic) and stitched to the garment.

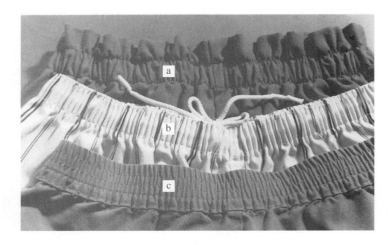

Figure 11–20   Elastic casings at waistline: (a) with header, (b) folded, with drawstring, and (c) formed with separate band of fabric.

Another method for making a casing involves attaching a separate band of fabric to the garment edge (Figure 11–20). In a single operation, the operator feeds a narrow band of fabric lengthwise into a folder, enclosing the elastic and seaming the folded band to the garment edge. This somewhat bulky method is sometimes required on unusually shaped edges but mainly is found in high-volume garments (for example, children's jeans and pull-on knit pants). The use of a separate band to form the casing results in more small pattern pieces than an attached edge casing, resulting in cost savings through better material utilization.

Casings Within Body of Garment. To create a casing within the body of a garment, often the operator stitches two seam allowances together or stitches the seam allowances to the garment to encase the elastic (Figure 11–19b). No stitches show on the outside of the garment if the seam allowances are stitched together. Another method for applying a casing within the body of the garment involves stitching a strip of fabric to the garment, enclosing the elastic. The fabric strip should be nonbulky and nonraveling.

Hemming Garments and Applying Other Edge Treatments

Operators hem and otherwise finish garment edges in a variety of ways (see Chapter 10). Hems are usually topstitched or blindstitched. Interestingly, some garment hems are among the first steps in the production process (pocket hems) while others are among the last (hems in tailored skirts). Other common edge treatments include serging, facings, bindings, bands, and plackets. These operations may also take place at different points in the production process depending on the particular garment and the sequence of construction planned by the spec technician.

SUMMARY

Preliminary garment assembly of parts and panels includes the operations that prepare small parts and those performed on garment panels before they are joined into three-dimensional pieces of the garment. Edges are serged. Labels are attached, either as cut-and-fold, single or loop, mitered, or four-side sew. Belt loops and other miscellaneous loops are constructed and sometimes applied during preliminary assembly. Rivets, bar tacks, and other reinforcements are applied to lend strength at key points of strain, either during parts and panel assembly, or later in the process. Garment parts and panels are often hemmed during preliminary assembly.

Stitching trims are ornamental stitchings. Topstitching is straight stitches that accent the garment. Embroidery stitches form a decorative design. Narrow fabric trims such as ribbon, lace, or braid may be sewn or glued on. Appliqués are fabric patches applied to garments, usually with fusing and satin stitches. Nonfabric trims such as beads and sequins must be securely attached.

In garments such as jeans, zippers are assembled after the stringers are applied to the garment. Operators apply assembled zippers by the slot, lapped, or invisible methods, identified by the number of rows of topstitching used to attach the zipper. Fly-front zippers are a form of lapped zipper used in pants. They can be constructed in a variety of ways. A fly shield and French fly are signs of quality. Zippers should be reinforced at the base and have a closure at the top to help absorb stress.

Patch pockets are easy to construct and attach, usually by topstitching them to the garment, sometimes through automation. In-seam pockets are concealed or exposed; the ends of the opening edges should be reinforced and the pocket bags should be double stitched for durability. Slashed pockets are costly to construct because of the fabric and labor requirements. Automation has reduced the cost and increased the consistency of slashed pockets. Slashed pockets include single- and double-welt pockets and upturned-flap pockets. Flaps may be added to any pocket type.

Operators apply interfacing most commonly by fusing it to the garment using appropriate time, temperature and pressure to avoid delamination and other problems. Some interfacings are sewn in. Interfacings in tailored garments may be pad stitched to add subtle shaping. Underlinings are applied, if applicable.

Garment shaping begins on panels. Darts should be accurately stitched, pleats and tucks parallel and on straight-of-grain, and gathers and ease evenly distributed. Seams should be sewn matching notches and ends. Patterns such as plaids and stripes should be matched at most seams of the garment; matched patterns indicate quality but add to fabric and labor costs. Seams sewn in the round are generally preferable to those sewn flat. Single-needle tailoring is also a mark of quality.

Elastic applied in the round is a sign of quality. Elastic is attached by applying it directly to the garment or in a casing; elastic may be required at the edge or within the body of the garment. The highest-quality garments allow the elastic to float freely in its casing. Lapped seams are superior to superimposed seams in elastic. Too many stitches in elastic weaken it.

Preliminary Assembly Quality Checklist

If you can answer yes to each of these questions regarding the garment you are evaluating, it was produced using high-quality preliminary garment assembly methods.

✓ Are care labels securely attached for the life of the garment?
✓ Are decorative trims even in width, fully and evenly gathered, and securely applied?
✓ Are trims mitered at corners to avoid bulk and eased or stretched around curves to avoid distortion?
✓ Are trims sewn on, not glued on?
✓ Are the ends of ribbons and other trims finished to prevent raveling?
✓ Is embroidery dense, smooth, and backed with interfacing?
✓ Is topstitching even and straight?
✓ Are the chain and tape of the zipper concealed?
✓ Is there a bar tack at the base of the fly zipper?
✓ Is zipper topstitching straight and even?
✓ Is there a closure located at the top of the zipper?

✓ As a quality extra, is the zipper hand picked?
✓ Does the fly zipper have a comfortable, durable, nonbulky underlap and overlap?
✓ Do men's pants contain a French fly with a lined fly shield?
✓ As a quality extra, is there a lingerie guard on the zipper in women's clothing?
✓ Are pockets positioned conveniently and attractively?
✓ Are pocket edges reinforced?
✓ Are applied pockets evenly shaped, with no raw edges exposed?
✓ Are large applied pockets interfaced and/or lined for smoothness and durability?
✓ Are in-seam pockets nonbulky, with the pocket bag concealed when the pocket gapes?
✓ Are slashed pockets even, on-grain rectangles that do not sag or spread?
✓ Are belt loops and other loops securely attached?
✓ Are there enough belt loops to support the belt, including one at the center back of pants and skirts?
✓ Is the application of interfacings, especially fusibles, smooth and nonbulky?
✓ Are sew-in interfacings in tailored garments pad stitched? As a quality extra in high-price lines, are they pad stitched by hand?
✓ Are darts flat, with no dimple or bubble at the tips?
✓ Are dart tips secured?
✓ Are pleats and tucks even and on-grain?
✓ Are gathers even and full?
✓ Is ease smooth and free of tucks, pleats, or gathers?
✓ Are linear patterns of more than 1/4 inch matched at all major seams where matching is possible?
✓ Was the garment hemmed before the opening edge was finished?
✓ Are facings, bindings, and bands applied in the round instead of flat?
✓ Does elastic remain flat, without rolling or twisting?
✓ Is elastic seamed with a lapped seam?
✓ As a quality extra in high-price lines, is elastic attached in the round?
✓ As a quality extra in high-price lines, is the casing made first and then the elastic inserted?
✓ If a superimposed seam in elastic is exposed, is it tacked down or covered with a label or small square of fabric?

New Terms

If you can define each of these terms and differentiate between related terms, you have gained a good working vocabulary for discussing the topics in this chapter. The terms are listed in the order in which they appeared in the chapter.

parts + panels = pieces
pieces + pieces = products
sequence of construction
preliminary assembly
ornamental stitching (OS)
topstitching/accent stitching
edgestitching
embroidery
monogram
cutwork
trapunto
hemstitching
fagoting
satin stitch
hand picked zipper
slot zipper
exposed zipper
wind flap
lingerie guard
lapped zipper
fly-front zipper
fly shield
French fly
invisible zipper application
template
pocket bag
concealed inseam pocket
exposed inseam pocket
belt loop
pad stitching
reinforcement
rivet
tack
bar tack
ticket tack
arrowhead tack
notch
flat versus in the round construction
seat seam
outseam
inseam
single-needle tailoring
applied elastic
elastic casing
free-floating elastic casing

Review Questions

1. Explain the equations "Parts + Panels = Pieces" and "Pieces + Pieces = Products."
2. How do notches aid the mass-production process?

3. Tell whether the following statement is true or false: "The opening edge should be finished first; then the garment should be hemmed." Justify your answer.
4. How are appliqués different from embroidery?
5. How is hemstitching different from fagoting?
6. How are rivets different from bar tacks?
7. What is the purpose of hanger loops?
8. How does flat versus in the round construction affect quality?
9. What is the advantage of single-needle tailoring?
10. What are the characteristics of a well-made dart?
11. Why are full, even gathers considered a sign of high quality? Do they always reflect higher costs?
12. What factors are important in applying fusible interfacing?
13. Why are pockets on basic garments often better executed than those on fashion garments?
14. Describe the various ways applied pockets are attached. What are the advantages and disadvantages of each?
15. Why are lapped seams superior to superimposed seams in elastic applications?

Activities

1. Visit an area apparel manufacturer's production facility. How closely do their methods follow the "parts to panels, pieces to products" sequence of construction?
2. Find examples of garments with narrow trims. Evaluate the application of the trims.
3. Find examples of the following stitching trims and evaluate them:
   a. topstitching
   b. edgestitching
   c. cutwork
   d. smocking
   e. shirring
4. Examine low-price and high-price garments with bows made of ribbon. Are the ends of the ribbons treated to prevent raveling?
5. Find garments with these zipper applications and evaluate them:
   a. lapped
   b. invisible
   c. exposed
   d. fly-front
   e. fly-front with French fly
6. Examine low-price and high-price pairs of jeans. Where are reinforcements used? Are there other locations where you would recommend that reinforcements be placed?

7. Examine low-price and high-price men's suit pants. Can you find any with heel guards? How many belt loops do the pants have? Do they have a belt loop sewn on at center back? Why or why not?

8. Evaluate the construction of the following pocket types in low-price and high-price garments:
   a. applied
   b. concealed in-seam
   c. exposed in-seam
   d. single-welt
   e. double-welt
   f. upturned-flap

   What differences, if any, do you find?

9. Examine garments made of plaid or other linear-design fabrics. Evaluate the pattern matching. Did the manufacturer try to minimize the need for pattern matching in any way?

10. Examine garments from your wardrobe that contain fusible interfacing. Evaluate the quality of the fusible applications.

11. Find examples of garments that illustrate flat versus in the round construction for
    a. elastic application
    b. facing
    c. hem
    d. band
    e. binding

12. Find examples of and evaluate garments with
    a. elasticized waistline at garment edge
    b. elasticized waistline within body of garment

Garment Assembly and Finishing: Pieces into Products

Chapter Objectives

1. Identify industry production flow process for garment assembly and finishing of manufactured garments.
2. Evaluate cost and quality of various assembly procedures.

The concept of *Parts, Panels, Pieces, and Products* was introduced in Chapter 4. Chapter 11 discussed the first part of the equation, "Parts + Panels = Pieces." Continuing along these lines, this chapter discusses the second part of the equation, "Pieces + Pieces = Products." During the main garment assembly process, partially assembled pieces are sewn to other partially assembled pieces to create finished garments. These products, when assembled, are ready for finishing. Finishing includes all the final steps necessary to get a product ready for shipping. Every step in the assembly and finishing process plays an important role in building quality into a product; all steps work together for a synergistic effect. (For more information, see Related Resources: Mass Production/Assembly.)

PIECE ASSEMBLY

As pieces are joined together, the garment begins to assume a readily recognizable appearance, whereas before seaming it might have looked like a jumble of parts and panels to the untrained eye (Figure 12–1). Piece assembly includes the construction of collars and necklines, sleeves, cuffs, waistlines and waistbands, and lining.

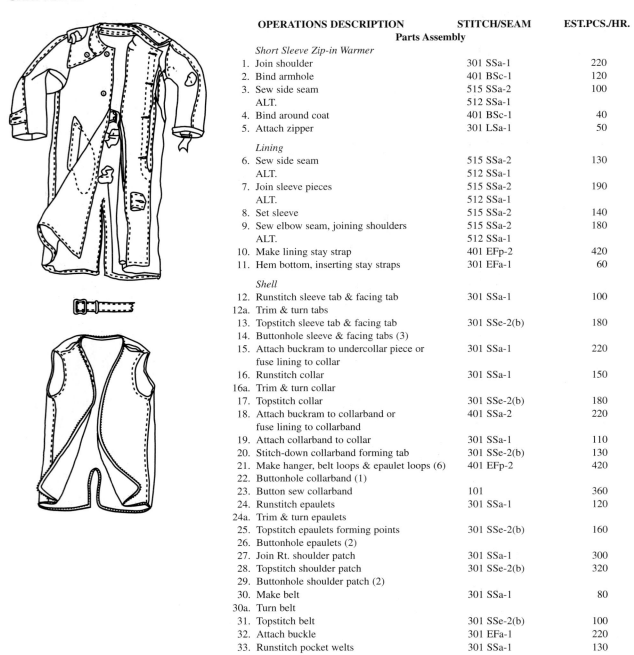

OPERATIONS DESCRIPTION	STITCH/SEAM	EST.PCS./HR.
Parts Assembly		
Short Sleeve Zip-in Warmer		
1. Join shoulder	301 SSa-1	220
2. Bind armhole	401 BSc-1	120
3. Sew side seam	515 SSa-2	100
ALT.	512 SSa-1	
4. Bind around coat	401 BSc-1	40
5. Attach zipper	301 LSa-1	50
Lining		
6. Sew side seam	515 SSa-2	130
ALT.	512 SSa-1	
7. Join sleeve pieces	515 SSa-2	190
ALT.	512 SSa-1	
8. Set sleeve	515 SSa-2	140
9. Sew elbow seam, joining shoulders	515 SSa-2	180
ALT.	512 SSa-1	
10. Make lining stay strap	401 EFp-2	420
11. Hem bottom, inserting stay straps	301 EFa-1	60
Shell		
12. Runstitch sleeve tab & facing tab	301 SSa-1	100
12a. Trim & turn tabs		
13. Topstitch sleeve tab & facing tab	301 SSe-2(b)	180
14. Buttonhole sleeve & facing tabs (3)		
15. Attach buckram to undercollar piece or fuse lining to collar	301 SSa-1	220
16. Runstitch collar	301 SSa-1	150
16a. Trim & turn collar		
17. Topstitch collar	301 SSe-2(b)	180
18. Attach buckram to collarband or fuse lining to collarband	401 SSa-2	220
19. Attach collarband to collar	301 SSa-1	110
20. Stitch-down collarband forming tab	301 SSe-2(b)	130
21. Make hanger, belt loops & epaulet loops (6)	401 EFp-2	420
22. Buttonhole collarband (1)		
23. Button sew collarband	101	360
24. Runstitch epaulets	301 SSa-1	120
24a. Trim & turn epaulets		
25. Topstitch epaulets forming points	301 SSe-2(b)	160
26. Buttonhole epaulets (2)		
27. Join Rt. shoulder patch	301 SSa-1	300
28. Topstitch shoulder patch	301 SSe-2(b)	320
29. Buttonhole shoulder patch (2)		
30. Make belt	301 SSa-1	80
30a. Turn belt		
31. Topstitch belt	301 SSe-2(b)	100
32. Attach buckle	301 EFa-1	220
33. Runstitch pocket welts	301 SSa-1	130

Figure 12–1 Sequence of construction for trench coat, with pieces sequence highlighted. *(Courtesy of Union Special Corporation Technical Training Center.)*

Constructing Collars

Necklines without collars may be finished by any edge treatment such as facing, binding, or banding. Some collar types finish all or part of the neckline edge; other collar types require an additional neckline finish such as a facing. The finish depends on neckline shape, fabric construction and weight, and cost considerations.

A collar is one of three types: flat, standing, or rolled (either partial or full roll) (see Chapter 5).

For flat collars, the inner edge of the collar is attached to the neckline edge of the garment. Then the neckline is finished with a binding, facing, stitching, or other edge finish. Standing collars are applied to the neckline with the raw edge of the garment neckline sandwiched between the collar layers as the collar is sewn on. However, if the neckline edge is not sandwiched between the collar layers, a neckline facing is required in addition to the collar to finish the neckline edge. This method produces a bulky neckline.

OPERATIONS DESCRIPTION	STITCH/SEAM	EST.PCS./HR.
Parts Assembly		
33a. Trim & turn welts		
34. Topstitch pocket welts	301 SSe-2(b)	140
Panel Assembly		
35. Hang pocket pieces inserting welts	301 SSa-1	120
36. Bag pocket	301 SSa-1	240
37. Stitch around pocket welts	301 SSa-1	100
38. Attach buckram to front panels or fuse	301 SSa-1	100
39. Join back panels & raise back seam	401 LSq-2(b)	50
40. Sew side seam & raise seam	401 LSq-2(b)	40
41. Join sleeve pieces	301 SSa-1	65
Pieces Assembly		
42. Set sleeve & raise seam in front & back	301 SSa-1	50
43. Sew elbow seam inserting tabs & joining shoulder	301 SSa-1	60
44. Raise elbow seam	301 LSq-2(b)	30
45. Bartack belt & epaulet loops		
46. Sew buttons to shoulder, sleeves & Rt. front		101
47. Make neck facing	301 SSa-1	210
48. Attach facing pieces	301 SSa-1	240
49. Attach zipper to facing	301 LSa-1	40
50. Make buttonhole fly	301 SSe-2(b)	240
51. Buttonhole button fly		
52. Bartack button fly to facing		
53. Edgestitch facing	301 OSf-1	60
54. Attach lining to facing, gathering lining at neck	301 SSa-1	50
55. Attach facing tab to Lt. front facing & tack down	301 LSq-2(b)	220
56. Attach belt loops	301 SSa-1	300
57. Attach facing to shell inserting hang loop & collar	301 SSa-1	50
58. Edgestitch coat	301 SSe-2(b)	60
59. Hem bottom of coat inserting lining stay straps	301 EFb-1	60
60. Tack vent	301 SSa-1	240
61. Attach lining at vent	301 SSa-1	140
62. Attach lining at cuff	301 SSa-1	100
63. Tack sleeve lining	301 SSa-1	180
Product Assembly/Finishing		
64. Sew buttons to Rt. front	101	
65. Stitch down buttonhole front	301 OSa-1	120
66. Attach size ticket	101	
67. Trim & inspect		
68. Press		

For cowl necklines, designers choose soft, lightweight, bias-cut or knit fabrics. Cowls have *no* interfacing so they are flexible and drapable. The neckline edge is faced after the cowl is sewn on, or the neckline seam is finished with an overedge stitch or flattened with a bottom-covering chainstitch.

The outer edges of a high-quality collar are smooth, even, and flat; points should be sharp and identical in both shape and length. Any trim such as lace or piping is even in width all around the collar and is applied without pleats or puckers. To achieve a quality appearance, operators are trained to miter trim at corners, stretching it slightly around concave curves or easing it around convex curves.

The collar is constructed as either a single ply or one, two, or three pieces that form a double ply plus interfacing. The more pieces involved, the more labor required and generally the higher the cost of the collar. Complex collars usually provide better-looking and more durable results on tailored garments, while simple collars are appropriate in casual sportswear styles.

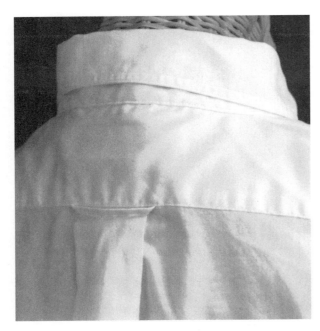

Figure 12–2 Collar exposes neckline seam. Also note locker loop and box pleat at center back below yoke.

The application of a collar to a jacket or coat with lapels requires extra labor and attention to detail. **Lapels** or **revers** are the pieces of the garment that roll or fold back above the front closure (Figure 5–24). The seam where the collar and lapel meet is the **gorge line.** The joining of the collar and lapels is critical to the appearance of a garment and is a good indicator of the care with which it was constructed. A skilled operator must accurately match the collar and lapels and stitch them together exactly to the gorge line but not beyond. Otherwise, a hole or puckering may form at the end of the gorge line. All excess bulk must be removed from the seam area formed by the collar and lapels for it to lie smoothly. In a loosely woven fabric, if too much of the seam allowance is removed, a hole may form.

The fall on a rolled collar should be long enough to cover the neckline seam of the garment. A skimpy, poorly designed collar often exposes the neckline seam where the collar is sewn to the garment (Figure 12–2). This is a mark of low quality.

Every rolled collar features a **roll line,** where the collar naturally tends to roll. Producers of better-tailored jackets and coats reinforce the roll line with a stay tape (twill tape) so it rolls more readily. Where the collar begins to roll depends on the level of the garment opening. The roll line of each lapel should not be artificially pressed in but should roll naturally on its own as a result of the interfacing and other shaping techniques that were used.

The interfacing of collars and lapels on better-tailored jackets and coats features pad stitching to help the collar and lapels roll smoothly. Pad stitching builds shape and support into the collar and lapels.

Single-Layer Collars. Sometimes a single layer of fabric is used as a collar, for example, lace collars or the knit collars used on most polo-style shirts. The fabric in a single-layer collar must have adequate body to lie smoothly. Although the labor cost involved in producing such a collar is low, the overall cost of the collar depends on the quality and cost of the raw materials used.

One-Piece Collar Construction. Most collars consist of two layers of shell fabric with interfacing between the plies; these collars may be formed from one, two, or three pieces of fabric. One-piece collar construction is simple and inexpensive. The operator folds a single piece of fabric in half lengthwise and sews the ends together, producing a two-ply collar. A one-piece collar is low in bulk because it has a fold rather than an enclosed seam at the outer edge. If nonfusible interfacing is used inside the collar, it should be secured with a line of stitches to prevent it from rolling.

One-piece collars are uncommon because the outer edge is a fold, which cannot be shaped; thus, only full-roll collars are made by this method because their outer edge is fairly straight. The outer edges of rolled collars made from one piece tend to curl upward because the slight shaping that could prevent curling is not possible at the folded edge. Another disadvantage is that trims such as lace or piping cannot be inserted in the folded edge of one-piece collars but must be topstitched on the outside. One-piece collars are mainly found on sportswear and sleepwear in low-price lines, and on inexpensive uniforms and smocks.

Two-Piece Collar Construction. Most collars are two-piece collars. Two-piece collars are made by sewing two plies of fabric, an **upper collar** and **under collar** (which becomes a facing for the collar) together using an enclosed seam. Interfacing is placed between the layers for shape and support. Two-piece collars require more labor but are often more fabric efficient than one-piece collars because they require two small fabric pieces rather than one large piece. On tailored garments, the under collar may be cut on the bias for a more pleasing roll (Figure 12–3b).

Collars on most men's suit jackets and sport jackets are **bluff-edge collars.** The under collar is made of *felt*, a nonwoven material with no grain (Figure 12–4). (Tailor's felt was originally a woven wool with a grain line that was felted so it would not ravel. Although

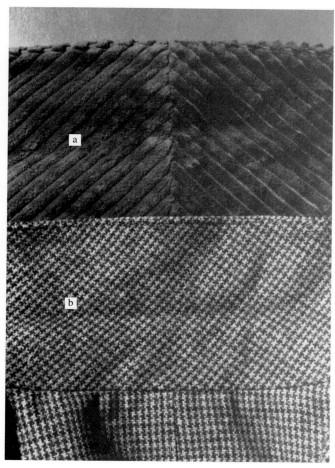

Figure 12–3   Under collars of two jackets: (a) three-piece collar with two-piece under collar cut on the bias and seamed at center back, and (b) two-piece collar with one-piece under collar cut on the bias.

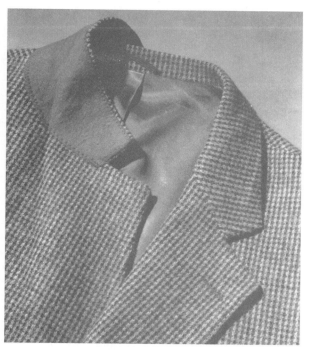

Figure 12–4   Bluff-edge collar with under collar made of felt. Also note ease pleat at center back of garment lining and decorative buttonhole on lapel.

tailor's felt is still available, nonwoven felt is now commonly used.) Because there is no grain difference in the two halves of felt used for the under collar, both sides roll identically, resulting in a sharp and graceful roll. Bluff-edge collars are so called because the felt has no seam allowances at the collar edges where it is stitched to the face of the upper collar; the raw edges of the felt are even with the turned-under edges of the upper collar. Felt, which does not ravel, makes the bluff-edge collar less bulky than other types because only the seam allowances of the upper collar are included in the seam at the collar edges. In high-quality jackets, the felt is stitched on by hand to create a less rigid, more flexible collar.

Three-Piece Collar Construction. The three-piece collar is composed of three pieces of fabric: an upper collar, and an under collar made of two halves with a seam in the center. A three-piece collar can be identified by the vertical seam in the middle of the under collar (Figure 12–3a). The under collar pieces are cut on the bias. The interfacing, if woven, is also cut in two pieces and on the bias. The bias cut aids the pleasing roll of the collar, because both halves of the finished collar roll identically since the grain of the two halves is identical. This is superior to an under collar cut on the bias all in one piece. Three-piece collars require more fabric and labor than the other collar types, increasing costs. They are mainly used on high-quality tailored garments.

On two- and three-piece collars, the under collar as well as the enclosed seam at the outer edge of the collar should not be visible. The spec technician may specify a control stitch for the enclosed seam to prevent the under collar from rolling out and showing; this stitch is a mark of better quality found in moderate- and high-price lines. Pressing the collar so the enclosed seam lies slightly under the edge and topstitching it in this position accomplishes the same result.

The under collars in better-tailored garments may be cut slightly smaller than the upper collars, and the operator then eases them to fit as they are sewn. This procedure, known as **slipping** or **bubbling,** prevents the under collar and the enclosed seam at the outer edge of the collar from slipping out and showing. Slipping pulls the seamline and the upper collar slightly under at the edge as the collar is sewn. Collars are rarely slipped in ready-to-wear because of the skilled labor required to smoothly join the two differently sized collar pieces. Slipping can also be used to improve the appearance of cuffs and other garment parts that are faced and have an enclosed seam at the edge. Without slipping, an enclosed seam in a heavy fabric may appear bulky and unattractive because the seamline and facing are noticeable at the edge.

Setting Sleeves

A sleeveless garment has no sleeves to finish its armhole edges. Consequently, the armholes of a sleeveless garment must be faced, bound, banded, edge-finish stitched, or otherwise treated to finish the raw edges.

Sleeves are either set-in, raglan, or kimono (see Chapter 5). Asymmetrical armscyes reflecting the forward pitch of the shoulders generally provide better fit than symmetrical armscyes. However, when pattern-makers plan armscye fronts and backs identically so the sleeve cap is symmetrical, fit becomes compromised for faster production and fewer sleeve-setting errors.

For most children's casual garments and sleepwear, and for low- and moderate-price men's shirts and womenswear with loosely fitting armscyes, symmetrical armscyes and sleeve caps have become the rule. Asymmetrical armscyes and sleeve caps are found only in better tailored garments.

Set-In Sleeves. Set-in sleeves fit the body more closely than any other sleeve type but still allow room for comfortable movement. This is accomplished through complex cutting and construction of both the bodice and sleeve. The sleeve has a shaped *cap* (the part above the biceps), cut larger than the armscye, that is eased into the armscye. This fits the cap to the rounded, upper part of the arm (see basic block Figure 5–5). Sleeves are correctly positioned in the armscye by matching notches, thus ensuring that the fullness is appropriately distributed.

An eased sleeve allows the sleeve to fit the rounded portion of the upper arm more smoothly than an uneased sleeve, which pulls and wrinkles, making the sleeve unattractive and uncomfortable. In addition, some set-in sleeves contain extra fullness in the cap, which is controlled by gathers or pleats. Gathered and pleated sleeves provide fitting ease plus design ease and are slightly easier to set than eased sleeves. In many low-price garments, the design provides for little ease because of the expense necessary to have a skilled operator set an eased sleeve into an armscye.

The closer the fit of the armscye and sleeve, the higher and more extreme the curve of the sleeve cap

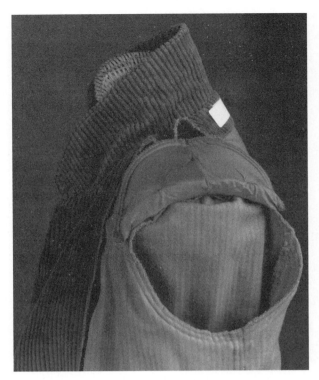

Figure 12–5   Sleeve set in the round.

and the more difficult to ease the sleeve cap into the armscye. The looser the fit of the armscye and sleeve, the flatter and more gradual the curve of the sleeve cap and the easier to set the sleeve cap into the armscye. Because the armscye seam is subjected to stress, especially in the lower half of the armscye, it should be stitched twice for maximum durability.

Setting sleeves set too far forward or too far back results in an off-grain sleeve that can bind, wrinkle, or twist. As little as half an inch of tilt can cause a problem in some sleeve styles. If the sleeve is set too far back, it pulls against the front of the arm. If the sleeve is set too far forward, it strains across the back of the arm. Correctly set sleeves are attractive, comfortable, and definitely an indicator of quality.

Sleeves can be set into armscyes in one of two ways: (1) in the round, with the underarm seam of the sleeve and side seam of the garment closed, or (2) flat, with the underarm seam of the sleeve and side seam of the garment open.

Set In the Round. Sleeves are traditionally *set in the round*. The underarm seam of the sleeve is sewn to create a tube, and the side seam and shoulder seam of the garment are sewn to create a round armscye. The tubular sleeve section is then set to the round armscye of the garment (Figure 12–5).

Sleeves set in the round can be recognized by examining the underarm seam intersection. If the sleeve is set in the round, the armscye seam is a continuous, unbroken circular seam. Setting a sleeve in the round provides for the closest, smoothest fit possible while still allowing movement. The sleeve must be designed with a high, very curved, narrow cap that fits the rounded, upper portion of the arm. A skilled operator eases the fullness of the sleeve cap to the armscye; the finished sleeve and armscye should appear smooth and closely fitted to the body. Tiny, unwanted pleats or puckers in the armscye seam resulting from inaccurate easing or too much fullness in the sleeve cap detract from the quality of a set-in sleeve.

Sleeves set in the round are comfortable to wear because the seam allowances follow the hollow of the underarm area from front to back. A sleeve set flat has seam allowances that protrude into the underarm from side to side and do not follow the contours of the body. Setting a sleeve in the round requires more time and expertise than setting it flat and therefore costs considerably more in labor. Sewing machines with programmable ease make the task more cost effective, but this operation still remains more dependent on operator skill than almost any other step in garment construction.

Sleeves set in the round look attractive in tailored and dressy clothes that require close, smooth-fitting armscyes. Because sleeves are costly to set in the round, this method is usually reserved for apparel in high-price lines.

Tailored coats and jackets often feature two-piece sleeves, which are always set in the round. The **two-piece sleeve** consists of two portions: the main sleeve piece and a second narrow, shaped sleeve piece under the arm. The seams that attach this second piece are dart substitutes that shape the elbow area so the sleeve follows the natural curve of the arm smoothly as it hangs in a relaxed position. Two-piece sleeves usually cost more to produce than one-piece sleeves because of the additional labor required, but they provide better quality through the improved fit.

Set in Flat. The least costly and most common way to set a sleeve is to stitch the sleeve to the garment while both are still open and flat. The tubular shape of the sleeve and garment body are then formed in one operation by sewing the side seam of the garment and the underarm seam of the sleeve in one long seam. A sleeve *set in flat* can be recognized by examining the intersection of the seams in the underarm area. If the sleeve was set in flat, the side seam and sleeve seam are a single, continuous seam (Figure 12–6).

Sleeves set flat do not fit as smoothly as sleeves set in the round. They tend to be cut looser than sleeves

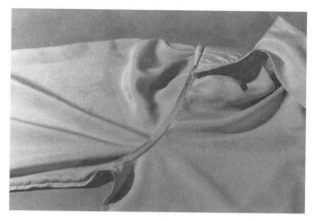

Figure 12–6   Sleeve set in flat.

set in the round to compensate for lower and less-shapely sleeve caps. Working with flat panels and small amounts of sleeve cap ease makes sleeves quick and easy to set flat and therefore less costly than sleeves set in the round. Because of the loose cut, sleeves set flat are comfortable to wear but often have wrinkles of excess fabric evident in the sleeve and in the garment near the sleeve.

All men's shirts at all price levels feature sleeves set flat; in fact, sleeves set flat are sometimes referred to simply as shirt-style sleeves. A jacket is usually worn over dress shirts, making a smooth fit less important.

Sleeves in sportswear for women and children, where comfort and low cost are more important than a close fit, are also commonly set flat. Sleeves set flat are also the most common type in low-price lines of dressy clothes for women and children; in dressy clothes, sleeves set flat often represent low cost and quality.

Kimono Sleeves.   Kimono sleeves are the simplest to construct because they are cut as one with the body of the garment. Because the sleeves are not separate pieces sewn to the garment, labor costs are minimized. However, garments with kimono sleeves may cost more than those with other types of sleeves because of poor material utilization. Material utilization is particularly low for garments with kimono sleeves because the pattern pieces are large and unusually shaped. Garments with kimono sleeves often have seams at center front and/or center back to reduce the size of the garment/sleeve pattern piece and thus reduce material costs. The kimono sleeve itself may be pieced or seamed to the body of the garment to improve material utilization; the sleeve qualifies as a kimono sleeve as long as the underarm curve is cut as part of the body of the garment.

When kimono sleeves fit close to the underarm, obvious wrinkles at the underarm appear. When the sleeve fits loosely, soft folds of extra fabric form in the underarm area. Both types are subject to strain in the underarm area when the wearer moves, but the more fitted kimono sleeves, which feature a higher underarm curve and/or a downward/angled shoulder seam, are especially prone to strain. The underarm seam of kimono sleeves must be adequately reinforced to withstand stress; the correct stitch type in the underarm area is a must. In high-quality garments, spec technicians reinforce the underarm seam with stay tape to strengthen it.

Sometimes designers or patternmakers add a triangular or diamond-shaped *gusset* (of bias-cut fabric) to the underarm of kimono sleeves (Figure 5–13). A gusset increases the roominess and comfort of the sleeve and allows the wearer to reach farther without straining the underarm seam. A gusset requires extra material and skilled labor to set into the underarm area. All the garment seams must match the points of the gusset, and the points should be sharp and free of unwanted pleats, puckers, or holes. Gussets may be added to any sleeve type to provide additional roominess but are most common in kimono sleeves. They are considered a mark of quality.

Raglan Sleeves. A raglan sleeve is recognizable by its characteristic diagonal seam, which runs from the underarm to the neckline of the garment. The diagonal seam attaches the tapered sleeve panel to the body of the garment (Figure 7–2).

A raglan sleeve may be set to the garment in one of two ways, flat or in the round. The most common and least expensive method is attaching the flat sleeve panels to the flat garment and then sewing the side seam of the garment and the underarm seam of the sleeve in one continuous and uninterrupted seam. The alternative in the round method requires sewing the side seams of the garment and then sewing the sleeves into tubes before joining them to the garment. In the round construction can be recognized by examining the seams in the underarm area; the armscye seam is continuous and interrupts the side seam and sleeve underarm seam. This method makes the sleeve more comfortable but is more costly than the flat method, so it is rarely used in low price lines. However, in the round application is used in all price lines for garments made of tubular knits without side seams (for example, sweatshirts and T-shirts) because there is no alternative way to join a raglan sleeve to these garments.

Designers use darts or dart substitutes to release fullness in the shoulder area of raglan sleeves to help the sleeve cover the rounded portion of the upper arm. *Split raglan sleeves* are made of two sleeve panels sewn together with a seam down the length of the

outer arm that shapes the sleeve to the shoulder and neckline. The seam is bias, and the operator must take care not to stretch it during production, or the seam may ripple and pucker. Darted and seamed raglan sleeves typically provide a tailored look but do not fit a wide range of people due to the close fit. Raglan sleeves gathered to the neckline are a better choice for fitting a wide range of sizes. However, gathers in a raglan sleeve provide a feminine look and are mainly used in women's and children's clothes, not in menswear. In sweatshirts and other knit garments, the stretch of the fabric serves as the dart substitute.

Adding Cuffs

While sleeves are usually sewn together and attached to the body of the garment during assembly, cuffs follow varying paths. Some are fully or partially made in preliminary assembly and then attached during the assembly process, and some are fully made and attached in assembly, depending upon cuff style.

Cuffs should be interfaced for smoothness and support unless they are rib knit bands intended to stretch over the hand for dressing and undressing. If sew-in interfacing is used, it should be caught in a seam or secured with a line of stitches at each edge to prevent the interfacing from rolling up during wear.

Cuff bands are constructed from a single ply of fabric folded in half or from two plies of fabric seamed together. One-piece cuff construction, identified by a fold at the lower edge, is less bulky and requires less labor but more fabric than two-piece cuffs. Two-piece cuffs are slightly more bulky than one-piece cuffs but are more fabric efficient because they use smaller fabric pieces. Two-piece cuffs cost less in materials but more in labor because they must be seamed together. Two-piece cuffs can be identified by the enclosed seam at the outer edge.

Cuffs should lie flat and have smooth, even curves and flat, sharp corners. Operators press and topstitch cuffs to prevent the cuff facing from slipping out and showing. In high-price garments, cuffs may be control stitched to accomplish this.

Open-Band Cuffs. Cuffs that have an opening require a placket in the sleeve that is usually buttoned closed; a zipper, tie, or other fastener may also be used. The cuff should lap, front over back, and fasten on the outer edge of the wrist or arm. If the operator accidentally sets the sleeves into the wrong armscyes or puts buttonholes in the underlaps, the cuffs will not button correctly.

Open-band cuffs are constructed first and then attached to the sleeves. Cuffs attached with two rows of stitches, one row to attach the cuff and a second row

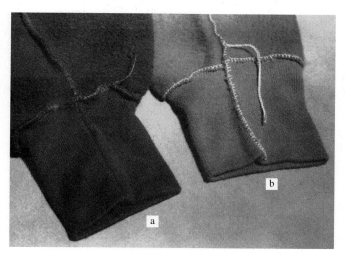

Figure 12–7 Order of band construction: (a) band joined to garment in the round costs more but looks better, than (b) band joined to garment flat.

to secure the cuff facing, usually look smoother and more attractive than when a single row of stitches attaches the cuff to the garment.

Low-price garments typically have one button per buttonhole on the cuff and few if any sleeve length variations available. Moderate-price garments may have two buttons per buttonhole on the cuff (Figure 10-37b). This allows the wearer to make the cuff smaller or larger so the sleeve can be pushed up or pulled down to fit varying arm lengths. High-price garments feature a single button per buttonhole on the cuff; the manufacturer produces a variety of sleeve lengths to fit various arm lengths precisely. The abundance of sleeve lengths increases costs because it requires more sizes to be produced by the manufacturer and carried in inventory by the retailer.

Closed-Band Cuffs. Closed-band cuffs are inexpensive because they do not require plackets or closures. Made of rib-knit fabric and then attached to the garment, closed-band cuffs are common in knit T-shirts and sweatshirts because they stretch over the hand and then contract to fit the wrist or arm. Closed-band cuffs of woven fabrics are designed so the cuff is large enough to pull over the hand without fitting the arm too loosely; they are found in low-end women's blouses.

Closed-band cuffs of high quality are set in the round after the sleeve underarm seam has been sewn, joining the sleeve into a tube. This method can be identified by the unbroken circular seam attaching the cuff. However, a low-cost method involves attaching the cuff to the sleeve while both are flat. Then the cuff and sleeve are joined into a tube with a single seam.

This method can be identified by the sleeve seam visible at the lower edge of the cuff (Figure 12–7).

Turned-Back Cuffs. Turned-back cuffs are produced in one of two ways. In the first method, the lower edge of the garment is deeply hemmed and the finished lower edge turned back to form a cuff. This method, because of the deep hem, requires over 4 extra inches of fabric length for a 2-inch cuff. The second method, used on sleeves or casual pants, is to hem the lower edge of the garment narrowly and roll it up repeatedly to hide the hem. This is attractive only if the fabric and seams are reversible. Both methods are performed in the assembly process.

Sometimes patternmakers apply a separate extension of fabric, which is hemmed or faced and then turned back to form the cuff. If the seam attaching the extension is made on the outside of the garment, the fold of the turned-back cuff conceals the seam. Producing a turned-back cuff of contrasting fabric requires a separate piece made of the contrasting fabric. Shaping turned-back cuffs to tapered or flared sleeves or pant legs also requires a separate extension, unless the garment edge is flanged (made as a mirror image) to fit the taper or flare. Applying a separate extension costs more in labor but less in fabric than cuffs that are extensions of the garment, so producers of low-price garments often use this technique.

Constructing Waistbands

The waistband is usually straight, although the waistline to which it is sewn is curved. The waistline is eased to the straight waistband so the garment fits the body. The curve of the waistline dips slightly lower in the back of women's clothing and rises slightly higher in men's clothing. While waistline seams are slightly curved, they appear straight when worn. Although a curved seam is more difficult to cut and sew, it fits the body better than a straight seam and is found in high-price garments. Some patternmakers plan straight waistlines on garments to simplify production methods. For example, elastic-waist shorts, pants, and skirts are easier to sew if the waistline is cut straight, but the resulting fit is less accurate than if the waistline is shaped into a slight curve.

Waistbands are interfaced for body and smoothness. The interfacing should be of adequate weight and stiffness to maintain the shape of the waistband but not so stiff that it is uncomfortable. Other waistbands are elasticized before they are sewn to the garment. Elasticized waistbands are common in low-price womenswear and in childrenswear. The operator folds the waistband over the elastic and sews the folded band to the waistline edge of the garment. Elasticized waistbands are a form of an elastic casing.

The ends of a waistband may be finished in various ways. However, the overlapping end of the waistband is almost always finished with an enclosed seam. This is the neatest-looking and generally the most durable finish, but it can be bulky. It is also the most costly method. Hemming the raw edge of the overlap creates bulk and is not a satisfactory finish in terms of appearance. If the overlap is decoratively shaped, the cost of finishing it is increased.

The underlapping end of the waistband in high-quality garments is usually finished with an enclosed seam. However, because its appearance is usually less critical than that of the overlap, the underlap may be treated in various ways to reduce costs without necessarily compromising quality. One inexpensive method is to overedge the raw edge of the underlap, making it non bulky and durable but not as finished looking as an enclosed seam. A slightly more durable and better-looking finish is hemming the raw edge of the underlap after overedging it, but this adds bulk.

Straight Waistbands. Straight waistbands, like straight waistlines, do not conform to the natural curves of the body. Straight waistbands are confined to locations at or near the natural waistline and are limited to a width of not more than 2 inches; most are about 1 1/2 inches wide. Straight waistbands wider than 2 inches either stand away where the body narrows, detracting from fit and appearance, or roll up where the body widens, causing the wearer discomfort. The waistband is cut with the lengthwise grain of the fabric going around the body because the lengthwise grain withstands more stress without stretching than the crosswise grain. A waistband extension provides a place for the application of a button, snap, or hook closure. Generally, the waistband extension is on the underlap side. An exception is at center front when an extension on the overlap side is used as a design feature.

A straight waistband is constructed of either one or two pieces of fabric. The one-piece waistband, made of a single, folded piece of fabric, can be identified by the fold at the outer edge. Although not as fabric efficient as the two-piece waistband, the one-piece waistband requires less labor. Because a one-piece waistband is less bulky, it is the more comfortable alternative when the garment fabric is bulky. Nonfusible interfacing inside one-piece waistbands may wrinkle and roll unless secured at the outer edge with a row of stitches.

Two-piece waistbands are made of two pieces of fabric, the waistband and its facing, seamed together. A two-piece waistband can be recognized by the enclosed seam at the outer edge. The raw edge of the waistband facing must be turned under, bound, overedged, or

Figure 12–8 (a) Curtained waistband. Also note (b) wide center back seam allowances, (c) French fly, and (d) exposed in-seam pocket.

otherwise treated to prevent raveling (unless the edge is cut on the selvage). Edges that are overedged or cut on the selvage create the least bulk. The finished edge is secured to the garment by topstitching or stitching in the ditch. Two-piece waistbands are found in high-price women's pants and skirts.

The facing of two-piece waistbands is usually self-fabric. However, in most men's dress pants, the waistband is faced with a **waistband curtain**, a prefabricated waistband facing that consists of a strip of firmly woven fabric attached to a bias-cut piece of interfacing. The lower edge of the curtain is a bias-cut fold of fabric. High-quality waistband curtains contain a stay of monofilament nylon or other material to add strength, stability, and shape retention without adding bulk. The bias cut of the curtain allows it to hug and fit the body contours (Figure 12–8). Some better women's slacks also feature curtains. The curtain is joined to the waistband with an enclosed seam and then tacked to pockets and seams to anchor it in place. A tack at center back is helpful because it flattens the bulk in that area. Between the tacks, a waistband curtain can be lifted to examine the inner construction.

A curtained waistband is the most costly waistline finish. Curtains may contain additional stays, decorative piping or other trim, or strips of rubber or elastic to help the pants stay up and to aid in gripping the shirttail so that it stays tucked in. The more elaborate the curtain, the more costly.

The operator applies the waistband curtain separately to the left and right halves of the garment; then the pants are seamed at center back. This makes the waistband easy to alter, because the waistline can be taken in or let out at the center back seam without removing the curtained waistband.

Contour Waistbands. Contour waistbands are shaped to fit the contours of the body (Figure 5–21). They are generally required when the waistband is lower than the natural waistline. For example, women's hip-hugger pants require a contoured waistband to fit the curve of the hip. If a straight waistband were used, it would stick out without hugging the body. Because of their unusual shape, contour waistbands not only reduce material utilization but require more labor to construct. Contour waistbands contain bias-cut areas, so they are not as stable as straight waistbands. Interfacing alone does not prevent a contour waistband from stretching out of shape, so a waistline stay is used.

Attaching Shoulder Pads

Shoulder pads should be carefully positioned to follow the lines of the body for a smooth look. For lined garments, shoulder pads are attached between the fashion fabric and the lining or fused as part of a fully fused front. In unlined garments, the shoulder pads are tacked to the shoulder and armscye seams; generally, the more tacks, the more secure the attachment. Tacking stitches should be inconspicuous from the outside of the garment. If the tacking stitches are too tight, they prevent the shoulder pad from conforming freely to the wearer's movements and distort the garment. On the other hand, if the tacking stitches are too loose, the shoulder pad is not secure. Consumers commonly complain that shoulder pads in blouses and dresses shift during wear, twist in washing, or fall out of the garment due to poor attachment. To avoid these problems, some shoulder pads are attached to the garment with hook-and-loop tape (Velcro®), which allows the shoulder pads to be easily removed when the garment is laundered and then replaced for wearing. However, hook-and-loop tape is too bulky for use on lightweight fabrics.

Applying Linings

Garments may either be lined to the edge or have linings attached at garment hems and facings. In a *lined-to-the-edge* garment, the lining is an exact duplication of the garment, extending to the outer edges of the garment. The raw edges are bound or finished by the enclosed seam joining the garment and lining. Unless the outer edges are bound, the lining will show from outside the garment at the edges. (Using control stitching or topstitching helps the lining remain hidden.) Self-fabric linings are least noticeable at edges but are too bulky unless the fashion fabric is lightweight. Sleeveless garments, such as vests, are often lined to the edge, as are garments made of bulky fabrics, which do not lend themselves to being faced. When individual garment parts are lined, they are usually lined to the edge.

Most regular linings do *not* exactly duplicate the garment. This is because the lining is cut narrower and shorter than the garment, sewn to the garment facings, and hemmed shorter than the garment. A lining should be large enough not to distort the hang or movement of the garment; skimpily cut linings are usually a sign of cost cutting. Patternmakers may intentionally cut the lining smaller than the garment so the lining absorbs the strain of wear, as in fitted skirts. In full or pleated garments, linings are usually cut smaller than the garment to reduce bulk.

Ease pleats should be added to the linings of jackets and coats. Vertical ease pleats in linings at the center back of garments such as jackets and coats provide adequate room for movement across the back and shoulders (Figures 5–17 and 12–4). Some garments feature additional vertical ease pleats in the lining at the shoulder seams. Horizontal ease pleats in the lining at sleeve and garment hems are also required for a smooth, easy fit. Ease pleats make the lining roomier and also help absorb the stress of movement, preventing distortion of the garment. Deep ease pleats indicate concern for quality. The absence of ease pleats reduces ease, decreasing the wearer's comfort as well as the durability of the garment. Sometimes strips of stretchy knit fabric are set in the lining to substitute for ease pleats in active sportswear.

Bagging the Lining. Manufacturers in all price lines apply linings by **bagging.** This method is the most common and least expensive way of inserting any lining that is attached around the outer edges of the garment. The lining and garment are constructed separately and then sewn, with right sides together, around the outer edges. An opening or gap is left in the stitching, forming a "bag." The entire garment is then turned through this opening in the "bag," and the opening is sewn shut. Although it may be inconspicuous, the location of the opening can be found in one of the sleeves or side seams of the garment.

Lining Attached at Armscyes. The linings in some moderate- and most high-price jackets and coats are attached not only around the outer edges but also around the armscyes. Operators construct the lining for the body and sleeves separately. During assembly, the lining for the body is sewn to the garment around the outer edges and armscyes, and then the sleeve linings are attached at the armscyes. Doing this prevents the lining from separating from the garment at the armscyes as it does when applied by bagging. Linings attached at the armscyes stay in position when the wearer moves, making the garment more comfortable to wear and less subject to abrasion. In the highest price lines and in couture apparel, hand stitches are used to attach the lining to the garment at the armscyes. Hand stitches yield soft, comfortable results and allow the operator to distribute ease smoothly throughout the sleeve cap. When linings are applied by bagging, tacks are sometimes used to join the garment and lining around the armscyes.

Free-Hanging Lining.   Linings are always attached to the hem of jackets. However, **free-hanging linings** or **slip linings** are used in dresses, skirts, pants, and coats. Because free-hanging linings are not attached to the garment hem, they do not inhibit the movement or drape of the garment. A free-hanging lining allows the consumer to examine the inner construction details of a garment. For this reason, consumers may consider free-hanging a sign of quality (compared with a lining sewn to the hem, which may hide poor-quality inner construction). For example, makers of fur coats often install free-hanging linings so the fine workmanship inside the coat can be examined.

A mark of quality in a garment with a free-hanging lining is the use of **French** or **swing tacks** (Figure 10–31). Swing tacks are about 1 1/2 long and are made of thread chains, strips of fabric similar to belt loops, or pieces of ribbon. They connect the lining hem and the garment hem at each seam allowance. Swing tacks allow the lining to move freely while preventing it from riding up or hanging below the hemline.

PRODUCT ASSEMBLY AND FINISHING

When all the major pieces of a garment are joined, the garment is now a product but not yet a finished product. Many detail operations have to be completed before the product is finished. These details include attaching buttons and buttonholes, snaps, hooks and eyes, decorative stitchings and trims; wet processing (if applicable); and finish pressing. (See Chapter 4 for details.)

Applying Buttons

Buttons are the most common garment closures. Buttons can make or break a garment, not only in type (see Chapter 8) but in positioning and attachment.

Button Placement.   *A button should be positioned at each horizontal stress point: bust/chest, waist, and hip levels.* Sometimes designers fail to locate buttons at these stress points. This becomes evident when a blouse with too few buttons gapes at the bust

Figure 12–9   Blouse opening gapes because it needs a button at bust level.

(Figure 12–9). (Gaping may also result when a wearer has a higher or lower bustline than that for which the garment is designed.) Designers sometimes eliminate the button at hip level on shirts for a variety of reasons. The lower button does not show when the shirttail is tucked. Eliminating the lower button reduces bulk and saves money. However, the lower button preserves a straight, undistorted center front line and helps the shirttail stay tucked. For these reasons, shirts with seven-button fronts are considered higher quality than shirts with six-button fronts.

Designers do not place a button at waist level if it interferes with the wearing of a waistband or belt. Custom decrees that a button should not be positioned on the hem of a garment; the lowest button usually falls at least 4 to 6 inches from the hem. The buttons on jacket sleeves are an exception; these buttons are set close together, with the lower button no more than 3/4 inch from the bottom of the sleeve. High-price men's suit jacket sleeves traditionally have four buttons while women's suit jacket sleeves have three buttons; men's sport coats often have only two buttons per sleeve.

Sometimes an *extra button/s* is provided with a garment in case a button is lost. These buttons may be sewn inside the garment or attached to a hang tag. Extra buttons are highly visible and consumers often associate them with quality, although manufacturers of low-price garments sometimes attach extra buttons as an inexpensive way to imitate high-price lines.

Button Attachment.   Secure button attachment is important to consumer satisfaction. Buttons are usually sewn to the garment with a machine stitch similar to a ticket tack. In highly mechanized operations, the buttons automatically feed from a hopper and are held in sewing position by a special machine attachment. In other operations, operators manually feed the buttons one at a time for sewing.

A common misconception about button attachment is that the more tightly a button is sewn on, the better. The fact is that a button sewn on too tightly is more likely to fall off, because the button cannot give as the body moves. The body motion abrades the tight threads until they break. Eyed buttons sewn tightly to a garment also tend to distort the buttonhole and dent the surrounding fabric, particularly if the fabric is heavy or bulky, giving the area a pulled or drawn look.

In general, the greater the number of stitches used to sew on a button, the more secure its attachment. For example, Huntington Clothiers and Shirtmakers advertises that the buttons on its shirts are "cross-stitched sixteen times." Equally important to the number of stitches are the type of machine and stitch type. Some button attaching machines are chainstitch type (Class 100) and others are lockstitch type (Class 300). Buttons sewn on with the chainstitch type machine can easily come off since there is no bobbin (bottom) thread to help stabilize the stitches (see Chapter 9). Buttons attached with a lockstitch are more secure and seldom fall off.

Some buttons are not sewn on but are mechanically attached to the fabric. The security of mechanically attached buttons is even more critical than that of sewn-on buttons. If a mechanically attached button falls off, the consumer has no means of replacing it. Mechanically attaching buttons tends to be a more secure attachment than sewing and is used primarily on heavy-duty apparel such as jeans and uniforms.

Buttons should be **in registration,** or properly oriented, when they are attached. For example, an elephant-shaped button should be attached so the elephant appears to stand on its feet, not on its head. Automatic button feeders (*hoppers*) feed registered buttons, eliminating the extra time and cost of manually registering buttons.

Applying Eyed Buttons. When an eyed button is attached, the stitches normally are parallel to the buttonhole. This allows the button to float in the buttonhole without distorting it. Four-eyed buttons are more securely attached than two-eyed buttons because they have twice as many stitches. Operators sew on four-eyed buttons with the holes stitched as independent pairs. Thread dragging from one pair of holes to the other can be considered aesthetically undesirable but is cost efficient due to equipment expense. (Such a

Figure 12–10 (a) Eyed button with thread shank, and (b) shank button.

thread is shown in Figure 12–12 later in this chapter.) For a decorative look, four-eyed buttons may be sewn on with stitches forming a square or an arrow pattern. Cross-stitching is the strongest method for sewing on a four-eyed button; however, it is not the most cost effective method. Large thread size and high stitch count are suggested for metal or shell buttons as they have sharp edges that can cut the thread through abrasion.

To prevent distortion of the buttonhole and surrounding fabric, eyed buttons on garments made of heavy or bulky fabrics can be sewn on with a thread shank. A wrapped **thread shank** is created when a button is sewn on loosely and extra thread is wrapped around the stitches between the button and the garment, suspending the button away from the fabric (Figure 12–10a). A thread shank allows the button to float above the buttonhole, and the button tends to stay on longer because it has freedom of movement. A special machine sews on the button and constructs a wrapped thread shank, but this method remains more costly than sewing a button on flat. Therefore, a thread shank is considered a mark of quality.

The shank should not be so long that the button droops when buttoned. A decorative button should not have a shank because it might droop. For example, on a double-breasted jacket with one row of functional buttons and one row of decorative buttons, the functional buttons should have thread shanks and the decorative buttons should not.

Applying Shank Buttons. Shank buttons require that the body fabric be folded in exactly the right place by the operator before the buttons are sewn on

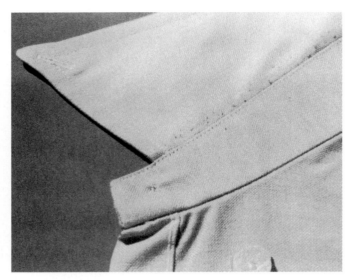

Figure 12–11   Circle of interfacing reinforces collar button on button-down collar shirt. Also note pilling on collar.

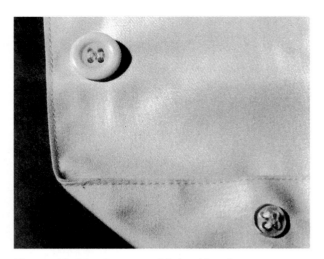

Figure 12–12   Button with backing button.

(Figure 12–10b). Ideally, the shank should be sewn on parallel to the buttonhole. A shank button has the same advantages of an eyed button with a thread shank. The button shank helps the button rise above the buttonhole without distorting it. The button gives with the wearer's movements rather than rubbing the thread away, so shank buttons stay on longer. Yet shank buttons found on extremely heavy or bulky fabrics may need a thread shank *in addition* to the built-in shank, a mark of cost and quality.

Some shanks, especially metal ones, sever the thread attaching the button to the garment; extra-strong thread may be required. For durability, a shank button may be attached with a metal toggle rather than sewn onto the garment, but this feature is found only in high-price lines. Nylon shanks are used increasingly because they are stronger, lighter, and cheaper than metal shanks, less likely to cut the thread, and do not rust in wet processing. Some shank buttons, such as those on denim jeans and work clothes, are mechanically attached to the garment without the use of thread.

Button Area Reinforcement.   Interfacing should be used in button areas to reinforce the buttons (Figures 5–15 and 5–16). For example, button-down collars on high-quality shirts feature small circles of interfacing beneath the collar buttons for reinforcement (Figure 12–11). The stress from a button sewn only to the fabric of the garment soon causes the fabric to tear. Two plies of fabric plus a ply of interfacing provide the ideal foundation for a button.

In button applications on most garments, sewing penetrates all fabric plies plus the interfacing for maximum strength. In high-quality coats and suits, buttons may be sewn through every ply except the facing. This technique trades some durability for aesthetics because it prevents stitches from showing on the inside of the garment when it is worn unbuttoned. Attaching buttons in this way is costly because it is done manually and requires skilled labor.

Backing Buttons.   When buttons are under heavy strain or are sewn to soft fabrics, the stress may be too great for just the fabric and interfacing alone to support. A flat, eyed **backing button** or **reinforcement button** may be sewn on with the button, under the fabric behind the button (Figure 12–12). The backing button rather than the fabric absorbs the stress, increasing the durability of the closure. Backing buttons, a sign of quality, are found mainly on coats. A square of fabric or ribbon may be substituted for a backing button in other types of garments (for example, blouses and dresses) for softer reinforcing and less bulk.

Buttonholes.   Buttonholes, while primarily functional, can also be decorative. Whether decorative or functional, they need to be smooth, even, and secure. A buttonhole should be long enough so the button can slip easily through the hole without strain or excessive wear. However, a buttonhole that is too long detracts from fit and appearance, and the button will not stay buttoned. The rule for establishing buttonhole length is that it should equal the diameter plus the thickness of the button (Figure 12–13). A *ball button,* a totally round button, requires a buttonhole with a length equal to the circumference of the button. If a button is rough or unusually shaped, the buttonhole requires additional length so the button slips through easily or may even require a snap fastener as the functional closure with the button sewn over the snap for decorative effect.

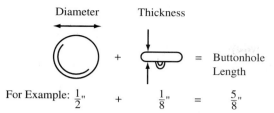

Figure 12–13   Formula for buttonhole length.

Buttonhole Reinforcement.   Buttonholes should be reinforced with interfacing. Buttonholes without interfacing are not durable; they become distorted and can tear away from the garment. If a strip of interfacing under a row of buttons interferes with the drape or hang of a garment made of a knit or other soft fabric, the spec technician may place individual pieces of interfacing under each buttonhole. Most spec technicians recognize the need for interfacing in button and buttonhole areas and seldom omit it. Figure 12–14 illustrates how a fabric with inadequate interfacing stretches and ripples in the buttonhole area.

Corded buttonholes are sometimes found in tailored garments. In a corded buttonhole, a narrow-diameter cording is buried in the buttonhole stitches as the buttonhole is stitched. The stitches of the buttonhole cover the cording, creating a decorative, raised effect and giving the buttonhole dimension. The cording absorbs some of the stress of use, reinforcing the buttonhole and preventing stretch.

Buttonhole Direction.   Horizontal buttonholes tend to stay buttoned. The button rubs against the end of the buttonhole, which absorbs the stress when the wearer moves. If the buttonhole is vertical, the button tends to slip out of the buttonhole when horizontal stress is applied. Large, vertical buttonholes are especially vulnerable to this problem. Thus, tight-fitting clothing or areas under stress require horizontal buttonholes to keep the garment buttoned; coats, jackets, neckbands, cuffs, pants plackets, and waistbands all use horizontal buttonholes. Horizontal buttonholes require more fabric than vertical ones because of the wider facing required.

Vertical buttonholes are appropriate when aesthetics is important, or when the area is loosely fitted and undergoes little stress. For example, most center front closures, especially button bands, look more attractive with vertical than with horizontal buttonholes. In garments made of knit fabrics, buttonholes parallel to the crosswise direction of the knit tend to stretch and ripple, so most buttonholes in knit-fabric garments are vertical.

Buttonhole Placement.   Garments lap where buttons and buttonholes are used. The portion of the lap

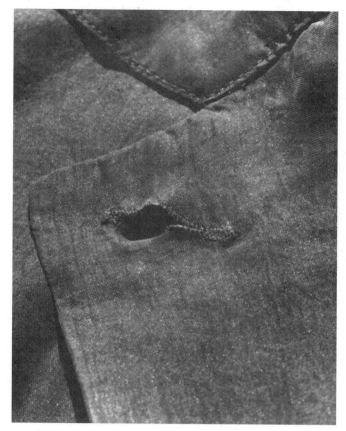

Figure 12–14   Inadequately interfaced buttonhole.

that extends beyond the button is the **underlap**; the part that extends beyond the buttonhole is the **overlap.** When the underlap and overlap are lapped, the garment fits properly. The width of these extensions depends on the size of the buttons and should equal the radius of the button plus 1/4 to 1/2 inch. In the case of large buttons, the underlap may need to be slightly wider. Narrow extensions conserve fabric but do not provide for adequate coverage of the opening, do not support the button well, and look unattractive if the button extends beyond the extension. Narrow underlaps and overlaps are a mark of low quality. In the United States, garments for females traditionally lap right over left and garments for males lap left over right.

Buttonholes should be spaced the same distance apart as the corresponding buttons to avoid strain or bubbling between buttonholes (Figure 12–15). This problem also arises when button loops, the two halves of snaps, or hooks and eyes are improperly aligned, or when the two sides of a zipper slider are unevenly attached.

Designers place buttonholes on the straight-of-grain of the fabric for maximum durability and shape retention. A horizontal buttonhole should begin 1/8

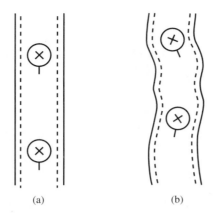

(a)   (b)

Figure 12–15 (a) Buttonholes should be spaced the same distance apart as the corresponding buttons to avoid the fabric straining or bubbling between buttonholes, as it does in (b).

inch beyond the center front, center back, or lap line and extend into the body of the garment. The corresponding button is located directly across from the buttonhole, on the center front line, center back line, or other lap line. A vertical buttonhole should be located exactly on the lap line. The corresponding button is located on the lap line and 1/8 inch below the top edge of the buttonhole. If these rules are followed, the lap lines of the buttoned garment align and the garment fits as intended (Figure 12–16). If these guidelines are ignored, as when buttons are placed in the middle of buttonholes, gravity and the stress of use cause the buttons to go to the ends of the buttonholes, and the garment will fit improperly.

Thread Buttonholes. Most buttonholes are made of thread. Special machines used to make thread buttonholes are programmed to stitch and then cut the buttonholes open automatically. Some of these machines can make up to six buttonholes in about 20 seconds. A sharp knife blade cuts the buttonholes open. If the knife blade dulls, the stitches of the buttonhole may be severed and the surrounding fabric may be damaged—knit fabrics run and woven fabrics exhibit pulls.

In general, the denser the stitches of a buttonhole, the more durable the buttonhole. Dense stitches withstand heavy use and prevent the fabric from fraying. The density of the buttonhole stitches is a direct clue to the cost of the equipment used and an indirect clue to the overall level of garment quality (Figure 12–17). A few quality-oriented manufacturers and retailers have advertised the number of stitches in their buttonholes to recommend the durability of their products. For example, Huntington Clothiers and Shirtmakers advertises that the buttonholes on the shirts it makes have "144 stitches for nonravel wearing," and Lands' End advertises a dress shirt with "130 locked stitches on each buttonhole." Lockstitch buttonholes are more durable than chainstitch buttonholes, which easily unravel.

Some fabrics are damaged by too-dense buttonhole stitches. For example, knits are prone to needle cutting due to dense stitches. Buttonholes must be completely surrounded with stitches. If not, fraying or tearing of the fabric is likely to occur during use.

Most thread buttonholes are rectangular, especially on shirts, blouses, and dresses (Figure 12–17).

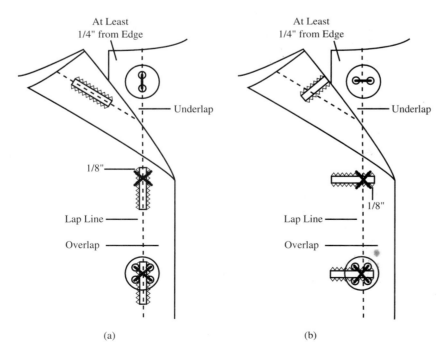

(a)   (b)

Figure 12–16 Placement of buttons and buttonholes.

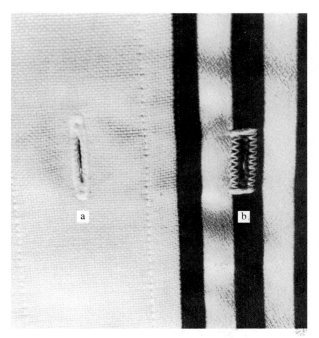

Figure 12–17 Buttonholes: (a) densely stitched, on band, and (b) sparsely stitched, on French front.

A rectangular buttonhole is formed by two rows of zigzag stitches, with bar tacks crossing each end to withstand the stress of use.

Oval (or **fan**) and **keyhole buttonholes** are named for their characteristic shapes (Figure 12–18b and c). The rounded ends allow the button to ride in the buttonhole without distorting the garment. Oval and keyhole buttonholes are used on tailored jackets and coats and on waistbands and pocket flaps of jeans and slacks. Oval and keyhole buttonholes are created with machine zigzag stitches or with machine stitches simulating the stitches in handworked buttonholes. When stitched with a plain machine zigzag stitch, an oval or keyhole buttonhole is not as durable as when stitched with a purled edge. Both types of buttonholes are often made with a strand of gimp thread applied under the stitching to increase durability. Stitching the buttonhole with a purled edge to imitate a hand-worked buttonhole increases the attractiveness and durability of oval and keyhole buttonholes. Buttonhole twist thread may be used to stitch a buttonhole, especially if the buttonhole has a purled edge. **Buttonhole twist** is a heavy, lustrous thread that reinforces the buttonhole and provides a decorative appearance.

Hand-worked (or **hand-purled**) **buttonholes** are increasingly rare, confined mainly to high-price menswear, fine imported baby clothes, and couture clothing. The purled edge consists of a series of individually knotted stitches. The stitches of hand-worked

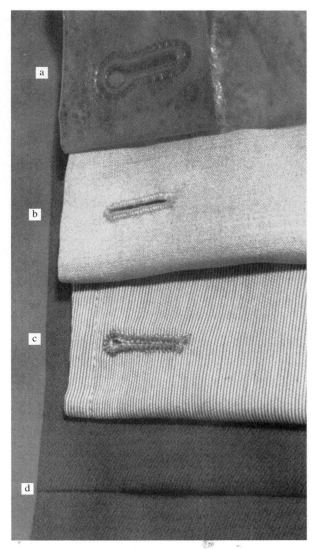

Figure 12–18 Types of buttonholes: (a) fused, (b) oval, (c) keyhole, and (d) inseam.

buttonholes are more irregular than machine-stitched imitations, but the two are difficult to tell apart. Because they are not as durable as machine imitations, there is no functional advantage to hand-worked buttonholes. But because they are very labor intensive and costly, hand-worked buttonholes may influence the consumer's perception of quality if attention is called to them.

Fabric Buttonholes. Buttonholes made of fabric are much less common than thread buttonholes. They are confined to high-price lines because of their labor intensity. They include bound, slit, faced slit, inseam, and fused buttonholes.

Bound Buttonholes. A **bound buttonhole** is a rectangular hole in the garment fabric which is bound or faced and backed with narrow strips of fabric that meet like lips to cover the opening. A bound buttonhole resembles a miniature double-welt pocket (Figure 5–27). The fabric lips abut, allowing a slit for the button to pass through. It requires many steps to complete. Even when automated, a bound buttonhole is much more costly to produce than a thread buttonhole.

A well-made bound buttonhole is a perfect rectangle with even lips that meet but do not overlap. The buttonhole should not fray or expose any raw edges. A bound buttonhole is not more durable than a thread buttonhole; its primary advantage is its neat, threadless appearance. In heavy fabrics, a bound buttonhole results in a smoother appearance than a regular buttonhole because it does not compress the fabric.

Bound buttonholes are prestigious because of their costly production. Bound buttonholes were once a common mark of quality in better lines of clothing. However, they are increasingly rare. They are found on some high-price and couture jackets and coats for women; seldom are they used in menswear.

Slit Buttonholes. Many fabrics require special buttonholes. Conventional buttonholes with dense stitches pierce vinyl, leather, and imitation leather too many times, thus weakening it. Because these fabrics do not ravel, **slit buttonholes** with raw edges are perfectly acceptable. A rectangle of machine stitching with a slit centered in the rectangle serves as a low-bulk buttonhole for leather garments. A rectangle cut in the fabric with narrow strips of the fabric glued to the back forms lips that resemble those of a bound buttonhole. Bound buttonholes are also appropriate for use in leather and leather-like garments.

A narrow **faced slit** is a buttonhole sometimes found in high-price European clothing. Faced slits, faced slashes in the fabric, require more steps and are therefore more costly to produce than thread buttonholes but are easier and less costly to make than bound buttonholes.

In-Seam Buttonholes. Another type of buttonhole is the **in-seam buttonhole** or *slot* buttonhole. In-seam buttonholes are rare because they are limited to designs with a seam in exactly the right location, directly over the buttons. The operator leaves the seam partially unstitched at intervals to create the buttonholes (Figure 12–18d). In-seam buttonholes are smooth, inconspicuous, and less costly to produce than other types of buttonholes. A disadvantage is that they cannot withstand as much stress as thread buttonholes.

Fused Buttonholes. Thermoplastic (heat-sensitive) fabrics may contain fused buttonholes. A **fused buttonhole** is formed by embossing the fabric with a hot

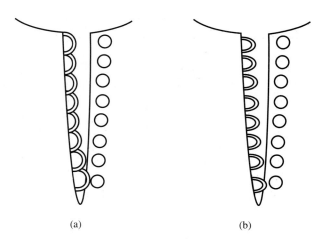

Figure 12–19 (a) Loops that are short and wide offer a more secure closure than do (b) loops that are long and narrow.

die which is patterned to resemble a stitched or bound buttonhole (Figure 12–18a). A slit in the fabric allows the button to slip through. In vinyls and other film fabrics, fused buttonholes are more durable than buttonholes with stitches, which would pierce and weaken the fabric.

Fused buttonholes are mainly confined to low-price lines, especially raingear or other garments made entirely of thermoplastic fabrics. They do not have good consumer acceptance in high-price lines or in other types of garments, perhaps because of the stiffness and the association with low-price lines.

Button Loops. Button loops may substitute for buttonholes. Button loops in a series should be evenly spaced and identical in size. To ensure this, some designers and spec technicians use presized, prespaced looping, for example, on the backs of wedding gowns with closely spaced loops. Loop closures are decorative as well as functional. However, they are suited only to areas that receive limited stress because they are unable to hold edges in place as precisely as do buttonholes. For this reason, loops are inappropriate as closures in areas where modesty is important.

Short, wide loops hold the edges together better than do long, narrow loops (Figure 12–19). When the operator sews loops into a seam, both ends of the loops should be caught securely. If not, when the loops are stressed by movement or a tight fit, they pull out of the seam. Careful placement of the corresponding buttons is important for attractive and functional loop closures.

Applying Snap Fasteners

Snap fasteners, most frequently used on children's clothing, offer a simple closure that is easier to handle than buttons. Snaps release more easily than buttons

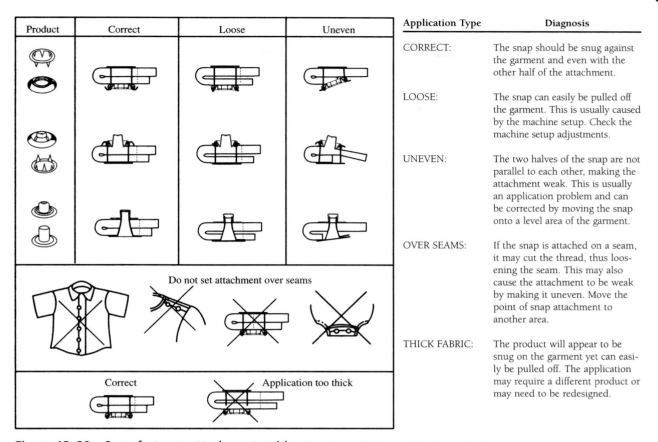

Figure 12–20 Snap fastener attachment guide. *(Courtesy of Universal Fasteners, Inc.)*

and therefore cannot be used in place of buttons in high-stress areas.

The stud portion of a snap is attached to the garment overlap because its thinner base does not distort the smooth surface of the overlap (Figure 12–20). The socket portion, which is indented to grip the stud portion, is attached to the underlap. Both parts of the snap should be evenly aligned.

Snap Fastener Placement. The appropriate placement and spacing for decorative and functional snaps are determined in the same way as the placement and spacing for buttons. Concealed snaps are similarly spaced but placed nearer the garment opening (1/8 to 1/4 inch from the edge). A concealed snap is never seen from the outside of the garment if correctly placed and attached.

Sew-On Snap Fasteners. Many snap fasteners are sewn on by machine. The number and type of stitches used affects the serviceability of machine-sewn snaps through wear and care. All four holes of a snap stud and socket should be sewn securely. Because of increased labor costs, hand-sewn snaps are used primarily when the expense of setting up a machine-sewn snap operation is not justified.

Garment edges that overlap require snaps sewn on flat. For abutting edges, hooks and eyes are usually substituted for snaps. In high-price lines, edges that abut may be joined by extending a snap socket from the edge or by hanging it from a thread chain.

Mechanically Attached Snap Fasteners. Snap fasteners are mechanically attached by using a pneumatic (air-pressure driven) machine or a foot-driven "kick press," or manually attached by an operator using hand-held dies and a hammer. No matter which method is used, the fabric should be adequately interfaced or reinforced, for example, with twill tape, to withstand the stress caused by repeated snapping and unsnapping. Unreinforced snaps tear away from the garment fabric during use and are a sign of low quality. Applying snaps over excessively thick or uneven areas (seam edges) of the garment prevents a secure attachment (Figure 12–20). Accurately attached snaps cannot be pried from the fabric. Mechanically attached snaps are best suited for medium- to heavyweight, firmly woven fabrics.

Snap Tape. The operator must carefully align both sides of the snap tape for the finished garment to fit properly. The lines of machine stitching used to attach snap tape are visible on the outside of the garment.

Applying Hooks and Eyes

For hooks and eyes that join abutted edges, the hook should be 1/16 to 1/8 inch from the edge of the opening, with the hook end toward the opening edge. If the closure laps, the hook should be attached to the overlap and the eye attached to the underlap for ease of fastening. If the eye is curved, it is placed with the curve toward the opening edge of the garment. A well-placed hook-and-eye closure is not visible from the outside of the garment. Because hooks and eyes absorb more stress than snap fasteners, they may be used in locations subject to considerable stress. However, greater stress requires a larger hook and eye, and the size of the hook and eye should not distort the fabric.

Sew-On Hooks and Eyes. Concealed hooks and eyes must be sewn on carefully so the stitches do not penetrate the outside of the garment. They should be sewn on with several stitches for durability. Ideally, the hook end of the hook should be sewn to the fabric to keep the hook flat against the garment when the closure is fastened. However, this step is usually seen only in high-price lines. Hook and eye closures subject to stress should be adequately reinforced with interfacing.

Mechanically Attached Hooks and Eyes. Large hooks and eyes may be mechanically attached (Figure 8–12). Mechanically attached hooks and eyes are used most frequently at waistbands. The hooks and eyes are attached through the unfinished waistband. Then the prongs of the hook and eye are bent over metal reinforcing plates to hold them in place, and the waistband is completed so the bent prongs are hidden. This closure looks neat in the finished garment. However, the hook and eye are attached to only one layer of the waistband. Separation of the waistband layers may occur unless the area around the hook and eye is secured with stitching through all layers. Hooks and eyes that are mechanically attached are not easily moved; the waistband must be opened up to move them.

Applying Miscellaneous Closures

A variety of other closures may be applied to garments in addition to the more traditional ones. These include hook-and-loop tape, drawstrings, and grommets and eyelets (see Chapters 5 and 8).

Hook and Loop Tape (Velcro). For consumer comfort, suppliers recommend attaching the hook portion of hook-and-loop tape to the underlap and the loop portion to the overlap of the garment. Machine stitches surround the tape and penetrate all plies of the garment for durable application, but the stitches show on the outside of the garment. Hook-and-loop tape is occasionally applied with adhesives, by heat or ultrasonically.

Drawstrings. Drawstrings require one or two openings in the casing so that each end of the drawstring can be brought to the surface and tied. Waistline drawstrings with one opening withstand stress better than those with two openings. On the other hand, two openings allow for a flatter knot to be tied in the drawstring. The ends of the drawstring should be capped or knotted so they do not get lost in the casing or pulled out of the casing, requiring rethreading. The drawstring may be stitched in place halfway through the casing to keep it in position.

Grommets and Eyelets. Grommets and eyelets, used for threading drawstrings, are mechanically attached to the fabric similarly to mechanically attached snap fasteners or hooks and eyes. They are most suitable for use on medium- to heavyweight fabrics. The area should be reinforced with interfacing and/or multiple plies of fabric to prevent the grommets or eyelets from tearing away from the garment. A securely attached grommet or eyelet cannot be separated from the fabric with fingernail pressure.

Finish Pressing

At this point, assembly is complete. Garments requiring garment dyeing, treatment for wrinkle resistance, or special-appearance finishes such as stonewashing or acidwashing, are sent to the wet process facility at this stage in the production process. (For more information on wet processing, see Chapter 4.) Garments not needing wet processing or garments that have already been wet processed now require finish pressing.

Off pressing or **finish pressing** can make or break the final appearance of any apparel product. (For more information on pressing, see Chapter 4.) Poor pressing can make even well-made garments appear to be low quality, while well-executed pressing can hide poor construction. When analyzing pressing, look for an overall smooth, undisturbed appearance. There should be an absence of shine, scorching, melting, clamp marks, and water marks. There should not be any unplanned creases or pleats, pressed wrinkles, or hems pressed to the wrong side. Inseams and side seams of pants and shorts should be pressed seam on seam with a smooth center crease. Skirts and dresses should not have any creases. Shirts and jean jackets will have a crease running down both sleeves but tailored jackets and coats will not have any sleeve creases.

When a garment is thoroughly finish pressed, it not only smoothes the garment and enhances the workmanship, it also helps the garment fit smoothly. High-quality garments are also **underpressed**, or pressed during construction, in addition to the final pressing. Because pressing requires extra labor, it is sometimes eliminated in an effort to reduce costs. But the importance of pressing is evidenced by the extensive use of hand-held steamers in retail stores to steam out shipping wrinkles in garments.

After pressing, any other needed finishing touches are added, such as belts or other accessories and advertising labels. Final inspection is conducted and then the garments are sent to fold and pack, after which they are subjected to a final audit. The complete "parts to panels, pieces to products" cycle is now complete!

SUMMARY

Pieces are joined to other pieces to create the garment. Collars are constructed either as a single ply or as one, two, or three pieces that form a double ply plus interfacing. Two-piece collars are most common, but three-piece collars with seamed, bias-cut under collars represent the highest cost and quality. High-quality collars cover the neckline seam. They are smooth and nonbulky, and the under collar does not show on the outside of the garment.

Set-in sleeves are used in most fitted and tailored garments. They fit more closely without wrinkling if they are set in the round rather than set flat. Sleeves set in the round cost more in labor than sleeves set flat. Set-in sleeves should be eased smoothly into the armholes without puckering, and the armhole should be stitched twice for durability. The underarm area of kimono sleeves should be reinforced and/or gusseted to reduce strain. Raglan sleeves provide the most room for movement.

Cuff bands may be open or closed. Open-band cuffs fasten, front over back, on the outer edge of the arm. Two buttons per buttonhole in moderate-quality garments enable the sleeve to fit a wider range of arm lengths than one button per buttonhole, which represents either lower or higher quality, depending on the number of exact sleeve lengths available. Turned-back cuffs on sleeve and pant legs also require extra fabric.

Waistbands are a popular band finish for waistline edges. They should be interfaced for smoothness. Straight waistbands may be faced with a curtain, the most costly waistband treatment. Contour waistbands should be stayed to prevent stretching.

Linings should have adequate ease pleats. Jacket linings attached at the armscyes and free-hanging linings with French tacks in skirts reflect high quality.

A closure should be located even with each horizontal stress point. Most buttons are sewn on; they should be attached using a number of stitches and tacking stitches. Mechanically attached buttons are very durable. Eyed buttons with four holes are most durable when cross-stitched. Buttons should not be sewn on too tightly to avoid distorting the fabric around them. A thread shank avoids this problem. Shank buttons have built-in shanks and are especially useful on heavy fabrics, but they may still require a thread shank on very heavy fabrics. Shank buttons are bulkier than eyed buttons and cost more to attach. Reinforcement buttons should be used on the backs of buttons on coats and jackets that will receive heavy use. Manufacturers sometimes provide an extra button(s) in case one is lost. Garments for females traditionally lap right over left and garments for males left over right (in the United States).

The length of the buttonhole is determined by the size of the button. Horizontal buttonholes tend to stay buttoned better than do vertical buttonholes. The overlap and underlap should be wide enough to support the buttons and buttonholes. The buttonhole should be carefully placed to align with its corresponding button. Most buttonholes are made of thread. Densely lockstitched buttonholes are most durable. Most buttonholes are rectangular, but some are oval or keyhole shaped to accommodate the shanks of buttons. In high-price lines, buttonholes may be hand-worked or bound. Faced slits, in-seam buttonholes, fused buttonholes, and special buttonholes in leather are variations of basic buttonholes.

Snaps and hooks and eyes should be carefully positioned. They may be manually sewn or mechanically attached to the garment, with mechanically attached closures generally being more durable.

Finishing the garment includes wet processing (if applicable) and a thorough finish pressing. After undergoing a final audit, the garment is shipped.

Assembly and Finishing Quality Checklist

If you can answer yes to each of these questions regarding the garment you are evaluating, it was produced using high-quality garment assembly and finishing methods.

✓ Is the collar flat and nonbulky, with smooth curves and sharp points?
✓ Is the collar interfaced with a suitable weight and type of interfacing?
✓ Is the under collar concealed?

✓ Does the roll of collar and lapels occur naturally, without being pressed in?

✓ Does a rolled collar cover the neckline seam?

✓ Is the gorge line free of bulk, wrinkles, and holes?

✓ On tailored garments, is the undercollar made of two pieces, each cut on the bias?

✓ Are sleeves eased or gathered evenly in the cap?

✓ Is the armscye seam stitched with the appropriate stitch type?

✓ Are closely fitted sleeves set in the round rather than set flat?

✓ Are kimono sleeves reinforced, or do they have gussets in the underarm area?

✓ Are sleeve seams sewn before the cuffs are attached?

✓ Do the cuffs lap, front over back, on the outer edge of the arm?

✓ Are the cuffs neatly finished?

✓ Is the waistline stayed to prevent stretching?

✓ Is the waistband interfaced for body and smoothness, avoiding wrinkling and uncomfortable stiffness?

✓ Is the waistband a comfortable width?

✓ Are the ends of the waistband nonbulky and finished neatly?

✓ In dress pants, are the center back seams of the garment and waistband sewn last?

✓ Does the lining feature generous ease pleats?

✓ Is the lining attached at the armscyes?

✓ If free-hanging, does the lining have swing tacks?

✓ Do the garment pieces line up evenly when closed?

✓ Are closures positioned at all stress points?

✓ Are buttons sewn on with multiple stitches?

✓ Are tacking stitches used to secure buttons?

✓ Are buttonholes the correct length for buttons?

✓ Are buttonholes stitched with lockstitches rather than chainstitches?

✓ Are buttonholes on straight-of-grain?

✓ Does interfacing reinforce all button and buttonhole areas?

✓ Are buttons not sewn on so tightly that they distort the fabric?

✓ Are the underlap and overlap on button closures wide enough?

✓ Are snaps and hooks and eyes securely and inconspicuously attached?

✓ Is the hook portion of hooks and eyes sewn flat to the garment?

✓ Are extra buttons provided?

✓ Do the buttons on garments made of heavyweight fabrics have thread shanks?

✓ Do buttons that will receive heavy use have reinforcement buttons?

✓ Are buttonholes densely and completely stitched?

✓ Are shoulder pads and other finishing details and devices positioned attractively and comfortably, and are they neatly and securely attached?

✓ Does pressing enhance the appearance of the garment?

New Terms

If you can define each of these terms and differentiate between related terms, you have gained a good working vocabulary for discussing the topics in this chapter. The terms are listed in the order in which they appeared in the chapter.

lapel/rever
gorge line
roll line
upper collar
under collar
bluff-edge collar
slipping/bubbling
two-piece sleeve
waistband curtain
ease pleat
bagging
free-hanging/slip lining
French/swing tack
in registration
thread shank
backing/reinforcement button
underlap
overlap
oval/fan buttonhole
keyhole buttonhole
buttonhole twist
hand-worked/hand-purled buttonhole
bound buttonhole
slit buttonhole
faced slit buttonhole
in-seam buttonhole
fused buttonhole
off pressing/finish pressing
underpressing

Review Questions

1. How does the construction of a collar (one-piece, two-piece or three-piece) affect its cost and quality?

2. List the criteria for a well-constructed collar.

3. Discuss the advantages and disadvantages of sleeves set in the round versus sleeves set flat.

4. What does the number of buttons per buttonhole on the cuff of a shirt tell you about its quality?
5. How does the construction of a waistband (one-piece or two-piece) affect its quality?
6. Why should a coat or jacket lining be attached at the armscyes?
7. Where should buttons be positioned on the garment?
8. How does a thread shank add to quality?
9. What is a reinforcement button?
10. What is the purpose of a keyhole buttonhole?

Activities

1. On a tailored jacket, label the parts of the collar and lapels.
2. Try on a garment with sleeves set in the round and another with sleeves set flat. How do they differ in appearance, comfort, and fit?
3. Examine cuffs in low-price and high-price garments. Do you see any differences in the quality of construction? Why or why not?
4. Examine low-price and high-price women's blouses.
   a. Evaluate the number of buttons and the button positioning.
   b. Is an extra button included?
   c. Evaluate how securely the buttons are sewn on.
   d. Evaluate the durability of the buttonholes.
   e. Repeat steps a through d for men's shirts.

5. Find an example of bound buttonholes in a women's garment. In what price line was the garment? How do the buttonholes affect the appearance of the garment?
6. Visit an apparel manufacturer. View how they attach buttons and make buttonholes and attach snap fasteners, hooks and eyes, and other closures.
7. Randomly select ten men's garments and ten women's garments with center front closures from a magazine or catalog. Are they lapped correctly according to tradition? How are unisex garments lapped?
8. Survey five friends. What are their pet peeves about buttons and buttonholes? zippers? snaps? hooks and eyes? hook-and-loop tape? other closures? Based on their answers, what changes would you suggest manufacturers make?
9. Visit an athletic apparel store or look at athletic apparel in a catalog. What kinds of sleeves does most athletic apparel have?
10. Examine a high-price, moderate-price, and low-price men's suit jacket. How is the inner construction the same? How is it different?
11. Study diagrams from the Union Special Corporation Technical Training Center's *Garment Construction Guide* (Figures 9–1, 11–1, 11–2, 11–16, and 12–1.) Explain how the suggested sequence of construction for a garment follows the "Parts to Panels to Pieces to Products" approach to garment assembly.

Related Resources

URLS FOR WORLD WIDE WEB SITES ON THE INTERNET

Note. Due to the rapidly developing and constantly changing nature of the World Wide Web, sites are coming and going every day. This list will provide at least a good starting point for your Internet search.

TRADE AND INDUSTRY-RELATED ORGANIZATIONS

American National Standards Institute (ANSI)
   http://www.ansi.org
American Society of Quality Control (ASQC)
   http://www.asqc.org
American Society of Testing and Materials (ASTM)
   http://www.astm.org
American Textile Manufacturers Institute (ATMI)
   http://www.atmi.org
Apparel Research Committee
   http://dama.tc2.com/arcnet.htm
British Textile Technology Group (BTTG)
   http://www.bttg.co.uk
Computer Integrated Textile Design Association (CITDA)
   http://www.citda.org
Fashion Group International (FGI)
   http://www.fgi.org
Garment Industry Development Corporation (GIDC)
   http://www.gidc.org
International Fabricare Institute (IFI)
   http://www.ifi.org
International Textiles and Apparel Association (ITAA)
   http://netserver.huec.lsu/itaahome.html
National Retail Federation (NRF)
   http://www.nrf.com
National Textile Center
   http://ntc.tx.ncsu.edu/
Textile/Clothing Technology Corporation (TC^2)
   http://dama.tc2.com/homepage.htm
Textile Institute
   http://www.texi.org
Uniform Code Council (UCC)
   http://www.uc_council.org

Union of Needletrades, Industrial and Textile Employees (UNITE)
   http://www.uniteunion.org

SOURCING

American Textile Exchange
   http://www.ameritex.com
America's Textiles International (ATI)
   http://www.billian.com/textile.htm
Apparel and Textile Network (AT-Net)
   http://www.at-net.com
Apparel Exchange
   http://www.apparelex.com
Apparel Industry Sourcing Site
   http://fashiondex.com
Apparel Manufacturer's Sourcing Web
   http://www.halper.com/sourcingweb.html
ApparelNet
   http://www.apparel.net
California Mart
   http://www.californiamart.com
Dallas Market Center
   http://www.the-center.com
Davison's Textile Blue Book
   http://dama.tc2.com/sourcing/davisntb.davisntb.htm
Embroidery and Garment Screen Printing (ESPonline)
   http://www.spyder.net/esp
FabricLink
   http://www.fabriclink.com
Fabric Stock Exchange
   http://www.fabrics.com
Fashion Directory
   http://www.convergentus.se/fashion/index.htm
The Mart: The Internet Showroom
   http://www.themart.com/
Silk and Rayon Printers and Dyers Association of America
   http://srpda.org
Technology Exchange
   http://www.webcom.com/tekguru/
Textile Information Management Systems (TIMS)
   http://www.unicate.com
Virtual Garment Center
   http://www.garment.com

FIBERS

Allied Signal
http://www.allied.com
BASF
http://www.basf.com
Cotton, Inc.
http://www.cottoninc.com
DuPont
http://www.dupont.com
Milliken
http://www.milliken.com/
Monsanto
http://www.monsanto.com
Natural Cotton Colours, Inc.
http://www.foxfibre.com
National Cotton Council of America
http://www.cotton.org
U.S. Cotton Exchange
http://www.cotton.com
Wool Bureau
http://www.woolmark.com

DESIGNERS AND MANUFACTURERS

Donna Karan
http://www.donnakaran.com
Georgio Armani
http://www.armaniexchange.com
Levi Strauss & Co.
http://www.levi.com
Nicole Miller
http://www.nicolemiller.com

MEDIA

Apparel Industry Magazine
http://www.svi-atl.com
Apparel Strategist
http://www.appstrat.com
Bobbin Magazine
http://www.bobbin.com
Daily News Record
http://www.dailynewsrecord.com
Elle
http://www.ellemag.com
Fashion U.K.
http://www.widemedia.com.fashionuk/
http://207.51.71.250.home.htm
Lumière
http://www.lumiere.com
Rags: Quarterly Reviews of Costume, Clothing, and Ethnic Textile Books
http://www.mcn.org/r/rags
Women's Wear Daily
http://207.51.71.250/home.htm

GOVERNMENT

American Textile Partnership (The AMTEX Partnership)
http://apc.pnl.gov:2080/amtex.www/amtex.html
Sweatshops
http://www.gov/nosweat.htm
U.S. Big Emerging Markets (BEMS)
http://www.stat-usa.gov/itabems.html
U.S. Customs Service (USCS)
http://www.ustreas.gov/treasury/bureaus/customs/customs. html
OR http://www.ustreas.gov/treasury/services/cusbbs.html
U.S. Department of Commerce (DOC)
http://www.ita.doc.gov.industry/textiles
U.S. Department of Justice (DOJ)
http://www.doj.gov
U.S. Department of Labor (DOL)
http://www.dol.gov
U.S. Environmental Protection Agency (EPA)
http://www.epa.gov
U.S. Federal Trade Commission (FTC)
http://www.ftc.gov
U.S. Global Market Information System (GEMS)
http://www.itaiep.doc.gov
U.S. International Trade Administration (ITA)
http://www.ita.doc.gov
U.S. National Institute of Standards and Technology (NIST)
http://www.nist.gov
U.S. Occupational Safety and Health Administration (OSHA)
http://www.osha.gov
U.S. Patent and Trademark Office (PTO)
http://www.uspto.gov
U.S. Superintendent of Documents
http://www.access.gpo.gov/su_docs

OTHER

Acts Testing Labs
http://www.acts-testing.com
CNN-Style
http://cnn.com
Fabricad
http://www.fabricad.com
Fashion
http://www.fashion.net
Fashion Angel
http://www.fashionangel.com
Fashion Internet
http://www.finy.com
Fashion Mall
http://www.fashionmall.com
First View
http://www.firstview.com
Gerber Garment Technology, Inc. (GGT)
http://www.ggt.com
Kurt Salmon Associates (KSA)
http://www.ksa.com

National Museum of Art
   http://www.nmaa.si.edu/
Smithsonian Institution
   http://www.si.edu/
Softworld's Sewing Resource Guide
   http://www.softworld.com/sewing/sewdir.htm
Your Image Plus
   http://www.yip.com

MAGAZINES AND JOURNALS

AATCC Textile Chemist and Colorist
American Demographics
Apparel Industry Magazine
ASTM Standardization News
Bobbin Magazine
Clothing and Textiles Research Journal
Daily News Record (DNR)
Journal of Applied Psychology
Journal of Consumer Affairs
Journal of Consumer Studies and Home Economics.
Journal of Home Economics
Journal of Marketing
Journal of Marketing Research
Journal of Retailing
The Needle's Eye
Women's Wear Daily (WWD)

GENERAL REFERENCES

AATCC Technical Manual. Research Triangle Park, NC: American Association of Textile Chemists and Colorists. Published annually.

Annual Book of ASTM Standards: Textiles. Philadelphia: American Society for Testing and Materials. Published annually.

ASQC Textiles and Needle Trades Division Transactions. Milwaukee, WI: American Society for Quality Control. Published annually.

Diamond, J., & Diamond, E. (1997). *The world of fashion.* New York: Fairchild.

Dickerson, K.D., & Jarnow, J. A. (1996). *Inside the fashion business* (6th ed.). Upper Saddle River, NJ: Prentice Hall.

Erwin, M.D., Kinchen, L.A., & Peters, K.A. (1979). *Clothing for Moderns* (6th ed.). Upper Saddle River, NJ: Prentice Hall.

Frings, G. S. (1996). *Fashion from concept to consumer* (5th ed.). Upper Saddle River, NJ: Prentice Hall.

Glock, R. E., & Kunz, G. I. (1995). *Apparel manufacturing: Sewn products analysis.* Upper Saddle River, NJ: Prentice Hall.

Kidwell, C. B., & Christman, M. C. (1975). *Suiting everyone: The democratization of clothing in America.* Washington, DC: Smithsonian Institution Press.

Proceedings of the Annual Meeting of the International Textiles and Apparel Association. Monument, CO: International Textile and Apparel Association. Published annually.

Stamper, A. A., Sharp, S. H., & Donnell, L. B. (1991). *Evaluating apparel quality* (2nd ed.). New York: Fairchild.

GLOBAL TRADE

Basic Guide to Exporting. (1992). Washington, DC: U.S. Department of Commerce.

Customs Regulations of the United States. (1995). Washington, DC: U.S. Customs Service.

Dickerson, K. G. (1995). *Textiles and Apparel in the Global Economy* (2nd ed.). Upper Saddle River, NJ: Prentice Hall.

The Export Trading Company Guidebook. (1987). Washington, DC: U.S. Department of Commerce.

Exporters' Encyclopedia. (1995). New York: Dun & Bradstreet.

Harmonized Tariff Schedule of the United States (HTSUS) Annotated for Statistical Reporting Purposes (8th ed.). (1996). Washington, DC: U.S. Customs Service.

Importing into the United States. (1994). Washington, DC: U.S. Customs Service.

International Apparel Buyers' Quality Guide. (1995). Hong Kong: Inchcape Testing Services.

International Business Practices. (1993). Washington, DC: U.S. Department of Commerce (in cooperation with the Federal Express Corporation and Delphos International).

King, R., Jr., (1988, May 16). Made in the U.S.A. *Forbes, 141,* 108.

Stone, E. (1994). *Exporting and importing fashion: A global perspective.* Albany, NY: Delmar.

REGULATIONS

Flammable Fabrics Act regulations, 16 C.F.R. 1602–1632, (1988).

Guidelines for drawstrings on children's outerwear. (1995). Washington, DC: U.S. Consumer Product Safety Commission.

Guides for the feather and down products industry. (1971). Washington, DC: U.S. Federal Trade Commission.

Regulations for toys and children's articles (1995). Washington, DC: U.S. Consumer Product Safety Commission.

Rules and regulations under the Fur Products Labeling Act. (1980). Washington, DC: U.S. Federal Trade Commission.

Rules and regulations under the Textile Fiber Products Identification Act. (1986). Washington, DC: U.S. Federal Trade Commission.

Rules and regulations under the Wool Products Labeling Act of 1939. (1986). Washington, DC: U.S. Federal Trade Commission.

Trade regulation rule: Care labeling of textile wearing apparel and certain piece goods. (1984). Washington, DC: U.S. Federal Trade Commission.

QUALITY

ANSI Z-1.4 Sampling procedures and tables for inspection by attributes. (1993). New York: American National Standards Institute. (Used as U.S. Military Standard)

Best, A., & Andreasen, A. R. (1976). *Talking back to business: Voiced and unvoiced complaints.* Washington, DC: Center for the Study of Responsive Law.

Besterfield, D. H. (1993). *Quality control* (4th ed.). Upper Saddle River, NJ: Prentice Hall.

Feigenbaum, A. V. (1983). *Total quality control* (3rd ed.). New York: McGraw-Hill.

ISO 9000 Compendium (6th ed.). (1996). Geneva: International Organization for Standardization.

Latture, W. E. (1981). Improving quality through the analysis of returned garments. *American Society for Quality Control Textile and Needle Trades Division Transactions, 50–59.*

Lester, R. H., Norbert, L. E., & Mottley, H. E., Jr. (1977). *Quality control for profit.* New York: Industrial Press.

Lund, A.K. (1994). *ISO 9000: The basics.* Overland Park, KS: Johnson County Community College.

Mehta, P. V. (1984). *An introduction to quality control for the apparel industry.* Tokyo: J.S.N. International.

Scherkenbach, W. (1992). *The Deming road to quality and productivity: Road maps and roadblocks.* St. Louis, MO: Washington University.

Sproles, G. B. (1977). New evidence on price and product quality. *Journal of Consumer Affairs,* 11 (1), 63–77.

CONSUMER BEHAVIOR

Ajzen, I., & Fishbein, J. (1980). *Understanding attitudes and predicting social behavior.* Upper Saddle River, NJ: Prentice Hall.

Galbraith, R. L. (1981). Consumer comments on textile and apparel quality. *American Society for Quality Control Textile and Needle Trades Division Transactions, 94–98.*

Howard, J. A., & Sheth, J. N. (1969). *The theory of buyer behavior.* New York: Wiley.

Jacoby, J., & Olson, J. C. (1985). *Perceived quality: How consumers view stores and merchandise.* Lexington, MA: D. C. Heath.

Kaiser, S. (1996). *The social psychology of clothing: Symbolic appearances in context* (2nd ed. rev.). New York: Fairchild.

Maynes, E. S. (1976). *Decision-making for consumers: An introduction to consumer economics.* Upper Saddle River, NJ: Prentice Hall.

Myers, J. H., & Alpert, M. I. (1968). Determinant buying attitudes: Meaning and measurement. *Journal of Marketing, 32,* 13–20.

Sproles, G. B. (1994). *Changing appearances: Understanding dress in contemporary society.* New York: Fairchild.

Swan, J. E., & Combs, L. J. (1976). Product performance and consumer satisfaction: A new concept. *Journal of Marketing, 40,* 25–33.

DESIGN AND STYLE

Amaden-Crawford, C. (1996). *The art of fashion draping* (2nd ed.). New York: Fairchild.

Davis, M. L. (1996). *Visual design in dress* (3rd ed.). Upper Saddle River, NJ: Prentice Hall.

Hollen, N. (1992). *Patternmaking by the flat pattern method* (7th ed.). Upper Saddle River, NJ: Prentice Hall.

Ireland, P. J. (1987). *Encyclopedia of fashion details.* London: B. T. Batsford.

Jaffe, H. & Relis, N. (1973). *Draping for Fashion Design* (2nd ed.). New York: Fairchild.

Kopp, E., Rolfo, V., Zelin, B., & Gross, L. (1991). *How to draft basic patterns* (4th ed.). New York: Fairchild.

Kopp, E., Rolfo, V., Zelin, B., & Gross, L. (1992). *Designing apparel through the flat pattern* (6th ed.). New York: Fairchild.

Mankey-Calasibetta, C. M. (1985). *Essential terms of fashion.* New York: Fairchild.

Mankey-Calasibetta, C. M. (1988). *Fairchild's dictionary of fashion* (2nd ed.). New York: Fairchild.

Miller, P. B. (1994). *AUTOCAD® for the Apparel Industry.* Albany, NY: Delmar.

Price, J., & Zamkoff, B. (1996). *Grading techniques for fashion design* (2nd ed.). New York: Fairchild.

Steinhaus, N. H., & Lott, I. M. *I CAD...CAN YOU? AutoCAD for apparel drafting and garment design.* Grand Rapids, MI: PW Publications.

Stipelman, S. (1996). *Illustrating fashion: Concept to creation.* New York: Fairchild.

Tate, S. L. (1998). *Inside fashion design* (4th ed.). New York: Harper & Row.

Watkins, S. M. (1984). *Clothing: The portable environment.* Ames, IA: Iowa State University Press.

SIZING AND FIT

Friese, P. (1985, August). Made-to-Measure Marvel. *Apparel Industry Magazine, 46,* 66–72.

Gioello, D. A., & Berke, B. (1979). *Figure types and size ranges.* New York: Fairchild.

McVey, D. C. (1984, February). Fit to be sold. *Apparel Industry Magazine, 45,* 24-26.

Rasband, J. A. (1994). *Fabulous fit.* New York: Fairchild.

Standard tables of body measurements. (various dates). Philadelphia: American Society for Testing and Materials.

Voluntary product standards: Body measurements for the sizing of apparel. (withdrawn 1983). Washington, DC: U.S. Department of Commerce.

FABRIC

Blackmon, A. G. (1975). *Manual of standard fabric defects in the textile industry.* Graniteville, SC: Graniteville Co.

Fortess, F. (1985, June). Objective evaluation of apparel fabrics. *Bobbin, 26,* 130–138.

Gioello, D. A. (1981). *Profiling fabrics: Properties, performance, and construction techniques.* New York: Fairchild.

Gioello, D. A. (1982). *Understanding fabrics: From fiber to finished cloth.* New York: Fairchild.

Hatch, K. L. (1993). *Textile science.* Minneapolis, MN: West.

Joseph, M. L. (1993). *Introductory textile science* (6th ed.). Austin, TX: Holt, Rinehart, & Winston.

Kadolph, S. J., Langford, A. L., Hollen, N., & Saddler, J. (1995). *Textiles* (8th ed.). Upper Saddle River, NJ: Prentice Hall.

Merkel, R. S. (1991). *Textile product serviceability.* Upper Saddle River, NJ: Prentice Hall.

Price, A., & Cohen, A. C. (1987). *Fabric science* (6th ed.). New York: Fairchild.

Rees, T. (1990, March). FAST fabrics. *Apparel Industry Magazine, 51,* 82-84.

Tortora, P. B. (1996). *Fairchild's dictionary of textiles* (7th ed.). New York: Fairchild.

Tortora, P. B. (1996). *Understanding textiles* (5th ed.). Upper Saddle River, NJ: Prentice Hall.

Worth street textile market rules. (1986). Washington, DC: American Textile Manufacturer's Institute.

STITCHES AND SEAMS

Mechanization of sewing. (n.d.). Huntley, IL: Union Special Corporation Technical Training Center.

Reader's Digest complete guide to needlework. (1979). Pleasantville, NY: Reader's Digest Association.

Stitch formation. (various pamphlets, various dates). Huntley, IL: Union Special Corporation Technical Training Center.

Technology of thread and seams. (n.d.). Glasgow, Scotland: J. P. Coats.

Thread consumption. (1974). Huntley, IL: Union Special Corporation Technical Training Center.

U.S. fed. std. no. 751a: Stitches, seams, and stitchings. (1965). Washington, DC: U.S. General Services Administration.

MASS PRODUCTION/ASSEMBLY

Garment construction guide. (1983). Huntley, IL: Union Special Corporation Technical Training Center.

Gioello, D. A., & Berke, B. (1979). *Fashion production terms.* New York: Fairchild.

Hudson, P. B. (1988). *Guide to apparel manufacturing.* Greensboro, NC: MEDIApparel.

Reader's Digest complete guide to sewing. (1978). Pleasantville, NY: Reader's Digest Association.

Shaeffer, C. (1997). *Sewing for the apparel industry: Industrial sewing techniques.* New York: Fairchild.

Solinger, J. (1988). *Apparel manufacturing handbook: Analysis, principles, and practice* (2nd ed.). New York: Van Nostrand Rinehold.

SALES AND MARKETING

Cohen, A. C. (1988). *Marketing textiles: From fiber to retail.* New York: Fairchild.

Kotler, P., and Armstrong, G. (1995). *Principles of Marketing* (7th ed.). Upper Saddle River, NJ: Prentice Hall.

Manning, G. L., and Reee, B. L. (1996). *Selling today* (6th ed.). Upper Saddle River, NJ: Prentice Hall.

Perna, R. (1987). *Fashion forecasting.* New York: Fairchild.

Popcorn, F. (1991). *The Popcorn report.* New York: Doubleday.

Popcorn, F., and Marigold, L. (1996). *Clicking: Sixteen trends to future fit your life, your work and your business.* New York: HarperCollins.

Russell, C. (1993). *The master trend.* New York: Plenum Press.

Winters, A. A., & Goodman, S. (1984). *Fashion advertising and promotion* (6th ed.). New York: Fairchild.

APPENDIX

Seams and Stitchings

Diagrams in *U.S. Fed. Std. No. 751a:*
Stitches, Seams, and
Stitchings

Schematic Index of Seams and Stitchings in Alphabetical Order by Class

Seam Class SS (Superimposed)

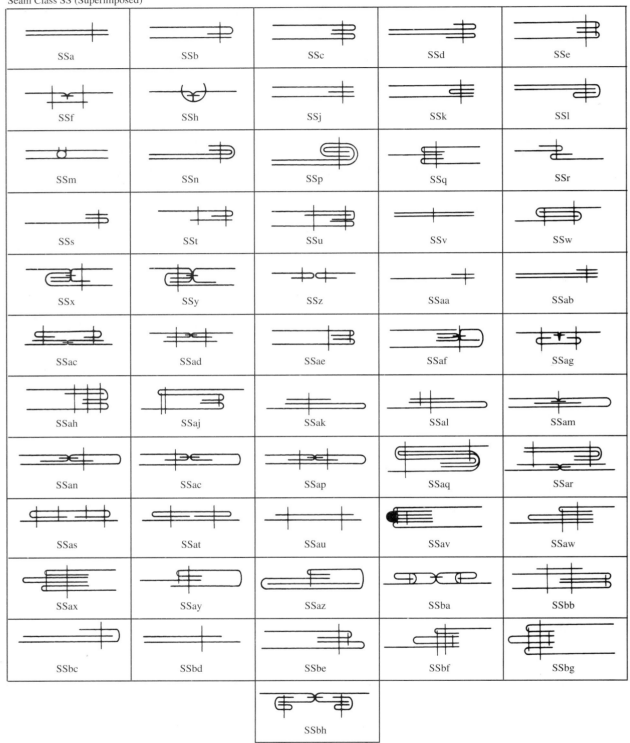

Seam Class LS (Lapped)

LSa	LSb	LSc	LSd	LSe
LSf	LSg	LSj	LSk	LSl
LSm	LSn	LSp	LSq	LSr
LSs	LSt	LSu	LSv	LSw
LSx	LSy	LSz	LSaa	LSab
LSac	LSad	LSae	LSaf	LSag
LSah	LSaj	LSak	LSal	LSam
LSan	LSap	LSaq	LSar	LSas
LSat	LSau	LSav	LSaw	LSax
LSay	LSaz	LSba	LSbb	LSbc
LSbd	LSbe	LSbf	LSbg	LSbh
LSbj	LSbk	LSbl	LSbm	LSbn

Seam Class LS (Lapped) (continued)

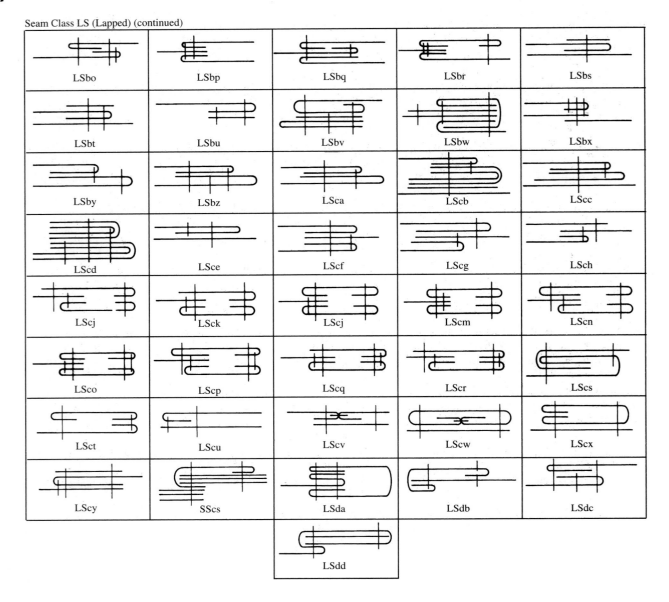

LSbo	LSbp	LSbq	LSbr	LSbs
LSbt	LSbu	LSbv	LSbw	LSbx
LSby	LSbz	LSca	LScb	LScc
LScd	LSce	LScf	LScg	LSch
LScj	LSck	LScj	LScm	LScn
LSco	LScp	LScq	LScr	LScs
LSct	LScu	LScv	LScw	LScx
LScy	SScs	LSda	LSdb	LSdc
	LSdd			

Seam Class BS (Bound)

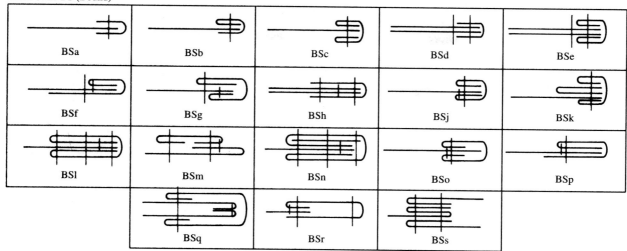

Seam Class FS (Flat)

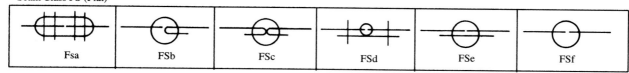

Seam Class OS (Ornamental)

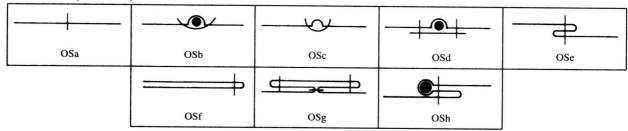

Stitching Class EF (Edge Finishing)

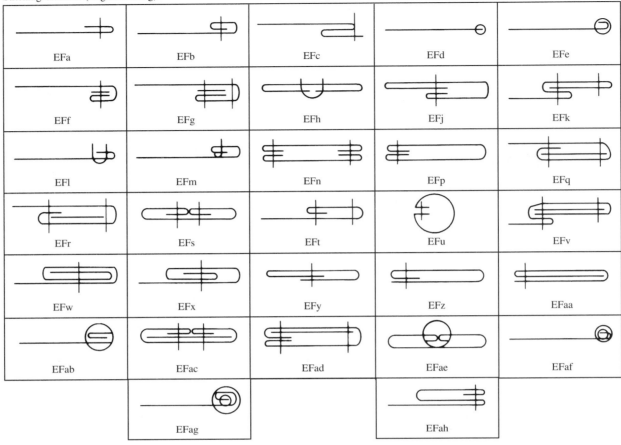

B

General Applications to Typical Operations

Applications of Stitches, Seams, and
Stitchings in *U.S. Fed. Std. No. 751a:*
Stitches, Seams, and Stitchings

Seam Type	Operation	Types of Standard Stitches Suitable
Superimposed Seams		
SSa–1	Basting	101.
	Seaming (straight)	301, 401.
	Seaming (zigzag)	304, 404.
	Seaming (overedge)	501 to 513.
	Seaming (using waxed thread)	101, 201, 301.
SSa–2	Seaming and serging	301, 401, 501 to 507, 602 515 to 519.
SSb–1 and SSb–2	Seaming (straight)	301, 401, 302, 402.
	Seaming (where similar stitch is essential on both surfaces)	301.
SSc–1 and SSc–2	Seaming	301, 401, 302, 402.
SSd–1	Seaming	301, 401.
SSe–2 and SSe–3	Seaming and edge finishing Making cuffs, collars, etc., and edge stitching on coats and shoes	301, 401, 302, 402.
SSf–3	Taping or staying	301, 401.
SSh–2	Cover seaming	302, 402, 406.
SSj–1	Seaming	201, 301, 401.
SSk–1	Seaming and cording	201, 301, 401.
SSl–1	Seaming	201, 301, 401.
SSm–1	Seaming or felling, where a blind stitch is required Padding lapels, felling tapes, etc.	103.
SSn–1	Seaming	101, 301, 401.
SSp–1	Seaming	301, 401.

Seam Type	Operation	Types of Standard Stitches Suitable

Superimposed Seams (Continued)

Seam Type	Operation	Types of Standard Stitches Suitable
SSq–2 and SSq–3	Seaming	301, 401, 302, 402.
SSr–1	Seaming	301, 401.
SSs–1 and SSs–2	Seaming and staying	301, 401.
SSt–2 and SSt–4	Seaming and taping	301, 401.
SSu–2 and SSu–4	Attaching elastic	301, 401.
SSu–2	Making pocket jettings	301.
SSv–1 and SSv–3	Quilting	301, 401.
SSw–2	Seaming	301, 401.
SSx–2	Seaming (crotch pieces and linings to trousers)	301, 401.
SSy–2	Seaming	301, 401.
SSz–3	Seaming	301, 401.
SSaa–1	Taping (coat fronts and armholes)	301.
SSab–1	Taping (coat fronts and armholes)	301.
SSac–3	Taping (crotch seams on trousers)	301.
SSad–3	Seaming and staying	301, 401.
SSae–2 and SSae–3	Seaming	301, 401.
SSaf–2	Seaming and staying	301, 401.
SSag–3	Seaming and staying	301, 401.
SSah–3 and SSah–4	Seaming	301, 401.
SSaj–3	Seaming	301, 401.
SSak–1	Attaching slide fasteners	301, 401.
SSal–2	Attaching slide fasteners	301, 401.
SSam–2	Seaming	301, 401.
SSan–2	Seaming	301, 401.
SSao–2	Seaming	301, 401.
SSap–3	Seaming	301, 401.
SSaq–2	Seaming	301, 401.
Ssar–3	Attaching end of left fly lining to crotch seam	301, 401.
SSas–4	Attaching buttonhole strips	301, 401.
SSat–2	Attaching buttonhole strips	301, 401.
Ssau–2	Staying	301, 401.
Ssav–2	Seaming and welting	301, 401.
Ssaw–2	Seaming and welting	301, 401, 504.
Ssax–2	Seaming and welting	301, 401, 504.
Ssay–2	Making waistbands	301, 401.
SSaz–1	Seaming neckties	104.
SSba–3	Book seaming	103 and 301 or 401.
SSbb–3	Seaming and staying	301, 401.
SSbc–1	Attaching interlining to cuff	103, 306.
SSbd–1	Seaming	301, 401.
SSbe–2	Seaming and edge finishing	301, 306, 401.
SSbf–3	Seaming and welting	301, 401.
SSbg–3	Seaming and welting	301, 401.
SSbh–3	Seaming	301, 401.

Lapped Seams

Seam Type	Operation	Types of Standard Stitches Suitable
LSa–1	Seaming knitted materials or underwear and similar garments	602, 603, 604, 605.
LSa–1 and LSa–2	Seaming	301, 401, 402, 406, 407.
	Seaming (using waxed thread)	101, 201, 301.
LSb–1 and LSb–2	Seaming	301, 401, 402, 406.

Seam Type	Operation	Types of Standard Stitches Suitable
LSc–1 to LSc–4	Seaming	301, 401.
LSd–1 to LSd–3	Attaching pieces to body of material	301, 304, 401.
LSe–1 to LSe–3	Seaming	301, 401.
LSf–1 and LSf–2	Seaming	301, 401.
LSg–2 to LSg–4	Facing (center plaits, stays, etc.)	301, 401.
LSj–2 and LSj–4	Facing (center plaits, stays, etc.)	301, 401.
LSk–2 and LSk–4	Facing (center plaits, stays, etc.)	301, 401.
LSl–2 and LSl–4	Facing and seaming (center plaits, stays, etc.)	301, 401.
LSm–2 and LSm–4	Facing (center plaits, stays, etc.)	101, 301, 401.
LSn–1	Facing (center plaits, stays, etc.)	301, 401.
LSp–2 and LSp–4	Joining with overlapping strip	301, 401.
LSq–2 and LSq–3	Seaming	201, 301, 401.
LSr–2	Seaming	301, 401.
LSs–2	Seaming	301, 401.
LSt–2	Seaming	301, 401.
LSu–2	Seaming	301, 401.
LSv–2	Facing and staying	301, 401.
LSw–4	Joining band (plain, elastic, etc.)	301, 401.
LSx–2 and LSx–3	Seaming	301, 401.
LSy–2 and LSy–3	Seaming	301, 401.
LSz–3 and LSz–4	Seaming	301, 401.
LSaa–3	Seaming	301, 401.
LSab–3 and LSab–4	Banding	301, 401.
LSac–2	Facing and binding	301, 401.
LSad–2	Facing and binding	301, 401.
LSae–1	Undersewing cushion	301, 401.
LSah–1	Seaming	301, 401.
LSaj–1	Seaming	301, 401.
LSak–2	Seaming	301, 401.
LSal–2 and LSal–4	Facing (center plaits, stays, etc.)	301, 401.
LSam–2 and LSam–4	Facing (center plaits, stays, etc.)	301, 401.
LSan–2 and LSan–4	Facing (center plaits, stays, etc.)	301, 401.
LSap–1	Finishing	301, 401.
LSaq–1	Finishing	301, 401.
LSar–2 to LSar–4	Facing and seaming	301, 401.
LSas–2	Seaming and gathering	301, 401.
LSat–2	Seaming and staying	301, 401.
LSau–2 to LSau–4	Seaming	301, 401.
LSav–4	Seaming and reinforcing	301, 401.
LSaw–3	Seaming	301, 401.
LSax–4	Seaming	301, 401.
LSay–4	Sewing-on band with elastic	301, 401.
LSaz–4	Seaming and staying	301, 401.
LSba–2	Seaming	301, 401.
LSbb–4	Seaming and staying	101, 301, 401.
LSbc–2 to LSbc–4	Facing	301, 401.
LSbd–2	Seaming	301, 401.
LSbe–2	Seaming	301, 401.
LSbf–2 to LSbf–4	Binding (center plait)	301, 401.
LSbg–2	Seaming	301, 401.
LSbh–1 and LSbh–2	Binding, inserting tape between binding and body material	301, 401.
LSbj–1	Attaching pieces to body material	301, 401.

Seam Type	Operation	Types of Standard Stitches Suitable
Lapped Seams (Continued)		
LSbk–2	Attaching pieces to body material	301, 401.
LSbl–2	Attaching pocket flaps and belt loops	301, 401.
LSbm–3 and LSbm–4	Seaming	301, 401.
LSbn–2	Seaming	301, 401.
LSbo–3	Seaming	301, 401.
LSbp–2	Joining yoke to shirt	301, 401.
LSbq–2	Joining yoke to shirt in loosely woven material	301, 401.
LSbr–3	Seaming	301, 401.
LSbs–1	Attaching slide fasteners	301, 401.
LSbt–2	Attaching slide fasteners	301, 401.
LSbu–2	Attaching slide fasteners	301, 401.
LSbv–3	Attaching slide fasteners	301, 401.
LSbw–3	Seaming and binding	301, 401.
LSbx–2	Forming welt on set-in pockets	301, 401.
LSby–2	Forming welt on set-in pockets	301, 401.
LSbz–2	Forming pocket welts	301, 401.
LSca–2	Forming pocket welts	301, 401.
LScb–2	Top edge of hip pocket with a stay and facing	301, 401.
LScc–2	Top edge of hip pocket	301, 401.
LScd–3	Top edge of hip pocket	301, 401.
LSce–2	Forming welt on bottom edge of set-in hip pockets	301, 401.
LScf–2	Attaching cuffs, waistbands or collars	301, 401.
LScg–2	Attaching cuffs, waistbands or collars	301, 401.
LSch–2	Attaching cuffs, waistbands or collars	301, 401.
LScj–3	Attaching cuffs, waistbands or collars	301, 401.
LSck–3	Attaching cuffs, waistbands or collars	301, 401.
LScl–3	Attaching cuffs, waistbands or collars	301, 401.
LScm–3	Attaching cuffs, waistbands or collars	301, 401.
LScn–3	Attaching cuffs, waistbands or collars	301, 401.
LSco–4	Attaching cuffs, waistbands or collars	301, 401.
LScp–4	Attaching cuffs, waistbands or collars	301, 401.
LScq–4	Attaching cuffs, waistbands or collars	301, 401.
LScr–4	Attaching cuffs, waistbands or collars	301, 401.
LScs–3	Attaching left fly to trouser fronts	301, 401.
LSct–2	Attaching waistband linings	301, 401.
LScu–2	Finishing bottoms of caps	301, 401.
LScv–3	Seaming curtains on waistbands	301, 401.
LScw–3	Making sewn-on belts or bands	301, 401.

Seam Type	Operation	Types of Standard Stitches Suitable
Lapped Seams (Continued)		
LScx–3	Making sewn-on belts or bands	301, 401.
LScy–3	Seaming and staying	301, 401.
LScz–2	Seaming	301, 401.
LSdb–2	Facing	301, 401.
LSdc–3	Trouser crotch seam	301, 401.
LSdd–2	Cut-on shirt front	301, 401.
Bound Seams		
BSa–1 and BSa–2	Binding, bound seaming	301, 401, 304, 404, 406.
BSb–1 and BSb–2	Binding, bound seaming	301, 401, 304, 404.
BSc–1 and BSc–2	Binding, bound seaming	301, 401, 304, 404.
BSd–2	Seaming and binding	301, 401.
BSe–2	Seaming and binding	301, 401.
BSf–2	Seaming and binding	301, 401.
BSg–2	Seaming and binding	301, 401.
BSh–3	Seaming and binding	301, 401.
BSj–1	Binding, bound seaming	301, 304, 401, 404, 406.
BSk–1	Binding and welting	301, 401.
BSm–3	Facing pockets	301, 401.
BSn–4	Binding flag headings	301, 401.
BSo–2	Binding, bound seaming	301, 304, 401, 404, 406.
BSp–2	Making pocket welts	301, 401.
BSq–2	Seaming and binding	301, 401.
BSr–2 and BSr–4	Seaming and binding	301, 401.
Flat Seams		
FSa–1	Seaming	304, 404, 606, 607.
	Attaching collars, cuffs, borders, etc. to knitted articles	602, 603, 606.
	Attaching edging, lace, etc.	601, 602, 603.
FSb–1	Seaming	304, 602, 603, 606.
FSc–1	Seaming	304, 404.
FSd–3	Seaming and staying	304, 404.
FSe–1	Seaming and staying	304, 404.
FSf–1	Hosiery toe closing	521.
	Seaming fur pelts, or seaming with overedge stitching where a flat butted seam is desired	501 thru 505.
Ornamental Stitching		
OSa–1 to OSa–3	Ornamental	101, 102, 104, 201, 203, 204, 301, 302, 303, 304, 305, 306, 307, 309, 310, 311, 312, 402, 403, 404, 405, 406.
OSb–1	Cording	102, 302, 402, 406.
OSc–1	Cording	102, 302, 402, 406.
OSd–2 and OSd–3	Cording	101, 301, 401.
OSe–1	Tucking or plaiting	101, 301, 401.
OSf–1	Tucking and mock seaming	101, 301, 401.
OSg–3	Making box or inverted plait	301, 401.
OSh–3	Welting	301, 401.

Seam Type	Operation	Types of Standard Stitches Suitable
Edge Finishing		
EFa–1 and EFa–2	Hemming (one fold)	101, 102, 301, 302, 401, 402, 406.
EFb–1 and EFb–2	Hemming (two folds)	101, 301, 401, 402, 406.
EFc–1	Blind hemming (woven)	301.
	Bind hemming (knit)	301, 401, 502, 503, 505.
EFd–1	Edge finishing (serging)	502, 503, 504, 505.
	Ornamental edge finishing	304, 502, 503, 504, 505, 601, 603, 604, 605, 607.
EFe–1	Ornamental edge finishing (zigzag)	304, 404.
EFf–1	Hemming with elastic tape	101, 301, 401.
EFg–2	Hemming with elastic tape	101, 301, 401.
EFh–1	Making loops or straps	406.
EFj–1 and EFj–3	Making straps	301, 401.
	Making straps (using waxed thread)	101, 301.
EFk–2 and EFk–4	Cut-on center plait (shirt fronts)	301, 401.
EFl–1	Blind hemming	103, 301, 306, 401, 502, 503.
EFm–1	Blind hemming	103, 301, 306, 401, 502, 503.
EFn–2 and EFn–4	Making straps or loops	301, 401.
EFp–2 and EFp–4	Making straps or loops	301, 401.
EFq–2	Inserting elastic in hems	301, 401.
EFr–2	Inserting elastic in hems	301, 401.
EFs–2	Making straps or loops	301, 401.
EFt–2 and EFt–4	Hemming shirt fronts	301, 401.
EFu–1	Making drawstrings or loops	301, 401.
EFv–2 and EFv–4	Cut-on center plait (shirt fronts)	301, 401.
EFw–1	Hemming (three folds)	101, 301, 401, 402, 406.
EFx–1	Hemming	101, 301, 401, 402, 406.
EFy–1 and EFy–3	Making straps or loops	301, 401, 406.
EFz–1 and EFz–2	Making straps or loops	301, 401, 406.
EFaa–1 and EFaa–2	Making straps or loops	301, 401, 406.
EFab–1	Hemming	502, 503, 504, 505.
EFac–2	Making straps or loops	301, 401.
EFad–2	Making straps or loops	301, 401.
EFae–2	Making straps or loops	103.
EFaf–2	Edge finishing	501, 502, 503, 504, 505.
EFag–2	Edge finishing	501, 502, 503, 504, 505.
EFah–1	Hemming	301, 401.

Glossary

Acceptable quality level (AQL)   The number of defective garments in a random sample below which the entire lot is accepted and above which the entire lot is rejected.

Ad valorem rate   Tariff charged according to percentage of the value of imported merchandise when it enters the U.S.

Aesthetic performance   The attractiveness of a garment; how well the garment meets aesthetic expectations.

American Apparel Manufacturers Association (AAMA)   A trade organization for U.S. apparel producers.

American Association of Textile Chemists and Colorists (AATCC)   An organization that publishes standard test methods relating to chemical processes and materials used in the textile industry.

American cut   Cut of a jacket that hangs from the shoulders and drapes loosely rather than fitting the body; also known as standard cut or natural-shoulder style.

American Fiber Manufacturers Association   Trade organization of U.S. fiber manufacturers.

American National Standards Institute (ANSI)   Privately funded federation of leaders from both the public and the private sectors that coordinates the U.S. voluntary consensus standards system.

American Society for Quality Control (ASQC)   A professional organization for people interested in quality control.

American Society for Testing and Materials (ASTM)   An organization that publishes standards and specifications for textiles and apparel.

American Textile Manufacturers Institute (ATMI)   A trade organization of U.S. textile manufacturers.

Apparel industry   Group made up of apparel manufacturers and contractors, garment wet processors, apparel wholesale representatives and direct importers who sell garments to retailers, and apparel retailers.

Apparel production cycle   Sequence of steps in the mass production of garments.

Apparel quality   Degree of excellence; conformance to requirements; the extent to which a garment meets expectations.

Applied elastic   Elastic stitched directly onto the garment to add shape where desired.

Appliqué   Decorative fabric patch applied to the garment.

Armscye   The armhole of a garment with sleeves.

Arrowhead tack   Decorative reinforcement shaped like an arrowhead.

Back tacking   Restitching at the beginning and end of a row of stitches.

Backing button   Flat, eyed button sewn on under the fabric behind a button to reinforce the button.

Backstitch   Secure form of stitching where one small stitch is taken backward for every large stitch taken forward.

Bagging   Inserting lining by attaching it to garment around outer edges and turning the garment through an opening left in the stitching.

Balance   As an element of fit, this refers to the garment being in equilibrium from side to side and from front to back.

Balanced tension   Equal tension on needle, bobbin, and/or looper threads.

Band   Straight (usually) piece of fabric seamed to the raw edge of a garment to extend and finish the edge.

Bar code   Black lines and spaces read by a laser beam; used to electronically identify a product.

Bar tack   Reinforcement consisting of several adjacent or overlapping zigzag stitches.

Basic block   Basic pattern used to produce a basic fitted garment.

Basting   Temporary stitches.

Belt   Decorative strip of fabric or other material that helps hold the garment in position and shapes it to the body at the waistline.

Belt loop   Narrow fabric strip or thread chain at the waistline to keep belt in position.

Bespoke   High-quality, custom-made; used to describe men's suits.

Better   Term that refers to the highest of the mass-merchandise price lines.

Bias   Any direction that is not the lengthwise or crosswise grain of a woven fabric.

Bias facing   Narrow bias strips of fabric used to face raw edges.

Bifurcated garments   Garments having two legs, for example, pants.

Binding   Strip of fabric that covers the raw edge of the garment and is visible from both inside and outside the garment; does not extend the edge.

Binding tariff classification ruling   U.S. Customs Service classification of a garment for import purposes; good for the life of its production.

Bleaching   Wet process using color-removing agents.

Blend   Two or more fiber types mixed together in a fabric.

Blind hem   Hem secured with nearly invisible blindstitches.

Blindstitch   Stitch that joins layers of fabric without the needle thread fully penetrating the top layer.

Bluff-edge collar   Collar with under collar made of felt and with no seam allowances at the collar edges.

Bobbin Magazine   Prominent periodical for apparel manufacturers; cosponsors Bobbin Show.

Bobbin Show™   Annual gathering of apparel manufacturers in Atlanta; showcases new apparel production equipment and technology and facilitates the exchange of ideas.

Bobbinless zigzag stitch   Stitch that resembles plain lockstitch zigzag on the face, but interloopings are visible on the back.

Bodies   Garment styles.

Body fabric   Main, outer fabric of a garment; also called fashion or shell fabric.

Boning   Stiff plastic strips sewn to garment seams to add shape and support.

Booked seam   Plain seam, butterflied, with the raw edges of the seam allowances folded under and blindstitched; also known as tailored seam.

Bottom-cover stitch   Stitch that features two or three parallel rows of straight stitches visible on the face side and many thread interloopings on the back side to flatten the area and conceal raw edges by covering them with thread.

Bound buttonhole   Rectangular hole in the fabric that is bound or faced and backed with narrow strips of fabric that meet like lips to cover the opening.

Bound seam (BS)   Seam made by using fabric binding strips to encase raw edges.

Bow   Ribbon or fabric strip tied into a decorative knot with loops and streamers.

Boys' sizes   Size classification for boys approximately 7 to 17 years old.

Bra size   The number equal to under-bust measurement plus 5 or 6 inches, whichever results in an even number.

Braid   Narrow trim formed by intertwining a set of yarns according to a definite pattern.

Branded apparel   Clothing developed by a manufacturer and sold to many retailers under the trademarked brand; also called name brand, national brand, or simply "brand."

Break-open stitch   Stitch that, because of the loose stitch formation, hinges open flat like a notebook.

Breakout   Written explanation of details in a sketch.

Bridge   Price line covering the gap between two price lines.

Bridle   Stay tape sewn at roll line of lapel to prevent gaping.

British cut   Jacket cut that falls between American cut and European cut.

Broken seam   Seam that has split apart because the stitches have broken.

Budget   Term that refers to the lowest of the mass-merchandise price lines.

Bulk continuous filament (BCF)   Texturized yarn.

Bundle   Like types of cut components grouped for assembly line production.

Bustle   Basket-like device used to expand and support added fullness in the back of a skirt.

Butterflied   Seam allowances that are pressed open, or busted.

Button loop   Fabric strip, cording, braid, or elastic that encircles a button; substitutes for a buttonhole.

Buttonhole twist   Heavy, lustrous thread.

Buying benefit   Performance advantage that results from the garment's physical features.

Canted   Pants legs with the backs cut slightly longer than the fronts, causing the hem to fall at an angle from the front to the back.

Carded yarn   Fuzzy, soft, loosely twisted yarn.

Care Labeling Rule   Federal law requiring that all apparel sold in the United States have a permanent label that provides full instructions for the regular care of the garment.

Casing   Tunnel of fabric through which elastic or a drawstring is threaded to provide shape to the garment.

Catchstitch   Stitch that looks like a series of uneven *X*s; a flexible, extensible stitch as well as a decorative one.

Certification   Seal of approval issued by a certifying agency. In the case of certification of supplier laboratories, it means the acceptance of performance test data from the supplier without in-house verification.

Chainstitch   Interlooped stitch.

Chapter 98   Provision 9802 in the Harmonized Commodity Description and Coding System allowing off-shore production; policy was formerly called Item 807.

Chargeback   Practice by which a running total of all defective merchandise is kept by the buyer, authorization for return is granted by the seller, and the appropriate amounts are subtracted from payments on future merchandise.

Chest piece   Pad used to fill out and smooth the hollow area below the shoulder near the armhole.

Children's sizes   Classification of clothing sizes for the child of approximately 3 to 6 years of age.

Childrenswear   Classification of clothing for children.

Circumvention   Avoiding trade regulations.

Clean finish   Edge treatment made by folding under the raw edge once and stitching it in place; essentially, a narrow hem on the edge; also called turned and stitched.

Clo   Unit of measure approximately equal to the insulation required to keep a resting person comfortable at room temperature.

Closed-band cuff   Unbroken ring of fabric large enough to fit over the arm.

Coil zipper   Continuous-element zipper with interlocking twisted, spiral strands of monofilament nylon.

Collar   Band applied to the neckline.

Collar slope   Vertical height of the collar.

Collar stay   Thin plastic strip inserted in collar to make it stay flat and to prevent the collar points from curling.

Color approval   Final choice of color.

Color service   Business that predicts color direction.

Color story   Cohesive use of color within a line or group of garments.

Colorfastness   Ability to retain original color.

Combed yarn   Smooth, lustrous, tightly twisted yarn.

Combination facing   Shaped facing combined with an extended facing.

Committee for Implementation of Textile Agreements (CITA)   Group that negotiates bilateral trade agreements for the United States; part of U.S. Department of Commerce.

Compound rate   Tariff charged according to a combination of ad valorem and specific rates.

Computer-aided design (CAD)   Computerized system used to enhance performance of design tasks.

Computer-aided manufacturing (CAM)   Computerized system used to enhance performance of manufacturing tasks.

Computed-integrated manufacturing (CIM)   System that links all computerized facets of a business electronically for efficient management.

Computer Integrated Textile Design Association (CITDA)   Professional organization for designers proficient in the use of computer-aided design.

Concealed in-seam pocket   Pocket hidden in a seam.

Consumer Product Safety Commission (CPSC)   U.S. government commission that oversees Flammable Fabrics Act, Regulations for Toys and Children's Articles, and Guidelines for Drawstrings on Children's Outerwear.

Construction   Methods used to assemble the garment.

Continuous-bound placket   Bound slash in the fabric perpendicular to the edge of the garment.

Contractor   Person or company hired by the manufacturer to do part or all of the work in producing a garment; also called outside shop.

Control stitching   Understitching used on enclosed seams; stitches the seam allowances to the lower ply to keep the seam flat and to prevent the lower ply from slipping out and showing.

Conventional zipper   Zipper that has a visible chain and one or both ends that remain together when it is unzipped.

Cord   Attached string or rope used as a closure.

Cording stitch   Stitch that secures creases; two rows of straight stitches appear on the top side with a looper thread underneath.

Corespun thread   Thread that consists of a spun core of polyester or nylon wrapped with cotton or other fibers.

Cost per wear   Purchase price divided by the number of times the garment is worn; assists in determining value.

Costing   Estimating the total cost of producing a garment.

Count   Number of yarns in one square inch of fabric; also called thread count or yarn count.

Counterfeit   Fake copy of currently popular branded apparel, accompanied by the illegal use of the rightful producer's brand name or trademark.

Country of origin   Nation in which a garment was produced.

Courses   Loops that run across the back of a plain knit fabric.

Couture   Term used to refer to high-price, designer-named ready-to-wear; true couture is high-quality custom-made clothing.

Crafted With Pride in U.S.A. Council   Organization that certifies and promotes garments made in the United States.

Crease   Pressed-in line.

Crocking Action of color rubbing off and transferring to other surfaces.

Cross-train To train operators for several jobs so they can work where needed most.

Crotch length Measurement of the crotch from the waistline in front to the waistline in back, as measured between the legs.

Cuff Banded or turned-back finish at lower edge of sleeve or pant leg.

Cup size The letter, ranging from AAA to F, that represents the difference between bra size and bust measurement at the fullest point.

Curing oven Device used to heat cure garments that have been treated with a resin finish to prevent wrinkling; also called heat tunnel.

Customs broker Intermediary who helps secure entry for imported goods.

Cut Number of loops per square inch of knit fabric; also called gauge.

Cut, made, and trim (CMT) contractor Contractor who performs all the production operations to produce a style.

Cutting Action of dividing fabric into garment components.

Cutwork Holes in a fabric, surrounded by embroidery.

D-ring Two d-shaped rings that work together with a fabric strip to create an adjustable closure.

Dart Triangular fold stitched to shape the flat fabric to the curves and bulges of the body.

Dart equivalents Dart substitutes that incorporate shape into the garment in a variety of ways.

Decitex (dtex) Term used to describe fine yarns; equals tex multiplied by 10.

Decorative chainstitch Stitch that is identical to 101 single-thread chainstitch except that chain appears on the face side of the fabric rather than the back side.

Defect guide Set of garment standards that aid in the monitoring and maintenance of quality levels during production and inspection.

Demographics Statistics that describe a population, including age, income, education, occupation, race, and geographic location.

Denier System used to designate fiber and yarn size; weight in grams of 9000 meters; the larger the number, the larger the fiber or yarn.

Denier per filament (DPF) Yarn denier divided by the number of filaments in the yarn.

Department of Labor (DOL) U.S. government department that oversees the Fair Labor Standards Act (FLSA).

Design The plan for the garment's style.

Design ease Extra ease in addition to fitting ease that gives a garment its style.

Designer Person who develops the style of a garment; in the highest sense, describes couture or haute couture apparel; as a price line, may include work by popular, high-price ready-to-wear designers as well as merchandise that bears the name of a nonexistent person.

Determinant attributes Features that have the greatest effect on the consumer's satisfaction.

Die Cutting device in the shape of piece to be cut; used to cut out small, complex pattern pieces.

Digitizer Device used to convert the hard pattern into a computerized format.

Dimensional stability Ability to maintain original shape and size.

Direct importer Agent that sells and monitors production exclusively from other countries.

Direct roller printing Process of applying a pattern by rolling it onto the fabric using a series of different color cylinders.

Directional stitching Sewing in the direction of the grain to minimize stretching.

Distribution center (DC) Place where merchandise is consolidated for shipment.

Double knit Knit fabric with two inseparable layers of loops.

Double ticketing Labeling clothing with both a junior size and misses size, for example, 5/6 or 11/12.

Drafting Process by which a pattern is drawn using body measurements.

Draping Placing fabric on a mannequin to design a garment.

Drawstring Narrow tube, cord, or strip of fabric inserted into casing and pulled up or tied to shape the garment to the body.

Dress size Womenswear outerwear size.

Drop In a suit, the difference between the measurement of the chest of the jacket and the waist of the pants.

Drop shipping Direct shipment from the vendor to the buyer.

Dual Technology Vendor Marking (DTVM) Including both Optical Character Recognition and Universal Product Code on the same ticket.

Dumping Method of trade rule circumvention that occurs when manufacturers sell goods for a lower price than their cost of production in order to gain a foothold in a new market, giving them an unfair advantage over competing producers in that market.

Dye lot Fabrics from same dye bath, producing color consistency.

Dyestuff Liquid colorant.

E-mail Electronic mail.

Ease Imperceptible fullness incorporated on one side of a seam and stitched in place; as an element of fit, it refers to the amount of roominess in a garment.

Ease pleat Pleat in the lining that provides adequate room for movement and a smooth, easy fit.

Edge finish stitching (EF) A series of stitches that finishes an edge.

Edge treatment A finish of the raw or cut edges of a garment.

Edgestitching Topstitching placed very close to an edge.

Elastic Fabric with a high degree of stretch and recovery.

Elasticity Fabric's ability to return to its original size after being stretched; also called memory.

Electronic data interchange (EDI) Exchange of information via computer linkages.

Embargo Denial of entry of goods into a country.

Embroidery Decorative stitching used to form designs and patterns.

Enclosed seam A seam in which the operator sews the fabric plies face sides together near the edge, opens out the plies and turns them back sides together to encase the seam allowances; occurs only at edges, where it appears as a line with no visible stitches along the edge.

End use Intended use of a garment.

Enterprise for the Americas Initiative (EAI) Proposed policy that would expand NAFTA to include Central and South American countries.

Environmental Protection Agency (EPA) U.S. government agency that enforces the Pollution Prevention Act, the Clean Air Act, and the Clean Water Act.

Equal Employment Opportunity Commission (EEOC) U.S. government commission that oversees the Civil Rights Act, the Age Discrimination in Employment Act, and the Equal Pay Act.

European cut Sleek, angular, highly shaped, and closely fitted cut of a jacket.

European Union (EU) Trading bloc of European countries.

Even plaid Plaid that contains a balanced arrangement of stripes on each side of the dominant horizontal and vertical bars of the plaid.

Export To sell goods to another country.

Export trading company (ETC) Entity that serves as an intermediary between the producer of the goods and the buyer of the goods in another country.

Exposed in-seam pocket Partially visible pocket in a seam.

Exposed zipper Zipper application in which zipper chain shows.

Extended facing Facing formed by extending the fabric at the edge to be faced and folding it under.

Extensibility Elongation or stretch.

Extrinsic attribute Feature that can be altered without changing the garment.

Eyed button Button that is sewn to the garment through holes in its face.

Eyelet Small reinforced hole in a garment.

Fabric Textile material from which garments are produced.

Fabric Assessment by Simple Testing (FAST) Simple fabric evaluation system that measures four main fabric characteristics critical to garment appearance and performance.

Faced placket Finish at an opening edge made by facing a slash in the fabric perpendicular to the edge of the garment.

Faced slit Slit in the fabric, faced to serve as a buttonhole.

Facing Piece of fabric used to finish raw edges of a garment; the facing is turned to the inside of the garment so that it backs or faces the garment at the edge.

Fagoting Decorative stitching that holds together two closely spaced folded edges of fabric with ornamental stitches.

Fair trade Policy that focuses on the need for trade practices that provide a level playing field for all global competitors.

Fallout Waste.

Fashion forecaster Business that analyzes fashion influences and predicts fashion direction.

Fax Facsimile of a document sent via computer linkage.

Federal Trade Commission (FTC) U.S. government commission that oversees the Textile Fiber Products Identification Act, the Care Labeling Rule, the Wool Products Labeling Act, the Fur Products Labeling Act, Guides for Feather and Down Products Industry, and Silk Labeling Regulations.

Felting shrinkage Reduction in size of fabric that occurs when fibers mat together.

Fiber Fine, hairlike structure; raw material from which fabrics are made.

Fiber content The percentage of each fiber in the garment; listed in order of predominance by weight.

Fiber dyeing Process of applying dye in the fiber stage of fabric production.

Fiberweb Fabric made directly from fibers; also called nonwoven.

Filament fiber Long fiber.

Filament yarn   Yarn composed of long filament fibers.

Fill   Yarns that run perpendicular to the selvages; in weaving, consists of yarns woven over and under the lengthwise yarns to create the fabric; also called crosswise grain, filling, or weft.

Filling knit   Interlooped fabric with yarns running horizontally across the fabric; also called weft knit.

Final audit   Quality inspection performed as the last stage in the manufacturing quality process or the first stage of the retailing in the retailing quality process; also called final inspection.

Findings   All materials other than fabric required to produce a garment. Also called notions or sundries.

Finish pressing   Pressing done at end of assembly process; also called off pressing.

Finishing   Final steps in the production of a garment; includes adding finishing details, trim and inspect, repair or rework of any defects, pressing, and folding and packing.

First pattern   Pattern for prototype garment.

Fit   How well the garment conforms to the three-dimensional human body.

Fit model   Individual who represents the figure type of the target customer and on whom fit is tested.

Fitting ease   Ease required for a comfortable fit.

500-class overedge stitches   Stitches formed, as the name implies, over the edge of the fabric, encasing the edge in thread interloopings; also called overlock, serge, overseam, overcast, or merrow.

Flagging system   Use of markers to alert spreaders to remove fabric flaws as they spread the cloth.

Flammable Fabrics Act   Law that establishes minimal flammability standards for apparel, with the strictest standards for children's sleepwear.

Flanges   Projections below the hemline cut as a mirror image of the garment above the hemline, enabling the hem allowance to lie flat and smooth against the garment when folded up.

Flap pocket   Pocket with piece of fabric extending down over pocket opening.

Flat collar   Collar that lies flat, or nearly flat, against the garment all around the wearer's neck.

Flat construction   Stitching pieces together while both are still open and flat; then forming tubular shapes by sewing the remaining seam in all pieces at once.

Flat seam (FS)   Joint in which raw edges are abutted (or sometimes slightly overlapped) and sewn together; also called butt seam or exposed seam.

Flat-bed press   Large, flat, table-type press. Also called buck press.

Flat-felled seam   Seam with the raw edges of both seam allowances folded under as the seam is stitched; a strong and durable seam.

Flexible manufacturing   Combination of various manufacturing techniques based on the product being produced.

Floor-ready merchandise (FRM)   Goods marked at the factory, enabling retailers to put them directly on the selling floor without passing them through a retail distribution center.

Fly-front/fly   Type of lapped-zipper application with wide topstitching; used at the center fronts of jeans and other garments.

Fly shield   Underlap beneath fly zipper that protects skin and undergarments from irritation by the zipper chain.

Focus group   Sample of target customers brought together to discover their wants and needs.

Folded hem   Hem with raw edge turned under and stitched to the garment.

Form fitting   Testing fit on a stationary three-dimensional form.

Form press   Press shaped like the garment. Sometimes called Paris® press.

400-class multithread chainstitches   Double-locked stitches formed by a needle thread passing through the fabric and interlooping with a looper thread.

Four Point System   The most popular fabric-grading system; used to assign penalty points to a fabric based on the number and size of defects.

Free-floating elastic casing   Tunnel in which elastic can move about freely.

Free-hanging lining   Lining not attached at the garment hem; also called slip lining.

Free trade   Policy favoring unrestricted imports in the interest of the free flow of goods between nations.

French fly   Tab or extension on fly-front underlap that buttons to the inside of the pants near the waist for a smoother look.

French seam   A "seam within a seam;" operator sews a narrow plain seam with the back sides of the fabric plies together and then sews a slightly wider plain seam with the face sides of the fabric plies together to encase the seam allowances of the first seam.

French tack   Thread chain, strip of fabric similar to a belt loop, or a piece of ribbon about an inch and a half long connecting the hem of a free-hanging lining and the hem of the garment at each seam allowance; also called swing tack.

Frog   Highly decorative button-and-loop closure made of elaborately coiled cord or braid.

Frosting   Use of a bleaching agent to remove color for a highlighting effect. Also called acidwashing.

Full-fashioned mark   Mark that represents increases or decreases in the number of stitches in a knitted garment section, a result of shaping the piece.

Fully-let-out   The most expensive type of fur garment, in which pelts are cut into narrow diagonal strips and sewn back together so that each pelt becomes a long, narrow panel that covers the length of the wearer's body.

Functional performance   Performance features other than appearance, namely, the garment's utility and durability.

Fur Products Labeling Act (FPLA)   Federal law regulating labeling of fur products.

Furnishings   Men's items other than clothing or sportswear, including shirts, ties, underwear, sleepwear, and accessories.

Fused buttonhole   Buttonhole formed by embossing the fabric with a hot die which is patterned to resemble a stitched or bound buttonhole, then slitting the fabric to let the button through.

Fusible   Item containing heat-sensitive adhesive for application using a hot press.

Garment dyeing   Dyeing the finished garment.

Garment rinsing/garment washing   Rinsing or washing the completed garment before it is sold to soften and preshrink the garment before it goes to the consumer.

Gathers   A series of small folds of fabric, controlled and held in place by stitches to provide visible fullness.

Gauntlet button   Button and buttonhole placed on a tailored placket to prevent it from gaping.

General Services Administration (GSA)   U.S. government office that publishes some federal documents.

General Agreement on Tariffs and Trade (GATT)   International agreement promoting free trade, currently being phased out.

Generalized System of Preferences (GSP)   Program under which exemptions from tariffs are granted to certain developing countries to encourage their economic growth.

Generic name   As established by the Federal Trade Commission, a name that denotes a family of fibers with similar chemical compositions.

Genuine/top grain leather   Top layer of a leather hide.

Girls' sizes   Classification of sizes fitting girls approximately 7 to 11 years old.

Godet   Triangular fabric piece set into a seam or slash, usually at the hem of a garment.

Gore   Vertical division within a garment, usually tapered panels seamed together to add shape to a garment.

Gorge line   Seam where collar and lapel meet.

Grade rules   Criteria establishing the amount of difference between clothing sizes for a particular manufacturer.

Graded nest   All sizes of graded patterns, superimposed on one another.

Grading   Increasing and decreasing the dimensions of a pattern to reflect the various sizes to be produced. Also refers to trimming the seam allowances of an enclosed seam, each to a slightly different length; this is also called blending, layering, or beveling.

Grain   As an element of fit, refers to need for lengthwise yarns to run parallel to length of body at center front and center back, down the center of the arm from shoulder to elbow, and down the center front of each pant leg; the crosswise yarns should run perpendicular to the length of the body at bust/chest, hip, and upper arm at bust/chest level.

Greige goods   Undyed, unfinished fabrics.

Group   Subdivision of a line of apparel.

Grommet   Large reinforced hole in a garment.

Growth tuck   Tuck in childrenswear that can be let out as child grows.

Guidelines for Drawstrings on Children's Outerwear   Guidelines to help prevent children from strangling or getting entangled in drawstrings at the neck and waist or bottom of clothing such as jackets and sweatshirts.

Guides for the Feather and Down Products Industry   Regulations for feather and down-filled products.

Gusset   Piece of fabric set into a seam or seam intersection to add shape and fullness to a garment.

Hand   Broad term for the tactile sensations resulting from touching, moving, or squeezing the fabric with the human hand.

Hand-worked buttonhole   Buttonhole with raw edges covered by hand-purl stitches; very labor-intensive, rare, and costly.

Hand overcasting   Series of evenly spaced diagonal stitches covering the seam or hem allowance edges to retard raveling.

Hand picking   Application, usually of a zipper, with hand pickstitches.

Harmonized System (HS)   International system of trade classification.

Harmonized Tariff Schedule of the United States (HTSUS)   Document that is part of the Harmonized System and is used to classify apparel imported into the United States.

Haute couture   Term for the most fashionable and exclusive couture apparel.

Heat setting   Process in which fabric is heated and then cooled in desired shape to maintain dimensional stability.

Heat transfer printing   Process of transferring a design from specially processed paper to the fabric using heat and pressure.

Heel guard   Layer of abrasion-resistant tape sewn in to reinforce the area at the back of the hem in high-quality pants; also called kick tape.

Hem allowance   Amount turned under in a hem.

Hemstitching   Pulling out a group of parallel yarns from a fabric and tying the remaining perpendicular yarns together with decorative stitches, or the machine imitation of this process.

Hong Kong binding   Very narrow, often color-contrasting bias strip used to decoratively bind seams, hem allowances, and other edges inside high-price tailored and couture garments.

Hook and eye   Interlocking closure consisting of a hook and a receptacle (eye).

Hook-and-loop tape/Velcro®   Fastener that consists of two separate tapes that interlock to create closure when pressed together.

Hoop   Plastic or metal ring used to support full skirts.

Horizontal placket   Finish at an opening edge of a garment, so named because the placket is parallel to the opening.

Horsehair braid   Braid that faces and stiffens hems in wedding and formal gowns with full skirts.

Hot goods   Goods sold or shipped in violation of the Fair Labor Standards Act.

Immigration and Naturalization Service (INS)   U.S. government service that enforces the Immigration Reform and Control Act.

Import   To buy goods from another country.

In-line inspection   Quality evaluation that takes place as the garment is being assembled.

In-process time   The time a product is having work done on it.

In registration   Precisely lined up.

In-seam buttonhole   Seam that is left partially unstitched to create a buttonhole.

In-seam placket   Finish at an opening edge of a garment made by leaving a seam unsewn for the last few inches of the edge.

In-seam pocket   Pocket that is set into a seam of the garment, usually the side seam of skirts, pants, dresses, and coats.

In-the-round construction   Creating tubes (for example sleeves) and then joining the tubular pieces together using a round seam.

Incoming acceptable quality level (IAQL)   Quality check performed by retailers on incoming goods.

Industrial flat iron   Like consumer flat irons, but much heavier and usually suspended from above for operator convenience and safety.

Infants'/babies' sizes   Classification of clothing sizes for infants from birth to approximately the age of 18 months, or old enough to walk.

Inseam   Inner leg seam of pants.

Inside shop   Manufacturer-owned-and-operated factories.

Inspection   Careful examination of fabric, garment parts, and completed garments at varying stages in the production cycle.

Interfacing   Supporting fabric usually hidden between garment and its facing; lends body, shape, and reinforcement to limited areas of the garment.

Interlining   Insulative layer applied strictly for additional warmth between the lining and the fashion fabric.

International Fabricare Institute (IFI)   Association of professional dry cleaners and launderers.

International Organization for Standardization (ISO)   An international organization with representatives from many nations that concentrates on international standardization.

Intrinsic attributes   Features that cannot be altered without changing the product itself.

Inventory   Goods in the factory waiting to be processed or in a warehouse waiting to be sold.

Investment dressing   The purchase of classic apparel such as coats and suits that can be worn several seasons.

Invisible zipper   Zipper constructed so that the chain is concealed beneath the tape when the zipper is closed.

ISO 9000 Certification   Certification that a company meets the ISO 9000 standards, a series of voluntary, private-sector standards.

Junior sizes   Size classification for short, slender women with youthful figures.

Just in time (JIT)   No wasted time between steps of production.

Kawabata Evaluation System for Fabrics (KES)   Fabric evaluation system that quantifies the statement of difficult-to-measure fabric performance specifications.

Keystone markup   Doubling the wholesale cost to obtain the retail price.

Keyhole buttonhole   Buttonhole with characteristic keyhole shape; rounded end allows button to ride in the buttonhole without distorting the garment.

Kimono sleeve   Sleeve cut as one with the body of the garment.

Kiosk   Self-contained video unit.

Knock off   The legal copy or near copy of the general idea of a design shown by another firm under a different brand name.

Lab dip   Dyed color samples from which the manufacturer can choose.

Lace trim   Narrow lace fabric.

Lacing   Cord or tie threaded through eyelets, grommets, or buttonholes, as on a shoe.

Lapels   Parts of the garment that roll or fold back above the front closure; also called revers.

Lapped seam (LS)   Seam made by overlapping the seam allowances of two or more fabric plies and sewing them together with the fabric plies extending in opposite directions.

Lapped zipper   Application characterized by only one line of visible stitching on the outside of the garment; the topstitching is on one side of the opening.

Latch tacking Technique of drawing the excess thread chain of 500- and 600-class stitches at the beginning of each row of stitches into the stitches to secure them.

Lay/layup Stack of fabric plies to be cut.

Lead time The time from order placement to receipt of the goods.

Lettered sizing The use of letters of the alphabet rather than numbers to designate size, for example, S, M, L, XL.

Lettuce-edge hem Hem created by stretching the edge as it is stitched so that it ripples attractively.

Licensing The process by which a manufacturer (the licensee) pays a fee to an individual or company (the licensor) for the privilege of affixing the licensor's name, trademark, or logo to the licensee's products.

Lignes Used to measure button size; 40 lignes are equal to a diameter of one inch.

Line Series of related designs (in this context, also called a collection); as an element of fit, it refers to the alignment of structural lines of the garment with the natural lines of the body.

Line development/lead-time calendar Chart containing the scheduling of key activities during all stages of the production cycle.

Line presentation board Groups of sketches for a line, on poster board for presentation to decision makers.

Lingerie Underwear, loungewear, and sleepwear; also called intimate apparel.

Lingerie guard Ribbon or fabric strip attached behind zipper chain so it cannot irritate wearer's skin or undergarments.

Lining A near replica of the garment, constructed of lightweight fabric and sewn inside the garment with seam allowances reversed to provide a finished inside appearance.

Lockstitch Interlocked stitch.

Lockstitch blindstitch The most durable type of blindstitch; used to secure hems in high-quality garments.

Loop Ring of cord, thread, or fabric used to hang the garment or to suspend articles from the garment.

Loss leader Style sold at a loss to attract buyers to a line.

Low labeling Recommending a more conservative care method than the garment requires.

Major defect Defect not acceptable in any situation; in fabric, a defect longer than nine inches and more than two inches from selvage.

Manufactured fibers Fibers formed through human effort; also called man-made fibers.

Manufacturer The person or company ultimately responsible for all the steps in producing garments and distributing them to retailers.

Manufacturing retailer One who serves the dual role of being the manufacturer responsible for producing garments and the retailer selling the finished goods to the consumer.

Marker Plan that indicates how all the pattern pieces of the garment are arranged on the fabric to achieve the most efficient layout.

Market potential price The highest price that the market will bear without dampening sales too much.

Market segmentation Dividing consumers into groups with common characteristics.

Material utilization (MU) Percentage of fabric utilized by a particular marker arrangement.

Materials The fabrics and other components used to produce garments.

Men's clothing Men's suits, jackets, pants, and coats.

Men's sizes Size classification for clothing that fits the average adult man.

Menswear Clothing for adult males.

Merchandiser Person who formulates the line for a manufacturer to satisfy the company's target market.

Metamerism Apparel change in color due to change in lighting.

Mill flaw Fabric defect.

Minor defect Defect that will not affect the use of the product but needs to be corrected in future production.

Misses sizes Size classification fitting the adult women of average proportions; also called missy sizes.

Mitering Seaming or folding a corner diagonally for sharper, less bulky corners.

Mock flat-felled seam Seam that imitates true flat-felled seam; also called mock fell seam.

Mock French seam Seam used to create the appearance of the true French seam but at a lower cost; also called false French seam.

Mock safety stitch Stitch resembling safety stitch but consisting of a single row of stitches rather than two individual rows; also called simulated safety stitch.

Model stock Merchandise assortment that reflects the anticipated demand for a particular store.

Modem Computer-linked device that converts information to audible tones that can be received and interpreted by another modem.

Moderate Term that refers to a middle-ground mass merchandise price line.

Modular manufacturing Technique that replaces the traditional assembly line; operators are grouped into teams, or modules.

Monofilament thread Clear thread resembling a fishing line made of a single filament of nylon.

Monogram Embroidery that forms the initials of the wearer's name.

Multifiber Arrangement (MFA) Under GATT, seeks an orderly growth in the openness of world trade in textiles and apparel; allows for tariffs and quotas.

Multifilament thread Several filament yarns twisted together to make a very strong thread.

Multiple-stitch zigzag stitch Stitch made in much the same way as a regular zigzag stitch except that each diagonal portion of the zigzag is made up of more than one stitch.

Nap-one-way (NOW) Fabric spread with each ply of fabric facing up.

Nap-either-way (NEW) Fabric spread face to face.

Nap-up-and-down (NUD) Napped fabric from alternate layers is sewn together so nap is consistent within each garment.

National Institute of Standards and Technology (NIST) U.S. government institute that formerly published voluntary standards for apparel sizing.

National Retail Federation (NRF) Trade organization of retailers.

Natural fibers Fibers that occur naturally in the environment.

Needle chewing Damage that occurs when a needle causes jagged, enlarged holes in the fabric.

Needle cutting Damage that occurs when the needle cuts, or severs, the yarns of the fabric rather than slipping between the yarns.

Needle heating Damage that occurs when sewing friction heats the needle, which then fuses or melts the finishes or fibers of the thread or fabric.

Nonfabric trim Decorative items made of plastic, metal, or other nontextile materials.

North American Free Trade Agreement (NAFTA) Policy creating a single North American market for goods originating in the United States, Canada, and Mexico.

Notch Small slit or wedge cut in the seam allowance that helps operators match parts and panels during assembly.

Number A style offered as part of a manufacturer's line.

Numbered sizing Sizing system based on numerals, for example, size 10.

Occupational Safety and Health Administration (OSHA) U.S. government administration that enforces the Occupational Safety and Health Act.

Off-grain Distorted fabric grain.

Off pressing Final pressing after construction.

Off-pricing/discounting Selling goods at lower prices than the manufacturers' suggested retail prices.

Offshore production Contracting with manufacturers in other countries to make goods.

100-class single-thread chainstitches Stitches interlooping one needle thread and having no underthread.

100 percent inspection Examination of every garment.

One-size-fits-all A garment that will stretch to fit many figure types and sizes.

Open-band cuff Cuff that has an opening so that the wearer can fit the cuff band over the hand and then fasten it to fit snugly.

Optical character recognition (OCR) System using a series of computer-read numbers without a bar code.

Ornamental stitching (OS) Series of stitches applied for decorative purposes.

Outsource To find a contractor outside the United States.

Outerwear Clothing seen by others when it is worn.

Outseam Outer leg seam.

Outside shop Independent contractor.

Oval/fan buttonhole Buttonhole with characteristic oval shape.

Overdye Dyeing one color over another.

Overhead costs Expenses of operating a business beyond the direct costs of producing garments.

Overlap Piece of fabric on top of a closure.

Oversized Designed with extra design or styling ease to create loose fit.

Pad stitching Tiny stitches made through the interfacing and barely catching the fashion fabric; softly and subtly shapes collars and lapels.

Panels Major garment sections.

Parts Minor garment parts.

"Parts, Panels, Pieces, Products" General order of garment assembly.

Patch pocket Piece of fabric attached, like a patch, to the outside of the garment; also called applied pocket.

Pattern design system (PDS) Computer system that enhances performance of pattern design tasks.

Pattern matching Lining up stripes, checks, plaids, and other linear patterns at seams.

Per sample buying Traditional buying in which buyers select from manufacturers' lines.

Perceived quality model Equation illustrating the process consumers use to evaluate the overall quality of a garment.

Performance features The garment's aesthetic and functional features that determine the standards it meets and how it benefits the consumer.

Petites Size classification for shorter-than-average women.

Physical features Attributes that provide the product's tangible form and composition.

Physical inventory Actual count of the merchandise.

Pickstitch Tiny, decorative backstitch; also called prick-stitch.

Pictograms Body measurements indicated on a sketch of the human body to communicate size internationally.

Piece dyeing Dyeing fabric in the fabric stage.

Piecework System in which operators are paid according to the number of garments they complete rather than by the hour.

Pieces Semicomplete sections of the garment.

Pilling Formation of fuzz balls of tangled fibers on fabric surface.

Pink To cut an edge with a serrated blade or scissors; pinking retards raveling.

Placket Finished structural opening in a garment that allows a body part to pass through for dressing and undressing.

Plain seam Simple, superimposed seam; appears as a line with no visible stitches on the outside of the garment, but the seam allowances are visible inside the garment; the most common seam for sewing structural garment seams.

Plain stitch A single, straight, continuous row of stitches that looks the same on both sides of the fabric; the stitch made by conventional home sewing machines; also called straight stitch.

Plain weave Weave in which filling yarns pass alternately over and under warp yarns; simplest and most common weave.

Pleat Fold of fabric folded back upon itself so that the pleat is comprised of three layers.

Plies Layers of fabric.

Pocket bag Pouch of fabric that forms the functional part of the pocket.

Point of sale (POS) The place and time at which the consumer purchases the product.

Poly bag Plastic bag.

Preclassification Classifying garments with U.S. Customs Service before their arrival.

Precost Preliminary estimate of what it will cost to produce a garment; also called quick cost.

Prepack Predetermined groupings of different sizes specified by the retailer.

Prepared for dye (PFD) Special white cloth from which garments are made that are to be garment dyed after assembly.

Preliminary assembly Parts line where as many small parts as possible are prepared for assembly.

Preproduction garments Trial units from every new style made using actual production techniques in the manufacturing plant.

Prêt-à-porter/prêt French term for ready-to-wear.

Price line Clustering of merchandise priced at the same price level; stores may carry low-price, moderate-price, and/or high-price lines.

Price point Specific dollar price amount.

Princess seam Dart-substitute seam that incorporates the bust and waist darts in womenswear.

Private label Brand developed by or for a specific retailer; also called private brand or store brand.

Product The finished garment.

Product comparison research Evaluation of competitors' products by measuring dimensions, conducting physical tests, comparing prices, and analyzing the results to determine value. Also called simply "comparisons."

Production costing Detailed, accurate costing that enables the manufacturer to accurately predict the cost of producing a garment.

Production pattern Pattern designed for optimal efficiency in mass manufacturing; also called hard pattern.

Profit improvement program Internal program initiated by employees to meet cost and quality challenges.

Progressive bundle system Production organized by keeping bundles of like components together. Each operator completes the same task on each garment in the bundle before passing it on to the next operator.

Prototype Trial model or item.

Prototype garment Experimental garment made from first pattern.

Psychographics Characteristics of people according to their lifestyle values—interests, attitudes, and opinions.

Pull Portion of the zipper that is grasped to operate the slider; also called tab.

Purled edge Series of raised loops, as a result of the interloopings of looper threads at an edge.

Put-up Amount of yardage on a roll.

Quality department Department in a company that monitors and maintains quality standards; also called quality assurance (QA) or quality control (QC).

Quick response (QR) Comprehensive business strategy consisting of computer linkages and interindustry partnerships based on trust and cooperation that substantially speed up the production and delivery of goods while at the same time enhancing quality.

Quick Response Leadership Committee (QRLC) Division of AAMA concentrating on Quick Response.

Quilting Stitching that joins the fashion fabric with a backing and an interlining; the stitches form a slightly puffy, raised design, often in a geometric or other decorative pattern.

Quota Limit on the quantity of items that may be imported.

Quota visa   Endorsement by the U.S. Customs Service, granting entry and proving that goods conform to quota limits for their classification and country of origin.

Raglan sleeve   Sleeve attached to the garment with a diagonal seam that runs from the underarm to the neckline of the garment.

Random sampling   Examining a representative sample rather than all; also called statistical sampling.

Raw edge   Hole in the seam caused by not stitching both seam allowances deeply enough.

Ready-to-wear apparel (RTW)   Clothing that is mass produced; in its broadest sense, includes any garment that is not custom-made for the wearer. May be used by some people to refer specifically only to women's clothing.

Reasonable basis   Proof that care label instructions provided are safe for the garment.

Refurbishing   Care of clothing, including laundering and dry-cleaning.

Registered number (RN)   Number registered with the U.S. government that identifies a specific manufacturer.

Regulations for Toys and Children's Articles   Laws that govern the safety of items intended for use by infants and children.

Reinforcement   Any device used to lend strength.

Reinforcement stitches   Small stitches used to help points of particular strain bear stress.

Relaxation shrinkage   Fabric shrinkage caused by fabric gradually relaxing to its original dimensions after being stretched.

Released dart   A dart left unstitched, resulting in a straight silhouette rather than a fitted garment.

Residual shrinkage   Additional shrinkage beyond initial shrinkage.

Retail price   The price retailers charge consumers.

Retailer   One who sells apparel to consumers.

Return to vendor (RTV)   Sending back defective products to manufacturer from retailer.

Rework   Repair of defective items.

Ribbon   Narrow woven fabric used as a trim and to make ties and bows.

Rise   Measurement from crotch level to the top of the waistband; also called crotch depth.

Rivet   Circular metal reinforcement.

Robotics   Use of robots.

Roll line   Area where the collar and lapel naturally tend to roll.

Rolled collar   Band of fabric that rolls fully or partially around the neck.

Rolled hem   Very narrow hem rolled up and stitched to the garment to enclose the raw edge of the hem.

Ruffle   Decorative gathered or pleated strip of fabric sewn to the garment; also called flounce.

Running stitch   Stitch made by the needle being passed up and down through the fabric, always moving forward, creating spaces between all stitches.

Saddle stitch   Decorative running stitch, 1/4 inch to 1/2 inch long.

Safety stitch   Stitch that combines a row of overedge stitches with an independent row of straight lockstitches or chainstitches.

Sample garments   First garments made in the production process; also called salesman samples or duplicates.

Sample room   Prototype lab where prototype garments are made.

Sandwashing   Wet process closely related to stonewashing but using particles of sand to gently soften the fabric.

Satin stitch   Smooth, dense zigzag stitches.

Satin weave   Weave in which filling yarns pass over or under several warp yarns at one time, creating a smooth-faced fabric.

Screen printing   Process of applying colored ink through a screen that has some areas blocked off to create a stencil.

Seam   Joint resulting when two or more fabric pieces are sewn together.

Seam allowance   Narrow width between the seam line and the raw edge of the fabric; also called seam margin.

Seam grin   Unsightly result that occurs when the seamline spreads open, exposing the stitches so that they appear similar to the teeth of a grin.

Seam line   Stitched line of a seam.

Seam pucker   Lack of seam smoothness that detracts from the appearance of the garment.

Seam slippage   Damage that occurs when the fabric pulls away from the stitches at the seamline.

Seat seam   Center back seam of bottoms.

Selling point   Physical feature of the garment that makes it desirable.

Selvages   Woven edges of the fabric.

Separating zipper   A zipper that unlinks at both ends and separates into two different halves when unzipped, unlike a conventional zipper that remains linked at one or both ends when unzipped.

Sequence of construction   Order in which a garment is assembled.

Set   As an element of fit, refers to smooth fit without undesirable wrinkles.

Set-in sleeve   A sleeve formed by sewing a tube of fabric into the armhole.

Sewing operator   Worker who sews garments together.

Shade approval   Final choice of acceptable variations of shade of the chosen color/s.

Shade bands   Long, narrow swatches of fabric cut from different dye lots, all with acceptable variations of shade, used to maintain consistency of coloration on incoming fabric.

Shading   Absence of color consistency.

Shade lot   Fabrics grouped together for color consistency.

Shadow panel   Extra layer of fabric at center of slip for modesty.

Shank button   Button with a stem of plastic, metal, or cloth built into the button.

Shaped facing   Facing shaped identically to the garment edges it is sewn to and which it faces.

Shaping methods   Devices that control the way the garment fits the contours of the body.

Shell hem   Hem that features a scalloped effect created by a decorative shell stitch that attaches the narrow folded hem allowance to the garment.

Shipping container marking (SCM)   Marking the shipping boxes with bar codes for faster and more accurate handling of goods.

Shirring   Permanent, parallel rows of gathers made in the body of the garment.

Shirttail hem   Narrow hem folded under twice and topstitched in place.

Shoulder pad   Shaping device for shoulder area of garment.

Shoulder slope   Angle that the shoulder seam makes as it slopes away from the neck.

Shrinkage   Reduction in size of garment or garment parts; usually occurs during laundering.

Silhouette   Outline or shape of the garment.

Silk Labeling Rule   Law that requires weighted silk to be so labeled.

Single knit   Knit fabric with one layer of loops.

Single-needle tailoring   Use of single needle sewing machine, even if seams have multiple rows of stitches; generally produces smoother, flatter, but more costly seams than using multiple-needle machines.

600-class cover stitches   Top-and-bottom-covering chainstitches with interloopings appearing on both the face and back; used to sew flat seams in which the fabric plies abut or overlap slightly and are interlocked by the stitches.

Size   System that suggests to consumers the suitability of a garment for their body dimensions.

Size classifications   Groups of sizes according to age and/or body types of consumers.

Sizing   Classification of the dimensions of garments.

Skew   Fabric grain distortion in woven fabrics when crosswise yarns slant from one selvage to the other.

Skin on skin   Method for making a fur garment in which whole pelts are sewn together.

Slashed pocket   Bound or faced slit within the body of the garment with the pocket bag sewn inside the garment.

Sleeve   Covering for the arm that is attached at or near the armscye.

Sleeve head   Layers of shaping fabric sewn into upper portion of armhole and extending out into sleeve; also called header.

Sleeve vent   Type of hemmed in-seam placket at the wrist of high-quality tailored suit and sport jacket sleeves.

Slider   Portion of the zipper that glides up and down the chain, engaging and disengaging the two halves of the chain.

Slipping   Cutting the under collar slightly smaller than the upper collar and easing the two together as they are sewn; also called bubbling.

Slipstitch   "Invisible" form of the running stitch, used to join a folded edge to another play of fabric with the stitches hidden in the fold.

Slit buttonhole   Buttonhole with raw edges; a slit in the fabric that serves as a buttonhole.

Sloper   A company's basic pattern; also called a basic block.

Slot seam   Decorative lapped seam in which the edges of the two fabric plies are folded under and nearly abutted; they are lapped over and stitched to a narrow fabric underlay, usually of a contrasting color.

Slot zipper   Application characterized by two visible rows of topstitching on the outside of the garment, one on either side of the zipper chain.

Smocking   Stitching that uses decorative stitches to hold the fabric in even, accordion-like pleats.

Snag   Pull in the fabric made when yarn catches on a sharp object.

Snap fastener/snap   Closure that interlocks when pressed together.

Snap tape   Strip of fabric into which snaps are mechanically attached by the supplier.

Solution dyeing   Dyeing of manufactured fibers before the fibers are formed, while they are still in the liquid stage; also called dope dyeing.

Source   To find a contractor.

Specific rate   Tariff charged according to a specified amount per unit of weight or other quantity

Specification (spec)   Defines specifically how, for a particular style of garment, to meet the company's standards.

Specification buying   Requesting goods made to meet buyers' requirements and standards rather than choosing from manufacturers' lines.

Split   Layers of a hide other than the top layer.

Sportswear Casual separates that can be mixed and matched.

Spread Distance from collar point to collar point.

Spreading Action of laying multiple plies of cloth on a table before the cloth is cut.

Spun thread Staple fibers spun into a yarn used for sewing.

Spun yarn Yarn composed of short staple fibers.

Square edge stitch Stitch with thread interloopings forming a square or box effect at the edge; also called box edge stitch.

Standard General guideline established by a company to reflect the overall quality level of its products.

Standard allowed minutes/SAMs Time required for a "100% operator" to perform the specified operation.

Standard cut Most conservative style of men's suits.

Standing collar Band extending straight up from the neckline edge and standing up around the neck.

Staple fiber Short fiber.

Stay Any stable, narrow, nonbulky tape, ribbon, fabric strip, or other device used to stabilize a seam.

Stitch Thread interlocking or interlooping that holds a garment together.

Stitched in the ditch Straight stitches placed in the crevice between the garment and a binding or band; also called crack stitched.

Stitches per inch (SPI) Measurement of stitch length.

Stitches per minute (SPM) Sewing speed.

Stitching Stitches applied to finish an edge or for ornamental purposes; does not join fabric pieces together as do seams.

Stock-keeping unit (SKU) Numbering system used by a company to identify a particular item.

Stockouts When a company runs out of an item.

Stonewashing Wet process that originally used real stones to soften the cloth, preshrink it, and make the garment look and feel used and broken in.

Stops Parts of the zipper that prevent the slider from leaving the chain at either end of the zipper.

Straight-of-grain Includes both lengthwise and crosswise grains, both of which follow the straight yarns of the fabric.

Strapped seam Seam with stay sewn over the completed seam on the outside of the garment.

Strikeoffs Print samples from which a manufacturer can choose.

Strike-through Unsightly result when adhesive from fusible interfacing leaks through the fashion fabric.

Stringer Length of zipper tape that comes on a roll with elements attached.

Stripped seam Seam with stay sewn over the completed seam inside the garment.

Style The cut and other identifying characteristics of a garment.

Subcontractor Contractor that performs highly specialized functions for other contractors and manufacturers.

Suede Napped leather with a fuzzy surface.

Superimposed seam (SS) Seam created by superimposing fabric plies, or stacking them on top of one another with edges even, and sewing them together near the edge.

Sweatshop Factory in which the owner reaps profits from the sweat of workers who are undercompensated.

Sweep Circumference of hem.

Systems approach Considering all items of apparel to be worn at once as integrated, and insuring that all items work well together to perform the needed function.

Tab Decorative fabric strip that sometimes serves as a functional closure.

Tack Reinforcement that consists of several overlapping zigzag stitches; used to sew on labels, secure facings and shoulder pads, and reinforce areas of high stress, for instance, at pocket corners, the base of zippers and in the attachment of belt loops.

Tailored Having trim, simple lines; usually refers to garments that are carefully structured and detailed, usually closely fitted and made of woven fabrics, for example, the classic business suit.

Tailored placket A bound slash; the overlap portion is bound with a topstitched strip of fabric and the underlap is bound with a narrower strip of fabric; also called shirt sleeve placket.

Tall Size for taller-than-average people.

Taped seam Seam with stay tape superimposed on the fabric plies and sewn in as part of the seam.

Target market Consumers in a particular market segment that a manufacturer aims to please with a particular product.

Tariff Duty or tax placed on imported apparel.

Tender goods Weak cloth.

Tensile strength Ability of the fabric to resist a pulling force; also called tenacity.

Testing Determining or confirming that the appropriate product quality level of fabric, findings and trim, and apparel is maintained.

Tex System used to designate fiber or yarn size; weight in grams of 1000 meters; the larger the number, the larger the fiber or yarn.

Textile industry Group made up of fiber, yarn, fabric, and some findings producers; converters that dye, print, and finish cloth; and wholesale representatives who sell fabrics and findings to apparel producers.

Textile and apparel pipeline Channel of distribution through which a garment passes, from the fiber producer all the way to the ultimate consumer.

Textile/Clothing Technology Corporation (TC)² Coalition of industry, education, government, and labor; concentrates on research and development into cutting-edge manufacturing techniques and training to advance apparel-manufacturing technology and enhance the competitiveness of the U.S. apparel industry; usually abbreviated (TC)2.

Textile Fiber Products Identification Act (TFPIA)| Federal law requiring that all apparel sold in the United States have a label that identifies fiber content, manufacturer, and country of origin.

Textiles Monitoring Body (TMB) Division of WTO that oversees the administration of WTO policy concerning textiles and apparel.

Texturized thread Thread processed to give it greater bulk, thus reducing luster, improving sewability and coverage, and increasing the wearer's comfort.

Thermoplastic Heat-sensitive; melts when exposed to high temperatures.

Thread shank Thread wrapped around the stitches between the button and the garment, suspending the button away from the fabric.

300-class lockstitches Stitches composed of a needle thread interlocked with a bobbin thread.

Ticket tack Version of bar tack used to attached paper label to apparel.

Tie Fabric strip or tube used as a closure.

Toddlers' sizes Classification of children's clothing sizes for the child from 18 months to approximately 3 years of age.

Toggle Decorative button-and-loop closure consisting of two loops; one has a rod-shaped button attached to it.

Tolerance The difference between the allowable minimum and maximum of a specification or standard.

Topstitching Visible, decorative stitching done on the outside of the garment; also called accent stitching.

Torque Fabric distortion in knits.

Trade deficit Situation that occurs when a country imports more goods than it exports.

Trademark A registered brand name or symbol.

Traditional retailer One who buys finished garments and sells them to consumers.

Transship Method of trade rule circumvention that involves sending goods to a country with a more favorable tariff or quota position.

Trapunto Form of embroidery that resembles quilting.

Trim Decorative material that adorns the garment.

Trim and inspect Examination of garments at the end of the production line for defects, and trimming of any excessively long, dangling threads.

True bias Fabric direction that occurs at a 45-degree angle to the lengthwise and crosswise grain of woven fabrics; has the highest degree of stretch of any fabric direction.

Tuck Stitched fold of fabric.

Tuck seam Decorative lapped seam stitched away from the edge to create a small flap of fabric.

Turned-back cuff Formed by turning back or rolling up the lower portion of the sleeve or pant leg.

Twill weave Weave in which filling yarns float over or under two or more warp yarns in a staggered progression; resulting fabric has diagonal ridges.

200-class stitches Stitches created by hand or on machines that pass a single thread through one side of the material and then the other.

Two-piece sleeve Sleeve consisting of two portions, the main sleeve piece and a second narrow, shaped sleeve piece under the arm.

Two-thread chainstitch The most common 400-class stitch; consists of a needle thread interlooping with a looper thread.

Under collar Facing of the collar.

Underarm shield Pad used to absorb perspiration in the underarm area; also called dress shield.

Underlining Lining each major piece of the garment individually and then handling the two plies as one as the garment is constructed.

Underpressing Pressing during construction.

Underwear Clothing worn beneath outerwear.

Uneven plaid Plaid that varies in the arrangement of stripes on each side of the dominant horizontal and vertical bars of the plaid.

Uniform Resource Locator (URL) World Wide Web site address.

Union of Needletrades, Industrial and Textile Employees (UNITE) Fourth-largest manufacturing union in the nation, fights for rights and job security for workers in the textile and apparel industry.

Unit production system (UPS) System that replaces the traditional assembly line; garments are sent to each operator's station via computer-controlled overhead transports, improving flow of garments through the factory and eliminating the time spent in handling bundles.

Universal Product Code (UPC) See Bar code.

Upper collar Visible portion of the collar.

Upright press Machine using clamps, hangers or both to hold garments in position for pressing; also called Colmac® press.

Upturned-flap pocket Flap attached to bottom of a finished slash, extending up and topstitched or slipstitched in place.

U.S. Fed. Std. No. 751a: Stitches, Seams, and Stitching Federal document that diagrams and defines the conformation of stitch, seam, and stitching types.

U.S. Patent and Trademark Office (USPTO) U.S. government office that registers trademarks, including brand names, words, or symbols, used to identify and distinguish one manufacturer's products from another's.

Vacuum table Table using suction to compress and stabilize multiple plies of fabric and hold them in place for cutting.

Value Relationship between price and quality.

Vanity sized Expensive lines cut large to appeal to consumers who desire to think of themselves as wearing a small-labeled size.

Vendor Raw materials source for manufacturer or garment source for retailer; also called supplier.

Vertical integration Situation that occurs when the same firm is responsible for multiple steps in the production or marketing of a product.

Voluntary Interindustry Commerce Standards (VICS) Standards for electronic data interchange for the apparel industry, established by a group with representatives from all facets of the industry.

Waistband curtain Prefabricated waistband facing that consists of a strip of firmly woven fabric attached to a bias-cut piece of interfacing; the lower edge of the curtain is a bias-cut fold of fabric.

Wales Loops that run up and down the face of a plain knit fabric.

Warp Yarns that run parallel to the selvages; consists of yarns held taut by the loom during weaving; also called lengthwise grain.

Warp knit Interlooped fabric made with the yarns running vertically.

Warranty Guarantee, either *implied* or *written,* that the product will perform in an acceptable manner for the purpose for which it is marketed.

Wear testing Wearing and caring for the garment under normal circumstances to determine in-use performance.

Wet process Procedure that adds a chemical finish to the assembled garment.

Weights Small, thin pieces of metal encased in fabric or chains tacked in place to perfect the drape of the garment.

Welt pocket Bound, slashed pocket.

Welt seam Decorative lapped seam with dimension created by a narrow seam allowance caught between the garment and a wider seam allowance by topstitching; the narrow seam allowance pads the area.

Wicking ability Rate at which a fabric diffuses moisture.

Wholesale price The price that manufacturers charge retailers.

Wholesale representative Agent of the manufacturer; sells finished garments to retailers for a commission; also called sales rep.

Wind flap Piece of fabric used to keep out the wind.

Women's sizes Size classification for adult women of average height with full, mature figures.

Womenswear Clothing for adult females.

Wool Products Labeling Act (WPLA) Federal law regulating the labeling of wool products.

Woolen yarn Carded wool yarn.

World Trade Organization (WTO) International group gradually phasing out and taking the place of the GATT.

World Wide Web (WWW) Part of Internet that enables easy access and retrieval of documents containing text and graphics from web sites anywhere in the world.

Worsted yarn Combed wool yarn.

Wrinkle resistance Wet process that helps garments maintain a pressed appearance after many washings and wearings.

Yarn Continuous strand of fibers; the thread used to make fabric.

Yarn dyeing Dyeing yarn prior to weaving or knitting the fabric.

Yarn number System used to designate staple-fiber yarn size; the larger the number, the smaller the yarn.

Yarn slippage Tendency of the yarns in a fabric to shift under stress.

Yoke Horizontal division within a garment; small, flat panel of fabric usually at the shoulder, waist, or midriff.

Young men's sizes Size classification designed for young men with developing builds.

Zigzag stitch Stitch made by the needle moving from side to side to produce a symmetrical zigzag pattern; the chief advantage is elasticity.

Zipper chain Part of the zipper that interlocks when the zipper is closed.

Zipper hump Unsightly defect that results when the zipper chain does not lie flat and smooth but instead creates waves in the fabric where the zipper is applied.

Zipper tape Fabric portion of a zipper.

Index

A-Squared. *See* American Association of Textile Chemists and Colorists
Abrasion resistance, 169, 195
Absorbency, 168
Accent stitching. *See* Topstitching
Acceptable quality level (AQL), 61
Acetate, 176
Acid washing. *See* Wet Processing
Acrylic, 176
Aesthetic performance, 38–39, 162, 172–194
Age Discrimination in Employment Act, 28
Amalgamated Clothing and Textile Workers Union (ACTWU), 32
American Apparel Manufacturers Association (AAMA), 3
American Association of Textile Chemists and Colorists (AATCC), 58–59, 170–172
American cut, 150
American Fiber Manufacturers Association, 173
American National Standards Institute (ANSI), 62
American Society for Quality Control (ASQC), 62
American Society for Testing and Materials (ASTM), 58, 158–159, 170, 180, 223
American Textile Manufacturers Institute (ATMI), 7, 158
ANSI. *See* American National Standards Institute
Antistatic finish, 188
Apparel Industry
   history, 1–2
   organization, 2–3
Apparel production cycle, 67–68
   related resources, 329
Appliqué, 201–202, 283
AQL. *See* Acceptable quality level
Armholes. *See* Armscyes
Armscyes, 147
Arrowhead tacks. *See* Tacks
Assembly line, 91
ASQC. *See* American Society for Quality Control
ASTM. *See* American Society for Testing and Materials
Athletic cut, 151

Attractiveness. *See* Aesthetic performance
Audit. *See* Inspection
Automation, 92

Babies'. *See* Infants'
Back tacking, 241
Backing buttons, 314
Backstitching, 112–113
Bagging. *See* Lining
Balance
   cost and performance, 51–52
   element of fit, 144
Balanced weave, 171
Bands, 268–269
Bar codes. *See* UPC
Bar tacks. *See* Tacks
Barré. *See* Fabric defects
Barrel cuffs. *See* Cuffs
Basic block, 74, 105
Basting, 225
Batting, 184
BCF yarns. *See* Yarns, bulk continuous filament
Beading. *See* Lace
Belt loops, 288
Belts, 214
Bespoke, 41
Better price line, 39–41
Bias, 102–104
Bias tape, 201, 255
Bifurcated, 148
Binding tariff classification ruling, 83
Bindings. *See* Seams, bound
   Hong Kong, 268
Bleeding, 195–196
Blends, 178
Blindstitches. *See* Stitches
Blocking, 164
Bobbins, 223
Bobbin Magazine, 97
Bobbin Show™, 97
Bodies, 72

Bonded fabric, 183
Boning, 215
Booked seams, 155
Bottom cover stitches. *See* Stitches
Bound buttonholes. *See* Buttonholes
Bound seams (BS). *See* Seams
Bowed fabric, 165
Bows, 124
Boys' sizes. *See* Sizes
Braid, 200
Brands, 4–5, 29–30
Bras, 137–138, 151, 215
Break, 150
Break open stitches. *See* Stitches
Breakouts, 83
Bridge price line, 40–41
Bridle, 215
Brightened, 188
British cut, 151
Brushed fabric, 187
BS. *See* Seams, bound
Bubbling. *See* Slipping
Buckles, 210
Budget price line, 40–41
Bulk continuous filament yarns. *See* Yarns
Bundles. *See* Progressive bundle system
Bursting strength, 171–172
Busted seams. *See* Seams, butterflied
Bustles, 215–216
Butterflied seams. *See* Seams
Button bands, 265
Button loops. *See* Loops, button
Buttonhole twist, 317
Buttonholes
    bound, 317–318
    fused, 318
    hand-worked, 317
    in-seam, 318
    keyhole, 317
    oval/fan, 317
    slit, 318
Buttons
    applying, 312–314
    eyed, 313
    shank, 313–314
Buying, 4
Buying benefits, 39

CAD. *See* Computer aided design
CAM. *See* Computer aided manufacturing
Canted, 150
Carded, 179
Care, ease of, 168, 196
Care Labeling Rule, 21–25, 178
Care symbols, 22–25

Casings, 110, 295–296
Catchstitches. *See* Stitches
Cellulosic fibers. *See* Natural fibers
Certification, 30–31
Chainstitches. *See* Stitches
Chapter 98 (Provision 9802), 8, 75
Chemical resistance, 169, 196
Chest pieces, 214
Chevron, 88
Childrenswear, 125, 151–152
CIM. *See* Computer integrated manufacturing
CITA. *See* Committee for Implementation of Textile Agreements
CITDA. *See* Computer Integrated Textile Design Association
Civil Rights Act, 28
Classification. *See* U.S. Customs Service
Clean Air Act, 28
Clean Water Act, 28
Clean finish, 263
Clo, 168
Clorox® color safe identifier, 31–32
Closures, 202–210
Coil zippers, 205
Collar fall, 119
Collar slope, 146
Collar spread, 146
Collar stand, 119
Collars, 146
    bluff edge, 304–305
    constructing, 302–305
    parts, 119
    stays, 215
    styles, 116–119
    under, 304
    upper, 304
Collection, 72
Color
    addition. *See* Wet processing
    approval, 82
    consistency, 162
    removal. *See* Wet processing
    services, 71
Colorfastness, 166, 195–196
Colorimeter, 162
Combed, 179
Comfort, 167–168, 196
Committee for Implementation of Textile Agreements (CITA), 8
Comparison shopping/research studies, 56, 71
Computer aided design (CAD), 72–73
Computer Integrated Textile Design Association (CITDA), 72
Computer aided manufacturing (CAM), 85
Computer integrated manufacturing (CIM), 12

Construction
    defined, 38
    sequence, 275–277
Consumer behavior, related resources, 328
Consumer Product Safety Commission (CPSC), 25
Contractors, 3–4, 75
Continuous bound plackets. *See* Plackets
Control stitching, 252
Cords, 210
Corespun thread. *See* Thread
Cost, 80–81
Cost per wear, 48–49
Costing, 75–79
Cotton, 174
Cotton Seal, 31
Count, 170–171
Counterfeit, 30
Country of origin, 19–20
Courses, 182
Couture, 40
Cover stitches. *See* Stitches
CPSC. *See* Consumer Product Safety Commission
Crack stitching, 256
Crafted With Pride, 31
Creases, 123
Crocking, 171, 195–196
Crockmeter, 171
Cross training, 92
Crotch
    depth, 148
    length, 148
Cuff links, 149
Cuffs
    construction, 308–309
    styles, 119–120
Curing oven, 95
Curtain, waistband. *See* Waistbands
Customs broker, 5
Cut. *See* Gauge
Cutting, 90
Cutwork, 281

D-rings, 210
Dart equivalents/dart substitutes, 106–107
Darts, 105–106
    constructing, 291
    released, 108
    well-fitting, 146
Decorative details, 277–278
Defect guides, 53–54
Degradation, 169–170, 196
Demographics, 46–47
Denier, 178, 180
Design, 38, 72–75
    related resources, 328

Designers, 41, 72, 326
Details
    decorative, 121–124
    functional, 124–126
Determinant attributes. *See* Quality
Development plans, 71–72
Dichroism, 162
Die cutting, 90
Differential feeding, 246
Differential shrinkage, 195, 246
Digitizer, 74
Dimensional stability, 164–166, 195
Direct importers, 4
Direct roller printing, 186–187
Directional fabric, 89
Discounting, 39
Distribution, 96–97
Double knit, 182
Double ticketing, 61
DPF. *See* Denier
Drafting, 74
Draping, 72
Drawstrings, 110, 320
Dress shields. *See* Underarm shields
Dress sizes. *See* Sizes
Dress styles, 116
Drill holes. *See* Marking
Drop, 151
Drop shipping, 96
Dry-cleanability, 169, 196
Dtex. *See* Tex
DTVM. *See* Dual Technology Vendor Marking
Dual Technology Vendor Marking (DTVM), 13
Dumping. *See* Trade regulations
Duplicates. *See* Sample garments
Durability, 39
Durable press. *See* Wet processing
Duties, 8–9
Dye lots, 162
Dyes/dyestuffs/dyeing, 184–186

EAI. *See* Enterprise for the Americas Initiative
Ease, 108, 144, 292
Edge finish stitchings (EF). *See* Stitchings
Edge finishes. *See* Edge treatments. *See also* Stitchings
Edge treatments, 116, 259–271
    performance, 259–260
Edgestitching. *See* Topstitching
Edging. *See* Lace
EDI. *See* Electronic data interchange
EEOC. *See* Equal Employment Opportunity Commission
EF. *See* Stitchings, edge finish
Elastic, 109–110, 213–214
    attaching, 294–295

Elasticity, 164, 195
Elbow patches, 290
Elderly. *See* Older adults
Electronic data interchange (EDI), 12–13
Elongation, 164–195
Embargo, 83
Embossed fabrics, 187
Embroidery, 280–281
Enclosed seams. *See* Seams
End use, 46
Enterprise for the Americas Initiative (EAI), 9
Environmental Protection Agency (EPA), 28–29
EPA. *See* Environmental Protection Agency
Equal Employment Opportunity Commission (EEOC), 28
Ergonomics, 27–28
Equal Pay Act, 28
ETCs. *See* Export trading companies
EU. *See* European Union
European cut, 150
European Union (EU), 9
Exports, 6–7
Export trading companies (ETCs), 5
Extensibility. *See* Elongation
Extrinsic attributes, 39
Eyed buttons, 203
Eyelet. *See* Lace
Eyelets, 210, 320

Fabric
    aesthetic performance, 162–172
    body, 111
    costs, 78–79
    defects, 160–162
    dyeing, 184–186
    ease of production, 158, 160
    fashion. *See* body
    fibers, 81–87
    finishing, 187–189
    functional performance, 157–162
    inspection, 59–60
    physical features, 172–189
    printing, 186–187
    related resources, 328–329
    shell. *See* body
    specifications, 158–162
    structure, 180–184
    testing, 82, 170–172
    weight, 171
    yarns, 87–89
Fabric assessment by simple testing (FAST), 160
Fabric production unit number (FPU), 25
Facings, 265–267
    bias, 267
    combination, 267

extended, 266
    shaped, 266–267
Fadeometer. *See* Weatherometer
Fading. *See* Colorfastness
Fagoting, 281–282
Fair Claims Guide for Consumer Textile Products, 49–50
Fair Labor Standards Act (FLSA), 27–28
Fair trade, 10
Fallout, 78, 82
Fashion forecasters, 71
Federal Trade Commission (FTC), 18
FAST. *See* Fabric assessment by simple testing
Felting. *See* Shrinkage
Fiber content
    elastic, 213
    fabric, 18–19, 178
    thread, 197
Fiber dyeing, 184
Fibers, 173–178
Fiberwebs, 183, 211
FIFO. *See* First in first out
Filament
    yarns. *See* Yarns
    thread. *See* Thread
Filling, 102–103, 181–182
Film fabrics, 183
Final audit. *See* Inspection
Findings, 79, 82, 193–216
Finish pressing. *See* Off pressing
Finishes
    chemical, 187–188
    defined, 38
    mechanical, 187
Finishing, 96
First in first out (FIFO), 96
First patterns, 74
Fit
    controlling, 104–141
    defining, 139–140
    elements, 141–144
    evaluating, 145–151
    models, 140–141
    forms, 140
    related resources, 327
Flagging defects, 160
Flammability, 168, 196
Flammable Fabrics Act, 25–26
Flat-felled seams. *See* Seams
Flat patternmaking, 74
Flat seams (FS). *See* Seams
Flaws. *See* Defects
Flax, 31, 174
Floor-ready merchandise (FRM), 13
Flexible manufacturing, 92

Flocked fabrics, 184
Flounces. *See* Ruffles
FLSA. *See* Fair Labor Standards Act
Fly shield, 285
Focus groups, 71
Forward stock, 96
Four Point System, 161–162
FPLA. *See* Fur Products Labeling Act
FPU. *See* Fabric production unit
Free trade, 10
French cuffs, 194
French darts, 106
French fly, 285
French front, 265
French seams. *See* Seams
French tacks. *See* Swing tacks
Fringe, 201
Frog, 203
Frosting. *See* Wet processing
FTC. *See* Federal Trade Commission
FRM. *See* Floor-ready merchandise
FS. *See* Seams, flat
Full-fashioned knits, 111
Fully fused front, 214
Fully-let-out fur, 189
Fume fading, 169, 196
Functional performance, 39, 157–162, 195–196
Fur, 189
Fur Products Labeling Act (FPLA), 20
Furnishings, 138–139
Fused buttonholes. *See* Buttonholes
Fusible interfacing/fusibles, 211

Galloon. *See* Lace
Garment dyeing, 94, 184–186
Garment production unit number (GPU), 25
Garment rinsing/washing. *See* Wet processing
Gathers, 108–109, 292
GATT. *See* General Agreement on Tariffs and Trade
Gauge, 170–171
Gauntlet buttons, 271
General Agreement on Tariffs and Trade (GATT), 8
General Services Administration (GSA), 223
Generalized System of Preferences (GSP), 9
Generic names, 18
Gentlemen's cut, 151
Gimp. *See* Braid
Girdles, 138
Girls' sizes. *See* Sizes
Global trade, 5–10
   related resources, 326
Glossary, 343–358
Godets, 110–111
Gore-Tex®, 183
Gores, 107–108

Gorge line, 119, 304
Government, related resources, 326. *See also* Regulations
GPU. *See* Garment Production Unit
Graded seams, 251
Grading patterns, 85
Grain, 102–104, 141–142
Graniteville System, 161
Green activities, 28–29
Greige goods, 184
Grommets, 210, 320
Grosgrain ribbon, 200
Group, 72
Growth tucks, 125
GSA. *See* General Services Administration
GSP. *See* Generalized System of Preferences
Guides for the Feather and Down Products Industry, 20
Gussets, 110, 308

Hand, 163
Hand stitches. *See* Stitches
Hand worked buttonholes. *See* Buttonholes
Handicapped. *See* Physical disabilities
Harmonized System (HS), 8
Harmonized Tariff Schedule of the United States (HTSUS), 8
Haute couture, 41
Heat resistance, 167, 196
Heat set, 167, 187
Heat transfer print, 187
Heat tunnel, 95
Heavy people, clothing for, 152
Heel guard, 290
Hem tape, 201, 261
Hemp, 174
Hems, 260–263
   attachment, 261
   blind, 261
   flanged, 262
   folded, 261
   lettuce-edge, 264
   rolled, 263
   scalloped, 265
   shell, 264
   shirttail, 263
   wedged, 262
   width, 262–263
Hemstitching, 281–282
Hook and loop tape, 209–210, 320
Hooks and eyes, 208–209
   applying, 320
Hoops, 215–216
Horizontal plackets. *See* Plackets
Horsehair braid, 216

HS. *See* Harmonized System
HTSUS. *See* Harmonized Tariff Schedule of the United States

IAQL. *See* Incoming acceptable quality level
IFI. *See* International Fabricare Institute
ILGWU. *See* International Ladies' Garment Workers Union
Immigration and Naturalization Service (INS), 28
Immigration Reform and Control Act, 28
Imports, 5–10, 19–20
Incoming acceptable quality level (IAQL). *See* Quality
In-process, 11
In-seam plackets. *See* Plackets
In-seam pockets. *See* Pockets
Incontinence, 153
Industry. *See* United States textile and apparel industry. *See also* Global trade
Infants' sizes. *See* Sizes
INS. *See* Immigration and Naturalization Service
Insect resistance, 169
Insertion. *See* Lace
Inside shops, 3. *See also* Manufacturers
Inspection, 58–61, 96–97
Insulation, 168
Interfacing, 112, 210
   application, 289–290
Interlining, 114, 213
International Fabricare Institute (IFI), 49–50
International Organization for Standardization (ISO), 62–63
International Ladies Garment Workers Union (ILGWU), 32
International trade. *See* Global trade
Internet, 12. *See also* World Wide Web
Intimate apparel. *See* Lingerie
Intrinsic attributes, 38
Inventory, 11, 13
Investment dressing, 46
ISO. *See* International Organization for Standardization
ISO 9000 certification, 62–63
Item 807. *See* Chapter 98

Jacket styles, 116, 150–151
Job titles, 69–71
Journals, related resources, 327
Junior. *See* Sizes
Just in time (JIT), 11

Kawabata Evaluation System (KES), 158, 160
Keeper, 289
KES. *See* Kawabata Evaluation System
Keystone. *See* Markup
Keyhole buttonhole, 242–243
Kick tape. *See* Heel guard

Kimono sleeves, 117, 119
Kiosks, 140
Knee patches, 290
Knits, 181–182, 211
Knock offs, 30

Lab dips, 82
Labels, 82–83, 197, 277
Lace, 183, 200–201
Lacing, 111
Lapels, 146–147, 304
Lapped seams (LS). *See* Seams
Laser-enhanced bonding (LEB). *See* Stitchless sewing
Latch tacking, 241
Latent defects, 44
Launderability, 169, 196
Launderometer, 169
Layouts/lays/lay-ups. *See* Spreading
Lead time
   calendar, 67–69
   considering, 75
Leather, 189
LEB. *See* Laser-enhanced bonding
Length of garment, 116, 149–150
Lettuce edge. *See* Hems
Licensing, 30
Life expectancy of apparel, 49–50
Light reflective, 168, 196
Lignes, 203
Line
   development calendar. *See* Lead time calendar
   element of fit, 143–144
   preliminary approval, 73
   presentation boards, 73
   series of related designs, 72
Linen. *See* Flax
Lingerie, 126, 137–138
Lingerie guards, 284
Lingerie strap keepers, 289
Lining, 112–113, 212
   application, 311–312
   attached at armscyes, 311–312
   bagging, 311
   to the edge, 311
Lockstitches. *See* Stitches
Loops
   belt, 288
   button, 203–204, 318
   hanger, 289
   locker, 289
   wrist, 289
Loss leader, 80
Low labeling, 22
LS. *See* Seams, lapped
Lyocell, 175–176

Magazines, related resources, 326–327
Manufactured fibers, 173
Manufacturers, 2–3, 20, 36, 47, 326
Marker making, 85–87
Marketing, related resources, 329
Marking, 90
Markup, 80
Market segmentation, 46
Masectomy, 126, 153
Mass production. *See* Apparel production cycle
Matching patterned fabrics, 87–89, 293
Material utilization (MU), 85–87
Materials, defined, 38
Maternity wear, 125, 152
Mature figures, clothing for. *See* Older adults
Medallion. *See* Lace
Media, related resources, 326
Menswear. *See* Sizes. *See also* Fit
Mercerization, 188, 197
Merchandisers, 72
Merrow. *See* Stitches, overedge
Metal fibers, 177
Metamerism, 163
MFA. *See* Multi-Fiber Arrangement
MFN. *See* Most favored nation
Mildew resistance, 169
Mill flaws. *See* Fabric defects
Mill week, 74
Misses'/Missy sizes. *See* Sizes
Mitering, 256, 268
Mock full-fashioned marks. *See* Full-fashioned marks
Modacrylic, 176–177
Model stock, 13
Moderate price line, 40–41
Modular manufacturing, 92
Moiré, 187
Moisture retention, 168
Monofilament thread. *See* Thread
Multifilament thread. *See* Thread
Monogram, 281
Most favored nation (MFN), 9
Moth repellent, 188
Multi-Fiber Arrangement (MFA), 8

NAFTA. *See* North American Free Trade Agreement
Name brands. *See* Branded
Nap. *See* Directional fabric
Napped finish, 187
National brands. *See* Branded
National Institute of Standards and Technology (NIST), 133
National Retail Federation (NRF), 4
Natural fibers, 173
Necklines, 116–117, 146
Needles, 240

chewing, 241
cutting, 240
heating, 240–241
NIST. *See* National Institute of Standards and Technology
NRF. *See* National Retail Federation
Nonwovens. *See* Fiberwebs
North American Free Trade Agreement (NAFTA), 9
Notches, 292–293
Notions. *See* Findings
Novelty yarns. *See* Yarns
Nylon, 176

OCR. *See* Optical Character Recognition
Occupational clothing, 126
Occupational Safety and Health Administration (OSHA), 27
Olefin, 177
Off-grain, 104
Off-pressing. *See* Pressing
Off-pricing. *See* Discounting
Off the rack. *See* Ready-to-wear apparel
Offshore production, 8
Older adults, clothing for, 125, 152
100% inspection, 60–61
Opacity, 163
Operators. *See* Sewing operators
Optical Character Recognition (OCR), 13
Ornamental Stitchings (OS), 280–282
OS. *See* Stitchings, ornamental
OSHA. *See* Occupational Safety and Health Administration
Outerwear, 136
Outside shops. *See* Contractors
Outsourcing. *See* Sourcing
Overcast/overlock/overseam. *See* Stitches, overedge
Overedge stitches. *See* Stitches
Overhead, 79
Overlaps, 285, 315
Oversized, 144

Pad stitching, 289–290
Panels, 91, 291–296
Pant lengths, 117
Pant styles, 115
Parchmentized, 188
Partial linings. *See* Linings
Parts, 91, 277–291
Parts, Panels, Pieces, and Products, 91, 275
Patch pockets, 121
Pattern design system (PDS), 74
Patternmakers, 74, 83–85
Payback, 81
PDS. *See* Pattern design system
Peplums, 124

Perceived quality model, 42–46
Performance features. *See* Quality
Permanent press. *See* Wet processing
Petites' sizes. *See* Sizes
PFD. *See* Prepared for dye
Physical disabilities, clothing for people with, 125–126, 153
Physical features. *See* Quality
Pickstitches. *See* Stitches
Picot-edge ribbon, 200
Piece dyeing, 184
Piece work, 91
Pieces, 91, 301–312
Pilling, 167
Pinking, 264
Piping, 201
Plackets, 269–271
    continuous bound, 270
    faced, 269–270
    horizontal, 269
    in-seam, 270
    slashed, 269
    tailored, 270–271
Plain seams. *See* Seams
Plain stitches. *See* Stitches
Plain weaves, 180
Plastic. *See* Vinyl
Pleats
    constructing, 291–292
    dart equivalents, 110
    types, 122–123
Plied yarns. *See* Yarns
Plies, fabric, 89
Pocket flaps, 121
Pockets
    constructing, 286–288
    styles, 120–121
Point of sale (POS) terminal, 13
Pollution Prevention Act, 28
Polyester, 176
POS. *See* Point of sale terminal
Preclassification. *See* United States Customs Service
Precosting, 77
Pregnant. *See* Maternity wear
Preliminary assembly, 91, 277
Prepacks, 79
Prepared for dye (PFD), 94–95, 185–186
Preproduction, 81–89
Pressing, 95, 320
Prêt à porter (Pret), 39
Price. *See also* Value
    cue to quality, 41–42
    lines, 39–41
    market potential, 80
    points, 40

    retail, 80
    wholesale, 80
Princess seams, 107
Printing, 186–187
Private labels, 4–5, 29–30
Production, 89–96
Production costing, 77–79
Production patterns, 83–85
Products, 91
Profit
    improvement programs, 80
    making, 80–81
Progressive bundle system, 91
Protectionism, 10
Protein fibers. *See* Natural fibers
Prototypes, 73–74
Psychographics, 47
Put-up, 160

Quality
    acceptable levels, 61, 97
    defined, 37
    determinant attributes, 44
    consumer perceptions, 42–46
    performance features, 2–3
    physical features, 2–3
    related resources, 327–328
Quality assurance (QA). *See* Quality department
Quality control (QC). *See* Quality department
Quality department, 12–14, 286–287
Quick costing, 32
Quick Response (QR), 39–41, 288
Quilting, 228–229

Raglan sleeves, 117, 119
Ramie, 174
Random sampling, 60
Raw edge, 247
Rayon, 175
Ready-to-wear apparel, 1
Ready made. *See* Ready-to-wear apparel
Reasonable basis, 21
Refurbishing, 21
Regenerated cellulosic fibers. *See* Manufactured fibers
Registered number (RN), 20
Registration, 186, 313
Regulations, 17–29
    related resources, 327
Regulations for Toys and Children's Articles, 26, 196
Reinforcement stitches. *See* Stitches
Reinforcements, 285, 290–291, 314–315
Related resources, 325–329
Relaxation shrinkage. *See* Shrinkage
Research
    fabric and findings, 74

market, 71–72
Reserve stock, 96
Residual shrinkage. *See* Shrinkage
Retail price, 34
Retailers
    traditional, 4
    manufacturing, 4–5
Return to vendor (RTV), 61–62
Returns, 61–62
Revers, 119
Ribbing, 182
Ribbon, 200
Rickrack. *See* Braid
Rise. *See* Crotch depth
Risers. *See* Yokes
Rivets. *See* Reinforcements. *See also* Trims
RN. *See* Registered number
Robotics. *See* Automation
Roll line, 119, 304
Rolled hem, 154–155
RTV. *See* Return to vendor
RTW. *See* Ready-to-wear apparel
Rubber fibers, 177
Ruching, 200
Ruffles, 124
Running stitches. *See* Stitches

Saddle stitches. *See* Stitches
Safety
    clothing, 168
    worker, 27
Safety stitches. *See* Stitches
Sales. *See* Marketing
Sales reps. *See* Wholesale representatives
Sample garments, 91
SAMs. *See* Standard Allowed Minutes
Sanforized,
Sanded, 187
Sandwashed. *See* Wet processing
Satin stitches. *See* Stitches
Satin weave, 180–181
SCM. *See* Shipping container marking
Screen printing, 186
Scrolling. *See* Braid
Seams
    allowances, 246
    bound seams (BS), 255–257, 267–268
    bulk, 246–247
    broken, 247
    classes, 248–249
    cracked. *See* broken
    dart equivalents, 107
    enclosed, 249–250
    flat seams (FS), 257
    flat-felled, 253–255

French, 252
general applications to typical operations, 337–341
labor costs, 249–250
lapped seams (LS), 253–255
mock flat-felled, 254–255
mock French, 252–253
performance, 245–248
plain, 249
related resources, 329
schematic diagrams, 332–335
slippage, 247–248
slot, 254, 256
stays, 215, 258
strapped, 259
strength, 247–248
stripped, 258
superimposed seams (SS), 249–253
tape, 201. *See also* Hem tape
taped, 258
types, 248–257
tuck, 254, 256
welt, 255–256
width, 257–258
Selling points, 39
Selvages, 102
Sequins. *See* Trim
Serge. *See* Stitches, overedge
Serviceability. *See* Durability
Set, 142–143
Set-in sleeves, 117, 119
Sewed out, 222
Sewing
    accuracy, 241, 258–259
    operators, 90
Shade approval, 82
Shade bands, 82
Shade lots, 162
Shading, 162–163
Shadow panel, 126
Shank buttons, 203
Shaping methods, 104–111, 291–296
Sheared, 187
Shell fabric. *See* Body fabric
Shell hems. *See* Hems
Shipping. *See* Distribution
Shipping container marking (SCM), 13
Shirring, 109
Shirt sleeve plackets. *See* Plackets
Shirttail hems. *See* Hems
Shoulder pads, 214, 311
Shrinkage, 164–165, 171, 187, 195, 246
Signature labels. *See* Branded
Silhouettes, 114–116
Silk, 174–175

washable, 188
weighting, 21
Silk Labeling Regulation, 21
Singed, 187
Single knits, 182
Single-needle tailoring, 145–146
Sizes
boys', 135
childrens', 135
childrenswear, 134
classifications, 132
dress, 136
expressed as body measurements, 133
girls', 135
infants', 134–135
junior, 137
lettered, 134
menswear, 138–139
misses/missy, 136
numbered, 132
one-size-fits-all, 134
outerwear, 136–137
petites, 136, 137
pictograms, 133–134
related resources, 327
talls, 136–137
toddlers', 135
underwear, 137–138
voluntary standards, 132–133
women's, 137
womenswear, 135–138
Sizing, 131–132
Skewed, 165
Skin-on-skin furs, 18987
Skipped stitches. See Stitches
Skirt
lengths, 114, 117
styles, 115
SKU. See Stock keeping unit
Sleeves
fitting, 147
heads, 214
kimono, 307–308
lengths, 149
raglan, 308
set-in, 306–307
styles, 118–119, 150–151
two-piece, 307
Slipping, 305–306
Slipstitches. See Stitches
Sloper. See Basic block
Slops, 2
Slot seams. See Seams
Smocking, 109
Snagging, 167

Snap crotch/inseams, 125
Snap tape, 208, 319–320
Snap fasteners, 207–208
applying, 318–319
Softened, 188
Soil release, 188
Sourcing, 8, 75, 77
related resources, 325–326
Soutache braid. See Braid
Specialty hair fibers, 175
Specifications, 51–56, 82, 158–162, 194
SPI. See Stitches, per inch
SPM. See Stitches, per minute
Sportswear
active, 126
men's, 138
women's, 136
Spreading, 89
Spun thread. See Thread
Spun yarns. See Yarns
SS. See Superimposed seam
Standard allowed minutes (SAMs), 91
Staple fibers, 173, 179
Static, 168
Statistical sampling. See Random sampling
Stays. See Seams
Stitches
basting, 225
chainstitches, 223–237
classes, 222–237
100 single-thread chainstitches, 225–226, 228
200 hand stitches and machine simulations, 225–227, 229, 264
300 lockstitches, 226–231
400 multithread chainstitches, 226, 229–233
500 overedge stitches, 226, 227, 231–236, 263–264, 277
600 cover stitches, 227, 235, 237
general applications to typical operations, 337–342
length, 236–239
lockstitches, 223–231
per inch (SPI), 236–239
per minute (SPM), 228–229, 232, 236
performance, 221–222
related resources, 329
skipped, 240
tension, 239–240
types, 222–237
width, 240
Stitching in the ditch, 143
Stitchings
edge finish (EF), 260–264, 336
general applications to typical operations, 341–342

ornamental (OS), 280, 335
related resources, 329
schematic diagrams, 335–336
Stitchless sewing, 222
Stock keeping unit (SKU), 13
Stone washing. *See* Wet processing
Straight-of-grain, 103
Strapped seams. *See* Seams
Strength. *See* Tensile strength. *See also* Bursting strength
thread, 197
trim and finding attachment, 196
Stretch. *See* Elongation. *See also* Comfort
Stretch panels, 125
Stride. *See* Crotch length
Strike through, 212
Strikeoffs, 82
Stripped seams. *See* Seams
Structural jamming. *See* Seams, pucker
Studs. *See* Trims and Findings
Styles, 114–124
related resources, 327
Style Fullness, 108
Suede, 189
Sueded, 187
Sundries. *See* Findings
Sunlight resistance. *See* Lightfastness
Superimposed seams (SS). *See* Seams
Suppliers, 3
Supporting devices, 114–115
Sweatshops, 27, 32
Sweep, 149
Swing tacks, 312
Synthetic fibers. *See* Manufactured fibers

Tabs, 124
Tacks, 291. *See also* Swing tacks, Back tacking, and Latch tacking
Tailored apparel, 102
Tailored plackets. *See* Plackets
Talls. *See* Sizes
Taped seams. *See* Seams
Target market, 46
Tariffs. *See* Duties
(TC)², *See* Textile/Clothing Technology Corporation
Ten Point System, 161
Tenacity, 168–169, 171–172
Tensile strength. *See* Tenacity
Tender goods, 95
Testing, 56–60, 82, 170–172
Tex, 178, 180, 199
Textile and apparel pipeline, 11
Textile/Clothing Technology Corporation (TC)², 97
Textile Fiber Products Identification Act (TFPIA), 18–20
Textile industry, 2–3
Textiles Monitoring Body (TMB), 9

Texturized thread. *See* Thread
Thermoplastic, 167
Thread, 197–199
corespun, 198
count. *See* Count
fiber content, 197
filament, 198
long and dangling, 241–242
monofilament, 198
multifilament, 198
spun, 198
strength, 197
texturized, 198
Ticket tacks. *See* Tacks
Tiers, 124
Ties, 210
Time and motion studies, 79
TMB. *See* Textiles Monitoring Body
Toddlers'. *See* Sizes
Tolerances, 55
Top-and-bottom-covering chainstitches. *See* Stitches
Top grain leather, 189
Top styles, 115
Topstitching, 280
Torque, 165
Trade. *See* Global trade
Trade and industry-related organizations, 325
Trade deficit, 6–7
Trade regulations, 8–10
Trademarks, 18–19, 29
Tranship. *See* Trade regulations
Trapunto, 281
Trend analysis, 71–72
Triacetate, 176
Trim and inspect, 60. *See also* Inspection
Trims, 193–196, 199–202, 282–283
Tuck seams. *See* Seams
Tucks, 110, 122
constructing, 291–292
Twill tape, 201
Twill weaves, 180
Two-piece sleeves, 119

UCC. *See* Uniform Commercial Code
Ultrasonic welding. *See* Stitchless sewing
Underarm shields, 216
Underlaps, 285, 315
Underlining, 113–114, 213, 290
Underlying fabrics, 111–114, 210–213
Underpressing. *See* Pressing
Understitching. *See* Control stitching
Underwear, 137–138. *See also* Lingerie
Uniform Commerical Code (UCC), 13
Uniform Resource Locator (URL). *See* World Wide Web

Union labels, 32
Union of Needletrades, Industrial, and Textile Employees, 32
Unit production system (UPS), 30
UNITE. *See* Union of Needletrades, Industiral, and Textile Employees
United States Government, 326. *See also* Regulations
United States Customs Service (USCS), 83
    classification, 83
    preclassification, 83–84
United States textile and apparel industry, 2–4
United States Fed. Std. No. 751a, 223–224, 248–249
United States Patent and Trademark Office, 29
Universal Product Code (UPC), 12–13
URL. *See* Uniform Resource Locator
USCS. *See* United States Customs Service
USPTO. *See* United States Patent and Trademark Office
UV protection, 168
Utility, 39

Value, 47–48
Vanity sized, 132
Velcro®. *See* Hook and loop tape
Vendor, 3
Vents. *See* Plackets
Vertical integration, 5
VICS. *See* Voluntary Interindustry Communications Standards
Vinyl, 183
Voluntary Interindustry Communications Standards (VICS), 13

Waistbands, 117, 148
    constructing, 309–311
    curtained, 310
Waistlines, 116–117, 147
Wales, 182
Warp, 102–103, 183
Warranties, 30
Wash and wear. *See* Durable press
Washability, 172
Water repellent, 188
Waterproof, 188
Wear Dated, 31
Wear tests, 56
Weatherometer, 172
Web. *See* World Wide Web
Wedged hems. *See* Hems
Weft. *See* Filling
Weights, 171, 216
Welt pockets, 121
Welt seams. *See* Seams
Wet processing, 92–95

Wholesale representatives/reps, 4
Wicking, 168
Wind flaps, 284
Women's. *See* Sizes
Womenswear. *See* Sizes
Wool, 175
    washable, 188
Wool Products Labeling Act (WPLA), 20
Woolen, 179
Woolmark, 31
World Trade Organization (WTO), 9
World Wide Web (WWW), 6, 12, 77, 325–327
Worsted, 179
Worth Street Textile Market Rules, 158
Wovens, 180–181, 211
WPLA. *See* Wool Products Labeling Act
Wrinkle resistance, 166–167
    finish. *See* Wet processing
WTO. *See* World Trade Organization
WWW. *See* World Wide Web

Yarn
    BCF. *See* bulk continuous filament
    bulk continuous filament, 179
    carded, 179
    combed, 179
    dyeing, 184
    fancy. *See* novelty
    filament, 179
    novelty, 179–180
    number, 180
    plied, 179
    size, 180
    slippage, 169
    spun, 179
    twist, 180
    wool, 179
    worsted, 179
Yokes, 107
Young men's. *See* Sizes, men's

Zigzag stitches. *See* Stitches
Zipper hump, 204
Zippers
    application, 283–285
        fly, 284–285
        invisible, 285
        lapped, 284
        slot, 284
    chain composition, 206
    length and size, 205–206
    parts, 204–205
    types, 206–207

About the Authors

Patty Brown originally wrote *Ready-To-Wear Apparel Analysis* to meet the needs of her fashion merchandising students. She is proud to see the second edition move closer to the industry, providing an excellent basis in both theory and current practice for understanding apparel production and quality, essential for success in the field.

Patty received her B.S. in Clothing and Textiles Retailing with an area of concentration in Business Administration as a Pershing Scholar at Truman State University, where she was a valedictorian. She received her M.S. in Clothing and Textiles as a Gregory Fellow while serving as a teaching assistant at the University of Missouri-Columbia. Her flawless academic record reflects her high standards and attention to detail.

Patty has worked in retail for Neate's Department Store and at the district level for Hancock Fabrics. She has served on the teaching faculties of Truman State University and Texas Christian University and currently is an adjunct instructor at Johnson County Community College. She operates Apparel Tech, a company that develops and markets educational materials in the area of textiles and apparel to colleges and universities. Patty is a member of the International Textiles and Apparel Association and Fashion Group International.

Janett Rice, a former educator, joined Patty Brown in the preparation of the second edition of *Ready-To-Wear Apparel Analysis* in order to share her industry experience with students of apparel merchandising, management, and design. Janett believes theory is most effective when complemented by practical, real-life examples. She contributed to this edition with this belief in mind.

Janett received her B.S. in Home Economics Education from the University of New Mexico and her M.S. in Clothing and Textiles Design from Colorado State University.

Janett's teaching career spanned nine years and included teaching on the faculties of The University of Manitoba and Iowa State University. Janett's apparel industry career spanned 13 years and includes managerial positions at The Lee Company (a division of VF Corporation) and Mervyn's (a division of The Dayton Hudson Corporation). Her responsibilities took her to domestic apparel manufacturers and contractors throughout the entire United States and textile testing labs throughout the world. For about 2 years, Janett operated TATR, a textile and apparel testing consulting service, which included clients such as ACTS Testing Labs and Textile Innovators. Presently Janett is the Director of Quality Assurance at Williams Sonoma, Inc., a retailer of products designed for home and garden use.

Janett is a member of Fashion Group International and is active in several industry professional organizations. She has received Certificates of Appreciation for her efforts from both ASTM and AATCC. Janett has continually maintained contact with the academic community through her service on advisory boards at four educational institutions and frequently provides guest lectures.